The Infinite Conversation

Theory and History of Literature
Edited by Wlad Godzich and Jochen Schulte-Sasse

For other books in the series, see p. 472

The Infinite Conversation

Maurice Blanchot

Translation and Foreword by Susan Hanson

Theory and History of Literature, Volume 82

University of Minnesota Press, Minneapolis and London

The University of Minnesota gratefully acknowledges the funding provided by the French Ministry of Culture for translation of this book.

Copyright 1993 by the Regents of the University of Minnesota
Originally published as *L'Entretien infini*. Copyright 1969 by Editions Gallimard.

Published by the University of Minnesota Press
111 Third Avenue South, Suite 290, Minneapolis, MN 55401-2520
Printed in the United States on acid-free paper

http://www.upress.umn.edu

Third Printing 1999

Library of Congress Cataloging-in-Publication Data

Blanchot, Maurice.
    [Entretien infini. English]
    The infinite conversation / Maurice Blanchot ; translation and foreword by Susan Hanson.
      p.   cm. — (Theory and history of literature : v. 82)
    Includes bibliographical references and index.
    ISBN 0-8166-1969-7 (acid-free paper).
    ISBN 0-8166-1970-0 (pbk. : acid-free paper)
    1. Literature—History and criticism—Theory, etc. I. Title. II. Series.
PN81.B54413 1993
809—dc20

92-16563

The University of Minnesota is an
equal-opportunity educator and employer.

Contents

II. THE LIMIT-EXPERIENCE

III. THE ABSENCE OF THE BOOK
(the neutral, the fragmentary)

This mad game of writing.
                                              (Mallarmé)

"But why two? Why two instances of
speech to say the same thing?"
— "Because the one who says it is always
the other."

"The neutral, the neutral, how strangely
this sounds for *me*."

"Because, for us, something might appear in the heart of the day that would not
be the day, something in an atmosphere of
light and limpidity that would represent the
shiver of fear out of which the day came?"

*Speaking is a fine madness; with it man
dances over and above all things.*
                                              (Nietzsche)

Note

[handwritten margin note: devotion to or emphasis on beauty or cultivation of the arts]

Certainly there are always books published in every country and in every language, some of which are taken as critical works or works of reflection, while others bear the title of novel, and others call themselves poems. It is probable that such designations will endure, just as there will still be books a long while after the concept of book is exhausted. Still, this remark must be made: since Mallarmé (reducing the latter to a name and the name to a reference point), what has tended to render such distinctions sterile is that by way of them, and more important than they are, there has come to light the experience of something one continues to call, but with a renewed seriousness, and moreover in quotation marks, "literature." Essays, novels, poems seem only to be there, and to be written in order to allow the labor of literature (now considered as a singular force or a position of sovereignty) to accomplish itself, and through this labor to allow formulation of the question "What would be at stake in the fact that something like art or literature exists?" This question is extremely pressing, and historically pressing (I refer here to certain texts of *The Space of Literature* and *Le Livre à venir*, as well as to the pages entitled "Literature and the Right to Death"), but it is a question that a secular tradition of aestheticism has concealed, and continues to conceal. *[handwritten: worldly]*

I will not say we have gotten past this moment: this would have scarcely any meaning. Whatever we do, whatever we write—and the magnificent surrealist experience has shown this—literature takes possession of it, and we are still in the civilization of the book. Yet literary work and research—let us keep this qualifying adjective—contribute to an unsettling of the principles and the truths that are sheltered by literature. In correlation with certain possibilities offered by knowledge, by discourse, and by political struggle, this labor has caused to emerge, although not for the first time (inasmuch as repetition, the eternal going over again, is its very origin) but rather in a more insistent manner and as affirmed in these works, the question of language; then, through the question of language, the question that perhaps overturns it and comes together in a word that today is apparently and easily accepted, even rendered ordinary, but that only a few dozen years ago in its neutral simplicity was considered nearly unreasonable, even the most unreasonable: *writing, "this mad game of writing."*

Writing, the exigency of writing: no longer the writing that has always (through a necessity in no way avoidable) been in the service of the speech or thought that is called idealist (that is to say, moralizing), but rather the writing that through its own slowly liberated force (the aleatory force of absence) seems to devote itself solely to itself as something that remains without identity, and little by little brings forth possibilities that are entirely other: an anonymous, distracted, deferred, and dispersed way of being in relation, by which everything is brought into question—and first of all the idea of God, of the Self, of the Subject, then of Truth and the One, then finally the idea of the Book and the Work— so that this writing (understood in its enigmatic rigor), far from having the Book as its goal rather signals its end: a writing that could be said to be outside discourse, outside language.

Yet another word of elucidation or obfuscation. When I speak of "the end of the book," or better "the absence of the book," I do not mean to allude to developments in the audio-visual means of communication with which so many experts are concerned. If one ceased publishing books in favor of communication by voice, image, or machine, this would in no way change the reality of what is called the "book"; on the contrary, language, like speech, would thereby affirm all the more its predominance and its certitude of a possible truth. In other words, the Book always indicates an order that submits to *unity*, a system of notions in which are affirmed the primacy of speech over writing, of thought over language, and the promise of a communication that would one day be immediate and transparent.

Now it may be that writing requires the abandonment of all these principles, that is to say, the end and also the coming to completion of everything that guarantees our culture— not so that we might in idyllic fashion turn back, but rather so we might go beyond, that is, to the limit, in order to attempt to break the circle, the circle of circles: the *totality* of the concepts that founds history, that develops in history, and whose development history is. Writing, in this sense—in this direction in which it is not possible to maintain oneself alone, or even in the name of all without the tentative advances, the lapses, the turns and detours whose trace the texts here brought together bear (and their interest, I believe, lies in this)—supposes a radical change of epoch: interruption, death itself—or, to speak hyperbolically, "the end of history." Writing in this way passes through the advent of communism, recognized as the ultimate affirmation—communism being still always beyond communism. Writing thus becomes a terrible responsibility. Invisibly, writing is called upon to undo the discourse in which, however unhappy we believe ourselves to be, we who have it at our disposal remain comfortably installed. From this point of view writing is the greatest violence, for it transgresses the law, every law, and also its own.

M.B.

± ± *His feeling, each time he enters and when he studies the robust and courteous, already aged man who tells him to enter, rising and opening the door for him, is that the conversation began long ago.*

A little later, he becomes aware that this conversation will be the last. Hence the kind of benevolence that emerges in their talk. "Have we not always been benevolent?" — "Always. Yet we are to be asked to bring proof of a more perfect benevolence, unknown to us as yet: a benevolence that would not be limited to ourselves." — "Nor that is content with extending itself to everyone, but maintains itself in face of the event in regard to which benevolence would not be fitting." — "The event that we promised to evoke today."

As always, one of the two awaits from the other a confirmation that, in truth, does not come, not because accord would be lacking, but because it was given in advance: this is the condition of their conversation.

± ± *He tells him to enter, he stays near the door, he is weary, and it is also a weary man who greets him; the weariness common to both of them does not bring them together.*

"As if weariness were to hold up to us the preeminent form of truth, the one we have pursued without pause all our lives, but that we necessarily miss on the day it offers itself, precisely because we are too weary."

± ± *They take seats, separated by a table, turned not toward one another, but opening, around the table that separates them, an interval large enough that an-*

other person might consider himself their true interlocutor, the one for whom they would speak if they addressed themselves to him: "Forgive me for having asked you to come to see me. I had something to say to you, but at present I feel so weary that I'm afraid I will be unable to express myself."—"You are feeling very weary?"—"Yes, weary."—"And this came upon you suddenly?"—"To tell the truth, no, and if I even took the liberty of calling you, it was because of this weariness, because it seemed to me that it would facilitate the conversation. I was even entirely sure of this, and still now I am almost sure of it. Only I had not realized that what weariness makes possible, weariness makes difficult."

He has to do with a person who expresses himself with such difficulty that for the moment he could not contradict him; besides, he does not wish to.

He asks him, he would like to ask him: "And if you were not as weary as you say you are, what would you say to me?"—"Yes, what would I say to you?" he repeats suddenly, almost gaily; a gaiety that he, in turn, cannot help pretending to share. Then, after what had seemed to him gaiety and is perhaps only liveliness, there follows a silence he must break. He would like to apologize for this pressure he exerts upon him in questioning him against his will, but he thinks he would exert it in any case, whether he question him or not, from the very moment he is present. "Yes," he resumes, "what would we say?" His interlocutor bows his head, as if he were growing heavy and preparing to sleep—and it is true that he gives the impression, because of his powerful frame, of being not weary but powerful, and also of giving to weariness the breadth of his power. A little later, and without raising his head, he asks: "What were we saying?" This time he appears wide awake.

"I'll come back. I believe you should rest just now."—"Yes, I need to rest, but we must first arrange to meet." Then he adds: "You are no less weary than I, perhaps more so." From which he concludes, smiling: "Weariness is generous."—"Yes, indeed it is; I wonder how we would get on otherwise; but do we get on?"—"One might ask oneself, and perhaps reply that, on the whole, we get on fairly well." Each of them laughs at this. "Yes, we get on fairly well." One of them stands up, as though strengthened by this reassurance; he turns aside almost abruptly, in a way that provokes a disturbance in the small room. He is turning toward the shelves where—one notices now—books are arranged in great number, in an order perhaps more apparent than rigorous, but which explains no doubt why even someone familiar with the room would not discover them at first sight. He does not touch a single volume, he stays there, his back turned and utters in a low but distinct voice: "How will we manage to disappear?"

In a low but distinct voice, as if night, settling around them with its rumor—it is broad daylight, he could recognize this—obliged him to reply: "Well, it would suffice for us . . ."—"No, it would not suffice . . ."

± ± From the instant that this word—a word, a phrase—slipped between them, something changed, a history ended; an interval should be placed between their

existence and this word, but the word always comprises this very interval, whatever it may be, and also the distance that separates them and separates them from it. They are always very conscious of this; it sometimes happens, through guile or through neglect, that they remain far from one another — it is easy, life keeps them apart. And when they stop seeing each other completely, when the city assigns them rounds of life that do not risk bringing them back together, they would be satisfied, if contentment were not also the manner in which the understanding of this word imposes itself upon them. They are not satisfied therefore, and this is enough to render vain both distance and forgetting.

± ± *There is a moment in the life of a man — consequently, in the life of men — when everything is completed, the books written, the universe silent, beings at rest. There is left only the task of announcing it: this is easy. But as this supplementary word threatens to upset the equilibrium — and where to find the force to say it? where to find another place for it? — it is not pronounced and the task remains unfinished. One writes only what I have just written, finally that is not written either.*

± ± *He remembers their conversation: he was questioning him in a weary manner; he seemed attentive, discreet, indifferent — he understood everything right away, this was visible; but on his face there was an expression of incuriosity, an inexpressive expression that was turning the words aside.*

± ± *"I asked you to come . . . " He stops an instant: "Do you remember how things happened?" The interlocutor reflects in turn: "I remember it very well." — "Ah, good. I was not very sure, finally, of having initiated the conversation myself." — "But how could I have come otherwise?" — "Friendship would have sent you." He reflects again: "I wrote to you, didn't I?" — "On several occasions." — "But did I not also call you on the telephone?" — "Certainly, several times." — "I see you want to be gentle with me. I am grateful. As a matter of fact, it's nothing new; the weariness is not greater, only it has taken another turn." — "It has several, I believe we know them all. It keeps us alive." — "It keeps us speaking. I would like to be able to state precisely when this happened, if only one of the characteristics of the thing did not make precision difficult. I can't help thinking of it." — "Well, then we must think of it together. Is it something that happened to you?" — "Did I say that?" And he adds almost immediately, with a force of decision that might justly be termed moving, so much does it seem to exceed his resources of energy: "Nothing that has happened," yet along with it this reservation: "Nothing that has happened to me." — "Then in my eyes it's nothing serious." — "I didn't say that it was serious." He continues to meditate on this, resuming: "No, it's not serious," as if he perceived at that instant that what is not serious is much more so. His interlocutor must feel it, and feel as well that he should do something to help him. "Well,*

*if it is not serious, then talking about it cannot be either." He looks at his friend—
two weary men, that is to say, not weary, but distant, as two weary men can be.
And no doubt this is what he awaits, that he tell him once more: "I am not weary,"
but the conversation brings him something else: "I have no secret for you, you
know this; it's just that I wasn't certain you would come."—"Yet I have never
missed a single meeting."—"Indeed, you have been the truest friend, but tell me
if you didn't happen to hesitate in coming."—"Now I might hesitate. But I came,
nothing else matters."—"Yes, you came." Each of them listens to this word spoken
with benevolence, with honesty. And both feel as though they are watched over
by the conversation's own benevolence, obliged—an obligation difficult in its
gentleness—to withdraw into it. Each time, they hear (how could they not hear
them?) these words that form for the instant the background against which all
words still stand out: weary or benevolent, we understand one another. Understanding that opens suddenly to this speech where nothing is expressed—hardly
more than a murmur: "I don't know what's to become of me." This reechoes softly.
It does not let itself be disturbed. And softly too he asks: "But tell me, what has
happened?" and in the same way receives the response: "What had to happen,
something that does not concern me." At once he is struck by the manner in which
this statement remains at a distance; it is not solemn, it makes hardly any call
upon him; it does not change the late morning light. He knows that it is, after all,
only a sentence, and that it would be better not to translate it into this other that
nevertheless he cannot refrain from offering: "Do you want me to understand that
this might concern me?"—"It concerns neither one of us." The silence has a
character to which he does not attend, given up entirely to the impression that
a threshold has been crossed, a force of affirmation broken, a refusal thrust aside,
but also a challenge issued—not to him, the benevolent interlocutor, but impersonally, or—yes, it is strange—to someone else, to the event in which precisely
neither one is involved. He would like to be able to keep himself at a distance in
order better to reflect on this, and it seems to him he will have the time for this,
as though he had been forgotten, that is, as though he had to confront this forgetting in order to think of it. It is true—does he think of it later, does he think of
it now?—that he feels temporarily abandoned by the conversation, of which there
subsists only the absence, an absence itself also benevolent. Perhaps this continues, but perhaps what follows comes immediately, what he is now ready to
hear: "This concerns neither one, this concerns no one."—"Is this what you wanted
to tell me?" The other gives him a pained look: "I didn't want to, and still now I
do not want to." After which he is silent in a way that can only mean: help me,
you must help me.*

*Both are thoughtful enough to realize that they should not remain there, one
(so he supposes) because he now feels the need to speak, the other for a reason
he does not delay in expressing: "Why did you not want to?"—"You know very
well," and then he adds softly: "I feared compromising you." For an instant he ac-*

cepts this idea, if only to make it lighter: "Well, now there is no place for that fear. Have we not, since we met, been engaged together, bound to lend assistance to one another, as before the same arbiter?"—"Engaged together?"—"Engaged in the same discourse."—"True, but because of this also we must take heed. I am aware of my responsibilities."—"As I am also, in regard to you."—"You are, it would be unfriendly not to recognize it, but up to a certain point." He questions himself about this limit, then he ceases to question: "You mean, inasmuch as we speak. That's right, speaking is the last chance remaining for us, speaking is our chance."—"You would not listen to me, if I spoke."—"But I listen." — "I too listen."—"Well, what do you hear?" They remain always facing one another, yet turned away, each looking at the other only from a great distance: "You asked me to come so that we might talk about it."—"I asked you to come in order not to be alone in thinking about it." "But," he adds with a faint gaiety, "I have never been alone since I have been thinking of it. I will never again be alone."—"I understand."—"Yes, you understand," he says sadly, adding almost immediately: "You know, I have been very weary for some time. You mustn't pay too much attention to what I might say. It is weariness that makes me speak; it is, at the very most, the truth of weariness. The truth of weariness, a weary truth." He stops, looking at him with a sly smile. "But weariness must not prevent you from having confidence in the one with whom you share this truth."—"You know very well that I have confidence in you; there is nothing else left to me."—"You mean that weariness perhaps also wears away the power to confide."

Speaking wearies him, it is visible. However, he would not speak (to me) were he not weary.

"It seems that, however weary you may be, you still accomplish your task, quite properly. One might say that not only does weariness not impede the work, but the work demands this being weary without measure."—"This is not only true of me, and yet, is it weariness or unwearying indifference to weariness?"—"To be weary, to be indifferent, they are no doubt the same thing."—"Indifference, then, would be something like the meaning of weariness."—"Its truth."—"Its weary truth." They each laugh at this again, the space freed for an instant, where he hears a bit later in the silence, and as though it had been necessary for him to be silent in order to say it: "Promise me you will not draw away too soon."

± ± The conversation, he notices, assists them with its own benevolence, however difficult it is to pursue on account of their mutual weariness. It assists them, it allows them to say nothing that preoccupies them. True, there remains the slight concern regarding their carefree conversation.

To be sure, their conversation is held at a distance from them, under the discreet supervision of general speech, the speech that bears the law and is such that no aggression, by intent or by deed, can arise against it.

± ± *"I suppose I should have been concerned about this situation earlier."—"It seems to me that you have always attended to it."—"In a certain way that is true, but in this unceasing preoccupation there was the concern over not having attended to it earlier."*

± ± *He recalls in what circumstances the circle was traced as though around him—a circle: rather, the absence of a circle, the rupture of that vast circumference from which come the days and nights.*

Of this other circle, he knows only that he is not enclosed within it, and, in any case, that he is not enclosed in it with himself. On the contrary, the circle being traced—he forgets to say that the line is only beginning—does not allow him to include himself within it. It is an uninterrupted line that inscribes itself while interrupting itself.

Let him admit for an instant this trace traced as though in chalk and certainly by himself—by whom otherwise?—or else by a man like him, he does not differentiate. Let him know that it disturbs nothing in the order of things. Let him sense, nevertheless, that it represents an event of a particular kind—of what kind he does not know, a game perhaps. Let him remain motionless, called upon by the game to be the partner of someone who is not playing . . .

And sometimes addressing himself to the circle, saying to it: Try once, indifferent circle, if only for an instant, to close up again, so that I know where you begin, where you end.

Be this circle—the absence of a circle—traced by writing or by weariness; weariness will not permit him to decide, even if it is only through writing that he discovers himself weary, entering the circle of weariness—entering, as in a circle, into weariness.

± ± *Everything began for him, when everything seemed to have come to an end, with an event from which he could not free himself; not that he was obliged to think of it constantly or remember it, but because it did not concern him. He only perceived, and no doubt well after it had come about—so long a time that he preferred to place it, and perhaps with reason, in the present—that something had happened—something apart from the glowing history, rich with meaning yet motionless in which everyone was taking part—by noting, among the innumerable facts and great thoughts that were soliciting him, the possibility that this had occurred, not without his knowledge—of necessity, he knew—but without his being interested.*

± ± *Everything begins for him—and at this moment everything seemed to have come to an end—with an event from which he cannot free himself, because this event does not concern him.*

An event: what nevertheless does not arrive, the field of non-arrival and, at the same time, that which, arriving, arrives without gathering itself in some definite or determinable point—the sudden arrival of what does not take place as either a single or a general possibility.

What, then, is this event before which, weary, he would remain weary?

± ± *He wanted to speak to me, he found nothing to say. He alluded to his weariness and he urged me to ask him questions. But to my surprise, I had to recognize that I had forgotten how to question. In order not to worry him, I told him that we were too close to question each other usefully. "Yes," he said, "too close, that's it." And he seemed to draw away infinitely.*

± ± *Implicated in a speech that is exterior to him. "When you are there and we speak, I become aware that when you are not there I am implicated in a speech that could be entirely exterior to me."—"And you would like to say it to me in order not to be implicated in it alone."—"But I am not alone in it: in a certain way, I am not in it."*

"What is troubling you?"—"The fact of being implicated in a speech that is exterior to me."

± ± *"If you were not there, I believe I could not bear the weariness."—"And yet I also contribute to it."—"That is true, you weary me very much, but precisely very much, within human limits. Nevertheless, the danger is not averted: when you are there, I still hold on, I have the desire to spare you, I do not give up appearances entirely. This will not last long. I ask you, then, to go. Out of respect for weariness."—"I will go then."—"No, don't leave yet."*

Why does he give the name weariness to what is his very life? There is a certain imposture there, a certain discretion. In the same way, he can no longer distinguish between thought and weariness, experiencing in weariness the same void, perhaps the same infinite. And when thought and speech disappear one into the other, identical, not identical, it is as though weariness passed into another weariness, the same, nevertheless, to which, ironically, he gives the name rest.

Thinking weary.

The weariness grows insensibly; it is insensible; no proof, no sign altogether sure; at every instant it seems to have reached its highest point—but, of course, this is a lure, a promise that is not kept. As though weariness kept him alive. For how long still? It is endless.

Weariness having become his sole way of living, with the difference being that the more he is weary, the less he lives, and yet living only through weariness.

If he rests, then weariness has already, in advance, taken possession of this rest.

It seems that at every instant he appears before his weariness: You're not as weary as all that, true weariness awaits you; now, yes, you are beginning to be weary, you are beginning to forget your weariness; is it possible for one to be as weary as this without offense? And never does he hear the liberating word: All right, you are a weary man, nothing but weary.

± ± *"The thought came to me that the reason for your friendship, perhaps its sole reason—and I could never say enough how constant, how disinterested it is—is what is most particular to me, my privileged part. But can one become attached to a weary man and only by reason of his weariness?"*

"I don't ask that weariness be done away with. I ask to be led back to a region where it might be possible to be weary."

± ± *"Friendship is given only to life itself."—"But it is a question of my life, which I do not distinguish from weariness, the difference being that weariness constantly goes beyond the limits of life." Weariness, so he calls it, but weariness does not leave him the resources that would allow him to call it thus legitimately.*

± ± *When he speaks of weariness, it is difficult to know what he is speaking of.*

Let us admit that weariness makes speech less exact, thought less telling, communication more difficult; does not the inexactitude proper to this state reach through all of these signs a kind of precision that would also finally serve exact speech by offering something to uncommunicate? But immediately this use of weariness again seems to contradict it, to render it more than false, suspect, which is in the way of its truth all the same.

Weariness is the most modest of misfortunes, the most neutral of neutrals; an experience that, if one could choose, no one would choose out of vanity. O neutral, free me from my weariness, lead me to that which, though preoccupying me to the point of occupying everything, does not concern me. —But this is what weariness is, a state that is not possessive, that absorbs without putting into question.

As long as you reflect upon what you call your weariness (1) you show complacency with regard to your weary self; (2) you miss your object, for you encounter no more than the sign of your intention; (3) you attenuate and efface it, drawing meaning and advantage from what is vain, you become interested instead of disinterested. —That is true, but only partially true: I do not reflect, I simulate reflection, and perhaps this manner of dissimulating belongs to weariness. I do not really speak, I repeat, and weariness is repetition, a wearing away of every beginning; and I not only efface, I increase as well, I exhaust myself in pretending to have still the strength to speak of its absence. —All of this is vain, quite true. You work, but at what is in vain. I leave you to work, then, since it is the only way for you to realize that you are incapable of working.

± ± *Do you really believe you can approach the neutral through weariness, and through the neutral of weariness, better hear what occurs when to speak is not to see? I do not believe it, in fact; I do not affirm it either. I am too weary for that. Only, someone says this close to me, someone I do not know; I let them talk, it is an inconsequential murmur.*

± ± *The neutral, the neutral, how strangely this sounds to* me.

± ± *The situation is like this: he has lost the power to express himself in a continuous manner, as one would properly, either by conforming to the coherence of a logical discourse through the succession of this intemporal time that belongs to a mind at work, to one seeking identity and unity, or by yielding to the uninterrupted movement of writing. This does not make him happy. Still, in compensation, he believes now and then that he has gained the power to express himself intermittently, and even the power to give expression to intermittence. Nor does this make him happy.*

It makes him neither happy nor unhappy, but seems to free him from any relation to a subject capable of happiness or liable to unhappiness.

When he speaks, he speaks like everyone, or at least so it seems to him; when he writes, he does so by following the paths that he has opened for himself, and without encountering more obstacles than in the past. What has happened then? He asks himself this, and from time to time he hears the reply: something that does not concern him.

± ± *The non-concerning. Not only what does not concern him, but what for itself is of no concern. Something illegitimate insinuates itself that way. As once, in the sadness of a knowing night, he could have evoked the foreign spirit simply by modifying a few terms; now he is himself evoked by a simple change in the play of words.*

± ± To live with something that does not concern him.

This is a sentence easily received, but in time it weighs upon him. He tries to test it. "To live"—is it really life that is involved? And "with"? Would not "with" introduce an articulation that precisely here is excluded? And "something"? Neither something nor someone. Finally, "this does not concern him" distinguishes him still too much, as though he were appropriating to himself the capacity to be discerned by this very thing that does not concern him. After that, what remains of the sentence? The same, immobile.

To live (with) what does not concern.

There are various ways of responding to this situation. Some say: we must live as though living did not concern us. Others say: since this does not concern, we must live without changing anything about life. But then others: you are changing, you are living non-change as the trace and the mark of that which, not concerning, could not change you.

± ± *This is a sentence of a somewhat enigmatic turn. He considers it to be scarcely coherent, uncertain, and of an insistence repugnant to him. It asks neither for acquiescence nor for refutation. In truth, that is its very mode of persistence: neither affirming nor withdrawing anything, despite the negative turn that puts him into difficulty with himself. All life has changed, life yet intact.*

He comes to understand that the sentence—which sentence is in question?—is there only to provoke intermittence, or through this intermittence to make itself signify, or give this intermittence some content; so that the sentence—is it a sentence?—besides its proper meaning, for it must surely have one, would have as its other meaning this intermittent interruption to which it invites him.

Interruption: a pain, a weariness.

While speaking to someone, he comes to feel the cold force of interruption assert itself. And strangely, the dialogue does not stop; on the contrary, it becomes more resolute, more decisive, yet so hazardous that their relation to the common space disappears between them forever.

± ± *You know very well that the only law—there is no other—consists in this unique, continual, universal discourse that everyone, be he separated from or united with others, be he speaking or silent, receives, bears, and sustains through an intimate accord prior to any decision; an accord such that any attempt to repudiate it, promoted or willed always by the very will of discourse, confirms it, just as any aggression makes it more sure and any arrest makes it endure. —I know. — You know, then, that when you speak of these interruptions during which speech would be interrupted, you do speak of them, immediately and even in advance returning them to the uninterrupted force of discourse. —When they occur I am silent. —If they occurred in such a way that you should once have to be silent, you would never again be able to speak of them. —Precisely, I do not speak of them. — Then what are you doing at this moment?—I am saying that I do not speak of them.*

I know all of this, I know it better than you, since if I am the supposed guardian of this speech, instituted and brought forth by it, you are but the guardian of this guardian, instituted and brought forth by him.

± ± *Of what do you complain, silence without origin? Why come here to haunt a language that cannot recognize you? What draws you among us, into this space where the brazen law has forever asserted itself? Is it you, that plaint not yet heard?*

± ± *The difficulty would be the following. This is not an incident of simple interruption, even if it offered itself at the start as accidental; it has, and, fundamentally, it has always had, a certain obligatory character; true, a very discreet obligation, one that does not impose itself. Still, it demands respect on account of its very discretion. A kind of interdict is asserted this way, without one knowing* whether the proscription of the interdiction does not already travesty, in decreeing it, the pure arrest. This is already a concern. But here is another: this interrup tion—perhaps merely an ancient accident, though with a certain obligatory character and bearing in an enigmatic way the interdict—presents itself also as interdicted, a regrettable exception, a breach opened in the circle; and no doubt it necessarily still belongs to the rule, if only as an anomaly, a hypocritical anomaly—how can one express oneself in any other way, without laying oneself under an interdict?—but he is aware that, despite this legitimation, it still continues, and every time as it has forever, to fall outside the rule that holds it nevertheless within the field of its force.

The pure arrest, the sentence that interdicts, in such a way that there should intervene, by an unappointed decision, the time of the inter-dicting.

± ± He was listening to the speech of the everyday, grave, idle, saying everything, holding up to each one what he would have liked to say, a speech unique, distant and always close, everyone's speech, always already expressed and yet infinitely sweet to say, infinitely precious to hear—the speech of temporal eternity saying: now, now, now.

How had he come to will the interruption of discourse? And not the legitimate pause, the one permitting the give and take of conversation, the benevolent, intelligent pause, nor that beautifully poised waiting with which two interlocutors, from one shore to another, measure their right to communicate. No, not that, and no more so the austere silence, the tacit speech of visible things, the reserve of those invisible. What he had wanted was entirely different, a cold interruption, the rupture of the circle. And at once this had happened: the heart ceasing to beat, the eternal speaking drive stopping.

Foreword
This Double Exigency:
Naming the Possible, Responding to the Impossible

Susan Hanson

The beauty of *The Infinite Conversation* perhaps lies principally in the rigorous, coherent turn of Maurice Blanchot's thought, a thought whose concerted advance sets forth an array of themes and concepts that would seem to exceed the limits of any one writer. But the reach and rigor of this thought are not that of the system; it is not a matter of developing a unified theory or of encompassing a body of knowledge. The *entretien* Blanchot names in his title consists rather in a series of singular encounters with writers whose concerns are as varied as those of Heraclitus and Beckett. Each of these critical essays, marked by an extreme attention to the matter and texture of the writings (or lives) under consideration, effectively interrupts the whole it advances. Together with the meditative essays and dialogues contained in this volume, they punctuate a unique path of reflection that forms what Blanchot describes as "an uninterrupted line that inscribes itself while interrupting itself."

The place *The Infinite Conversation* occupies in Blanchot's work is itself singular. To be sure, it follows "Literature and the Right to Death," *The Space of Literature*, and *Le livre à venir* (as Blanchot remarks in his introductory Note), citing and continuing the reflections of these earlier texts with an almost astonishing persistence. But it also breaks with them in significant ways. This break is signaled most clearly by the emergence of the problematic of *autrui*—by the *address* of *autrui* as Blanchot responds to it throughout the text.[1] While the carefully worked through terms of the question of reflection that Blanchot brings out in his earlier critical writings in fact prepare the space of encounter with *autrui*, the thematization of *autrui* in this collection signals the intrusion of otherness with an urgency that is not heard in the earlier volumes. *The Infinite Conversation* therefore seems closer to Blanchot's fiction than do the earlier critical writings, as is also suggested by the essays written in the form of dialogue with a friend, an other, whose enigmatic presence adds yet another voice (or voices) to the conversation. Still another shift is marked by the fact that the dialogue between philosophy, ethics, and the space of literature here occupies a central site, marking a *between*-two or rift, out of which arises the appeal of *autrui*, and concerning not only thought, the work of the concept and of language, the writer and the work of art, but also the relations of human beings in the world.

Since the question of *autrui* will be taken up again further on, let us for the moment simply state that the encounter with the *other* can only take place "outside" discourse, inasmuch as this encounter is accompanied by (and entails) a "curvature of space" that alters the very nature of *being in relation*. As a consequence, relations of reciprocity and equality that tend toward unity (the unity guaranteed by that of the concept and the self-subject), hold in *the Infinite Conversation* only up to a certain point. The terms and interlocutory voices thereby encounter, or prompt—saying something that is heard again and again, not quite heard—a strangeness, an event, that the categories of reflection will measure, but are unable to account for. In order to situate the stakes of such an event, let us sketch out the part that specific other interlocutors, in fellowship and in friendship, have in its coming about.

It should first be said that Blanchot's thought, as that of other contemporary French thinkers whose names are now widely known, situates itself against the background of the concept of reflection as it develops from Descartes to Husserl. More precisely, it situates itself in relation to a rupture in the metaphysics of subjectivity that is discernible in various forms in the writings of Marx, Nietzsche, Freud, and Heidegger, and marked most demonstratively by the motifs of the "death of God" and the "death of man"—"ends" that both World Wars demonstrated in their frightening ways in the twentieth century.

One of the approaches Blanchot offers to this excess lies in the relations he defines between philosophy, poetry, and the space of literature. Let us take "The Great Refusal" (the fourth essay of the volume) as a beginning point—not fortuitously, as it stages explicitly a movement between philosophy and literature. In the course of a discussion that recalls the terms of "Literature and the Right to Death" (*death* and *negation* in particular), Blanchot names what he calls "the loss of death," a loss that poetry is said to respond to, and, in responding, affirms. Yet this loss is not simply a loss, nor the forgetting of the fact that we are mortal. The loss of death that occurs in naming and in the movement of the concept is a loss of the immediate, a loss of the presence of "what is," which is thus present only in its disappearance. A great deal is involved here; for one thing, each time I speak I affirm my power to do away with what I name, by naming it I master it, and cause it to disappear. My speech thus attests to the secret violence that haunts it, and that it sets loose in the world. Having introduced death into thought, I have also closed up the space where there might be a place for dying. What I have nonetheless gained is the power of the negative, the capacity to render absent, and this, as Blanchot writes, "in favor of a clear and defined coherence of notions, relations, and forms—the work of tranquil man." The "loss of this singular end" thereby entitles the life of the mind, the work of the concept. Death interiorized is now a power, the movement "through which meaning comes toward us, and we toward it."

It has long been the fate of philosophy to fear the unknown that inhabits this space opened by speech between being and a formless immediate, or between word and thing, but let us not go all the way back to Plato; Blanchot's interlocutors are for the moment Hegel, Bonnefoy, Heidegger, and Hölderlin, each of whom will question and respond to the others in the passages of "The Great Refusal" that concern us. By way of their dialogue, death will be linked to speech and to thought, and poetry will be shown to respond to the question that philosophy asks: the question of the whole, but also the question of the lack that is fundamental to speech, that speech turns into a power of thought, a thought in its turn captive to the One, to Unity.

The question Blanchot reads in Bonnefoy's commentary on the task (and the hope) of poetry is the following:

> The fact remains . . . that what "is" has disappeared: something was there that is there no longer. How can I find it again, how can I, in my speech, capture this prior presence that I must exclude in order to speak, in order to speak it? And here we will evoke the eternal torment of our language when its longing turns back toward what it always misses, through the necessity under which it labors of being the lack of what it would say.

What exactly disappears? The response initially offered to poetry's question is now accompanied by the names Baudelaire, René Char, and Hölderlin: "The sacred is 'immediate' presence"—"this body that passes," "this simple life flush with the earth": "the reality of sensible presence." But is this the answer? Is sensible presence what the speech of poetry seeks to capture? Heidegger, commenting on Hölderlin, will offer a further definition: "the immediate is the very thing that offers neither any hold nor stopping point, the terror of the immediate that defeats every grasp, the shattering of chaos."

Following Heidegger now, Blanchot suggests that what poetry affirms, in responding to this "loss," this "nothing" lost, is nothing other than poetry's response, its desire and capacity to respond. What it affirms is its imperative to say the "now,"[2] an event that no light, no day can illuminate, for the coming and the place of this now of speech is inaccessible to vision, to sight, except as a *between*: a space or a rift, once again, that opens between the affirmation of speech (poetry's speech) and that to which that affirmation responds (which forms the object of philosophy's question).

Perhaps after remarking this space, we now have a better sense of the "infinite" of *The Infinite Conversation*'s title, and of the "gifts" exchanged in the movement of questioning, responding, and affirming. In the case of poetry and philosophy, each works in the other's stead, suspending the identity of the other, interrupting their contrariety and setting it aside or out of work (*désoeuvré*). Affirmation and negation also slip from their place, past one another and away from us, nonetheless not saying the same thing (even if negation now affirms in its inability to negate itself) nor in the same way. The sign ($\pm \pm$),[3] then, of a manner saying, a writing *otherwise* that would have no stopping point. Thought will not give up nor will speech, as neither knows any rest.

In the Note to the reader, Blanchot characterizes *writing* as "the aleatory force of absence": it is a "writing that remains without identity, and little by little brings forth possibilities that are entirely other: an anonymous, distracted, deferred, and dispersed way of being in relation by which everything is brought into question." Let us borrow this affirmation regarding writing and being in relation to describe the moves of exchange we just read in "The Great Refusal" in relation to death and the immediate, philosophy and poetry—noting that if we are to speak of an exchange, we must think of it as an exchange withdrawn from all exchange inasmuch as such a writing *of* and *in* this space between corresponds to "a writing that could be said to be outside discourse, outside language." "Outside discourse" would mean that what occurs in this "now" of the "between-two" pitches the interlocutors into a speech that is itself anonymous (neutral); into a dialogue where for the subject who speaks it is not a matter of winning, of seeking to settle the differences between the speakers, or to fuse them into one. This is a speech that does not tend toward unity, does not unify. Nor is it a matter of convincing the other, of having the last word so as to prevail or bring the conversation to an end: *infinite*, then, in the sense that each turn the *entretien* takes interrupts it, and moves it elsewhere, reopens it to an otherness that haunts the very limits of language. (*Conversation* is thus understood as a turning toward and with, while *entretien* in French suggests a holding up, a supporting and maintaining, a between that is rigorously held to: a keeping up of speech, that is, a keeping to the rift or opening that both permits and interrupts speech—its gift but also its shadow.)

Let us determine more clearly what would set us "outside discourse," "outside language." This space of the outside, in Blanchot's terms, is defined by the work that language and discourse accomplish in the world; a world governed by the light of the day, and that tends toward unity, identity, and the attendant notions of dialectical struggle and accomplishment.[4] By contrast, an infinite holding to a plural (anonymous and neutral) speech would open onto an outside of speech and language wherein these would abandon their work, and no longer answer to the demand for unity (or homogeneity) of the concept and the self-subject. The between of the several discursive spaces of "The Great Refusal" thus points to a truth that is *other*; in passing from interlocutor to interlocutor, never dwelling or detained, it continues on, but each time setting out anew. Blanchot can thus affirm that a limit has been passed: the limit at which "the idea of a Self, of the Subject, then of Truth and the One, then finally the idea of the Book and the Work" are abandoned.

Recalling the relation of speech to death, it is notable that this infinite and plural holding to speech that *The Infinite Conversation* makes heard in a strangely insistent *"now"* brings the book itself to the limit at which it encounters its own "death," the limit beyond which it disappears. As it happens, the heartbeat of one of the interlocutors of the first untitled dialogue will cease, soon after one (looking around the room, full of books, in which two men are speaking of weariness) asks the other, "How will we manage to disappear?"

Let us set next to the question concerning disappearance this other one, which is very like it: "Would man have to disappear in order to communicate?" The word *communication*—pointing to a linguistic structure outside or beyond what we mean by this term as it is generally used—recalls by their common radical, and by the strange temporality that accompanies them, the word *communism*, which sounds so strangely in the Note to the reader: it, too, having already occurred, already passed or passing, not yet having come, still to come. Death or disappearance—that of man, consequently of men—can also be understood as a kind of promise, a fervent vow or exigency: "the unhoped for of all hope" that is tied to "the impossible," that to which "the day breaks" of Hölderlin's desiring speech (the "gift" of poetry) responds.

"The Great Refusal" would in this sense announce the chapters that follow it and that conclude Part I. Each of these is written in response to the thought of Lévinas; indeed, we may say that Blanchot's reading of *Totality and Infinity* moves the *entretien* to one of its central concerns: the exigency of *autrui*, and the attendant notions of the "non-concerning," the neuter or the neutral. But the encounter with *autrui*, prepared in the opening chapters of the volume, also reappears in the central essays of Part II, which hold to the same path of thought. "The same path," once again, that consists in holding to a *between* of speech that in its multiple divergences gives this path an almost musical complexity. What is said by the return of refrains and chords is repeated again and again, but each time as a fragment referring to no whole or system. As the melody turns it disappears, only to return again, so as to make something like a song audible beyond hearing.

It is perhaps in this sense also that nearly every phrase of the untitled opening dialogue is cited in the essays that follow it (unless it can be said to cite in advance what is to come), thereby finally ruining the idea of accord or beginning, except as an endless replaying or reworking of a movement or refrain. As though to take up the beating of the heart that ceases keeping time at the end of the first dialogue, the text continues to speak—thus remarking the death or the limit experience to which it attends.

But let us begin again, taking up the question of the place of *autrui*, which in the central chapters of Part II seems essential. I shall not dwell long on this, for *autrui* and the thematic branching out that this word entails should be left to radiate at the center of the volume. To speak too simply, too long, or too eloquently would in any case place too much or too little value on what cannot be separated out from the movement of thought and of writing that are inseparable from Blanchot's considerations of *autrui*. The fact that this site is also not one, but consists in a moving outward, a *rayonnement* from a point always central and always moving, makes the search for a center an infinite task. Let us nonetheless say that the question of *autrui* cannot be posed apart from the question of human relations: "of what there is between man and man when nothing brings them together or separates them but themselves." The question of "man" would therefore be a "universal" question, but also a question—*man* as a question—that situates this thought at a turning point: a "now," however mobile it may be, wherein what are often called "the master narratives" have more or less fallen into ruin.

I shall take Blanchot's phrase "man is the indestructible that can [nonetheless] be destroyed" as a sign that the "question of man" (or the question of the human) indicates also the nature of the difficulty of the appeal that comes to man from *autrui*. For *autrui* is both man and other than "man." Since he has fallen below even the level of need, he is the one from whom we seem not to be able to get free, despite the fact that, on the whole, "man" is "getting on."

If "man" can be said to be "passing"—"getting on passably well" or "disappearing," depending on how one hears this expression—man as a *question* seems to call up a burden that a "we" collectively bears each time consideration is brought to the idea of the human, and when we consider the relations that exist between human beings in the world. In attempting to answer the question "who is *autrui* in relation to man?" one must perhaps say that *autrui* is "man," is still a human being, yet also an *other* to man, and other than any particular man or woman. These statements that fail to support one another are in fact irreconcilable, irreducible one to the other. As are the terms of the phrase "man is the indestructible that can be destroyed." Let us try to clarify this affirmation. It means two things. First, that humankind is capable of anything in its power to construct the world. Second, that "man" is a presence that persists even in the face of the greatest affliction; "man," human presence, in this sense cannot be done away with, even though individuals (and peoples) can be destroyed by other individuals. Man, then, is also capable of everything, since in harnessing and unleashing nuclear and other forms of energy (and in the power afforded by other technological advances) man has become capable of doing what, some fifty years ago, only the stars could do. But he is not capable of attaining the presence of the human itself.

What then of *autrui*? Inasmuch as *autrui* is the stranger, the unknown, the absolutely foreign, he offers no approach: beyond all horizon, he either looms over me or is situated so low that he becomes absolutely *other*. "Lost" through terror and oppression, he effectively disappears into the very conditions of affliction. He cannot appear as a subject and is bereft of even the power to struggle against the forces that render him powerless. *Autrui* addresses me, but as a "subject" he or she is essentially mute, outside speech as a power and invisible to the eye of justice.

Let us now return to the two formulations we set side by side: "Man is the indestructible that can [nonetheless] be destroyed" and "Would man have to disappear in order to speak?" Would this not suggest (to put it much too simply, and without reserve) that in the encounter with *autrui* no self-subject would be able to be present, as such? For my *self* is not able to respond to the appeal that *autrui* addresses to me unless I am set outside the horizon bounded by the world and by the categories that attend the relations that dialectical struggle and discourse imply. If *autrui*, having fallen away from his or her self, deported and deprived of speech, has already disappeared, that is, is no longer a self-subject, able to speak in the first person, then by the same token I, too, am only able to hear his appeal "outside" the first-person subject pronoun. Seized by the infinite distance that I am from what I can neither "think" nor "recognize," my" self" is disarmed, infinitely vulnerable and claimed by an otherness (by this *other*) that absolutely exceeds my power.

Autrui is "man without horizon," he who, coming from no land and errant, is dispossessed of any belonging, and he who, in his very dispossession—and herein lies the chance of this encounter and also of speech—dispossesses me. Since *autrui* is a stranger, also the guest, "the one who is coming," the encounter with *autrui* opens the space in which the unknown is encountered *as* unknown. *Autrui* "cites," calls up, the site of a between-two, between appearing and disappearing.

The essay "Being Jewish" presents a particular instance of the question of the relation to *autrui* inasmuch as it raises the question of the "relation of man with man," which, as Blanchot states, "defines in an implicit manner the relation of every man to himself." The terms *exodus* and *exile*, marking a relation to language, truth, and thought, are defined here by way of biblical reference, citation, and a reading of Judaic history. In the first part of the essay "The Indestructible," he writes: the idea of exile and the initiative that is exodus (which for Blanchot situate "being Jewish") exist "so that the experience of strangeness may affirm itself close at hand as an irreducible relation; it exists so that, by the authority of this experience, we might learn to speak." The event of a setting out, of beginning, is thus tied to the experience of strangeness, and placed at the very origin of speech—a speech that would not work to secure, like the concept, a dwelling place, but rather open a relation to the other and deliver humankind to a nomadic truth.

Lévinas, in *Sur Blanchot*, draws out this contrast or contrariety between a "rootedness in the land" (which he also terms "a paganism") and the movement of exile or exodus. While the themes of the pagan and the nomad require a more careful development, we may summarize Blanchot's use of this difference by noting that these words strike a particular chord or motif in Heidegger's work, as does the value Blanchot gives to exile or to the movement of setting out (a stepping *outside*), which breaks with, or brings out a difference with, Heideggerian thought.

The world, for Blanchot, the world *in* which, also *by* which I am necessarily in relation, always entails relations of force, power, and possession (exclusion and inclusion with homogeneity in view: one truth, one land, one people or horizon). A nomadic truth would therefore set itself outside relations of a firmly established property and identity, that is to say, also, outside the relations by which the self-subject—if only by the grasp that is comprehension, and through the security afforded by the homogeneity of the concept and of discourse—would secure its reign and its name.

> To be pagan is to be fixed, to plant oneself in the earth, as it were, to establish oneself through a pact with the permanence that authorizes sojourn and is certified by certainty in the land.

In contrast:

> There is a truth of exile and there is a vocation of exile; and if being Jewish is . . . a call to a sojourn without place, . . . it also ruins every fixed relation of force [and] answers to a foreign truth.

A "foreign truth," a truth causing us to set out and wander from home, would not, in Blanchot's terms, signify a privation. Rather, it would engage us in "an authentic manner of residing . . . that does not bind us to the determination of place or to settling close to a reality forever and already founded, sure, and permanent." Blanchot's distance from Heidegger at this point becomes more clearly articulated with the following question: "Why does errancy substitute for the domination of the Same an affirmation that the word Being—in its identity—cannot satisfy?" Inasmuch as identity and possession belong to a same principle or concept (are governed by a same law) there are human relations to which the law of the same, its rights and privileges—those of possession—do not answer.

As Blanchot recalls in "The Suppliant," the other, like *autrui*, comes from another country: he or she is without origin, foreign, but in this protected by the power of the divine. Precisely inasmuch as the stranger's or the guest's identity is open and unknown, he cannot be put out. He comes bearing a strange truth that one may not wish to receive, but a truth that cannot be set aside or done away with, precisely because it cannot enter the categories of the "known" or the "to be known."

Have we now come before the irreducible, the event of strangeness? Although this laborious attempt to name it has inevitably caused it to disappear, this is not the case in *The Infinite Conversation*. Its own dispersal and repeated return to the now of its speaking is the very space of *encounter*; a space whose reserve and silences give the text the breathing space, the pauses and interruptions whose infinite allows the text to say everything there is to say, but in an infinite curvature of space. A time between speaking wherein the world for an instant falls silent, and in whose disarming silence the reader is claimed by the appeal, the presence of something radically *other*. *Autrui*'s appeal to "man," "the infinite and infinitely silent presence of *autrui*," makes an address that by its questioning and disappearing presence haunts the text and the reader: a shadow on the wall, a plaint, a cry or a murmur, a desire—perhaps the unhoped for of hope that arises out of friendship for another human being, and out of a hope for what Blanchot has named "the impossible."

This appeal of the other that speech must bear, as it arises in a voice that is plural, and as an event that is impossible to say—and this is the gift of Blanchot's speech—can only arise in a neutral, intransitive speech, thus in a silence or reserve of speech that is heard only in an infinite speaking.

Notes

1. The word *autrui* has been left untranslated to distinguish it from *l' autre* (the other). *Autrui* designates other people, neighbor (*prochain*), fellow man. It is most generally used in French as a complement.

2. Hölderlin's lines, from "As on a holiday . . . ," "Wie wenn am Feiertage": "*But now the day breaks! I waited and saw it come. / And what I saw, the holy be my word.*"

3. We read in "Literature and the Right to Death": "this original double meaning, which lies deep inside every word [has the] strange effect [of] attract[ing] literature to an unstable point where it can indiscriminately change both its meaning and its sign . . . ; . . . but this disintegration is also a construction, if it suddenly causes distress to turn into hope and destruction into the element of the indestructible" (*Gaze of Orpheus*).

4. It must be emphasized that Blanchot in no way wishes to deny the essential place of discourse (that of dialectical accomplishment, of the whole), which must also be struggle in the world. We read in "The Indestructible": "the one who is dispossessed must be received not only as '*autrui*' in the justice of speech, but also placed back into a situation of dialectical struggle. . . . We always come back, then, to this double exigency." That is, to the exigency of *autrui*, but also to "the instance of a Self-Subject": "to the possibility of a Self become not only conscious of affliction as though this Self were in [*autrui*'s] place, but become responsible for it by recognizing in it an injustice committed against everyone"; thus to a "Subject who affirms itself as being the representative of a collective structure" and who can "find in this injustice the point of departure for a *common demand*."

Translator's Acknowledgments

I would like to thank those to whom this translation owes so much. Mary Beveridge and Kristin Strohmeyer of Drake University and Hamilton College libraries generously gave untold hours to the pursuit of elusive references. Christopher Dadian, Dennis Schmidt, and Richard Lockwood offered invaluable assistance with puzzling questions, making available to me the kinds of knowledge and informed hunches that come only from long devotion to a field of study. Without their expertise, and that of many others, countless puzzles would have remained without solution. My thanks go most of all to Christopher Fynsk, whose thoughtful attention to the manuscript as a whole could have been given by no other reader. I thank also the deans of Hamilton College and the Center for the Humanities at Drake University for the funds they provided for preparation of the manuscript. Without those who so generously gave of their time and support, this translation could not have come about.

I

PLURAL SPEECH

the speech of writing

I

Thought and the Exigency
of Discontinuity

Poetry has a form, the novel has a form;[1] research, the research in which the movement of all research is in play, seems unaware that it does not have a form or, worse still, refuses to question the form that it borrows from tradition. "Thinking," here, would be the same as speaking without knowing in which language one speaks or which rhetoric one employs, and without even sensing the meaning that the form of this language and this rhetoric substitutes for what "thought" would determine for itself. Specialized terms are sometimes used, concepts are forged for the sake of a particular field of knowledge, and this is legitimate. But the manner of conveying what is in question in research remains, generally, that of exposition. The scholarly, academic dissertation is the model.

These remarks hold above all, perhaps, for modern times. There have been important exceptions; one should first recall them, then attempt to interpret them. A task worthy of a long study. I will cite as examples, and as chance permits a memory that is not erudite, the ancient Chinese texts (which are among the most significant), certain texts of Hindu thought, and the early Greek language, including that of the dialogues. In Western philosophy, the *Summa* of Thomas Aquinas — through the rigorous form of a determinate logic and a mode of questioning that is actually a mode of answering — realizes philosophy as an institution and as a form of teaching. In contrast, Montaigne's *Essays* escape the demands of the thought that claims to have its place in the University. As for Descartes, if the *Discourse on Method* is important, be it only in its freedom of form, it is because this form is no longer that of a simple exposition (as in scholastic philosophy), but rather describes the very movement of a research that joins thought and existence in a fundamental experience: this being the search for a mode of progressing, that is, a method; this method being the bearing, the mode of holding oneself and of advancing of one who questions.

Let us pass over this history. Such inquiry, which I recommend to researchers, would be very instructive. But I will note something that is valid for the most diverse epochs: the form in which thought moves to encounter what it is seeking is often tied to teaching. This was the case for the most ancient thinkers. But Heraclitus not only teaches; it may well be that the sense of the *logos* that offers itself when he speaks is contained in the word "lesson," "the intelligent conversation," where something is said to several persons in view of all — a dialogue that nonetheless must take its place in the sacred institutional framework.[2] Socrates, Plato, Aristotle: here, teaching is philosophy. And what happens is that philosophy institutionalizes itself and then takes its form from the preestablished institution in whose framework it becomes instituted: Church and State. The seventeenth and eighteenth centuries demonstrate this with their striking exceptions, which are significant, among other reasons, for the fact that they mark a break with philosophy-as-teaching. Pascal, Descartes, and Spinoza are dissidents who do not have the official function of learning while teaching others. Pascal indeed writes an apology, a unified and coherent discourse designed to teach the truths of Christianity and to persuade the libertines of them, but his discourse, in the twofold dissidence of thought and death, reveals itself to be a dis-cursus — a broken, interrupted course that for the first time imposes the idea of the fragment as a form of coherence. In the eighteenth century (at least in France), it is the writer who will bear the destiny of philosophy itself. To write is to philosophize. Teaching is now the lively exchange of letters (as is already the case in the preceding century), the rapid circulation of libels, the distribution of pamphlets. Rousseau, finally, is the great philosopher, and a part of his discourse is dedicated to modifying pedagogical habits, for it is no longer man but nature that teaches.

The high period of philosophy, that of critical and idealist philosophy, will confirm the relations maintained with the University. From Kant onward, the philosopher is primarily a professor. Hegel, in whom philosophy comes together and accomplishes itself, is a man whose occupation is to speak from the height of a university chair, to prepare courses, and to think in conformity with the demands of this magisterial form. I say this without disparaging intent. The encounter of wisdom and the University has great significance. And it is clear that the necessity of being a philosopher in the capacity of professor, that is, of giving philosophical research the form of a continuous and developed exposition, is not without consequences. But what about Kierkegaard? Nietzsche? Yes, of course. Nietzsche, too, was a professor, but he then had to give up being one for various reasons, one of which is revealing: how could his venturous thought, a thought that realizes itself in fragments — in separate affirmations that demand separation — how could *Thus Spoke Zarathustra* have found a place in teaching and adapted to the requirements of academic speech? That noble manner of being together and thinking together according to the division of master and disciple, which the University (perhaps mistakenly) claims to maintain, is here refused. With Nietzsche, something unwonted comes to light,[3] as something unwonted had come to light when philosophy took up the mask of Sade, representing no longer the man *ex cathedra*, but the hidden man of the prisons. And yet the philosopher can no longer avoid being a professor of philosophy. Kierkegaard engenders great Academics. When, in 1929, Heidegger poses the question: "What is metaphysics?" he does so in an inaugural lesson at the University of Freiburg, and while bringing into question the community of professors and students formed by the technical organization of the Faculties (which he thereby challenges). And a large part of his writing is made up of courses and work for the university.[4]

One could reduce to four the formal possibilities that are available to the man of research: (1) he teaches; (2) he is a man of science and his knowledge is bound to the always collective forms of specialized research: psychoanalysis (a science of non-knowing), the social sciences, and basic scientific research; (3) he combines his research with the affirmation of political action; (4) he writes. Professor; man of the laboratory; man of praxis; writer. Such are his metamorphoses. Hegel, Freud and Einstein, Marx and Lenin, Nietzsche and Sade.

To say that these four ways of being have always been related (that Pythagoras teaches, elaborates a unitary theory of the universe and founds a kind of religious and political party), and thus to suggest that nothing ever changes, is to say nothing at all. Let us avoid this kind of weak association. It would be more important, and more difficult as well, to question the long-standing and constant relations of philosophy and teaching. At first sight one might respond: teaching is speaking, and the speech of teaching corresponds to an original structure, that of the master/disciple relation. On the one hand, it is a matter of oral communication in its specificity; on the other, a matter of a certain anomaly affecting what one might call (guarding against any suggestion of realism) interrelational space. We should understand that the philosopher is not merely one who teaches what he knows; and we should not be content with attributing to the master the role of example, or with defining his bond with the student as an existential one. The master represents a region of space and time that is absolutely other. This means that, by his presence, there is a dissymmetry in the relations of communication; this dissymmetry means that where he is the field of relations ceases to be uniform and instead manifests a distortion that excludes any direct relation, and even the reversibility of relations. The presence of the master reveals a singular structure of interrelational space, making it so that the distance from student to master is not the same as the distance from master to student—and even more, making it so that there is a separation, a kind of abyss between the point occupied by the master, point A, and the point occupied by the disciple, point B: a separation that will hereafter be the measure of every other distance and every other time. Let us say more precisely that the presence of A introduces for B, but consequently also for A, a *relation of infinity* between all things, and above all in the very speech that assumes this relation. The master is destined, then, not to smooth out the field of relations but to upset it, not to facilitate the paths of knowledge, but above all to render them not only more difficult, but truly impracticable—something that the Oriental tradition of the master shows rather well. The master offers nothing to be known that does not remain determined by the indeterminable "unknown" he represents, an unknown that affirms itself not through the mystery, the prestige, or the erudition of the teacher, but through the *infinite distance* between A and B. Knowing by the measure of the "unknown," approaching the familiarity of things while preserving their strangeness, relating to everything by way of an experience of the very *interruption* of relations is nothing other than hearing speech and learning to speak. The relation of master to disciple is the very relation of speech when the incommensurable becomes measure therein, and irre-lation, relation.

But, as one can well imagine, a double alteration threatens the sense of this strange structure. Sometimes the "unknown" is limited to being the whole of things not yet known (or nothing more than the object of science itself). At other times the "unknown" merges with the person of the master: then it is his own qual-ity, his value as example, his virtues as guru or zaddik (his master's transcen-dence), and no longer the form of the interrelational space of which he is but one of the terms, that become the source of wisdom. In both cases teaching ceases to correspond to the demands of research.

*

Let us retain from the preceding remarks two points. The unknown that is at stake in research is neither an object nor a subject. The speech relation in which the unknown articulates itself is a relation of infinity. Hence it follows that the form in which this relation is realized must in one way or another have an index of "curvature" such that the relations of A to B will never be direct, symmetrical, or reversible, will not form a whole, and will not take place in a same time; they will be, then, neither contemporaneous nor commensurable. One can see which solutions will prove inappropriate to such a problem: a language of assertion and answer, for example, or a linear language of simple development, that is to say, *a language where language itself would not be at stake.*

But what is striking, and also comprehensible, is that solutions are sought in two opposing directions. One entails the demand for absolute continuity and a lan-guage that might be called spherical (as Parmenides first proposed). The other en-tails the exigency of a discontinuity that is more or less radical, the discontinuity of a literature of fragments (this solution predominates in the Chinese thinkers, as in Heraclitus; Plato's dialogues also refer to it; Pascal, Nietzsche, Georges

Bataille, and René Char demonstrate its essential persistence and, what is more, the decision that paves its way). That these two directions should impose themselves in turn finally becomes quite understandable. Let us return to the master/disciple relation, insofar as it symbolizes the relation that is at stake in research. This relation is such that it involves the absence of a common measure, the absence of a common denominator, and thus, in some sense, the absence of relation between the terms: an exorbitant relation. Hence the concern for marking either the interruption and the rupture or the density and the plenitude of this field resulting from difference and tension. One can see as well, however, that continuity risks being merely the continuity of simple development, thus eliminating the irregularity of the "curvature," or that discontinuity risks being the simple juxtaposition of indifferent terms. Being merely a continuity of surface rather than volume, continuity is never continuous enough; and discontinuity, never arriving at more than a momentary discordance rather than an essential divergence or difference, is never discontinuous enough.

With Aristotle the language of continuity becomes the official language of philosophy. But this is the continuity, on the one hand, of a logical coherence reduced to the three principles of identity, contradiction, and excluded middle (it is consequently a coherence of simple determination); on the other hand, this continuity is neither really continuous nor simply coherent insofar as the Corpus of knowledge instituted by Aristotle is but a poorly unified whole, a disparate sum of expositions assembled together.[5] One must therefore await the Hegelian dialectic for continuity—a continuity engendering itself, moving from the center to the periphery, from the abstract to the concrete, being no longer simply the continuity of a synchronic whole, but adding to itself the "parameter" of duration and history—to constitute itself as a totality that is finite and unlimited, that moves according to the circular demand corresponding at once to the principle of understanding, which is satisfied only by identity through repetition, and to the principle of reason, which requires an overcoming through negation. Here, as one can see, the form of the research and the research itself coincide, or should coincide, to the closest degree. Moreover, the speech of dialectics does not exclude, but seeks to include the moment of discontinuity: it moves from one term to its opposite, for example, from Being to Nothingness. But what is *between* the two opposites? A nothingness more essential than Nothingness itself—the void of an interval that continually hollows itself out and in hollowing itself out becomes distended: the nothing as work and movement. Of course the third term, that of synthesis, will fill this void and close the interval; in principle, nonetheless, it does not do away with it (since everything would be immediately arrested), but rather maintains it by accomplishing it, realizes it in its very lack, and thus makes of this lack a capacity, another possibility.

A manner of progressing so formally decisive that philosophy seems compelled to come to rest in its movement. Nonetheless, several difficulties immediately shatter this form. First, the role of discontinuity is revealed to be insufficient. Two opposites, because they are simply opposed, are still too close to one another—contradiction does not represent a decisive separation: two enemies are already bound in a relation of unity, while the difference between the "unknown" and the familiar is infinite. Therefore, in the dialectical form, the moment of synthesis and reconciliation always ends by predominating. Formally, this elimination of discontinuity translates into the monotony of a three-step development (replacing the classical rhetoric of the three parts of discourse), while institutionally it leads to the identification of Reason and State and to the coincidence of Wisdom and the University.

This last trait is not secondary. The fact that the Sage agrees to disappear into the institution, the *Universitas* as it is organized in the nineteenth century, is significant. The University is now nothing more than a sum of determinate bodies of knowledge having no relation with time other than that of a program of studies. The speech that instructs is in no way the speech that the master/disciple structure revealed to us as liable to open upon a fundamental rupture; it is rather content with a tranquil discursive continuity. The competent master speaks before an interested audience, that is all. Evoke the leveling of relations that the slightly elevated position of the lecturer before a group of docile students introduces into philosophical language, and one will begin to understand how the philosopher, now a professor, brings about an impoverishment of philosophy so visible that dialectics cannot fail to break with what appears to it to be the idealism of speech in order to arrive at the more serious divisions of revolutionary struggle.

*

One of the questions posed to the language of research is thus bound up with this demand for discontinuity. How can one speak so that speech is essentially plural? How can the search for a plural speech be affirmed, a speech no longer founded upon equality and inequality, no longer upon predominance and subordination, nor upon a reciprocal mutuality, but upon dissymmetry and irreversibility so that, between two instances of speech, a relation of infinity would always be involved as the movement of signification itself? Or, again, how can one write in such a way that the continuity of the movement of writing might let interruption as meaning, and rupture as form, intervene fundamentally? For the moment, we will put off approaching this question. Let us simply remark that any language where it is a matter of questioning rather than responding is a language already interrupted—even more, a language wherein everything begins with the decision (or the distraction) of an initial void.

But let us note as well that writing—whether of an essay or a novel—runs the risk of contenting itself with a supposed continuity that will in fact be nothing but a pleasant interlacing of upstrokes and downstrokes. In the text I am writing at this moment, sentences follow one another and link up more or less as they should. The paragraph divisions are no more than convenient breaks; there is a sustained movement designed to facilitate the course of reading, but this movement cannot pretend to correspond to a true continuity. Let us recall that, in modern literature, the preoccupation with a *profoundly* continuous speech is what first gave rise—with Lautréamont, with Proust, then with surrealism, then with Joyce—to works that were manifestly scandalous. An excess of continuity unsettles the reader, and unsettles the reader's habits of regular comprehension. When André Breton opens the space of our books to what he terms *"absolute continuity,"* and when he calls upon the writer to trust *"the inexhaustible character of the murmur,"* if he thus disrupts our manner of reading it is because the mind, with its measured and methodical gait, cannot stand up to the immediate intrusion of the totality of the real (a real that is precisely the impossible continuity of the "real" and the "imaginary"). Yes, as always, the surrealist ambition helps us a good deal in understanding what is at stake in this play. Automatic writing would assure the immediate communication of what is. It not only assures it—in its substantial continuity, automatic writing is the absolute continuity of what is. It is this imaginarily; a marvelous search for immediation. (From this, perhaps, arises the misunderstanding that has related this movement to the Hegelian movement, though no philosopher is more hostile to the seductions of the immediate than Hegel; it remains nonetheless true that both movements seek continuity, except that, for surrealist poetry, continuity can only be given immediately, while for Hegel it can only be attained: it is produced as a result.)[6] But one discerns as well the postulate that would appear to correspond to such an aspiring to absolute continuity: that reality itself—the ground of things, the "what is" in its essential depth—should be absolutely continuous. A postulate as ancient as thought.

This is the great Parmenidean sphere of Being, it is Einstein's model of the universe. From which it would follow that it is only the modalities of our knowing, the structures of our senses, of our instruments and the forms of our mathematical and non-mathematical languages, that force us to tear or to cut up this beautiful seamless tunic. But what does this mean? That one must see in discontinuity a sign of the adversity of understanding and analytic comprehension, and, more generally, an imperfection in the human structure, a mark of our finitude? Or should we dare an entirely different and very troubling conclusion that might be formulated in this way: why should not man, supposing that the discontinuous is proper to him and is his work, reveal that the *ground of things*—to which he must surely in some way belong—has as much to do with the demand of discontinuity as it does with that of unity? A troubling and an obscure conclusion that we will immediately try to make more precise by adding the following. When we speak of man as a non-unitary possibility, this does not mean that there would remain in him some brute existence, some obscure nature irreducible to unity and to the labor of dialectics: this is out of the question here. It means that, through man, that is, not through him but through the knowledge he bears, and first of all through the exigency of speech that is in advance always already written, it may be that an entirely different relation announces itself—a relation that challenges the notion of being as continuity or as a unity or gathering of beings; a relation that would except itself from the problematic of being and would pose a question that is not one of being. Thus, in this questioning, we would leave dialectics, but also ontology.[7]

II

The Most Profound Question

1

We ask ourselves about our time. This questioning is not pursued at privileged moments, but goes on without pause; it is itself part of time, harrying in the harrying manner that is proper to time. Scarcely a questioning, it is a kind of flight. Upon the background noise constituted by our knowledge of the world's daily course, which precedes, accompanies, and follows in us all knowledge, we cast forth, waking or sleeping, phrases that are punctuated by questions. Murmuring questions. What are they worth? What do they say? These are still more questions.

Where does this concern for questioning come from? And the great dignity accorded to the question? To question is to seek, and to seek is to search radically, to go to the bottom, to sound, to work at the bottom, and, finally, to uproot. This uprooting that holds onto the root is the work of the question. The work of time. Time seeks and tries itself in the dignity of the question. Time is the turning of times. To the turning of time corresponds the power to turn oneself back into question, into a speech that, before speaking, questions through the turn of writing.

In a certain way, then, it is time — the movement of time and the historical epoch — that questions? Time, but time as a question, as that which through time, and at a certain moment in time, brings forth the questions as a whole, and history as the whole of these questions. Freud more or less says that all of the questions randomly posed by children turn on and serve as relays for the one they do not pose, which is the question of the origin. We question ourselves about everything in the same way, in order to sustain and advance the passion of the question; but all questions are directed toward one question alone — the central question, or the question of the whole.

The question of everything as a whole, the question that bears all the questions combined.[1] We do not know whether these questions form a whole, nor if the question of everything, the one that includes all of the questions combined, is the ultimate question. The turning of time is the movement through which the question of everything is released. By emerging, by coming to the surface, the question uproots itself; and thus, having become superficial, it hides once again and preserves the most profound question.

We do not know whether these questions form a whole, but we know that they seem to question only when questioning in the direction of this whole whose meaning is not given, even as a question. To question, then, is to advance or to back up toward the horizon of every question. It is thus to place oneself in the impossibility of questioning by partial questions, to experience the impossibility of questioning in particular, despite the fact that every question is particular and even all the better posed the more firmly it answers to the particularity of its position. Every question is determined. Determined, it is the very movement by which the undetermined, in the determination of the question, still reserves itself.

A question is movement, the question of everything is a totality of movement and movement of everything. In the simple grammatical structure of interrogation, we already feel this opening of questioning speech — there is a demand for something else; incomplete, the speech that questions affirms that it is only a part. In which case, contrary to what we just said, the question would be essentially partial, it would be the place where speech is always given as incomplete. What would the question of everything signify, then, if not the affirmation that in the whole is still latent the particularity of everything?

The question, if it is incomplete speech, rests upon incompleteness. It is not incomplete as a question: on the contrary, it is speech that is accomplished by having declared itself incomplete. The question places the full affirmation back into the void, and enriches it with this initial void. Through the question we give ourselves the thing and we give ourselves the void that permits us not to have it yet, or to have it as desire. The question is the desire of thought.

*

Let us take two modes of expression: *"The sky is blue," "Is the sky blue? Yes."* One need be no great scholar to recognize what separates them. The "Yes" does not at all restore the simplicity of the flat affirmation; in the question the blue of the sky has given way to the void. The blue, however, has not dissipated. On the contrary, it has been raised dramatically up to its *possibility*: beyond its being and unfolding in the intensity of this new space, certainly more blue than it has ever been, in a more intimate relation with the sky, in the instant—the instant of the question where everything is in instancy. Yet hardly is the Yes pronounced, and even as it confirms in its new brilliance the blue of the sky brought into intimacy with the void, we become aware of what has been lost. Transformed for an instant into pure possibility, the state of things does not return to what it was. The categorical Yes cannot render what was, for a moment, only possible; still more, it withdraws from us the gift and the richness of possibility since it now affirms the being of what is, but affirms it in response, thus indirectly and in a manner that is only mediate. So in the Yes of the answer we lose the direct, immediate given, and we lose the opening, the richness of possibility. The answer is the question's misfortune, its adversity.

This means that it makes the adversity that is hidden in the question appear. This is even the unpleasant trait of the answer. It is not in itself unfortunate; it retains an assurance, its sign is a kind of haughtiness. The one who answers is implicitly superior to the one who questions. One says of a child who forgets the status of childhood that he talks back. Answering back is the question's maturity.

And yet the question demands a response? Certainly there is a lack in the question that seeks to be made up for. But this lack is of a strange kind. It is not the severity of negation: it does not do away with, it does not refuse. If it is a power wherein something negative exerts itself, this power takes up at a stage before the negative has reached a fully negative determination: *The sky is blue, is the sky blue?* The second phrase withdraws nothing from the first, or it is a withdrawal in the mode of a sliding, like a door turning upon its silent axis. The word "is" is not withdrawn; it is only lightened, rendered more transparent, committed to a new dimension. In some languages the interrogative is marked precisely by the promotion of the verb, which suddenly comes to the fore: *Is the sky blue? Ist der Himmel blau?* Here, with a kind of violence and suspect valor, the light falls upon being, which "comes into question" and by which the light of the question strikes all the rest. A rise in rank that resembles that of the stars, whose brilliance augments just before its end. The illuminating force that brings being to the fore, and that is like the appearance of a previously unapparent being, is at the same time what threatens to dissolve it. Questioning is the movement wherein being veers and appears as the suspension of being in its turning.

Hence the particular silence of interrogative sentences. It is as though being, in questioning itself—the "is" of the questioning—had abandoned its part of resounding affirmation, its decisive, negating part, and had freed itself, even where it emerges foremost, from itself: opening itself, and opening the sentence in such a way that, in this opening, the sentence seems no longer to have its center in itself but outside itself—in the neutral.

One might say that this is true of every sentence: each one pursues and completes itself in another. But the question is not pursued in the answer. On the contrary, it is terminated, closed again by the answer. The question inaugurates a type of relation characterized by openness and free movement; and what it must be satisfied with closes and arrests it. The question awaits an answer, but the answer does not appease the question, and even if it puts an end to the question, it does not put an end to the waiting that is the question of the question. Question, answer; between these two terms we find the joining of a strange relation: strange insofar as the question calls up what is *foreign* to it in the answer, and at the same time wants to maintain itself in the answer as the turn of the question that the answer arrests so as to put an end to this movement and allow rest. But the answer, in answering, must again take up within itself the essence of the question, which is not extinguished by what answers it.

2

We ask ourselves about our time. This questioning has its own characteristics. It is pressing: we cannot for an instant do without questioning. It is total, seeking only to bring to light in everything the question of everything. It bears upon our time, which bears it. Finally, we question ourselves in questioning this time.

This last trait has been brought into sharp relief. Every question refers back to someone who questions, that is to say, to the being we are and for whom alone exists the possibility of questioning, or of coming into question. A being like God (for example) could not put himself in question—he would not question; the word of God needs man to become the question of man. When after the Fall Jahweh asks Adam "Where are you?" this question signifies that henceforth man can no longer be found or situated except in the place of the question. Man is from now on a question for God himself, who does not question.

But why is it that, far from feeling ourselves questioned in this pressing, always total questioning—a questioning that bears upon our time and that is our possibility, coming from us and directed at us in every regard—we are, rather, caught in an unmeasured movement from which all questioning character seems to have disappeared? Why is it that when we question, it is already to the inordinate force of the question (a question that is no one's and that leads us to identify with no one) that—in the best of cases—we are responding? This is our experience of the most profound question. It calls us to task without concerning us. We bear it, we who are preeminently the bearers of the question, and yet it acts as though it had no bearing upon us. It is as though, in the question itself, we had to contend with what is other than any question; as though, coming only from us, it exposed us to something entirely other than us. A questioning that does not question, wants no response, and that seems to draw us into the irresponsibility and evasion of tranquil flight.

This can be indicated in another way: the personal capacity to question does not suffice. Mastery ceases to be an authentic manner of facing it. Even when expressed, this question is always implicit and handled rather than considered—disposing of us as we dispose of it and transforming us into its unskilled laborers. At the same time, it does not hide; questions abound, as do responses—everyone takes part. But this evidence and this multiplicity seem to be there only in order to turn us away from the whole of the questions, which then reaches us only through the suspicion we have of this very detour. (The question questions us in this detour that turns us from it, and from ourselves.)

Hence, when the question manifestly comes to affirm itself as the total question in all of the great dialectical movements that belong to our time, it disappoints us with its abstract poverty, a poverty that immediately reverses itself to become an exigency. For this abstraction is ourselves, it is our very life, our passion and our truth, each time it forces us to bear, impersonally, toward the general question that we bear. We suffer from this abstract, impersonal force; we are tormented by it, unhappy; we deem it poor, and it is poor. Even our abstract language exerts upon us a constraint that separates us cruelly from ourselves—and yet we must answer for this abstraction. And in it we recognize, questioning us, our general truth.

This does not suffice: this general truth, poor and abstract, making us poor and abstract, does not reach us as truth but as question, and in this question something more profound seems always to be at work: the most profound question, present in the very detour that turns us away from it and from ourselves. In other words, when we arrive at the end-point that is the question of everything, this question once again dissimulates itself in the question of knowing whether the question of the whole is the most profound.

*

This dispute between the question of the whole and the most profound question is the dispute that brings the dialectic into question. From the point of view of the dialectic these proceedings still belong to it: the most profound question is but a moment of the general question, the moment when the question believes that it is in its nature to elaborate an ultimate, a final question—question of God, question of being, question of the difference between being and what is. But for the dialectic there is no last question. Where we finish, we begin. Where we begin, we do not truly begin unless the beginning is once again at the term of everything, that is, unless the beginning is the result—the product—of the movement of the whole. This is its demand for circularity. Being unfolds as a movement turning in a circle; and this movement goes from the most interior to the most exterior, from the undeveloped interiority to the exteriorization that alienates it, and from this alienation that exteriorizes up to an accomplished and reinteriorized plenitude. A movement without end and yet always already completed. History is the infinite accomplishment of this movement that is always already realized.

reasoning
debate
discussion

The dialectic is thus always ready to begin with any particular question, just as one can begin speaking with any word. We have always already begun, always already spoken. This "always already" is the meaning of every beginning that is only a beginning again. Nevertheless, when we ask ourselves about our time, questioned in time and by time, we experience the impossibility of holding ourselves, in beginning, to a particular question. Today every question is already the question of everything. This general question—a question that leaves nothing out and constantly confronts us with everything, obliging us to interest ourselves in everything and only in everything with an exhausting, abstract passion—is present for us in all things; it is the sole presence, substituting itself for everything that is present. We no longer see men, we no longer handle things, we do not speak in particular words or singular figures; where we see men, it is the question of the whole that stares at us—this is what we are handling and what is handling us. It is what reaches us in every word, making us speak in order to put in question all of language, not allowing us to say anything without saying everything and everything together. When, therefore, we ask ourselves about our time, we first of all come up against the question of everything—which comes down to saying that the first question, the question against which we bear ourselves, head bowed rather than held high, is the question of the dialectic, the question of its validity and of its limits, or, to take up again the title of Sartre's book: the critique of dialectical reason.

An essential question and, rigorously speaking, even the only one—hence its rigor and its cruelty. But at the same time, it is not at all privileged, it is even challenged by the dialectic itself as a particular question. The dialectic, of course, does not have to be justified, just as it will not accept being given but a part: everything comes to it—it is this coming about of the whole. It is unjustified, then, in the sense that, being the movement through which it engenders itself by dissolving every particular justification, every demand for theoretical or immediate intelligibility, it affirms itself as the putting into question of everything—which cannot itself be put to the question since everything that contests it comes from it and falls back within this contestation whose self-accomplishing movement it is: a going beyond that cannot be gotten beyond.

But if every possibility passes by way of the dialectical imperative and passes only by way of it, what then of the most profound question? It is not at all disturbed by such omnipotence. It even requires that the dialectic have taken possession of everything, for it is most nearly itself when the whole, in order to be affirmed, has been withdrawn from it. *It is the question that is not posed.* When the dialectic reigns, gathering all things up in the one general question, when through its accomplishment everything has become question, then the question that is not posed poses itself. On the one hand, this question is only the shadow of the question of everything, the shadow of a question—the illusion that there is still questioning to be done when there is nothing more to be said; in this sense, the most superficial, the most misleading. On the other hand, this question is the most profound, because it seems that it can be thought and formulated only if we do not cease taking a step back toward that which still demands to be thought, even when everything, the whole, is thought.

This is just why "the most profound question" is always held back: held in reserve until that turning of time when the epoch falls and discourse is complete. With each change of epoch this question appears, momentarily, to emerge. With each revolution, it seems to merge so intimately with the historical question that it is beyond question: in one moment everything is affirmed, everything said – the general truth is there, deciding everything. But when, on the contrary, it becomes the object of a special problematic, when, as ultimate question, it is posed openly as the question of God or the question of being, this preeminence instead signifies its setting aside, its entry into a region where what is grasped of it allows it to escape. Thus we understand why today, when the dialectic takes possession of everything, this necessity of questioning that presses upon us by bearing us toward the question of the whole also presses upon us by insistently drawing us into this question that is not posed; a question we will call, in defiance, in derision and with rigor, the most profound question – or the question of the neutral.

3

If the Greeks were able to elaborate a form of question that has retained its value and authority for thousands of years, it is because the most profound question and the general question mutually seize and obscure one another therein.

Let us for a moment evoke the Sphinx as question and man as response. The being that questions is necessarily ambiguous: ambiguity itself questions. Man, when he questions, feels himself questioned by something inhuman and feels himself at grips with something that does not question. Oedipus before the Sphinx: at first appearance, this is man before non-man. All of the work of the question aims at leading man to the recognition that before the Sphinx, non-man, he is already before himself. Is the question thus posed – a question poised between the playful, the enigmatic, and the menacing, a question lacking seriousness yet backed up by the seriousness of what is at stake – the most profound question? In any case, a profound question. The profound question is man as Sphinx; that dangerous, inhuman, and sacred part that, in the face to face confrontation of an instant, arrests and holds arrested before it the man who with simplicity and self-satisfaction calls himself simply man. Oedipus's response is not only a response. It is the question itself, though with a change of meaning. When the Sphinx speaks in the language of lightness and danger that belongs to it, it is to give voice to the most profound question; when Oedipus answers, saying with assurance the one word that fits, it is to oppose to it man as the "question of everything." A memorable confrontation of the profound question and the general question.

We can recognize here some of the traits of both. The profound question is frivolous and frightening; it is distracting, attractive and mortal. Since it demands more than reflection it is addressed not only to the mind, and yet the head is what is aimed at: one must respond, the stakes being no less than capital. This is sensed immediately. It is fascinating, it reigns by the lure of its presence, which is the presence of something that should not be there—in *truth*, that is not there—and before which one cannot be, cannot abide, cannot hold oneself erect: the presence of an image that transforms you into the enigma of an image. The most profound question is such that it does not allow one to understand it; one can only repeat it, let it reverberate on a plane where it is not resolved but dissolved, returned to the void from which it arose. This is its solution: it dissipates in the very language that comprehends it.

An important victory. In an instant, the air clears. The crossroads, where open the paths descending toward the perfidious depths, give way to the space of sovereignty and a tranquil human reign. Nevertheless, we know what follows. The most profound question has disappeared, but disappeared into the man who bears it and into that word—man—by which he had answered. In responding humanly, Oedipus drew into the question of man the very horror to which he wanted to put an end. Certainly, he *knew* how to answer, but this knowing did no more than affirm his ignorance of himself, his answer being possible only by reason of this profound ignorance. Oedipus knows man as a general question because he is ignorant of man—ignorant of his ignorance—as a profound question. He attains, on the one hand, abstract clarity, that of the mind, but on the other hand, he plunges concretely into the abominable ignorance of his depth. Later, too late, he will put out his eyes in an attempt to reconcile clarity and obscurity, knowledge and ignorance, the visible and the non-visible, the two opposing regions of the question.[2]

From this confrontation we learn that there is one question for which an accurate response does not suffice: if this question disappears and is forgotten, if it is taken at its word, ostensibly vanquished by discursive mastery, it is then that it prevails. Even when it presents itself in a clear form that seems to call for an answer that would conform to it, we cannot meet it except by recognizing that it poses itself as the question that is not posed. Even manifest, it still flees. Flight is one of its ways of being present in the sense that it unceasingly draws us into a space of flight and irresponsibility. To question in this profound mode, or to question it, is therefore not to question profoundly; it is, just as much, to flee (to accept the detour of this impossible flight). Yet perhaps this flight brings us into relation with something essential.

*

Let us try to designate this new relation more precisely. To question is to make a leap in the question. The question is this call to a *sault* that does not let itself be held back by a *result*. In order to leap there must be a free space, there must be firm ground, and there must be a force that, starting from a secure foothold, changes the movement into a jump. The freedom to question is a leap starting from, and moving away from, all firmness. However, in the depths of the flight in which we flee, questioning, there is nothing sure, nothing firm. Everything is already filled with our very flight. The flight into which the profound question draws us transforms the space of the question into an empty plenitude where, obliged to respond to an idle question and with our head on the line, we can neither grasp nor escape it. What in the world of mastery, truth, and power is a general question, in the space of profundity is a panic question.

The similarity between these words in ancient Greek involves more than word play. The question of everything and the panic question have this in common: each draws "everything" into its play. But in the first, "everything" is with regard to the same (for example, the same that is the singular identity of the one who questions, or the principle of unity), and if this question always refers back to everything, it does so always in order to come back to the same, and finally, to reduce everything to the same. With the second question, "everything" is with regard to the other—not content with being everything, but designating what is other than everything (what is absolutely other and has no place in the whole), thus affirming the Entirely Other where there is no longer any return to the same.

This dimension of the profound question, where in everything there is no longer place for the same, this panic relation whereby it questions everything by way of what would be outside of everything, questioning the "world" by way of a "non-world" where the question no longer has a question's value, dignity, or power, is not at all exceptional. On the contrary, it is constant; it simply slips away. It reaches us constantly as what constantly gets away from us and allows us to get away. In all the great movements in which we exist only as interchangeable signs, the panic question is there, designating us as anyone at all, and depriving us of all power to question. In a crowd our being is that of flight. But the crowd still has a determinate reality; it gives proper meaning to what has as its mode impropriety and indetermination.

Opinion, the opinion without material basis that one reads in the newspapers—but never in any particular one—is already closer to the panic character of the question. Opinion settles and decides by way of a speech that does not decide and that does not speak. It is tyrannical because no one imposes it, no one is accountable for it. The fact that there is no answering for it (not because no guarantor is to be found, but because it asks only to be spread, not affirmed or even expressed) is what constitutes it as a question never brought to light. The power of rumor is not in the force of what it says, but in the fact that it belongs to the space where everything that is said has always already been said, continues to be said, and will not cease being said. What I learn through rumor I have necessarily already heard, it being what is simply related and what, for this reason, requires no author, no guarantee or verification. Rumor is what abides no contestation since its sole, its incontestable truth is to be related in a neutral movement wherein the relating seems reduced to its pure essence—a pure relation of no one and nothing.

Assuredly, opinion is nothing but a semblance, a caricature of essential relation, if only because it is a system organized on the basis of utilizable means, instruments of the press and pressure, the broadcast media and centers of propaganda that transform into an active power the passivity that is its essence, into a power of affirmation its neutrality, into a power of decision the sense of impotence and indecision that is opinion's relation to itself. Opinion does not judge or opine. Radically unavailable because foreign to any position, it is all the more at one's disposal. This justifies every criticism. Nevertheless, its panic movement escapes those critics who stress precisely opinion's seductive and tranquilizing alienation, for its movement constantly dissipates this power by which everything is alienated into a nullity or an inalienable indetermination. He who believes that he has rumor at his disposal rapidly loses himself in it. Something impersonal is always in the process of destroying in opinion all opinion. This is the vertigo of uprooting. The insipid ideas and linguistic banalities that serve as its vehicles dissimulate the way it sinks into profundity, the diversion that plunges into the vortex of flight. Opinion is thus never opinion enough (this is precisely what characterizes it). It is content with being its own alibi. But the fact that rumor, even while being only a semblance, appears capable of opening in such a way as to afford us a distance from which we might discover something more important—this play of illusion is also the trait it has in common with the play of the most profound question.

*

With this latter, it seems that we question more than we are able to question, more than the power of questioning allows, and thus beyond the reach of any question. We will never have done with the question, not because there is still too much to question, but because, in this detour of profundity that is proper to it—a movement that turns us away from it and from ourselves—the question places us in relation with what has no end. Something in the question necessarily exceeds the power of questioning; but this does not mean that there are too many secrets in the world that provoke questions: it is rather the contrary. When being is finally without question, when the whole becomes socially or institutionally realized, at that time and in an unbearable manner, the excess of questioning with respect to the power of questioning will make itself felt for the bearer of the question: the question will be felt as the impossibility of questioning. In the profound question, impossibility questions.

Every true question opens onto the whole of questions (a whole that is the accomplishment of this "opening" that is the meaning of the question). Hence its moving force, its dignity, its value. But now we see that there is in it, more "profoundly," a detour that diverts questioning from being able to be a question, and from being able to bring about an answer. This detour is the center of the profound question. Questioning places us in relation with what evades every question and exceeds all power of questioning. Questioning is the very attraction of this detour. What shows in the questioning of the profound question, even as it slips away in the detour of speech, is that which cannot be seized by an affirmation, nor refused by a negation, nor raised up to possibility by interrogation, nor restored to being through a response. *It is speech as detour.* Questioning is this detour that speaks as a detour of speech. And history at its turning is like the accomplishment of this movement of turning and slipping away in which, realizing itself completely, it would slip away completely.

*

Since the movement of flight also gives us an idea of the nature of this turning aside, we might seek to learn something about questioning through it. Man flees. First he flees something, then he flees all things through the unmeasured force of flight that transforms everything into flight. Then when flight has taken hold of everything—making of everything what must be fled as much as what one cannot succeed in fleeing—flight makes the whole, by a repulsion that attracts, slip away in the panic reality of flight. In panic flight it is not that everything declares itself to be what should be fled or what is impossible to flee: it is the very category of the whole—the one borne by the general question—that is unseated and made to falter. We are here at the juncture where the experience of the *whole* is shaken, and, in this shaking, gives way to panic profundity.

When we flee we do not flee each thing one at a time and one after another, according to a regular and indefinite enumeration. For each thing, equally suspect, has collapsed in its identity as a thing, and the whole of things has collapsed in the slipping movement that steals them away as a whole. Flight now makes each thing rise up as though it were all things and the whole of things—not like a secure order in which one might take shelter, nor even like a hostile order against which one must struggle, but as the movement that steals, and steals away. Thus flight not only reveals reality as being this whole (a totality without gap and without issue) that one must flee: flight is this very whole that steals away, and to which it draws us even while repelling us. Panic flight is this movement of stealing away that realizes itself as profundity, that is, as a whole that steals away and from which there is no longer any place to steal away to. And thus it accomplishes itself finally as the impossibility of flight. This is Phaedra's movement:

The sky, the whole world's full of my forefathers.
Where may I hide? Flee to infernal night.
How? There my father holds the urn of doom.

Flight is the engendering of a space without refuge. Let us flee. This should mean: let us seek a place of refuge. But rather it says: let us flee into what must be fled, let us take refuge in the flight that takes away all refuge. Or again: there where I flee, "I" do not flee, only flight flees, an undefined movement that steals, steals away and leaves nothing into which one might steal away.

*

Here, between the crowd and flight (and also rumor), we might rediscover this reversal of relations that the profound question seems to hold out to us. If, in the crowd, being is in flight, it is because belonging to flight makes of being a crowd, an impersonal multiplicity, a non-presence without subject: the unique self that I am gives way to an indefiniteness that is paradoxically always growing, that sweeps me along and dissolves me in flight. At the same time, the empty self that is undone in the crowd in flight remains solitary, without support, without contour, fleeing itself in everyone who flees: an immense solitude of flight where no one accompanies anyone else. All speech then belongs to flight, precipitates flight, orders all things upon the confusion of flight—and this is a speech that, in truth, does not speak, but flees whoever speaks, drawing him into a still more rapid flight.

A flight, moreover, that is stationary, tranquil; a flight that makes a given epoch, a given people, into a simultaneity without constancy, a fleeting unreality.

Yet this immensity, disoriented and deprived of a center, this immobile dispersal of movement, would turn into that which turns strangely around if out of its depths it were to succeed in reconstituting itself as a whole, a power to be everything and to gather everything unto itself in the face of something else that it flees. Let us assume this were possible. It would "suffice" that the alteration that is flight—the becoming-other that it is—be cast outside, incarnated and affirmed in a reality that is other, in an adversity such that one might flee it, and thus also combat it (as soon as one *can* flee something one has already regained the power to combat it). This movement is what occurs in the overturning that is called revolt, at times revolution. The abject disorganization of the crowd, that immense common powerlessness that is not even lived at first in common, turns into an exigency. It is dispersal itself—disarrangement—that by turning about now affirms itself as the essential, reducing to insignificance every power already organized, suspending any possibility of reorganization and yet giving itself, outside every organizing organ, as the space between: the future of the whole where the whole withholds itself.

A turning about that accomplishes itself in and through speech.

Speech is this turning. Speech is the place of dispersion, disarranging and dis-arranging itself, dispersing and dispersing itself beyond all measure. For the speech that sets into flight, therein becoming flight, preserves in this very flight the movement of stealing away that is not content with desperate or even panic flight, and thus retains the power of stealing away from it.

What sort of power is this? Is it still a power? Speech flees more rapidly, more essentially than flight does. It holds in it the essence of flight in the movement of stealing away; this is why speech speaks it, pronounces it. When someone, in flight, begins to speak, it is as though the movement of stealing away suddenly took to speech, suddenly took form and appearance, came to the surface and re-stored depth as a whole, but a whole without unity in which the irregularity of disarray is still decisive.

Naturally, when this speech becomes petrified in a watchword, "flight" simply ends and everything returns to order. But flight can also, even while maintaining itself as an infinite power of dispersal, recapture in itself this more essential movement of stealing and turning away that originates in speech as detour. This detour is equally irreducible to affirmation and to negation, to question and to re-sponse; it precedes all these modes, speaking before them and as though in turn-ing away from all speech. Even if it tends to determine itself as a power to say no, particularly in the movements that manifest themselves in revolt, this no that challenges all constituted power also challenges the power to say no, designating it as what is not founded in a power, as irreducible to any power and, by virtue of this, unfounded. Language lends itself to the movement of stealing and turning away — it watches over it, preserves it, loses itself there and confirms itself there. In this we sense why the essential speech of detour, the "poetry" in the turn of writing, is also a speech wherein time turns, saying time as a turning, the turning that sometimes turns in a visible manner into revolution.

*

Let us temporarily conclude these remarks. Man has in all times turned away from himself as a profound question, and above all when he has endeavored to seize this as an ultimate question: the question of God, the question of being. To-day, he seems to approach the very essence of stealing and turning away by ap-proaching, through the opposing force of dialectical exigency, man as a general question. But what steals away steals away profoundly, and profundity is still but an appearance that steals away. No one could say, without being inconsistent: man *is* what steals away. Nor would it suffice to turn this affirmation into a question — in whatever form one might wish. For example: is man part of the movement of stealing away? Is it through man that being is what steals away? Is that which steals away the being of man — does it come to be in man? Profound questioning by no means finds its measure in a question, even if in this question it is the movement of slipping and stealing away that seeks to come into question.

Can we at least delimit the experience of this *neutral turn* that is at work in turning away? One of the characteristic traits of this experience is that it cannot be assumed by the one to whom it happens, by a subject in the first person; it only realizes itself by introducing into the field of its realization the *impossibility* of its accomplishment. This is an experience that, even while escaping all dialectical possibility, refuses to fall into some realm of evidency or into an immediate grasp, just as it has nothing to do with a mystical participation. An experience, therefore, in which the disputes of the mediate and the immediate, subject and object, intuitive knowledge and discursive knowledge, the cognitive relation and the love relation, are not transcended but left aside. The most profound question is this experience of being diverted in the mode of a questioning that is foreign, anterior, or posterior to any question. Man is turned by the profound question toward what turns aside—and turns itself aside.[3]

III

Speaking Is Not Seeing

"I would like to know what you are searching for.

— I too would like to know.

— This not knowing is rather carefree, is it not?

— I'm afraid it may be presumptuous. We are always ready to believe ourselves destined for what we seek by a more intimate, a more significant relation than knowing. Knowledge effaces the one who knows. Disinterested passion, modesty, invisibility: these are what we risk losing by not just knowing.

— But we will also lose certitude, a proud assurance. Behind the face of the man of science, impersonal and as though effaced, there is the terrible flame of absolute knowledge.

— Perhaps. Nonetheless, this flame does not fail to glimmer everywhere there are eyes. I see it even in the unseeing eyes of statues. Uncertainty does not suffice to render modest men's efforts. But I admit that the ignorance in question here is of a particular kind. There are those who seek, looking to find — even knowing they will almost necessarily find something other than what they are searching for. There are others whose research is precisely without an object.

— I remember that the verb 'to find' [*trouver*] does not first of all mean 'to find,' in the sense of a practical or scientific result. To find is to turn, to take a turn about, to go around. To come up with a song is to turn a melodic movement, to make it turn. No idea here of a goal, still less of a stopping. To find is almost exactly the same word as 'to seek' [*chercher*], which means to 'take a turn around.'

— To find, to search for, to turn, to go around: yes, these are words indicating movement, but always circular. It is as though the sense of searching or research lay in its necessary inflection in turning. 'To find' is inscribed upon the great celestial 'vault' that gave us the first models of the unmoved mover. To find is to seek in relation to the center that is, properly speaking, what cannot be found.

— The center allows finding and turning, but the center is not to be found. Research would be, perhaps, that rash seeking determined always to reach the center instead of being content to act in response to its point of reference.

— A hasty conclusion all the same. It is true that the turning movement of research resembles the movement of a dog that, when its prey is motionless and menacing, believes it has captured its prey by encircling it, while in fact it remains solely under the fascination of the center to whose attraction it submits.

— The center, as center, is always safe.

— Searching and error, then, would be akin. To err is to turn and to return, to give oneself up to the magic of detour. One who goes astray, who has left the protection of the center, turns about, himself adrift and subject to the center, and no longer guarded by it.

— More accurately, he turns about—a verb without complement; he does not turn around some thing or even around nothing; the center is no longer the immobile spur, the point of opening that secretly clears the space of advance. One who goes astray moves steadily ahead and stays at the same point; he exhausts himself while under way, not advancing, not stopping.

— And he is not at the same point, although being there by returning. This is worth considering. The return effaces the point of departure; being without a path, error is that arid force that uproots the landscape, ravages the wilderness, ruins the site.

— An advance in the frontier regions and along the frontier of the march.

— Above all, an advance that opens no path and corresponds to no opening; error designates a strange space where the hiding-showing movement of things has lost its directing force. Where I am through error there no longer reigns either the benevolence of welcome or the rigor, itself reassuring, of exclusion.

— I think of the aged Empedocles: *driven* by the heavens to the sea, *spit* from the sea to the earth, *spit out again* toward the sun and *thrown back* by the sun to the heavens; *'exiled from god and in error for having trusted myself to the frenzy of irritation.'*

— But to measure up to such an ordeal, one must be a daimon, a lesser daimon, the promise of man. There still, the exile remains one of exclusion; the exclusion takes place within a closed world where, through the play of the four corners that endlessly divide him, the being in exile nonetheless lives as though he were outside. The biblical exile is more essentially that departure and recognition of the outside where the covenant originates. Error, it seems to me, neither closes nor opens; nothing is enclosed and yet there is no horizon—unbounded, it is not in open sky. A snow-covered expanse evokes the space of error, as Tolstoy and Kafka sensed.

— With the term 'error,' you mean to say that things neither show nor hide themselves, not yet belonging to the 'region' where there is a place for unveiling and veiling.

— Did I say that? I would say rather: error is an obstinacy without perseverance that, far from being a rigorously maintained affirmation, pursues itself by diverting the affirmation toward what has no firmness. Essential error is without relation to the true, which has no power over it. Truth would dispel error, were they to meet. But there is an error of sorts that ruins in advance all power of encounter. To err is probably this: to go outside the space of encounter.

— I confess to not understanding well your 'error.' There would be two kinds: one being the shadow of the true; the other—but this other, I wonder how you can speak of it.

— This is perhaps the easiest. Speech and error are on intimate terms.

— I see nothing but banter here: as though you were recalling that one would not deceive if one did not speak. Speech, we well know, is the resource and, etymologically, even the origin of the devil.

— Of the words ball and ballistics as well—all diabolical works. Note that etymologies—important because they show the facetious force of language, and the mysterious play that is an invitation to play—have no other purpose than to close the word rapidly up upon itself again in the manner of those shelled creatures that withdraw as soon as one inspects them. Words are suspended; this suspense is a very delicate oscillation, a trembling that never leaves them still.

— And yet, they are also immobile.

— Yes, of an immobility that moves more than anything moving. Disorientation is at work in speech through a passion for wandering that has no bounds. Thus it happens that, in speaking, we depart from all direction and all path, as though we had crossed the line.

— But speech has its own way, it provides a path. We are not led astray in it, or at most only in relation to the regularly traveled routes.

— Even more than that perhaps: it is as though we were turned away from the visible, without being turned back round toward the invisible. I don't know whether what I am saying here says anything. But nevertheless it is simple. Speaking is not seeing. Speaking frees thought from the optical imperative that in the Western tradition, for thousands of years, has subjugated our approach to things, and induced us to think under the guaranty of light or under the threat of its absence. I'll let you count all the words through which it is suggested that, to speak truly, one must think according to the measure of the eye.

— You don't wish to oppose one sense to another, hearing to sight?

— I would not want to fall into that trap.

— Especially since writing—which is your own way, and no doubt the first way—would be lacking to you in this case.

— To write is not to give speech to be seen. The game of common etymology makes of writing a cutting movement, a tear, a crisis.

— This is simply a reminder that the proper tool for writing was also proper for incising: the stylet.

— Yes, but this incisive reminder still evokes a cutting operation, if not a butchery: a kind of violence — the word flesh is found in the family, just as graphy is a scratch. Higher and further back, to write and to curve meet. Writing is the curve that the turn of seeking has already evoked for us and that we find in the bending of reflection.

— In each word, all words.

— Yet speaking, like writing, engages us in a separating movement, an oscillating and vascillating departure.

— Seeing is also a movement.

— Seeing presupposes only a measured and a measurable separation: to see is certainly always to see at a distance, but by allowing distance to give back what it removes from us. Sight is invisibly active in a pause wherein everything holds itself back. We see only what first escapes us by virtue of an initial privation, not seeing things that are too present, and not seeing them if our presence to things is pressing.

— But we do not see what is too distant, what escapes us through the separation of distance.

— There is a privation, an absence, precisely through which contact is achieved. Here the interval does not impede; on the contrary, it allows a *direct* relation. Every relation of light is an immediate relation.

— To see is thus to apprehend *immediately* from a distance.

— . . . immediately from a distance and through distance. To see is to make use of separation, not as mediating, but as a means of immediation, as immediating. In this sense too, to see is to experience the continuous and to celebrate the sun, that is, beyond the sun: the One.

— And yet we do not see everything.

— This is sight's wisdom, though we never see only one thing, even two or several, but a whole: every view is a general view. It is still true that sight holds us within the limits of a horizon. Perception is a wisdom rooted in the ground and standing fixed in the direction of the opening; it is of the land, in the proper sense of the term: planted in the earth and forming a link between the immobile boundary and the apparently boundless horizon — a firm pact from which comes peace. For sight, speech is war and madness. The terrifying word passes over every limit and even the limitlessness of the whole: it seizes the thing from a direction from which it is not taken, not seen, and will never be seen; it transgresses laws, breaks away from orientation, it disorients.

— There is a facility in this liberty. Language acts as though we were able to see the thing from all sides.

— And then begins perversion. Speech no longer presents itself as speech, but as sight freed from the limitations of sight. Not a way of saying, but a transcendent way of seeing. The 'idea,' at first a privileged aspect, becomes the privilege of what remains under a perspective to which it is tributary. The novelist lifts up the rooftops and gives his characters over to a penetrating gaze. His error is to take language as not just another vision, but as an absolute one.

— Do you want us not to speak as we see?

— I would want, at least, that we not give ourselves in language a view that is surreptitiously corrected, hypocritically extended, deceiving.

— We should choose then: speech, sight. A difficult choice, and perhaps unjust. Why should the thing be separated into the thing seen and the thing said (written)?

— An amalgam, in any case, will not remedy the split. To see, perhaps, is to forget to speak; and to speak is to draw from the depths of speech an inexhaustible forgetfulness. Let me add that we do not await just any language, but the one in which 'error' speaks: the speech of detour.

— An unsettling speech.

— A differing speech, one that carries here and there, itself deferring speech.

— Obscure speech.

— Clear speech, if the word clarity, being the property not of visible but of audible things, does not yet have a relation to light. Clarity is the exigent claim of what makes itself clearly heard in the space of resonance.

— Hardly speech, it discloses nothing.

— Everything in it is disclosed without disclosing anything.

— That is nothing but a formula.

— Yes, and not too sure. I am seeking a way, without getting there, to say that there is a speech in which things, not showing themselves, do not hide. Neither veiled nor unveiled: this is their non-truth.

— A speech wherein things would be said without, for the fact of this saying, coming to light?

— Without arising in the place where there is always a place for appearing, or failing that, for refusing to appear. A speech such that to speak would no longer be to unveil with light. Which does not imply that we would want to go in search of the joy, or the horror, of the absence of the day: just the contrary; we would want to arrive at a mode of 'manifestation,' but a manifestation that would not be one of unveiling-veiling. Here what reveals itself does not give itself up to sight, just as it does not take refuge in simple invisibility.

— This word reveal, I fear, is not quite suitable. To reveal, to remove the veil, to expose directly to view.

— Revealing implies, in fact, that something shows that did not show itself. Speech (at least the one we are attempting to approach: writing) lays bare even without unveiling, and sometimes, on the contrary (dangerously), by reveiling in a way that neither covers nor uncovers.

— Is it not this way in dreams? The dream reveals by re-veiling.

— There is still something like a light in the dream, but in truth we would not know how to qualify it. It implies a reversal of the possibility of seeing. To see in a dream is to be fascinated, and fascination arises when, far from apprehending from a distance, we are apprehended by this distance, invested by it and invested with it. In the case of sight, not only do we touch the thing, thanks to an interval that disencumbers us of it, but we touch it without being encumbered by this interval. In the case of fascination we are perhaps already outside the realm of the visible-invisible.

— So it is, then, with the image, which seems to hold us at the limit of these two domains.

— Perhaps. Of the image, too, it is difficult to speak rigorously. The image is the duplicity of revelation. The image is what veils by revealing; it is the veil that reveals by reveiling in all the ambiguous indecision of the word reveal. The image is image by means of this duplicity, being not the object's double, but the initial division that then permits the thing to be figured; still further back than this doubling it is a folding, a turn of the turning, the 'version' that is always in the process of inverting itself and that in itself bears the back and forth of a divergence. The speech of which we are trying to speak is a return to this first turning—a noun that must be heard as a verb, as the movement of a turning, a vertigo wherein rest the whirlwind, the leap and the fall. Note that the names chosen for the two directions of our literary language accept the idea of this turning; poetry, rightly enough, alludes to it most directly with the word 'verse,' while 'prose' goes right along its path by way of a detour that continually straightens itself out.

— But these words designate only the exterior aspect of these two literary forms: prose, a continuous line; verse, an interrupted line that turns about in a coming and going.

— No doubt, but the turning must already be given for speech to turn about in the torsion of verse. The first turn, the original structure of turning (which later slackens in a back and forth linear movement) is poetry. Hölderlin said (according to Saint Clair and Bettina): *'Everything is rhythm; the entire destiny of man is a single celestial rhythm, just as the work of art is a unique rhythm.'*

— Well, here we have explained rhythm—and rhyme, which follows from it.

— You are right to recall us to some reserve. Nothing is explained, nothing laid out; rather, the enigma is again bound up in a word. I wanted, with too much haste, to trace this speech of detour that holds in it the errancy of seeking. And yet we were advised against haste by our very subject. The detour is not a short-cut. And in the speech that responds to it, the essential is vicissitude. It is a matter of holding to it, holding up and keeping up, between us.

— Hence, perhaps, the meaning of the conversation we are holding.

— In this turn that is rhythm, speech is turned toward that which turns aside and itself turns aside. This is a rare speech; it knows no precipitation, just as it does not know the refusal to go on, or oscillating doubt. It is most open in its obliqueness, through interruption always persisting, always calling upon detour, and thus holding us as though in suspense between the visible and the invisible, or on the hither side of both.

— Here again is something that is understood only with difficulty. What does this mean? What is not visible must surely be held to be invisible.

— Perhaps there is an invisibility that is still a manner of something letting itself be seen, and then another that turns aside from everything visible and everything invisible. Night is the presence of this detour, particularly the night that is pain and the night that is waiting. Speaking is the speech of the waiting wherein things are turned back toward latency. Waiting: the space of detour without digression, of errancy without error. There is no question of things either showing or hiding themselves in this space, at least inasmuch as these movements would entail a play of light. And in the speech that responds to this waiting there is a manifest presence that is not an act of the day, a disclosure that discloses before any *fiat lux*, disclosing the obscure through the detour that is the essence of obscurity. The obscure, in stealing away, offers itself to the turn that originally governs speech.

— Despite your efforts to avoid having to evoke light in speaking of the obscure, I cannot help but refer everything you say back to day as the sole measure. Is it because our language has become abusively — necessarily — an optical system that speech speaks well only to our sight? I wonder whether Heraclitus, when he says of sacred speech that it *neither exposes nor conceals, but gives a sign*, is not saying something about this. Might one not lend him the idea you wish to present: that there is a language in which things neither show nor hide?

— It is perhaps not for us to lend this idea to Heraclitus, but he may be the one to lend it to us. The speech here in question is the one that is questioned at Delphi: it speaks in the manner of those oracles that are oracles through signs, scorings and incisions — writing — in the text of things. Nevertheless, at Delphi, we do indeed have to do with a language, a language that escapes the necessity of showing, in escaping that of hiding. In this language such a difference does not arise: it neither covers nor uncovers.

— Speaking without either saying or being silent.

— Speaking by virtue of a difference other than that of the words *legei-kruptei*, a difference that is bound up in the single word *sêmainei*, which we translate by *to indicate* or *to give a sign*. This difference that suspends and contains all others is the difference that is also conveyed by the word 'turn.' In this turn that turns toward that from which it turns away, there is an original torsion in which is concentrated the difference whose entanglement every mode of speaking, up to and including dialectic, seeks to slacken, to put to use, to clarify: speech/silence, word/thing, affirmation/negation—all the enigmas that speak behind every language that is spoken live in these. For example: speech is speech against a ground of silence, but silence is still no more than a noun in language, a manner of speaking; or, the noun names the thing as being different from the word, and this difference can only be brought forth with the name. I won't belabor the point. This amounts to saying that we speak by way of this difference, which makes it so that in speaking we defer speaking.

— This is simply a play on words.

— Yes, and why should it not be? It plays with the idea of time, reminding us that time necessarily has a part in this difference, and suggesting to us that the turn of speech is not foreign to this turning that is the turning of 'history,' and that essentially accomplishes itself now apart from any present. Then too, it plays with the idea that we speak only through the difference that holds us at a distance from speech, it speaking only because we speak, and nonetheless not yet. This 'not yet' does not refer back to an ideal speech, to the superior Word of which our human words would be but an imperfect imitation; it rather constitutes, in its non-presence, the very decision of speech, this still to come that all speech that we hold to be present is and that is all the more insistent for designating and engaging with the future—a future that is also a future to be spoken, the non-speech that belongs to language and that nevertheless places us outside language each time we speak essentially, just as we are never closer to speaking than in the speech that turns us aside from it.

— So here again is the peculiarity of that turning toward . . . which is detour. Whoever would advance must turn aside. This makes for a curious kind of crab's progress. Would it also be the movement of seeking?

— All research is crisis. What is sought is nothing other than the turn of seeking, of research, that occasions this crisis: the critical turn.

— This is hopelessly abstract.

— Why? I would even say that every important literary work is important to the extent that it puts more directly and more purely to work the meaning of this turn; a turning that, at the moment when it is about to emerge, makes the work pitch strangely. This is a work in which worklessness, as its always decentered center, holds sway: the absence of work.

— The absence of work that is the other name for madness.

— The absence of work in which discourse ceases so that, outside speech, outside language, the movement of writing may come, under the attraction of the outside."

IV

The Great Refusal

1

1

The outside, the absence of work; I hold such words in reserve, knowing their fate is bound up with the writing outside language that every discourse, including that of philosophy, covers over, rejects, and obscures through a truly capital necessity. Which necessity? The one to which everything in the world submits. It is therefore fitting to name it at once, without ostentation, without hesitation, and also without precaution, for it is death; that is, the refusal of death — the temptation of the eternal, all that leads men to prepare a space of permanence where truth, even if it should perish, may be restored to life. The concept (therefore all language) is the instrument in this enterprise of establishing a secure reign. We untiringly construct the world in order that the hidden dissolution, the universal corruption that governs what "is" should be forgotten in favor of a clear and defined coherence of notions and objects, relations and forms — the work of tranquil man. A work that nothingness would be unable to infiltrate and where beautiful names — all names are beautiful — suffice to make us happy. And is this not an important task, the fitting response to an untenable destiny? To be sure. Once the gods, once God, helped us not to belong to the earth where everything passes away, and helped us, our eyes fixed upon the unperishing that is the superterrestrial, to organize meanwhile this earth as a dwelling place. Today, lacking gods, we turn still more from passing presence in order to affirm ourselves in a universe constructed according to the measure of our knowledge and free from the randomness that always frightens us because it conceals an obscure decision. There is, however, defeat in this victory; in this truth of forms, of notions and of names, there is a lie, and in this hope that commits us to an illusory beyond, to a future without death or to a logic without chance, there is, perhaps, the betrayal of a more profound hope that poetry (writing) must teach us to reaffirm.[1]

1. *We have lost death*

For, struggling in a superb manner and with extraordinary resources, it is not possible that we should not have sacrificed something; lost, in order to save ourselves, the truth of that from which it was our task to keep ourselves secure. But here we enter into a more secret realm, saying with words that betray: we have lost death. Lost death? What are we seeking to say here? Have we forgotten that we are mortal? Do we not at every instant name what makes us mortals? We name it, but in order to master it through a name and, through this name, finally rid ourselves of it. All of our language—and therein lies its divine nature—is arranged to reveal in what "is" not what disappears, but what always subsists, and in this disappearance takes form: meaning, the idea, the universal. In this way language retains of presence only that which, escaping corruption, remains the mark and the seal of being (its glory as well), and therefore *is* not truly either. The drawing back before what dies is a retreat before reality. The name is stable and it stabilizes, but it allows the unique instant already vanished to escape; just as the word, always general, has always already failed to capture what it names. Of course, we have words that designate this too since I have just (and with what ease) referred to it. We speak of sensible reality, we say the presence of what is present, the being of an instant in a fortuitous place or, as does all poetry that is banality's accomplice, "what one will never see twice." But—and here Yves Bonnefoy runs up painfully against Hegel—scarcely have I said *now*, saying in this single word at one and the same time every "now" in its general form and in its eternal presence, and this now itself, this unique now, has slipped away into the word, carrying with it the proper enigma of what dissolves there, and around which I can very well multiply singularities, but without doing anything other than altering it still more in trying to particularize it with the help of universal traits and in trying to catch it disappearing with a hold that eternalizes it. We thus find ourselves caught in the treachery of I know not what trap. And it is from here that Yves Bonnefoy, through images and the summons he knows how to hear in them, will seek in a sustained effort, for himself and for us, the path of return—seeking to recapture the act of presence, the true place, that site where there gathers in an undivided unity what "is": this broken leaf of ivy, this bare stone, a step fading in the night.

*

But I will stop here, not to criticize this approach—it has a force of attraction and a noble meaning that we must not avoid—but to see better what is at stake in such a movement. I will say simply that Yves Bonnefoy was perhaps wrong to follow Hegel and at the same time flee him as though in secret. When he speaks of the concept, it is of philosophy as it comes together in Hegel that he is speaking; but when he speaks of the concept as the instrument through which thought has contrived to refuse and to forget death, he is then expressing himself in a manner that situates poorly, I think, his opposition. For (I repeat this hastily, this knowledge is now so profoundly inscribed in us) the force of the concept does not reside in refusing the negation that is proper to death, but on the contrary in having introduced it into thought so that, through negation, every fixed form of thought should disappear and always become other than itself. Language is of a divine nature, not because it renders eternal by naming, but because, says Hegel, "it immediately overturns what it names in order to transform it into something else," saying of course only what is not, but speaking precisely in the name of this nothingness that dissolves all things, it being the becoming speech of death itself and yet interiorizing this death, purifying it, perhaps, in order to reduce it to the unyielding work of the negative through which, in an unceasing combat, meaning comes toward us, and we toward it.

I will not betray the author of *L'improbable* by situating his defiance precisely at this juncture. For through an astonishing vocation, mind and language have succeeded in making a *power* of this death; but at what price? By idealizing it. What in fact is it now? No longer an immediate dissolution in which everything disappears without thought, but the infamous death that is the beginning of the life of the mind. And how could we not be led to claim that what is lost in this idealizing denaturation is obscurity itself, and the dark reality of this indescribable event—turned by us, thanks to an astonishing subterfuge, into a means of living and a power of thought? We again find ourselves, therefore, before what must be called "the great refusal," the refusal to stop beside the enigma that is the strangeness of this singular end.

Around the already decomposing remains of Lazarus, there is a curious assembly of sages and a kind of struggle, in the end almost laughable, yet analogous to that "struggle of giants" over being of which Plato has spoken in his irony. Which is the true death? One will answer that the gift forever courageous, presence of mind, lies with he who, without being engulfed in cadaverous reality and even while looking steadily at it, is able to name it, "comprehend" it, and, by this understanding, pronounce the *Lazare veni foras* through which death will become a principle, the terrible force in which the life that bears it must maintain itself in order to master it and find there the accomplishment of its mastery. The temptation of rest, cowardly surrender, and abdicating laziness consists, in this sense, in falling back to the level of nature and in losing oneself in thoughtless nothingness, that empty and meaningless banality.

To which another, in a more subdued voice and more obscurely, will respond: But what does this Lazarus saved and raised from the dead that you hold out to me have to do with what is lying there and makes you draw back, the anonymous corruption of the tomb, the lost Lazarus who already smells bad and not the one restored to life by a force that is no doubt admirable, but that is precisely a force and that comes in this decision from death itself? But which death? That death comprehended, deprived of itself, become pure privative essence, pure negation; the death that, in the appropriated refusal that it constitutes for itself, affirms itself as a power of being, and as that through which everything is determined, everything unfolds as a possibility. And perhaps this is indeed the true death; death become the movement of truth. But how can one not sense that in this veritable death, the death without truth has entirely slipped away: what in death is irreducible to the true, to all disclosure, what never reveals itself, hides, or appears? And, certainly, when I speak, I recognize very well that there is speech only because what "is" has disappeared in what names it, struck with death so as to become the reality of the name; the life of this death—this is indeed what the most ordinary speech is admirably, as is the speech of the concept at a higher level. But the fact remains—and this is what it would be blindness to forget and weakness to accept—that what "is" has in effect disappeared: something was there that is there no longer. How can I find it again, how can I, in my speech, recapture this prior presence that I must exclude in order to speak, in order to speak it? And here we will evoke the eternal torment of our language when its longing turns back toward what it always misses, through the necessity under which it labors of being the lack of what it would say.

2. *The question, torment of the immediate*

But what is it lacking? Can we, now that we have as it were encircled and tracked down this strange prey, always a shadow as soon as we seize it, and now leaning with Yves Bonnefoy over this emptiness—perhaps empty because of its plenitude—that is not only the most ancient tomb, but every sensible thing in its fresh newness—can we, having so resolutely *sacrificed* what we can find again only by rejecting it, finally come upon, perhaps throw light upon, what is at stake in this contest that is no longer a Crusade or a Dispute over the empty Sepulcher, but the "struggle over origins?" In a word, we can—on condition that we ask it of the one for whom in his speech and even his life this *sacrifice* was the tearing of discovery, and who once affirmed:

> But now the day breaks! I waited and saw it come,
> And what I saw, the holy be my word.[2]

Das Heilige, the Sacred, an august word charged with lightning and as though forbidden, serving perhaps only to conceal with the force of a too-ancient reverence the fact that it can say nothing. But let us bring it together with what Bonnefoy often indicates directly; and will we not be brought before a knowledge so simple that it cannot but disenchant us, saying in our turn, and refusing to say: the Sacred is "immediate" presence. It is this body that passes, is pursued and nearly grasped even unto death by Baudelaire, *this simple life flush with the earth* that René Char announces. The Sacred is then nothing other than the reality of sensible presence. Yes, this is truly an easy knowledge, tranquil, within our reach — and yet a "bitter knowledge," for holding onto our affirmation we must immediately reverse it and restore to it its enigmatic force, now saying: presence, this is the Sacred — the very thing "that offers neither any hold nor stopping point, the terror of the immediate that defeats every grasp, the shattering of chaos."[3]

If this approach is justified, and even if we do not yet know precisely what we have approached, we understand better why this *"real presence"* to whose promise Yves Bonnefoy wants to return us — and about which at times he speaks so easily, at times refuses to say anything, placing this unpossessable gift in our hands as he withdraws it from us — obliges us, even as we have it, to await it still in an immobile search, by a progression of trials in which life is consumed. For here it is no longer a matter of that somehow technical or abstract difficulty we delimited above (to the extent one can). Because in the difficulty of our approach we have a presentiment that, in turning ourselves about through an impossible movement in order to see face to face what we are authorized to look at only by turning away from it, what we will see, what in truth we have always already seen, call it the sensible or the earthly body — is the divine itself, what men have always indistinctly had in view with this name. This, then, is the entire secret. Bonnefoy will thus speak of negative theology, of initiatory realism and, using a word that is indeed dangerous, will promise us salvation — even when it is only a question *"of glimpsing, on the side of some mountain, a window pane in the evening's sun."*[4]

*

We thus find ourselves once again at the heart of the most serious debate, where perhaps our destiny is at stake. Must we affirm with Hegel that this immediate, this immediate singularity (intuition or ineffable vision) is nothing, the most vain and banal of platitudes — or rather that, inviolate and safe, it is, has long been, and has always been being itself in its very secret? Must we affirm, still with Hegel or perhaps with Marx, that we will recover what is of value in the immediate not at the beginning, but at the end, and in the entire development of our history, our language, and our action — namely, as the concrete Universal, the object of an incessant struggle: not what is given, but what is conquered through the work of mediation? Or must we claim that if there is not some kind of "experience," some kind of vocation of presence (an unwarranted guarantor of everything that is present), that we will give ourselves over still more to the great refusal, losing sight of that on the basis of which alone we can begin to see, and perhaps to speak? Or, finally, we can certainly speak of what Bonnefoy favors too much by calling it what *is*, the originary immediate—this is easy; but can we say it? And is there poetry because the one who would have *seen* being (the absence of being through the mortifying gaze of Orpheus) will also, when he speaks, be able to hold onto its presence, or simply make remembrance of it, or keep open through poetic speech the hope for what opens on the hither side of speech, hidden and revealed in it, exposed and set down by it?

So many questions. But might there not be still another? That is, another way of putting these questions into play without reducing them to the form to which we are bound by the obligation to choose between a dialectical speech (that refuses the immediate in order to rely solely upon the mediating force) and a vision (a speech of vision, also visionary, that speaks only insofar as one sees, entering through speech into sight, and, through sight, immediately drawn into the being that would be an opening of light)? There cannot be an immediate grasp of the immediate (Hölderlin says this with the dreadful force that is his in the fragment entitled "The Most High"). The immediate excludes everything immediate: this means all direct relation, all mystical fusion, and all sensible contact, just as it excludes itself—renounces its own immediacy—each time it must submit to the mediation of an intermediary in order to offer access.

So we find ourselves denied as though on all sides. Let us reflect, nonetheless, on this strangeness: "the immediate excludes everything immediate." Let us try to understand that what is in question is not a simple contradiction between presence and access to presence or to representation. "The immediate excluding everything immediate, as it does every mediation" tells us something about presence itself: immediate presence is presence of what could not be present, presence of the non-accessible, presence excluding or exceeding any present. This amounts to saying: the immediate, infinitely exceeding any present possibility by its very presence, is the infinite presence of what remains radically absent, a presence in its presence always infinitely other, presence of the other in its alterity: non-presence. What can we conclude from these propositions? Nothing, for the moment. Except this: (1) that when we question about immediate presence, attempting to retain the immediate in thought as a fundamental shaking, it is not in order to privilege a direct relation, be it a mystical or a sensible contact, a vision or effusion; (2) that if *"the immediate is for mortals as well as for immortals, strictly speaking, impossible,"* it is perhaps because impossibility—a relation escaping power—is the form of relation with the immediate; (3) finally, and we approach here the decisive question, that if the immediate is infinitely absent, exceeding and excluding any present, the only relation with the immediate would be a relation reserving in itself an infinite absence, an interval that nevertheless would not mediate (that should never serve as intermediary).

3. *The desiring call, speech*

Perhaps now we ought to return to Hölderlin's words. They give us no answer. But in their sober and simple rigor, we find gathered everything that has just come into question. To begin with, the *now* that Bonnefoy proposed to us as what is at stake in poetry, and that irrupts from the beginning of the line with the impatience of a first light: *But now day breaks!* Then, immediately after the burst of this present in which the day dawns, we fall back, having lost it, to the past, and we must again live the infinite of waiting, the time of distress and destitution without companionship: *I waited.* A waiting without a term, existence reduced to a fruitless waiting without a present that is nevertheless also a waiting rich and full of the presentiment in which the coming and the vision of what always comes is prepared: *I waited and saw it come.* What is seen? The coming. But what is it that comes? This remains undetermined, or better, is said in the mode of the neuter, even though in this undetermined and in this neutral there is certainly understood the approach of the "now" in which day dawns, but that could not be seen directly, is only seen as a coming, being what dispenses everything that can come to pass.

> *But now day breaks! I waited and saw it come.*

Just as, in this first line, we have an alternance and an opposition of tense, being sent back from the burst of the present to the pain of the waiting without present, in the second line and in the same way, we pass again from a time remembered to a present, but to another kind of present in whose nuance, it seems to me, our entire poetic destiny is at stake:

> *And what I saw, the holy be my word.*

I will limit myself to two remarks. The first uncertainty: *what I saw.* It is indeed affirmed that something occurred, that vision took place: what is the viewed of this vision? We might think: the holy. This is generally what French translations specify, punctuating the text in this manner: "And what I saw, the holy, may it be my word." But it is not this way in the original where, at the moment of breaking the seal and finally revealing what we were destined to see, once, through the poet's intervention, the line interrupts itself, becoming silent for an instant before gathering impetus to give form with an urgent force to a new present; but which one? The present of desire (in which, therefore, absence presents itself), of poetic desire in its highest form: *the holy be my word.* May my word be the holy. Here, in this sort of exclamatory prayer and desiring appeal, is all that is given to us of the relation that holds between the poet, speech, and the Sacred. Hölderlin does not say that he saw the holy—this he could not say—he can only, having seen, give himself in a movement that evokes and invokes to the future of the fundamental wish: *the holy be my word.* We perceive, on the one hand, the extent of the ambition: it is not only a matter of speaking of the Sacred, or around the Sacred—the Sacred must be speech, and, even more, my very speech. A demand that must be qualified as mad, strictly speaking. But on the other hand, we see the extreme restraint of the ambition, since all is limited to the exigency of a fervent wish so that, finally, "what I saw" is perhaps nothing more than the present of this wish, this provoking resolution that gathers in an intimacy of belonging and through an already sacrilegious contact the Sacred and speech in the space of the extremity of desire.

This is an outcome we will once again be tempted to find disappointing if, at the moment when the sacred present declares itself for us in its now, we have with it no other relation than that of desire and are still only able to reach, in the very name by which we establish it, our fervent wish to name it. Desire is very little. And is it not an entirely subjective impulse? But perhaps it is much more, as we sense when, with the same movement with which Hölderlin's line opens, René Char says: "*The poem is the realized love of desire that has remained desire.*" But perhaps we would do well to take our distance from these divisions—subject, object—borrowed from the knowledge that is proper to this world in which truth is constructed. In the same way, when Yves Bonnefoy rises up against the clarity of the concept, decisively taking the part of the sensible, he well knows that by entering into the play of oppositions and determinations that are elaborated precisely by the rational order, he is still thinking and speaking within, and in favor of, this conceptual order whose value he seeks to challenge, or at least delimit.

*

But the text we are considering also calls this desire hope. "I would like to bring together, I would like almost to identify poetry and hope." What does this hope want? What does it say? What is its relation with poetry and with the act or the place of poetry?

2
How to Discover the Obscure?

This hope is not just any hope. Just as there are two poetries, "the one chimerical, deceiving and fatal," "there are two hopes." Poetic hope is to be reinvented, or to put this another way: it is up to poetry to "found a new hope." Even as hope is all but identified with poetry—so that the reality of poetry would be that of hope—hope appears, coming after it, as the gift that poetry would offer us. Poetry would be the medium of this new hope. Hence the affirmation: poetry is a means and not an end.[5]

Hope is to be reinvented. Would this mean that what this hope aims at is to be obtained through invention, a beautiful utopian future, or through the splendor of the imaginary that certain romantics are said to have had as their horizon? Not at all. The hope that passes by way of the ideal—the lofty heavens of the idea, the beauty of names, the abstract salvation of the concept—is a weak hope. Hope is true hope insofar as it aspires to give us, in the future of a promise, what is. What is is presence. But hope is only hope. There is hope when, far from any present grasp, far from any immediate possession, it relates to what is always yet to come, and perhaps will never come; hope says the hoped-for coming of what exists as yet only in hope. The more distant or difficult the object of hope is, the more profound and close to its destiny as hope is the hope that affirms it: I hope little when what I hope for is almost at hand. Hope bespeaks the possibility of what escapes the realm of the possible; at the limit, it is relation recaptured where relation is lost. Hope is most profound when it withdraws from and deprives itself of all manifest hope. But at the same time we must not hope, as in a dream, for a chimerical fiction. It is against this that the new hope appoints itself. Hoping not for the probable, which cannot be the measure of what there is to be hoped for, and hoping not for the fiction of the unreal, true hope—the unhoped for of all hope—is an affirmation of the improbable and a wait for what is.

On the first page of his book, one of the most beautiful, Yves Bonnefoy has written: "*I dedicate this book to the improbable, that is to say, to what is. To a spirit of vigil. To the negative theologies. To a poetry longed for, of rains, of waiting and of wind. To a great realism that aggravates instead of resolving, that designates the obscure, that takes clarity for clouds that can always be parted. That has concern for a clarity high and impracticable.*"

Why the improbable? And how would what is be the improbable? The improbable escapes proof, not because it cannot be demonstrated for the time being but because it never arises in the region where proof is required. The improbable is what arises in a way other than through the approbation of proof. The improbable is not simply that which, remaining within the horizon of probability and its calculations, would be defined by a greater or a lesser probability. The improbable is not what is only very slightly probable. It is infinitely more than the most probable: "*that is to say, what is.*" And yet what is remains the improbable.

What does such a word seek to tell us? I would like to clarify it by translating it in this way: were there a meeting point between possibility and impossibility, the improbable would be this point. But what do these two new names indicate to us?

4. *Possibility: language as power*

They belong to our everyday vocabulary. We say something is possible when a conceivable event does not run up against any categorical impediment within a given horizon. It is possible: logic does not prohibit it, nor does science or custom object. The possible, then, is an empty frame; it is what is not at variance with the real, or what is not yet real, or, for that matter, necessary. But for a long time we have been alert to another sense. Possibility is not what is merely possible and should be regarded as less than real. Possibility, in this new sense, is more than reality: it is to be, plus the power to be. Possibility establishes and founds reality: one is what one is only if one has the power to be it. Here we see immediately that man not only has possibilities, but is his possibility. Never are we purely and simply, we are only on the basis of and with regard to the possibilities that we are; this is one of our essential dimensions. The word possible becomes clear, then, when it is placed in relation with the word power [*pouvoir*], first in the sense of capacity, then in the sense of a power that is commanded or a force [*puissance*]. (I am simplifying a great deal.) To what extent is power as a force an alteration, to what extent a definition of possibility? With this latter, at least, power [*puissance*] comes to be, and the appropriation that is accomplished by possession receives its determination. Even death is a power, a capacity. It is not a simple event that will happen to me, an objective and observable fact; here my power to be will cease, here I will no longer be able to be here. But death, insofar as it belongs to me and belongs to me alone, since no one can die my death in my stead or in my place, makes of this non-possibility, this impending future of mine, this relation to myself always open until my end, yet another power [*pouvoir*]. Dying, I can still die, this is our sign as man. Retaining a relation to death, I appropriate it as a power: this is the utmost limit of my solitary resolution. And we have seen that death seized again as a power, as the beginning of the mind, is at the center of the universe where truth is the labor of truth.

From this perspective, our relations in the world and with the world are always, finally, relations of power [*puissance*], insofar as power is latent in possibility. Let us restrict ourselves to the most apparent characteristics of our language. When I speak I always exercise a relation of force [*puissance*]. I belong, whether or not I know it, to a network of powers of which I make use, struggling against the force that asserts itself against me. All speech is violence, a violence all the more formidable for being secret and the secret center of violence; a violence that is already exerted upon what the word names and that it can name only by withdrawing presence from it — a sign, as we have seen, that death speaks (the death that is power) when I speak. At the same time, we well know that when we are having words we are not fighting. Language is the undertaking through which violence agrees not to be open, but secret, agrees to forgo spending itself in a brutal action in order to reserve itself for a more powerful mastery, henceforth no longer affirming itself, but nonetheless at the heart of all affirmation.

Thus begins that astonishing future of discourse wherein secret violence, disarming open violence, ends by becoming the hope and the guarantee of a world freed from violence (and all the same constituted by it). This is why (I say this in passing, and these things can only be said in passing) we are so profoundly offended by the use of force that we call torture. Torture is the recourse to violence – always in the form of a technique – with a view to making speak. This violence, perfected or camouflaged by technique, wants one to speak, wants speech. Which speech? Not the speech of violence – unspeaking, false through and through, logically the only one it can hope to obtain – but a true speech, free and pure of all violence. This contradiction offends us, but also unsettles us. Because in the equality it establishes, and in the contact it reestablishes between violence and speech, it revives and provokes the terrible violence that is the silent intimacy of all speaking words; and thus it calls again into question the truth of our language understood as dialogue, and of dialogue understood as a space of force exercised without violence and struggling against force. (The expression "We will make him see reason" that is found in the mouth of every master of violence makes clear the complicity that torture affirms, as its ideal, between itself and reason.)

5. *The thought (of) the impossible: the* other *relation*

As soon as we are in relation within a field open to possibility, and opened by possibility, force threatens. Even comprehension, an essential mode of possibility, is a grasp that gathers the diverse into a unity, identifies the different, and brings the other back to the same through a reduction that dialectical movement, after a long trajectory, makes coincide with an overcoming. All these words – grasp, identification, reduction – conceal within themselves the rendering of accounts that exists in knowledge as its measure: reason must be given. What is to be known – the unknown – must surrender to the known. But then comes this apparently innocent question: might there not exist relations, that is to say a language, escaping this movement of force through which the world does not cease to accomplish itself? In this case, such relations, such a language, would also escape possibility. An innocent question, but one that is already questioning at the margins of possibility and that, in order to guard its dignity as a question, must avoid disintegrating in the ecstasy of a response without thought, to which it may well lead.

We sense, of course, that impossibility – now employing this word as though by chance – could not be an easy movement, since we would see ourselves drawn by it away from the space in which we exercise power, if only in a negative manner, by the simple fact of living and dying. Likewise, if the thought of the impossible were entertained, it would be a kind of reserve in thought itself, a thought not allowing itself to be thought in the mode of appropriative comprehension. This is a dangerous direction, and a strange thought. It must be added, however, that the impossible is not there in order to make thought capitulate, but in order to allow it to announce itself according to a measure other than that of power. What would this other measure be? Perhaps precisely the measure of the *other*, of the other as other, and no longer ordered according to the clarity of that which adapts it to the same. We believe that we think the strange and the foreign, but in reality we never think anything but the familiar; we think not the distant, but the close that measures it. And so again, when we speak of impossibility, it is possibility alone that, providing it with a reference, already sarcastically brings impossibility under its rule. Will we ever, then, come to pose a question such as: what is impossibility, *this non-power that would not be the simple negation of power*? Or will we ask ourselves: how can we discover the obscure?; how can it be brought out into the open? What would this experience of the obscure be, whereby the obscure would give itself in its obscurity?

And, continuing to question, will we ask ourselves further: if there is possibility—because, always being able, we are the being that is fixed toward the future, always ahead of itself and even in the delay it also is, forewarning and anticipating itself—would we not be fortunate to be drawn into an entirely other experience, if it happened that this experience were that of a time out of synchrony and as though deprived of the dimension of passing beyond, henceforth neither passing nor ever having had to pass?

This is an experience we do not have to go very far to find, if it is offered in the most common suffering, and first of all in physical suffering. No doubt, where it is a matter of a measured suffering, it is still endured, still, of course, suffered, but also brought back into our grasp and assumed, recaptured and even comprehended in the patience we become in the face of it. But it can lose this measure; it is even of its essence to be always already beyond measure. Suffering is suffering when one can no longer suffer it, and when, because of this non-power, one cannot cease suffering it. A singular situation. Time is as though arrested, merged with its interval. There, the present is without end, separated from every other present by an inexhaustible and empty infinite, the very infinite of suffering, and thus dispossessed of any future: a present without end and yet impossible as a present. The present of suffering is the abyss of the present, indefinitely hollowed out and in this hollowing indefinitely distended, radically alien to the possibility that one might be present to it through the mastery of presence. What has happened? Suffering has simply lost its hold on time, and has made us lose time. Would we then be freed in this state from any temporal perspective and redeemed, saved from time as it passes? Not at all: we are delivered over to another time—to time as other, as absence and neutrality; precisely to a time that can no longer redeem us, that constitutes no recourse. A time without event, without project, without possibility; not that pure immobile instant, the spark of the mystics, but an unstable perpetuity in which we are arrested and incapable of permanence, a time neither abiding nor granting the simplicity of a dwelling place.

We must admit that, considered in this light, this experience has a pathetic appearance, but on condition that one also give the word pathos its non-pathetic sense. It is a question not of that paroxysmic state where the self cries out and is torn apart, but rather of a suffering that is almost indifferent, not suffered, but neutral (a phantom of suffering) insofar as the one who is exposed to it, precisely through this suffering, is deprived of the "I" that would make him suffer it. So now we see it: the mark of such a movement is that, by the fact that we experience it, it escapes our power to undergo it; thus it is not beyond the trial of experience, but rather that trial from which we can no longer escape. An experience that one will represent to oneself as being strange and even as the experience of strangeness. But if it is so, let us recognize that it is this not because it is too removed. On the contrary, it is so close that we are prohibited from taking any distance from it—it is foreign in its very proximity.

But we have a word that designates what is so close that it destroys all proximity—a word before which we once again find ourselves. I am referring to the immediate: the immediate that allows no mediation, the absence of separation that is absence of relation as well as infinite separation because this separation does not reserve for us the distance and the future we need in order to be able to relate ourselves to it, to come about in it.

Thus we can begin to surmise that "impossibility"—that which escapes, without there being any means of escaping it—would be not the privilege of some exceptional experience, but behind each one and as though its other dimension. And we can surmise as well that if possibility has its source in our very end—which it brings to light as the power most proper to us, according to Hölderlin's demand: "For what I want is to die, and it is for man a right"—it is from this same source that "impossibility" originates, though now sealed originarily and refusing itself to all our resources: there where dying means losing the time in which one can still come to an end and entering into the infinite "present" of a death impossible to die; a present toward which the experience of suffering is manifestly oriented, the suffering that no longer allows us the time to put a limit to it—even by dying— since we will also have lost death as a limit.

6. *The passion of the outside*

Here we will have to ask ourselves whether we have reached a point from which we might become attentive to what until now has offered itself to us merely as the other side of possibility. This is hardly certain. Nevertheless, we have arrived at a few characteristics. First this one: in impossibility time changes direction, no longer offering itself out of the future as what gathers by going beyond; time, here, is rather the dispersion of a present that, even while being only passage does not pass, never fixes itself in a present, refers to no past and goes toward no future: *the incessant*. A second trait: in impossibility, the immediate is a presence to which one cannot be present, but from which one cannot separate; or, again, it is what escapes by the very fact that there is no escaping it: the *ungraspable that one cannot let go of*. Third trait: what reigns in the experience of impossibility is not the unique's immobile collecting unto itself, but the infinite shifting of dispersal, a non-dialectical movement where contrariety has nothing to do with opposition or with reconciliation, and where the *other* never comes back to the same. Shall we call it becoming, the secret of becoming? A secret that stands apart from every secret and that gives itself as the diverging of difference.

If we hold these traits together—the present that does not pass, while being only passage; that which cannot be let go of, while offering nothing to hold onto; the too-present to which access is denied because it is always closer than any approach, reversing itself to become absence and thus being the too-present that does not present itself, yet without leaving anything in which one might absent oneself from it—we perceive that in impossibility it is not only the negative character of the experience that would make it perilous, but also "the excess of its affirmation" (what in this excess is irreducible to the power to affirm). And we perceive that what comes into play in impossibility does not withdraw from experience, but is the experience of what no longer allows itself to be withdrawn; what accords neither distance nor retreat, and without ceasing to be radically different. Thus we could say (very approximately and provisionally) that what is obscure in this movement is what it discloses: what is always disclosed without having had to disclose itself, and has always in advance reduced all movement of concealing or self-concealing to a mode of the manifest. A present in which all things present, including the self that is there present, are suspended, and yet a present exterior to itself, the very exteriority of presence. Finally, we perceive here the point at which time and space would rejoin in an originary disjunction: "presence" is as much the intimacy of instancy as the dispersal of the Outside. More precisely, it is intimacy as the Outside, the exterior become an intrusion that stifles, and the reversal of both the one and the other; what we have called "the vertigo of spacing."[6]

But all of these traits tend to delimit, in its limitlessness, the fact that impossibility is nothing other than the mark of what we so readily call experience, for there is experience in the strict sense only where something radically *other* is in play. And here is the unexpected response: radical non-empirical experience is not at all that of a transcendent Being; it is "immediate" presence or presence as Outside.[7] The other response is this: impossibility, which escapes every negativity, does not cease to exceed, in ruining it, every positivity; impossibility being that in which one is always already engaged through an experience more initial than any initiative, forestalling all beginning and excluding any movement of action to disengage from it. But we know, perhaps, how to name such a relation, which is the hold over which there is no longer any hold, since it is again what we have tried to designate (confusedly) by the term *passion*. So we shall be tempted to say provisionally: impossibility is relation with the Outside; and since this relation without relation is the passion that does not allow itself to be mastered through patience, impossibility is the passion of the Outside itself.

These remarks once again assembled, we see that the situation with regard to our questioning at the beginning has reversed itself. It is no longer impossibility that would be the non-power: it is the possible that is merely the power of the no. Should we then say: impossibility is being itself? Certainly, we must! Which amounts to recognizing in possibility the sovereign power to negate being: man, each time that he is on the basis of possibility, is the being *without* being. The struggle for possibility is this struggle against being.

But must we not also say: impossibility, neither negation nor affirmation, indicates what in being has always already *preceded* being and yields to no ontology? Certainly, we must! Which amounts to the presentiment that it is again being that awaits in possibility, and that if it negates itself in possibility, it is in order better to preserve itself from this *other* experience that always precedes it and is always more initial than the affirmation that names being. This would be the experience that the Ancients no doubt revered under the title of Destiny: that which diverts from every destination and that we are seeking to name more directly in speaking of the *neutral*.

But what does such a whirlwind of rarefied notions, this abstract storm, signify? That we have just been toyed with by the indefinite overturning that is the "attraction" of the impossible relation, a relation to which those extraordinary Ancients had also become attentive in their encounter with Proteus. As men of measure through knowledge of the lack of measure that was close to them, did they not recommend that Proteus be held firmly and bound in order that he should agree to declare himself truthfully in the most simple form? Simplicity is, in fact, what alone answers to the duplicity of the enigma. When, for example, Simone Weil says simply, "Human life is *impossible*. But misfortune alone makes this felt," we understand very well that it is not a question of denouncing the unbearable or the absurd character of life—negative determinations that belong to the realm of possibility—but of recognizing in impossibility our most human belonging to immediate human life, the life that it falls to us to sustain each time that, stripped through misfortune of the clothed forms of power, we reach the nakedness of every relation: that is to say, the relation to naked presence, the presence of the other, and in the infinite passion that comes from it. In the same way, Simone Weil writes: "Desire is impossible." And now we understand that desire is precisely this relation to impossibility, that it is impossibility become relation—*separation* itself, in its absolute—that becomes alluring and takes form. And we will begin also to understand why, in inspired words, René Char has said: "*The poem is the realized love of desire that has remained desire.*" And finally, if ever we were to declare imprudently that communication is impossible, we should understand that such a sentence, so clearly rash, is not meant to negate scandalously the possibility of communication, but to alert us to that other speech that speaks only when it begins to respond to the other region that is not governed by the time of possibility. In this sense, yes, we must for an instant say it, if only to forget it just as immediately: "communication" (to take up again a term that is here out of place since there is no longer any common measure) exists only when it escapes power and when impossibility, our ultimate dimension, announces itself in it.

7. *Naming the possible, responding to the impossible*

Let us leave this path of reflection. We ought not count on a simple confrontation of words to prove that poetry might orient us toward another relation — a relation with the obscure and the unknown that would be a relation neither of force [*puissance*], nor of comprehension, nor even of revelation. We sense even that it is not the role of language, be it literary or that of poetry, even true poetry, to bring to light or to the firmness of a name what would affirm itself, unformulated, in this relation without relation. Poetry is not there in order to say impossibility: it simply answers to it, saying in responding. Such is the secret lot, the secret decision of every essential speech in us: *naming* the possible, *responding* to the impossible. A lot that nevertheless must not lead to a kind of allotment, as though we were free to choose between a speech for naming and a speech for responding; as though, finally, between possibility and impossibility there were a frontier, perhaps moving, but always determinable according to the "essence" of the one and the other.[8]

Naming the possible, responding to the impossible. Responding does not consist in formulating an answer, in such a way as to appease the question that would obscurely come from such a region; even less in transmitting, in the manner of an oracle, a few truth contents of which the daytime world would not yet have knowledge. It is poetry's existence, each time it is poetry, that in itself forms a response and, in this response, attends to what is addressed to us in impossibility (by turning itself away). Poetry does not express this, does not say it, does not draw it under the attraction of language. But it responds. Every beginning speech begins by responding; a response to what is not yet heard, an attentive response in which the impatient waiting for the unknown and the desiring hope for presence are affirmed.

V

Knowledge of the Unknown

"What is a philosopher?

— That is perhaps an anachronistic question. But I will give a modern response. In the past one might have said it is a man who stands in wonder; today I would say, borrowing words from Georges Bataille, it is someone who is afraid.

— Philosophers are numerous then, excepting Socrates and Alain—both famous for having been good combatants and for having drunk hemlock without trembling (the first at least, but also on occasion the second). But perhaps philosophical fear is of a more noble character.

— Not at all. Fear, whether it be cowardly or courageous, is intimate with what is frightening, and what is frightening is what makes us leave peace, freedom, and friendship all at the same time. Through fright, therefore, we leave ourselves, and, thrown outside, we experience in the guise of the frightening what is entirely outside us and other than us: the outside itself.

— Then common fear would be philosophical fear insofar as it gives us a kind of relation with the unknown, thereby offering us a knowledge of what escapes knowledge. Fear: anguish. And we thus approach philosophies that themselves are not unknown. Yet there is in this experience a movement that collides as though head-on with philosophy. The fearful man, in the space of his fear, participates in and unites with what makes him afraid. He is not only fearful, he is fear—that is, the irruption of what arises and is disclosed in fear.

— You mean that this is an irrational movement?

— To say it is irrational would be saying very little. We are past the point of reducing philosophy to reason, or reason to itself, and we long ago found the means for recuperating sense—the power of comprehension—from the movements of sensibility. But if your definition of the philosopher is to be challenged, it is because fear—anguish—either does not make the one who experiences it go beyond his limits, being always a fear experienced by a Self in the world, or it does make him go beyond them, destroying his power to be still himself (lost in anguish, we say). But in this latter case, what happens in fear and trembling constitutes an ecstatic, properly speaking, a mystical movement: there is an intense pleasure and a fruition, a union in and through repulsion; a movement one might revere or denigrate, but that one cannot call philosophical, any more than a divine union could come about under the supervision of a metaphysics.

— Why? Let us leave aside God—the name is too imposing. Why should the contact with the unknown that is determined by fear—that way of being the unknown brought to us by fear—not be of central concern to philosophy? Perhaps being afraid, searching for what is reached in fear, putting oneself at stake in the shaking that is fear is not philosophy. And yet, does not the thought that is afraid, the thought that is the thought of fear and the fear of thought, bring us closer to a decisive point that, if it escapes philosophy, does so because something decisive escapes philosophy?

— But is it thought that can be afraid? Are you not already using here a language that is symbolic, full of imagery or 'literary?' It is the thinker who becomes frightened; he is frightened of what threatens his thought. And what does he fear, as a man of thought? Nothing other than fear.

— The philosopher, in this case, would be someone who is afraid of fear.

— Afraid of the violence that reveals itself in fear and that threatens to transform him from a frightened man into a violent man; as though he feared less the violence he suffers than the violence he might exercise. Why is this so? But let us first reflect on the question concerning *contact* with the unknown and why it would not belong to philosophy. Note that we are here tacitly admitting that philosophy—or anything you wish to imply by this name—is essentially knowledge of the not-known, or, more generally, relation with the unknown.

— Let us admit this for the time being.

— But as I am saying the unknown *as* an unknown, perhaps we will not be so quick to affirm it. For if the unknown is to remain unknown in the very knowledge we have of it—not falling under our grasp, and irreducible not only to thought alone, but also to every manner of seizing it in our power—do we not risk being obliged to conclude from this that we have knowledge only of what is close to us: of the familiar and not of the foreign?

— One could easily object that in speaking of the unknown it is the unknowable that we aim for; but knowledge of the unknowable is a monster that critical philosophy exorcised long ago. I will add that if we are able to have commerce with this unknowable, it is precisely in fear or in anguish, or in one of those ecstatic movements that you just refused as being non-philosophical; it is there that we have some presentiment of the Other—it seizes us, staggers and ravishes us, carrying us away from ourselves.

— But precisely in order to change us into the Other. If in knowledge—even dialectical knowledge, and through any intermediary one might want—there is appropriation of an object by a subject and of the other by the same, and thus finally a reduction of the unknown to the already known, there is in the rapture of fright something worse; for it is the self that is lost and the same that is altered, shamefully transformed into something other than myself.

— I see nothing shameful there—unless one should be ashamed of fearing this shame—if such a shameful movement were to permit us to relate ourselves finally to what is outside our limits.

— The unique dignity of the relation philosophy proposes I entertain with what would be the unknown (and which in any case escapes my power, being that over which I have no hold) consists in its being a relation such that neither myself nor the other ceases to be, in this very relation, preserved from everything that would identify the other with myself, that would confuse me with the other, or alter both of us through a middle term: it being an absolute relation in the sense that the distance separating us will not be diminished but, on the contrary, produced and maintained absolutely in this relation.

— A strange relation that consists in there being no relation.

— That therefore consists in preserving the terms that are in relation from what would alter them in it; a relation that excludes, therefore, ecstatic confusion (that of fear), mystical participation, but also appropriation, every form of conquest, and even, when all is taken into account, the seizing that comprehension always is.

— I think this is another approach to the question we once formulated like this: how can we discover the obscure without exposing it to view? What would this experience of the obscure, in which the obscure offered itself in its obscurity, be?

— Yes, we were seeking then to circumscribe the affirmation of impossibility, this non-power that would not be a simple negation of power. And in asking ourselves what thought it might be that could not be thought in the mode of power and of appropriating comprehension, we came to say that 'impossibility is the passion of the Outside itself,' and also that 'impossibility is the experience of non-mediate presence.' A response (if to give affirmative force to a question is to respond) that philosophy has the right to despair of.

— But we must not despair of philosophy. In Emmanuel Lévinas's book—where, it seems to me, philosophy in our time has never spoken in a more sober manner, putting back into question, as we must, our ways of thinking and even our facile reverence for ontology—we are called upon to become responsible for what philosophy essentially is, by entertaining precisely the idea of the Other in all its radiance and in the infinite exigency that are proper to it, that is to say, the relation with *autrui*. It is as though there were here a new departure in philosophy and a leap that it, and we ourselves, were urged to accomplish.[1]

— The idea of the other: is it so new? Do not all contemporary philosophies accord this idea a place that is more or less privileged?

— Indeed, more or less — which means more or less subordinated. For Heidegger, being-with is approached only in relation to Being and because it bears, in its way, the question of Being. For Husserl, if I am not mistaken, only the sphere of the ego is original, that of *autrui* is for me only 'ap-presented.' Generally speaking, almost all Western philosophies are philosophies of the Same, and when they concern themselves with the Other it is still only with something like another 'myself,' being at best equal to me and seeking to be recognized by me as a Self (just as I am by him) in a struggle that is sometimes a violent struggle, at other times a violence appeased in discourse. But we are led through the teaching of Lévinas before a radical experience. *Autrui* is entirely Other; the other is what exceeds me absolutely. The relation with the other that is *autrui* is a transcendent relation, which means that there is an infinite, and, in a sense, an impassable distance between myself and the other, who belongs to the other shore, who has no country in common with me, and who cannot in any way assume equal rank in a same concept or a same whole, cannot be counted together with the individual that I am.

— Well, this *autrui* is strangely mysterious.

— This is because he is in fact the Stranger, that Unknown with regard to whom we supposed, in beginning, that the relation with him was philosophy itself: metaphysics, says Lévinas. The Stranger comes from elsewhere and is always somewhere other than where we are, not belonging to our horizon and not inscribing himself upon any representable horizon whatsoever, so that his "place" would be the invisible — on condition that we hear in this expression, following a terminology we have sometimes used: what turns away from everything visible and everything invisible.

— But is this not to propose a philosophy of separation, a kind of solipsism? There is myself, and, separated from me, this lowly *autrui* without residence, wandering on the outside or confused with the destitution or the strangeness of an outside that is inaccessible.

— This seems to me to be the contrary of solipsism, and yet it is indeed a philosophy of separation. I am definitely separated from *autrui*, if *autrui* is to be considered as what is essentially other than myself; but it is also through this separation that the relation with the other imposes itself upon me as exceeding me infinitely: a relation that relates me to what goes beyond me and escapes me to the very degree that, in this relation, I am and remain separated.

— We come back, then, to that strange relation of which we had begun to speak. I confess that I see nothing more uncertain or more abstract.

— On the contrary, nothing is more real. One of the strongest aspects of Lévinas's book is to have led us, through the beautiful, rigorous, vigilantly con-

trolled, and yet trembling language that is his—but in a manner for which we ourselves feel responsible—to consider *autrui* from the basis of separation. We are
led to entertain this relation that might be called impossible along four paths that
differ through the movement of the analysis alone. The first takes up again the
Cartesian idea of the Infinite. The finite self thinks the infinite. In this thought,
thought thinks what goes infinitely beyond it and what it cannot account for on
its own; it thinks, therefore, more than it thinks. A unique experience. When I
think the infinite, I think what *I am not able* to think (for if I had an adequate
representation of it, if I comprehended it, assimilating it and making it equal to
myself, it would be a question only of the finite). I therefore have a thought that
goes beyond my power; a thought that, to the very extent that it is a thought of
mine, is the absolute exceeding of the self that thinks it—in other words: a relation
with what is absolutely outside myself: the other.

— I'm sorry, but this remains very abstract.

— What the abstraction hides here is perhaps not at all abstract, but a movement almost too consuming. Here is another approach to it: the thought that thinks
more than it thinks is Desire. Such a desire is not the sublimated form of need,
any more than the prelude to love. Need is a lack that awaits fulfillment; need
is satisfied. Love wants union. The desire that one might call metaphysical is a
desire for what we are not in want of, a desire that cannot be satisfied and that
does not desire union with what it desires. It desires what the one who desires
has no need of, what is not lacking and what the one who desires has no desire
to attain, it being the very desire for what must remain inaccessible and foreign—
a desire of the other as other, a desire that is austere, disinterested, without satisfaction, without nostalgia, unreturned, and without return.

— Wouldn't René Char's superb words be fitting here: '*The poem is the realized love of desire that has remained desire*'?

— Lévinas mistrusts poems and poetic activity, but when Simone Weil writes
'Desire is impossible'—which we commented upon by saying 'Desire is precisely
this relation to the impossible, it is impossibility become relation'—perhaps such
a manner of speaking would not be out of place.

— Is this philosophical desire not akin to the Platonic Eros?

— That it may owe it its name I would readily grant, but Eros did not serve
as its model, or only by way of its difference from it. Eros is still the nostalgic
desire for lost unity, the movement of return toward true Being. Metaphysical desire is desire for that with which one has never been united, the desire of a self
not only separated but happy with the separation that makes it a self, and yet still
in relation with that from which it remains separated and of which it has no need:
the unknown, the foreign, *autrui*.

— Then let us say a bit brusquely that this Desire is the desire for a strict transcendence that has taken *autrui* as what it aims for, and that makes *autrui* the
Transcendent.

— Let us say it attentively and soberly, for it may be that everything that can be affirmed of the relation of transcendence—the relation of God to creature—must be first (for my part, I would say only) understood on the level of the social relation. The Most High would be *autrui*.

— This name seems to mean something to me. But if *autrui* is the Most High—and this not in an approximate way but in an original sense—*autrui*, eluding all manifestation, risks being as far from me as the sky from the earth, as uncertain and as empty.

— As far from, yes, one can say that. But this extreme remoteness is not only able to manifest itself, it presents itself to us face to face. In the visage whereby it offers itself to me openly, in the frankness of a gaze, in the nakedness of an approach that nothing prevents, it is presence itself; and Lévinas gives precisely the name *visage* to this 'epiphany' of *autrui*. When *autrui* reveals himself to me as what is absolutely outside and above me—not because he would be the most powerful, but because there my power ceases—there is the visage.

— Here, finally, is a more tangible reality. Although I suspect that this visage is not a simple part of the body. But are we not to understand at least that, through the visage, *autrui*, whom you were elevating as though outside the world, falls suddenly into the domain of visible things? The visage is necessarily a way of approach that, coming about through sight, depends both upon the light by which it comes forward, and upon my power to look, that is to say, to unveil by light.

— The visage—but I admit this name creates difficulties—is on the contrary a presence that I cannot dominate by my gaze, that always exceeds both the representation I might make of it and any form, any image, any view, any idea by which I might affirm it, arrest it, or simply let it be present. The visage—here is the essential, it seems to me—is that experience I have when, facing the face that offers itself to me without resistance, I see arise 'out of the depths of these defenseless eyes,' out of this weakness, this powerlessness, what puts itself radically in my power and at the same time refuses it absolutely, turning my highest power into im-possibility. In front of the visage, Lévinas emphasizes, *I am no longer able*. And the visage is that before which the impossibility of killing—the 'thou shalt not kill'—is decided on the very basis of what exposes itself completely to my power to bring death. Or again, facing the visage, I come up against the resistance of what in no way resists me. And this resistance, at least as Lévinas characterizes it, is ethical. This is why, if metaphysics is the transcendent relation with *autrui*, and as this transcendence is first of all of a moral order—measured by an impossibility that is an interdiction—it must be said that the first philosophy is not ontology (the care, the question, or the call of Being) but ethics, the obligation toward *autrui*.

— Unexpected and moreover courageous assertions in a time when no one expects anything 'good' to come from morals. And the precipitous manner in which you present them makes them all the more fierce.

— Because the only fitting approach to morals cannot but be abrupt. Is the general name 'ethics' in keeping with the impossible relation that is revealed in the revelation of *autrui*, which, far from being a particular case, precedes any relation of knowledge? And does the experience of impossibility, if it can take secondarily the form of a 'thou shalt not' come down, ultimately, to a prohibition? These are questions of such gravity that we must, for the moment, leave them aside. What to my mind remains decisive is that the manner by which *autrui* presents himself in the experience of the visage, this presence of the outside itself (of exteriority, says Lévinas), is not the presence of a form appearing in light or its simple retreat in the absence of light; neither veiled nor unveiled.

— So, here we are again at grips with what cannot be grasped.

— But without being reduced to effusions of the heart, for *autrui* speaks. *Autrui* speaks to me. The revelation of *autrui* that does not come about in the lighted space of forms belongs wholly to the domain of speech. *Autrui* expresses himself, and in this speaking proposes himself as other. If there is a relation wherein the other and the same, even while holding themselves in relation, *absolve themselves* of it (being terms that thus remain *absolute* within the relation itself, as Lévinas firmly states), this relation is language. When I speak to the other, I call out to him. Before all else, speech is this address, this invocation in which the one invoked is beyond reach, in which, even when disparaged or respected, and even when called upon to be silent, he is called to the presence of speech. The other is not reduced to what I say of him, to the theme of a discourse or the subject of a conversation, rather he is the one who is always outside and beyond me, exceeding me and looming over me since I appeal to him, unknown, to turn toward me, and stranger, to hear me. In speech, it is the outside that speaks in giving rise to speech, and permitting me to speak.

— So that the interlocutors would not speak except by reason of their preliminary strangeness and in order to give expression to this strangeness?

— Yes, fundamentally. There is language because there is nothing in 'common' between those who express themselves: a separation that is presupposed—not surmounted, but confirmed—in all true speech. If we had nothing *new* to say to one another, if through discourse there did not come to me something foreign, something capable of instructing me, there would be no question of speaking. This is why man—or so one may suppose—would lose both his visage and his language in a world where nothing would reign but the future of dialectical accomplishment, the law of the same.

— So language acquires here an exceptional signification?

— All the more so as it is language that founds and gives all signification. I am not saying this in order to shock. But what must be clearly understood is that it is not a matter of just any language, but solely of the speech whereby I enter into relation with the Other in his dimension of height; when *autrui* presents himself face-on, beyond the reach of my powers, when he is present in his speech that is his presence, and when, by this infinite presence, he teaches me and teaches me what exceeds me absolutely: the thought of the infinite. As *Autrui* is the Master, all true speech is magisterial. Whence it follows that oral discourse alone would be a plenitude of discourse.

— Socrates already affirmed that.

— Lévinas often invokes Socrates on this point, recalling the well-known pages of Plato where the pernicious effects of writing are denounced. But I wonder whether this comparison doesn't introduce into Lévinas's thought some ambiguity—unless it be a necessary ambiguity. On the one hand, language is the transcendent relation itself, manifesting that the space of communication is essentially non-symmetrical, that there is a kind of curvature of this space that prevents reciprocity and produces an absolute difference of levels between the terms called upon to communicate; I believe this is what is decisive in the affirmation we must hear and must maintain independently of the theological context in which it presents itself.[2] *Autrui* is not on the same plane as myself. Man as *autrui*, always coming from the outside, always without a country in relation to me, a stranger to all possession, dispossessed and without dwelling place, he who is as though 'by definition' the proletarian (the proletarian is always the other) does not enter into dialogue with me. If I speak to him, I invoke him and speak to him as the one I can neither reach nor place at my disposal; when he speaks to me, he speaks to me by way of the infinite distance he is from me, and his speech announces precisely this infinite, thereby inviting me, through his powerlessness, his destitution, and his strangeness, to a relation that is 'incommensurable with a *power* exercised, a conquest, a joyful possession or a knowledge.' All true discourse, Lévinas says solemnly, is discourse with God, not a conversation held between equals.

— How are we to understand this?

— In the strongest sense, as one always must. And in remembering, perhaps, what is said in Exodus of God speaking: as one man to another. But here, I believe, is the ambiguity. This speech of eminence, which speaks to me from very far away, from very high above (or very far below), is the speech of someone who does not speak with me on an equal footing and such that it is not possible for me to address myself to *autrui* as though he were another Myself—yet, suddenly, this speech once again becomes the tranquil humanist and Socratic speech that brings the one who speaks close to us since it allows us, in all familiarity, to know who he is and from what country, according to Socrates' wish. Why, then, does oral discourse seem to Socrates (and to Lévinas) to be a manifestation without peer? Because the man who speaks can assist his speech; he is always ready to answer for it, to justify and clarify it, contrary to what happens with what is written. Let us for a moment admit this, though I hardly believe it. We see, in any case, that the privilege of spoken language belongs *equally* to *Autrui* and to the Self, and thus makes them equal; furthermore, we see that this is a privilege attributed to the vigilance of the self who speaks in the first person, that is, with the privilege attributed to all subjectivity and no longer to the incommensurable presence of the visage. But it is not at all certain that in such a rigorous conception of the relation with *autrui* one can speak of the Self and of the Other in the common terms of subjectivity. No, one cannot. No more than one could say of the one and of the other that they are *equally* existent beings or are *equally* men, if it is understood that *Autrui* can never enter with the Self into the identity of any name or any concept.

— Unless we are to understand precisely that the relation of man to man is such that the concept of man, the idea of man as a concept (even dialectical), could not account for it.

— That is perhaps so. Nevertheless, the thought that recognizes in *Autrui* this dimension of radical exteriority with respect to the Self cannot at the same time ask of interiority that it furnish a common denominator between the Self and *Autrui*, any more than it can seek in the (subjective) presence of the 'I' to its speech what would make language a manifestation without peer. First, because it is the property of all language — spoken, but also, and perhaps to a higher degree, written language — always to lend assistance to itself, never saying only what it says but always more and always less. Moreover — as we have had occasion to affirm, and as we find authoritatively confirmed in the analyses of Lévinas — language's center of gravity is as follows: 'Speaking turns away from everything visible and everything invisible. To speak is not the same as to see. Speaking frees thought from the optical imperative that for thousands of years in the Western tradition has subjugated our approach to beings and induced us to think only under the guarantee of light or under the threat of its absence.'

— Yes, I remember that we were following the idea that to speak is to break originarily with all sight and no longer to refer back to clarity (or to the lack of clarity) as the sole measure. And we said that there is in speech a manifest presence that is not brought about by the light of day; a discovery that dis-covers, before any *fiat lux*, a speech that we now sense would be the revelation of *autrui*. But this *autrui*, I confess, remains for me a mystery.

— It is a mystery.

— But also an enigma. What is it then? The Unknown, the Stranger, the Proletarian, but also the Most High, or again, the Master. Now and then, in listening to you, I wondered whether *autrui* were not simply the locus of some truth necessary to our relation with the true transcendence that would be the divine one.

— There is this inclination in Lévinas's thought: as when he says that *Autrui* must always be considered by me as being closer to God than myself. But he says also that man alone can be absolutely foreign to me. In any case, what must be kept in mind is that the privilege I am to recognize as belonging to *autrui*, and whose recognition alone opens me to him, this recognition of height itself, is also the one thing that can teach me what man is, and what is the infinite that comes to me from man as *autrui*. What ensues from such an assertion? We perceive that it could engage us in a denunciation of all dialectical systems, of ontology, and even of nearly all Western philosophies, at least those that subordinate justice to truth or only take as being just a reciprocity of relations.

— So this philosophy could well signify, in its turn, the end of philosophy.

— And the approach of what we would name in its terms prophetic eschatology, that is to say, the affirmation of a power of judgment capable of wresting men from the jurisdiction of history.

— The interruption of history, prophetic eschatology: this is what happens when morality is awakened.

— Would you fear the shaking that can come to thought by way of morality?

— I fear the shaking when it is provoked by some Unshakable. But I recognize that today there is nothing that ought to give more cause for reflection.

— Let us reflect and give ourselves some time."

VI

Keeping to Words

"Since our last conversation, I've been thinking that if what you say points in the right direction, the human relation, as it affirms itself in its primacy, is terrible.

— Most terrible, but without terror.

— It is most terrible because it is tempered by no intermediary. For in this view there is between man and man neither god, nor value, nor nature. It is a naked relation, without myth, devoid of religion, free of sentiment, bereft of justification, and giving rise neither to pleasure nor to knowledge: a neutral relation, or the very neutrality of relation. Can this really be asserted?

— It can also be said more soberly. One can say that the relation I have with *autrui* does not pass by way of being (be it as God or as the whole, or as the 'Heideggerian' being). Being, totality, and all the concepts that are connected with these terms are not only ill-suited for defining this relation, but also (perhaps) undone by it. Or, to put this in different terms that rejoin your own, my relation with *autrui* is irreducible to any measure, just as it excludes any mediation and any reference to another relation that would include it.

— Yes, this is just what I was saying: it is terrible.

— Why this word 'terrible'?

— Between this *autrui* and 'myself' the distance is infinite, and yet, at the same time, *autrui* is for me presence itself; the presence of the infinite. A presence diverted from any present, thus what is most impoverished and least protected.

— But a presence infinitely other.

— Yes, these two traits must always be retained together. Only man is absolutely foreign to me; he alone is the unknown, he alone the other, and in this he would be *presence*: such is man. (Presence that rests neither on being nor on having; a presence that one might call immediate, if mediate and immediate were not unsuitable words here.) Each time we project strangeness onto a non-human being or refer the movement of the unknown back to the universe, we disburden ourselves of the weight of man. We sometimes imagine in a very impoverished fashion our frightened encounter in the sky of the planets and the stars with a different and superior being, and we ask ourselves: what would happen? A question to which we can perfectly well respond, for this being has always been there: it is man, man whose presence gives us all measure of strangeness.

— What is so terrible in this relation?

— I would just as soon call it grave. And because of this gravity that should in the first place govern our words, we must try not to hurry. Several movements need to be separated out here. One is almost clear. Every relation in the world is established by means of the world: we meet around a table, we gather together around a task, we find one another around truths and values. Companions are not face to face; they have in common the bread that they earn, share, and eat in common. These are relations whereby men, when they go to meet one another, do not go directly but in working toward the affirmation of a common day. This is the law, that is to say, the accomplishment of the whole that then holds them together. Dialectical fulfillment is at work, and this is necessary. Naturally, a relation of this sort is a relation of struggle and of violence. In the world, bound to negation, we know how to make of negation a possibility, as we know how to make of death a power; this negation, barring accident, is partial, limited, hidden by the affirmation of what is accomplished thanks to it. Extended in time, compensated by time, negation is time itself building upon its ruins. But in this instant we are trying to delimit, the density of things is no longer between us. The walls have fallen: those that separate us, those too that permit us to communicate, and those, finally, that protect us by keeping us at a distance. In a sense, man is now the inaccessible, but the inaccessible is in a sense the immediate; what exceeds me absolutely is absolutely at my mercy. Here is man come forth in his presence; that is to say, reduced to the poverty of presence. I say this encounter (which is not fortuitous, but originary) is terrible, for here there is no longer either measure or limit. My intervention—that of the self—will not be limited to the partial violence of work, nor to the limited and veiled negation of refusal; there, if I assert myself still as a power, my power will extend to death, and this not a partial but a radical death. Indeed, how could I take on presence in its simplicity without the risk of making it disappear? How could I even grasp it, if only by way of my gaze? Let us once again recall Orpheus and Eurydice. Eurydice is the strangeness of the extreme distance that is *autrui* at the moment of face-to-face confrontation; and when Orpheus looks back, ceasing to speak in order to see, his gaze reveals itself to be the violence that brings death, the dreadful blow.

— One would have to say, then, that man facing man like this has no choice but to speak or to kill.

— It is perhaps, in fact, the summary brutality of this alternative that would best help us approach such an instant: should the self ever come under this command—speech or death—it will be because it is in the *presence* of *autrui*.

— But we would also have to say, then, that the absolute distance that 'measures' the relation of *autrui* to me is what calls forth in man the exercise of absolute power: the power to give death. Cain killing Abel is the self that, coming up against the transcendence of *autrui* (what in the other exceeds me absolutely and that is well represented in biblical history by the incomprehensible inequality of divine favor), attempts to confront it by resorting to the transcendence of murder.

— But are these two transcendencies of the same order? And what can their conflict mean? Cain says to Abel: your dimension as infinite and absolutely exterior, that by which you claim to surpass me, that which puts you beyond my reach—I will show you that I am its master; for as a man of power, I am master also of the absolute and I have made death into my possibility.

— This is because Abel's infinite presence stands in Cain's way like a thing that is thus truly a thing belonging to Abel and of which Cain must deprive him. And, in a sense, this is not false: this presence is also Abel's good fortune, the blessing, the flock that multiplies. As soon as the presence of the other in *autrui* is not received by me as the movement through which the infinite comes to me, as soon as this presence closes around *autrui* as a property of *autrui* established in the world, as soon as it ceases to give rise to speech, the earth ceases to be vast enough to contain at the same time *autrui* and myself, and it is necessary that one of the two reject the other—absolutely.

— I notice that Cain says to Abel, when he wants to have it out with him: 'Let's go outside,' as though he knew that the outside were Abel's place, but also as though he wanted to lead him back to the destitution, to the weakness of the outside where every defense falls away.

— Perhaps. Only it is through Cain, that is, through the approach of mortal threat, at the very instant when presence is reduced to the nakedness of presence without defense, that presence also reveals itself to be what death as a power destroys but is unable to reach.

— What death can indeed make radically disappear, but cannot grasp.

— What it changes into absence but does not touch. Power has no hold over presence. On the contrary, what the decisive hold of the mortal act reveals is that presence, reduced to the simplicity of presence, is what presents itself but cannot be seized: what slips away from every grasp.

— Thus intact, but not intangible. Just the same, let us not give this assertion too facile a meaning. If it is true that mortal violence can neither take hold of presence, nor take in presence, it has at least the power to reduce it to insignificance.

over simplified

And if violence knows of presence only the insignificance to which it can reduce it, this is because presence is also always at the limit of insignificance insofar as it precedes all signification, or perhaps gives signification, but does not itself have the truth of a reality already constituted, rich in meaning, signified; it is therefore unsignified. — *w/ no sign*

— Such would be the speech that measures the relation of man placed face to face with man when there is no other choice than to speak or to kill. A speech as grave, perhaps, as the death it diverts. The alternative speech/murder is not the simple exclusion of the one by the other, as though it were a matter of choosing once and for all between a good speech and a bad death. What sort of speech is this?

— This isn't the moment for us to give an account of it. But I will say two things: first, if speech is weighty, it is because, being bare presence, it is what lays presence bare, what thus exposes it to radical violence in reducing it to the fragility of what is without power. To speak at the level of weakness and of destitution—at the level of affliction—is perhaps to challenge force, but also to attract force by refusing it. And second: in this situation, either to speak or to kill, speech does not consist in speaking, but first of all in maintaining the movement of this *either . . . or*; it is what founds the alternative. To speak is always to speak from out of this interval *between* speech and radical violence, separating them, but maintaining each of them in a relation of vicissitude.

— From which we must conclude that if the relation of man placed in the presence of man is terrible, it is because it confines us within this alternative: either speak or kill, and because, in this alternative, speech is no less grave than death, with which it is conjoined as its reverse side. But I would now like to pursue this thought along another line. In speaking of the infinite presence of *autrui*, we say that when the relation of man to man is the direct relation of *autrui* to myself, the approach is particularly grave, because it is face to face. This expression is misleading, and doubly so. In the first place because such a *vis-à-vis* is not an encounter between two faces, but rather access to man in his strangeness through speech. In the second place because, in such a facing-off, what makes capital the movement by which man presents himself directly to man (before all representation) is that there is no reciprocity of relations. I am never facing the one who faces me; my way of facing someone who comes before me is not that of an equal confrontation of presences. This inequality is irreducible.

— Yes. When *autrui* turns toward me, he, being essentially exterior to me, is as though infinitely diverted; and *autrui* is this movement of turning toward— there where detour reigns. The presence turned toward me is thus still a presence of separation, of what to me is presence even as I am separated from it, distant and turned away. And, for me, to be facing *autrui* is always to be in the abrupt presence, without intermediary, of the one who turns toward me in the infinite approach of the detour.

— The vis-à-vis of a diverted presence, in a sense. But what speaks in speech, precisely — what this essential turn that is speech measures in its turning — is the immeasurable irregularity of this movement that by disjoining joins, yet without bringing back together, and that consists first of all in the non-correspondence of the interlocutors (their absolute difference of level, their un-equalness or inequality). Speech affirms the abyss that there is between 'myself' and '*autrui*,' and it passes over the impassable, but without abolishing or reducing it. Moreover, without this infinite distance, without this abysmal separation there would be no speech, so it is accurate to say that all veritable speech recalls the separation by which it speaks. But what is the meaning of this 'unequalness'? Of what order is it? I don't see it.

— I don't see it well either. Emmanuel Lévinas would say that it is of an ethical order, but I find in this word only secondary meanings. That *autrui* should be above me, that his speech should be a speech of height, of eminence — these metaphors appease, by putting it into perspective, a difference so radical that it escapes any determination other than itself. If he be higher, *autrui* is also lower than I am, but always Other: the Distant, the Stranger. My relation to him is a relation of impossibility, eluding power. And speech is the relation whereby the one whom I cannot reach becomes present in his inaccessible and foreign truth.

— The word truth is perhaps premature. Let's keep it nonetheless. And let us repeat ourselves by saying that speech is the relation with no common measure between *autrui* and myself, a relation in which speech is not for me a means of knowledge, or a way of seeing, of having, of being able to do something. And I will add: no more than it is a way of speaking between equals. Here we are again before the difficulty.

— There is, in fact, something difficult to say here, as though when we speak of it, something kept us apart from this very speech. How can one say unequalness by means of what tends to equalize? How can one affirm the non-community of terms in the very movement and in the name of their communication? The language we are using at this moment can only send us back to speech as a dialectics — the only 'legitimate' speech, let us not forget. Yet what we are seeking to express in affirming the inordinate relation beyond measure of '*autrui*' to 'the self' is a non-dialectical experience of speech. The inequality in question signifies perhaps nothing other than a speech that would speak without leveling, without identifying, that is, without tending toward the identity implied by satisfaction and full understanding.

— That is to say, a speech that would maintain in its irreducible difference a foreign truth, that of the Stranger who, in his very speech, is the presence of strangeness.

— Yes, but let's watch where we are heading. When, in speech, *autrui* speaks to me as the Stranger and the Unknown, this speech is not of the kind that might enter into discussion, having no need, in order to come about, to come up in dialogue against an opposing affirmation; it is absolutely other and is itself without other, being the other of all speech. In this it is non-dialectical. It escapes contestation.

— It is outside contestation, without being incontestable. For I can always take exception to it, exclude it. I can even do away with it altogether. Nothing is easier: it suffices not to hear it—this is strictly my right.

— I can and I cannot; we would need to see the consequences more clearly. But I recognize nonetheless that such a speech eludes contestation in the same way that it escapes certitude, initiating signification but signifying nothing, or nothing determined; thus lacking a signified, as we were saying a moment ago or, more precisely, withdrawing, always turning away from the signified that 'I' am led to attribute to it. Hence, in some sense, its superiority, its altitude, what situates it above—or before—any horizon and the exigency of always having to hear in what it says more than it says, and more than any saying.

— Still, it must enter into the play of communication.

— It enters into it, but as a speech that is not in play—or whose play may assuredly be grasped by the play, but only at the risk of neglecting what comes from it by forgetting what, in the accord of discourse, makes it hold to its disaccord. A speech without concordance.

— Thereby affirming the determinant discontinuity of every relation that is always both implied and hidden in the relation between man and man. Speech says: infinite distance and difference, a distance to which speech itself attests and that holds it outside all contestation, all equality, and all commerce.

— *Autrui* is thus unequal in relation to me, revealing himself to me only through the hiatus of inequality. We come back, then, to our question. For it is of the nature of dialectical accomplishment to refuse such inequality inasmuch as it works toward affirming the whole wherein each one must recognize himself in the other as another myself. Nothing is more important.

— Nothing, indeed. But it may be that I cannot give the measure of equality its true sense unless I maintain the absence of common measure that is my relation to *autrui*. An equality of what is nevertheless radically unequal. Just as 'everything' would have to be known to me in order that my relation with the Unknown that is man should present itself to me in all its authenticity and as the very weight of the Outside. I will add, though, that these two experiences of speech, these two movements that must be maintained together—one being the work of equalization in which everything unequal is always destined to be included, the other being what in advance excludes itself from this equal truth—are also necessarily irreconcilable. For while the one wants to be everything, being the passion, the realization, and the speech of the whole, the other speaks before and outside the whole.

— The one is a speech of power, of confrontation, of opposition and of negation in order to reduce everything opposed, and in order that the truth be affirmed in its entirety as silent equality.

— The other is a speech beyond opposition, beyond negation, and does nothing but affirm; but it is also outside affirmation, because it says nothing but the infinite distance of the Other and the infinite exigency that is *autrui* in its presence; that which eludes all power to negate and to affirm.

— A speech that nevertheless never names *autrui* but calls upon him, so that, unknown, he may turn toward me.

— Through this essential turn that is speech and in whose movement man receives man in that from which he turns away.

— A speech that is other than any speech already said and thereby always new, never heard: to be precise, a speech beyond hearing and to which I must nonetheless respond.

— Such, then, would be my task: to respond to this speech that surpasses my hearing, to respond to it without having really understood it, and to respond to it in repeating it, in making it speak.

— To *name* the possible, to *respond* to the impossible. I remember that we had designated in this way the two centers of gravity of all language.

— This response, this speech that begins by responding and that in this beginning says over again the question that comes to it from the Unknown and the Stranger—here is what lies at the basis of the responsibility that is subsequently expressed in the hard language of exigency: one must speak.

— Speak without power, speak without power to.

— Hold to one's word. Engage with speech."

VII

The Relation of the Third Kind
Man without horizon

"I think we should try to be more open.

— More clear as well.

— More frank and more clear, two things that don't always go together. In the meantime, let us try to say what relation, among all those that exist, human experience and human exigency have allowed us to conceive among men. We can define, for example, more or less arbitrarily, three sets of relations. In the first reigns the law of the same. Man wants unity, he observes separation. What is other — be it some other thing or some other person — he must work to render identical. Adequation and identification, with mediation as their means, that is to say, struggle and labor in history, provide the paths by which he aims to reduce everything to the same, but also to give to the same the plenitude of the whole that it must in the end become. In this case, unity passes by way of totality, just as truth is the movement of the whole — the sole truth being an affirmation of the whole.

— The second kind of relation would be, it seems to me, the following: unity is always not only demanded, but immediately attained. In a dialectical relation, the I-subject, either dividing itself or dividing the Other, affirms the *Other* as an intermediary and realizes itself in it (in such a way that the I is able to reduce the Other to the truth of the Subject). In this new relation the absolutely Other and Self immediately unite: this relation is one of coincidence and participation, sometimes obtained through methods of immediation. The Self and the Other lose themselves in one another: there is ecstasy, fusion, fruition. But here the 'I' ceases to be sovereign; sovereignty is in the Other who is the sole absolute.

— And the Other, in this case, is still no more than a substitute for the One.

Be the relation mediate, immediate, or infinite, thought, like a magnetic needle, index of the north, always points toward unity.

— Even more than Being, even more than the Same, the rigor of the One holds thought captive. And surely it is not some gentle madness that will free us from the One; nor are we in any way rejecting this work toward unity — on the contrary, we are working as much as is in our power toward the affirmation and the accomplishment of the world considered as a unity of the whole. And as we will continue to repeat, this is the task of each one in working and speaking. But each time, too, we will add: we must try to think the Other, try to speak in referring to the Other without reference to the One and without reference to the Same.

— We must try; and in this way will we turn toward the third kind of relation, a relation about which one must simply say: it does not tend toward unity, it is not a relation from the perspective of unity or with unity in view, not a relation of unification. The One is not the ultimate horizon (even if beyond every horizon), any more than is Being, thought always (even in its retreat) as the continuity, the gathering, or the unity of being.

— But toward what are we venturing? I am frightened and am resisting. Are we not going to become guilty of a parricide — one in regard to which Plato's would be an act of pious filiation? It is no longer here simply a matter of raising our hand against Being or decreeing the death of God, but of breaking with what has always, in all laws and in all works, in this world and in every other, been our guarantee, our exigency, and our responsibility.

— Therefore we will only go forward with caution; not forgetting in any case that it is not from coherent thought that we would seek to break away, and that we do not seek to rid ourselves all at once of unity — what a joke that would be; rather, speaking, and speaking necessarily under the authority of a comprehensive thought, we will try to come to a sense of another form of speech and another kind of relation wherein the Other, the presence of the other, would return us neither to ourselves nor to the One.

— A relation, then, not of fiction or of hypothesis, but one that, though diverted and caught up in the (real) relations between men, is always in play as soon as they speak and encounter one another.

— A relation we are designating as multiple only inasmuch as it is not determined by the One. A mobile-immobile relation, untold and without number, not indeterminate but indetermining, always in displacement, being without a place, and such that it seems to draw-repel any 'I' into leaving its site or its role — which, nonetheless, the 'I' must maintain, having become nomadic and anonymous in an abyssal space of resonance and condensation.

— Let's go back then. I am — to begin with what is most common — necessarily in relation with someone. This relation can be instrumental or objective, as when I seek to use someone as I might an object or even simply study him as an object of knowledge and of truth. Or I can look at him in his dignity and his liberty, seeing in him another myself and wanting him to make my self freely recognized by him, being myself a self only in this free recognition that is both equal and reciprocal — a movement that is not accomplished by the sole impetus of the *belle âme*, but through the labor, the discourse, and the liberating action of history. This is a long labor, an action that transforms nature into a world and, in the world, lays claim to transparency; here, the whole supposedly accomplished, the reign of liberty would substitute itself for the reign of necessity — and we already know what measure of blood, sweat, and tears is required for this. Or again, I can desire to become immediately one with you in the instant through the rapture of communication and draw the other into me in an effusion where there remains neither the one nor the other. Desire — a certain desire — be it an illusion of truth or the truth of illusion, tends toward this immediate unitary relation, just as all the other relations aim at establishing between beings and between things, but in a manner that is only mediate, a form of unity or identity. We begin to have a sense, then, of what we have called the relation of the third kind (the first being a mediate relation of dialectical or objective identification, the second a relation demanding immediate unity). Now what 'founds' this third relation, leaving it still unfounded, is no longer proximity — proximity of struggle, of services, of essence, of knowledge, or of recognition, not even of solitude — but rather the *strangeness* between us: a strangeness it will not suffice to characterize as a separation or even as a distance.

— Rather an interruption.

— An interruption escaping all measure. But — and here is the strangeness of this strangeness — such an interruption (one that neither includes nor excludes) would be nevertheless a relation; at least if I take it upon myself not to reduce it, not to reconcile it, even by comprehending it, that is, not to seek to consider it as the 'faltering' mode of a still unitary relation.

— And such would be the relation of man to man when there is no longer between them the proposition of a God, the mediation of a world, or the subsistence of a nature.

— What there would be between man and man, if there were nothing but the interval represented by the word 'between' — an empty space all the more empty as it cannot be confused with pure nothingness — is an infinite separation, but offering itself as a relation in the exigency that is speech.

— Let us suppose this, and ask ourselves what it means.

— Yes, what does this mean? It means first that, in this relation, man is what is most distant from man, coming toward him as what is irreducibly Distant; in this sense, far more separated from him than he is from the limit of the Universe or than he would be from God himself. This means also that this distance represents what, from man to man, escapes human power — which is capable of anything. This relation founded by a pure lack in speech is designated there where my power ceases, there where possibility falls away.

— In other words, the pure interval between man and man, this relation of the third kind, would be on the one hand what relates me to nothing but man, but yet in no way relates me to myself, to another myself; on the other hand, it is what does not arise from possibility and does not declare itself in terms of power.

— Yes, but let's not be content with so little; let us try to open a path for ourselves, patiently, and without being afraid of the possibility of making no headway. I have in this relation with man a relation with what is radically out of my reach; and this relation measures the very extent of the Outside. This tells us that true exteriority is not that of objects, nor that of an indifferent nature or the immense universe (which it is always possible to attain through a relation of power by keeping it within the realm of my representation, the horizon of my knowledge, my view, my negation, and even my ignorance); nor is it this personal exteriority that distinguishes men by holding them to be interchangeable, but that also holds them with regard to one another under the judgment—the joinder—of a set of common values. True strangeness, if it comes to me from man, comes to me from this Other that man would be. He alone, then, is the ex-centric; he alone escapes the circle of vision from which my perspective unfolds, and this not because he would constitute in his turn the center of another horizon, but because he does not turn toward me from the basis of a horizon that is proper to him. The Other: not only does he not fall within my horizon, he is himself without horizon.

— Man without horizon, and not affirming himself on the basis of a horizon— in this sense a being without being, a presence without a present, thus foreign to everything visible and to everything invisible—he is what comes to me as speech when to speak is not to see. The Other speaks to me and is only this exigency of speech. And when the Other speaks to me, speech is the relation of that which remains radically separate, the relation of the third kind affirming a relation without unity, without equality.

— Does this mean that communication with '*Autrui*,' such as it is marked in speech, is not a transsubjective or an intersubjective relation, but inaugurates a relation that would not be one of subject to subject or of subject to object?

— I think we should make the decision to say this. When *Autrui* speaks to me he does not speak to me as a self. When I call upon the Other, I respond to what speaks to me from no site, and thus am separated from him by a caesura such that he forms with me neither a duality nor a unity. It is this fissure—this relation with the other—that we ventured to characterize as an interruption of being. And now we will add: between man and man there is an interval that would be neither of being nor of non-being, an interval borne by the Difference of speech—a difference preceding everything that is different and everything unique.

— Here I would like to return to our point of departure, when one of us proposed trying to be more open. It seems to me that we have done no more than prepare ourselves for frankness through some rather devious detours.

— Because to be open is to speak after having crossed over some limit; a movement that is better accomplished when it is not done directly.

— I had the feeling, in fact, that we'd just passed some threshold, particularly at the moment when we said: 'When *Autrui* speaks to me, he does not speak to me as a self' and 'The relation of this *Autrui* to myself is not a relation of subject to subject.' I confess that in saying and in hearing this, I experienced a feeling of fear: as though we were coming directly up against the unknown, or perhaps as though the alibi of our relations were about to be exposed.

— Clearly there is a question here that has continued to bear upon us, and whose pressure made us cross the threshold. This question might be: Who is '*Autrui*'?

— I wonder whether we can draw '*Autrui*' into such a question. I wonder if this very word does not deceive us; it carries with it a hint of the term *altruism* created by Auguste Comte. On this basis morality can easily lay claim to it.

— *Autrui* is not, in fact, the word one would want to hold onto. Yet it comes from afar and was already used in epic language. *Autrui* is the Other in the objective case and on the model of the word '*lui*' [him], which was used at that time only as a verbal complement. According to certain supercilious grammarians, *autrui* should never be used in the first person. I can approach *autrui*, *autrui* cannot approach me. *Autrui* is thus the Other when the other is not a subject. Using this linguistic particularity as a reminder, we could say that *Autrui* is lacking an ego; but this lack, nonetheless, does not make him an object.

— When we ask ourselves 'Who is *autrui*?' we question in such a way that the question necessarily distorts what it means to call into question. *Autrui* cannot designate a nature, it cannot characterize a being or an essential trait. Or, to express this crudely, *autrui* is not a certain type of man whose task it is to occupy this role—in the manner of the saints and prophets, delegates of the Most High—opposite the clan of the 'I's'. This must be recalled (even if such a precaution is somewhat ludicrous) because our language substantifies everything.

— Yet there is still another difficulty: if it is true that *autrui* is never for me a self, for *him* the same is true of me. This means that the Other who looms up before me—outside my horizon and as one coming from afar—is *for himself* nothing but a self who would like to be heard by the Other, be received by the Other and stand in my presence, as if I were the Other and because I am nothing other than the Other: the unidentifiable, the 'I'-less, the nameless, the presence of the inaccessible. Whence a tangling of relations that seems necessarily to set us back up again under the exigency of dialectical accomplishment.

— Indeed this is one of the traps laid out for us. For the moment, we shall have to make two remarks, and say first of all that this redoubling of irreciprocity—the reversal that makes me apparently the other of the other—cannot, at the level at which we are situating our analysis, be taken over by the dialectic, for it does not tend to reestablish any equality whatsoever; on the contrary, it signifies a double dissymmetry, a double discontinuity, as though the empty space between the one and the other were not homogeneous but polarized: as through this space constituted a non-isomorphic field bearing a double distortion, at once infinitely negative and infinitely positive, and such that one should call it neutral if it is well understood that the neutral does not annul, does not neutralize this double-signed infinity, but bears in it the way of an enigma. And then too, we ought to say the following: if the question 'Who is *autrui?*' has no direct meaning, it is because it must be replaced by another: 'What of the human "community," when it must respond to this relation of strangeness between man and man—a relation without common measure, an exorbitant relation—that the experience of language leads one to sense?' And yet this question does not signify that the Other—*autrui*—would be simply a way of being, that is to say, an obligation that each in turn would either fulfill or avoid, whether knowingly or not. There is infinitely more at stake. In this relation, the other—but which of the two of us would be the other?—is radically other, is solely the other and, as such, a name for the nameless whose momentary position on the board—a board upon which he plays when he speaks, and in speaking puts himself at stake—causes him to be now and again designated by the word 'man.' (Just as the pawn can become every piece except the king.) The Other: the presence of man precisely insofar as he is always missing from his presence, just as he is missing from his place.

— Man, that is to say, men. I will translate our preceding remarks, then, by saying more simply: in responding to this other relation—a relation of impossibility and strangeness—which we experience as soon as we speak (and at a certain still poorly situated level of speech), we, as speaking beings, also experience man as the absolutely Other, since the Other cannot be thought either in terms of transcendence or in terms of immanence. We must not be content to say in regard to this experience that language simply expresses or reflects it, for it originates only in the space and the time of language—there where language, through writing, undoes the idea of an origin.

— An experience in which the Other, the Outside itself, exceeding any positive or any negative term, is the 'presence' that does not refer back to the One, and the exigency of a relation of discontinuity where unity is not implied. The Other, the *He*; but only insofar as this third person is not a third person and brings the neutral into play.

— The neutral, the neutral, how strangely this sounds for *me*.

— *Me*, myself: can one then still speak of a self? We have to do, perhaps, with an I without a self, a non-personal punctuality oscillating between no one and someone, a semblance that only the exigency of the exorbitant relation invests silently and momentarily with this role, or establishes in the position of the Self-subject with which it can then be identified in order to simulate the identical—so that, on this basis, through writing, the mark of the absolutely non-identical in the Other might announce itself.

— Perhaps, also, it is time to withdraw this term *autrui*, while retaining what it has to say to us: that the Other is always what calls upon 'man' (even if only to put him between parentheses or between quotation marks), not the other as God or other as nature but, as 'man,' more Other than all that is other.

— Therefore, and before we delete it, let us keep in mind that *autrui* is a name that is essentially neutral and that, far from relieving us of all responsibility of attending to the neutral, it reminds us that we must, in the presence of the other who comes to us as *Autrui*, respond to the depth of strangeness, of inertia, of ir-regularity and idleness [*désoeuvrement*] to which we open when we seek to re-ceive the speech of the Outside. *Autrui* would be man himself, through whom comes to me what discloses itself neither to the personal power of the Subject nor to the power of impersonal truth. All the mystery of the neutral passes, perhaps, by way of the other, and sends us back to him; passes, that is to say, through this experience of language in which the relation of the third kind, a non-unitary rela-tion, escapes the question of being as it does that of the whole, leaving us exposed to 'the most profound question,' that questioning of the detour through which the neutral—which is never the impersonal—comes into question.

— And let us add that every notion of alterity already implies man as the other, and not the inverse. Only, it follows from this that the Other man who is '*autrui*' also risks being always Other than man, close to what cannot be close to me: close to death, close to the night, and certainly as repulsive as anything that comes to me from these regions without horizon.

— We well know that when a man dies close by, however indifferent his exis-tence might be to us, in that instant and forever he is for us the Other.

— But remember that the Other speaks to me; the decisive interruption of rela-tion speaks precisely as an infinite relation in the speech of the Other. You are not claiming that when you speak to *autrui* you are speaking to him as though to a kind of dead person, calling to him from the other side of the partition?

— When I speak to the Other, the speech that relates me to him 'accomplishes' and 'measures' that inordinate distance (a distance beyond measure) that is the in-finite movement of dying, where death puts impossibility into play. And, in speaking to him, I myself speak rather than die, which means also that I speak in the place where there is a place for dying."

*

I listen in turn to these two voices, being neither close to the one, nor close to the other; being, nevertheless, one of them and being the other only insofar as I am not me—and thus, from the one to the other, interrupting myself in a manner that dissimulates (simulates only) the decisive interruption. How can one pretend to receive the enigmatic force that comes from the interruption that becomes in-finite relation in speech, and that we betray with our insufficient means?

Let us again repeat:

(1) Language, the experience of language — writing — is what leads us to sense a relation entirely other, a relation of the third kind. We will have to ask ourselves in what manner we enter into this experience, assuming that it does not repel us, and ask ourselves if it does not speak to us as the enigma of all speech.

(2) In this relation that we are isolating in a manner that is not necessarily abstract, the one is never comprehended by the other, does not form with him an ensemble, a duality, or a possible unity; the one is foreign to the other, without this strangeness privileging either one of them. We call this relation neutral, indicating already in this manner that it cannot be recaptured, either when one affirms or when one negates, demanding of language in this way not an indecision between these two modes, but rather a possibility of saying that would say without saying being and without denying it either. And herein we characterize, perhaps, one of the essential traits of the "literary" act: the very fact of writing.

(3) The neutral relation, a relation without relation, can be indicated in yet another manner: the relation of the one to the other is doubly dissymmetrical. We have recognized this several times. We know — at least we sense — that the absence between the one and the other is such that the relations, if they could be unfolded, would be those of a non-isomorphic field in which point A would be distant from point B by a distance other than point B's distance from point A; a distance excluding reciprocity and presenting a curvature whose irregularity extends to the point of discontinuity. [1]

(4) In making explicit this relation, we cannot avoid representing it as taking place between two terms, *and as a consequence, we seem to give ourselves the right to consider them as having, outside this relation, their own reality and determinations. In a certain sense we are justified in doing so. First of all, because even if the two men who are present in a room and who speak are nothing but the site of a set of possible relations, we have recognized that among these relations certain ones make each of them exist as a distinct, objective reality, or as a Self-subject: a unique existence, a center centered upon a radiating unity, finally a history by which all of their truth passes through the world that is being made. Many difficulties are assembled in these few words. Nevertheless, we will resolutely disregard them in order to hold to the relation upon which we are reflecting. Here too, it seems we were not mistaken in speaking of terms between which a relationship could take place, and as though these terms could claim to affirm themselves in this very relation as distinct from the relation — and not only as distinct but as separated by a difference and a distance that are infinite. For such would be its meaning: to be an infinite double separation. Yes, let us remember this. It is of the nature of such a strange relation to designate an* infinite *double absence. But then, in this case, we could say — and it is necessary to say — that the Other, this "Other" in play in the third kind of relation, is no longer one of its terms; it is neither the one nor the other, being nothing other than relation it-*

self, a relation of the one to the other that requires infinity. Nevertheless, as we well sense, we cannot content ourselves with the simplicity of this affirmation. The Other is not only said of the relation, *designated as a relation of foreignness be-tween man and man; for in this other relation, and through it, the other is for me the very* presence *of the other in his infinite distance: man as absolutely other and radically foreign; he who does not yield to the Same nor is exalted in the unity of the Unique. Or again, for myself, and insofar in myself as I am (momentarily and by function) the one, I undergo the experience of the Other, not as a strange relation with a man like myself, but as man in his strangeness — that which escapes all identification, be it that of an impersonal knowledge, of a mediation, or of a mystical fusion: the outside or the unknown that is always already beyond the aim of my sight, the non-visible that speech bears. This amounts to saying that for me the other is at one and the same time the* relation *of inaccessibility to the other, the other that this inaccessible relation sets up, and, nonetheless, the inaccessible* presence *of the other — man without horizon — who becomes relation and access in the very inaccessibility of his approach.*

It is as though in the time-space of interrelation it were necessary to think un-der a double contradiction; to think the Other first as the distortion of a field that is nevertheless continuous, as the dislocation and the rupture of discontinuity — and then as the infinite of a relation that is without terms and as the infinite termi-nation of a term without relation.

VIII

Interruption
As on a Riemann surface

The definition of conversation (that is, the most simple description of the most simple conversation) might be the following: when two people speak together, they speak not together, but each in turn: one says something, then stops, the other something else (or the same thing), then stops. The coherent discourse they carry on is composed of sequences that are interrupted when the conversation moves from partner to partner, even if adjustments are made so that they correspond to one another. The fact that speech needs to pass from one interlocutor to another in order to be confirmed, contradicted, or developed shows the necessity of interval. The power of speaking interrupts itself, and this interruption plays a role that appears to be minor — precisely the role of a subordinated alternation. This role, nonetheless, is so enigmatic that it can be interpreted as bearing the very enigma of language: pause between sentences, pause from one interlocutor to another, and pause of attention, the hearing that doubles the force of locution.

I wonder if we have reflected enough upon the various significations of this pause that alone permits speech to be constituted as conversation, and even as speech. We end up by confining someone who speaks without pause. (Let us recall Hitler's terrible monologues. And every head of state participates in the same violence of this *dictare*, the repetition of an imperious monologue, when he enjoys the power of being the only one to speak and, rejoicing in possession of his high solitary word, imposes it without restraint as a superior and supreme speech upon others.) But let us take the most steady conversation, the conversation least exposed to chance caprice; even if its discourse is coherent, it must always frag-

75

ment itself by changing protagonists. Moving from one to the other interlocutor, it interrupts itself: interruption permits the exchange. Interrupting for the sake of understanding, understanding in order to speak.

It is clear, however, that the stops that punctuate, measure, and articulate dialogue are not always of the same kind: some block conversation. Kafka wondered at what moment and how many times, when eight people are seated within the horizon of a conversation, it is appropriate to speak if one does not wish to be considered silent. But such silence, even if disapproving, constitutes the part that moves discourse. Without it, one would not speak, or only to ask oneself belatedly if one had not mistaken the interlocutor's attitude and if it had not been the other who made you speak (just as, in other circumstances, one might reproach the host for having made you drink—it is, after all, the same intoxication). And even when remaining silent is a refusal it is rarely abrupt; it takes part in the discourse, inflecting it with its nuances, contributing to the hope for, or the despair of, a final concord. Silence is still only a deferred speech, or else it bears the signification of a difference obstinately maintained.

*

Interruption is necessary to any succession of words; intermittence makes their becoming possible, discontinuity ensures the continuity of understanding. There would certainly be a great deal to conclude from this. But for the moment, I would like to show that the intermittence by which discourse becomes dialogue, that is to say dis-course, presents itself in two very different ways.

In the first case, the arrest-interval is comparable to the ordinary pause that permits the conversation's "each in turn." Here, discontinuity is essential since it promises exchange—essential, but relative. What it aims at, be it later or never, and yet at the same time starting from today, is the affirmation of a unitary truth where coherent discourse will no longer cease and, no longer ceasing, will merge with its other, silent side. From this perspective, rupture still plays into the functioning of common speech, even if it fragments it, thwarts it, or impedes it. Not only does rupture give meaning, but it also brings common sense forth as a horizon. It is the respiration of discourse. In this category could be grouped all the forms of speech that belong to a dialectical experience of existence and of history—from everyday chatter to the highest moments of reason, of struggle and of practice. Interrupting for the sake of understanding.

But there is another kind of interruption, more enigmatic and more grave. It introduces the wait that measures the distance between two interlocutors—no longer a reducible, but an irreducible distance. Having mentioned this often in these investigations, I will simply allude to it again. Within an interrelational space, I can seek to communicate with someone in a number of ways: first, by considering him as an objective possibility in the world, according to the ways of objectivity; another time, by regarding him as another self, perhaps quite different, but whose difference passes by way of a primary identity, that of two beings each equally able to speak in the first person; and a third time, no longer by a mediate relation of impersonal knowledge or of personal comprehension, but by attempting to achieve an immediate relation wherein the same and the other seek to lose themselves in one another or draw near to one another through the proximity of a familiar address that forgets or effaces distance. These relations have in common the fact that all three tend toward unity: the "I" wants to annex the other (identify the other with itself) by making of it its own thing, or by studying it as a thing, or, yet again, in wanting to find in it another myself, whether this be through free recognition or through the instantaneous union of two souls. There remains another modality (without a mode). This time, it is no longer a question of seeking to unify. In the other I no longer want to recognize one whom a still common measure — the belonging to a common space — holds in a relation of continuity or unity with me. What is in play now is the foreignness between us, and not only the obscure part that escapes our mutual knowledge and is nothing more than the obscurity of the self's position — the singularity of the singular self; this foreignness is still very relative (a self is always close to a self, even in difference, competition, desire, and need). What is now in play, and demands relation, is everything that separates me from the other, that is to say the other insofar as I am infinitely separated from him — a separation, fissure, or interval that leaves him infinitely outside me, but also requires that I found my relation with him upon this very interruption that is an *interruption of being*. This alterity, it must be repeated, makes him neither another self for me, nor another existence, neither a modality or a moment of universal existence, nor a superexistence, a god or a non-god, but rather the unknown in its infinite distance.

An alterity that holds in the name of the neutral.

To simplify, let us say that through the presence of the other understood in the neutral there is in the field of relations a distortion preventing any direct communication and any relation of unity; or again, there is a fundamental anomaly that it falls to speech not to reduce but to convey, even if it does so without saying it or signifying it. Now it is to this hiatus — to the strangeness, to the infinity between us — that the interruption in language itself responds, the interruption that introduces waiting. But let us understand that the arrest here is not necessarily or simply marked by silence, by a blank or a gap (this would be too crude), but by a change in the form or the structure of language (when speaking is first of all writing) — a change metaphorically comparable to that which made Euclid's geometry into that of Riemann. (Valéry once confided to a mathematician that he was planning to write — to speak — on "a Riemann surface."[1]) A change such that to speak (to write) is *to cease thinking solely with a view to unity*, and to make the relations of words an essentially dissymmetrical field governed by discontinuity; as though, having renounced the uninterrupted force of a coherent discourse, it were a matter of drawing out a level of language where one might gain the power not only to express oneself in an intermittent manner, but also to allow intermittence itself to speak: a speech that, non-unifying, is no longer content with being a passage or a bridge—a non-pontificating speech capable of clearing the two shores separated by the abyss, but without filling in the abyss or reuniting its shores: a speech without reference to unity.

*

The difference between these two kinds of interruption, as I have just schematized them, is theoretically very firm. It corresponds to the two kinds of experience we have with speech: one is dialectical, the other is not. One is the speech of the universe, tending toward unity and helping to accomplish the whole; the other, the speech of writing, bears a relation of infinity and strangeness. This decisive difference is nonetheless always ambiguous: when two persons speak, the silence that permits them to speak in turn as they speak together is still no more than the alternating pause of the first degree; but in this alternance there may also, already, be at work the interruption by which the unknown announces itself.[2] Yet there is something more grave; when the power of speech is interrupted, one does not know, one can never know with certainty, what is at work: the interruption that permits exchange, the interruption that suspends speech in order to reestablish it at another level, or the negating interruption that, far from still being a speech that recovers its wind and breathes, undertakes—if this is possible—to asphyxiate speech and destroy it as though forever. When, for example, interruption arises out of fatigue, out of pain or affliction (all forms of the neutral), do we know to which experience it belongs? Can we be sure, even though it may be sterilizing, that it is simply barren? No, we are not sure (and this, moreover, adds to the fatigue and the affliction). We sense as well that if pain (fatigue or affliction) hollows out an infinite gap between beings, this gap is perhaps what would be most important to bring to expression, all the while leaving it empty, so that to speak out of fatigue, out of pain or affliction [*malheur*], could be to speak according to the infinite dimension of language. And can we not go still further? Let us suppose an interruption that would in some sense be absolute and absolutely neutral; let us conceive of it as being no longer within the sphere of language, but exterior and anterior to all speech and to all silence; let us call it the ultimate, the hyperbolical. Would we have attained with it the rupture that would deliver us, even if hyperbolically, not only from all reason (this would be little), but from all unreason, that is, from the reason that madness remains? Or would we not be obliged to ask ourselves whether from out of such an interruption—barbarity itself—there would not come an exigency to which it would still be necessary to respond by speaking? And would we not even have to ask whether speech (writing) does not always mean attempting to involve the outside of any language in language itself, that is to say, speaking within this Out-side, speaking according to the measure of this "outside," which, being in all speech, may very well also risk turning speech back into what is excluded from all speaking? To write: to trace a circle in the interior of which would come to be inscribed the outside of every circle . . .

Let us go no further and summarize. We have, first of all, two important dis-tinctions: one corresponding to a dialectical, the other to a non-dialectical ex-igency of speech: the pause that permits exchange, the wait that measures infinite distance. But in waiting it is not simply the delicate rupture preparing the poetic act that declares itself, but also, and at the same time, other forms of arrest that are very profound, very perverse, more and more perverse, and always such that if one distinguishes them, the distinction does not avert but rather postulates am-biguity. We have "distinguished" in this way three of them: one wherein empti-ness becomes work; another wherein emptiness is fatigue, affliction; and the other, the ultimate, the hyperbolical, wherein worklessness (perhaps thought) in-dicates itself. To interrupt oneself for the sake of understanding. To understand in order to speak. Speaking, finally, only to interrupt oneself and to render possi-ble the impossible interruption.

IX

A Plural Speech

I think of what Apollo affirms when, through the mouth of the poet Bacchylides, he says to Admetus: *"You are a mere mortal; therefore your mind must harbor two thoughts at once."* In other words, a multiplicity of speech in the simultaneity of one language.

It is all very well for a god, bearer of the one and unitary thought, to scorn and pity us for the duality with which he charges us. To us falls the responsibility of extending it to the furthest reaches of a reign from which the heavens do not escape, even the one no longer inhabited by Apollo. To speak is always to put into play an essential duplicity from which one draws advantage—this is the ambiguity, the indecision of Yes and No—by claiming to reduce it through the rules of logic. But to speak according to the necessity of an irreducible plurality, to speak as though each word were its own indefinite echoing within a multiple space, is too heavy a burden for one to bear alone. Dialogue must help us share this duality; we double up in order to bear this double speech, now less weighty for being divided, and above all for having been made successive through the alternance that unfolds in time. Being two, thinking and speaking by twos in the intimacy of dialogue, would be an ingenious means for Admetus, given his status as a mortal condemned to simultaneous thoughts, to make himself Apollo's equal and even his superior, since this ever present duality, be it that of two persons, maintains the movement of thought that is necessarily excluded from a being that is one.

A perfect solution, then. Yet we must ask ourselves—as soon as we have set aside the alibis of good conscience with which it provides us—why the solution

80

of dialogue remains insufficient, and why Admetus would have been wrong to see in it a fitting answer to the god's malediction. It is because dialogue is founded upon the reciprocity of words and the equality of speakers; only two "I"s can establish a relation of dialogue, each one acknowledging in the second "I" the same power to speak as his own, each considering himself equal to the other and seeing in the other nothing other than another "Self." This is the paradise of decorous idealism. But we know, first of all, that there is almost no sort of equality in our societies. (It suffices, in whatever regime, to have heard the "dialogue" between a man presumed innocent and the magistrate who questions him to know what this equality of speech means when it is based upon an inequality of culture, condition, power, and fortune. But each of us, and at every moment, either is or finds himself in the presence of a judge. All speech is a word of command, of terror, of seduction, of resentment, flattery, or aggression; all speech is violence—and to pretend to ignore this in claiming to dialogue is to add liberal hypocrisy to the dialectical optimism according to which war is no more than another form of dialogue.) But there is more to be said. Even if speaking equally were possible, even if speaking ensured this equality and worked toward this identity, something no less essential would be missing from speech. Let us return to Admetus. To Admetus is extended the burden of thinking, the burden, that is, of speaking doubly in one act of speaking; he believes he can escape by unfolding this duplicity and sharing it out between two men who speak on equal terms. We have, then, two words in one speech, two that are different and yet identical. Yes, let us once again acknowledge that this is an impressive feat. But something has been lost in this admirable turn of affairs. It is *difference* itself; a difference that nothing should simplify, nothing can equalize and that alone, mysteriously, gives voice to two instances of speech by keeping them separate even as they are held together only by this separation.

Admetus, the founder of dialogue, still falls victim to the terror of a god. Subject to the god's ideal, he has only unity in view, as though in aiming for the same the One had to be the truth of all comprehension, the goal of every relation human and divine. This is not the case. In the interrelational space, dialogue, and the equality dialogue presupposes, tend to do nothing other than increase entropy, just as dialectical communication, requiring two antagonistic poles charged with contrary words and provoking a common current through this opposition, is itself, after brilliant bursts, destined to die out in entropic identity. Dialogue is a plane geometry wherein relations are direct and remain ideally symmetrical. But let us suppose that the field of relations rests upon some anomaly analogous to what physicists would call a curvature of the universe; that is, a distortion preventing any possibility of symmetry and introducing between things, and particularly between man and man, a relation of infinity.

Let us suppose with regard to this spatial knot, this point of abrupt density, this polarization, this fundamental irregularity that hollows out and swells extension and duration in such a way that there would be nothing equal in them, and nothing simply unequal either—let us suppose that it falls to speech not to reduce it, not to turn away from it by declaring it unsayable, but rather to present it, that is (just the same), give it form. Yes, let us suppose this, and let us agree to acknowledge the full reach of the exigency that is given to us by this supposition. First of all, that to speak is certainly to bring the other back to the same in a search for a mediating speech; but it is also, first of all, to seek to receive the other as other and the foreign as foreign; to seek *autrui*, therefore, in their irreducible difference, in their infinite strangeness, an empty strangeness, and such that only an essential discontinuity can retain the affirmation proper to it. What, fundamentally, is the god asking of Admetus? Perhaps nothing less than that he shake off the yoke of the god and finally leave the circle in which he remains enclosed by a fascination with unity. And this is no small thing, certainly, for it means ceasing to think only with a view to unity. And this means therefore: not fearing to affirm interruption and rupture in order to come to the point of proposing and expressing—an infinite task—a truly plural speech. Precisely speech that is always in advance destined (and also dissimulated) in the written exigency.

It is toward this Difference that we are initially turned—torn from every particular, different thing, and through a mysteriously alternative form—by one of the first works in which thought was called to itself through the discontinuity of writing, a work time has broken in on as though to render accidental its fragmentary presence. Dissuading, in this way, rather than persuading, the broken texts of Heraclitus come toward us.

II

THE LIMIT–EXPERIENCE

I

Heraclitus

Clémence Ramnoux has written that if, when reading Heraclitus, we translate "Day Night" or "Lightning Speech" with the common nouns of the modern world we already go against their meaning because modern nouns have not been formed in the same way.[1] Nonetheless, we are obliged to translate (for it must be done); at least first in seeking the linguistic tradition and the kind of discourse in relation to which the invention of a new form comes to situate itself—a form that seems eternally new, and is yet necessarily in a relation of belonging and rupture with other ways of saying. Here erudition comes in, but it bears less upon the hard to grasp and always malleable facts of culture than upon the texts themselves: witnesses that do not lie should one decide to be faithful to them. A reading of Hesiod (one of the great early names to which Heraclitus responds by a sovereign opposition) suggests that in these more ancient times the Greeks had at their disposal two sorts of discourse for saying sacred things. One was a vocabulary of divine names with a corpus of fascinating legends, immemorial traditions, terrible mythic accounts ("children thrust back into their mother's womb, fathers castrated by their sons, struggles with monsters . . . "), and another vocabulary having a more ambiguous destination that names the Forces at work in the accounts of genesis, thereby introducing the first questioning concerning origin. These names of Forces—Chaos (the primordial breach or the void), Earth understood as the primordial firmness, Night that divides into night and day, the Children of the Night, Death, Sleep—are names that are certainly still sacred, but also signs of the stirring, extreme, and often contrasting experiences that nonetheless belong to the most intimate human experience. Hesiod's cosmogony already employs names and sometimes structures that will furnish a model for later teachings.

Does this mean that when (around the sixth century B.C.) there appears among those traditionally entitled to speak an entirely new kind of master of speech—those who invented the discourses of nature, and for us this means first Heraclitus—this appearance would have been less unexpected or less decisive for being in continuity with the past? On the contrary; it is all the more mysterious that the rarest of inventions should take form and place close to the traditional formulations it modifies from within to tell the secret of things: a language that is suddenly "sober and severe." A prodigious event; not only a new manner of speaking, but one that invents simplicity, discovers the richness of poor words and the illuminating power of a speech that is brief, deprived of images, and, in a sense, ascetic. That the decisive deepening of human language should be brought about by an attention suddenly given to a few, very ordinary words (verbs as common as the verbs to speak, to be), and by the role accorded to these words that are recognized as being more important and charged with more secrets than the loftiest sacred names—so much so that they become superior in dignity and able to challenge any notion of equivalence with them[2]—this is the surprise and truly divine teaching that continues to be of the highest value.

Clémence Ramnoux rightly speaks of a mutation. A new man is born here. And this birth occurs at little cost. One can technically read its signs in just a few characteristics. Sacred discourse becomes a discourse of *physis*: first, by doing with a few divine names that are handled always more soberly and taken for signs of some other Thing, more secret or more difficult to name; also, through the strong meaning accorded to very common words (static verbs, to be there, not to be there; and dynamic verbs, to gather, to disperse, to approach, to depart); then through the choice of the singular neuter to designate, by a sort of non-designation, what we are tempted to emphasize by calling it the essential ("the wise Thing," "the One," "the common [Thing]," "the Thing not to be expected");[3] and then through the decision to employ, in the singular and with a great heightening of meaning, a word such as *logos*, ordinarily used in the plural; most generally, through the privileged use of a severe type of formulation.

With Heraclitus, we grasp this transformation at the moment when it carries at once all the gravity of the sacred language on the basis of which it is formed, and all the opening force of the severe language it offers to a future of truth. We have, therefore, a first double meaning—the initial possibility of a double reading, on whose basis Heraclitus's language, in a manner strangely concerted and with a conscious knowledge of its resources, will deploy the enigmatic power that is its own in order to seize in the network of its duplicities the disjointed simplicity to which the enigma of the variety of things corresponds.

*

Heraclitus the Obscure: so he has been qualified since ancient times, and so he is. Not fortuitously, and certainly not (as claimed some Greek critics, already as frivolous as some of Mallarmé's commentators) so as to pass as more profound, but with the resolute aim of making answer to one another in writing the severity and the density, the simplicity and the complex arrangement of the structure of forms — and, on this basis, to bring into correspondence the obscurity of language and the clarity of things, mastery over the double sense of words and the secret of the dispersion of appearances: in other words, perhaps, dis-course and discourse.

In nearly all of Heraclitus's sentences, such as time's memory has kept them in their fragmentation, one can read through their transparency the strict configurations to which they submit: at one moment the same form filled with different words; at another, the same words composing themselves in different configurations; and at another, the schema remaining empty or calling attention to a hidden word called forth by one that is present and with which it forms elsewhere a visible couple. Life-Death, Wakefulness-Sleep, Presence-Absence, men-gods: these words, coupled and held together by their reciprocal contrariety, constitute interchangeable signs with which the most subtle scriptuary game is tried out in multiple, mysterious combinations, at the same time (but this is also essential) as the structure of alternance is put to the test: a relation of disjunction that, from couple to couple, finds itself the same and nonetheless different — for "All-One," this goes without saying, is not of the same structural relation as "Day-Night" or "men-gods." [4]

We must not be afraid to conclude that a very lofty play of writing is going on here. Each sentence is a cosmos, a minutely calculated arrangement whose terms are in relations of extreme tension, never indifferent to their place or figure, but rather disposed as though aiming at a secret Difference they do no more than indicate by showing, in the form of a measure, the changes and visible conversions of which the sentence is the isolated site. A closed arrangement therefore: each formulation is tacitly sufficient, each unique, but one with the silence that both opens and closes it and that gathers in a virtual manner the dangerous sequence of the as yet unmastered alternations. Naturally, it is understood that in the archaic tradition, word games, riddles, and verbal jugglery constitute a manner of speaking that pleases the gods and of which they themselves, whether for good or for ill, make ample use; furthermore, in divine as in human things, the Greeks passionately loved these games and this language between speech and silence, jest and mystery. This is quite certain. Heraclitus is Greek (to the point of serving as an enigma for the Greeks); he belongs to the age in which the gods still speak and speech is divine. But it is of great consequence that this severe language, which opens as though for the first time onto the depth of simple words, should reintroduce and reinvest the power of enigma and the part allotted to the sacred in writing; then, equally so, that this obscurity to which all understanding is joined should be affirmed here in this first example as a necessity of mastery, as a sign of rigor and an exigency of the most attentive and most contained speech, supremely balanced between the contraries that it tests, faithful to double meaning, but only out of fidelity to meaning's simplicity, and in this way calling upon us never to be content with a reading that would have a single sense or direction.[5]

*

But if the man awake is the man who remembers to read doubly, one would have to be sleeping and reading at the same time to see in the words Heraclitus so rigorously arranges no more than an arrangement of words. We are constantly reminded that when Heraclitus is there, things are there. When he speaks of the river whose waters flow over us, never the same, this is not an example given by a professor. The river itself is teaching us in an immemorial fashion through its call to enter into the secret of its presence: to enter it, but never twice and not even once, as into a sentence that has always already closed upon itself as soon as we pretend to keep our footing there and hold onto it. The teachings of the river, of fire, of the lowest and the highest of things. Almost every one of these formulations is thus written in proximity to neighboring things, coming to terms with them by a movement that goes from things to words, then from words to things, according to a new relation of contrariety we are powerless to master once and for all, but that makes us hear in concrete fashion the mysterious relation existing between writing and the logos, then between the logos and men; a relation according to the double direction of "coming together-going apart": when they approach they move away from one another. *"They are separated from the logos with which they are in the most continuous contact; and the things they meet with every day seem foreign to them"* (fragment 72). A formula in which separation is inscribed in the logos itself as that which has always previously destined it to the disjunction of writing.

The contrariety of "(it) approaches-departs," and the other of "(it) gathers-disperses," is also what measures our understanding of what is in what is said, be it a matter of the manner in which things speak to the Master, or the Master to his disciples; a sort of conversation, both strange and familiar, amicable and hostile, understood and misunderstood, that Clémence Ramnoux is perhaps inclined to place at the level of Socratic dialogue—Heraclitus thus becoming the direct precursor and as though the first incarnation of the inspired, untimely, prosaically divine and garrulous speaker whose merit (assuredly of the first order, according to Plato) consisted in turning back on his steps so that "by thousands and thousands of turns and without taking a single step ahead he always came back to the same point."[6] And it is true that Heraclitus's movement does not advance along the one straight path, as tradition would have it of Parmenides, but rather makes us move, almost without our knowing it and even in the most diverse places, by way of the same crossing: to that point where the paths lead us, according to ever different itineraries, toward the Thing not to be found, not to be expected and to which there is no access.[7]

It is clear to me that Heraclitus was familiar with things, no less than with words. I mean first that he was not interested in closing himself up in an "aesthetics of speech for speech's sake," even if the rigor with which his sentences are constructed is such as to make us content with them and with this newly won austerity. I again cite Clémence Ramnoux: "His characteristic advance *comes and goes* between event and discourse. He has not yet disassociated unseizable event and autonomous discourse. Even less does he let discourse slip from his attention. He lives in the combat of things and words, working to compose a discourse that *resembles* and is not a discourse of pure semblance. Such would be the situation of man between things and words." This is a prudent way to orient our reading. Yet I wonder if the advice given to us to seek to capture this coming and going from words to things and from things to words does not risk leading us to arrest this movement and to establish a distance—a distance that would be of our own making—between what is and what is said. Does Heraclitus truly want to compose a *discourse of resemblance*? Resembling what? And would not the very idea of resemblance, of imitation—an idea that sets us in the wake of Platonism—place speech not only in a state of submission, but also in an irreversible dependency? Would this not serve merely to authorize a one-way exchange rather than that indefatigable reciprocity through which the relations (relations of contrariety, of difference, but in the mode of "moving apart-coming together") of things to words and of words to things give themselves in such a way that reversal is always possible and so one can begin and can end at times with the word, at other times with the thing?

A physician of antiquity reproached Empedocles for having borrowed his manner of conceiving the composition of the cosmos from the plastic arts. A very shrewd criticism (even if it is not certain that the art of painting might then usher us into an aesthetics of resemblance). But between Empedocles and Heraclitus, who precedes him by perhaps fifty years, there is much more than a difference of generation. After Heraclitus everything changes because with him everything begins. One might be tempted to say, however, that if the art of painting permitted Empedocles to compose the world, it is from the art of speech that Heraclitus borrowed the structures that allow him to enter into an understanding of things. First of all, the idea of a changing configuration that, says Emile Benveniste, is equivalent to the word *rhythm* taken in its archaic sense; then, the use of a rigorous proportion, understood by analogy with the carefully calculated relations between words and even parts of words; finally, the very mystery of the *logos*, which, even if it gathers unto itself more than can be said, nonetheless finds in scriptural language its elected domain. Yes, this is a tempting view: that poetic rigor gave man the first idea (perhaps one that cannot be gotten past) of a natural rigor; that the arrangement of words would have constituted the first cosmos, the first order—secret, powerful, enigmatic, and upon which man, in the name of the gods, conspired to exercise a mastery capable of extending to other orders; and finally, that the first physicists would have entered into a prodigious new future by beginning to create a language: men of *physis* because men of this new speech. There is doubtless nothing in this perspective that does a grave wrong to truth. But it also arrests and freezes its movement.

*

Heraclitus—this is his obscurity, his clarity—admits speech no less from things than from words (and in order to return it to them in a kind of reversed form), speaking both with the one and with the other and, even more, holding himself between the two. Speaking—writing—by way of their divergence and this between-two that he does not immobilize but dominates, because he is oriented toward a more essential difference: a difference that is certainly manifest but not exhausted in the distinction that we who are attached to the dualism of body and soul too decisively establish between words and what they designate. Obviously Heraclitus is far from any primitive confusion—no one is further from this than he; but with the vigilance of a man to whom a knowledge of what is double has been imparted, he watches over the secret alterity that governs difference, but governs it by preserving it against the indifference wherein all contrariety would be annulled.

Thus, under the sovereignty of this mysterious Difference, things and names are in a state of unceasing reciprocity. At one moment it is the thing that represents movement toward dispersion, the name saying unity (the river in which we bathe is never the same river, except by the noun that identifies it). At another, it is the name that puts in the plural the thing that is one, and language, far from gathering, disperses (a god is variously named according to the law of each one who names). Occasionally there is a rigorous disparity between name and thing (fragment 48: "*The bow's name is life* [*bios*], *its work is death*"). Yet this game of words, a game of an oracular sort, is there not to disqualify language, but rather to establish the secret relation between contraries that is beyond contrariety: "Life and Death are one: example, the Bow." In this formulation, perhaps customarily used in Heraclitean circles in the manner of a game (the first surrealist game), we observe that the word is not quartered within language, but that both the name and the work of a thing belong to the logos as the site of difference, as much by their discord as by their accord; that is, by the tension of their always reversible belonging (there being a kind of meaning beyond meaning). We also observe that when the irreducible separation between word and thing is affirmed, this separation neither arrests nor separates but, on the contrary, gathers; for it signifies, at once signifying itself and making a sign in the direction of what would not otherwise appear: here the essential couple Life-Death, directed perhaps toward Unity, perhaps already beyond it.

Fundamentally, what is language for Heraclitus, what speaks essentially in things, in words, and in the crossed or harmonious passage from the one to the other, and, finally, in everything that shows itself and everything that hides, is Difference itself; mysterious because always different from what expresses it, and such that there is nothing that does not say it and in saying does not refer back to it, but such also that everything speaks because of this difference that remains unsayable.

From this difference, which makes it so that in speaking we defer speech, the most ancient Greeks drew the presentiment that this was the hard, the admirable necessity in the name of which everything is ordered. But on condition that the initial indifference, diversity without direction, without form and without measure, had been initially reduced to a first, horizontal difference—an equalization of the for and the against, a rigorous equation of the diverse reasons for acting in one way or another; and then that this difference was in its turn put in question by a prior difference—the vertical difference represented by the duality of the divine and the human.[8] René Schaerer expressed this very convincingly in his book *L'homme antique*. The golden scales of the eighth book of the *Iliad* express this view: it is the great moment of Western discovery. Zeus, having decided to bring the Trojan conflict that was troubling everything to an end, brings the gods together and relieves them of all personal initiative (thus gathering unto himself all divine power). Then he ascends to Mount Ida and from this highest point, an immobile gaze at the summit of the world, he is nothing more than ascendancy and pure contemplation. This divine gaze, from daybreak to noon, surveys the field of battle with an empirical eye, observing with a nonpreferential equanimity the exactly equal forces up to the moment when the decisive action is taken: setting up the scales, placing the two mortal fates in the balance, Zeus raises justice up by the middle. Schaerer comments: "Each side's chances first had to be equal, otherwise the weighing would have been useless. But it is first of all important to note that it is at this instant that Zeus's gaze moves from the battlefield to the scales, and that empirical observation gives way to speculative vision; a vision still contemplating the conflict, but this time formalized, reduced to pure alternative." The four Greek words of line 72: "He balanced [his golden scales] by the middle," mark the highest point of divine ascension and affirmation. The scales pronounce.[9] This image of the scales, Schaerer observes, joins organically the horizontal plane of the arm that oscillates with the scales' two pans and the vertical axis of the divine gaze that observes. It is, in other words, the essentially unstable composition of two differences, which itself obeys a difference more hidden: that of the "All-One" that is unfolded in its turn, and as though in its difference, by *"the wise Thing set apart from all."*

*

Let us recall that Apollo, through the mouth of the poet Bacchylides, said one day to Admetus: "You are a mere mortal; therefore your soul must harbor two thoughts at once." That Heraclitus should have been charged with unfolding this duality—forcing it in its reserve and never leaving it at rest, seeking always what it hides and the retreat of what hides it—this is what gives to each of his words its clarity, its obscurity, and the fascinating audacity we each time experience with the same surprise. A language that speaks through enigma, the enigmatic Difference, but without complacency and without appeasing it: on the contrary, making it speak and, even before it be word, already declaring it as *logos*, that highly singular name in which is reserved the nonspeaking origin of that which summons to speech and at its highest level, there where everything is silence, *"neither speaks nor conceals, but gives a sign."*[10]

II

Measure, the Suppliant

From Homer to the tragic poets, the suppliant is one of the great figures of Greek poetry. We read in the *Odyssey*: *"Zeus the quest god, who stands behind all strangers with honors due them, avenges any wrong toward strangers and suppliants. . . . It is Zeus the Protector who goes with them and would that they be respected."* We are quite familiar with this: Thetis before Zeus, Priam before Achilles, Ulysses and Nausicaä, later *The Suppliants*. But let us limit ourselves to the most ancient tradition.[1]

Supplication is a rite that shows two persons face to face: the suppliant and the one being supplicated, then invisible and out of play, but present in an almost immediate presence, the divinity itself. The suppliant gathers into himself, as though withdrawn from space and retired into his initial simplicity, as he pronounces the ritual formulas: "I clasp your knees. Take pity on me and respect the gods." The suppliant's posture and request bring into play a double meaning: they exalt the one being supplicated, who dominates as he looks down from above. The latter is in possession of everything—authority, force, the power of decision, freedom; thus it is a matter of firmly establishing the fact of inequality, and even more, the fact that there is no common measure between the two limit-terms facing each other. Through his humiliation, the suppliant carries out a psychological maneuver of appeasement, but at the same time lets it be understood (and often proclaims) that being thus separated from all force, he escapes power's jurisdiction and answers to another law: a law affirmed by his truth as a stranger, and that the god's close presence in his invisibility renders manifest.[2] The suppliant and the stranger are one; both are cut off from the whole, being deprived of

93

the right that founds all others and alone establishes one's belonging to the home. Edmond Beaujon reminds us that the proper sense of the Greek word that we translate by "suppliant" is "he who comes." The suppliant is thus the man who is coming, always on the move because without a place and of whom one must therefore ask the most mysterious of questions, that of the origin. Hence the response: he who comes from elsewhere comes from Zeus. The stranger, the suppliant, troubles the man of the household, even the most powerful. The *Iliad* says: "When a mortal . . . unexpectedly arrives at a rich man's house from a foreign land, a wonder seizes those who approach him." Even Achilles, although forewarned by his mother, loses his composure when Priam, an enfeebled and worn out old man who has succeeded in crossing the enemy lines, appears to confront the slayer of his sons; Priam's presence in and of itself troubles the order of things. Later, in Pindar's fourth Pythian Ode, it is Pelias the king who, in front of Jason, an unescorted traveler, falls into a state of utter confusion and loses his bearings. Beaujon expresses this in the strongest terms: every new arrival proposes a truth that must not be turned away; but who knows where it will lead should it be welcomed?

It is said that the rite of supplication has to be linked to the Greek search for measure. As soon as force exceeds the limit, thereby compromising equilibrium, another force intervenes that reverses the situation of power in favor of the man without means (the man cast out, outside-the-law, as Aeschylus will say in *The Eumenides*); thus "the law protecting those whom force would crush merges with the law that holds the world in equilibrium and whose symbol is the scales of Zeus." Let us suppose this. But what of these words *measure, excess* that are so hard for us to grasp? We can see (at first glance) that, contrary to the romantic meaning of the term with which we are most familiar, unmeasure is for the Greeks human; it expresses the audacity of the man who trusts to his own forces, whereas measure is divine: an opening upon the divine and relation with a mysterious point—the center—that moreover does not fall within our means. One can still speak of measure on this basis, and in the most diverse senses. When the later Greeks, in their famous address to the Meletians, want to persuade them that they do not have the right to invoke justice because there is too great a difference of force between the two adversaries, the Greeks make a perverse but legitimate use of the law of equilibrium: when one is very weak, it is strictly dishonest and impious to appeal to justice, which is only valid when forces are nearly equal. An entire tradition confirms this; one must not ask too much of the gods: this is measure. And if Athena saves Orestes by intervening in his favor at the moment of the vote of the Areopagus, it is because an equally divided number of human votes had previously been cast. As we have just seen, this is what Schaerer commented upon in saying: it falls to man first to equalize the for and the against while waiting for the heavens to tip the balance; and the heavens, in order to make the scales tip, wait until man has equalized them.

What is the suppliant's place, and what recourse might he have from such a perspective? It is in changing perspective. Measure not only measures force by rendering it equal; it opens another Dimension, another Measure with which, in measuring itself, force must come to terms. The suppliant is not weaker or the weakest, he is so low he is utterly beyond reach: separate, sacred. His moves are religious because in himself he belongs to a region of separation; and no doubt his gestures are ritual, but the rite's incantatory powers in no way suffice to make it effective inasmuch as the suppliant supplicates without certainty and without guarantee, never sure whether or not he will be brought back within the system of rights that constitutes justice. What then, finally, gives him a chance? It is the fact that he speaks. The suppliant is, par excellence, the one who speaks. Through speech, he, the very low, is in relation to the very high and, without breaking down the distance, makes his powerful interlocutor enter into a space they do not yet have in common but that is between them. This between-two (empty and sacred) is the very space of the middle, the mysterious "median thing." Speech is measure—not, however, just any speech at all. At the same time as the speech of entreaty gives voice to the one who speaks out of his pain, it manifests the presence of the god in his invisibility: a speech attending the invisible, and by way of the invisible reminding us that if Zeus is the one who comes from afar he is also "omphaios," the master of voices. The stranger, lacking all common language, is paradoxically the one who is present solely through his speech; just as it is when everything is lacking that the man engulfed in misfortune has the means to speak, for therein is his true measure. It is after speech—speech having arranged this space between-two where men meet who are separated by everything—that life once again becomes possible. Such is the great lesson of the *Iliad*. After having listened to the old man, then wept with him and having spoken in his turn, Achilles will not rest until Priam has eaten: "*Now then, divine old man, you too must think of a meal.*" Hospitality consists less in nourishing the guest than in restoring in him a taste for food by recalling him to the level of need, to a life where one can say and stand hearing said: "*And now, let us not forget to eat.*" Sublime words. So much so that when Priam still refuses to take his place at the table, Achilles, again becoming furious, comes very close to killing him.[3] There is really no third term: you shall be either benevolent host or murderer. This too is measure: when there is no middle. And the rigor of the dilemma is in no way lessened, but rendered more essential by supplication. From which one might conclude that to supplicate is to speak when speaking is maintaining, in all its severity and its primary truth, the alternative: speech or death.

III

Tragic Thought

Pascal does not stop with the idea, as is generally said, that contrariety derives from the play of opinion. If there is a dialectic it is that of reality itself, founded upon a creation originally corrupt, and founded upon the more dazzling and more august mystery of the union of two natures in Jesus Christ. Because Jesus Christ is God and is man—affirmations that are indissolubly linked, yet averse to one another—we ought to expect to find the mark of truth in their aversion and contradiction; and we will not only have to entertain these opposing affirmations, maintaining them firmly together, but also take them as true because of their opposition, which will oblige us to demand a higher order that founds them.[1]

Reason, therefore, does not begin in the light of an evidency by which it would seize itself, but rather in an obscurity that itself is not manifest and whose discovery, seizure, and affirmation alone put thought to work, causing it to find and to extend its own light. *"Without this mystery, the most incomprehensible of all, we are incomprehensible to ourselves." "The beginning, after having explained incomprehensibility."* Let us note well that all the contradictions in which we exist—the misfortune of a thought that has nothing with which to begin and dissipates from one infinite to the other; the ambiguity by which we are scattered, not dwelling, incessantly coming and going, always here and there and yet nowhere, curious with regard to everything in order not to stop anywhere; a world in which nothing is either present or absent, where there is neither proximity nor distance, where everything escapes, leaving us the illusion of having everything—all this is the consequence of a dispersing, pervasive, and errant obscurity that we have not had the force to fix in place.

This play of equivocal light is diversion.

Where everything is unsettled one can only live in perpetual detour, for to hold to one thing would suppose that there were something determined to hold onto; it would presuppose, therefore, a neat division of light and shadow, of sense and nonsense, and, finally, of fortune and misfortune. But inasmuch as the one is always the other, and we know it (but by way of a kind of ignorance that dissuades us without enlightening us), we seek only to preserve uncertainty and obey it, inconstant through a want of constancy that is in things themselves, leaning upon nothing because nothing offers support. And this flightiness responds to the truth of our ambiguous existence, which is rich only in its ambiguity—an ambiguity that would immediately cease were it to seek to realize itself, it never being anything but possible.

Interpretations of Descartes have doubtless changed a great deal, but not like those of Pascal. This is because Descartes has remained the property of wise philosophers while Pascal has fallen into the hands of reckless literary types: thus he was impious in the eighteenth century, pathetic and prophetic in the nineteenth, and in the twentieth century, existential. But this genius of the heart for which he is known (through a misunderstanding that leads to opposing reactions) is not the only thing that has fascinated literature. That there should be no writer more brilliant surely plays a role in this fascination, but there is still another reason for it. One might perhaps say that in naming and in justifying diversion, Pascal gave to the literary art of the future one of its privileged categories. No doubt, it is the everyday course of existence he has in mind; the inauthentic and almost senseless existence in which, half awake, half deceitful, we hold ourselves suspended in an illusion that, through blind skill and a lazy stubbornness, we do not cease to render lasting. *"So life slips away."* But, at the same time, Pascal does not condemn diversion because he knows that the thought explaining and judging this movement already belongs to the vicissitudes of a diverted life, and simply gives evidence of a senseless inconsistency that augments the mystification. *"And finally, others tire themselves to death in order to remark all these things, not to become wiser thereby, but only to show that they know them, and these are the most foolish of the lot—since they are so knowingly . . . " "and I who write this . . . and perhaps my readers . . . "* There can therefore be no knowledge of diversion: being as it were the very essence of diversion, this sort of infinite regression, this bad infinity ruins the knowledge that would apply to it and makes it so that knowledge, in so applying itself, also alters and ruins it. If one wishes to be faithful to the truth of diversion one must not know it, nor take it to be either true or false for fear of making disappear the essential, which is ambiguity: that indissociable mixture of true and false that nonetheless marvelously colors our life with ever-changing nuance.[2]

Thus everyday man will be the most consequent and the most wise. But Pascal clearly opens up another possibility: being unable to know our ambiguous life, will we not be tempted to "describe" it, to write it? Might not written description be the sole mode of presentation that does not disturb the strange enchantment of appearances and disappearances in which we exist?; a presentation that would not render impurity pure, but would give us the infinite unreality of our life for what it is: unreal, and yet for all this very real? And naturally we will not be content with a surface description: we will descend into the depths, as does Pascal himself, finding them always more profoundly superficial, always more ambiguous, clear but falsely so, obscure, but with a dissimulating obscurity that always further dissembles itself; and thus we will obey the sole rule, which is to save this ambiguity, without arresting its movement and without pause, so that what is deprived of all final meaning will not cease to appear to us full of meaning, and so that, in this manner, we may be in accord with the discordant traits of human existence. The terrible vanity of art would thus come from the fact that it alone does justice, without justifying it, to what is vain: following diversion all the way through, accomplishing it in its incompletion and without our either being able or desiring to elude it. How will Pascal himself escape art's ambiguity?

One might say: by another form of art that seeks its coherence in a tragic vision of the world. But here we must follow a path opened by Lucien Goldmann, one of the first commentators to apply in his reading and study of Pascal certain principles of dialectical materialism.[3] Goldmann borrows the elements of this conception of the tragic from Georg Lukács's analyses in *Soul and Form*, a book that appeared some fifty years ago; but in applying it to Pascal, Goldmann gives it a rigor that transforms it. How to move from this equivocal state that is the senseless sense of the world, and that we ought not mistake, to the absolute truth, that pure and total light whose exigency I find in myself? How to entertain the ambiguity and not accept it; how to live in the diverting confusion of vague and brilliant instants and, faced with this "anarchy of the *clair-obscure*,"[4] hold myself to a contrariety so exclusive that it transforms into an essential affirmation that which is essentially without firmness? It seems that Pascal's efforts, his discovery and his conversion (which was also philosophical), tend to take up and gather all obscurity into a higher region where it becomes mystery, situating it in such a way that the incomprehensible becomes a source of comprehension and gives a power of understanding — and this without yielding in any way to the "mysticism" of the irrational. The obscurity must be held fast; and by going back to that superior region, by overtaking it with a leap, one must above all disclose — not tone down — the hidden divisions of the world in such a way that they become illuminated and sharpened by the mystery's initial obscurity: irreconcilable contraries, affirmations that exclude one another, exigencies that are opposed. One must disclose the exigency of their opposition and the more exigent exigency of the necessity of their truth in the whole.

The man of the world lives in nuance and by degrees, he lives in a mixture of light and shadow, in confused enchantment or irresolute mediocrity: in the middle. Tragic man lives in the extreme tension between contraries, going from a yes and no confusedly merged back to a yes and a no that are clear and clearly preserved in their opposition. He does not see man as a passable mixture of middling qualities and honest failings, but as an unendurable meeting of extreme grandeur and extreme destitution, an incongruous nothingness in which the two infinites collide.

But how does man become tragic man? And what does he gain by it? What he loses is evident: ease, forgetfulness, tranquil malaise, dull pleasures, a tender inconstancy, and an almost agreeable nausea, neither truth nor lies, but the illusion of both—a mystified life that some might charge is not a life, but that is a life of appearances one will do anything not to lose. But tragic man is one whose existence has *suddenly* become transformed: from a play of light and shadow it has become both an exigency of absolute clarity and an encounter with heavy darkness, the summons to a true speech and the trial of an infinitely silent space. Finally, it has become the presence of a world incapable of justice and offering only derisory compromise when it is the absolute, and the absolute alone, that is required: hence an uninhabitable world in which one is obliged to dwell. For tragic man, everything has instantly hardened, everything is the face to face of incompatibilities. Where does this come from? Whence this sudden metamorphosis?

It comes from the fact that, having sought, he has encountered infinitely outside and above himself that which holds gathered within an initial event the greatest clarity and the greatest obscurity; an incomprehensible unity in the face of which he will from now on hold himself, everything in him and around him changed by this measure of extreme contrariety that makes disappear the equivocacies nonetheless destined to render life possible. This event is the union in Christ of divinity and humanity, of all grandeur and all baseness, as in man it is the mystery of original sin and, finally, higher, or at least the instance beyond which we cannot rise: the mystery of the presence of the hidden God.

In the Lafuma edition (which claims to restore, if not the order that might have belonged to the completed *Pensées*—for this order is perhaps unthinkable—at least the classification of bundles and notebooks in which Pascal gave a provisional ordering to his work), what comes in the beginning, as the principle from which all else is to follow, is the name and the thought of the *Deus absconditus*: "*the presence of the God that hides.*" This, in effect, is a sure point of departure for everyone for, unlike the *Cogito*, this principle gathers within itself absolute certitude and absolute incertitude, itself saying it is certain only in that it can only be uncertain. The doubter who would refuse this beginning, maintaining that, for him, God is not there and he does not see him, would do no more than demonstrate his agreement with the idea of God's invisibility and bear witness to God's distance, as to the darkness in which men dwell. This is doubtless no more than a point of departure by which nothing yet begins; nonetheless, something essential has already been acquired because consciousness of this obscurity is the difficult point that, separating compromise from the play of light and shadow, puts us at the same time in touch with the fact that in the world there is no true light, that man nonetheless wants light, wants it totally and wants it to be total. This is why Pascal will vigorously affirm: "*Atheists ought to say things perfectly clearly.*" But as they find it impossible to do so—it being "*inconceivable that God should exist and inconceivable that he should not exist; that there should be a soul in the body, that we should have no soul; that the world should have been created, that it should not, etc.; that there should be original sin, and that there not be*"— we are led, not reasonably but by a very particular movement, to bind together, into bundles as it were, these terrible incomprehensibilities whose incompatible nature nonetheless joins them two by two, and to elevate them to the point where they are the most incompatible and impose themselves with a force become infinite: in the supreme incertitude of the supremely certain, the presence of the absent God. *Vere tu es Deus absconditus.*

*

Thus it becomes comprehensible that if tragic man should come into the light that is the hidden God, this light would metamorphose everything, make nuance vanish and transform the happy mean into the harsh encounter of being and nothingness. The means for living at the mean are no more. One must live without pause in the restless tension of exclusive exigencies; live grandly with one's baseness and reduced to nothing by a memory of greatness, like a righteous man who is but a sinner—precisely the righteous sinner whose prayer is necessary, but not necessarily answered. Yes, the world is henceforth discredited. But will it not be possible for us—assuredly not easy, but possible—to refuse the world and to take refuge in the certainty of another world and a God under whose gaze we will hold ourselves in hope and in waiting for the final reconciliation? Would not tragic man thereby become the "spiritual" man whose faith in God furnishes him with the beginning of a response to these anguishing questions?

But this is what he will be unable to become, for he cannot forget—unless he forgets everything—that if all clarity and all obscurity are gathered together in God it is not in order that they may neutralize each other in a happy harmony from which we would immediately derive appeasement and happiness. Perhaps, in truth, it shall be this way, but now, at this very moment on earth, it is not so. And what we have gained is not a light making all obscurity vanish, not a certainty enveloping all uncertainty, but the hard mystery of both the one and the other, which is expressed in this God always present and always absent: a permanent presence and a permanent absence that make the hidden God—hidden because manifest, present in his absence—a certainty and an uncertainty that are equal and equally absolute.

It must be understood that the mystery of this fundamental opposition ought not rewaken ambiguity. God's present-absence is not ambiguous. Our certitude and our incertitude in regard to him render him neither doubtful nor probable but as certain as he is uncertain. The obscurity of our position in relation to him, and that of his will in relation to us, makes it our duty to act as rigorously as we would if we had clear knowledge of our ends. But here is another consequence: for tragic man, the presence of God is such that he can no longer be in any way satisfied with the world in which he knows that nothing of value will ever be accomplished; but, at the same time, the absence of God is such that he cannot find refuge in God, any more than he can unite mystically with the infinite as with the sole substantial reality. So now he is thrown back into the world, which he nevertheless refuses; a refusal that henceforth changes meaning, for it is within the world and within its limits that he must oppose it, becoming through this opposition conscious of what man is and what he would wish to be.

Tragic man, in front of the presence-absence of the hidden God, and deriving from the incomprehensible union of contraries a power of understanding that is always neither sure nor doubtful, must therefore learn to "*live*" in the world "*without taking part in it and without acquiring a taste for it*"; he must also learn to know the world by his very refusal — a refusal that is not general and abstract but constant and determined, and that serves knowledge better than any rationalist optimism insofar as this reason frees him from the mystifications of a false knowledge.[5] Thus man, comprehending the world and comprehending himself on the basis of what is incomprehensible, is on the way toward a comprehension more reasonable, more exigent, and more far-reaching that can be called tragic: entertaining ambiguity without accepting it, and, more precisely, returning from diversion and ambiguity — from the intimacy of a mingled yes and no — to the paradox of a yes and a no simultaneously affirmed, each being absolute, each without mixture and without confusion, yet always equally posed together inasmuch as their truth is in their simultaneous clarity and in the obscurity that this simultaneity makes appear in each as a reflection of the other's light.

*

God is therefore hidden at the center of tragedy. This thought creates difficulties for Pascal, but these difficulties are in any case inevitable and in a sense constitute the particular strength of Pascal's thought. An uncertain certitude — which is as foreign to doubt as it is distinct from an immediate evidency or from a mystical apprehension — introduces at the heart of reason an affirmation that reason will never master, and to which it lends itself only by an assent whose risky nature it measures at every moment. Will it be possible for this new tragic reason to arrive, in a manner that is neither irrational nor intellectual, at this paradoxical affirmation to which there indeed seems to be no means of access? It is here that Pascal discovers as essential to this reason the new mode of approach that is constituted by the wager.

There is in the wager an effort to utilize the rigor of a mathematical form and the constraint of a calculation in order to move beyond both this form and this constraint. Here we see to what extent Pascal is hardly one to abandon thought. He is bold enough to sense in these pure, amusing speculations the seriousness of a future science; bolder still not to fear putting a reasoning suited to frivolity in service of what is the highest and, for him, the most venerable. And he is a Jansenist.

One has to take risks; that is to say, uncertainty has to be worked for. And this is the wager's first objective: to make us conscious of this imperative to which we have been consigned without our knowledge. Then, from the moment we must wager consciously, we must wager reasonably. Hence, a double effort meant to increase consciousness and make us carry out the folly of the leap in such a way that this folly shall be a lucid act that reason illuminates, bears, and supports as far as possible.

There is in the wager something that sweeps reason along and scandalizes it. "Machine of an enormous power," Etienne Souriau says in his forceful study.[6] The wager's centrality, and the fact that it has value not only for the libertine who loves games of chance but also for Pascal, is seen in several passages;[7] these show, moreover, the imperious movement of the unparalleled dialogue in which we are engaged despite ourselves — being, in any case, this dialogue's respondents, where everything is set into place to clarify, assure, and nonetheless surprise our decision. Perhaps all bets are placed from the moment he writes "*Yes, but wager you must . . . you have embarked on it. So which will you have?*" This is the essential moment at which tragic reason intervenes: one must wager, one must choose. One must, that is, renounce the ambiguity that refuses choice; does not even refuse it, but only takes it as being possible and never accomplishes it. (Here we are perhaps failing to do justice to that ambiguity by which meaning is always on the *hither side* of the moment at which the alternative is posed and requires a choice. In this case, ambiguity occupies a position the wager will not be able to attain; it is not that ambiguity does not wish to be engaged, but there seems to be a region where the impossibility of choosing and the necessity of not choosing impose themselves, not out of concern for the possible, but because the possible is essentially lacking. Here, courage and morality consist in standing watch over the indecision of being and in reawakening it as soon as it begins to slip.) For Pascal we have always already wagered in advance; tragic reason obliges us to become conscious of the wager's inevitability, and to assume the risk it introduces into thought and makes inseparable from each of its moves.

We must, therefore, wager: engage our certain action for something that is certainly uncertain. But for which uncertainty? God, nothingness, the fulfillment of human destiny, the classless society? Here it is as though tragic reasoning were seconded by a mathematical reasoning that, because it believes it can master chance (the experience of chance, as André Breton saw it, is the experience of a kind of immanent transcendence of an unknown nature), acquires a power of surpassing by which we are pushed reasonably to a leap whose essence, nonetheless, is to put reason at risk. A risk that is calculated but escapes all measure.

There is an equivocation here that is perhaps no longer in keeping with the rigor of tragic thought. It might be expressed as follows: let us suppose that the wager leads us, as hope's reckoning invites us, to choose God. Won't such a manner of choosing be incompatible with this God we choose? Or, as Souriau says: "What will happen if certain ways of opting for the infinite render us unfit for the infinite?" Furthermore, continues Souriau: if our reckonings are good and if God — the God that hides — is truly present at the end of the game, is he not responsible for this iniquitous game he obliges us to play?; iniquitous because God offers an enormous advantage to the one who plays in a certain manner — one's hand, as it were, is forced; iniquitous also because we are obliged to toss a coin in order to settle the uncertain existence of he who thus puts it "up to chance." Now it is the entire thought of "the God that hides" that becomes scandalous — and this scandal is not foreign to the essence of tragic thought. It is a scandal so outrageous that it would seem that the only means of justifying God, and justifying the moral bankruptcy represented by the wager's necessity, is the wager's possible failure. As though God's having put himself at stake could be justified solely on condition that he not exist. One might say that by the human force of the wager alone, and by this path that necessarily diverts us from being, we always place our wager on nothingness, no matter how the bet is finally called: a nothingness we sometimes call God, sometimes the world and where, in either case, what will have won is indeed the infinite, but the infinite of nothingness.[8]

The uncertain certainty of God's existence makes us unable to prove either that God is or that he is not; nor can we doubt the one or the other (our life, moreover, always represents a living affirmation for or against God). We must therefore affirm both and always set truth in the rigorous asperity that divides our thought as soon as it thinks this sovereign contrariety. It is for this reason that the wager itself is double. The wager of tragic reason: one must wager and become conscious of the fact that one lives solely by wagering. This lucid and constant, rigorous consciousness makes the wager — accomplished with full knowledge of the risk and with a presentiment of its failure — an infinite act that, rendering us now capable of the infinite, allows us thereby to opt for an infinite that, though determined, remains infinitely aleatory. The wager of mathematical reason: this second wager intervenes by the objective calculation of chance so as to keep the infinite of the risk and the uncertainty of the decision from reducing our choice to an arbitrary act; it is not simply a matter of tossing a coin, but of playing seriously by engaging in the game not only all of being, but also the reason that calculates coldly and that, by its calculations, succeeds in establishing a link between the finite and the infinite.

But God, reached by wager, is nonetheless such that he ought to make this wager scandalous and impossible.

From this angle (in the sense that Pascal is unable to stand by the God of the wager—a God whose one face is being, the other nothingness—and moves to a God with whom relations are spiritual or mystical), we touch the point at which thought reaches its greatest exigencies, and reaches them perhaps no longer in Pascal, nor in anyone. Infinitely separated from God and separated from the world, but living solely *for* this God it can reach only in separation, and living solely *in* this world it knows only by the insufficiencies it refuses—such a tragic consciousness is exposed to two temptations from which it must escape. One is the way out offered by spirituality: "the progressive detachment from the world . . . the soul's movement toward God," where tragic consciousness finds the interior life, the promise of perfection and joy; the other, still more formidable, is that of a mystical experience where infinite separation becomes union with the infinite, and the presence-absence of God an absence that offers itself ecstatically as the rapture of a presence. Temptations that are perhaps inevitable.

It must be noted that the thought of the *hidden God* is a thought the Scriptures inherited from negative theology, and always ready to give way to a mystical movement. The great merit of Goldmann's analysis is to have in a sense purified this thought, and to have conceived of it as an endless movement between the opposed poles of presence and absence; "a movement that never advances because, eternal and instantaneous, it is foreign to a time in which there are progress and retreat." This is important. But does the thought of a God that hides present itself in this way to Pascal? He says that God reveals himself to those who seek him and hides from those who test him. And he adds that God is partly hidden and partly revealed (not totally hidden and totally manifest). Each man, it is true, is never simply a man who seeks; this is why God, should man discover him, is always a hidden God, for there are light and obscurity even for the elect. "*There is light enough to enlighten the elect, and darkness enough to humble them. There is darkness enough to blind the reprobates and light enough to damn them.*" To know God without knowing man's misery is dangerous, just as it is dangerous to know one's misery without knowing God. But if one knows God and knows one's misery, one knows that one can only know the remoteness of God, God manifest insofar as he is distant. Or, one knows that one cannot find God but only seek him; or again, that one cannot possess God but only desire him. However, when Pascal says "*that God established in the Church sensible signs by which those who seek Him in sincerity should know Him, at the same time so hiding them that He can only be perceived by those who seek Him with all their hearts,*" the thought of the hidden God he is expressing here (and it is in this form that he most often does so)[9] ceases to be a tragic thought (God speaking only by his silence), just as there is a point, as Lucien Goldmann remarks, at which Pascal says yes without adding to it the contrary no: the point at which he affirms the correspondence between the paradoxical nature of man and the paradoxical content of Christianity. Here, the Christian religion is not relatively true but entirely true since, accounting for the incomprehensible without dissipating it, making of obscurity a mystery and of mystery a light—a new light—it holds the key to all possible truth.[10]

*

The hidden god: in one of his last poems, Hölderlin also gave voice to this thought: *"Is God unknown? Is he manifest as the sky? This rather I believe."* And in another fragment: *"What is God? unknown, yet/rich in qualities is the aspect/of him the sky offers us. For the lightnings/are the wrath of a God. Is all the more/invisible, what adapts itself to strangeness."*[11] Here we have the movement proper to the thought of the God that hides. God is unknown and nonetheless manifest. There where he is manifest, he has the qualities that render him, unknown, familiar to us. Familiar, he destines himself (adapts himself) to what is foreign to him, and the more a thing is invisible the more it is destined to this manifestation of strangeness. But it becomes foreign to itself thereby, and foreign in the strangeness that renders it familiar to us; hidden as soon as manifest, hiding there where it shows itself. God is unknown, God is manifest. Unknown and open as the sky, he reveals himself in that which, showing him hidden, lets him appear as he is: Unknown.[12]

But what is such a thought? Is it mystical? Is it dialectical? Is it tragic?[13]

IV

Affirmation (desire, affliction)

1

Those who find Simone Weil's thought so irritating that it seems to them scarcely a thought reproach her for a lack of rigor that is all the more troublesome for the certainty of the rigorous exigency to which it responds. Yes, it is a thought often strangely surprised. But in this, too, worthy of attention and rich in truth, even if this truth is not entirely her own — perhaps close to her just the same. And to say that her thought lacks coherence is to rid oneself rather quickly of what one is saying. Where, then, is this lack situated? In what does it consist? It is certainly not where it is most visible, in these affirmations that are blindly at odds: one must become uprooted, one must take root; God is perfectly absent, he is the only presence; the world is evil, the order of the world is the good itself.

We are in the habit of valiantly withstanding the shock and the constraint of such contradictions, and I do not see why Simone Weil alone would be disqualified as a thinker because she accepted within herself as legitimate the inevitable opposition of thoughts. Perhaps instead we should ask why this division of which she is conscious (since she tries to theorize it), but to which she also often pays little heed, would in her case be more serious, revealing a refusal to choose and to become aware that — given her life, her experiences, the force of her sincerity, and the steadfastness of her orientation — might on the contrary take on all the more importance and contain a singular meaning.

Those who speak of contradiction run up against those who speak of unity. Unity, understood as a uniformity of direction analogous to the oscillating indication of a compass needle, at times disoriented but always certain of the pole (even if the latter proves to be unsituatable) is, in fact, much more visible. There is even something quite striking in the fact that this young intellectual, without any religious ties and as though naturally atheist, should almost suddenly, at about age twenty-nine, be the subject of a mystical experience of a Christian nature, without this event seeming in any way to modify either the movement of her life or the direction of her thoughts.

A singular case that cannot be compared to that of Claudel. Simone Weil did not convert, nor will she ever do so, despite entreaties both from within and from without. The experience of what cannot be grasped through experience does not even give her faith. She only perceives that as an atheist—"professing to be an atheist"—she was then no less turned toward the same light than she is now that she has (dangerously) at her disposition a religious vocabulary that is more precise. And the word conversion is not a word she uses willingly, except in the sense of this word that she finds in the texts of Plato. The violence of a decisive turnabout, a capital break, are instead events to be mistrusted because of the illusory hopes their vividness cannot fail to bring forth, just as seeking God and finding God are unsuitable expressions, which, at the most, indicate that we have found a false God and that in seeking have forgotten what cannot be sought. Conversion cannot but be silent, invisible, perfectly secret; it requires of the one in whom it is accomplished only the same attention and the same immobility to which it was the brief, illuminating response.

*

The Christian interpretations that were immediately applied to Simone Weil's thought are legitimate; she herself called them forth. And if it is difficult not to feel her to be irreducibly at the margin, this margin, when defined in relation to the Christian religion and Christian mysticism, is soon absorbed by them. Even if this marginal position is often respected by her commentators (out of honesty or antipathy) it is nonetheless, in their view, Christian thought that gives meaning to her bearing and to the latitude that constitutes it. This is no doubt inevitable. It is also perhaps what has veiled, I will not say the originality of this thought—she in no way wished to be original—but what in it is irregular, an irregularity that is not easy to grasp.[1] Yet how can one not be struck, in reading certain of her writings (at least those having a certain volume), by the tone that is hers and by the manner in which she makes her assertions: with a certitude so remote from herself, so distant from all proof and all guarantee, yet so restrained and nearly effaced that one indeed feels one cannot refuse her a hearing, without hoping in return ever to be heard by her. Not that she would be unable to listen or attend to the words of others; but it is certain she will always respond in this blank and monotone voice, and with the authority that, while imposing itself without the least violence, will nonetheless never yield inasmuch as impersonal truth is incapable of making concessions.

What is surprising, among other traits in this discourse, is the quality of the affirmation and the transparency of the certitude. We, believers and non-believers, are less in the habit of doubting than questioning. We enter into thought, and especially our own, only by questioning. We go from question to question to the point where the question, pushed toward a limit, becomes response – the response then being, according to a famous expression, no more than the question's last step. Such a way of proceeding is foreign to Simone Weil. Even in her notebooks questions are rare, doubts almost unknown. Is she, then, so sure of her thoughts? Not entirely. But it would seem that she first responds to herself, as though for her the answer always came first, preceding every question and even every possibility of questioning: there is an answer, then another, and then again another answer. These answers often do not coincide, and even profoundly contradict one another (hence the uneasiness of many readers); but she leaves them as they are, without seeming to renounce any of them, much less bring them into agreement. Affirming is often for Simone Weil a way of questioning or a way of testing.

It must be added that through her mentor and teacher, Alain, she had become familiar with this way of thinking and proceeding not by proof or by doubt, but by affirming and by holding firmly without wavering to the movement of affirmation that by a pact unites thought, will, and truth. But this itinerary is different with Simone Weil. The kind of invisible effort by which she seeks to efface herself in favor of certitude is all that remains in her of a will as she advances from affirmation to affirmation. It is true that at times, and without knowing it, she is still very present by the grip she imposes upon herself in order to maintain the calm and even course of her diction. And sometimes – for example, in *L'Enracinement* [*The Need for Roots*] or when she touches upon obsessional subjects – the affirmation stiffens and hardens to the point of becoming an empty force: then certitude, no longer abiding in its inaccessible firmament, descends to coerce rather than persuade us – and so the intolerance of spirit begins. But this inflection is almost rare. It is, on the contrary, remarkable that all the while living with certitude in relations that exceed it, she can still maintain the distance this very certitude requires; a certitude that has no power over us and is without relation with us until we have renounced everything we hold to be certain.

*

We shall have to consider the nature of this certitude, and her surprising incapacity to counteract it. No one has doubted less than she did; and if, as is said, there are saints for whom the idea of God in difficult moments becomes obscured, Simone Weil represents someone who was not only incapable of doubting the

Good, but also incapable of thinking this doubt through. Here, too, in our modern world of beliefs she is an exceptional figure. Nonetheless, she sometimes attempted to put her thought and the pressure such an invincible certitude exerted on her into form. In the notes published under the title *La connaissance surnaturelle* [*First and Last Notebooks*], she comes back to this subject three times, and formulates what is for her a sort of Pascalian Wager, very superior (she says) to Pascal's. I choose the last of these formulations, which seems to me the best, or at least the most significant: "*If I avert my desire from all things of this world as being false goods I have the absolute, unconditional certainty of being in accord with truth. . . . To turn away from them — that is all. . . . But, it will be asked, does this good exist? What does it matter? The things of this world exist, but they are not the good. . . . And what is this good? I have no idea — but what does it matter? It is that whose name alone, if I attach my thought to it, gives me the certainty that the things of the world are not the good. . . . But is it not ridiculous to abandon what exists for something which, perhaps, does not exist? By no means, if what exists is not the good and if what perhaps does not exist is the good. But why say what perhaps does not exist? It makes no sense to say the good exists or the good does not exist; one can only say the good.*"[2]

If one reflects upon this astonishing Wager (whose object is to eliminate both wager and risk), one will see that all its force comes not from the old ontological argument, but from the force and the purity of desire — a desire incapable of being satisfied and of coming to rest in anything — and, even more, from the extraordinary and sovereign attraction that the name of the Good exercises upon Simone Weil. This is singular. And in this sense if it is true that she is a Christian, she owes it to Plato, for it is first of all in Plato that she found the Good, and it is through the beauty of the Greek texts that the name of the Good revealed itself to her as the sole reality, the unique response capable of illuminating the true reality of her desire and the unreality of all the rest.

It is certain that Simone Weil was extremely touched by the beauty of texts. She was in a sense "converted" by an English poem: it was during its recitation that, according to the terms she uses (and that one does not reproduce without discomfort), "*Christ came down and took possession of me*"; later, in reciting the Greek Lord's Prayer, whose exceptionally beautiful form she always admired, she was again, and several times, enraptured and transported. Revealing the power reading had upon her, she says: "*For me the proof, the miraculous thing, is the perfect beauty of the accounts of the Passion joined with a few fulgurating words by Isaiah and Saint Paul; this is what constrains me to believe.*" Again and again she asserts that we know nothing of the Good and nothing of God save the name. She assures us that "*through the name of God we can orient our attention toward the true God, who is beyond our reach and is unconceivable by us. — Without the gift of this name we would have only a false, earthly God, conceivable by us. The name alone permits us to have a Father in the Heavens, about which we know nothing."*

This is perhaps a surprising affirmation. Did Simone Weil, without knowing it, come under the influence of the Jewish religious traditions—particularly that of the Cabala—for which the secret name of God is the object of a special reverence and can even, through the contemplation and combination of letters, ecstatically engage us in the divine mystery? Does she know that "the world of letters is the true world of beatitude?" Yet she does not believe that some substantial power attaches to God's name. It is rather a kind of sacrament. Just as, according to convention, the least bit of matter can enclose the divine presence, so by convention can any assembling of syllables become the name of God. Convention is arbitrary in its form, but it gives to this arbitrary form its necessity when we consent to it as simply as though it were ratified by God himself: then God does in effect ratify it. God's name is therefore his real name only if we renounce everything in thinking it. Yet in her view, this name does not give itself as an indifferent pretext that the purity of meditation alone would render pure. God truly gave his name to us and in this way gave himself over to us: *"God has placed the skies between him and us in order to hide himself; he gave to us only one thing, his name. This name is truly given to us. We can do what we will with it. We can attach it like a label to any created thing. But in so doing we profane it, and it loses its virtue. It has virtue only when it is spoken without our imagining any representation of it."*

"*It has virtue only . . .* " We first had the idea of a Good, then the name of the Good, then the name of God. ("*That God is the good is a certainty. It is a definition.*") Do we not feel as though we have already dangerously slipped since the initial certitude (when the Good was a certitude only as an idea)? For it is quite another certitude we have acquired, having, through the affirmative richness that the ambiguous use of God's name puts at our disposal, regained possession of a large part of the traditional thought about God: ready henceforth to think of him as real, and real because present and existent. If indeed there was a sliding, how can it be justified?

*

We can represent it in this way: no one felt a more rigorous exigency than Simone Weil. There is in her an impulse that prompts her to render the thought of the absolute and the desire that oriented her toward it ever and always more pure. It is categorically and almost with horror that she rejects all the diversions offered by faith: the idea of salvation, the belief in a personal immortality, the conception of a beyond, and, in general, all that would allow us to bring close to us what has truth for us only if we love it, all the while becoming disinterested in all that for us is true. We can never put enough distance between ourselves and what we love. To think that God is, is still to think of him as present; this is a thought according to our measure, destined only to console us. It is much more fitting to think that God is not, just as we must love him purely enough that we could be indifferent to the fact that he should not be. It is for this reason that the atheist is closer to God than the believer. The atheist does not believe in God: this is the first degree of truth, providing he does not believe in any kind of God; if this is so, if he is in no way idolatrous, he will believe in God absolutely even while being unaware of it and by the pure grace of his ignorance. Not to "believe" in God. Not to know anything of God. And to love in him only his absence so that this love, being a renouncing of God himself, may be a love that is absolutely pure and "the emptiness that is plenitude." But we must not know even this, or we risk consenting to emptiness only in the hope of being filled with it.

This movement, as we see, is of an exigency such that it authorizes no affirmation whatsoever, and such that the one who follows it seems never able to rest either in God or in the thought of God, in the thought of God's abandonment, or in anything—not even in the thought of death. Simone Weil is familiar with this movement. Nonetheless, it is a fact that she does not follow it out to its end and seems to be constantly unfaithful to it. One finds in one of her *Notebooks* this remark: "*Not to speak about God (not even in an inner language of the soul); not to pronounce this word*, except when one is not able to do otherwise ('*able' is obviously used here in a particular sense*)." The word God is in other passages replaced by the word nothing: "*Obedience to God, that is to say, since God is beyond all that we can imagine or conceive, to nothing.*" But these reservations are rare. She speaks constantly of God and she does so without prudence, without reserve, and with the facility that universal tradition has accorded her. Why is this?

It is not simply a weakness, but one of the singular traits of her experience. We should speak here of the kind of faith and of the conception of faith that was hers. When Simone Weil speaks of the Good as of a certitude, this certitude is too lofty and too certain to be an object of faith. It is outside faith, as it is above everything. Nothing will cause her to waver on this point. But the more lofty a certitude the idea of the Good becomes (a certitude only at this point of extreme height where it is inaccessible), the more does this other idea—the idea that we have no relation with the Good and no hope of ever approaching it—impose itself. The cost of this certitude of certitude should be eternal despair.

Simone Weil just escapes this, but she does so completely. She herself knows very well why, and she says it clearly: since adolescence she has not ceased to believe in the spiritual efficacy of desire. She believed that any human being whatsoever will enter the realm of truth, if one only desires the truth and perpetually concentrates on attaining it. Here is how she was led to this hope. At about age fourteen, having persuaded herself of the mediocrity of her mind, she was overcome by despair. Close to her was her brother who, due to his mathematical precocity, was compared to Pascal. Believing she was without genius, she thought herself forever excluded from the transcendent domain to which only those who have great intelligence and are able to find the truth have access. "After months of inner darkness" she came "suddenly and forever" to the certitude that, even if one's faculties are of no account, the pure good—truth, virtue, beauty—will be accorded to those who purely desire it. She never departed from this new certitude. This for her was faith. *"That every thought of mine which is a desire for good brings me nearer to the good; this is an object of faith. Only through faith can I have this experience."*

There is a relation of necessity, then, between desire and the good. But what sort of relation, and what is the necessity that allows me to affirm: "When one desires bread one is not given stones"? Here we approach the moment at which we will get hold of Simone Weil's fundamental indecision, an indecision she seems not to notice, perhaps because it is impossible for her to put it aside. The belief that I, a being who is without relation to God and incapable of doing anything to approach him on my own (for everything that brings me close to him immediately distances me from him), can nevertheless live in such a way that I will die in God's presence, and even in this life unite myself with him—this thought seems to mark the point at which intervenes an assistance that is foreign, gratuitous, yet indispensable, and that allows us to rise above our earthly weight. This support bears a well-known name, for it is grace. Apparently nothing less than grace will diminish this frightening distance between we who know nothing of the Good and can do no more than desire it, and the "reality" of the Good.

There is a good part of Simone Weil's thought that must be interpreted as a meditation on grace. At a certain moment, in extreme affliction, if we hold onto the possibility of loving, infinite love responds to us and plants in us *"a tiny seed"*—an infinitesimal, divine seed for which we must become a place of reception and nurture. That is all. *"From that moment, God has no more to do; neither have we, except to wait"* (but waiting is a very important thing). We see, even here, that Simone Weil reduces as much as possible God's personal intervention, for which she feels an extreme distaste. Yet even this is still too much. And having given everything over to God, she nonetheless, through an entirely different impulse in her thought, seeks to do without his agency in order to make possible his impossible approach. Not through an excessive confidence in human means, quite the contrary. But just as the world in which mechanical necessity reigns and that is absolutely empty of God is also, by the purity of this very emptiness, what is closest to the divine essence, so, in the same way, what in us is nature is always ready to reverse itself into a surnature, to the extent that we consent to bear its weight. Then we will suffer. Then the suffering and affliction will divide us in such a way that a part of us will be in distress while another part will consent to this distress and, continuing to desire the Good, will become capable of it. This division by suffering divides us exactly into nature and surnature. Through natural affliction we witness a kind of genesis of the surnature within us.

*

Desire and painful suffering are the givens of Simone Weil's experience. She did not invent or discover them in her thought, but in her life. She felt them fundamentally and underwent them as the necessary and sufficient conditions of salvation. Affliction, as Jacques Cabaud observes, is for her a kind of natural redemption.[3] But it is also the strange path toward a damnation without sin, since those who are struck by affliction become fortuitously incapable of receiving God and are in danger of passing the limit beyond which there is no hope of salvation. Yet even in extreme affliction love (desire) is perhaps never entirely lost. Through desire we can orient ourselves toward the good. And desire for the good produces the good. Some of her formulations have a disquieting rapidity: *"Therefore, God exists because I desire him: this is as certain as my own existence."* Yet what she understands by this is in many texts more precise: that the desire for the good, being pure, is not a desire to possess it but only to desire it (I know nothing of the good, and I desire it too purely to appropriate it for myself). I am thus filled by my very desire: I constantly have the good when I desire it, since I desire only to desire it and not to have it.

She says this in many ways. But we also find the following statement, which shows the constant equivocacy of her thought: *"If desire for the good equals possession of the good, desire for the good is productive of the good, that is to say, it produces the desire for good. Outside me there is a good which is superior to me and which influences me for the good every time I desire the good. As there is no possible limit to this operation, this external good is infinite; it is God."* This is an assembling of notions that mixes together without rigor residues of the ontological argument and Platonic realism. It is no longer my desire in itself that produces the good: rather it is the great Good that each time responds to my desire and influences me. A conclusion one can only arrive at by a leap. Let us nonetheless admit it. But if I have such a certitude, will my desire not lose its disinterestedness, its purity? And ceasing to be pure, it will be empty; no good will respond to it. We are therefore condemned to this essential contradiction: thought of the truth alone is enough to falsify the truth, just as knowing the rules required for salvation is enough to make one no longer capable of observing them *"because the very fact of thinking about them already constitutes their violation."* Which once again shows either our absolute powerlessness and the impossibility of any salvation, or else obliges us to place our hope solely in divine mercy. Thus everything constantly reverses itself.

The strange thing is that in such extreme difficulties Simone Weil seems never to despair or to doubt, even if at times the feeling of man's affliction tears at her.

Here again, at a time when faith and doubt, thought and anguish seem interchangeable—to such an extent that one can just as well take the one for the other—Simone Weil offers us an example of certitude that, neither passing by way of her person nor owing anything to she who is nothing, remains beyond the reach of the uncertainties that thought is always ready to bring back to life so we can set our mind on avoiding them. In a manner that is almost calm, equable, and unbending, she keeps always pure the affirmation she nonetheless cannot affirm. A strange affirmation that eludes the obscurities of faith, as well as the contradictions of salvation, and to which she does not succeed in giving form or even introduce into her thought; and yet an invincible affirmation. Thus the question returns, still there: where does this certitude come from?

2

There is a simple answer to the questions one may ask oneself about "Simone Weil's certitude": mystical in origin, it is an echo of the ecstatic experiences during the course of which she was several times in contact with "the unconditional good," and that she thereby knew through experiential knowledge, having each time *"felt, without being in any way prepared, a presence more personal, more certain and more real than that of a human being; a presence inaccessible to the senses as well as to the imagination and analogous to the love that is glimpsed through the most tender smile of a loved one."* Her thought thus refers us back to that mystical knowledge upon whose obscure foundation she believes she is thinking a certitude that, in thought itself, is already nothing more than uncertainties: uncertainties she then does not perceive, or about which she is not concerned to the same degree as we are because of all she has and all that we do not: the plenitude of her implicit faith, her implicit hope, a belief that God is love and that a sincere waiting cannot be disappointed. Affirmations that were all experientially confirmed, and that do not cease to support her uncertain reasons.

This answer is to a certain extent true but it does not suffice. First of all, it must be observed that the more she uses God's name with indiscretion, the better she keeps—with an exemplary restraint, and even from herself—the secret of the gift that was bestowed upon her, never speaking of it in her notes, even less using it as an authority or as proof.[4] She does not betray herself, nor does she betray the secret. Because she knows also that such instants, exceptional as they may be, and because they represent the exception, prove nothing, guarantee nothing, and, themselves without guarantee, are thus all the more useless. How altered they would be if one claimed to make them serve some certainty. Besides, when one would wish to give proof, it would no longer be the experience that is present but its memory. The memory of a mystical event is not mystical—rather, it reintroduces the uncertainties of time and discourse into the ungraspable certitude of which memory is but a reflection. Or to state this more precisely, a memory is valid only through the transformation of those who remember and to the extent to which they would be able to become entirely that of which there is memory. But then they would no longer remember. They would be forgetting, empty—a pure nothing for them and for us.

True knowledge is surnatural. All Simone Weil's writings and all her thoughts are oriented toward this affirmation. Except that the word *surnatural* must be read in a constantly ambiguous manner; in such a way that it indicates, perhaps, the approach of the only veritable "reality," but in no way indicating that in order to approach it anything surnatural is needed, at least anything that would not have as its principles and conditions some general givens: desire, attention, obedience, renunciation. Even experience of the transcendent does not seem to entail making the part of grace any greater, or the decision of a suprahuman intervention any more necessary. This is what is remarkable. Did she not, then, in a lightning flash, escape gravity and earthly law? Was she not touched by a surnatural presence? Yet what tore her from herself was not herself.

Most certainly. No one has set aside more firmly all forms of power, even spiritual power. Man can do nothing, and he is excepted from truth each time he exercises power (or has the illusion of doing so). But God can do no more than man. He is not the All-Powerful that our idolatry hastens to adore so we can adore the power in ourselves. On the contrary, he is the absolute renunciation of power: he is abdication, abandon, the consent to not being what he could be, and this in the Creation as well as in the Passion. God is not *able* to do anything for us; as long, at least, as we are still ourselves, encompassed by ourselves. *"In this world God is a dissolvent. Friendship with him confers no power."* We come back to the question: if what tore her from herself is not herself and is not God, then what is it? One must answer: this tearing itself. This response, though she does not quite (but very nearly) give it this form, is what sustains her entire life and her entire thought. All the certitude comes together here. There is in us something that must be called divine, something by which we already dwell close to God: it is the movement by which we efface ourselves, it is abandon—the abandonment of what we believe to be, a retreat outside ourselves and outside everything, a seeking of emptiness through the desire that is like the tension of this emptiness and that, when it is the desire for desire (then a surnatural desire), is the desire of emptiness itself, emptiness desiring.

This, as she says, is perfectly simple. We have but little force; if we renounce it, if we consent to everything, we become all-powerful. We have but little being, a semblance of being; if we renounce it we will surely be extinguished, but by the plenitude of being. *"God created me as a non-being which has the appearance of existing in order that through love I should renounce this apparent existence and be annihilated by the plenitude of being."* Yes, this is simple. But, one will ask, why the plenitude of being and not simply nothingness without plenitude?

Because this abdication, this loving consent to be nothing, this immobile impetus of desire toward an anticipated death is, in Simone Weil's profound conviction, the absolute itself, absolute certitude; or to use a language closer to hers, it is, already in the world, our common trait with God, our equality with him. *"God abdicated from his divine omnipotence and emptied himself. By abdicating from our small human power we become, as regards emptiness, equal to God."* (We cannot but sense that there is in this humbling a great spiritual pride.)

It follows that we are in the surnatural by all that, within us and outside us, naturally disposes us to this abdication we will call divine. Outside us: affliction, time, aimless necessity. Within us: the consent to affliction, obedience to time, the desire finally without hope; a desire that desires nothing but this nothing it is. *"If we desire non-being we have it, and all we have to do is be aware of the fact." "To become something divine I have no need to get away from my misery, I have only to adhere to it."* All this—affliction, desire—is natural, and so too can be liberation. But all this is at the same time surnatural and, one must perhaps add, very mysterious. For how, being nothing, are we to consent to being nothing? How can necessity, which is everywhere, become in us obedience and attention? How can time become an acceptance of time, how can it become waiting, patience, and, by a transmutation of patience, eternity? Things are not easy on God's side either. For why did God play this trick on us; why did he give us a semblance of being, a deceptive appearance that, at the price of infinite suffering, we must bring back to the truth of the nothingness that it is by falling back to the nothingness from which, unfortunately, we were made to come out of: or rather, that we were allowed to believe we had left? We are an illusion. And we have to find the means for making the illusion vanish. This is the whole problem of salvation. "This joke of God is what we are." "Creation is God's fiction."

*

Simone Weil conceived of creation in a manner that may seem strange and, in any case, foreign to tradition. It is an interesting conception. First, because it once again reveals to us the true sources of her certitude, but also because this conception puts her, without her knowing it, back into the Jewish tradition from which she turned away with such violence and often such obstinate incomprehension; a mystical tradition, it is true. In fact, it is Isaac Luria (a saintly man and profound thinker of the sixteenth century, whose influence we know was great) who, interpreting an idea from the ancient Cabala (the *Tsimtsum*), recognized in the creation an act of abandonment on the part of God. A forceful idea. In creating the world God does not set forth something more, but, first of all, something less. Infinite Being is necessarily everything. In order that there be the world, he would have to cease being the whole and make a place for it through a movement of withdrawal, of retreat, and in "abandoning a kind of region within himself, a sort of mystical space."[5] In other words, the essential problem of creation is the problem of nothingness. Not how something can be created out of nothing, but how nothing can be created in order that, on the basis of nothing, something can take *place*. There must be nothing: that the nothing exists is the true secret and the initial mystery, a mystery that begins painfully with God himself—through a sacrifice, a retraction, and a limitation, a mysterious consent to exile himself from the all that he is and to efface and absent himself, if not disappear. (It is as though the creation of the world, or its existence, would have evacuated God from himself, posed God as a lack of God and therefore had as its corollary a sort of ontological atheism that could only be abolished along with the world itself. Where there is a world there is, painfully, the lack of God.) A profound thought indeed.

Now this is the thought Simone Weil rediscovered, for nothing permits us to say she borrowed it. The numerous formulations she employs are well known: *"For God, Creation consisted not in extending himself, but in withdrawing." "On God's part creation is not an act of self-extension but of retreat, of renunciation. . . . By this creative act he denied himself, as Christ has told us to deny ourselves." "God, in a sense, renounces being the whole." "Because he is the creator, God is not all-powerful. Creation is abdication. But he is all-powerful in the sense that his abdication is voluntary." "The Creation is an abandonment. In creating what is other than himself, God necessarily abandoned it."* This means two things: God renounced both himself and us. Abandonment: the fact of abandoning and of being abandoned, by its double signification and with its negative and positive aspects, is the initial certitude and the unique truth, which, in God as well as in us, indicates all we ought to believe and all it is necessary for us to have in order that we may once again find everything and become again like God: in order that we may recognize God in us, in this renunciation that he is, by which he makes us be, and through which we become him by restoring unto him the being we are not.

The only truth: abandonment, renunciation. Through renunciation God created the world; through renunciation we de-create the world. Renunciation is truly God in us.[6] And through him, when we transform this passive abandonment—the fact of being abandoned—into an active abandonment—the fact of giving ourselves in abandoning—we can constantly recapture all that we lack, and all the more so as we lack it. For example: the world is absolutely bereft of God since God in a sense absented himself and emptied himself of his divinity in order that the world may be. But as nothing in God is more divine than this abdication, nothing can render God more present to us than this absence that is his most admirable gift, and that the world represents for us, essentially "is." So that Simone Weil can say: *"The World, inasmuch as it is entirely empty of God, is God himself,"* or again: *"The abandonment in which God leaves us is his own way of caressing us. Time, our single misery, is the very touch of his hand. It is the abdication by which he makes us exist."*

Thus in everything and everywhere we "have" God, as much in his absence as in his presence, which is only the eminent form of his absence. Hence an invincible certitude. A certitude, however, that is always ready to turn about. For from the moment I *know* this, the detachment through which alone I can reunite with truth, the renouncing that is my divine part, ceases to be pure and I renounce nothing, having the certitude that in renouncing I will be everything and more: God himself. So that the ultimate conclusion should be: one must dwell in ignorance, in illusion, and lose oneself in incomprehensible affliction. Certitude, become once again inaccessible and nearly confounded with the emptiness of the sky, might, on this basis, recover its "reality."

(The manner in which Simone Weil conceives of creation surely renders it difficult to aver. For Isaac Luria, creation requires a double act: one is an act of retreat, the other an act of unfolding. The first consists in making emptiness and obscurity; the second in making of the emptiness a clearing by sending light into it—a double effort of withdrawal and of bursting forth, of obscurity and revelation. But Simone Weil retains only the idea of negation and divine reflux. What, then, can the degree of reality of the world be if it seems to correspond to no positive act? At times she thinks there is in us an increate part, the non-created depth of the soul, and this, within the soul, is so close to God that it is the divine essence itself. She borrows this idea from Meister Eckhart, to whom she is closer than to any other mystic (he also believes that desire and emptiness suffice to oblige God to give himself to us). Thus everything that in creation is "real" would come from what is uncreated in it. Beyond this increate part, creation is nothing and nothing good.

This is because creation is unjustifiable. Its only justification is that it leaves us the possibility of destroying it by renouncing it. In weighty terms Simone Weil writes, *"God's great crime against us is to have created us; it is the fact of our existence. And our existence is our great crime against him." "Why is creation, being inseparably linked to evil, a good? In what way is it good that I exist and not God alone? That through this miserable intermediary God should love himself? I cannot understand it."* This is probably the most serious doubt she has expressed, and the question remains without response. It is true that she adds: *"But God suffers all that I suffer."* Here, she is close to conceiving of the creation in terms of exile; as though, through the creation, something of the divine being had been exiled from it, thus giving us the task of working for the restoration of harmony and unity by taking upon ourselves this exile that is ourselves and our very essence, and by carrying it out to its end. But this idea of exile, while so close to her thought, remained alien to her.)

*

When one reads Simone Weil's notebooks, it is not the difficult coherence nor the refusal to think things all the way through that one might take as ground for complaint. It is another regret one feels. She says that we can reach truth only in secret: *"truth is secret,"* love this very secret itself. *"God is always absent from our love as he is from the world, but he is secretly present in pure love." "The heavenly Father dwells only in secret." "Our Father which is in secret."* She nonetheless lacks this secrecy. No thought has more rigorously sought to maintain God's remoteness, the necessity of knowing that we know nothing of him and that he is truth and certitude only when he is hidden, the hidden God. But she does not cease to speak openly of this hidden God, with assurance and with indiscretion, forgetting that this indiscretion renders nearly all her words vain.

It may be (and are we not continually having this experience?) that the further thought goes toward expressing itself, the more it must maintain a reserve somewhere within itself, something like a place that would be a kind of uninhabited, uninhabitable non-thought, *a thought that would not allow itself to be thought.* A presence-absence with which thought torments itself and over which it watches painfully, with suspicion and negligence, only able to turn away from this non-thought if all that brings it closer to thought also separates it from it. Forgetting this non-thought might be the most appropriate measure, inasmuch as forgetfulness has perhaps its origin in this initial lacuna, and as it alone gives us a presentiment of this "immediate" reality. Let us forget it, then, so as to remember it only through forgetting. But it happens, rightly or wrongly, that this sort of blind spot of thought—this *impossibility* of thinking that thought is for itself in its reserve—can appear to us to be not only present in all things, in all speech and all action in a certain negligible way, but also, by this negligible presence, able to take up always more space, to extend itself to all experience and, little by little, alter it completely. A strange and perilous situation against which we are tempted to react. From this come various methods of struggle (a fierce effort to think only *against* this un-thought) and compromises (one might, by a pact, circumscribe regions of influence, raise Chinese walls, isolate it in the great Castle); or again—and this has always been the most tempting and easy solution—instead of leaving the empty part empty, one can name it and, in a word, fill it by obscuring it with the strongest, the most august and most opaque name that can be found.

We know what this name is for Simone Weil. We also know that she loved this name, indeed imposing, loved it for itself and loved in it only itself, its transparency (not its gravity), its secrecy (not its capacity to divulge the secret). Perhaps, having discovered it by inspiration, she knew how to preserve in it the purity of the discovery, and pronouncing it in the beautiful Greek language that for her was beauty par excellence, in repeating it, her mind empty, she felt assured that it would not suppress in her the emptiness whose entire place it served to occupy.

Yet the emptiness must remain. The commentator who allowed himself to be misled by the cumbersomeness of the name, and who saw no more than the name, would commit an error, nearly a falsification. Everything interesting about Simone Weil's thought, and also the friendship one cannot fail to feel for her, comes from the pure force with which she preserved this emptiness, maintaining it and attempting to abide by it in two forms.

*

One is affliction, the other attention. I cannot pause long here over these two things encountered in her experience. They are essential. The thought of affliction is precisely the thought of that which cannot let itself be thought. Affliction is an "enigma." It is of the same nature as physical suffering, from which it is inseparable. Physical suffering, when it is such that one can neither suffer it nor cease suffering it, thereby stopping time, makes time a present without future and yet impossible as present (one cannot reach the following instant, it being separated from the present instant by an impassable infinite, the infinite of suffering; but the present of suffering is impossible, it being the abyss of the present).[7] Affliction makes us lose time and makes us lose the world. The individual who is afflicted falls beneath every class. The afflicted are neither pathetic nor pitiable; they are ridiculous, inspiring distaste and scorn. They are for others the horror they are for themselves. Affliction is anonymous, impersonal, indifferent. It is life become alien and death become inaccessible. It is the horror of being where being is without end.

Having in some sense indicated this, Simone Weil understood that affliction, far more than anguish, holds in it the limit from which we should assume a perspective on the human condition—a movement that hinders precisely all perspective.[8] In the space of affliction we have very close to us, and almost at our disposition, all that religion, in inverting it, projected up into the heavens. We are not above but beneath time: this is eternity. We are not above but beneath the person: this is the impersonal, which is one of the traits of the sacred. We are outside the world: this is not the beyond but the before, not the purity of nothingness or the plenitude of being, but being as nothingness.

"For me who deliberately, and almost without hope, chose to take the point of view of those who are at the bottom . . . " What Simone Weil says of herself we should say of thought. Thought cannot but be fraudulent unless it is thought from out of the baseness of this affliction: from out of base impersonality, base eternity (which is only time become the loss of time), and from this impossibility that affliction "is" for itself and that it lays bare for us (without ceasing to cover it over anew). To think through affliction is to lead thought toward this point at which force is no longer the measure of what must be said and thought; it is to make thought one with this impossibility of thinking that thought is for itself, and is like its center. *"Thought finds affliction as repugnant to think about as living*

flesh finds death repugnant." In this way the center of thought is that which does not let itself be thought.

*

What is attention? Affliction has a relation to time. Through affliction we endure "pure" time, time without event, without project and without possibility; a kind of empty perpetuity that must be borne infinitely, and at every instant (just as fatigue and hunger must be borne in the extreme destitution of need). Let it be over. But it is without end. Deprived of ourselves, deprived of the I upon which we naturally lean, deprived of the world that in normal times exists in our place and disburdens us of ourselves, we are time, indefinitely endured. Attention is this same relation to time. Attention is waiting: not the effort, the tension, or the mobilization of knowledge around something with which one might concern oneself. Attention waits. It waits without precipitation, leaving empty what is empty and keeping our haste, our impatient desire, and, even more, our horror of emptiness from prematurely filling it in. Attention is the emptiness of thought oriented by a gentle force and maintained in an accord with the empty intimacy of time.

Attention is impersonal. It is not the self that is attentive in attention; rather, with an extreme delicacy and through insensible, constant contacts, attention has always already detached me from myself, freeing me for the attention that I for an instant become.

In impersonal attention, the center of attention, the centering point around which are distributed perspective, sight, and the order of what is to be inwardly and outwardly seen disappears. Personal and impersonal attention are in this way distinguishable. Average, personal attention organizes around the object of attention everything one knows and sees, the entire inner and outer landscape that seems to come out of the object, enriching itself through it, and enriching it. This average attention, then, remains a means. The other attention is as though idle and unoccupied. It is always empty and is the light of emptiness.

If we evoke this thought that does not allow itself to be thought and that thought always holds in reserve as a non-thought within thought; if we call it a mystery (but the mystery is nothing, even as a mysterious nothing), we might say that the essence of this mystery is its being always on the hither side of attention. But then we will be saying that the essence of attention is its capacity to preserve, in and through itself, that which is always before attention and is in some way the source of all waiting: the mystery. Or again, mystery is the center of attention when attention, being equal and perfectly equal to itself, is the absence of any center: thus beyond all regularity, all evenness. Attention is the reception of what escapes attention, an opening upon the unexpected, a waiting that is the unawaited of all waiting.

*

Simone Weil does not express herself exactly this way. But I do not believe I am distorting her thought in using this language.[9] It would be false to conclude hastily that, according to her, attention is affliction already redeemed and transfigured through its own agency, and that there is a way of transforming the empty time of affliction into the empty time of attention. Simone Weil knows, and by way of experience, that extreme affliction is without relation to anything that would make it cease being what it is. God could not do this, for affliction removes God, making him *absent, more absent than someone who is dead, more absent than light in a dark cell.* The relation between attention and affliction is the relation that only the plenitude of love can reestablish with the afflicted one. It is love alone — love become the immobility and the perfection of attention — that, by way of the gaze of the other who is *autrui*, opens a way toward the closing off of affliction. Under this gaze of love and attention the afflicted allow themselves to be looked at. *"Knowing how to let a certain gaze take them in. This gaze is first of all an attentive gaze by which the soul empties itself of all its own content so as to receive in itself the being that it is looking at, such as it is, in all its truth."* Affliction is inattention's extreme. Attention is an attention that makes itself bearable to the affliction that cannot bear being attended to.

Simone Weil's relation to attention is itself mysterious. She does not give the outward impression of having been capable of the immobility that she recommends to thought. She was rather restless, attending to many things, unable to keep herself from doing first one thing, then another, worrying those she met with questions, always wanting to experience everything so as to test herself and at times strangely unaware of the reserve that is the first need of the other [*autrui*], blind to *autrui* in her efforts to devote herself to and recognize herself in them. Even on her deathbed she continues to discuss and argue, astonishing and wearying the priest who comes to visit her. The habit of debating may seem to be a relic of the schools and small circles she so liked to frequent. Perhaps. But this restlessness must also be recognized as the impossibility of remaining in place that comes with the experience of affliction. Affliction is the loss of a dwelling place, the unceasing disquiet — a cold and indifferent disquiet — with regard to what is never there. Agitated and uneasy in the details of existence,[10] Simone Weil gave in her thought the example of certitude and, in her works, the model of an even expression, almost calm and as though perfectly at rest in its movement. For attention, at times absent from the surface of her life, is present as much as is possible in the depth of her language, for which she is, in her radiance, the uneven evenness. Through attention, language has with thought the same relation thought would like to have with this lacuna in it — this affliction — that thought is and that it cannot render present to itself. Language is the place of attention.

V

The Indestructible

1
Being Jewish

Attention, waiting. Waiting, affliction. To reflect historically upon these words that are so difficult to pronounce, all the while maintaining their abstract simplicity, is to expose oneself to the even greater difficulty of undergoing the ordeal of a history to which Simone Weil was obliged (by what necessity of thought, what pain in thinking of it?) to close her eyes. Why must she, too faithful to Greek clarity, forget that every reflection upon a fundamental injustice passes by way of the condition that has for thousands of years been allotted to the Jews? Why, in turn, are we so uneasy as we reflect upon it? Why, in reflecting upon it, do we stop our reflection at a certain moment; accepting, if we must, what is negative in the Jewish condition—once again enlightened (assuming that it is a question of light) about a negative extremity—but thereby missing the positive significance of Judaism? Is it, perhaps, through fear of playing into the hands of nihilism and its most vulgar substitute, anti-Semitism? But perhaps this fear is the very way in which such forces still impose themselves upon us, and even by our refusal. We will not cease to see this equivocation at work.

The Jew is uneasiness and affliction. This must be clearly said even if this assertion, in its indiscreet sobriety, is itself unfortunate. The Jew has throughout time been the oppressed and the accused. He is, he has been, the oppressed of every society. Every society, and in particular Christian society, has had its Jew in order to affirm itself against him through relations of general oppression. One

123

could say—borrowing this expression from Franz Rosenzweig—that there is a movement of history that makes every Jew the Jew of all men, which means that every man, whoever he may be, has a particular relation of responsibility (a relation not yet elucidated) with this "Other" that is the Jew. "To be Jewish," says Clara Malraux, "means that nothing is given to us." Heine said: "Judaism? Do not speak to me about it, doctor, I would not wish it even upon my worst enemy. Injury and shame is all it brings: it is not a religion, it is an affliction." Being-Jewish would be, then—we are coming to it—essentially a negative condition; to be Jewish would be to be from the outset deprived of the principal possibilities of living, and in a manner not abstract, but real.

Still, is Jewish existence only this? Is it simply a lack? Is it simply the difficulty of living that is imposed upon a certain category of men by the hateful passion of other men? Is there not in Judaism a truth that is not only present in a rich cultural heritage, but also living and important for the thought of today—even if this thought challenges every religious principle? There is an astonishing sign of barbarity in the fact of having to ask such a question, and also in the audacity felt in asking it. Albert Memmi wonders why the Jew should always have to disavow himself, why he is refused the right to be different.[1] Is anti-Semitism so embedded in our ways of being that in order to defend those it assails, we can find no other means than to take from them the entirety of their existence and truth, making them disappear in an unreal human abstraction, which, moreover, is later held against them? "A Jew is nothing but a man like any other! Why speak of the Jews?" And if one calls him by name one seems to be lacking reserve, to be pronouncing a dangerous, even injurious word, as though being Jewish could have only a pejorative meaning rather than designate a grave truth and an exceptionally important relation.

Sartre described anti-Semitism rigorously. He showed that the portrait-accusation drawn up against the Jew reveals nothing about the Jew but everything about the anti-Semite, inasmuch as the anti-Semite projects the force of his injustice, his stupidity, his base meanness, and his fear onto his enemy. But in affirming that the Jew is no more than a product of the others' gaze, and is only Jewish by the fact of being seen as such by the other (which thereby obliges him either to deny or to claim his identity), Sartre tends to recognize Jewish difference, but merely as the negative of anti-Semitism. It is certainly true that anti-Semitism has modified Jewish existence (if only by threatening it, making it more scarce, and at times exterminating it); and perhaps it has affected the idea that particular Jews have of themselves—but this on the ground of a prior "historical" reality and authenticity one has to call Judaism, and that defines in an implicit manner the relation of every man to himself. Being Jewish, therefore, cannot be the simple reverse of anti-Jewish provocation; nor is it a break with the incognito into which the Jew must vanish, not only to be secure but in some sense to be himself—absence thus being at the same time his refuge and his definition. Being Jewish signifies more, and doubtless something it is essential to bring to light.

This can only be the fruit of long work and a meditation more personal than erudite. There is a Jewish thought and a Jewish truth; that is, for each of us, there is an obligation to try to find whether in and through this thought and this truth there is at stake a certain relation of man with man that we can sidestep only by refusing a necessary inquiry. Certainly, this inquiry will not be entertained here as proceeding from a religious exigency. Let us acknowledge this beforehand. Let us also declare that it is not a question of the interest we bring to facts of culture. Finally, let us acknowledge that what the Jewish experience can tell us at this level cannot pretend to exhaust the meaning that gives it its richness. Each one understands what he can. Moreover, the principal thing is perhaps not to be found in a lengthy development, but already and almost entirely in the words themselves: being Jewish.

When in his turn Pasternak asks "What does being Jewish signify? Why does it exist?" I believe that among all the responses there is one in three parts that we cannot avoid choosing, and it is this: it exists so the idea of exodus and the idea of exile can exist as a legitimate movement; it exists, through exile and through the initiative that is exodus, so that the experience of strangeness may affirm itself close at hand as an irreducible relation; it exists so that, by the authority of this experience, we might learn to speak.

Reflection and history enlighten us on the first point with a painful evidence. If Judaism is destined to take on meaning for us, it is indeed by showing that, at whatever time, one must be ready to set out, because to go out (to step outside) is the exigency from which one cannot escape if one wants to maintain the possibility of a just relation. The exigency of uprooting; the affirmation of nomadic truth. In this Judaism stands in contrast to paganism (all paganism). To be pagan is to be fixed, to plant oneself in the earth, as it were, to establish oneself through a pact with the permanence that authorizes sojourn and is certified by certainty in the land. Nomadism answers to a relation that possession cannot satisfy. Each time Jewish man makes a sign to us across history it is by the summons of a movement. Happily established in Sumerian civilization, Abraham at a certain point breaks with that civilization and renounces dwelling there. Later, the Jewish people become a people through the exodus. And where does this night of exodus, renewed from year to year, each time lead them? To a place that is not a place and where it is not possible to reside. The desert makes of the slaves of Egypt a people, but a people without a land and bound by a word. Later, the exodus becomes the exile that is accompanied by all the trials of a hunted existence, establishing in each heart anxiety, insecurity, affliction, and hope. But this exile, heavy as it is, is not only recognized as being an incomprehensible malediction. There is a truth of exile and there is a vocation of exile; and if being Jewish is being destined to dispersion—just as it is a call to a sojourn without place, just as it ruins every fixed relation of force with *one* individual, *one* group, or *one* state—it is because dispersion, faced with the exigency of the whole, also clears the way for a different exigency and finally forbids the temptation of Unity-Identity.

André Neher recalls these stages of Jewish presence (the presence of a non-presence) in one of his books. First of all, of course, the Jew has the right to the name Jew (I know none more worthy of being claimed); but one must not forget that before being Jewish the Jew was an Israelite, that before being an Israelite he was a Hebrew (today becoming an Israeli), and that to be Jewish is thus to bear without bending the weight and the fullness of all these names. Here I will rapidly take up again André Neher's remarks.[2] The Jewish man is the Hebrew when he is the man of origins. The origin is a decision; this is the decision of Abraham, separating himself from what is, and affirming himself as a foreigner in order to answer to a foreign truth. The Hebrew passes from one world (the established Sumerian world) to something that is "not yet a world" and is nonetheless this world here below; a ferryman, the Hebrew Abraham invites us not only to pass from one shore to the other, but also to carry ourselves to wherever there is a passage to be made, maintaining this between-two-shores that is the truth of passage. It must be added that if this memorial of the origin that comes to us from so venerable a past is certainly enveloped in mystery, it has nothing of the mythical about it. Abraham is fully a man; a man who sets off and who, by this first departure, founds the human right to beginning, the only true creation. A beginning that is entrusted and passed on to each of us but that, in extending itself, loses its simplicity. The Hebrew himself will not remain Hebrew. The relation with the Unknown one can know only by way of distance, through migration and march, becomes, with the filing out of Jabbok and in the night of Penuel, enigmatic contact: the struggle about which one knows nothing since what is at stake is the truth of the night, that which is not to be retained when day breaks. Jacob runs headlong into the inaccessible outside whose partner he becomes, struggling not to overcome it, but to receive it in the very night of the word that he firmly stands up to until the moment when it comes to him as benediction. Thus marked, the Hebrew, becoming Israel, becomes the one who is not like the others; election is an alteration. The one who is subject to the brusque interpolation of the Foreign, the one who is responsible for the ambiguous choice that sets him apart, is at the mercy of this strangeness that he risks making into a power, a privilege, a kingdom, and a State. Israel's solitude—a sacerdotal, a ritual, and also a social solitude—comes not only from the passions of the men who live adjacent to it, but also from this particular relation with itself that placed this extreme, infinite distance, the presence that is other, in its proximity. Thus is born the Jew. The Jew is the man of origins; he who relates to the origin not by dwelling but by distancing himself from it, thus saying that the truth of the beginning is in separation. Israelite, he is in the Kingdom. Jew, he is in Exile, and is as though destined to make of exile a kingdom. André Neher says: "How can one be in Exile and in the Kingdom, at the same time vagabond and established? It is precisely this contradiction that makes the Jewish man a Jew." (A contradiction that Neher is perhaps too inclined to translate into dialectical terms, whereas it signifies a contrariety for which dialectics is unable to account.)

Let us insist now upon a single point. The words *exodus, exile* — as well as those heard by Abraham, "Leave your country, your kinsmen, your father's house" — bear a meaning that is not negative. If one must set out on the road and wander, is it because, being excluded from the truth, we are condemned to the exclusion that prohibits all dwelling? Or would not this errancy rather signify a new relation with "truth"? Doesn't this nomadic movement (wherein is inscribed the idea of division and separation) affirm itself not as the eternal privation of a sojourn, but rather as an authentic manner of residing, of a residence that does not bind us to the determination of place or to settling close to a reality forever and already founded, sure, and permanent? As though the sedentary state were necessarily the aim of every action! As though truth itself were necessarily sedentary!

But why this refusal to found the "concept" of the true on the need to dwell? Why does errancy substitute for the dominion of the Same an affirmation that the word Being — in its identity — cannot satisfy? It is not simply a question of privileging becoming; nor is it a question of introducing a purely idealist claim in rejecting all that is terrestrial. It is with the Greeks that we find the primacy of the world of ideas — a primacy that is nonetheless simply a way for the visible to reign invisibly. It is with the Christians that we find the disavowal of the here below, an abasement of life, a scorn for presence. To leave the dwelling place, yes; to come and go in such a way as to affirm the world as a passage, but not because one should flee this world or live as fugitives in eternal misfortune. The words exodus and exile indicate a positive relation with exteriority, whose exigency invites us not to be content with what is proper to us (that is, with our power to assimilate everything, to identify everything, to bring everything back to our I). Exodus and exile express simply the same reference to the Outside that the word existence bears. Thus, on the one hand, nomadism maintains above what is established the right to put the distribution of space into question by appealing to the initiatives of human movement and human time. And, on the other hand, if to become rooted in a culture and in a regard for things does not suffice, it is because the order of the realities in which we become rooted does not hold the key to all the relations to which we must respond. Facing the visible-invisible horizon Greek truth proposes to us (truth as light, light as measure), there is another dimension revealed to man where, beyond every horizon, he must relate to what is beyond his reach.

Here we should bring in the great gift of Israel, its teaching of the one God. But I would rather say, brutally, that what we owe to Jewish monotheism is not the revelation of the one God, but the revelation of speech as the place where men hold themselves in relation with what excludes all relation: the infinitely Distant, the absolutely Foreign. God speaks, and man speaks to him. This is the great feat of Israel. When Hegel, interpreting Judaism, declares, "The God of the Jews is the highest separation, he excludes all union" or "In the Jewish spirit there is an insurmountable abyss," he is merely neglecting the essential, which, for thousands of years, has been given expression in books, in teaching, and in a living tradition: this is the notion that if, in fact, there is infinite separation, it falls to speech to make it the place of understanding; and if there is an insurmountable abyss, speech crosses this abyss. Distance is not abolished, it is not even diminished; on the contrary, it is maintained, preserved in its purity by the rigor of the speech that upholds the absoluteness of difference. Let us acknowledge that Jewish thought does not know, or refuses, mediation and speech as mediating. But its importance is precisely in teaching us that speaking inaugurates an original relation in which the terms involved do not have to atone for this relation or disavow themselves in favor of a measure supposed to be common; they rather ask and are accorded reception precisely by reason of that which they do not have in common. To speak to someone is to accept not introducing him into the system of things or of beings to be known; it is to recognize him as unknown and to receive him as foreign without obliging him to break with his difference. Speech, in this sense, is the promised land where exile fulfills itself in sojourn since it is not a matter of being at home there but of being always Outside, engaged in a movement wherein the Foreign offers itself, yet without disavowing itself. To speak, in a word, is to seek the source of meaning in the prefix that the words *exile, exodus, existence, exteriority*, and *estrangement* are committed to unfolding in various modes of experience; a prefix that for us designates distance and separation as the origin of all "positive value."

Assuredly, it would be rash to claim to represent Judaism by allowing God's name to vanish into thin air — although the discretion with regard to this name and the silence that measures it, in so many important texts, authorize the interpreter not to pronounce it if he can do without it. With regard to Greek humanism, Jewish humanism astonishes by a concern with human relations so constant and so preponderant that, even when God is nominally present, it is still a question of man; of what there is between man and man when nothing brings them together or separates them but themselves. The first word that comes to Adam from on high after he has lapsed is: "Where are you?" It falls to God to express the preeminent human question: "Where is man?" — as though, in some sense, there had to be God in order that the questioning of man might reach its height and its breadth; but a God speaking a human language, so that the depth of the question concerning us is handed over to language. Inquiring about the nature of the commandments, Franz Rosenzweig makes this remark: "I could not venture to present any of the commandments as human. . . . But neither can I present the divine nature of the Torah in its entirety in a manner other than does Rabbi Nobel: 'And *God* appeared to Abraham; Abraham raised his eyes and he saw three *men*.' "[3] Let us recall Jacob. He has just struggled with his opponent of the Night, who said to him in an already significant manner: "You wrestled with Elohim as with men"; and Jacob, giving this place the name Penuel, says: "I have seen God [*Elohim*] face to face and my life is preserved." Then, a little later, he meets his brother Esau, whom he has much reason to fear, and says to him: "If I have won favor in your sight, then accept this gift from me; for I have seen your face as one sees the face of God, and you were pleased with me." An extraordinary expression. Jacob does not say to Esau "I just saw God as I see you" but "I see you as one sees God," which confirms the suggestion that the marvel (the privileged surprise) is indeed human presence, this Other Presence that is *Autrui*—no less inaccessible, separate, and distant than the Invisible himself. It also confirms the terrible character of such an encounter, whose outcome could only be approbation or death. Whoever sees God risks his life. Whoever encounters the Other can relate to him only through mortal violence or through the gift of speech by receiving him.

As arbitrary as it may be to limit ourselves to these remarks, I do not think the direction they take alters the truth. And this truth is that whoever wishes to read the meaning of the history of the Jews through Judaism ought to reflect upon the distance that separates man from man when he is in the presence of *Autrui*. Jews are not different from other men in the way racism would have us believe; they rather bear witness, as Lévinas says, to this relation with difference that the human face (what in the visage is irreducible to visibility) reveals to us and entrusts to our responsibility; not strangers, but recalling us to the exigency of strangeness; not separated by an incomprehensible retribution, but designating as pure separation and as pure relation what, from man to man, exceeds human power—which is nonetheless capable of anything. Anti-Semitism, in this sense, is in no way accidental; it gives a figure to the repulsion inspired by the Other, the uneasiness before what comes from afar and elsewhere: the need to kill the Other, that is, to submit to the all-powerfulness of death what cannot be measured in terms of power. One could perhaps say that anti-Semitism has three characteristics: (1) it turns all the "positive" values of Judaism into negatives and, first of all, the primary affirmation of the distance that is "infinite," irreducible, impassible (even when it is passed over), with which Judaism confronts us; (2) it transforms into fault (into an ethically and socially condemnable reality) this being-negative to which it reduces the Jew; (3) it does not restrict itself to a theoretical judgment, but calls for the actual suppression of the Jews in order better to exercise against them the principle of denial with which it has invested their image. A denial so absolute, it is true, that it does not cease to *reaffirm* the relation with the infinite that being-Jewish implies, and that no form of force can have done with because no force is able to meet up with it (just as one can kill a man who is present, and yet not strike down presence as an empty never-present presence, but rather simply cause it to disappear). The anti-Semite, at grips with the infinite, thus commits himself to a limitless movement of refusal. No, truly, excluding the Jews is not enough, exterminating them is not enough; they must also be struck from history, removed from the books through which they speak to us, just as the presence that inscribed speech is must finally be obliterated: the speech before and after every book and through which, from the farthest distance where all horizon is lacking, man has already turned toward man — in a word, destroy *"autrui."*[4]

2
Humankind

"Each time the question: Who is *'Autrui'*? emerges in our words I think of the book by Robert Antelme, for it not only testifies to the society of the German camps of World War II, it also leads us to an essential reflection.[5] I don't mean to imply that his book spells out a full response to the question. But even without taking into account the time or the circumstances it portrays (while nonetheless taking them into account), what impels this work toward us is what remains of the question's interrogative force. Through reading such a book we begin to understand that man is indestructible and that he can nonetheless be destroyed. This happens in affliction. In affliction we approach the limit where, deprived of the power to say 'I,' deprived also of the world, we would be nothing other than this Other that we are not.

— Man is the indestructible that can be destroyed. This has the ring of truth, and yet we are unable to know it through a knowledge that would already be true. Is this not merely an alluring formulation?

— I believe Robert Antelme's book helps us advance in this knowledge. But we must understand how heavily such a knowledge weighs. That man can be destroyed is certainly not reassuring; but that because of and despite this, and in this very movement, man should remain indestructible — this fact is what is truly overwhelming: for we no longer have the least chance of seeing ourselves relieved of ourselves or of our responsibility.

— As though the inexorable affirmation in man that always keeps him standing were more terrible than universal disaster. But why the indestructible? Why can he be destroyed? What relation is there between these two words?

— I read in Antelme's book: *'But there is no ambiguity; we remain men and will end only as men. . . . It is because we are men as they are that the SS will finally be powerless before us . . . [the executioner] can kill a man, but he cannot change him into something else.'* Here is a first response: human power is capable of anything. This means that man has power over what has to do with the whole and with the power that resides in me: power, in other words, over the Self-Subject itself. In this sense, alienation goes much further than is said by those who, through a need for logical security, hold on to the *ego cogito* (understood as the inalienable foundation of every possibility of being alienated). Man can do anything; and first of all, he can deprive me of myself, take from me the power to say 'I.' In affliction—and in our society affliction is always first the loss of social status—the one who suffers at the hands of men is radically altered. Having fallen not only below the individual, but also below every class and every real collective relation, the person no longer exists in his or her personal identity. In this sense the one afflicted is already outside the world, a being without horizon. And he is not a thing; even useless, a thing is precious. The deported person is not a thing belonging to the SS: when still working as a laborer, his work gives him, however little, the value of a man exploited; but for the essentially deported person, the one who no longer has either a face or speech, the work he is forced to do is designed only to exhaust his power to live and to deliver him over to the boundless insecurity of the elements. Nowhere any recourse: outside the cold, inside hunger; everywhere an indeterminate violence. '*The cold, SS*,' Antelme says profoundly. In precisely this way he blocks the enemy's endeavor. What force would want is to leave the limits of force: elevate itself to the dimension of the faceless gods, speak as fate and still dominate as men. With an unfaltering instinct, Antelme holds himself at a distance from all natural things, keeping himself from seeking consolation in the serene night, the beautiful light, the splendor of a tree: '*By looking at the sky, everywhere black, the SS barracks, the mass of the church and the farm, the temptation could come upon one to confound everything on the basis of the night. . . . History mocks the night that would do away instantly with contradictions. History closes in more relentlessly than God; its exigencies are far more terrifying. On no account does history serve to give peace to one's conscience.*' And in another passage: '*Francis wanted to talk about the sea, I resisted. . . . The sea, the* water, *the sun, made you choke when bodies were decomposing. It was with these very words . . . that one risked no longer wanting to take a step or get up.*' This is what bears meditation: when through oppression and terror man falls as though outside himself, there where he loses every perspective, every point of reference, and every difference and is thus handed over to a time without respite that he endures as the perpetuity of an indifferent present, he has one last possibility. At this moment when he becomes the unknown and the foreign, when, that is, he becomes a fate for himself, his last recourse is to know that he has been struck not by the elements, but by men, and to give the name *man* to everything that assails him.

So when everything ceases to be true, 'anthropomorphism' would be truth's ultimate echo. We should, therefore, complete Pascal's thought and say that man, crushed by the universe, must know that in the last instance it is not the universe but man alone who kills him. But it is precisely in affliction that man has always already disappeared: the nature of affliction is such that there is no longer anyone either to cause it or to suffer it; at the limit, there are never any afflicted—no one who is afflicted ever really appears. The one afflicted no longer has any identity other than the situation with which he merges and that never allows him to be himself; for as a situation of affliction, it tends incessantly to de-situate itself, to dissolve in the void of a nowhere without foundation.

— This is the trap of affliction. But here Antelme's book teaches us a great deal. The man of the camps is as close as he can be to powerlessness. All human power is outside him, as are existence in the first person, individual sovereignty, and the speech that says 'I.' It is truly as though there were no Self other than the self of those who dominate and to whom he is delivered over without appeal; as though his own self, therefore, having deserted and betrayed him, reigned among those who predominate, leaving him to an anonymous presence without speech and without dignity. And yet this force that is capable of everything has a limit; and he who literally can no longer do anything still affirms himself at the limit where possibility ceases: in the poverty, the simplicity of a presence that is the infinite of human presence. The Powerful One is the master of the possible, but he is not master of this relation that does not derive from mastery and that power cannot measure: the relation without relation wherein the 'other' is revealed as '*autrui.*' Or, if you will, the relation of the torturer to his victim, about which so much has been said, is not simply a dialectical relation. What limits his domination first of all is not his need of the one he is torturing, be it only to torture him; it is rather that this relation without power always gives rise, face to face and yet always infinitely, to the presence of the Other [*l'Autre*] as that of the Other being who is *Autrui*. Hence the furious movement of the inquisitor who wants by force to obtain a scrap of language in order to bring all speech down to the level of force. To make speak, and through torture, is to attempt to master infinite distance by reducing expression to this language of power through which the one who speaks would once again lay himself open to force's hold; and the one who is being tortured refuses to speak in order not to enter through the extorted words into this game of opposing violence, but also, at the same time, in order to preserve the true speech that he very well knows is at this instant merged with his silent presence—which is the very presence of *autrui* in himself. A presence no power, even the most formidable, will be able to reach, except by doing away with it. It is this presence that bears in itself and as the last affirmation what Robert Antelme calls *the ultimate feeling of belonging to mankind.*

— So that, fallen away from my self, foreign to myself, what is affirmed in my place is the foreignness of the other who is *autrui*: man as absolutely other, foreign and unknown, the dispossessed and the wandering or, as René Char puts it, the unimaginable man by whose presence passes the affirmation of an infinite exigency.

— '*Our horror, our stupor,*' Antelme states, '*was our lucidity.*'

— But what happens nonetheless to the one who is no longer a presence—a terrifying transformation—in the first person? Destroyed as a Subject, that is, in this sense, essentially destroyed, how can he respond to this exigency that is the exigency of the presence in him?

— Here again Antelme's book gives us the right response, and it is the book's most forceful truth. When man is reduced to the extreme destitution of need, when he becomes 'someone who eats scraps,' we see that he is reduced to himself, and reveals himself as one who has need of nothing other than need in order to maintain the human relation in its primacy, negating what negates him. It must be added that need now changes; radicalized in the proper sense of this term, it is now no more than a need that is barren, without pleasure and without content: a naked relation to naked life where the bread that one eats answers immediately to the exigency of need, just as need is immediately the need to live. Lévinas, in various analyses, showed that need is always at the same time pleasure, which is to say that in eating I not only nourish myself in order to live, but already have taken pleasure in life, affirming myself and identifying with myself in this first satisfaction. But now what we encounter in Antelme's experience, the experience of man reduced to the irreducible, is the radical need that relates me no longer either to myself or to my self-satisfaction, but to human existence pure and simple, lived as lack at the level of need. And it is still no doubt a question of a kind of egoism, and even of the most terrible kind, but of an *egoism without ego* where man, bent on survival, and attached in a way that must be called abject to living and always living on, bears this attachment to life as an attachment that is impersonal, as he bears this need as a need that is no longer his own need proper but as a need that is in some sense neutral, thus virtually the need of everyone. 'To live,' as he more or less says, 'is then all that is sacred.'

— One can therefore say that when, through oppression and affliction, my relation with myself is altered and lost—making of me this foreigner, this unknown from whom I am separated by an infinite distance, and making of me this infinite separation itself—at this moment need becomes radical: a need without satisfaction, without value, that is, a naked relation to naked existence; but this need also becomes the impersonal exigency that alone bears the future and the meaning of every value or, more precisely, of every human relation. The infinite that is the movement of desire passes by way of need. Need is desire and desire becomes confounded with need. It is as though in nourishing myself at the level of subsistence it is not I whom I nourished; it is as though I received the Other [*l'Autre*], host not to myself but to the unknown and the foreign.

— Yet we must not believe that with need everything is already saved: it is with need that everything is at stake. In the first place, man can fall below need; he can be deprived of this lack, dispossessed of dispossession.[6] But more must be said. Even at the level of this need that is sustained without satisfaction, at a level where, rather than a self-possessed will, there is in me a quasi-impersonal affirmation that alone sustains the fact of being dispossessed; when, therefore, my relation with myself makes me the absolutely Other [*l'Autre*] whose presence puts the power of the Powerful radically into question, this movement still signifies only the failure of power—not 'my' victory, still less 'my' salvation. For such a movement to begin truly to be affirmed, there must be restored—beyond this self that I have ceased to be, and within the anonymous community — the instance of a Self-Subject: no longer as a dominating and oppressing power drawn up against the 'other' that is *autrui*, but as what can receive the unknown and the foreign, receive them in the justice of a true *speech*. Moreover, on the basis of this attention to affliction without which all relation falls back into the night, another possibility must intervene: the possibility that a Self outside me become not only conscious of the affliction as though this Self were in my place, but become responsible for it by recognizing in it an injustice committed against everyone — that is, it must find in this injustice the point of departure for a *common demand*.

— In other words, through the intermediary of an exterior Subject who affirms itself as being the representative of a collective structure[7] (for example, class consciousness), the one who is dispossessed must be received not only as '*autrui*' in the justice of speech, but also placed back into a situation of dialectical struggle so he may once again consider himself as a force,[8] the force that resides in the man of need, and, finally, in the 'proletarian.' We always come back, then, to the exigency of this double relation.

— Yes, and this is what Antelme's book expresses explicitly on several pages that should be cited, were it not fitting to preserve their entire meaning by leaving them within the general movement that belongs to reading. I would like to add that the significance of this book ought now to appear more clearly. It is not, as I have said, simply a witness's testimony to the reality of the camps or a historical reporting, nor is it an autobiographical narrative. It is clear that for Robert Antelme, and very surely for many others, it is a question not of telling one's story, of testifying, but essentially of *speaking*. But which speech is being given expression? Precisely that just speech in which '*Autrui*,' prevented from all disclosure throughout his or her entire stay in the camp, could, and only at the end, be received and come into human hearing.

Let us once again recall that during their stay, all of them found themselves (in a movement that was necessarily painful, partial, unfinished, and impossible to realize) deprived as it were of a self and constrained to be the other [*autrui*] for themselves. Among those who were deported there were doubtless relations that allowed them to reestablish an appearance of society, that therefore allowed each one the occasion to feel himself or herself momentarily a self vis-à-vis someone in particular, or even to maintain a semblance of force in confronting those who were the Powerful (if only because the political struggle continued in the rest of the world and was preparing a new day). Had it been otherwise, everything would have immediately given way to a death without end. But what in this situation remains essential, its truth, is the following: the camp confined no more than a bondless entanglement of Others [*hommes Autres*], a magma of the other [*autrui*] face to face with the force of a Self that kills, and that represents nothing but the untiring power to kill. Between these deported persons who are Other and this Self of Force no language is possible; but neither is there any possibility of expression between these Others. What is then said is essential, but in *truth* heard by no one; there is no one to receive as speech (save through the momentary exchanges in which, through camaraderie, a self comes back to life) the infinite and infinitely silent presence of *autrui*. Now each one has no relation with words other than the reserve of speech, which he must live in solitude, and must also preserve by refusing any relation of false language with the Powerful, for such a relation could only definitively compromise the future of communication.

To speak in refusing, but in reserving speech.

So now we understand this reserved speech of *autrui*; a speech unheard, inexpressible, nevertheless unceasing, silently affirming that where all relation is lacking there yet subsists, there already begins, the human relation in its primacy. It is this truly infinite speech that each of those who had been handed over to the impossible experience of being for himself or herself the 'other' [*autrui*] felt called upon, now back in the world, to represent to us in speaking endlessly, without stopping, for the first time. Antelme says this, saying immediately the essential from the first words of his book: '*During the first days that followed our return, we were all, I think, seized by a veritable delirium. We wished to speak, to be heard at last.*'

— Yes, one had to speak: to entitle speech in responding to the silent presence of the other that is *autrui*. The unique authority of this speech coming directly from this very exigency.

— It was, in fact, the most immediate exigency that can be. I have to speak. An infinite demand that imposes itself with an irrepressible force. And it was as well an overwhelming discovery, a painful surprise: I speak, am I speaking? Could I now truly speak? Nothing more grave than this being able to speak from the basis of the impossible, the infinite distance to be 'filled' by language itself. '*And yet,*' says Robert Antelme, '*it was impossible. We had hardly begun to speak and we were choking.*'

— Why this wrenching? Why this pain always present, and not only here in this extreme movement but already, as I believe it is, in the most simple act of speaking?

— Perhaps because, as soon as two individuals approach one another, there is between them some painful formulation of the kind we expressed in beginning. They speak, perhaps, in order to forget it, to deny it, or to represent it.

— That man is the indestructible that can be destroyed? I continue to be wary of this formulation.

— How could it be otherwise? But even if we are to delete it, let us agree to keep what it has most plainly taught us. Yes, I believe we must say this, hold onto it for an instant: man is the indestructible. And this means there is no limit to the destruction of man.

— Is this not to formulate a radical nihilism?

— If so I should be quite willing, for to formulate it would also perhaps already be to overturn it. But I doubt that nihilism will allow itself to be taken so easily."[9]

VI

Reflections on Nihilism

1
Nietzsche, today

What about Nietzsche, today? This question is first of all anecdotal: it concerns history, and the petty details of history. It also has to do with Nietzsche's German and French interpreters and their interpretations. Let us note that as always it is a matter of the most important names: Jaspers, Heidegger, Lukács, Karl Löwith, Bataille, Jean Wahl; more recently, Fink in Germany and in France, Foucault, Deleuze, and Klossowski. This question will help us consider why the thought of nihilism, which retains all its historical, political, and literary vigor, seems — and even because of the verifications time accords it — almost naive and like the still tranquil dream of a "better" age.

In publishing a new edition of Nietzsche and in revealing the conditions under which it had come about, Karl Schlechta created a great stir.[1] He said nothing that had not been known in a vague sort of way, but he said it with the proof that had been lacking. When in 1934 he entered the Nietzsche Archives to work on a critical edition, he scarcely foresaw what awaited him. Nietzsche had been delivered over to lies; lies that were conscious, resolute, at times refined, and that went from the use of a free thought for anti-Semitic ends to the fabrication of a weighty mythology organized by a pseudo-religious ambition. But the "true" Nietzsche, in the guise of a mass of unpublished documents, was resting quietly in the very house where this absence of scruples and the need to show oneself off to advantage reigned. In order to make his way to him, Schlechta had to enter "the den of the old lioness," Nietzsche's fatal sister, who had not delayed in hoisting the flag of her brother over the battlements of Hitler's millennial empire, and who received in her lair as the most welcome guests "some of the great carnivores of the day." Working under such conditions, scholars (among whom Schlechta was not alone in proposing and finally preparing, without preconceived notions, an edition of the whole of Nietzsche's works) had less the impression of being peaceful philosophers than conspirators.

This sinister but simplistic and superficial falsification, like all political falsification (Hitler had not the least notion of Nietzsche and cared very little about him), would be of only mediocre interest, had it not been the sequel to a falsification more serious bearing upon the work itself, and that had been evolving for more than thirty years.

From 1895 on, Mme. Förster-Nietzsche had acquired from her mother all the rights, even the financial ones, over the papers that constituted the immense heritage of a thought she was to exploit with energy. First, she dismissed all her brother's true friends and worked relentlessly to render them suspect, keeping by her side only the weak Peter Gast, who, being the only one able to decipher the illegible manuscripts, became the reluctant artisan of her unbounded ambitions. Dr. Horneffer, one of those who had been collaborating with her and Peter Gast, had already revealed in 1906 the unreasonable conditions under which she obliged them to work. The mass of the unpublished texts was immense. The first concern, before any attempt at publication, ought to have been at last to read and recopy them all. But this demanded too much time. It was necessary to publish as fast as possible, and always more volumes: the need for money, a taste for exhibition, the feverish urge to gain renown by way of this great name that had to be made fashionable gave her no rest.

But she wanted more. Her main concern was to make Nietzsche a true philosopher, in the common sense of this word, and to enrich his oeuvre with a central piece where, within a systematically organized whole, all his positive assertions would find their place. Since this work did not exist, she made use of a title and a plan chosen among several others and asked her collaborators to channel into this framework, by chance so it seems, the mass of posthumous notes taken from the most varied notebooks—a good number of which represented texts that Nietzsche had separated out from his previously published works. Thus was born *The Will to Power*, whose first edition was made up of 483 aphorisms, and the second, significantly enriched, 1,067: this is the work that in fact, and in part thanks to the brilliance of its title, ended by imposing itself as one of the principal works of modern times.

The Will to Power is therefore not Nietzsche's book. It is a work fabricated by its editors and it is a false work, in the sense that what Nietzsche had written at various moments over the course of years traversed by the most diverse intentions, without order or system, is presented to us as the material of a systematic work that he had prepared and intended as such. Schlechta has shown that this fabrication was arbitrary and the order adopted unjustifiable. It sets before us fortuitous notes from which no one had the right to create a whole. The only honest method of presentation would have involved doing away with the ordering of the material that had been invented by its previous editors and returning the manuscripts to their original state by following their own chronological order. This is what Schlechta attempted, but in a manner still very open to criticism. In volume three of Nietzsche's *Works*, published under Schlechta's supervision, we for the first time lose sight of this great false work that had been created by an act of violence, and around which the ideological inveigling of an essentially ungraspable thought had been organized.[2]

*

Why was it Nietzsche's fate to be delivered over to forgers? Why had this mind—which above all prized probity in research—laid itself open to maneuverings against which Nietzsche had in advance protested when he said: "Above all, do not mistake me for . . . " "I am often taken for someone else. It would be to render me a great service to defend me from such confusion." But he also said: "Every profound thinker is more afraid of being understood than of being misunderstood." Where does the sort of trickery that permitted (not without good faith) an editor's compilation to impose itself as the essential work arise from? It comes from bias, and first of all from the bias alleging that there is no great philosopher without a great systematic work. Of course, Mme. Förster-Nietzsche showed her incapacity to grasp the measure of such a thought when she wished it to find expression in a good solid work rather than in those books rendered in her view frivolous by their too literary form. As though Nietzsche's manner of thinking and writing had not been fragmentary in principle. Schlechta wrote on this subject remarks that are to some extent appropriate: Nietzsche possessed a nearly infinite capacity for precise ideas that were separate and rigorously formulable, each one of them alive in the manner of a tiny organism. The very loose unity of all these thoughts resided in the secret gathering intention that remained always present to Nietzsche alone: a hidden and tormenting presence. This is expressed by a certain direction that is perceptible in each text and that orients it. But, by the gravitational force of a "title," it sometimes happens that several of these organisms unite in a larger ensemble that they in turn render living. This process is accomplished with extraordinary rapidity: as though formed by the secretions of a supersaturated seawater [*eau-mère*] become crystalline, the work instantaneously becomes visible and present. A crystallization that often fails to occur. If a plan is abandoned, this does not preclude its reemergence many years later, although other works have used the materials for which the plan had first been envisioned. This is what happened with *The Will to Power*, which had been announced on the cover page of *Beyond Good and Evil* and then abandoned for the "polemical" works of the last years. (I shall later propose, nonetheless, an entirely different interpretation of "fragmentary writing.")

Now one better understands the extent to which the editors lacked scruples, and also subtlety, in so unceremoniously taking Nietzsche's place and in substituting, without even realizing it, the crude work of compilation for the creative process of crystallization. Likewise with their claim to bring his philosophy forward by establishing a dominant work he would always have had in mind and for whose completion he had only lacked time. There being nothing of the sort in the posthumous papers, the travesty is therefore undeniable and without the least justification—except, in my opinion, for the following: at times Nietzsche himself also yielded to the common prejudice and, as though having suffered from the exigency of the fragmentary, seems to have been tempted, in the years when he wanted to make himself better understood, to express himself in a more traditional language and a more systematic form. At least so he stated, and he was taken at his word. This is his responsibility.

If *The Will to Power*, which is not Nietzsche's—and where there is not a single central thought that had not already been expressed in a manner just as rich, as profound, and more supple in the works that appeared during his lifetime[3]— asserted itself with such power, it is precisely because, not being Nietzsche's (but just the same authorized by him), this book led to the success of affirmations that its very form made more accessible, even to the point of permitting the simplified interpretations that over time were imposed by the Nietzsche legend. Almost all the posthumous writings, says Schlechta, lack that second voice, so precious in the secret dialogue that Nietzsche carries on with himself; they render everything more brutal, more simple, hence their influence. This judgment, naturally, is itself overly simple. But it is true that Nietzsche was a victim of the inordinate interest we bring to works that come into our possession not by life, but by the death of their author. How strange that the greatest literary glories of our time should be born of entirely posthumous works: Kafka, Simone Weil, Hopkins; or of works partially posthumous, as is the case with Hölderlin, Rimbaud, Lautréament, Trakl, Musil, and, in an even crueler sense, Nietzsche. One would like to recommend to writers: leave nothing behind, destroy everything you wish to see disappear; do not be weak, have confidence in no one, for you will necessarily be betrayed one day. In Nietzsche's case, the madness that had abruptly delivered him over to others, and delivered over to the night a mass of writings of all kinds, is precisely what gave an astonishing value and a false nocturnal brilliance to his surviving words, as though they held the very secret and the truth for which he had become mad. One can see that very different prejudices come together to make triumph in Nietzsche the Nietzsche that he himself did not leave to us: first of all, the idea that he had succeeded in giving to his thought the dogmatic expression capable of making it influential; then the idea that it is beyond clearsightedness and reason, and with the prophetic authority of a voice rising out of the tomb that this philosophy, in the name of destiny, speaks to us.[4]

*

Jaspers was the first to advise us of the principles that every interpretation of Nietzsche must respect, if it does not wish to make him complicitous with the forces he did not cease to combat. The essential movement of Nietzsche's thought consists in self-contradiction; each time it affirms, the affirmation must be put in relation with the one opposing it: the decisive point of each of its certitudes passes through contestation, goes beyond it, and returns to it. Such contradiction does not proclaim some sort of caprice or confusion in Nietzsche's mind: no one could be less skeptical or more further removed from tranquil negation; because of the terrible seriousness, the constant will of the Yes—this will that goes in search of the true in the depths where truth is no stranger to contradiction—everything must at a certain moment turn around.

In Nietzsche's work there is nothing that might be called a center. There is no central work, no *Hauptwerk* at all. But since what he conceives that is essential manifests itself also in what is apparently accidental, none of it can be neglected or scornfully rejected, including the posthumous writings, on the pretext that they would merely give another form to thoughts already expressed. Still, when his books are read in chronological order, one becomes aware of an obsessive monotony, despite the variety of preoccupations and the changing color of formulation. Something fundamental is seeking expression: an identical theme, not identical, a constant thought, something like the summons of a non-centered center, of a whole beyond everything that is never attained but endlessly supposed, interrogated, and at times demanded. This "whole" is neither a concept, nor a system. The incomparably instructive force of Nietzsche's thought is precisely in alerting us to a non-systematic coherence, such that all that relates to it seems to press in from all sides in order to resemble a coherent system, all the while differing from one. In order not to miss this whole, says Jaspers, one must always maintain thought and existence together: knowledge wants to entrust itself to every possibility, and thus go beyond each of them; but Nietzsche is not content with knowing, he has to become that of which he speaks. Yet at the same time he would not know how to remain there. He knows this inexorable going beyond is his strongest virtue, and he knows it is the greatest danger: "I am always over an abyss." The exigency that does not allow Nietzsche to restrict himself to realizing his thought through a simple ideal movement, but makes it imperative that he move through all these positions with all his being and in a living manner, is the "real dialectic" proper to him.

Every interpretation of Nietzsche should, then, remain faithful to these principles: remain unsatisfied until one has found that which contradicts what one has asserted about him; maintain amidst the contradictions the exigency of the whole that is constantly present, though constantly dissolved by them; never conceive of this whole—which is non-unitary—as a system, but as a question, and as the passion of the research in its impetus toward the true, one with the critique of all that has been acquired in the course of the research; grasp anew "the real dialectic": thought as the play of the world, text as fragment.

Whoever reads Nietzsche with this restless, suspicious gaze will not be tempted to make use of Nietzsche. Yet even Jaspers, so taken up with recognizing in his person the exception and in his work the force of the untransmissible, runs the risk of betraying him and precisely for this reason—be it only in favor of a philosophy of existence for which Nietzsche appears, by the same rights as Kierkegaard, as one who announces and reveals. When Heidegger on the contrary, and not without energy, declares that we must learn to read *Zarathustra* with the same rigor we bring to a treatise by Aristotle, and also that this way of thinking is neither less firm nor less substantial than that of the Greek philosopher, he is suggesting there is a way of setting Nietzsche apart that makes us forget what is important in his thought. His works are great, even exceptional, not because they situate themselves apart from what has been expressed in Western history since Descartes, Leibniz, Kant, Schelling, and Hegel, but because they accomplish it. "To link Nietzsche with Kierkegaard is to misread him essentially. . . . Nietzsche *never* thought existentially, he thought metaphysically." And the unique force of his thought consists in its being not a metaphysical doctrine among others, but the final completion of metaphysics: that region where for a long time the central event that Nietzsche himself named nihilism has announced itself. He gave himself the title of the last philosopher. This also means that, in his eyes, he is still a philosopher. To meditate upon his philosophy is to meditate upon this end of philosophy, but in taking it seriously and in taking seriously what he says when he speaks of the Will to Power, the Overman, and the Eternal Return, without contenting oneself with seeing in these terms literary images or formulas meant to express certain incommunicable existential experiences.

*

This call for rigor is a reminder of Nietzsche's true greatness. The political use that was made of his thought is less painful to observe than the aura of false fervor and the sentimental exaltation that, in some circles, transformed the authority of the freest mind into a religion. If Lukács, in a hasty essay,[5] denounces in Nietzsche the precursor of a Fascist aesthetics, consenting to read him with the same eyes as Nietzsche's Third Reich thurifers, it is because he does not resist considering him through the ecstatic language of a Bertram, whom he complacently and cruelly cites. For Lukács, too, Nietzsche is at the end of one world and at the beginning of another. The constant oppositions of his thought are not simply the sign of a research willing to attempt anything, they reflect the contradictions that characterize Europe on the eve of its imperialist period. In combating the culture and the art of his age, Nietzsche is above all carrying on the romantic tradition. Like all the romantic critics, he combats the fetishism of modern civilization in order to oppose to it a culture that is economically and socially more primitive. But he does not restrict himself to this point of view. He detests the civilization of his time because its fundamental principle lies in the degrading realities of capitalism (mechanization, the division of labor); but he detests this capitalism no less for being, it seems to him, still insufficiently developed. He is thus at the same time the elegiac romantic of past ages and the herald of imperialist development, desiring neither narrow corporatism nor patriarchal relations between owners and workers, his ideal being rather the dominion of the evolved, cultivated capitalists, a domination that would exercise its power over an army of workers as sober as soldiers.

The central experience for Nietzsche, as for romanticism, in this view, is man's degradation by capitalism, which tends to reduce everything to the mode of the thing. This alteration of the human by capitalism liberated a superabundance of anarchic feelings, without root and without use, at the same time as it impoverished affective life, brought about excessive intellectualization and a general spiritual abasement.

Lukács sees Nietzsche's entire philosophy, then, as a psychology blown up into the myth of a personal history: the reversal of a man who was first taken hostage by contemporary decadence (the veneration for Schopenhauer and Wagner; illusions about Bismarck's empire), who then suffered the error of his ways, and finally sought to surmount them. Nietzsche does no more than generalize his own experience — a search in sickness for health — into a philosophy of history and culture. Hence the tone of sincerity and authenticity. But, objectively, behind this experience, there is nothing in it other than the illusion of being able to surmount the contradictions of real capitalism by means of the myth of a developed capitalism: imperialism. This mythicization, however, is not without power; it allows Nietzsche to dissimulate the capitalist nature of his utopia (Overman, Will to Power) and to present it as an enterprise of struggle against capitalism itself. Thus it seems to be something historically new, with a certain revolutionary force that found its measure precisely in the events of the twentieth century. Nietzsche is no doubt not responsible for the vile content with which his myth has been filled, but in myth content is unimportant; this is precisely what the myth says: the creative feat alone counts, a work without discourse, the imperative language of a violence without language. In freeing the force of myth, Nietzsche thereby authorized everything that was able to make his own myth effective, which was then rapidly reduced to a myth of heroes, then to that of the active personality, then Hitler . . .

*

That the critique of Nietzsche finally should have become the critique of the Nietzsche myth is a movement from which he can only draw advantage. Lukács has shown that one of Nietzsche's merits, as a thinker of high rank, is not to have attenuated the decisive opposition his thought entails, but to have brought the contradictions of his time to the truth of paradox; contradictions his time did not want to perceive and that have remained our own, those of the modern age. However, if he has above all acted through his positive ideas, travestied in myth, it is precisely to the degree that this myth made it possible to forget the force of his critique and the rigor with which it unmasked the world—our world; showing not what in this world is mediocre and weak, its beliefs and its prejudices, but what in it is strong and essential: its concern with the true, its demand for knowledge, and the universal mastery toward which it tends. Those who want science must also want the consequences of science, and must therefore in the end want nihilism; this is the warning Nietzsche gave his contemporaries, who used the Nietzsche myth in order not to hear it. Heidegger said in a moving way: one of the most silent and timid of men suffered the torment of being obliged to cry out and, enigma following upon enigma, what was a cry risked becoming idle chatter. Nietzsche's admonition, "the written cry of his thought"—a cry that took form in the disagreeable book that is *Zarathustra*—in fact came to be lost in two ways: it was not heard, it was heard overly well; nihilism became the commonplace of thought and of literature. Still, when suddenly, and with what surprise, we perceive that the danger to which knowledge exposes us is not the danger of a style and when, at the same time (with what hypocrisy), we endeavor to preserve all the advantages of science, but in refusing its risks, it would perhaps be useful to summon the rational courage and the pitiless probity of Nietzsche's mind.

2
Crossing the Line

It seems that Nietzsche's influence, in France and doubtless in other countries more preponderant than ever, has diminished in Germany. It has been noted that students there almost never elect to work on him when they are free to choose their subject. Why this distance? One might perhaps think that the discredit that struck the former political regime has also fallen on the name it had mobilized for its own propagandistic ends. Lukács says that efforts are being made today to de-Nazify Nietzsche, as was done for Schlacht and Guderian. This polemical remark falls short. It was not after Hitler's fall but during his reign that Jaspers, Löwith, and Heidegger, in their courses and publications in Germany, sought to shield Nietzsche from falsification and pointed out that his thought is a thought essentially free. Jaspers in particular demonstrated a tranquil courage and a freedom he drew precisely from Nietzsche himself. Thus one can say that during Hitler's time Nietzsche's work was indeed marshaled under his banner and yet struggled against him. The name that was officially celebrated remained nonetheless the symbol of a non-official truth and the rallying word of a thought that had not fallen in line. This ambiguity, one that is proper to Nietzsche, does not relieve him of responsibility but rather offers its measure. It must be added that if in Germany his work has known—but at what level?—a certain disfavor, the heavily lavished favor he received during those political times in no way favored the reading of his work. Nietzsche's official commentators were read; one was careful not to read Nietzsche. Schlechta had this curious experience: when in 1938 the first volume of letters of the critical edition appeared—where clear allusion was made to the maneuverings of Mme Förster-Nietzsche, who just two years before had been treated at her national funeral as a heroine of the regime—the editors expected the worst. But nothing happened, no one noticed anything (with the exception of a Swiss professor, who remained silent), because even the Nazi Nietzsche specialists did not read him and wished to know nothing more about him. Very little is read. This is the fact dissimulated by the enormous diffusion of authors and books.

*

Nietzsche's thought remains associated with nihilism, a word he no doubt borrowed—an ironic detour—from Paul Bourget,[6] but that he examined enthusiastically and fearfully: sometimes through simple and radical statements, at other times with a hesitating, uncertain approach and through a thought impossible to think, treating it finally as an extreme that cannot be gotten beyond and yet is the only path of a true going beyond, the principle of a new beginning. These oscillations are not to be attributed to Nietzsche's unstable genius, or to his "shortcomings." They are the very sense of his thought. Certainly the question "What is nihilism?" can be answered without difficulty, and Nietzsche has given many clear responses, for example, this one: "That the highest values devaluate themselves." He no less clearly indicates the origin of this decline: "God is dead." This event, which acquired a sort of tiresome celebrity by the dramatic form he gave it, does not aim at the personal phenomenon of unbelief. Kierkegaard's Christianity and, more especially, Dostoyevski's, like the atheism of Nietzsche or the young Marx ("I hate all gods"), belong to that turning point in the history of the world from which the light of the divine has withdrawn. God is dead; God means God, but also everything that, in rapid succession, has sought to take his place— the ideal, consciousness, reason, the certainty of progress, the happiness of the masses, culture: everything that, not without value, nonetheless has no value of its own; there is nothing man can lean upon, no thing of value other than through the meaning, in the end suspended, that man gives to it.

This analysis can no longer move us, so familiar has it become. Would this be nihilism? A mere humanism!: the recognition of the fact that, from now on deprived or freed of the ideal of some absolute meaning conceived on the model of God, it is man who must create the world and above all create its meaning. An immense, intoxicating task. Nietzsche, with a joy only he felt so purely and expressed so fully, saw in this movement of infinite negation that withdraws from us every solid foundation the sudden opening on a space of unlimited knowledge: *"At last the horizon seems open once more . . . every audacity of knowledge is again permitted to the discerner; and the sea, our sea, again lies open before us."* *"There is yet another world to be discovered—and more than one! Embark, philosophers!"* We could fill pages with citations. Nietzsche is inexhaustible in expressing this happiness in knowing and seeking freely, infinitely, with everything at risk and without having the sky as limit, or even truth, the all-too-human truth, as measure. One cannot read Nietzsche without being swept up with him by the pure movement of the research. If anyone denigrates him, it is because he has become insensitive to this movement, a movement that is in no way a call to some vague, irrational awareness, but the affirmation of a rigorous knowledge, "clear, transparent, and virile"—the kind that is particularly manifest in the natural sciences. *"And that is why: long live physics! And even more, what compels us to arrive at that: our probity!"*

Here, then, is a first approach to nihilism: it is not an individual experience, not a philosophical doctrine, nor is it a fatal light cast over human nature, eternally destined to nothingness. Rather, nihilism is an event accomplished in history that is like a shedding of history—the moment when history turns and that is indicated by a negative trait: that values no longer have value in themselves. There is also a positive trait: for the first time the horizon is infinitely open to knowledge, "Everything is permitted." This new authorization given to man when the authority of values has collapsed means first of all: knowing everything is permitted, there is no longer a limit to man's activity. *"We have a still undiscovered country before us, the boundaries of which no one has seen, a beyond to all countries and corners of the ideal known hitherto, a world so over-rich in the beautiful, the strange, the questionable, the frightful."*

Nietzsche, we are told, had only a mediocre acquaintance with the sciences. That is possible. But in addition to the fact that he had been professionally trained in a scientific method, he knew enough about science to have a presentiment of what it would become,[7] to take it seriously, and even to foresee—not to deplore—that from now on all that is serious in the modern world would be entrusted to science, to scientists, and to the prodigious force of technology. On the one hand, he saw with a striking force that since nihilism is the possibility of all going beyond, it is the horizon upon which every particular science, as well as every exigency of knowledge, opens—in order to hold themselves in the very movement of this opening. On the other hand, he saw no less clearly that when the world no longer has any meaning, or when it becomes the pseudo-meaning of some great possible non-sense, what alone can overcome the disorder of this void is the cautious movement of science; its power to give itself precise rules and to create meaning, but of a sort that is limited, and in this sense operational — thus the power at once to extend to the furthest limits and to restrict most closely its field of application.

*

Agreed. And here, once again, is something that reassures us. At the moment when nihilism shows us the world, its counterpart, science, creates the tools to dominate it. The era of universal mastery opens. But there are consequences. First, science cannot but be nihilist; it is the meaning of a world deprived of meaning, a knowledge that is founded on the last ignorance. One can respond that this reservation is only theoretical, a reservation of principle. But we must not hasten to disregard this objection, for science is essentially productive: knowing that the world is not to be interpreted, science transforms it, and through this transformation there passes the nihilistic exigency that is proper to it — the power of nothingness that science has made into the most effective of tools, but with which it plays a dangerous game. Knowledge is fundamentally dangerous. Nietzsche has given the most brutal formulation of this danger: *"We experiment on truth! Perhaps humanity will be destroyed by it! Well, so be it!"* This is what the scientist is liable to say, and must say if he renounces the hypocrisy of deploring catastrophe, which is one of the results of science. For one cannot construct the universe without the possibility of its being destroyed. Destruction and creation, when they bear upon the essential, says Nietzsche, are hardly distinguishable: the risk, therefore, is immense. Moreover, with its probity and measured steps, science bears this very contradiction within itself: it can produce a world in which scientists would no longer continue to exist as such, a world in which they would no longer be permitted to work according to the objectivity of knowledge, but rather only according to the arbitrary sense of the new world. In other words, by making science possible, nihilism becomes science's possibility — which means that, by it, the human world can perish.

Another consequence is the following: to the void made by nihilism corresponds the movement of science; to the achievement of science, the domination of the earth. The greatest force of surpassing is set into motion. Now what happens to man when this transformation is realized and history turns? Does he become transformed? Has he set out to go beyond himself? Is he ready to become what he is, the lucid man who can rely on nothing and who is going to make himself master of all? No. Man, such as he is, the bourgeois at the end of the nineteenth century that Nietzsche knew, is a man of small aims, small certainties, conniving and inadequate, a man who still knows nothing of the event that is in the process of being accomplished through his intervention; an event, as it were, beyond him, an event that is going to give him infinite powers, and impose upon him duties as extreme as he has ever known since he must freely create the meaning of the world and create himself in proportion to this world without measure.

I will pass over the succession of upheavals, the "formidable logic of terror," and the vast wars that Nietzsche foresaw to be the appanage of the twentieth century and the immediate consequence of a disequilibrium: present-day man believes himself to be definitive, stable in his nature and happy in the small circle he has closed around himself, committed to the spirit of vengeance; yet, impelled by the impersonal force of science and by the very force of the event that frees him from values, he possesses a power that exceeds him, but without his ever seeking to surpass himself through this power. Present-day man is man of the lowest rank, but his power is that of a being who is already beyond man. How could this contradiction not harbor the greatest danger? But instead of holding to the conservative attitude and condemning knowledge in order to safeguard the eternal in man (the man of his time), Nietzsche sides with science and with the being of exceeding, which is the becoming of humanity.

In several commentaries, Heidegger has indicated that such is the meaning of the overman: the overman is not the man of today elevated disproportionally, nor a species of man who would reject the human only to make the arbitrary his law and titanic madness his rule; he is not the eminent functionary of some will to power, any more than he is an enchanter destined to introduce paradisiacal bliss on earth. The overman is he who alone leads man to be what he is: the being who surpasses himself, and in whose surpassing there is affirmed the necessity of his passing.

If such is the case (but is it?), we see why the overman could be considered as the first decisive affirmation to follow the extreme negation of nihilism—without, however, himself being anything other than this consequent negation: the overman is the being who has overcome the void (created by the death of God and the decline of values), because he has known how to find in this void the power of overcoming, a power in him that has not only become a power, but will—the will to overcome himself. Freed from all that represses, diverts, or degrades the will in its capacity to will, and free of all reactive will, there is no longer anything negative in what he wills: by a free act, he commands himself and decides the extent of his destiny.

The figure of the overman, however, even interpreted in this way, remains ambiguous. As the end of human becoming, self-surpassing is thereby negated in this very figure. And if this figure is *not* the end, it is because there is still something to overcome. His will, therefore, is not free of all external meaning; his act of willing is still a Will to Power. With the overman, Nietzsche may well have had a presentiment of a man who is indistinguishable from present-day man except for his negative characteristics, and thus qualitatively different—poorer, simpler, more sober, more capable of sacrificing himself, slower in his resolutions, quieter in his speech. Nonetheless, his essential trait, the will, would make him, in his pure rigor and his harshness, the very form of nihilism for, according to Nietzsche's clear statement, *"the will would rather will nothingness than not will."* The overman is he in whom nothingness makes itself will and who, free for death, maintains this pure essence of will in willing nothingness. This would be nihilism itself.

*

Enthusiastically and with categorical clarity, Zarathustra announces the overman; then anxiously, hesitatingly, fearfully, he announces the thought of eternal return. Why this difference in tone? Why is the thought of the eternal return, a thought of the abyss, a thought that in the very one who pronounces it is unceasingly deferred and turned away as though it were the detour of all thought? This is its enigma and, no doubt, its truth. I want to note here that for a long time nearly all of Nietzsche's commentators, whether on the right or the left (Bäumler, the official Nazi interpreter, eliminates the theory of eternal return), have been troubled by this "doctrine," which seemed to them arbitrary, useless, mystical, and, furthermore, very antiquated, since it has been around since Heraclitus. It is perhaps conceivable that a modern man could come up with such an idea, but that he should be seized with such terror in approaching it, that he should see it as the most weighty of thoughts, the most anguishing and the most properly able to overturn the world, here was an absurdity that one hastened to avoid, concluding that it derived all its force for Nietzsche precisely from the ecstatic vision in which he had grasped it. One of the changes in the interpretation of Nietzsche is that this idea should be taken seriously. Karl Löwith, to whom we owe several important books, has contributed a good deal to making us more attentive to this idea; as has also, no doubt, the very spirit of our age, which has led us to reflect on time, on the circularity of meaning, and on the end of history: on the absence of being as recommencement.[8]

The thought of the eternal return remains strange in its antiquated absurdity. It represents the logical vertigo that Nietzsche himself could not escape. It is the nihilist thought par excellence, the thought by which nihilism surpasses itself absolutely by making itself definitively unsurpassable. It is therefore the most able to enlighten us as to the kind of trap that nihilism is when the mind decides to approach it head-on. Nietzsche (or Zarathustra) said with perfect clarity that when the will becomes liberating it collides with the past. The rock of accomplished fact that the will (however forceful and willing it may be) cannot displace is what transforms all *sentiment* into *ressentiment*: the spirit of revenge consists in the movement that turns the will back into a counter-will, a willing-against, when the will stumbles on the "it was." But so long as man is characterized by *ressentiment*, he will remain at the level of his present complacency, seeking only to degrade all earthly things, and himself, and time in the name of some absolute ideal, far from the highest hope. He must, then, no longer be limited in his temporal dimension by the necessity of an irrecuperable past and an irreversible time: he needs time as total accomplishment.

But the reversal of time lies outside the possible, and this impossibility takes on here the highest meaning: it signifies the defeat of the overman as will to power. The overman will never be capable of the extreme. Eternal return is not of the order of things that are in our power. The experience of the eternal return entails a reversal of all these perspectives. The will that wills nothingness becomes the will that wills eternity—and in this process, eternity, without either will or end, returns to itself. Personal and subjective all-powerfulness is transformed into the impersonal necessity of "being." Transvaluation does not give us a new scale of values on the basis of the negation of every absolute value; it makes us attain an order to which the notion of value ceases to apply.

Having thus recovered the idea of eternity, and the idea of "being," love of the eternal and knowledge of the depth of "being," does it not seem that we are definitively sheltered from nihilism? In fact, we are at the heart of nihilism. With the incisive simplicity that is proper to him (and that leads Lukács to call him barbaric), Nietzsche expressed it in this way: "Let us think this thought in its most terrible form: existence, as it is, without meaning or aim, yet recurring inevitably without any finale of nothingness: the eternal recurrence"—"the most extreme form of nihilism." What do we learn from this remark? Until now we thought nihilism was tied to nothingness. How ill-considered this was: nihilism is tied to being. Nihilism is the impossibility of being done with it and of finding a way out even in that end that is nothingness. It says the impotence of nothingness, the false brilliance of its victories; it tells us that when we think nothingness we are still thinking being. Nothing ends, everything begins again; the other is still the same. Midnight is only a dissimulated noon, and the great Noon is the abyss of light from which we can never depart—even through death and the glorious suicide Nietzsche recommends to us. Nihilism thus tells us its final and rather grim truth: it tells of the impossibility of nihilism.

This has the air of a joke. But if we will grant that all modern humanism, the work of science, and planetary development have as their object a dissatisfaction with what is, and thus the desire to transform being—to negate it in order to derive power from it and to make of this power to negate the infinite movement of human mastery—then it will become apparent that this sort of weakness of the negative, and the way in which nothingness unmasks itself in the being that cannot be negated, lays waste at one stroke to our attempts to dominate the earth and to free ourselves from nature by giving it a meaning—that is, by denaturing it. But this is no more than a first way of translating the strange account of the abyss; one that in part explains Zarathustra's distress in understanding that he will never definitively go beyond man's insufficiency, or that he will only be able to do so, paradoxically, by willing his return. But what does this return mean? It means what it affirms: that the extreme point of nihilism is precisely there where it reverses itself, that nihilism is this very turning itself, the affirmation that, in passing from the No to the Yes, refutes nihilism, but does nothing other than affirm it, and henceforth extends it to every possible affirmation.[9]

*

In the dialogue between Jünger and Heidegger, which marked the double celebration of their sixtieth birthday and took the form of a treatise on nihilism, Jünger leads one to believe, by the very title of their exchange ("Over the Line"), that the crossing of the critical zone was being accomplished, or could be accomplished. But Heidegger, more rigorously and in giving another meaning to the same title,[10] immediately remarks that the movement of nihilism, as it comes to an end, is to leave what it means to reach the end undecided: end or accomplishment? Also undecided is the meaning of such an accomplishment: either passage into the nullity of nothingness or into the region of a new turning of being. By the same token, he observes, it is very dangerous to describe the action of nihilism, for the description already belongs to the action; and yet, if to want to give "a *good* definition" of nihilism is a bizarre pretension, to renounce this temptation is to leave the field open to what in it is perhaps essential: its gift of travesty, its refusal to avow its origins, its power to slip away from every decisive explication. We speak of man's passage through the critical zone, but man is not simply a passerby who would have only a geographical relation with what he crosses; he does not merely hold himself in this zone, he is himself, though not by or for himself alone, this zone and this line. Let us therefore be circumspect. Let us handle these provocative notions with prudence and not allow these words to speak with the realist efficacy they have acquired; let us gently lead them back toward the silence from which they come. Heidegger suggested — and this was his principal contribution to the examination of this strange adversary — that we would henceforth be well advised in writing both the word being and the word nothingness only as crossed out with a Saint Andrew's cross: being, nothingness.

It is certainly appropriate to meditate on this invitation, but by returning to quite another reflection that would ask whether all the preceding interpretations do not tend to forget Nietzsche by placing him back into a tradition that he himself was not content simply to put into question (contestation does not suffice; it always keeps one within the horizon of the same interrogation): the tradition of the logical discourse issuing from the *logos*, of thought as a thought of the whole, and of speech as a relation of unity — a relation that would have no other measure than light or the absence of light.

With Nietzsche philosophy is shaken. But is this only because he would be the last of the philosophers (each one always being the last)? Or because, summoned by a very different language, the writing of effraction (whose vocation it would be to take "words" only as set apart, struck or crossed out by the movement that separates them, but which holds them through this separation as a site of difference), he must face an exigency of rupture that constantly turns him away from what is in his *power* to think? What, then, would be this exigency, supposing that we ourselves who are held by it are able to designate it without interrupting it and without being interrupted by it?

3
Nietzsche and fragmentary writing

± ± It is relatively easy to bring Nietzsche's thoughts into a coherency that would justify their contradictions, either by lining them up according to a hierarchy or by making them dialectical. There is a possible—a virtual—system whereby the work, abandoning its dispersed form, would give rise to a continuous reading. To useful, necessary discourse. Now we understand everything, without obstacles and without weariness. We are reassured that such a thought, tied to the movement of a research that is also the seeking of becoming, can lend itself to a general exposition. Moreover, this is a necessity. Even in its opposition to dialectic, it must arise out of a dialectic. Even disengaged from a unitary system and engaged in an essential plurality, this thought must still designate a center on the basis of which the Will to Power, the Overman, the Eternal Return, nihilism, perspectivism, tragic thought, and so many other separate themes go toward one another and reach harmony according to a single interpretation: even if this occurs precisely as the diverse moments or stages of a philosophy of interpretation.

± ± There are two kinds of speech in Nietzsche. One belongs to philosophical discourse, the coherent discourse he sometimes wished to bring to term by composing a work of great scope, analogous to the great works of the tradition. Commentators strive to reconstitute this. His broken texts can be considered as elements of this ensemble or whole. The whole keeps its originality and power. It is in this great philosophy that we find the assertions of a terminal thought, assertions brought to a high point of incandescence. Thus it is possible to ask whether it ameliorates or refutes Kant, what it owes to or retracts from Hegel, if it is dialectical or antidialectical, if it ends metaphysics or replaces metaphysics, if it prolongs an existential mode of thinking, or if it is essentially a Critique. All of this, in a certain sense, belongs to Nietzsche.

Let us admit this. Let us admit as well that such a continuous discourse may be behind these divided works. It remains nonetheless true that Nietzsche does not content himself with such a continuity. And even if a part of these fragments can be brought back to this kind of integral discourse, it is manifest that such a discourse—philosophy itself—is always already surpassed by Nietzsche; that he presupposes it rather than gives it exposition, in order, further on, to speak according to a very different language: no longer of the whole but of the fragment, of plurality, of separation.

± ± It is difficult to grasp this speech of fragment without altering it. Even what Nietzsche says of it intentionally leaves it covered over. There is no doubt that such a form marks his refusal of system, his passion for the unfinished and his belonging to a thought that would be that of *Versuch* or of *Versucher*; there is no doubt also that this form is linked to the mobility of research, to the thought that travels (to the thought of a man who thinks while walking and according to the truth of the march). It is also true that it seems to be close to aphorism, since it is agreed that the aphoristic form is the form in which Nietzsche excels: "*The aphorism, in which I am the first master among Germans, is a form of eternity; my ambition is to say in ten sentences what everyone else says in a book—what everyone else does not say in a book.*" But is this truly his ambition?; and does the term aphorism meet the real measure of what he is seeking? "*I myself am not narrowminded enough for a system—not even for my own.*" The aphorism works as a force that limits, encloses. A form that takes the form of a horizon: its own. We can see from this what is attractive about it, always drawn back into itself and with something somber, concentrated, obscurely violent about it, something that makes it resemble the crimes of Sade. Entirely opposed to the maxim, that sentence designed for the beau monde and polished until it becomes lapidary, the aphorism is as unsociable as a stone (Georges Perros) (but a stone of mysterious origin, a grave meteorite that, scarcely fallen, would like to volatilize). A speech that is unique, solitary, fragmented, but, by virtue of being a fragment, already complete in the breaking up from which it proceeds and of a sharpness of edge that refers back to no shattered thing. It thus reveals the exigency of the fragmentary, which is such that the aphoristic form could never suit it.

± ± Fragmentary speech does not know self-sufficiency; it does not suffice, does not speak in view of itself, does not have its content as its meaning. But neither does it combine with other fragments to form a more complete thought, a general knowledge. The fragmentary does not precede the whole, but says itself *outside* the whole, and after it. When Nietzsche affirms "*Nothing exists apart from the whole,*" he means to lighten the burden of our guilty particularity and also to challenge judgment, measure, and negation ("*for* one cannot *judge, measure or compare the whole, to say nothing of denying it*"); but he still thereby affirms the question of the whole as the only valid one and reinstates the idea of totality. Dialectic, system, and thought as a thought of the whole recover their rights, founding philosophy as a finished discourse. But when he says "*It seems to me important that we should get rid of the* Whole, *of Unity;* . . . *we must shatter the universe, un-*

learn our respect for the Whole," he then enters into the space of the fragmentary, and risks a thought no longer guaranteed by unity.

± ± This speech that reveals the exigency of the fragmentary — a non-sufficient speech, but not through insufficiency, unfinished, but because foreign to the category of completion — does not contradict the whole. On the one hand, the whole must be respected; and if one does not say it, one must at least accomplish it. We are beings of a Universe and thus turned toward a still absent unity. Our wish, says Nietzsche, is *"to bring the universe under our control."* But there is another thought and a very different wish that in truth is not one. It is as though everything were now already accomplished: the universe is our lot, time has ended, we have left history through history. What, then, is there still to say, what is there still to do?

± ± The fragmentary speech that is Nietzsche's does not know contradiction. This is strange. We noted, after Jaspers, that one cannot understand Nietzsche or do justice to Nietzsche's thought unless one seeks, each time it affirms with certitude, the opposed affirmation with which this certainty is in relation. And, in fact, this thought does not cease to oppose itself, without ever being content either with itself or with this opposition. But, here again, we must make distinctions. There is the work of a critique: the critique of Metaphysics, principally represented by Christian idealism but also present in all speculative philosophy. The contradictory affirmations are a moment of this critical work: Nietzsche attacks the adversary from several points of view at the same time, for plurality of viewpoint is precisely the principle that the adverse thought fails to recognize. Nietzsche, however, is not unaware that he is obliged to think from where he is, and obliged to speak on the basis of the discourse he is challenging. He still belongs to this discourse — we all belong to it; thus the contradictions cease to be polemical, or even only critical. They aim at him, he himself, in his thought; they are the expression of this energetic thought that cannot be content with its own truths without putting them to the test, assaying them, going beyond them, and then again coming back to them. The Will to Power will therefore sometimes be a principle of ontological explanation, saying the essence, the foundation of things, and at other times saying the exigency of all going beyond, and going beyond itself as an exigency. At times the Eternal Return is a cosmological truth, at times the expression of an ethical decision, and at other times the thought of being understood as becoming, etc. These oppositions say a certain multiple truth and the necessity of thinking the multiple if one wants to say what is true in accordance with value — but this multiplicity is still in relation with the one, still a multiplied affirmation of the One.

± ± Fragmentary speech does not know contradiction, even when it contradicts. Two fragmentary texts may be opposed: they are simply posed one after another, one without relation to the other, or related one to another by this indeterminate blank that neither separates nor unites them but brings them to the limit they designate, which would be their meaning—if, precisely, they did not thereby, hyperbolically, escape a speech of signification. The fact of being always posed in this way *at the limit* gives to the fragment two different traits: it is first a speech of affirmation, affirming nothing but this plus, this surplus of affirmation that is foreign to possibility; and yet it is nonetheless in no way categorical, neither fixed as a certainty nor posited in a relative or an absolute positivity, still less saying being in a privileged manner, or saying itself on the basis of being but rather already effacing itself, slipping outside itself by a sliding that leads it back toward itself in the neutral murmur of contestation.

There where opposition does not oppose but rather juxtaposes, where juxtaposition gives together what escapes all simultaneity, without becoming a succession, there a non-dialectical experience of speech is proposed to Nietzsche. Not a manner of saying and thinking that would claim to refute or to express itself against the dialectic (Nietzsche, on occasion, does not fail to salute Hegel or even recognize himself in him, as he also does not fail to denounce the Christian idealism that carries him forward); this is rather a speech that is other, separate from discourse, neither negating nor (in this sense) affirming, and yet allowing the unlimited in difference to play between the fragments by its interruption and arrest.

± ± The fact that Nietzsche takes his leave from the thought of the One God, that is to say, from the god of Unity, must be taken seriously. Yet for him it is not simply a matter of contesting the categories that govern Western thought. Neither is it enough to arrest the opposition of contraries before the synthesis that would reconcile them, or enough even to divide the world into a plurality of centers of vital domination whose principle, still one of synthesis, would be the Will to Power. Here Nietzsche is tempted by something more bold, something that draws him, in the strict sense of the term, into the maze of detour before exalting him to the height of the enigma of return: thought as the affirmation of chance, the affirmation wherein thought relates to itself necessarily, infinitely, by way of that which is aleatory (not fortuitous); a relation wherein thought gives itself as a thought that is plural.

Pluralism is one of the decisive traits of the philosophy elaborated by Nietzsche; but, here again, there is philosophy and there is what will not be content with philosophy. There is philosophic pluralism, very important, of course, since it reminds us that meaning always comes severally and that there is an overabundance of signification; that *"One is always wrong,"* whereas *"truth begins at two."* Hence the necessity of an interpretation that does not consist in the unveiling of a truth that is unique and hidden, or even ambiguous, but rather entails the reading of a text in several senses at once, with no other meaning than *"the pro-*

cess, the becoming" that is interpretation. There are therefore two kinds of pluralism. One is a philosophy of ambiguity, the experience of being as multiple. Then there is this other, this strange pluralism; a pluralism neither of plurality nor of unity that the speech of the fragment bears in itself as the provocation of language—a language still speaking when all has been said.

± ± The thought of the overman does not first of all signify the advent of the overman, but rather the disappearance of something called man. Man disappears, he whose essence is disappearance. Man thus continues to exist only insofar as one can say he has not yet begun. "*Humanity still has no goal or end* (kein Ziel). *But . . . if humanity suffers from the lack of an end, would this not be because there is not yet a humanity?*" Scarcely does man enter into beginning than he enters into his end, begins to end. Man is always man of the decline, a decline that is not a degeneration but, on the contrary, a lack that one can love; a lack that, in separation and distance, makes "human" truth one with the possibility of perishing. Man of the last rank is the man of permanence, of substance, the man who does not want to be the last one.

Nietzsche speaks of the man who *synthesizes, who totalizes and justifies*. Remarkable expressions. This man who totalizes and who therefore has a relation to the whole, either because he establishes the whole or because he masters it, is not the overman but higher man. Higher man, properly speaking, is a man who is integral, the man of the whole and of synthesis. This is "*the goal humanity needs.*" But Nietzsche also says in *Zarathustra*: "*Higher man is a failure* (missgeraten)." He is not a failure because he has failed; he has failed because he has succeeded, has reached his goal ("*Once you have reached your goal . . . , precisely upon your height, Higher Man, will you stumble*"). We may ask: what is the language of the higher man, or what would it be? The answer is easy. It, too, is an integral discourse, the logos that says the whole, the seriousness of philosophic speech (the characteristic proper to higher man is the seriousness of his probity and the rigor of his veracity): a speech that is continuous, without intermittence and without blanks, the speech of logical completion that knows nothing of chance, play, or laughter. But man disappears; not only failed man, but superior man, that is to say successful man, the man wherein everything, the whole, is realized. What, then, does this failure of the whole signify? The fact that man disappears—the man to come who is the man of the end—finds its full meaning because it is also man as a whole who disappears, the being in whom the whole in its becoming has become being.

± ± Speech as fragment has a relation with the fact that man disappears; a fact more enigmatic than one might think, since man is in a sense the eternal or the indestructible and, as indestructible, disappears. Indestructible: disappearance. And this relation, too, is enigmatic. One can perhaps understand—and this can even seem evident—that what speaks in this new language of brisure only speaks through waiting, through the announcement of this indestructible disappearance. It is necessary that what one calls man have become the whole of man and the world as a whole; and it is necessary that, having made of his truth the universal truth and made of the Universe his already accomplished destiny, he engage himself with all that is, and even with being itself in the possibility of perishing in order that, free of all the values proper to his knowledge—transcendence (that is to say, also, immanence), the other world (that is, also, the world), God (that is, also, man)—the speech of the outside can be affirmed: that which is said beyond the whole and beyond language inasmuch as language, the language of consciousness and of acting interiority, says the whole and the whole of language. It is not nothing that man should disappear, but this is no more than a disaster within our measure; thought can bear this. It seems that one can accommodate oneself to, and even rejoice in, the idea that truth and every possible value, even the very possibility of value, should cease to have currency and be swept away, as though with a casual gesture: thought is also this lighthearted movement that tears itself from the origin. But what about thought, when being—unity, the identity of being—has withdrawn without giving way to nothingness, that too easy refuge? What about thought when the Same is no longer the ultimate meaning of the Other, and Unity no longer that in relation to which the multiple is said? When plurality is said, without referring back to the One? Then, perhaps then, one might have a sense of the exigency of fragmentary speech, not as a paradox but as a decision: speech that, far from being unique, is not predicated of the one and does not say the one in its plurality. Language: affirmation itself, that which no longer affirms by reason of, nor with a view to Unity. An affirmation of difference, but nonetheless never differing. Plural speech.

± ± The plurality of plural speech: a speech that is intermittent, discontinuous; a speech that, without being insignificant, does not speak by reason of its power to represent, or even to signify. What speaks in this speech is not signification, not the possibility of either giving meaning or withdrawing meaning, even a meaning that is multiple. From which we are led to claim, perhaps with too much haste, that this plurality designates itself on the basis of the between [*l'entre-deux*], that it stands a sort of sentry duty around a site of divergence, a space of dis-location that it seeks to close in on, but that always dis-closes it, separating it from itself and identifying it with this margin or separation, this imperceptible divergence where it always returns to itself: identical, non-identical.

However, even if this sort of approach is in part justified—we are still unable to decide—let us keep in mind that it is not enough to replace the continuous with the discontinuous, plenitude with interruption, gathering with dispersion, in order to bring us close to the relation we claim to receive from this other language. Or, to state this more precisely, discontinuity is not the simple reverse of the continuous, nor, as occurs in dialectics, a moment within a coherent development. Discontinuity, the arrest of intermittence, does not arrest becoming; on the contrary, it provokes becoming, calls it up in the enigma that is proper to it. This is the great turning in thought that comes about with Nietzsche: becoming is not the fluidity of an infinite (Bergsonian) *durée*, nor the mobility of an interminable movement. The first knowledge is knowledge of the tearing apart—the breaking up—of Dionysus, that obscure experience wherein becoming is disclosed in relation with the discontinuous and as its play. The fragmentation of the god is not the rash renunciation of unity, nor a unity that remains one by becoming plural. Fragmentation is this god himself, that which has no relation whatsoever with a center and cannot be referred to an origin: what thought, as a consequence—the thought of the same and of the one, the thought of theology and that of all the modes of human (or dialectic) knowledge—could never entertain without falsifying it.

± ± Man disappears. This is an affirmation. But this affirmation immediately doubles into a question. Does man disappear? Does the disappearance he bears and that bears him liberate knowledge?; does it free language of forms and structures, or of the finalities that define our cultural space? With Nietzsche, the response falls with an almost terrible decisiveness, and yet it also holds back, remaining in suspense. This is translated in several ways, and first by a philosophical ambiguity of expression. When, for example, he says man is something that must be surpassed, man must be what is beyond man; or, in a more striking manner, Zarathustra himself must overcome himself; or again, nihilism, vanquished by nihilism, the ideal, ruin of the ideal—it is almost inevitable that this exigency of going beyond, this use of contradiction and negation for an affirmation that maintains what it does away with while developing it, should place us back within the horizon of dialectical discourse. One has to conclude from this that far from debasing man, Nietzsche still exalts man by giving him as task his true accomplishment: then the overman is but a mode of man; man freed from himself and aiming at himself through the summons of the greatest desire. This is correct. Man stands for a self-suppressing that is nothing but a self-surpassing; he is the affirmation of his own transcendence. Many texts (the greater part of them) authorize us to hear this with the guarantee of a still traditional philosophical knowledge. The commentator who Hegelianizes Nietzsche cannot, in this sense, be refuted.

And yet we know that Nietzsche follows an entirely different path, even if he does so against himself, always aware, to the point of suffering, of a rupture within philosophy so violent that by it philosophy is dislocated. Going beyond, creation, the creative exigency—we may become enchanted by these terms and open ourselves to their promise; but they tell, finally, of nothing but their wearing away inasmuch as they keep us still close to ourselves, under the infinitely prolonged sky of men. Going beyond means going beyond without end, and nothing is more foreign to Nietzsche than such a future of continuous elevation. Would the overman, in the same way, be man ameliorated, man carried to the extremity of his knowledge and his own essence? In truth, what is the overman? We do not know and, properly speaking, Nietzsche does not know. We know only that the thought of the overman signifies: man disappears; an affirmation that is pushed furthest when it doubles into a question: does man disappear?

± ± Fragmentary speech is not a speech in which the site would already be designated, as though in filigree—white on white—where the overman would find his place. Fragment speech is speech of the *between*-two. This between-two is not the intermediary between two times, the time of man already disappeared—but does he disappear?—and that of the overman in whom the past is to come—but does it come, and by what coming? The speech of fragment does not form a joinder from one to the other, it rather separates them; as long as it speaks, and in speaking remains silent, it is the moving tear of time that maintains, one infinitely distant from the other, these two figures wherein knowledge turns. Thus, on the one hand marking rupture, this speech hinders thought from passing by degrees from man to overman; that is, from thinking them according to the same measure or even according to measures that are merely different; that is, it keeps thought from thinking of itself according to the measure of identity and unity. On the other hand, fragment speech marks more than rupture. If the idea of going beyond—whether understood in a Hegelian or a Nietzschean sense, a creation that does not preserve but destroys—is insufficient for Nietzsche; if thought is not only a going beyond; if the affirmation of Eternal Return is understood (first) as a failure of this going beyond, then does fragmentary speech open us to this "perspective," does it permit us to speak in this sense? Perhaps, but in an unexpected manner. This is not the speech that announces "*the dance over every here and there and over there.*" It is not annunciatory. In itself, it announces nothing, represents nothing: it is neither prophetic nor eschatological. When it speaks everything has already been announced, including the eternal repetition of the unique, the most vast of affirmations. Its role is still more strange. It is as though, each time the extreme is said, it called thought outside (not beyond), designating to thought by its fissure that thought has already left itself, that it is already outside itself: in relation—without relation—with an outside from which it is excluded to the degree that thought believes itself able to include this outside and, each time, necessarily, does truly make the inclusion by which it encloses itself. And it is still saying too much of this speech to say that it "calls forth" thought, as though it possessed some absolute exteriority and as though its function were to make this exteriority resound as a never situated site. This extreme speech does not say, in relation to what has been said, anything new. And if, for Nietzsche, it suggests that the *Eternal Return* (where all that is affirmed is eternally affirmed) could not be the ultimate affirmation, it is not because this speech would affirm something more, it is because it repeats the ultimate affirmation in the mode of fragmentation.

In this sense, fragmentation is bound up with the revelation of the Eternal Return. The eternal return says time as an eternal repetition, and fragment speech repeats this repetition by stripping it of any eternity. The eternal return says the being of becoming, and the repetition repeats it as the incessant ceasing of being. The eternal return says the eternal return of the Same, and the repetition says the detour wherein the other identifies itself with the same in order to become the nonidentity of the same and in order that the same become, in the return that turns it aside, always other than itself. The eternal return, in a speech strangely, marvelously scandalous, says the eternal repetition of the unique, and repeats it as a repetition without origin, as the re-beginning where what has not yet begun begins again. And thus repeating repetition ad infinitum, this speech renders repetition in some sense parodic, but also withdraws it from everything that has the power of repeating: both because this speech says repetition as an affirmation that is unidentifiable and unrepresentable, an affirmation impossible to recognize, and because it ruins repetition by giving it back, in the guise of a sort of indefinite murmur, to the silence that speech in turn ruins by giving silence to be heard as the speech that, from the most profound past, from the furthest future, has always already spoken as a speech ever yet to come.

± ± I would note that the philosophy of Nietzsche takes its distance from dialectical philosophy less in contesting it than in repeating it, that is, in repeating the principal concepts or moments that it deflects: i.e., the idea of contradiction, the idea of going beyond, the idea of transvaluation, the idea of totality, and above all the idea of circularity, of truth or of affirmation as circular.

± ± Fragmentary speech is barely speech—speech only at the limit. This does not mean that it speaks only at the end, but that in all times it accompanies and traverses all knowledge and all discourse with another language that interrupts speech by drawing it, in the turn of a redoubling, toward the outside where the uninterrupted speaks, the end that is never done with. In Nietzsche's wake, then, it too always alludes to the man who disappears, not disappearing; to the overman who comes without a coming and, inversely, to the overman who has already disappeared, to the man not yet come: an allusion that is the play of the oblique and the indirect. To put one's trust in this speech is to exclude oneself from all faith, all trust, all confidence: that is to say from all defiance, including even the force of the challenge itself. And when Nietzsche says: *the desert grows,* fragment speech takes the place of this desert without ruins, except that in it the devastation always more vast is always reconfirmed within the dispersion of limits. A becoming of immobility. That this speech may seem to play the game of nihilism and lend to nihilism, in its unseemliness, a suitable form—this it will never deny. And yet how far it leaves this power of negation behind. It is not that in playing with it negation undoes it. To the contrary, it leaves this power of negation a free field. Nietzsche recognized—this is the meaning of his untiring critique of Plato—that being is light, and he submitted the light of being to the labor of the most severe suspicion.[11] A decisive moment in the destruction of metaphysics and, even more, of ontology. Light gives pure visibility to thought as its measure. To think is henceforth to see clearly, to stand in the light of evidence, to submit to the day that makes all things appear in the unity of a form; it is to make the world arise under the sky of light as the form of forms, always illuminated and judged by this sun that does not set. The sun is the overabundance of clear light that gives life, the fashioner that holds life only in the particularity of a form. The sun is the sovereign unity of light—it is good, the Good, the superior One that makes us respect as the sole true site of being all that is "above." At first Nietzsche criticizes in ontology only its degeneration into metaphysics: the moment at which, in Plato, light becomes idea and makes of the idea the supremacy of the ideal. His first works—and there is a trace of his first preferences in nearly all his works—maintain the value of form, and in the face of an obscure Dionysian terror, the calm luminous dignity that protects us from the terrifying abyss. But just as Dionysus, in dispersing Apollo, becomes the unique force without unity in which everything divine holds back, so does Nietzsche little by little seek to free thought by referring it back to what does not allow itself to be understood either as clarity or as form. Such is finally the role of the Will to Power. It is not as a power [*pouvoir*] that the will to power [*puissance*] imposes itself in principle, and it is not as a dominating violence that this force becomes what must be thought. But force escapes light: it is not something that would simply be deprived of light, an obscurity still aspiring to the light of the day. Scandal of scandals, it escapes every optical reference; and thus, while it may only act under the determination and within the limits of a form, form—an arrangement of structure—nevertheless always allows it to escape. Neither visible nor invisible.

± ± "How can one understand force, or weakness, in terms of clarity and obscurity?" observes Derrida.[12] Form allows force to escape, but it is not received by the formless. Chaos, the indifference without shore from which every gaze is averted, this metaphoric site that organizes disorganization, does not serve as its matrix. If force—without relation to form, even when form seeks shelter in the amorphous depths, refusing to let itself be reached either by clarity or by non-clarity—exercises upon Nietzsche an attraction for which he also feels distaste ("*Blush before power*"), it is because force interrogates thought in terms that will oblige it to break with its history. How to think "force," how to say "force?"

Force says difference. To think force is to think it by way of difference. This is first to be understood in a quasi-analytical fashion: whoever says force says it always as multiple; if there were a unity of force there would be no force at all. Deleuze expressed this with a decisive simplicity: "All force is in an essential relation with another force. The being of force is plural, it would be absurd to think it in the singular." But force is not simply plurality. The plurality of forces means that forces are distant, relating to each other through the distance that makes them plural and inhabits each of them as the intensity of their difference. ("*It is from the height of this feeling of distance,*" says Nietzsche, "*that one arrogates to one-self the right to create values or to determine them: what matter utility?*") Thus the distance that separates forces is also their correlation—and, more characteristically, is not only what distinguishes them from without, but what from within constitutes the essence of their distinction. In other words, what holds them at a distance, the outside, constitutes their sole intimacy; it is that by which they act and are subject, "the differential element" that is the whole of their reality, they being real only inasmuch as they have no reality in and of themselves, but only relations: a relation without terms. But then what is the Will to Power? "*Not a being, not a becoming, but a pathos*": the passion of difference.

The intimacy of force resides in its exteriority. The exteriority thus affirmed is not a tranquil spatial and temporal continuity, a continuity whose key is provided by the logic of the *logos*—a discourse without *discursus*. Exteriority—time and space—is always exterior to itself. It is not correlative, a center of correlations, but instead institutes relation on the basis of an interruption that does not bring together or unify. Difference is the outside's reserve; the outside is the exposition of difference; difference and outside designate the originary disjunction—the origin that is this very disjunction itself, always disjoined from itself. Disjunction, where time and space would rejoin by their mutual disjoining, coincides with that which does not coincide, the non-coinciding that in advance turns away from all unity.

Just as high, low, noble, ignoble, master, slave have neither any meaning nor any established value in themselves, but affirm force in its always positive difference (this is one of Deleuze's unerring remarks: the essential relation of one force with another is never conceived as a negative element), so the force that is always plural seems—if not to Nietzsche, at least to the Nietzsche that fragmentary writing calls forth—to propose itself only in order to put thought to the test of difference; the latter not being derived from unity, any more than it would imply it. A difference, however, that one cannot call primary, as though, inaugurating a beginning, it were to refer back, paradoxically, to unity as secondary. This is rather a difference that always defers, and thus never gives itself in the present of a presence nor allows itself to be seized in the visibility of a form. It defers, as it were, from differing, and in this redoubling that withdraws it from itself, affirms itself as discontinuity itself, difference itself: the difference in play where there is dissymmetry as space at work, discretion or distraction as time, interruption as speech, and becoming as the "common" field of these three relations of dehiscence.

± ± One can suppose that if, with Nietzsche, thought had need of force conceived as a *"play of forces and waves of forces"* in order to think both plurality and difference, even if it entails exposure to all the difficulties of an apparent dogmatism, it is because force supports the presentiment that difference is movement; or, more exactly, that difference determines the time and the becoming in which difference is inscribed, just as the Eternal Return will make it be felt that difference is experienced as repetition and that repetition is difference. Difference is not an intemporal rule, it does not have the fixity of law. As Mallarmé discovers at about the same time, difference is space—space inasmuch as *"it spaces and disseminates itself"*—and time: not the oriented homogeneity of becoming, but becoming when it *"becomes scansion and intimation,"* when it interrupts itself and, in this interruption, does not continue, but dis-continues itself. One must conclude from this that difference, the play of time and of space, is the silent play of relations, *"the multiple disengagement"* that governs writing—which amounts to saying that difference, essentially, writes.

± ± *"The world is deep: deeper than the day can comprehend."* Nietzsche does not content himself here with calling up the Stygian night. He suspects more and he interrogates more profoundly. Why, he asks, this relationship between day, thought, and world? Why do we say confidently of lucid thought the same thing we say of the day, and thus believe we have in our grasp the power to think the world? Why would light and seeing furnish us all the modes of approach that we would like to see thought provided with in order to see the world? Why is intuition—intellectual vision—proposed to us as the great gift that men are lacking? Why do we see essences, Ideas, and God? But the world is more profound. And perhaps one will respond that, when one speaks of the light of being, one is speaking metaphorically. But then why, among all possible metaphors, does the optical metaphor predominate? Why this light that as metaphor has become the source and the resource of all knowing, and thus subordinated all knowledge to the exercise of (a primary) metaphor? Why this imperialism of light?

± ± These questions are latent in Nietzsche, sometimes suspended, as when he elaborates the theory of perspectivism, that is to say, point of view; a theory he ruins, it is true, by pushing it to its term. Latent questions, questions that are at the bottom of the critique of truth, of reason, and of being. Nihilism is invincible as long as, submitting the world to the thought of being, we entertain and seek truth on the basis of the light of its meaning, for it is perhaps in light itself that meaning is dissimulated. Light illuminates—this means that light hides itself: this is its malicious trait. Light illuminates: what is illuminated by light presents itself in an immediate presence that discloses itself without disclosing what makes it manifest. Light effaces its traces: invisible, it renders visible; it guarantees direct knowledge and ensures full presence, all the while holding itself back in that which is indirect and suppressing itself as presence. Light's deception, then, would be in the fact that it slips away in a radiating absence, infinitely more obscure than any obscurity, since the absence proper to light is the very act of its light, its clarity, and since the work of light is accomplished only when light makes us forget that something like light is at work (thus making us forget, in the evidency in which it holds itself, all that it supposes—the relation to unity to which light returns and that is its true sun). Clarity: the non-light of light, the non-seeing of seeing. Light is thus (at least) doubly deceptive: because it deceives us as to itself, and deceives us in giving as immediate what is not immediate, as simple what is not simple. The light of the day is a false day, not because there would be a truer day, but because the truth of the day, the truth about it, is dissimulated by it; we see clearly only because light is clear and does not offer itself in the clarity it provides. But the most serious problem—in any case, the one with the gravest consequences—remains the duplicity by which light causes us to have confidence in the simplicity of the act of seeing, proposing im-mediation to us as the model of knowledge whereas light itself, out of sight and in a hidden manner, acts only as a mediator, playing with us through a dialectic of illusion.

It would seem that Nietzsche thinks, or, to be more exact, writes (when he gives himself over to the exigency of fragmentary writing) under the sway of a double suspicion that inclines toward a double refusal: refusal of the immediate, refusal of mediation. It is from the true—this true that is in some sense inevitable, whether it be given to us by way of a developed movement of the whole or in the simplicity of manifest presence, whether it come forth at the end of a coherent discourse or is immediately affirmed in a speech that is linear, continuous, and univocal—that we should attempt to withdraw, "*we, philosophers of the beyond, of the beyond of good and evil, if you please,*" if we wish to speak, to write in the direction of the unknown. Double rupture, all the more dominant for never being accomplished, or only accomplished by way of suspicion.

± ± "*And do you know what 'the world' is to me? Shall I show it to you in my mirror?*" Nietzsche thinks the world: this is his concern. And when he thinks the world, be it as "*a monster of energy,*" "*this mystery-world of twofold voluptuous delight,*" "*my Dionysian world,*" or as the play of the world, this world here below, the enigma that is the solution to every enigma, it is not being that he is thinking. On the contrary. Whether rightly or wrongly, he thinks the world in order to free thought as much from the idea of being as from the idea of the whole, as much from the exigency of meaning as from the exigency of the good: in order to free thought from thought, obliging it not to abdicate but to think more than it can, to think something other than what for it is possible. Or, again, to speak in saying this "more," this "surplus" that precedes and follows all speech. One can criticize this way of proceeding; one cannot renounce what is announced in it. For Nietzsche, being, meaning, aim, value, God, day and night, and the whole, and unity, have validity only within the world; but the "world" cannot be thought, cannot be said as meaning or as a whole, even less as a world-beyond. The world is its very outside: the affirmation that *exceeds* every power to affirm and, in the endlessness of discontinuity, is the play of its perpetual *redoubling* — will to power, eternal return.

Nietzsche expresses himself in still another way: *"The world: the infinite of interpretation (the unfolding of a designation, infinitely)."* Hence the obligation to interpret. But who, then, will interpret? Is it man? And what sort of man? Nietzsche responds: *"One may not ask: 'who then interprets?' for interpretation itself is a form of the will to power, it exists (not as a 'being' but as a 'process,' a 'becoming') as affect."*[13] A fragment rich in enigmas. One can take it to mean — and this happens to Nietzsche — that philosophy should be a philosophy of interpretation. The world is to be interpreted, interpretation is multiple. Nietzsche will even say that *"to understand everything"* is to *"misunderstand the essence of knowledge,"* for totality is not of the same measure as what there is to be understood, any more than it exhausts the power to interpret (interpreting implies there is no term). But Nietzsche goes even further: *"Unsere Werte sind in die Dinge hineininterpretiert; our values are introduced into things by the movement that interprets."* Then would we have before us an integral subjectivism wherein things have meaning only insofar as the subject who interprets them gives them meaning, and according to his pleasure? *"There are no facts in themselves,"* Nietzsche says again, *"but one must always begin by introducing meaning in order for there to be facts."* Yet in the fragment we saw earlier, Nietzsche dismisses the "who?,"[14] authorizes no interpreting subject, and recognizes interpretation only as the neutral becoming — without subject and without complement — of interpreting itself, which is not an act but a passion and, by this fact, holds in itself *"Dasein"* — a *Dasein* without *Sein*, Nietzsche immediately adds. Interpreting, the movement of interpretation in its neutrality — this is what must not be taken as a means of knowing, an instrument thought would have at its disposal in order to think the world. The world is not an *object* of interpretation, any more than it is proper for interpretation to give itself an object, even an unlimited object, from which it would distinguish itself. The world: the infinite of interpreting; or again, to interpret: the infinite: the world. These three terms can only be given in a juxtaposition that does not confound them, does not distinguish them, does not put them in relation, and that thus responds to the exigency of fragmentary writing.

± ± *"We others, philosophers of the beyond . . . who in reality are interpreters and malicious soothsayers, we to whom it has been given to be placed, as spectators of things European, before a mysterious and as yet undeciphered text . . . "* One can understand that the world would be a text whose exegesis must only be carried out well in order that its proper meaning be revealed: the work of philological probity. But written by whom? And interpreted in relation to what previously given signification? The world does not have meaning, meaning is within the world; the world: that which is exterior to sense and non-sense. Here, since it is a matter of an event within history—of things European—we admit this contains some sort of truth. But what if it is a matter of the "world"? And what if it is a matter of interpretation, of the neutral movement of interpreting that, having neither subject nor object, is the infinite of a movement that relates to nothing but to itself? (And this is saying still too much, for it is a movement without identity.) A movement, in any case, that has no preceding thing to which it relates and no term capable of determining it. Interpreting, being without being; the passion and the becoming of difference? This text, then, indeed deserves to be called mysterious: not because it would contain some mystery as its meaning but because, if this is a new name for the world (this world, enigma and solution of all the enigmas), if it is the difference that is at stake in the movement of interpreting and is in a sense what prompts it always to differ, to repeat by differing or deferring, if, finally, in its infinite scattering (in this sense, Dionysus), in the play of its fragmentation, and even more precisely, in the exceeding of what withdraws it, it affirms this plus of affirmation that does not hold to the exigency of clarity or light or give itself in the form of a form, then it is a text that is certainly not already written, any more than the world is produced once and for all time, but, not separating itself from the neutral movement of writing, is what gives us writing; or rather, through it, writing gives itself as that which, turning thought away from all things visible and invisible, is able to free thought from the primacy of signification understood either as light or as the retreat of light and able, perhaps, to liberate it from the exigency of unity, that is to say, from the primacy of all primacy, since writing is difference, since difference writes.

± ± In thinking the world, Nietzsche thinks it as a text. Is this a metaphor? It is a metaphor. Thinking the world at this depth that is not reached by the light of the day, he substitutes for it a metaphor that seems to restore to the day all its prerogatives. For what is a text? A set of phenomena that hold themselves in view; and what is writing if not bringing into view, making appear, bringing to the surface? Nietzsche does not think highly of language: *"Language depends upon the most naive prejudices. If our reading of things discovers problems and disharmonies, this is because* we think only *in the form of language—and thus believe in the 'eternal truth' of 'reason' (for example: subject, attribute, etc.). We cease to think when we refuse to do so under the constraint of language."* Let us set aside the objection that it is still in the form of language that Nietzsche denounces language. Let us also not respond by indicating speech's power to falsify, that goodwill of illusion that is speech's and that would also be art's. The first objection throws us back into dialectics; the second gives us over to Apollo, who, having already become long ago dispersed in Dionysus, will no longer be able to keep us from perishing, were we ever to come up against the true. (*"We possess art lest we perish of the truth."* Words that would be most scornful of art, if they did not immediately turn around in order to say: But do we have art? And do we have truth, even if it causes us to perish? And do we, dying, perish? *"But art is of a terrible seriousness."*)

The world: a text; the world: *"divine play beyond Good and Evil."* But the world is not signified in the text; the text does not render the world visible, legible, able to be grasped in the moving articulation of forms. Writing does not refer back to this absolute text that would have to be reconstituted on the basis of fragments, in the lacuna of writing. Nor is it through the breaks in what is written, in the interstices thus delineated, in the pauses thus arranged and the silences thus reserved that the world, always exceeding the world, would testify to itself in the infinite plenitude of a mute affirmation. For it is now, when we risk becoming complicitous with an ingenuous and indigent mysticism, that we must laugh and withdraw, saying by our laughter: *Mundus est fabula.* In *Twilight of the Idols*, Nietzsche explains his suspicion with regard to language; it is the same suspicion as with regard to being and unity. Language implies a metaphysic, the metaphysic. Each time we speak, we tie ourselves to being, we say being, be this only by implication, and the more brilliant our speech the more it shines with the light of being. *"Nothing, in fact, has hitherto had a more naive power of persuasion than the error of being . . . , for every word, every sentence we utter speaks in its favor."* And Nietzsche adds, with a profundity that does not cease to surprise us: *"I fear indeed that we shall never rid ourselves of God because we still believe in grammar."* There is, however, this *"hitherto."* Are we to conclude from this qualification that we are at a turning point—a turning of necessity—where, in place of our language and by the play of its difference, up to now folded back into the simplicity of sight and equalized in the light of a signification, another sort of exteriorization would come forward, and such that, in this hiatus opened in it, in the disjunction that is its site, there would cease to live these guests who are unwonted because too habitual, unreassuring because too sure, masked but endlessly exchanging their masks: divinity in the form of logos, nihilism in the guise of reason?

The world, text without pretext, interlacing without woof or texture. If the world of Nietzsche is not handed over to us in a book, and even less in the book imposed upon him by an infatuation with culture and known by the title *The Will to Power*, it is because he calls us outside this language that is the metaphor of a metaphysics, a speech in which being is present in the double light of a representation. It does not result from this that the world is unsayable, nor that it can be expressed in, or by, a manner of speaking. It simply advises us that if we are sure we can never hold the world either within speech or outside of speech, the only destiny from now on fitting is that language, in perpetual pursuit and perpetual rupture and without having any other meaning than this pursuit and this rupture, should indefinitely persist (whether silent, whether speaking—a play always in play and always undone), and persist without concern for having something to say—the world—or someone—man with the stature of overman—to say it. It is as though Nietzsche had no other chance of speaking of the "world" than by speaking (of) himself in accordance with the exigency that is his, which is to speak without end, and in accordance with the exigency of difference, always to defer speaking. The world? A text? The world refers text back to text, as the text refers the world back to *affirmation* of the world. The text: certainly a metaphor; but if it no longer claims to be the metaphor of being, neither is it the metaphor of a world free of being: at most, the metaphor of its own metaphor.

± ± This pursuit that is rupture, this rupture that does not interrupt, this perpetuity of both the one and the other, the perpetuity of an interruption without stop and of a pursuit without attainment: neither the progress of time nor the immobility of a present—a perpetuity that perpetuates nothing, not enduring, not ceasing, the return and the turning aside of an attraction without allure: Is this the world? Is it language? The world that cannot be said? Language that does not have the world to say? The world? A text?

± ± Marks of breakage [*brisées*], fragments, chance, enigma: Nietzsche thinks these words together, especially in *Zarathustra*. His effort is thus double. First, wandering among men, he feels a kind of pain at seeing them only in the form of debris, always in pieces, broken, scattered, and thus as though on a field of carnage or slaughter; he therefore proposes, through the effort of a poetic act, to carry together and even bring to unity—the unity of the future—these chaotic pieces, shards, and accidents that are men. This will be the work of the whole, a work that will accomplish the integral. *"Und das ist mein Dichten und Trachten, dass ich in eins dichte und zusammentrage, was Bruchstück ist und Rätsel und grauser Zufall; And the whole dense aim of my poetic act is to bring together, gathering poetically to unity, what is no more than fragment, enigma, horrendous chance."* But his *Dichten*, his poetic decision, takes as well a very different direction. Redeemer of chance is the name he claims for himself. What does this mean? Saving chance does not mean returning it to a series of conditions; this would be not to save it, but to lose it. To save chance is to safeguard it from everything that would keep it from being affirmed as dreadful chance: what the throw of the dice could never abolish. And, by the same token, to decipher (to interpret) the enigma—is this simply to make the unknown pass into the category of the known or, on the contrary, to will it as enigma in the very speech that elucidates it, to open it, beyond the clarity of meaning, to this other language that is not governed by light nor obscured by the absence of light? Thus these marks of breakage, these fragments, should not appear as moments of a still incomplete discourse but rather as the language, the writing of effraction by which chance, at the level of affirmation, remains aleatory and by which the enigma frees itself from the intimacy of its secret so that, in writing itself, it might expose itself as the very enigma that writing maintains, because writing always takes it up again in the neutrality of its own enigma.

± ± When Nietzsche writes, *"And when my eye flees in vain from 'now' to 'then,' it always discovers the same thing: debris, fragments, horrible chances – but nowhere men,"* he obliges us once again to examine ourselves, not without terror: would the truth of the fragment and the presence of men be incompatible? Is it prohibited, where there are men, to maintain the affirmation of chance, writing without discourse, the play of the unknown? What does this incompatibility, if it is one, signify? On the one hand, the world, presence, human transparency; on the other, the exigency that makes the earth tremble *"when words, creative and new, ring out and the gods throw the dice."* Or, to state this more precisely, would men in some sense have to disappear in order to communicate? A question that is only posed and, in this form, is not yet even posed as a question. All the more so if one pursues it as follows: would not the Universe (that which is turned toward the One), and the cosmos (which presumes the existence of a physical time that is oriented, continuous, homogeneous although irreversible, obviously universal and even superuniversal), far from reducing man by its sublime majesty to the nothingness that frightened Pascal, not rather be the safeguard and the truth of human *presence?* Not because men, conceiving it in this way, would still construct the cosmos according to a reason that is only their own, but because there is no cosmos, Universe, or the whole except through the submission to light that human reality represents when it is *presence* – whereas where "knowing," writing, and, perhaps, speaking come about, it is a question of a very different "time" and of an absence such that the difference that governs it unsettles, disconcerts, and decenters the very reality of the universe – the universe as a real object of thought? To put this another way, there would not only be incompatibility between man and the power to communicate that is man's most proper exigency, but incompatibility as well between the Universe – substitute for a God, guarantee of human presence – and the speech without traces wherein writing nonetheless calls us and calls to us as men.[15]

± ± Interpreting: the infinite: the world. The world? A text? The text: the movement of writing in its neutrality. When we posit these terms – positing them with a concern for holding them outside themselves, without however making them leave themselves – we are not unaware of the fact that they still belong to the preliminary discourse that at a certain moment has allowed them to be put forward. Thrown out ahead, they do not yet leave the whole. They prolong it by their rupture; they say this pursuit-rupture by virtue of which they say themselves, disjoined in their movement. They are isolated as though out of discretion, but this is a discretion already indiscreet (too marked); they follow one another, but in such a way that this succession is not one, since, with no relation other than that of a sign that punctuates, a sign of space by which space indicates itself as a time of indication, they also dispose themselves, and as though having previously done so, in a reversible-irreversible simultaneity; succeeding one another but given together; given together, but apart, without constituting a whole; interchanging themselves according to a reciprocity that equalizes them and according to a non-reciprocity always ready to reverse itself: thus at the same time bearing and refusing all the ways of becoming, as they bear and refuse all positions of spatial plurality. For they write: designated here by writing, it is writing they designate explicitly, implicitly, coming from this writing that comes from them, returning to writing as though turning away from it by this difference that always writes.

± ± Juxtaposed words, but words whose arrangement is entrusted to signs that are modalities of space, and that make space a play of relations wherein time is at stake: we call these signs of punctuation. Let us understand that they are not there to replace sentences from which they would silently borrow meaning. (Nonetheless, one might perhaps compare them to Spinoza's mysterious *sive: deus sive natura, causa sive ratio, intelligere sive agere*, which inaugurates an articulation and a new mode, namely in relation to Descartes even if it seems to be borrowed from him.) Whether they be more indecisive, that is to say, more ambiguous, is not important either. Their value is not one of representation. They figure forth nothing, except the void they animate without declaring it. For, in effect, it is the emptiness of difference they retain by their accentuation, preventing it, though without giving it form, from being lost in indetermination. On the one hand, their role is to give an impetus; on the other (and it is the same), to suspend. But the pause they institute has the remarkable character of not posing the terms whose passage they both ensure and arrest, and neither does it set them aside; it is as though the alternative of positive and negative, the obligation to begin by affirming being when one wants to deny it, were here, at last, enigmatically broken. Signs, of course, that have no magical value. Their entire worth (even if they were done away with or not yet invented, and in a certain way they always disappear in the accessory or accidental aspects of a graphics) derives from discontinuity—an absence that is unfigurable and without foundation—whose power [*pouvoir*] they bear up under rather than carry, there where lacuna becomes cesura, then cadence, and perhaps juncture. To articulate the void by a void, to structure it as a void by drawing from it the strange irregularity that always from the outset specifies it as empty; it is in this way that the signs of space—punctuation, accent, scansion, rhythm (configuration)—which are the preliminary to all writing, lend themselves to difference and engage in its play.

Not that they serve to translate this void or render it visible in the manner of a musical notation: on the contrary, far from keeping the written at the level of the marks writing leaves or the forms it concretizes, their property is to indicate in it the tearing, the incisive rupture (the invisible tracing of a trait) through which the inside turns eternally back into the outside, while what designates itself there, to the point of giving meaning, and as its origin, is the gap that removes it from meaning.

± ± Difference: the non-identity of the same, the movement of distance; that which carries, by carrying off, the becoming of interruption. Difference bears in its prefix the detour wherein all power to give meaning seeks its origin in the distance that holds it from this origin. The "to differ/deferring" of difference is borne by writing, but never inscribed by it—demanding of writing on the contrary that, at the limit, it not inscribe; a becoming without inscription, that it describe a vacancy, an irregularity that no trace can stabilize (or inform): a tracing without trace that is circumscribed only by the endless erasure of what determines it.

Difference: it can only be a difference of speech, a speaking difference that permits speech, but without itself coming directly to language—or coming to it and then referring us back to the strangeness of the neutral in its detour, to that which does not let itself become neutralized. A speech that always in advance, in its difference, is destined to the exigency that is written. To write: trait without trace, writing without transcription. Writing's characteristic trait will never be the simplicity of a trait capable of tracing itself and merging with this trace; it will be rather the divergence on the basis of which begins, without beginning, this pursuit-rupture. The world? A text?[16]

VII

Reflections on Hell

1

One can reflect on this situation. It can happen that someone is very close to us, not close: the walls have fallen. Sometimes still very close, but without relation: the walls have fallen, those that separate, and also those that serve to transmit signals, the language of prisons. Then one must once again raise a wall, ask for a little indifference, that calm distance by which lives find equilibrium. A naive desire that takes form after having already been realized. But from such an astonishing approach to an other, one retains the impression that there was a brief moment of luck; a moment bound not to the favor of the look that may have been exchanged, but to something like a movement that would have preceded us both, just before our encounter. At this instant it seems that *he* was truly our companion in an infinite and infinitely deserted space where, by a marvelous chance, he had suddenly appeared at our side; so it was and so it was going to be, inexplicable, certain, and marvelous. But who was *he?* Only the desert, perhaps? The desert become our companion? Marvelous, this remains marvelously desolate, and then the companion has once again disappeared—there is nothing but desert. But in its harsh truth and arid presence it is suddenly close to us, familiar, a friend. A proximity that at the same time says to us: *"the desert is growing."*

One could perhaps compare this movement to the movement of the absurd experience to which, for a time, Albert Camus attached his name. In many respects, this experience—and it could not be otherwise—was properly his. Personal, also, was the way in which he moved through analyses and ideas, and personal the demands he brought forward: that of unity, for example, or the passion to endure, the aspiration to the eternal. In *The Rebel, An Essay on Man in Revolt*, he writes: *"Perhaps, without this insatiable need to endure, we would better understand earthly suffering—if we knew it to be eternal. At times it seems that great souls are less terrified by pain than by the fact that it does not endure. Lacking an untiring happiness, a long suffering would at least constitute a destiny. But no, our worst tortures one day cease."* Is this what great souls desire? Perhaps only a reflection on suffering could speak in such a way. Extreme suffering, first of all physical suffering, speaks otherwise. When it calls upon death it is still bearable, for it hopes; it places its hope in the end and this hope signifies an alliance with the future, the promise of time. Man then remains master of his destiny, free to have done with his suffering: he suffers and bears up under it, he dominates it by this end to which he appeals. But there is a suffering that has lost time altogether. It is the horror of a suffering without end, a suffering time can no longer redeem, that has escaped time and for which there is no longer recourse; it is irremediable.

This inquiry does not pertain to a limited aspect of our condition. Would suffering be greater in our time? A vain question. But we must not doubt that suffering weighs more heavily on us to the extent that our estrangement from religious consolations, the disappearance of the other world, and the breaking up of traditional social frameworks deprive the one who suffers of all distance and more clearly expose him to the truth of suffering—a truth that consists in withdrawing from him the space that suffering requires, the little time that would make his suffering possible. One can assert that suffering is an ordeal of the individual that does not bring our common destiny into play; also that, rather than the commentaries of thought, it calls for medical intervention, the latter happily undoing what does not let itself be undone. It is in this sense that Albert Camus chose in *The Plague* to make a doctor the symbol of an action that still remains just. A reasonable decision one is astonished to hear scornfully criticized, for it answers to the energetic will of the modern age: the will to maintain man as a power in the face of impossibility, to respond to the excesses of what has caused us to lose the world with a stubborn effort to slowly expand and affirm it, even while this affirmation touches nothing firm.

Nonetheless, what has been said of suffering and of an individual destiny must be said all the more of affliction, oppression, and misery. The man who is altogether unhappy, who is reduced by abjection, hunger, sickness, or fear, becomes what no longer has any relation to itself or to anyone: an empty neutrality, a phantom wandering in a space where nothing happens, a living being fallen below the level of need. This affliction may be particular, but it first of all concerns the majority. Those who are alone in their hunger and live deprived of justice in the midst of a world still happy or tranquil have a chance of being committed to a violent solitude, to the sentiments we call evil—envy, shame, the desire to take revenge, to kill oneself or another—where there is still hope. The hunger of which Knut Hamsun speaks is a hunger that can be fed by pride. The truth of this other kind of misfortune seems to reside in the untold number of those who suffer from it. There is said to be community in misfortune, but there is a point at which what is suffered in common neither brings together nor isolates, only repeating the movement of an affliction that is anonymous, neither belonging to you nor making you belong to a common hope or to a common despair. One speaks of an equality in misfortune, but this is an infinite dissimilarity, an oscillation without any level, an equality without anything being equal. And it is not certain that in order to approach such a situation we must turn to the vast, overwhelming upheavals produced in our time. There is a weariness from which there is no rest; it consists in no longer being able to interrupt what one is doing, in working always more, and, in sum, for the common good: one can no longer be weary, separate oneself from one's fatigue in order to dominate it, put it down and find rest. So it is with misery, affliction. It becomes invisible and in a sense forgotten, disappearing into the one whose disappearance it has brought about (without doing anything to the fact of his existence). It is intolerable but always borne, because the one who bears it is no longer there to undergo it in the first person.

Those who are suffering and those afflicted or subjected to misery have become strangers to the master-slave relationship, which, from the perspective of their situation, has an almost attractive status. The slave has the good fortune of having a master; the master he serves today is the one against whom he will rise up tomorrow. There are also slaves without masters, their slavery such that they have lost every master and every relation with the master, thus all hope of emancipation, as well as all possibility of revolt. Losing the master because he has become nameless—a pure, irresponsible, and undiscoverable power—is already an extremely difficulty situation, but abstract powers can still be named; the most distant and hard to grasp will one day be called God, and God's omnipotence ends by holding out the promise of a decisive combat. Still more grave is the slavery that consists in the absence of the slave, a bondage to shadows, itself seemingly as light as a shadow: a destiny without weight and without reality. Albert Camus said, "I am in revolt, therefore we are," placing all the decision of a solitary hope in a word. But those who have lost the power to say "I" are excluded from this word and from this hope.

Men have always had some idea of hell. They have sensed that where there is man there is hell. Damnation is not an easy thought to deal with. It is striking that a sort of dark dignity has been reserved for the damned. They are of noble origin and the hell that would humble revolt is, on the contrary, exalted by it. The formidable mouth that Dante made speak incessantly repeats—in Arab, it is true—"Honor my splendor in the abyss as it has shone in the world." Damnation still remains a rich but terrible movement. It is sometimes identified with the fiery sentiments of hate, resentment, and envy (the damned eternally contemplate what they abhor), at other times with despair, lost happiness, estranged love; but in every case there still exists, although passing through nothingness and abjection, a relation with the world above. Hell cannot weaken this relation. The damned seem always able to love God by way of their damnation. This possibility remains open to them; their damnation consists in refusing it, but in damnation and in the repetition of this refusal the possibility is still present. It seems that hell ought to have become for the world of faith the pure site of atheism and a symbol of its mystery. Are not the damned, being not only those cut off from God, but also those from whom God has withdrawn absolutely, the only true atheists? Hell is then the extreme space that is empty and free of God, and yet where such an abandon, such a falling outside being, far from measuring itself by this nothingness, pursues and affirms itself in the torment of an infinite time.

One can imagine that saving the damned might be the obsessive concern hovering around belief. More strange would be the thought that asks of the damned the secret and the path of salvation for us all. Yet this is what an entire part of our world has sought to do. Not through misguided sentiment or out of an affection for what is base. Nor is it because one has sought to save the suffering, rather than simply the individual who is suffering (with a pretension we might easily call Hegelian), or to save him by means of his suffering, thinking that he cannot be really and completely saved unless he is saved by this extreme suffering that leaves him no issue either on the side of life or on the side of death. Perhaps we do secretly think this, but things are not so simple. The concern with turning ourselves toward an extreme and necessarily obscure moment—a moment beyond which man, or the possibility of thinking man, seems to disappear—is itself an obscure concern. It does not mean only, as simplicity would lead us to suppose, that it is at the moment when man escapes us that the truth of man would be seized; we would thereby be left leaning over an empty hole, rather than filling it in and making it the seat of a veritable dwelling place.

The search for a beginning firm enough so that what is affirmed from there would not be invisibly absorbed by the uncertainty of an unstable and unknown region—a region situated in an anterior infinity that would secretly ruin our steps—is quite an ambiguous one. The dizzying hope that seized the world when Marx (according to a long-standing interpretation) suggested that history—old, weighty, dialectical history—was coming about as though by itself, and precisely today, for a man ready to begin—a man as close as can be to nothing, deprived of all of history's values and of every form of power, a man having nothing, but also for this reason ready to assume all power and all history in the most just manner—gives proof of the force of this exigency. So it is with the obsession with nihilism. Albert Camus says in the preface to one of his books "*We are beginning to leave nihilism behind us.*" Yes, but however assured this affirmation may be, it leaves in its wake a doubt it has not overcome. It is true, we have left nihilism; but this—perhaps—is because we have never even come into it, at least as concerns its collective form rather than the experience of an exceptional self. Even Marx's proletariat seems to exclude the proletariat in rags, as it excludes the man fallen below need, the shadow of the slave exiled from slavery who labors outside a formative relation with work. And to return to the experience of Camus, it is perhaps in this fact that we should seek a reason for the kind of resistance that has kept us from putting our trust in *The Rebel.*

If Sisyphus, happy-unhappy man of hell, brought a light to the dark days of our time, it is because he and "the stranger" were an image of this extreme limit — we will not say on the side of nothingness, for it is precisely one of the painful discoveries of our experience that nothingness is not the extreme, or is so only insofar as it deceives us. Sisyphus is a man who still works, but uselessly; deprived of the work of time, but not freed from the absence of time, he is given over by this absence to the measurelessness of an eternal rebeginning. And this naked man (who is not a man, but the space of nudity and emptiness he would produce if he had always already and as though in advance disappeared) gives rise to a joyful affirmation that, in silence, says the joy and the force of man naked and bereft. This is a movement, at least in its exigency, that is very close to that of Marx's proletariat. But if what makes Sisyphus interesting is this "light" he casts upon what would be behind man, if it is in the vehemence of his effort to bring us back toward a man infinitely behind man (who nonetheless pushes and maintains him), can we say that *The Rebel* preserves for us this image and sets out from it as from a true beginning? And if so many readers have been struck by the distance that separates the two books, is it by reason of their different conclusions — which, perhaps, differ very little? Is it not rather because of their different points of departure? Is it not because the elementary presence that is Sisyphus and the slave in revolt are already worlds apart, or are separated precisely by the world? One thing is certain: to pass from one to the other one must make a leap.

Camus states that he drew the revolt, whose nature, decisions, and limits *The Rebel* would simply develop and undergo, from the experience of Sisyphus. But the revolt of Sisyphus and that of the slave who says "no" are situated at very different levels. The slave is a man who has already succeeded — an infinite progress — in encountering a master; he thus has this master to rely upon, although, in fact, the analysis of the "No" of the man in revolt will lead Camus to affirm between the two a common measure that in the end holds both of them outside servitude and outside mastery. Sisyphus is a solitude deprived of a center not because he is alone, but because he is without relation to himself. And above all: his revolt, this volte-face with which everything (re)commences, is the about-face of the rock. All the truth of Sisyphus is bound to his rock; a beautiful image of the "elementary" that is within him and outside him, the affirmation of a self that accepts being entirely outside itself, delivered over and boldly entrusted to the strangeness of the outside. How far does this affirmation extend? What was being affirmed by it? The book does not tell us, but it left us with an image; an image is generous, it can say a great deal, promise and give. But what it did not promise is the hope of the slave capable of saying "no" to his master: one cannot pass from this empty hell, this space of dispersion, to the moment of real community and revolt in the first person without flying over a veritable abyss.

But if it is true that such an interval exists between these two figures, which in these two moments of Camus's reflection seek to represent the limits of the man bereft, we must reflect upon this distance, imagine that it is neither arbitrary nor simply introduced by the impatience of a man anxious to conclude. Even if it represents a lacuna that one seems able to get out of only by sinking into it and justifying it, it poses a problem so deceptive that one is tempted to solve it by ignoring it: that is to say, by an implicit but resolute refusal. So it is with the one who believes he meets a companion in the desert of communication: he cannot, without great peril, stop at the moment when what had appeared to him as absolute proximity (as the volatilization of obstacles and the certainty of immediate presence) also reveals itself to be absolute distance—the loss of all relation and the ruin of those partitions by which, up to now, he could still communicate. Would he not, at this point, be justified in once again raising a wall, thus avoiding the mirage and returning to a more stable and clearly defined form of communication? Must he not at a certain moment, and if only in order not to lose it, escape from such an experience? There is perhaps no experience more dangerous, more doubtful, but also, perhaps, more essential; for what it suggests to us is that the proximity and the force of communication depend—to a certain extent, but to what extent?—upon the absence of relation. What it also suggests is that one must be—to a certain extent, but this is precisely an extent without measure—faithful to this absence of relation and faithful also to the risk one runs in rejecting all relation. As though, finally, this fidelity—a fidelity where faithfulness is not possible—this risk, this migration without rest across the space of the desert and the dispersion of hell could also bloom in the intimacy of a communication.

2
Logical victory over "the absurd"

We must begin. Albert Camus says clearly that the movement of the absurd is the equivalent of methodical doubt; he also says that the No of the man in revolt, this word that means "I am in revolt, therefore we are," corresponds to the "Cogito" of Descartes. These two connections shed light upon the exigency of beginning. The "Cogito" was that firm, unshakable, beginning word, and apparently without anything to support it but its own evidency; truly a first word, alone capable of stopping the moving march of the desert, in this case, doubt. That the "Cogito" should in turn be shaken by the unsatisfied exigency of a beginning still more beginning is a long story that would be out of place here; it moreover leaves intact everything this word, by its suddenness and its imperious beginning force, gathers in the way of brilliance and decision. When, in a word, the beginning has spoken, we see it still illuminated by the light of the "Cogito."

We must, therefore, begin: affirming the limit to which we cannot fail to come back in order to confirm by it the rectitude of our steps, but back behind which all return will henceforth be prohibited. The limit itself interdicts such a return, and this is what marks it as initial, the companion to every new initiative. But why is the limit that Sisyphus represents, why is the region that this figure comes close to indicating, unable to furnish us a beginning? Why would the No of the slave and the speech of revolt in the first person—and not the Yes of Sisyphus—constitute this first affirmation that ought not cease speaking to us? Why is Sisyphus, a tragic hero whose whole truth consists in abiding by his situation without issue, suddenly reduced to an episodic role and, still further, reduced to being employed as a methodical servant, employed as a ruse of reason, and later dismissed by reason when he becomes troublesome? Camus says that it is in the nature of this hero to efface himself; it is in the nature of the absurd to be but a passage and immediately reject whoever encounters it. Then the truth of "the absurd" would be in the fact that it turns out he who seems to be held by it, and in the fact that it disappears beneath the thought that would seize it, leaving in its place a void that speech can then come to fill; a word by which, this time, everything begins.

Let us reflect upon such a moment. With his response, and on his own account, Camus takes up the objection that was made to him at the outset: the absurd cannot speak, cannot affirm itself without destroying itself. That which excludes all value becomes, by its affirming itself, a value; it proposes a value judgment and escapes the absurd. A peaceful and logical victory that reassures us with regard to the absurd—or with regard to what is behind this too-clear word. A disquieting victory. For if it delivers us from the absurd so easily, perhaps it does so in order to give us over to the threat of forgetting the absurd—or, much more grave, to forgetting the place where this word is situated and the importance that attaches to this place. Even the term value thereby becomes suspect. It has marvelously and magically exorcised nihilism; but what is it then? Perhaps the mask of nihilism itself. It may be, in fact, that what we call nihilism has been at work in this obscure constraint that turns us away from it; that it was the very thing that hides it, the *movement of detour* making us believe we have always already put nihilism aside. A doubly ruinous movement: the victory over the absurd would have the principal effect of closing it up within the intimacy of our logic and under cover of our happy reason. But, to our mind, there is something even more grave. We not only turn away from a dangerous experience that holds and maneuvers us by this very detour; we at the same time deprive ourselves of an experience whose scope we are thereby incapable of ever again grasping. Perhaps nihilism is the nihilism of destruction and sterile violence only because we agree to protect ourselves from it by this detour and the subterfuge it offers. If, perhaps, we were able to draw it out into a space where the world would no longer shelter it, where values would cease to serve as its mask, we might succeed in turning this adversary into an ally and, holding firm before this force, succeed in recapturing the chance to reach a dimension of ourselves whose measure would no longer be force.

Perhaps. But this "perhaps" does not exclude another risk; on the contrary, it contains it within itself. For this naive concern with tearing the veil might not be the sign of our free desire to see clearly; this supposed lucidity could itself be fascinated, the work of fascination. To look face-on at nihilism in order to seize it is also what it would be waiting for in order to seize us. All the hardy adventurers who have attempted to undergo this ordeal have run the risk of losing themselves in the desert (and without getting any closer to it) through the tormented passion that sometimes metamorphoses the desert into a companion, at other times into an abyss. Hence, surely, the leap that leads Camus to establish such an interval between the beginning — the true beginning that marks the opening of possibility, and through the No of the revolt opens the world — and what we will call, in accordance with a terminology that can be used provisionally, the region of non-origin: that region of infinite rebeginning toward which Sisyphus is turned, and where the possible is lacking. It seems that one must not only establish this interval, but also refuse to elaborate on it since perceiving it is already to make it vanish: only the decision of an implicit refusal can keep the desert at a distance.

*

Is death at the center of Camus's reflection, as his commentators affirm, speaking of death where he himself speaks of the sun? Let us leave thought to its own intimacy and take a look at the books. The essay on Sisyphus examined suicide; the essay on the man in revolt examined murder — not the exceptional crime or the crime of passion, not the moral prohibition against killing, but death as history, as the means and the labor of truth in history. The first essay dismisses suicide because the passion of the absurd — the absence of an issue — cannot accept taking one's own life as a way out. The passion of the absurd can only be a passion that affirms, upholds, and lifts to the point of joy the recommencement of the absurd for which there is no end; this, in fact, is what Sisyphus represented.

The essay on revolt is also a revolt against the power of death that history seems to become, either in abandoning itself to the hypocrisy of values (values that are not equally valid for everyone), thus a pretense under cover of which the most unjust violence is at work, or because the movement of revolution, no longer passing by way of the limits of the person in revolt (under an empty sky, and in a world without value), yields a power over this nothingness that is man in order methodically to raise him to the whole and to the truth of power. There is between these two books, then, the continuity of the same research: a reflection willing to leave to mortal violence its irreducible part, but that will not agree to making it right; on the contrary, Camus's reflection claims mortal violence is wrong, when it is exercised refuses it, and in this refusal founds revolt. We have come back, then, to our question: why is Sisyphus, who does not want to ally himself with suicide, not also the man in revolt who does not want to ally himself with murder? Why are the two separated by such an interval?

It is because the response of the absurd man is only on the face of it the firm answer we think we hear; more profoundly, his response draws us toward an entirely different reading. What does Sisyphus say? He does not at all say that he does not want to take his life; he says rather that he does not want to because he cannot. Having left precisely the space of possibility, he has left the world where dying is possible. Sisyphus is the approach to this region where even the one who commits suicide by an act that is personal and a will that is resolute collides head-on with death as with a density no act can penetrate and that cannot be proposed as an end or a goal. A region that is announced by extreme suffering, by extreme affliction, by the desolation of shadows; a region approached in life by all who, having lost the world, move restlessly *between* being and nothingness: a swarming mass of inexistence, a proliferation without reality, nihilism's vermin: ourselves.

In *The Death of Empedocles*, Hölderlin named the human exigency: "For what I want is to die, and it is for man a right." This right to death, when it is lost, marks the moment at which the non-origin becomes our place of sojourn, causing us to slide toward the space where the figure of Sisyphus is outlined. We understand, then, that this figure cannot represent the limit and the firm decision against death that one would have to rely upon in order to begin; itself under the fascination of dying, it is the image of this between-two where one belongs neither to one nor to the other shore. Albert Camus's sure instinct, his alert aversion for the obscure regions, advised him that the Yes of Sisyphus is the circle of enchantment. A strange Yes that merely takes from the No the purity of its negation; a Yes that affirms nothing, it being the flux and reflux of indecision on the basis of which nothing begins, but from which, without beginning and without end, everything begins again; a Yes that takes from us even the certainty of nothingness and is, as it were, the secret kernel of the No when the No no longer denies by a pure and decisive force, but is rather that which cannot deny itself, that which says always and ever again Yes in the No itself: the Yes in which the No is dissimulated, is dissimulation.

And now we have an inkling that it is on this very doubtful Yes that, in the face of the absurd, the tranquil logical victory is based; the logic of the logos that, in its incapacity to seize the absurd in its neutral form, discovers the reassuring sign of the mastery of thought, which needs only to affirm itself to exterminate "the absurd." But in this case thought exterminates nothing, sets nothing aside. Here, the absurd, or if one prefers, nihilism, has as its sole blind accomplice the arrogant logic of reason, which is content to say: "Logos signifies the impossibility of the absurd. The proof is that each time I speak I tell of meaning and of value and always finally affirm, even if only to deny." So thought echoes within itself the essence of "the absurd," which consists in wanting to *remain "un-thought"* and *"un-said"* in order to be the depth of the neutral that steals into the Yes, dissimulating itself there, and therein dissimulating its own dissimulation.

One could say, therefore, that one of the errors of *The Rebel* is that, on the pretext of rapidly putting nihilism out of play, it in reality plays into nihilism's hands by accepting its own self-effacement, the autodisappearance that is but its visage and the seduction this visage exercises. But one can at the same time understand why this book, faced with the advance of the reason we call dialectic and of history conceived as its movement, declares its mistrust of this reason, which to it seems to be a kind of colonialization of the mind by the absurd; that is to say, the invisible labor of Sisyphus at the center of this thought where he found shelter. This can be said, however, with the following reservation: the dialectic is perhaps, in fact, the greatest effort the logic of reason has ever shown in order to make use of the Yes-No of the "absurd," but in accordance with a deliberate, methodical design. The goal of dialectical reason is to make an alliance with the "absurd," to seek in the "absurd" the very principle of its movement and, through a theoretical and practical development, convince it that it is itself already reason and that the shadows of its dissimulation, in spite of themselves, tell of the light of the day, promise this day, the whole, and the richness of a day that will finally account for the night.

One understands as well that in combating this disproportionate reason whose servant Sisyphus would seem overtly to have become (becoming a functionary and a policeman of this reason), that is, in reestablishing, almost unbeknown to himself, a certain distance between the region of non-origin and the beginning of revolt, Camus is first of all seeking to eliminate from death this lack of measure that appears to come from its accord with the right and reason of legality, but in fact comes more profoundly from the relation that death maintains with a region that is non-originary, and where what speaks in death is without determination and without measure.

The task of culture has always been to restore a kind of purity to death, to make it authentic, personal, proper — but also to make it possible. We feel instinctively, all of us, the danger of seeking man's limit too low, where it nonetheless is: at the point at which, through suffering, misery, and despair, existence seems so deprived of "value" that there death finds itself rehabilitated and violence justified. When history and thought seek the beginning at the level of extreme baseness, it is inevitable that the violence of death itself should also become degraded and attain the lack of measure that is particular to it; here the violence of death joins forces with the ease of numbers and becomes the height of horror in becoming that which draws neither horror nor even interest, becoming as insignificant as "the act of cutting a head of cabbage or drinking a glass of water." How could a movement of rebellion that situates its point of departure at the level of the nether world (where beings have fallen below the "dignity" of death) take into account the protestations of those who enjoy life nobly, who have made values into what is most of worth for them, and made of death itself an event that is important, pure, personal, and in a sense sanctified? For infernal revolt these protestations are insignificant and, moreover, false, since they do not tell even the truth of the end about itself, but tell only of the travesty of a death that is warded off, embellished and dressed up by fear and consoling illusions. It is at the level of hell that one can see the "true" face of death. There, too, one learns to pay without bargaining — the price being death — for the hope of a humanity that has left hell, because there death was measured for its weight and found to be light.

*

There is a natural movement of repulsion that turns us away from hell and thereby puts us in its keeping. The wall of China is the defense that one would first wish to raise against the desert. It is not Camus, but Marx, who sees in the wasted element of the proletariat — the man stripped by oppression of his resistance to oppression — the dead weight that does not further, but delays, the movement of the proletarian revolution. It is not Camus, but Lenin, who entrusts the direction and initiative of the revolution to the proletariat's avant-garde, which he also calls the highest grouping of the proletarian classes: the one having "consciousness, self-mastery, a spirit of sacrifice and heroism," all qualities that are infinitely beyond the limit of the man who has been stripped (reduced). And Hegel, in his turn, cannot, without a leap that remains the enigma of enigmas, pass from the primordial Yes-No — from the movement that we have called "error," a movement of infinite migration where one is no more than errant — to the force of mediation and the progression of the so-called real dialectic (supposing, in Hegel's case, that it is real, and not marked by a double idealism that is at the same time speculative and empiricist). These are, perhaps — but not everything has been said when the word "dialectic" is pronounced — the conditions without which there would be no world, and that the one struggling to make the world possible cannot lose sight of. In a certain sense, then, Sisyphus must be killed; he is that part of us we must deny if we want to begin, become at least slaves, engage in revolt. Killing, here, would be the means of ceasing to kill, the means of opening a path to a world in which, if one does not escape death, one endeavors at least to submit it to a measure whose lack one rejects, arrests, and condemns.

But the problem remains: how can one make disappear what has disappearance as its essence?

3
You can kill that man

Kafka — who also engaged in a solitary combat against what he would not have called the absurd[1] — was able to bring into image a reasoning very close to that of Camus, when Camus says (in the introduction to *The Rebel*) that all thought of non-signification, as soon as it is expressed, lives by way of a contradiction. "Manage, if you can," Kafka says, "to make yourself understood by the wood louse. If you once succeed in questioning him on the goal of his work, you will by the same stroke have exterminated the population of wood louses." This is quite the same movement. "Understanding," a thought that has always already posited ends and values, is in and of itself the force that exterminates the absurd, the movement by which the absurd, if it allows itself to become engaged in it, is exterminated. Kafka, it is true, says more precisely: "If you are able, if you succeed . . . "; he does not say this attempt ought to succeed, rather he suggests (but this is not asserted either: Kafka, of course, suspects dialogue is impossible, but for this reason we must engage in it)[2] that confrontation between thought and the absurd is itself absurd. The would-be dialogue with the population of wood louses entails a language in which solely our will to clarity speaks — a will to clarity that is a will to exterminate. This last word causes us to reflect. There is in Kafka's image something that brings to light a disquieting violence. It is a matter of exterminating, of doing away with; and speech would be what brings death to the inhuman, that which is in possession of nothingness and destruction.

Let us agree that this is so. But why? Is it, as Camus says and also, with more nuance, Sartre, because speech is always a speech of representation or of signification? But then speech would in no way make disappear that which, escaping meaning, always escapes speech and always precedes it. Or is it because it may happen that, in speaking, speech speaks outside all power to represent or to signify? In which case, what is speech if not the very site where the vermin, this people of the underworld that men of all times have rejected by calling them lemures, restlessly move about: something very abject and very deceptive, which is to say, once again, the desolation of hell. This would be a speech in which the vermin disappear, but precisely because it is this very disappearance that defines vermin, just as it defines speech, or at least a certain, strange speech.

Elsewhere, Kafka expresses himself in a like, yet nonetheless different, manner: "*Crows claim that a single crow could destroy the sky. This is no doubt so, but it proves nothing about the sky for the sky signifies precisely: the impossibility of crows.*" Crows, here, are men and their idle and pretentious thoughts; the pretentious "logical" and "humanist" thought that asserts that a single thought will destroy the absurd. This is no doubt so, but it does not affect the sky of the absurd for the absurd signifies the impossibility of (logical) thought. Such a response, without advancing the conversation very much, nonetheless brings us before this adverse region regarding which human thought, the thought in which the power of logos speaks, is not cast out of "reality" but rather enters into impossibility. There may therefore be a region—an experience—where the essence of man is the impossible; where, were he able to make his way into it, if only by a certain speech, he would discover that he escapes possibility; where, also, speech would disclose itself as that which lays bare this limit of man that is no longer a power, not yet a power. A space from which what is called man has as if in advance always already disappeared.

*

We seem to have been directed back to the hell into which Orpheus made his way, or back to the meeting with the desert we evoked at the start of these reflections. When in the immense, always more empty emptiness—the *desert is growing*—we encounter the equivocal companion who suddenly appears at our side, everything would advise us—if we do not wish to perish in the fascinating illusion of absence and if we wish to avoid the mirage that suddenly causes us to encounter the desert in the figure of a companion—to make him undergo the extreme questioning whose horizon is death. This is the decisive test. Whoever has reached the desert where there reigns the absence of relations exposes himself to this test, and exposes to it the one he encounters: here you must kill the companion (or let him kill you, happily the choice exists) in order to recognize and verify his presence, seize in him the moment when the absence of relation becomes the pure relation of that which is nonetheless not the "immediate." But let us try to see more precisely what this denouement is; let us not allow its simplicity to impress us, for where the sword cuts the knot still remains essentially intact.

This moment, which is the moment of *"encounter,"* at the same time precedes the encounter and situates itself at the moving limit where, from the bottom of the non-originary depths—a region always other, a space of emptiness and dispersion—this void and this nudity become the naked visage of encounter and the surprise of the face to face. Such is Eurydice in the underworld at the instant when Orpheus is about to touch her with his gaze, when he sees her such as she is and sees who she is: hell, the horror of absence, the boundlessness of the night that is *other*. And yet, by this chance, he sees that the void is also the naked visage of Eurydice such as the world had always hidden it from him. It is true, the gaze of Orpheus, this gaze of possession and appropriative violence, immediately disperses it. But before the destructive (and knowing) gaze that has made the void and exterminated the cadaveric illusion (which, in obedience to the vocabulary of diurnal wisdom, we are not afraid to call vermin), there is another movement we must not neglect and that the myth principally refers to. This movement that is not yet a gaze is speech, when speech speaks outside all power to represent and to signify. It is the song of Orpheus: a language that does not push hell back, but makes its way into it, speaking at the level of the abyss and thereby giving word to it; giving a hearing to what can have no hearing.

This speech, spoken by no one, no doubt leads to the gaze of Orpheus, he who loses what he seizes. But because this speech—and this is of some consequence—precedes his gaze, because it is itself this gaze, only anterior to it (the gaze before light that is other than any vision), it is essentially tied to the moment when, before Eurydice's naked visage vanishes into radical death, the very nudity that is her visage is revealed: the non-transparency that escapes being, escapes the power of being and the power of the violence that forces and seizes. As though the proximity of absolute power, the power of death, were required to strip the clothed figure of living beings (always dressed by the world), in order to lay it bare and assure an encounter with it; but also, at the same time, in order to discover that this nakedness is what one encounters but does not seize, it being what slips away from every hold. As though the exercise of absolute power were required, therefore, in order to encounter the limit of this power, no longer solely in its negative form, but as the strange affirmation that escapes being and the negation of being. It is at this limit that the absence of relation—the inaccessible, the unseizable desolation of the desert—becomes, in and through the speech that establishes itself at this level, the experience of the outside. After which (naturally, this "after" is not chronological) everything risks falling under the violence that annihilates and into insignificance.

It cannot be denied that this movement may be the risk itself. There, speech is surrounded by empty horror, the error of empty night. Speech lies under the shadow of the violence that makes death possible and under the enchantment of death as impossibility. It is linked to both: to patience and impatience, to the violence of impatient desire, to the violence of Orpheus's gaze that seizes and puts to death, and to the unmeasured passion that makes him *"infinitely dead,"* an Orpheus divided into pieces and scattered. Speech is bound to these two spaces of death; it is the intimacy of their double violence, the space in which this double violence itself seems to become neutralized, *seems* for a moment to become calm, like the extreme immobile movement at the center of the maelstrom.

*

If in his work and his reflections Albert Camus accorded a place to those he called "the Just"—those young Russians who, as Brice Parain reminds us, were "derisively" called nihilists[3]—it is perhaps because he recognized that they were obsessed by an action at once invisible and striking, and into which they sought to disappear in order to identify themselves with its disappearance. Why does the history of these men who have been excluded by our time seem to concern us in a way that remains secret? Is it because, demanding, as did Rimbaud, *"the flight of tyrants and demons,"* they were themselves the heroes of a negative resolve?

But were they heroes? Were they not, on the contrary, strangers to all that makes the individual glorious and visible? Of course some of them—Kaliayev, Jeliabov, Sazonov—are familiar to us. These are names and also faces, but what they name is anonymous, what they display has no form. Nor were they saints; those tormented by ambition or renown were not absent from their ranks, neither were the authoritarians who wanted to win in accordance with their own laws. But the singularity of their story resides in the fact that ambition, reputation, the perversities of collective violence, and even the beauty of heroic actions have all dissolved into an impersonal transparency. This story, told by a few striking acts and by an immense, nameless misfortune, is but the accomplishment of the fact that each of them, in affliction or exaltation, almost succeeded in being no one.

And they were, there is no doubt, men of a negative resolve. But how does it happen that through this force—negation of themselves and negation of others—the simplicity of an innocent affirmation came to be expressed? What does this expression tell us? This is hardly easy to bring to light, for what it says is not said clearly; simplicity speaks in it, but simplicity itself—tears and blood joined together, distress and hope, love and rigor—refuses to become what for us in the world is a speech that can be grasped. What it says is not only the terrible necessity of violence, or the tension that must be maintained when one has broken with the security of right in order to make just what can no longer be justified. Their story says this, but not only or exactly this: this would be little, perhaps only the mantle of another illusion. "To die," says Camus in setting forth Jeliabov's and Kaliayev's thoughts, "to die annuls the culpability and the crime itself." Perhaps. But not with regard to the truth of the world. Kaliayev kills the Grand Duke Sergei, then Kaliayev dies and in a sense freely, by premeditated consent. For us Kaliayev represents freedom, all that we hold dear. The grand duke represents "despotism," all that weighs upon the world and darkens it. And yet the death of Kaliayev cannot buy back the death of the grand duke. It does not "annul" it, does not purify it, and rather than making it lighter makes it more heavy; it adds to it, it being the same death, the open parentheses that at the same time close upon two beings, as though the same being had died twice over. But this no longer concerns morality (morality will never justify Kaliayev, nor will it understand his innocence; it places itself at a level where one death, no matter which death it may be, never balances out another). Here it is a matter of an entirely different necessity. Camus again cites Kaliayev's words, spoken after the assassination: *From the moment I was behind bars, I never for one moment had the least desire to stay alive.* Because he knows, and does not shirk from this knowledge, that from the instant he brought death into the world by his own initiative, he, too, entered into death; in bringing about this breach in a universe of reflections, pretense, and lies, he lost the world, lost his consolation, his happy light, lost all "possibility" of living.

This is the understanding that the nihilists had of their action; an exigency difficult to determine, but not a moral one. It is not a matter of personally claiming a terrible action whose consequences one will accept. And it is not a matter of astonishing history by dying courageously: for many, it was a matter of living, obscurely and desperately, in the space of death they had opened and in which they had to remain, deprived of every justification and every recourse. Many men are able to die courageously; courage is the companion the world sends us, the energy life delegates to us in order to make death an event still tied to the values of the world and to respect for life. But to descend with lucidity and fidelity into the space opened by death, to remain there and to die there in one's turn, sometimes to live there and bear the sentence of one's own violence—this is a decision that goes beyond all courage, a decision that remains secret and tells not only of devotion, heroism, and faith in the future. Savinkov says of Dora Briliant, who prepared the assassination of the grand duke of Plehve and of many others: "*Terror weighed on her like a cross. . . . She was not able to reconcile herself to murder, and yet she had agreed to spill blood. She sought a way out and did not find one.*" When she was told that the attempt on the Grand Duke Sergei's life had been successful, "*She bowed her head and I saw her tears, I heard the sobs she could no longer hold back. . . . 'The grand duke has been killed! My God, it's we who have killed him, It's I! Yes, I am the one who killed him!' She wanted to give her life, and it is another's death that was being offered her. She did not want to kill, she wanted to die, but she was obliged to live and her life was a torment without measure, without issue.*"

In the play Camus wrote on the death of the Grand Duke Sergei, Dora, before the assassination, says to Kaliayev (who, assisted by his dreamy, joyful nature, assures her he will not waver): "*I know. You're brave. That is what makes me anxious . . . throwing the bomb, the scaffold, dying twice over, that is the easier part. Your heart will see you through. But standing in the front line . . . you'll be standing in front, you'll see him. . . . —See whom?—The grand duke.—Scarcely for a moment. —A moment during which you will look at him!*" We know that, the first time, Kaliayev did not have the force to kill because he saw the grand duke's wife and children sitting in the carriage next to him. Savinkov, who had organized the assassination, relates in his *Memoirs* what Kaliayev said to him just after that moment: "*Understand. I fear this is a crime against all of us, but I couldn't do otherwise. Understand, I wasn't able. When I saw that woman, those children, my hand stopped . . . I couldn't, and now, too, I cannot.*" A few days later the grand duke was alone and Kaliayev executed him without hesitating.

Perhaps such an episode helps us approach this simple word whose affirmation, in the midst of terror, nihilist history has succeeded in keeping open. We sense that the recoil of violence—its arrest in front of the children's weakness, Kaliayev's "*I cannot*"—coincides with the moment at which violence lays bare the visage and makes man this extreme destitution before which death draws back because it cannot reach it, because this weakness is this arrest, this drawing back itself. The children and the wife, their innocence, are nothing other than the visage of the grand duke, the naked visage that Dora had made Kaliayev see in advance: nothing other than the nakedness that is man in proximity with death's revelation, nothing other than the *"moment at which you will look at him."* What we are left with is this moment. This is the *time* of the word, the moment at which speech begins, lays bare the human visage, says the encounter that is this nakedness and says man as the encounter with the extreme and irreducible limit. *"Understand, I could not, and now, too, I cannot."* *"I cannot"* is the secret of language where, outside all power to represent and to signify, speech would come about as what always differs from itself, and, as difference, holds back. It does not merge with the moral interdiction against killing, nor with the fact that one cannot really kill. *"I cannot"* is death speaking in person, an allusion that death formulates when, in the act of killing, it comes up against the evidence of the visage as though it were its own impossibility; a moment that is death's own drawing back before itself, the *delay* that is the site of speech, and where speech can take place.

This is a speech, assuredly, of which we are not directly aware and, it must be said again, a speech that is infinitely hazardous, for it is encompassed by terror. Radical violence is its fringe and its halo; it is one with the obscurity of night, with the emptiness of the abyss, and so doubtful, so dangerous that this question incessantly returns: why the exigency of such a language? What have we to do with it? What does it bring us in the frightening silence that announces extreme violence but is also the instant at which violence goes silent, becomes silence? What is this communication without community that no power—that is to say, no comprehension—no human or divine presence can anticipate? Would it not be, alluring without attraction, *desire* itself?: the desire become song that opens hell up to Orpheus when what becomes *embodied* is the absolute of separation, all the while remaining the depth and the detour of interval? Let us examine this inexhaustible myth one more time.

4
Orpheus, Don Juan, Tristan

Orpheus seems to be separated from Eurydice by the underworld. But if hell is nothing but the space of dispersion, it is nonetheless this space that makes Orpheus the one toward whom separation, dispersion itself, advances under the veil of the invisible and as the shadow of a person. This is indeed one aspect of the myth. Who follows Orpheus in the underworld? Absolute distance, the interval that is always facing the other way. But is it Eurydice? A question that transforms Eurydice into an empty site, and impossibility into powerlessness. It is not Eurydice insofar as it is Orpheus, insofar as Orpheus is still the master speech that would grasp the ungraspable and bring the depth of passion into action. So it is no more than illusion, insignificance, unreality; it is empty, cruelly empty. But this emptiness is nonetheless the naked visage of Eurydice, the moving encounter that takes place only through the force of strangeness and irregular chance. The desire that carries Orpheus forward, and that compels Tristan, is not an impetus able to clear the interval and pass over absence, even the absence of death. Desire is separation itself become that which attracts: an interval become *sensible*, an absence that turns back into presence. Desire is this turning back when in the depth of night, when everything has disappeared, disappearance becomes the density of the shadow that makes flesh more present, and makes this presence more heavy and more strange, without name and without form; a presence one cannot then call either living or dead, but out of which everything equivocal about desire draws its truth.

From this perspective, desire is on the side of "error," the infinite movement that always begins again, but whose recommencement is sometimes the errant depth of what does not cease, at other times the repetition wherein what always returns is still newer than any beginning. Hence, to the extent that the Christian world has not spiritualized it, the myth of Don Juan. Like Sade's characters, Don Juan has decided in favor of numerical repetition;[4] with an admirable effrontery he accepts the pleasure of enumeration as a satisfying solution. Desire is pleased endlessly to add encounter to encounter, to make a number of the innumerable. This is why, as Micheline Sauvage has noted,[5] the myth of Don Juan essentially presupposes the "lista numerosa," the Catalog whereby joyful desire recognizes itself in numbers, and in these recognizes what is stronger than eternity since eternity could no more exhaust desire than it could succeed in ending its count with a final figure.

And yet—inevitable episode—Don Juan runs up against the Commander. What is he? Desire's other face. The Commander is not a representative of God or even of the other world beyond death. He is always and still desire, but desire's nocturnal face; when it is separation that becomes desire, the inaccessible that would be the "immediate." Whoever desires is not only bound to the repetition of what always begins again; the one who desires enters into the space where the remote is the essence of proximity—where what unites Tristan and Isolde is also what separates them: not only the limit of their bodies that are closed and off-limits, the inviolable reserve of their solitude that rivets them to themselves, but the secret of absolute distance.

Don Juan is the man of the possible. His desire is a force [*puissance*], and all his relations are relations of power [*pouvoir*] and possession; that is why this is a myth of modern times. But this is to speak only of appearance. Because Don Juan is a man of desire, he lives in the field of the fascination that he himself exercises, uses, and enjoys, all the while preserving through mastery and its incessant renewal this desiring freedom that he does not wish to cease being. Don Juan knows very well that along with desire he admits impossibility; but he affirms that impossibility is nothing but the sum of the possible and that it can therefore be mastered numerically—whether the count be "a thousand and three" or more or less is unimportant: Don Juan could perfectly well limit himself to a single woman whom he might possess only once, but on condition that he desire her not as a woman who is unique, but as a unity entailing the infinite of repetition.

Another trait: Don Juan is not a man who desires in order to have or to possess. His list is not that of Alexander's conquests. He desires—that is all. Of course this desire seizes and captures, but it does so with a joyful force and the rapture of desire, without second thoughts, without concern, and with a somewhat shameless innocence that is astonished by the objections made to it. It is certain that he desires; he is not simply a man who, by fascinating, would indirectly enjoy the passion he has inspired. He himself enters into the game, and his caprices, being those of desire, have the suddenness, the youth, the ardor, and, to say it once more, the gaiety of a desire that is necessarily happy. Nothing is more joyous or more "healthy" than Don Juan, as Micheline Sauvage says; he is truly a superb hero, a man of the sword and of courage, a man who introduces the vivacity and the energy of day into night. Only he has a weakness, if it is one, an invincible bias; he wants at the same time to be desire and freedom, desiring freedom—the man who, weighed down by fascination, would remain lightness, sovereign action, mastery. The consequence is the Commander. And the Commander is the encounter of passion become coldness, the impersonality of night; precisely the night of stone that Orpheus's singing desire succeeds in opening.

Is this because he found himself opposite Anna, who is his equal? Is it because his liberty failed him before her? Or because he encountered in that enigmatic Anna an Isolde who turns him into a Tristan? One can at least say that the Commander, or the rendezvous with him, is a rendezvous with the space of desire in which Tristan wanders: a space that is the desire for night, but a night that is necessarily empty for one who wants to hold onto the fullness of personal mastery. A night that opposes the impersonality and the coldness of stone to he who attacks it with the sword and with signs of provocation and power. All the nights of Don Juan are gathered up into this night that he does not know how to desire and wants only to combat—a man, up to the end, of initiative where boundless indecision reigns.

It is remarkable that this myth, formed in a Christian universe in which everything would lead to embodying the final force that seizes Don Juan (the man of earthly pleasure) in a grandiose and spiritually rich presence, should have made this image of transcendence into something cold, empty, and terrifying, but terrifying due to its coldness and its empty unreality. This does not mean that the myth is finally atheist, but that Don Juan encounters something even more extreme than the other world. What he encounters is not the All-Powerful, a meeting that would finally have pleased him, this man of war, of power and combative desire; what he meets is not the extreme of the possible but rather impossibility—the abyss of non-power, the icy, frozen excess of the *other* night. At the bottom of the myth there remains the enigma of the stone statue, which is not only death but something colder and more anonymous than Christian death: the impersonality of all relation, the outside itself. And the last meal with the Commander, a courtly ceremony that ironically borrows the forms of a highly socialized life, represents the defiance of Don Juan, who is resolved to treat the *other* as though the *other* were still himself, refusing to sense in this *other* with whom no relation is possible what the bias of his mutilated desire has definitively dismissed from his commerce with those who are living. And now what he seizes is an icy hand. What he perceives, he who chose not to look at the naked visage of the beings he desired, is the emptiness this nakedness has now become.

*

We all end in the underworld; but Don Juan's hell is Tristan's heaven. A hell, an obscurity that even the obscurity of death cannot cover over. And yet, in a sense, it is the same desire. Don Juan is perhaps a myth, just as Tristan and Orpheus are mythical figures, but precisely to the extent that myth distinguishes between them, and as though it would be more unreal to be Don Juan alone, to be mutilated passion, than to be, in the contradiction that divides them, all at once Don Juan and Tristan and Orpheus.

Yes, all desire has the spring, the youth, and the joyous insouciance of Don Juan, for whom the interminable is each time the identical novelty of another term; he cannot be bound any more than he can rest, being the resource of what never sleeps. And thus he is already at the frontier of Tristan's passion—Tristan who cannot let go, but because he is not bound either, not by a true bond, by those relations of the day that are formed through struggle, work, and community, a possible relation. Tristan's and Isolde's passion escapes all possibility. This means first that it escapes their power, escapes their decisions and even their "desire." This is strangeness itself; it has no regard either for what they are capable of, or for what they want; it *pulls* them into the space of the strange where they become strangers to themselves in an intimacy that also makes them strangers to each other. The inaccessible that has become the "immediate" is more than sudden: Don Juan's most prompt desire appears slow, prudent, and wily next to the limitless trembling where Isolde does not even have to give herself and Tristan does not have to take, where, dispossessed of themselves, they take body from, as they give body to, the distance of absolute separation; each of them night without term, neither merged nor united in it but forever dispersed by it insofar as it is the error of the other night, the absence of unity, the time that is other.

This is why these lovers, who touch each other not only by their beautiful presence but also by the fatal attraction of absence, these lovers without hesitation, without reservation, and without doubt, also give the impression of an intimacy that is absolute yet absolutely without intimacy, given over as they are to the passion of the outside that is the erotic relation par excellence. Bound together by the absence of a bond, they seem less close to each other than would be anyone in the world and an indifferent passerby. This is precisely because the world has collapsed,[6] and because it is impossibility alone that holds them: the potion that drinks them in as soon as they touch it to their lips.[7] Would they be, then, eternally separated? Neither separated nor divided: they are inaccessible to one another and, in the inaccessible, in infinite relation.

In like manner, this passion whose rapidity evokes the lightning bolt of love at first sight also seems what is most slow. The years pass. Everything is consumed and everything drifts in the vacancy of the unaccomplished. Without future, without past, without present, it is a desert where they are not and where those who seek them only find them lost in the sleep of their incomprehensible absence. Thus it is ridiculous to say they are faithful: to be faithful one must be one with oneself, have time at one's disposal and enter into time through the allegiance of a real relation. One day, when Milena and Kafka met in Gmünd, she asked him whether he had not been unfaithful to her in Prague. *"Was this a possible question?,"* Kafka writes to her. *"But this was still not enough, and I made it even more impossible. I said that indeed I had been faithful."* Isolde might question Tristan in the same absurd way. For the episode of the other Isolde is but an allusion to such a faithless fidelity in this realm of fascination where beings have the duplicity of an image. A dream world bereft of sleep where one comes and goes without taking hold of anything, yet nonetheless an abyss where the sudden is decisive—as when Tristan, by a marvelous leap that is missing from the story of Don Juan, jumps from his bed to that of the inaccessible Isolde.

*

We shall not forget one of the most significant episodes of this story: the herbed wine the two lovers drink by mistake is a love philter carefully composed so it will only have effect for three years. The three years having passed, they come to a sort of awakening; they see the harshness of their life, the desert in which they wander, the joys of the world they have lost. They part, each one returning to the existence of everyone. Is everything over then? Not in the least. On the contrary, everything begins all over again. They are separated, but only in order to reunite; they are far from each other, but one in this distance across which they do not cease to call to one another, hear one another, and return to a proximity. Chroniclers and poets have been puzzled by this contradiction without daring to resolve it; it is as though the lovers' passion had at the same time to be passing and remain the site of the indefinite, the movement of the interminable. Their passion arises in time, the encounter takes place in the world; it begins and comes to an end, it lasted three years. This is the way the story is seen and is told. But passion, limited in accordance with the time of the day, does not know these limits in the night to which it belongs. The two lovers live in a duplicity and under a constraint that nothing explains. On the one hand, since the world rediscovers them, they continue their worldly existence without obstacle; Tristan thus once again becomes a useful man, wields a glorious sword, and finally marries: this is the rule. But the marriage that is sumptuously celebrated in the light of day can only dissipate at night, for at night the new Isolde, Isolde of the white hands, is never present; night is still always the night of the desert, the pale day of the forest of Morois or, more accurately, a night without anyone and given over solely to images — the paintings that Tristan, with a sure instinct, brought forth in a place set outside the world.

The chronicle might have stopped at the commonplace: they loved each other with an eternal passion. But the secret we sense here is deeper. After three years Tristan and Isolde awake from their desire. Three years, after which they forget each other. But in this forgetting they approach the true center of their passion, which, interrupted, perseveres. Hence their malaise. It is true, they no longer love one another, the time for this is past; yet all their new encounters seem as unreal as a tale that would go on without them. They no longer love each other in this time but this is unimportant, for passion has little concern for this time that cannot be redeemed or appeased by the work of time. This does not mean they relive their history, and, henceforth without love, are led back by the nostalgia of their memories to days they can no longer live and that take from them the taste for living new days: it is not a matter of psychology. Their vicissitudes refer above all to another movement. When the absolute of separation has become relation it is no longer possible to be separated. When desire has been awakened by impossibility and by night, desire can indeed come to an end and an empty heart turn away from it; in this void and this end, in this passion that has cloyed, it is the infinite of the night itself that continues to desire night — a neutral desire that takes into account neither you nor me, that appears, then, as a mystery wherein the happiness of private relations founders. A failure nonetheless more necessary and more precious than any triumph, if it holds hidden and in reserve the exigency of another relation.

Perhaps this shadow behind the story of Tristan and Isolde must be grasped. Forgetting is the mute and closed space where desire endlessly wanders; where someone is forgotten he or she is desired, but this forgetting must be a profound forgetting. Forgetfulness: the movement of forgetting: the infinite that, with forgetting, opens up in closing upon itself — on condition that it be received not by the lightness that frees memory from memory but, within remembrance itself, as the relation with what hides and that no presence can hold. The Ancients had already sensed that *Lethe* is not merely the other side of *Aletheia*, its shadow, the negative force from which the knowledge that remembers would deliver us. *Lethe* is also the companion of Eros, the awakening proper to sleep, the distance from which one cannot take one's distance since it comes in all that moves away; a movement, therefore, without a trace, effacing itself in every trace, and nonetheless—the expression must be used, however faultily—still announcing itself and already designating itself in the lack of writing that writing—*this senseless game*—remembers outside memory as its *limit* or its always prior illegitimacy.

VIII

Forgetting, Unreason

On forgetting

Forgetting: non-presence, non-absence.

To open to forgetting as accord with what hides. Forgetting, with each event forgotten, is the event of forgetting. To forget a word is to encounter the possibility that all speech could be forgotten, to remain close to all speech as though it were forgotten, and close also to forgetting as speech. Forgetting causes language to rise up in its entirety by gathering it around the forgotten word.

In forgetting there is what turns away from us and there is the detour that comes from forgetting itself. There is a relation between the detour of speech and the detour of forgetting. From this it follows that, even saying the thing forgotten, speech does not fail forgetting but speaks on its behalf.

*

The movement of forgetting.

(1) When we are missing a forgotten word it still indicates itself through this lack; we have the word as something forgotten, and thus reaffirm it in the absence it seemed made to fill and whose place it seemed made to dissimulate. We seize in the word forgotten the space out of which it speaks, and that now refers us back to its silent, unavailable, interdicted and still latent meaning.

In forgetting a word, we sense that the capacity to forget is essential to speech. We speak because we have the power to forget, and all speech that works in a utilitarian manner against forgetting (all speech of recall, encyclopedic knowledge) runs the risk—a risk nonetheless necessary—of rendering speech less telling. Speech ought therefore never forget its secret relation to forgetting; which means that it ought to forget more profoundly, hold itself, in forgetting, in relation to the sliding that belongs to forgetfulness.

(2) When we perceive that we speak because we are able to forget, we perceive that this ability-to-forget does not belong solely to the realm of possibility. On the one hand, forgetting is a capacity: we are able to forget and, thanks to this, able to live, to act, to work, and to remember—to be present: we are thus able to speak usefully. On the other hand, forgetting gets away. It escapes. This does not simply mean that through forgetting a possibility is taken from us and a certain impotency revealed, but rather that the possibility that is forgetting is a slipping outside of possibility. At the same time as we make use of forgetting as a power, the capacity to forget turns us over to a forgetting without power, to the movement of that which slips and steals away: detour itself.

*

The time of affliction: a forgetting without forgetting, without the possibility of forgetting.

*

"To forget what holds itself apart from absence and apart from presence, and nonetheless causes both presence and absence to come forth through the necessity of forgetting; this is the movement of interruption we would be asked to accomplish. — To forget everything, then? — Not simply everything; and how could one forget everything, since 'everything' would also include the very 'fact' of forgetting, which would as a consequence be reduced to a determinate act and deprived of an understanding of the whole? — To forget everything would perhaps be to forget forgetting. — Forgetting forgotten: each time I forget, I do nothing but forget that I am forgetting. To enter into this movement of redoubling, however, is not to forget twice; it is to forget in forgetting the depth of forgetting, to forget more profoundly by turning away from this depth that lacks any possibility of being gotten to the bottom of. — Then we must seek elsewhere. — We must seek the same thing, arrive at an event that would not be forgetting, and that nonetheless would be determined only by forgetting's indetermination. — Dying might appear to be a good answer. The one who dies is done with forgetting, and death is the event that becomes present in the accomplishment of forgetting. — To forget dying is sometimes to die, sometimes to forget, and then it is to die and to forget. But what is the relation between these two movements? We do not know. The enigma of this relation is the enigma of impossibility."

*

To forget death is not to relate oneself in a rash, inauthentic, and evasive manner to this possibility that would be death; on the contrary, it is to enter into an event that is necessarily inauthentic, a presence without presence, an ordeal without possibility. Through the movement that steals away (forgetting), we allow ourselves to turn toward what escapes (death), as though the only authentic approach to this inauthentic event belonged to forgetting. Forgetting, death: the unconditional detour. The present time of forgetting delimits the unlimited space where death reverts to the lack of presence.

To hold oneself at the point where speech allows forgetting to gather in its dispersal and allows forgetting to come to speech.

The Great Confinement

The relation of desire to forgetting as that which is previously inscribed outside memory, a relation to that of which there can be no memory, that always comes before and yet effaces the experience of a trace—this movement that excludes itself, and through this exclusion designates itself as being exterior to itself, thus necessitates an exteriority that is never articulated: inarticulate. But this *inarticulation of the outside* nonetheless seems to offer itself in the most closed of structures; it is this inarticulation that makes internment into a structure and structure into an internment when, through an abrupt decision (that of a certain culture) saying sets apart, places at a distance and *interdicts* what exceeds it. The demand to shut up the outside, that is, to constitute it as an *interiority* of anticipation or exception, is the exigency that leads society—or momentary reason—to make madness exist, that is, to make it *possible*. An exigency that has become almost clear to us since the publication of Michel Foucault's book, a book in itself extraordinary, rich, insistent, and through its necessary repetitions almost unreasonable. (Moreover, as a doctoral thesis, it brought us before a significant collision between the University and unreason).[1] I shall first recall the marginal idea that came to be expressed in this book, which is not so much a history of madness as a sketching out of what might be "a history of *limits*—of those obscure gestures, necessarily forgotten as soon as they are accomplished, by which a culture rejects something that, for it, would be the Exterior." It is on this basis—in the space established between madness and unreason—that we have to ask ourselves if it is true that literature and art might be able to entertain these limit-experiences and thus, beyond culture, pave the way for a relation with what culture rejects: a speech of borders, the outside of writing.

Let us read, or reread, this book from such a perspective. During the Middle Ages, the demented are interned in a more systematic fashion than before. But we observe that the idea of internment is inherited; it follows in the wake of the movement of exclusion that had previously induced society to sequester those with leprosy and then, when leprosy (almost suddenly) disappeared, to maintain the necessity of cutting humanity's dark side off from the rest of society. "Often, and in the same places, the formulas of exclusion will be strangely similar: the poor, the convict, and the mentally deranged will assume the role abandoned by the leper." This would seem to be an interdict of a singular nature. Absolutely separated, and yet kept by this margin in a fascinating proximity, the inhuman possibility that mysteriously belongs to men is affirmed and exhibited.[2] One can therefore say it is this obligation to exclude—exclusion as a necessary "structure"— that discovers, calls forth, and consecrates those beings who must be excluded. It is not a matter of a moral condemnation, nor of a simple, practical separation. The sacred circle encloses a truth, but one that is strange and dangerous: the extreme truth that menaces every power to be true. This truth is death, whose living presence is the leper. Then, when the time of madness comes, it is still death, but a death more interior, unmasked even in its seriousness: the empty head of the idiot substituted for the macabre skull, the laughter of the demented instead of the funerary rictus, Hamlet opposite Yorick, the dead buffoon, twice buffoon. An unapproachable truth, the force of a fascination that is not simply madness but is expressed through madness and that gives rise, as the Renaissance approaches and extends itself, to two kinds of experience. One can be called tragic or cosmic (madness reveals a staggering depth, a subterranean violence, a knowledge that is boundless, devastating, and secret); the other is a critical experience that assumes the aspect of a moral satire (life is fatuity, a mockery; but if there is a "mad madness" from which nothing can be expected, there is also a "wise madness" that belongs to reason and has the right to ironic praise).

This is indeed the Renaissance, the Renaissance as it liberates mysterious voices, all the while tempering them. *King Lear*, *Don Quixote*: it is the great day of madness. Montaigne meditates before Tasso, admiring him and wondering whether the latter's pitiful state were not due to a too great clarity that blinded him, "to that rare aptitude for the exercises of the soul that left him without capacity [*exercise*] and without soul." The classical age arrives; two movements are being determined. Descartes, "by a strangely forceful blow," reduces madness to silence; this is the solemn break of the first Meditation: the refusal of any relation with extravagance that is required by the advent of the *ratio*. It comes about with an exemplary severity: "But what, these are madmen, and I would be no less extravagant were I to guide myself by their example." This is asserted in a simple sentence: If, awake, I can still suppose that I am dreaming, I cannot, through thought, suppose myself to be mad, since madness is irreconcilable with the exercise of doubt and with the reality of thought. Let us listen to this sentence, as we have here a decisive moment of Western thought. Man—as the accomplishment of reason, as the affirmation of the sovereignty of the subject who is capable of the true—is himself the *impossibility* of madness. Of course, there may be men who are mad, but man himself, the subject in man, cannot be so; for only he can be man who realizes himself through affirmation of the sovereign *I* and in the initial choice he makes against Unreason: to fail to make this choice, in whatever way, would be to fall outside human possibility, to choose not to be man.

The "Great Confinement" that occurs as though on cue (one morning in Paris six thousand persons are arrested) confirms this exile of madness by giving it a remarkable compass. Those who are insane are shut up, but at the same time and in the same places are also confined (by an act of banishment that mixes them together) the poverty-stricken, the idle, the profligate, the impious, and the libertines, those who do not think in the right way. Later, during the progressive eras, this confusion will arouse indignation or derision, although it is no laughing matter. Rich in meaning, this movement indicates rather that the seventeenth century does not reduce madness to madness but, on the contrary, perceives the relations that madness maintains with other radical experiences: experiences that touch upon sexuality, religion (atheism and sacrilege), or libertinage—in other words, as Foucault says in summary, experiences that touch on the relations that are being established between free thought and a system of passions. To put this another way, what is being constituted in silence—in the seclusion of the Great Confinement, and through a movement that answers to the banishment pronounced by Descartes—is the very world of Unreason: a world of which madness is but a part and to which classicism annexes sexual prohibitions, religious interdicts, and all the excesses of thought and of the heart.

Such a moral experiment with unreason, which is the other side of classicism, is tacitly carried out and becomes manifest in giving rise to this almost socially invisible arrangement: the closed space where dwell side by side the insane, the debauched, the heretical, and the disorderly—a sort of murmuring emptiness at the heart of the world, a vague menace from which reason defends itself with the high walls that symbolize the refusal of all dialogue: ex-communication. There is no relation with the negative; kept at a distance, disdainfully rejected, it is no longer the cosmic specter of preceding centuries but what is insignificant, banal non-sense. And yet, for us—and in part for that century itself—this sequestration by which all the unreasonable forces are contained, this hemmed-in existence that is reserved for them, also obscurely preserves these forces and restores to them the extreme "sense" that belongs to them. Within the limits of this narrow enclosure something beyond measure is lying in wait: in the cells and the dungeons, a freedom, in the silence of seclusion, a new language, the speech of violence and of desire without representation and without signification. And the proximity that is prescribed for madness will also have consequences: just as the highest negative forces are marked by a scarlet letter, so will those who are mad, comrades in chains of the depraved and the licentious, remain their accomplices under the common sky of the Fault. This relation will never be entirely forgotten; the scientific knowledge of mental illness will never repudiate the groundwork that was constituted for it by the moral demands of classicism. But, reciprocally, as Michel Foucault states, the fact that "it is a certain liberty of thought that furnishes a first model for mental alienation" will contribute to sustaining the secret force of the modern concept of alienation.

This is not the case, however, in the nineteenth century, when the relationship between the "alienation" referred to by physicians and the "alienation" of the philosophers is undone. The communication between them, represented (up until the Pinel reform) by the practice of placing unreasonable beings into contact with beings without reason, this silent dialogue between madness related to license and madness related to illness, is now broken off. Madness gains specificity; it becomes pure and simple, it falls into truth, it renounces being a negative strangeness and instead takes its place in the calm positivity of things to be known. This positivism (which moreover remains tied to the forms of bourgeois morality) seems, in the guise of philanthropy, to master madness more definitively through the constraints of a determinism more exhaustive than all the previous mechanisms of correction. What is more, to reduce madness to silence, whether by rendering it, in effect, mute (as in the classical age) or by confining it in the rational garden of a species (as in all the ages of enlightenment), is the constant move of every Western culture concerned with maintaining a line of partition.

*

One must turn to the great somber works of literature and art to hear the language of madness—to hear it, perhaps, anew. Goya, Sade, Hölderlin, Nietzsche, Nerval, Van Gogh, Artaud—these existences fascinate us by the attraction to which they themselves were subject, but also by the relation that each of them seems to have maintained between the obscure knowledge of Unreason and what the clear knowledge of science calls madness. Each in his own way, and never in the same way, leads us back to the question onto which Descartes's choice opens and that defines the essence of the modern world: if reason, if this thought that is power excludes madness as *the impossible* itself, would it not be because when thought seeks to experience itself more essentially as a power without power—seeking to bring back into question the affirmation that identifies it with possibility alone—it must, as it were, withdraw from itself, turn away from a mediating and patient labor and turn instead toward a searching that is distracted and astray, without labor, without patience, without result and without works? Is it possible that thought cannot arrive at what is, perhaps, the ultimate dimension without passing through what is called madness and, passing by way of it, falling into it? Or again, to what extent can thought maintain itself in the difference between unreason and madness if what becomes manifest in the depth of unreason is the appeal of *indifference*: the neutral that is also difference itself; that which differentiates itself in nothing? Or, to return once more to the words of Michel

Foucault: what, then, would condemn to the realm of madness those who once undertook the ordeal of unreason?

One may wonder why it is writers and artists (strange names, always already anachronistic) who have borne such questions in a privileged manner and forced others to become attentive to them. The response is at first almost easy. "Madness" is the absence of work, while the artist is one who is preeminently destined to a work—but also one whose concern for the work engages him in the experience of that which in advance always ruins the work and always draws it into the empty depths of worklessness, where nothing is ever made of being.[3]

Can one say that this absolute denunciation of (the) work (and in a sense of historical time, of dialectical truth)—a denunciation that at times opens onto the literary work, at times confines itself to aberration, and at other times affirms itself in both—designates precisely the point at which there would be an exchange between aberration and creation, where, between mere idle chatter and originary speech, all language would still hesitate; where time, turning away from time and into the absence of time, would offer through its brilliance the image and the mirage of the Great Return that Nietzsche might, for an instant and before sinking into darkness, have held before his eyes? Naturally, one cannot say this. However, if one is never sure of being able to define this confrontation between unreason and madness or between madness and the work from the basis of its worklessness other than as a sterile relation, and if, in the same man (be this a Nietzsche), one can do no more than leave in their place—consigned to a strange face-to-face meeting and to a mutism that is pain—the being of tragic thought and the being of insanity (identical and without relation), there is nevertheless an event that has come to confirm, for culture itself, the value of this bizarre experience of un-Reason that the classical age, without knowing it, took upon itself (or exempted itself from). This event is psychoanalysis.

Here, too, Michel Foucault says with clarity and with depth what must begin to be said. For after the aggregate joining insanity, violence of the mind, frenzies of the heart, solitary disorder, and all the forms of a nocturnal transcendence comes progressively apart, after positivist psychiatry has imposed upon mental alienation the status of an object and thus definitively alienated it, there comes Freud: Freud who attempts to "bring madness and unreason back together and restore the possibility of dialogue." Once again something seeks to speak that for a long while had been silent or had no language other than lyrical fulguration, no form other than the fascination of art. "In psychoanalysis it is no longer a matter of psychology, but rather of the very experience of unreason modern psychology was meant to mask." Hence, also, the kind of complicity that links writers and those seeking a new language—a complicity that is not without misunderstandings inasmuch as psychoanalysts are reluctant to abandon some of the demands of the knowledge we call scientific, which wants to situate madness in a manner progressively more precise in the substantiality of a nature, and within a temporal, historical, and social framework (in reality, it is not yet a matter of science).

This reluctance is important, for it reveals one of the problems psychoanalysis comes up against: as though in confronting unreason and madness it were necessary to take into account two opposed movements. One of these points to a course back toward the *absence of time*—the return to a non-origin, an impersonal dive (this is the knowledge of Unreason); the other, on the contrary, develops in accordance with the sense of a history and repeats this history in certain of its moments. This duality is found in a few key notions, which, more or less successfully, are given currency by the various psychoanalytic schools. To this it must be added that the new orientation of psychoanalytic work undertaken in relation to Hegel, Heidegger, and linguistic research may perhaps find its reason (in spite of this apparent heterogeneity of reference) in a parallel question that we might formulate as follows: if madness has a language, and if it is even nothing but language, would this language not send us back (as does literature, although at another level) to one of the problems with which our time is dramatically concerned when it seeks to keep together the demands of dialectical discourse and the existence of a non-dialectical language, or, more precisely, a non-dialectical experience of language? This is an obscure and violent debate that Sade, following *Rameau's Nephew*, immediately brought into the light of our time. Meeting Unreason in one of the cells where he was confined with it, he delivered it up and proclaimed it, after more than a century of silence and to everyone's horror, to be speech and desire; a speech without end, desire without limit—and both offered, it is true, by way of an accord that does not cease to remain problematic. Yet it is nonetheless only on the basis of this enigmatic relation between thought, impossibility, and speech, that one can attempt to grasp the *general* importance of the *singular* works of art that culture rejects even as it receives them, just as culture denies, by objectifying them, the limit-experiences—works that therefore remain solitary, almost anonymous, even when one speaks of them. I am thinking of one of the most solitary works, the one to which, as though out of friendship and in play, Georges Bataille lent his name.

IX

The Limit-Experience

1
Affirmation and the passion of negative thought

Permit me, in thinking of Georges Bataille, to think in proximity to an absence rather than claiming to set forth what everyone should be able to find in his books—books that in no way constitute a minor part, the simple trace of a presence that has disappeared. They say the essential and they are essential. Not only by their beauty, their brilliance, and their literary force, which finds its equal in no other writer, but also by their relation to the research to which they bear witness. It is even surprising that a thought so removed from booklike coherence should without betrayal have been able to affirm itself to this extent in a work that reading still has the power to reach. That reading can reach, providing it grasp the work in the entirety of its expression and retain as its center (next to the *Interior Experience*, *Guilty*, and *Part Maudite*) the books Georges Bataille published under a name other than his own, and whose force of truth is without comparison: I am thinking especially of *Madame Edwarda*, of which I have spoken in the past, calling it rather feebly "the most beautiful narrative of our time."

A reading such as I suggest ought to efface the epithets by which one seeks to make what one is reading interesting. To be sure, bringing the words mysticism, eroticism, and atheism together attracts attention. To speak of a contemporary writer as a man who went into ecstasy, engaged in irreligion, praised debauchery, replaced Christianity with Nietzscheanism and Nietzscheanism with

202

Hinduism, after having hung around surrealism (I resume some well-intentioned accounts), is to offer thought as a spectacle and create a fictional character with little concern for the niceties of truth. Where would this need to seek the true solely at the level of anecdote and by way of a false picturesque come from? Of course each of us, as we know, is menaced by his Golem, that crude clay image, our mistaken double, the derisory idol that renders us visible and against which, living, we protest by the discretion of our life, but once we are dead perpetuates us. How can it be kept from making our disappearance (even the most silent) the moment at which, condemned to appear, we must precipitately answer to public interrogation by admitting to what we were not? And sometimes it is our closest friends, with the good intention of speaking in our place and so as not to abandon us too quickly to our absence, who contribute to this benevolent or malevolent travesty through which we will from now on be seen. No, there is no issue for the dead, nor for those who die after having written. In the most glorious posterity I have never discerned anything but a pretentious hell where critics—all of us— figure as rather poor devils.

I have reflected upon this at length, and I reflect upon it still. I do not see how to evoke in the proper terms a thought as extreme and as free, should one be content to repeat it. In general this is true of all commentary. The commentator is not being faithful when he faithfully reproduces; words, sentences, by the fact that they are cited, become immobilized and change meaning, or, on the contrary, take on too great a value. The very forceful expressions that Georges Bataille is allowed to employ belong to him, and under his authority they retain their measure; but should we happen to speak after him of despair, of horror, of ecstasy, of transport, we can only experience our own awkwardness—even more, our lies and falsification. I do not mean to say that employing an entirely different language, one deprived of these guiding words, would bring us closer to the truth, but at least the reading would remain intact by its more innocent accord with a thought that is preserved.

From this perspective, I think the work of an accompanying discourse—a work that should lean toward modesty—might limit itself to proposing a point from which one would better hear what only a reading can bring forth. This point, moreover, may vary. Let us seek a way to place ourselves so that the limit-experience, which Georges Bataille called the "interior experience," whose affirmation draws his own search to its greatest point of gravity, will not simply offer itself as a strange phenomenon, as the singularity of an extraordinary mind, but keep for us its power to question. I shall briefly recall what this experience is concerned with.

The limit-experience is the response that man encounters when he has decided to put himself radically in question. This decision involving all being expresses the impossibility of ever stopping, whether it be at some consolation or some truth, at the interests or the results of an action, or with the certitudes of knowledge and belief. It is a movement of contestation that traverses all of history, but that at times closes up into a system, at other times pierces the world to find its end in a beyond where man entrusts himself to an absolute term (God, Being, the Good, Eternity, Unity)—and in each case disavows itself. Let us note, however, that this passion of negative thought does not merge with skepticism, or even with the moves of a methodical doubt. It does not humble the one who bears it, does not strike him with powerlessness, does not judge him incapable of accomplishment. On the contrary; but here let us be more careful. It may be that the exigency of being all is fully realized in man. At bottom, man is already everything! He is so in his project, insofar as he is all the truth to come from that whole of the universe that holds only through him; he is so in the form of the sage whose discourse includes all the possibilities of a finished discourse; he is so from the perspective of a society freed from servitude. Should we not say that now and henceforth history is in some sense at its point of *completion?* This does not mean that nothing more will happen, nor that man, the individual man, will no longer have to endure the suffering and blindness of the future. But man, man as universal, is already master of all the categories of knowledge; he is capable of everything and he has an answer for everything (though it is true, only for everything, not for particular difficulties; and to this he also responds by prompting the particular to renounce itself, for the particular has no place in the truth of the whole). Of course, this is quickly said, and doubts can be raised as to this end of history to which we look forward. Some doubts, perhaps. But let us reflect still further: who in us is doubting? The small self that is weak, insufficient, unhappy, knowing almost nothing and closed up in the obstinacy of its ego. For this small self there is obviously only the end that is its own, one it regrets all the more for the fact that, in its egoism, this end does not have as its horizon everyone else's. This small reason either makes the self quickly renounce every reasonable way out, throwing it into the complacent torments of absurd existence,[1] or prepares it for hope of another life where it will recognize itself in God. So I repeat. For all of us, history, in one form or another, approaches its end ("save the denouement"). It approaches its end for the man of great reason because he thinks of himself as the whole and because he works without pause to make the world reasonable; for the man of small reason because, in a furious history deprived of an end, the end is as though at each moment already given; for the believer because, from now on, the beyond brings history gloriously and eternally to term. Yes, when we reflect upon this, we see that we all live more or less from the perspective of a terminated history, already seated beside the river, dying and being reborn, content with the contentment of the universe, and thus of God, through beatitude and knowledge.

Now the passion of negative thought admits this proud outcome that promises man his own end. It not only admits it, but works toward it; the action that engages us in this future is, in fact, nothing other than the "negativity" through which the man in us, negating nature and negating himself as a natural being, makes himself free through his bondage to work and produces himself in producing the world. This is admirable; man achieves contentment by deciding to be unceasingly discontent; he accomplishes himself because he carries through completely all his negations. Ought we not say that he touches the absolute since he would have the power to exercise totally, that is, *transform into action*, all his negativity? Let us say so. But scarcely having said this, we run up against this very assertion, as against the impossible that throws us backward; as though in saying it we were at the same time running the risk of effacing discourse. For it is here that the decisive contestation steps in. No, man does not exhaust his negativity in action; no, he does not transform into power all the nothingness that he is. Perhaps he can reach the absolute by making himself equal to the whole and by becoming conscious of the whole. But then more extreme than this absolute is the passion of negative thought; for faced with this response, negative thought is still capable of introducing the question that suspends it, and, faced with the accomplishment of the whole, still capable of maintaining the other exigency that again raises the issue of the infinite in the form of contestation.

Let us attempt to "clarify" this moment further. We are supposing man to be essentially satisfied; as universal man he has nothing more to do. He is without need, and even if individually he still dies, he is without beginning and without end, at rest in the becoming of his immobile totality. The limit-experience is the experience that awaits this ultimate man, the man who one last time is capable of not stopping at the sufficiency he has attained: the desire of he who is without desire, the dissatisfaction of he who is "wholly" satisfied, pure lack where there is nonetheless accomplishment of being. The limit-experience is the experience of what is outside the whole when the whole excludes every outside; the experience of what is still to be attained when all is attained and of what is still to be known when all is known: the inaccessible, the unknown itself. But let us see why we are able to lend to man what we will still call, inappropriately, this "possibility." It is not a matter of extorting an ultimate refusal from the vague discontent that accompanies us up to the end; it is not even a matter of the power to say no by which everything in the world is done—each value, each authority being overturned by another that is each time more far-reaching. What our proposition implies is something very different. Precisely this: there belongs to man, such as he is, such as he will be, an essential lack from which this right to put himself in question, and always in question, comes.[2]

So we have returned to our preceding remark: man is the being that does not exhaust his negativity in action. Thus when all is finished, when the "doing" (by which man also makes himself) is done, when, therefore, man has nothing left to do, he must, as Georges Bataille expresses it with the most simple profundity, exist in a state of "negativity without employ." The interior experience is the manner in which this radical negation, a negation that has nothing more to negate, is *affirmed*. One might well say that man has at his disposal a capacity for dying that greatly and in a sense infinitely surpasses what he must have to enter into death, and that out of this excess of death he has admirably known how to make for himself a power. Through this power, denying nature, he has constructed the world, he has put himself to work, he has become a producer, a self-producer. Nonetheless, a strange thing, this is not enough: at every moment he is left as it were with a part of dying that he is unable to invest in activity. Most often he does not know this, he hasn't the time. But should he come to sense this surplus of noth-ingness, this unemployable vacancy, should he discover himself to be bound to the movement that causes him, each time a man dies, to die infinitely, should he allow himself to be seized by the infinity of the end, then he must respond to an-other exigency—no longer that of producing but of spending, no longer that of succeeding but of failing, no longer that of turning out works and speaking use-fully but of speaking in vain and reducing himself to worklessness: an exigency whose limit is given in the "interior experience."

Now we are perhaps more fairly placed to recognize what is at stake in such a situation, and why Georges Bataille has captured it with the thought of sover-eignty. For at first glance one would have the right not to let oneself be taken in by the exceptional nature of these surprising states. A man becomes ecstatic. Al-though this may be an extraordinary gift, how would the fact of having reached such a state impart anything to those to whom it would remain foreign; and how would it modify, perhaps extend, human space? Would we not be submitting to the attraction that the word mystical holds for us? And would not the stirring of interest that surprises us when someone speaks of ecstatic transport come from a religious legacy whose trustees we remain? Mystics have always benefited from a special status in the church, and even outside it: they unsettle dogmatic comfort and are troubling. They are sometimes strange, sometimes scandalous; but they are apart, not only because they remain the bearers of an evidency beyond any-thing visible, but because they participate in and contribute to the ultimate act: the unification of being, the fusion of "earth" and "heaven." We ought, then, to be wary of these marvels. And we ought to say that the severe and untiring chal-lenge to every religious presupposition—as well as to every revelation and spiritual certainty that is implied by the "mystical" inclination—belongs essen-tially and in the first place to the movement we are describing.

Whoever has bound himself through the most firm decision to the passion of negative thought will at the very least begin by not stopping at God any more than at God's silence or absence, and, more important still, will not let himself be tempted by the repose offered by Unity, no matter what form it may take. We can represent things in still another way: in the schema I have used to speak rather figuratively of the end of history, let us understand that the entire meaning ex-pressed by the name of the highest is again taken up by human activity where it burns with a clear flame in the fire of Action and Discourse. At the point to which we have come, "the end of time," man has in a sense already rejoined the point omega. This means that there is no longer any Other other than man, and that there is no longer any Outside outside him since, affirming the whole by his very existence, he includes and comprehends the whole of everything as he includes and comprehends himself as being within this closed circle of knowledge.

Thus, at present, the problem brought forth by the limit-experience is the following: how can the absolute (in the form of totality) still be gotten beyond? Having arrived at the summit by his actions, how can man—he the universal, the eternal, always accomplishing himself, always accomplished and repeating himself in a Discourse that does no more than endlessly speak itself—not hold to this sufficiency, and go on to put himself, as such, in question? Properly speaking, he cannot. And yet the interior experience insists upon this event that does not belong to possibility; it opens in this already achieved being an infinitesimal interstice by which all that is suddenly allows itself to be exceeded, deposed by an addition that escapes and goes beyond. A strange surplus. What is this excess that makes the conclusion ever and always unfinished? Whence comes this movement of exceeding whose measure is not given by the power that is capable of everything? What is this "possibility," after the realization of every possibility, that would offer itself as the moment capable of reversing or silently withdrawing them all?

When Georges Bataille responds to these questions in speaking of *the impossible*, one of the last words he made public, he must be rigorously understood; it must be understood that possibility is not the sole dimension of our existence, and that it is perhaps given to us to "live" each of the events that is ours by way of a double relation. We live it one time as something we comprehend, grasp, bear, and master (even if we do so painfully and with difficulty) by relating it to some good or to some value, that is to say, finally, by relating it to Unity; we live it another time as something that escapes all employ and all end, and more, as that which escapes our very capacity to undergo it, but whose trial we cannot escape. Yes, as though impossibility, that by which we are no longer able to be able, were waiting for us behind all that we live, think, and say—if only we have been once at the end of this waiting, without ever falling short of what this surplus or addition, this surplus of emptiness, of "negativity," demanded of us and that is in us the infinite heart of the passion of thought.[3]

Here we begin to discern what I will name (without the least disparagement) the intellectual importance of the limit-experience, and also why this importance does not come from its singularity, but from the movement that leads up to it and from which it is inseparable since its singular traits do no more than express, in a single movement and even as a kind of flash, the infinite of putting into question. This is what first must be said again: the ecstatic "loss of knowledge" is nothing but the grasping seizure of contestation at the height of rupture and dispossession. The experience is not an outcome. It does not satisfy, it is without value, without sufficiency, and only such that it frees all human possibilities from their meaning:

every knowledge, every speech, every silence, every end, and even this capacity-for-dying from which we draw our last truths. But, here again, we must keep from concluding lightly by ascribing it to some sort of irrationalism or by relating it to a philosophy of the absurd. This non-knowledge, said to *communicate ecstasy*, in no way takes from knowledge its validity, any more than non-sense, momentarily embodied in experience, would turn us away from the active movement by which man tirelessly works to give himself meaning. On the contrary, let me insist again: it is only beyond an achieved knowledge (the knowledge affirmed by Lenin when he announces that "everything" will one day be understood) that non-knowledge offers itself as the fundamental exigency to which one must respond; no longer this non-knowledge that is still only a mode of comprehension (knowledge put in brackets by knowledge itself), but the mode of relating or of holding oneself in a relation (be it by way of existence) where relation is "impossible."

This said, there remains something difficult. Let me recall a preceding proposition: interior experience is the manner in which the radical negation that no longer has anything to negate *is affirmed*. This is what we have just attempted to clarify by stating that this experience cannot be distinguished from contestation. But then what kind of affirmation has it fallen to such a moment to bring forth? In what way can we claim that it affirms? It affirms nothing, reveals nothing, communicates nothing. Then one might be content to say that the affirmation is this "nothing" communicated, or the incompletion of the whole seized in a feeling of plenitude. But in this case, we run the risk of substantializing this "nothing," that is, we risk substituting for the absolute-as-a-whole its most abstract moment: the moment at which nothing immediately passes into the whole and in turn unduly totalizes itself. Or are we to see here a last dialectical reversal, the last degree (but a degree pertaining to no scale) on the basis of which man, this intellect accomplished in proportion to the universe, would send the entire edifice back into the night and, doing away with this universal intellect, still receive from this ultimate negation a light, a supplementary affirmation that would add to the whole the truth of the sacrifice of the whole? Despite the nature of such a movement — so immoderate that one cannot pretend to refuse it (assign to it a meaning precise enough to enable one to reject it, it not being deniable) — I would like to say that the limit-experience is still more extreme.

For this act of supreme negation we have just supposed (and that for Georges Bataille was no doubt for a time represented by the research of *Acéphale*) still belongs to the possible. Power, the power that is capable of everything, is able even to do away with itself as a power (the explosion of the nucleus itself being one of the extremes of nihilism). Such an act will in no way make us accomplish the decisive step, the step that would deliver us over — in a sense without ourselves — to the surprise of impossibility by allowing us to belong to *this non-power that is not simply the negation of power*. For thought, the limit-experience represents something *like* a new origin. What it offers to thought is the essential gift, the prodigality of affirmation; an affirmation, for the first time, that is not a product (the result of a double negation), and that thereby escapes all the movements, oppositions and reversals of dialectical reason, which, having completed itself before this affirmation, can no longer reserve a role for it under its reign.

This event is hard to circumscribe. The interior experience affirms; it is pure affirmation and it does nothing but affirm. It does not even affirm itself, for then it would be subordinate to itself: it rather affirms affirmation. It is for this reason that Georges Bataille can consent to saying that this affirmation, after having discredited every possible authority and dissolving even the idea of authority, holds within itself the moment of authority. This is the decisive Yes. Presence without anything being present. Through this affirmation, an affirmation that has freed itself from every negation (and consequently from every meaning), that has relegated and deposed the world of values, that consists not in affirming, upholding, and withstanding what is, but rather holds itself above and outside being, and that therefore does not answer to ontology any more than to the dialectic, man sees himself assigned—between being and nothingness, and out of the infinite of this between-two that is entertained as relation—the status of his new sovereignty: the sovereignty of a being without being in the becoming without end of a death impossible to die. Thus the limit-experience is experience itself: thought thinking that which will not let itself be thought; thought thinking more than it is able by an affirmation that affirms more than can be affirmed. This more itself is the experience: affirming only by an excess of affirmation and, in this surplus, affirming without anything being affirmed—finally affirming nothing. An affirmation by way of which everything escapes and that, itself escaping, escapes unity. This is even all one can say about it: it does not unify, nor does it allow its own unification. Hence it would appear to be in play on the side of the multiple, and in what Georges Bataille names "chance"; as though in order to put it *into play*, one not only had to attempt to give thought over to chance (an already difficult gift), but also (in a world in principle unified and stripped of all accident) had to give oneself over to the sole thought that would issue another *throw of the dice* by thinking in the only affirmative manner and at the level of pure affirmation: that of the interior experience.

Such an affirmation cannot be maintained. It cannot maintain itself, and even always runs the risk, in placing itself in the service of force, of turning against the sovereignty of man by becoming an instrument of his domination, going so far as appearing to grant to an "I" who thinks it has attained it the arrogant right to call itself henceforth the great Affirmer. The pretension of the "I" is the sign of its imposture. The self has never been the subject of this experience. The "I" will never arrive at it, nor will the individual, this particle of dust that I am, nor even the self of us all that is supposed to represent absolute self-consciousness. Only the ignorance that the I-who-dies would incarnate by acceding to the space where in dying it never dies in the first person as an "I" will reach it. Thus it is necessary to indicate one last time the strangest and most weighty trait of this situation. We speak as though this were an experience, and yet we can never say we have undergone it. An experience that is not lived, even less a state of our self; at most a *limit-experience* at which, perhaps, the limits fall but that reaches us only at the limit: when the entire future has become present and, through resolution of the decisive Yes, there is affirmed the ascendency over which there is no longer any hold.

The experience of non-experience.

Detour from everything visible and invisible.

If man did not in some sense already belong to this detour that he most often employs to turn himself away from it, how could he set out along this path that soon disappears—having in view the attainment of what escapes both aim and sight, advancing as though backward toward a point he only knows he will not reach in person, a point at which nothing of him will arrive and where, forever absent, he will not even find the night as a response (the night with its nocturnal privileges, its vanishing immensity, its calm empty beauty) but rather the *other* night, false, vain, eternally restless and eternally falling back into its own indifference? How could he desire this? How, desiring it with a desire that is without hope and without knowledge, making him a being without horizon, a desire for what cannot be attained, a desire that refuses all that might fulfill it, a desire therefore for this infinite lack, this indifference that desire is; a desire for the impossibility of desire, bearing the impossible, hiding it and revealing it, a desire that, in this sense, is the blow of the inaccessible, the surprise of the point that is reached only insofar as it is beyond reach and where the proximity of the remote offers itself only in its remoteness—how could thought, supposing that it might for an instant have affirmed itself there, ever return from such a blow and bring back, if not a new knowledge, at least what thought would need in order to hold itself, at the distance of a memory, in its keeping?

The response is unexpected. It is not perhaps the one that Georges Bataille would have wished to give, or even have ratified. And yet it is he himself, his books, the surprise of his language, the often unique tone of this silent discourse that permit us to propose it: speech entertains what no existent being in the primacy of his own name can attain; what existence itself, with the seduction of its fortuitous particularity, with the play of its slipping universality, could never hold within itself. And not only does speech retain what decidedly escapes in this manner, but it is on the basis of this always foreign and always furtive affirmation—the impossible and the incommunicable—that it speaks, finding there its origin, just as it is in this speech that thought thinks more than it can. And no doubt this is not just any speech. It does not contribute to discourse, it does not add anything to what has already been formulated; it would wish only to lead to what, outside all community, would come to "communicate" itself if, finally, when "everything" was consummated, there was nothing more to say: saying at this point the ultimate exigency.

Experience is this exigency, is only as exigency, and is such that it never offers itself as accomplished since, going beyond all memory, no memory could confirm it and since forgetting—the immense forgetting that is borne by speech—is alone proportionate to it.

It belonged to Georges Bataille to be the respondent of this affirmation that is the most transparent and the most opaque (the obscure by way of a transparency), an affirmation of which man has no memory, but that remains in the waiting attention of language. To him fell the task of holding open the relation to it and of alerting us, almost despite ourselves and from a distance, to this relation that was his sole measure, a measure of extreme pain and extreme joy. I would add that, far from claiming to keep it solely for himself, his constant concern was that it should not be affirmed in solitude but communicated, although it is also an affirmation of solitude. He once called it *friendship*, the most tender of names. Because his entire work expresses friendship, friendship for the impossible that is man, and because we receive from it this gift of friendship as a sign of the exigency that relates us infinitely and sovereignly to ourselves, I would like to say again what, citing Nietzsche's judgment of Zarathustra, I wrote many years ago when the *Interior Experience* appeared, and that twenty years of thought, of attention, of recognition and friendship have rendered always more true for me: "This work is entirely apart."

2
The play of thought

I would like to attempt to complete the preceding reflections by taking them up again in another form, starting with the following: in a manner perhaps unique in our society, Georges Bataille had the power to speak no less than the power to write. I allude not to the gift of eloquence, but to something more important: the fact of being present through his speech and, in this presence of speech, through the most direct conversation, of opening attention even unto the center. Not that he was prepared to play a Socratic role, initiate some sort of teaching, or even act in the subtle fashion that the words one utters will allow. Even less than Nietzsche would he have wished to move on the impulse to be right or to exercise influence, whether by the intermediary of signs or by example.

For independently of both content and form, what this power of saying made manifest to every interlocutor is that speaking is a grave thing: as soon as one speaks, even in the most simple manner and of the most simple facts, something unmeasured, something always waiting in the reserve of familiar discourse is immediately at stake. Here is the first gift this true speech gave us: speaking is our fortune, our chance, and to speak is to go in search of chance, the chance of a relation "immediately" without measure. There is another gift linked to this gravity: speaking is levity itself. Most often when we speak, and also when we hear someone else speaking, we do not fail afterward to experience a feeling of discomfort, as though some shame were attached to using words, whether to say important or insignificant things; in the first case, because we have betrayed them by speaking too adroitly or too awkwardly, in the second, because we have betrayed the seriousness of speech itself. I do not mean to say that every conversation with Georges Bataille was free of this feeling, but rather that speech then took up its own malaise, and as soon as it was sensed, assumed it and respected it in such a way as to offer it another direction. Here speech's lack interceded on speech's behalf, becoming the way that, through a decision each time renewed, one turned toward the other so as to respond to the frankness of a presence (just as the eminence of being, its height, cannot be separated from its decline).

We should come back to this idea of a presence that is tied to the act of speaking. This presence is rare. It is not to be confused with the traits of a particular physical reality. Even the visage in its unforgettable, visible affirmation is not manifest as speech can be when presence announces itself in it. The theatrical magic of the voice, the premeditated wiles of expression, and even the immediate manifestation of any perceptible movement must be excluded here. What is present in this presence of speech, as soon as it affirms itself, is precisely what never lets itself be seen or attained: something is there that is beyond reach (of the one who says it as much as of the one who hears it). It is between us, it holds itself between, and conversation is approach on the basis of this between-two: an irreducible distance that must be preserved if one wishes to maintain a relation with the unknown that is speech's unique gift.

The movement of the most simple communication therefore has its own proper conditions, for in each word uttered everything is already in play. We never speak without deciding whether the violence of reason that wants to give proof and be right or the violence of the possessive self that wants to extend itself and prevail will once again be the rule of discourse. In the precaution from which Georges Bataille never considered himself free, even when speaking with a very old friend, there was no prudence nor even simply a concern for the interlocutor. There was much more: a silent appeal to attention so as to confront the risk of a speech spoken in common, also an accord with this reserve that alone allows one to say everything, and, finally, an allusion to a movement toward the unknown to which, almost immediately, two persons together who are bound by something essential are as though obliged to bear witness. A precautionary speech, turned toward the interior, and by this precaution designating the impossible central thought that does not let itself be thought.

*

Here we should consider the proper meaning of such an oral movement, since it fell to Georges Bataille to give it a specific character of depth. Why speak rather than write? What comes to thought by way of this exigency that is carried out or missed when one speaks in a manner that involves thought directly? Let us recall that it is not a matter of teaching something or of extracting the truth by going from one interlocutor to another, as did Socrates in order to keep seeking the true through the vicissitudes of an unyielding conversation. But let us also recall that neither is it a matter—at least at this level—of what Jaspers calls a dialogue of existences; that movement by which two human beings enter into relation in a perceptible fashion, where indiscretion now becomes obligatory, and mystery presents itself only to be violated and profaned. If speaking requires this precaution that is a putting on alert rather than on guard it is because for thought there is no familiarity: what calls upon it is always the non-familiar. Thought does not recognize what it is aiming for; each time there is a new beginning and a decision to offer itself up to the non-known whose intention thought sustains. And yet this non-familiarity that the strangeness in speech preserves is also the intimacy of thought; it passes by way of this abrupt and silent, I mean implicit, intimacy that is destined to open within the known and frequentable space between two interlocutors another space where the habitual possibilities steal away. This other space opened by the non-familiar intimacy of thought is the space of attention. But let us immediately specify that it is not simply an attentive listener that the one speaking would have need of. This attention is between the one and the other: center of the encounter, sign of the between-two that brings close as it separates. Attention empties the site of all that encumbers it and renders it visible. This is a profound and at times painfully hollowed out absence on the basis of which, and in coinciding with it, the presence of speech is able to affirm itself. In the sense that this attention is the attention of no one, it is impersonal; but it is also, through speech and between those who are there, the very waiting for what is in play. Yet this attention also responds to an accord between two beings, each one carried forward by the decision to sustain the same movement of research and thus to be faithful (without faith and without guarantee) to this same rigorous movement. Here a mutual promise is made that commits the play of thought to a common openness in this game in which the players are two speaking beings and through which thought is each time asked to affirm its relation to the unknown.

Let us understand that what is at stake in this game is the essential: the reaching of an infinite affirmation. Let us also understand that, being deprived of all the rules and procedures of a game, including those of rhetoric, and with no resource other than the movement of the most simple speech, it could never for the participants be a question of winning, that is, of arguing or giving proof in view of some truth to be known. The players—I maintain this figure of speech, though it may lend itself to misunderstanding—are called upon, through the pursuit of this match (a match that for them is simply an endgame, but whose constant renewal plays with them in an unforeseeable manner) to become the momentary respondents of this thought of the unknown. Let us understand, then, why it can happen that speaking does not bow to writing. Speech bears in it the fortuitous trait that binds thought to chance through the game. Speech depends immediately upon life, on the humors and fatigues of life, and it opens to them as its secret truth: a weary player may be closer to the game's attention than the brilliant player who is master of himself and of his attention. Above all, speech is perishable. Scarcely said, it is effaced, lost without recourse. It forgets itself. In the intimacy of this speech forgetting speaks — not only a forgetting that is partial and limited but the profound forgetting out of which all memory arises. Whoever is speaking is already forgotten. Whoever speaks, almost without premeditation, gives himself over to forgetfulness in tying the movement of reflection — meditation, as Georges Bataille sometimes calls it — to this necessity of forgetting. Forgetting is master of the game.

*

Speaking with simplicity and with speech's light gravity, present through his speech not because he used it to express the pathos of a sensibility, but to affirm with reserve and caution the concern from which his interlocutors never heard him depart, Georges Bataille linked the detours of conversation to the unlimited play of thought. I would like to insist on this point. Generally, when we speak, we want to say something we already know — whether to share it with someone else because it seems true to us or, in the best case, to verify it by submitting it to a new judgment. Still more rare is a speech that reflects while expressing itself; perhaps because the disposition to speak does not favor reflection, which has need of silence and also of time, an empty, monotonous, and solitary time that one could not without discomfort share with another interlocutor who would in turn be silent. Yet in a certain kind of dialogue, this reflection may chance to come about by the sole fact that speech is divided and doubled: what is said a first time on one side is said again a second time on the other and is not only reaffirmed, but also (because there is repetition) raised to a new form of affirmation whereby, changing place, the thing that is said enters into relation with its difference and becomes sharper, more tragic: not more unified, but, on the contrary, tragically suspended between two poles of attraction. It is precisely to such a form of dialogue that a speech engaged in the game of thought leads: the speech Georges Bataille made present to us by a movement that was his own. The thought that plays with and has as its stakes the unlimited in thought — reaching an infinite affirmation — does not come about in the form of an invitation to question and answer, even less to affirm and then contest. It excludes all discussion and disregards all controversy (the work by which two men whose views are at variance bring their differences together, confronting one thesis with another in view of a dialectic reconciliation). In the dialogue we are considering, it is thought itself that puts itself at stake by calling upon us to sustain, and in the direction of the unknown, the limitlessness of this play—that is, when thinking, as Mallarmé would have it, is to issue a throw of the dice. In this movement it is a matter not of one or another way of seeing or conceiving, however important these may be; it is rather always a matter of an affirmation that is unique, the most far-reaching and the most extreme, even to the extent that once affirmed, it ought, exhausting thought, to relate it to an entirely different measure: the measure of what does not allow itself to be reached or be thought. This affirmation can only remain latent, withdrawn in relation to all that can be affirmed of it; not only because one cannot master it but because, bearing with it the infinitely distant relation from which comes all that is affirmed, it escapes all unity. A terrifying relation, says Georges Bataille; a relation that opens onto fear and yet to which speech, through its play, constantly engages us to respond: *"fear . . . yes the fear, which only the unlimited in thought can reach."*

On this basis, let us attempt to make more precise the nature of the dialogue that results from this situation. Rather than dialogue, we should name it plural speech. Plural speech, inasmuch as in its simplicity it is the seeking of an affirmation that, though escaping all negation, neither unifies nor allows itself to be unified but rather always refers to a difference always more tempted to defer. This is a speech that is essentially non-dialectical; it says the absolutely other that can never be reduced to the same or take a place in the whole. As though it were a matter of speaking only at the moment when, by previous decision, "the whole" is supposed to have already been said. Hence, it seems to me, the interlocutors' strange situation: they are bound by the essential yet they are not together since, properly speaking, where they are no whole is possible. Speaking in the same direction, they say the same thing, for they neither discuss nor speak of subjects able to be approached in diverse ways. Being the bearers of a speech that speaks in view of this unique affirmation that exceeds all unity, they do not oppose one another, nor are they in any way distinguishable as to what they have to say; and yet the redoubling of affirmation, its reflection, differentiates this affirmation always more profoundly, bringing to light the hidden difference that is proper to it and is its always unrevealed strangeness. Hence an understanding that, growing unceasingly more profound, is nonetheless an accord without accord, founded upon a hiatus that must not allow itself to be filled or even denounced.

One could say of these two speaking men that one of them is necessarily the obscure "Other" that is *Autrui*. And who is *Autrui*? The unknown, the stranger, foreign to all that is either visible or non-visible, and who comes to "me" as speech when speaking is no longer seeing. One of the two is the Other: the one who, in the greatest human simplicity, is always close to that which cannot be close to "me": close to death, close to the night. But who is me? Where is the Other? The self is sure, the Other is not—unsituated, unsituatable, nevertheless each time speaking and in this speech more Other than all that is other. Plural speech would be this unique speech where what is said one time by "me" is repeated another time by "*Autrui*" and thus given back to its essential Difference. What therefore characterizes this kind of dialogue is that it is not simply an exchange of words between two Selves, two beings in the first person, but that the Other speaks there in the presence of speech, which is his sole presence; a neutral speech, infinite, without power, and where the unlimited in thought, placed in the safekeeping of forgetting, is at stake.

*

Perhaps it is apparent why this form of expression goes beyond the very movement of communication. It exceeds all community and is not meant to communicate anything; nor does it establish between two beings a common relation, even by the intermediary of the unknown. (The unknown, as neutral, cannot serve as an intermediary inasmuch as every relation with it—this infinite affirmation—falls outside all relation.) This is also why such a plural speech, insofar as it aims neither at equality nor at reciprocity, could not pass for a simple dialogue. Certainly, the interlocutors would speak to one another as equals were they to speak to one another, but inasmuch as they respond to *Autrui*, whose speech at times coincides with the speaking of the one and at times with that of the other, there is each time between them an infinite difference that cannot be evaluated in terms of superiority or predominance. And, at the same time, let us not forget that this game of thought cannot be played alone; there must be two partners in play and they must engage in the game with the same decision, the same frankness, and the same relation to the stakes. To state this still more precisely, one could say that the conversation they hold, this movement of turning together toward the infinite of affirmation, is similar to the dialogue that occurs between two persons throwing dice: they dialogue not through the words they exchange—they are passionately silent—but through the dice each casts in turn, facing the immense night of unseizable chance that each time responds to them unpredictably. Here the two partners are not playing against each other; rather, by way of a game that separates them and brings them still closer, each plays for the other. And if, in this case, speech is the dice that are tossed out and fall again by a double movement in the course of which is accomplished the redoubling of affirmation we have evoked,[4] the dialogue will entail only two players playing a single time by a single throw of the dice, and with no gain other than *the very possibility of playing*; a possibility that does not depend on our capacity to attain anything when what is brought into play, through speech, is the unlimited in thought.

> *O the dice played*
> *from the depth of the tomb*
> *with fingers of fine night*
>
> *dice of birds of the sun*

I will not push any further our understanding of such an intense proposition. I shall only say, from the same perspective, that the non-familiar intimacy of thought between two men speaking who are bound by the essential establishes a distance and a proximity beyond measure. As exists perhaps between two gamblers. A non-personal intimacy from which the particularities of each person cannot be entirely excluded but, in principle, does not take them into account. Indeed each player may bring his particular existence into play, but as a player he is without particularity, introduced by the game into anonymity and reduced to the abstract truth of the infinite risk that takes from him all determined social reality: without history, without anecdote, himself an unknown through this relation with the unknown wherein he affirms himself, and each time asking (as though it were an implicit rule) that all that is known of him be forgotten, or at least not brought into the game. Relations that are strange, privileged, sometimes exclusive, and that can only with difficulty withstand being shared with others; relations of invisibility in full light that are guaranteed by nothing, and when they have endured over a lifetime represent the unforeseeable chance, the unique chance in view of which they were risked.

3
Insurrection, the madness of writing

(1) Sade is hard to read. His writing is clear, his style natural, his language without detour. Laying claim to logic, he reasons and is concerned solely with reasoning; free of prejudice, this reason speaks in order to convince and by appealing to truths to which it gives universal form. These truths seem to it so evident that every objection is energetically ascribed to superstition. Such is Sade's certainty. He aspires to reason, and it is reason that engrosses him; a reason he proposes to everyone and that will be seemly for everyone.

I believe Sade's relation to some manner of reason must not be forgotten (hence the demonstrative character of even his lesser writings, all derided by the standard-bearers of morality). And indeed how could the reader forget it, inasmuch as this claim to reason, a reasonable demand, is immediately encountered? But how could we not forget it, since we also immediately encounter everything that would belie it: the most shameless contradictions, arguments that cancel one another out, propositions that fail to stand up, an incoherency of vows and principles by which one may be either violently or imperceptibly surprised? Each one can verify this for himself. I shall cite only a general example, borrowed from the celebrated treatise entitled *Philosophy in the Bedroom*.[5] In the part dealing with religion, the author claims that if we want to have good citizens, good fathers, and good husbands, religion must be rejected; the reason being that frightened, ignorant, and servile men (as are all believers) are unable to fulfill their civic duties, having lost all sense of liberty. But in the second part of the treatise an entirely different ideal is recommended to us; it is proposed that children should be fatherless, it is decreed that men and women should live communally, and finally it is affirmed in the strongest of terms that the family should be abolished: *"Do not suppose you are fashioning good republicans so long as children, who ought to belong solely to the republic, remain immured in their families."*

Fine, we are convinced. At the same time or elsewhere, however, we become aware of a very different thought: children without fathers, yes, but not for the greatness of the republic, rather for the convenience of debauchery; women in common for men (and men in common for women), not for an honest communism of mores, but to facilitate recruitment for the establishments whose purpose is libertinage. As for the family, if at present there is no longer any haste to do away with it, this is better to preserve adultery as well as all the deviations that would be lost with the family — beginning with incest, about which Sade writes with his imperceptible humor: *"I dare to assert that incest ought to be the law of every government based upon fraternity."* Let us stop there. Persuaded of the author's unreason, one reader will put down the book; another will keep reading because of this unreason itself. I believe both would be wrong. Sade is perhaps mad (as we all must be in our beautiful nocturnal hours), but what he writes cannot fall under such a categorical judgment. The sign of this is that we come away from reading Sade less troubled in our sensibilities than belied in our manner of thinking. It is not that we are convinced; rather, we are offered as it were to a manner of understanding that escapes us and nonetheless draws us on. And thus despite ourselves and despite our desire for a simple logic, we again take up our reading, carried along by a movement there is no stopping.

(2) Something is being sought in Sade's writing. This search for a new lucidity does not proceed in the interrogative mode, but by clear, assured, and always-decisive assertions. This movement is proper to it. Analytical reason, with its postulates and demonstrative promptitude, is here put in service of an ultimate principle that cannot be discovered and whose allure takes no account of the determinations of the analysis. A combination of clarity and obscurity, this alliance is what troubles us, complicating our reading and making it inwardly violent. This violence is much stronger than that of the characters' cruel adventures, which serve as much to divert us from it as to represent it. Of course, one can say that Sade is content to receive this tranquil positive reason from his time, just as he receives from it his clear language, his linear and shadowless writing; and one will add that somehow or other he makes these serve truths and justifications with which they do not square. This has been said, and it can be supported. But I believe things must be put differently. The exigency of excess, which is what is extreme in Sade's thought and in his experience, does not only affirm its right to reason, nor is it simply content with knowing itself in accord with the principles

of a positive reason (atheist materialism), for it knows it is more reasonable than positive reason inasmuch as it pushes further than this reason the movement that inhabits it, and never allows itself to be frightened by any of the consequences. With Sade it is always a question of logic. He feels that his writing is more rigorous and even more coherent (a coherence that includes incoherence) than that of others; and the frenzy he lets invade his writing is most often that of a reason held in check, arrested in a progression that risks precipitating it into the abyss. One of Sade's truths is that reason is capable of an energetic becoming and is itself always in the process of becoming, being essentially movement. And one can say as well that this is the impulse that moves his work—an impulse that is certainly inordinate, but because to be reasonable is first of all always to be so excessively.

(3) Reason is excessive. I will not insist upon the various ways in which Sade's work explores this excessiveness. Counting them, to simplify, one might say there are three:

— One is of an encyclopedic nature. It is a matter of compiling an inventory of possibilities, precisely those that are held to be disordered and the most forceful manifestations of energy: those without which reason would cease being natural (cease being the fire kindled by nature, where nature burns and is incorruptibly consumed).

— The second is of a dialectical nature. We know now that this is one of the strongest traits of Sade's work. I refer here to the essay entitled "La Raison de Sade," as well as to the profound reflections of both Georges Bataille and Pierre Klossowski. When it is asserted that this gentleman libertine did no more than seek easy arguments in positive materialist principles capable of justifying his wicked behavior, when one adds that he is a phenomenon of his age and belongs to his time, one says what is true, even if one is obviously using Sade to discredit materialist atheism and at the same time hastening to reduce to the immorality of an epoch what in Sade is extreme. One says what is true, but only when it is recognized, first, that Sade in no way seeks to justify his conduct in his books—a conduct that always seemed to him quite ordinary; and, secondly, that had he sought to do so, this justification would in any case be senseless since it would only tend to show him virtually guilty of the enormous crimes he never came close to committing. But it is indeed the case that he seeks a meaning for the thought he does not distinguish, and rightly so, from the force of his imagination; it is true that he asks himself, in the affirmative mode: why am I able to think this, and to what excess of imagination can I go? What is the signification of these transports, this formidable movement that is perhaps unique, but, as such, in no way reserved solely for me and whose principle resides in a hidden reason? It is true that this is his preoccupation, and also that, present in all his work, it is always affirmed there as the work of a greater reason—a reason either preparing itself, modifying itself, or preparing itself by its own ruin. But why is this dialectical? Would there not be a certain complacency, or imprudence, in advancing this word that is destined to such a great future? Sade is not Hegel, not by any means. Nonetheless, I see no anachronism in calling dialectical, in the modern sense of this term, the essentially sadistic pretension to found the reasonable sovereignty of man upon a transcendent power of negation, a power that Sade does not fail to recognize in the principle of the most clear and simple positive reason. I refer to the infinite power of negation that expresses, and then by turns and by a circular experience annuls, the notions of man, of God, and of nature, in order, finally, to affirm the integral man, "the man unique in his genre"; also to the way in which an infinite negation, by coinciding with all the moments of its experience—a coincidence that is not a reconciliation but a flashing event—comes to seize itself once again as an affirmation, it, too, infinite. I believe that one cannot read Sade without recognizing that here indeed is the truth of the disordered movements that work themselves out in and by an enormous oeuvre.

— This truth seeks itself through the movement of writing: the third form that reveals the measure of an immoderate reason. Writing is the madness proper to Sade. It is not to be found in what Sade himself, and without hesitation, called the irregularity of his morals, which he saw in one regard as the simple effect of his constitution and, in another, more remarkably, as the sign of his freedom; a freedom that, setting him apart, liberated him from the prejudices of his society—to the point that he could affirm that the day society should no longer oppose them he would fervently give them up. A remarkable declaration. But he very quickly ceased to differentiate between himself and the solitude of his prison. From this buried solitude that horrified him (and doubly so: in itself, and through the sanction it represented), and from this horror turned into attraction, there originated and grew the irrepressible necessity of writing; a terrifying force of speech that would never be calmed. Everything must be said. The first liberty is the liberty to say everything. So he translates, in the form of a demand that for him will henceforth be inseparable from a true republic, the fundamental exigency. But let us note that the "whole" that is at stake in this freedom to say everything is no longer simply the universality of an encyclopedic knowledge (be it the knowledge of our perverse possibilities); nor is it the totality of an experience wherein meaning is accomplished by the movement of a negation pushed to its term—a circular discourse, closed and achieved, that affirms mastery of the whole.

This saying everything, which is heard in his books as the prodigious repetition of an eternal speaking—eternally clear and eternally empty—goes still further. Here it is no longer the whole of the possible that is offered and expressed. Nor is it, as has been too readily believed, the set of values that a religion, a society, and a morality have prohibited us from asserting. Interdiction certainly plays its role as a limit that must, in this movement of illimitation, be gone beyond. But this is in no way the ultimate limit. And Sade may very well experience pleasure, a simple and healthy pleasure, in the forceful scenes he imagines, in which all the truths of his time are flouted, where he says all that is not to be said and recommends the unspeakable. The blasphemy to be uttered, the evil to be exalted, the criminal passions to be sustained: for him these are the least of the things of which he will not be deprived, but with which it is not a question of being content. Something more violent comes to light in this frenzy of writing, a violence that cannot be either exhausted or appeased by the excesses of a superb and ferocious imagination, but that is nonetheless always inferior to the transports of a language that will not tolerate stopping any more than it can conceive of a term. All the more forceful for being simple, this violence is affirmed by a speech without equivocation, without ulterior motive, saying everything without further ado and leaving nothing dissimulated, thus speaking purely—pure of the dishonest obscenity that the majestic emotions of a Chateaubriand will soon impose upon language, and without any law to denounce it. Sade's major impropriety resides in the simply repetitive force of a narration that encounters no interdict (the whole of this limit-work recounting the interdict by way of the monotony of its terrifying murmur) because there is no other time than that of the interval of speaking [*l'entre-dire*]: the pure arrest that can be reached only by never stopping speaking.

(4) Writing is the madness proper to Sade. Liberation from prison does not free him from this madness that was acquired in prison, or at least came in prison to be what it is, an always clandestine and subterranean force; liberty rather redoubles it by another madness that will make him believe that such a madness can be affirmed in the light of the day and as the reserve or the future of a common possibility. Thus for an instant, the moment when revolution encounters philosophy in chains,[6] these two hiatuses in history, certainly very different, coincide; the one founding an era and opening history, the other being that from which history will always want to close itself off.

I will not enter into an examination of Sade's political conduct during the course of those years, when (to the great dismay of the virtuous souls of the revolution, and to the great satisfaction of those of the counter-revolution) he was an "active citizen," spoke and wrote against the king, spoke and wrote in tribute to Marat, appeared at the Convention where he moreover took the floor, presided over the Piques Section (that of Robespierre), proposed a cult without gods, supported and had adopted his own ideas regarding sovereignty, gave revolutionary names to the streets of Paris, and was even (not without pleasure) a prosecuting magistrate. One might untiringly discuss whether he acted sincerely or hypocritically, whether his sentiments were in accord with his comportment and outward declarations. I do not believe there is much mystery here. He himself changed opinion. This was true of them all, even Saint-Just and Robespierre (who were not the first to demand the fall of the monarchy), simply because the truth of events always outdistanced thought. He was prudent, yet without real prudence and always something less than unstable, showing an instability that was a fidelity to the swiftness of becoming. Whether prudent or not, nothing would have hindered him from remaining apart or attempting to flee; he could have done so. Even taking into account all the other reasons that may have kept him in Paris, there is hardly any doubt that he took the most lively interest in events, and that an entire part of him recognized itself in what was happening. Which part? That obscure (extravagant) part that, without succeeding in making of him a true (a socially plausible) writer, condemned him to write endlessly. I think the word coincidence is the most fitting. With Sade—and in a very high form of paradoxical truth—we have the first example (but is there a second?) of the way in which writing, the freedom to write, can coincide with the movement of true freedom, when the latter enters into crisis and gives rise to a vacancy in history. A coincidence that is not an identification. For Sade's motives are not those that had set the forces of revolution into motion; they even contradict them. And yet without them, without the mad excess that the name, the life, and the truth of Sade have represented, the revolution would have been deprived of a part of its Reason.

(5) To arrive at an idea of Sade's political conceptions, it will, I think, suffice to cite only a few texts. Marked by an invisible irony, the very title of the treatise already referred to, "Yet Another Effort, Frenchmen . . . ," speaks to us clearly enough. It says that living in a republic will not suffice to make a republican, nor will a republic be made by having a constitution, nor, finally, will laws make this constitutive act that is the creative power endure and maintain us in a state of permanent constitution. We must make an effort, and still always another—this is the invisible irony. Hence the conclusion, barely hinted at, that the revolutionary era is only just beginning. But what kind of effort will it be? Who will require it of us? Sade calls this permanent state of the republic insurrection. In other words, a republic knows no state, only movement—in this it is identical to nature. This perpetual perturbation is necessary, first of all, because the republican government is surrounded by enemy governments that hate it and are jealous of it (the thesis of being closed in); there is no peace for man once he has been roused: revolutionary vigilance excludes all tranquility, thus the only way to preserve oneself henceforth is never to be conservative, that is to say, never at rest. A situation that Sade judges irreconcilable with ordinary morality, which is no more than inertia and sleep: *For the state of a moral man is one of peace and tranquility, while the state of an immoral man is one of a perpetual unrest that pushes him to, and identifies him with, the necessary insurrection in which the republican must always keep the government of which he is a member.*

This is a first reason, but there is another given to us by way of a very bold reflection: today all the nations that want to govern themselves as republics are not only threatened by violence from without, but also, because of their past, are themselves already inwardly violent or, according to the terminology of the time, criminal and corrupt. How can they surmount this somber inherited violence if not by a violence that is stronger and also more terrible because it is without tradition and, in a sense, originary? The virtue that all its legislators place at the basis of the Republic would be in keeping with it only if we were able to achieve it without the past—outside history and beginning history with it. But he who is already in history is already in crime, and will not escape from it without increasing both the violence and the crime. (A thesis we may well recognize—but calling it Hegelian and being scandalized by it does not suffice to keep it from being true.) But will we ever depart from it? And what will the difference be? What will we have gained? First of all, a change in vocabulary: what we used to call crime will be called energy; an insignificant change, yet one of great consequence. The world to come will not be a world of values. Neither good and evil nor virtue and vice will constitute its poles; rather, a relation to the principle to which affirmation and negation answer when they are pushed to their fullest measure and identify with one another. When Sade writes *"All is good when it is excessive,"* this excess (which is different from the state of effervescence that passes through what Dolmancé calls apathy) designates a state of high tension and clear insensibility that is the sole morality of energetic man; it also designates the kind of sovereignty he can lay claim to in this movement of liberty that, even in self-concentration, causes him to feel himself no longer distinct from the dissolution that is the common trait of the whole. Excess, energy, dissolution: these are the key words of the new epoch.[7]

(6) Let us reread now, in their entirety, the two passages to which I just alluded. I think we will grasp them better on the basis of this general idea of the whole in which they find their place. *"The Greek legislators had perfectly appreciated the necessity of corrupting the member-citizens in order that, their moral dissolution having an effect upon that dissolution useful to the machine of government, there would result the insurrection that is always indispensable to a political system of perfect happiness, which, like the republican government, must necessarily excite the hatred and envy of all its surrounding neighbors. These wise legislators believed that insurrection was not a moral state, but that it ought to be the permanent state of a republic; hence it would be no less absurd than dangerous to require that those who are to insure the perpetual immoral perturbation of the governing order themselves be moral beings: for the moral state of man is one of peace and tranquility, whereas the state of immoral man is one of perpetual unrest that pushes him to, and identifies him with, the necessary insurrection in which the republican must always keep the government of which he is a member."* And here is the second text, no less striking: *"A most singular thought comes to mind, but if it is audacious it is also true, and I will mention it. A nation that begins by governing itself as a republic will only be sustained by virtues because, in order to attain the most, one must always start with the least. But an already old and corrupt nation that courageously casts off the yoke of its monarchical government in order to adopt a republican one will only be maintained by many crimes; for it is criminal already, and if it were to wish to*

pass from crime to virtue, that is to say, from a violent to a tranquil state, it would fall into an inertia whose result would soon be its certain ruin."[8]

I grant, in rereading this passage, that here the word crime is entirely necessary and ought to conserve its power both to evoke and to provoke. Crime has the brilliant force, the defiant freedom, and the beauty of an appeal that always causes Sade's speech, as well as his heart, to rise up, as it does to no less a degree the austere language of the Revolution. Is it Sade or Saint-Just who wrote *"Nothing resembles virtue like serious crime"*? And there is this affirmation, more enigmatic than it seems: *"Virtue embraces crime in times of anarchy."* And this recommendation, destined to resound severely at the Society of the Jacobins, *"Arm virtue with the dexterity of crime against crime,"* where, with a spirit of frankness, it would suffice to substitute violence for dexterity (how could the rectitude of the act here be anything but violent?) to find once again what is essential in Sade. Finally, when Saint-Just from his very first speech praises energy by saying *"Energy is not force,"* he says something that Sade's entire work also seeks to say more passionately. (The last moral of *Justine and Juliette* comes to mind: it is not in accordance with the greater or lesser degree of virtue or vice that human beings are happy or unhappy, but according to the energy they display; for *"happiness is proportionate to the energy of principles; no one who endlessly wavers would ever be capable of experiencing it."*) Let us again read Saint-Just: *"The solution is in the real insurrection of minds."* And Sade: *"Insurrection . . . ought to be the permanent state of the republic."* What is it that distinguishes, I will not say these two men, who are as foreign and as close as two contemporaries can be, but these two equally absolute sentences? It is clear. For Sade, insurrection ought to be as much an insurrection of morals as an insurrection of ideas; it ought to reach all men and the whole of every man; still more, it ought to be permanent, all the while being excessive. Subversion should constitute the only permanent feature of our life; it should always be carried to its highest point, that is to say, always closer to its term, since where there is energy as a reserve of force, there is energy as an expenditure of force: an affirmation that is accomplished only by the greatest negation. I understand that one will wish here to denounce this utopia, and the danger of utopia (which at least has the advantage of being not simply a utopia of evil). But let us leave judgments aside.

(7) A third text ought to help us orient our interpretation still further. I borrow it from part four of *The Story of Juliette: "The reign of laws is vicious; thus lawful rule is inferior to anarchy; the greatest proof whereof is the government's obligation to plunge the State into anarchy whenever it wishes to reframe a new constitution. To abrogate its former laws it is driven to establish a revolutionary regime in which there are no laws at all: from this regime new laws finally emerge. But this second State is necessarily less pure than the first, since it derives from the earlier one, and since in order to achieve its goal, constitution, it had first to install anarchy."* A text apparently very clear, and moreover illuminated by many

others in which Sade affirms that there does not exist a single free government. And what is the reason for this? Because man everywhere is, and will be, the victim of laws. Laws are capable of an injustice that always makes them more dangerous than any individual impulse. The dangerous passion of a single man may do me harm, but within the limits determined by my own passion. Against the law, which everywhere constrains me, there is no recourse: the law wants me always to be deprived of myself, always without passion, that is to say mediocre, and before long stupid. Hence these critiques that recur in countless forms: the law is unjust because it holds power and usurps sovereignty, which, in its essence, must never be delegated; invented to curb the passions of my neighbor, the law will perhaps preserve me from them but it leaves me without guarantee against its own affirmations, which are the most corrupt and most cruel because they never represent anything free but only a force that is cold and without liberty; finally, they weaken and render false the just relations of men, whether these be with nature or with the future of knowledge: *"But for laws and religion there is no imagining the degree of grandeur and glory human knowledge would have attained today; no imagining how these infamous curbs have held back progress. . . . Priests dare inveigh against the passions; lawyers dare to fetter them with laws. . . . It is to strong passions alone that invention and artistic wonders are due. . . . Those individuals who are not moved by strong passions are but mediocre beings; man becomes stupid as soon as he is no longer impassioned."*[9] This series of certainties comes to a close with this impressive affirmation: *"It is only at the moment when the law is silent that great actions burst forth."* But as it is clear that such an affirmation will remain beyond the reach of most, better to conclude with a compromise: if we must have laws, let them be few and mild; if the law must "chastise" those one persists in calling guilty, let it not claim to improve them; finally, never let the law encroach upon life itself, on this point compromise is impossible: for how can a people delegate its right to exist, that is, finally, its right to death, if it cannot communicate its right to be sovereign? *"Whatever veneration J.-J. Rousseau's authority imposes upon me, I cannot forgive you, oh great man, for having justified the right to give death."* A challenge, in fact, that does not come from Sade, but, once more, from Saint-Just. This does not mean that the latter would have taken up as his own the petition for anarchy. Nothing would have horrified him more. The word *law*, when pronounced by Saint-Just, has the same strange resonance and the same purity on his lips, it seems to me, as does the word *crime* on Sade's. Nonetheless, precisely because the law is always above any particular law and always vilified by precepts, Saint-Just, too, demands that there be few of them (*"where there are too many, the people are slaves"*); he asserts that laws that are too lengthy are a public calamity, and refuses whatever might, in the name of the law, make sacred the force of civil repression, of which he says with his sublime inflexibility: *"I will not consent to submit to any law that supposes me intractable and corrupt."* And elsewhere, in a concise sentence that expresses almost everything: *"The citizen first has relations only with his conscience and morality; should he forget them, he has a relation with the law; should he scorn the law, he is no longer a citizen: here begins his relation with power."* As a result, the law is but the beginning step in a long process of degradation at the end of which authority, become oppressive, will drown in laws, as happened under the monarchy. *"It is not evident that the law must be obeyed." "Too many laws, too few civil institutions." "If you want to found a Republic, take from the people as little power as possible." "If you want to return man to freedom, make laws only for him, do not crush him under the weight of power."* Under the monarchy *"the law made a crime of the purest of penchants"* — a declaration in alexandrine form that Sade would have readily accepted, just as he would have always recognized that *"tyranny has an interest in the softness of the people."* The reason being that tyranny is strong only through a dwindling of energy, for energy, in Sade's view the sole true principle, is alone capable of limiting tyranny.

(8) Sade therefore calls the pure time of suspended history marking an epoch a revolutionary regime; it is the time of the between-times where, between the old laws and the new, there reigns the silence of the absence of laws, an interval that corresponds precisely to the suspension of speech [*l'entre-dire*] when everything ceases, everything is arrested, including the eternal speaking drive, because then there is no more interdiction. Moment of excess, of dissolution, and of energy; a moment during which — Hegel will say this some years later — being is nothing other than the movement of the infinite, which suppresses itself and is endlessly born in its own disappearance: "bacchanal of truth when no one can remain sober." Always pending, this instant of silent frenzy is also the instant at which man, by a cessation wherein he affirms himself, attains his true sovereignty; he is no longer only himself, not only nature (natural man), but that which nature never is: consciousness of the infinite power of destruction — that is, of negation — through which consciousness ceaselessly makes and undoes itself.

This is the extreme point of Sade's thought; a point to which he does not always hold, but toward which he tends and arrives notably in volumes eight and nine of *La Nouvelle Justine* where, with magnificent cries, Juliette rejects nature no less forcefully than she had the law, morality, and religion. Nature, she says, has no more truth than God himself: *"Ah! you bitch, you deceive me perhaps, as in times past I was deceived by the vile deific chimera to which they said you were subordinate; we depend no more upon you than upon him." "Yes, my friend, yes; I abhor nature."* Thus for an instant, an instant of prodigious suspense for which Sade reserves the title revolutionary, the laws are silent. Social, moral, and natural laws give way not to the tranquility of some nothingness — for example, to a time before birth — but rather to this power of dissolution that man bears within himself as his future; a power of dissolution that is the joy of flagrant insult and outrage (there is nothing somber, finally, nothing but what is superb and laughing in the approach of this supreme turbulent moment): a need to go beyond that is the heart of reason. This reason is certainly dangerous, terrible, and, properly speaking, terror itself, but nothing ill-fated is to be expected from it—on condition, however, that one "*never lack the force necessary to go beyond the further- most limits.*" As Saint-Just says, with a word that trembles in its brevity: "*A repub- lican government has as its principle virtue, if not terror.*"

(9) Freed in April of 1790, arrested as suspect in December of 1793, Sade par- ticipated for nearly four years in the advent of the republic, and during sixteen months took part in the Revolution, not in the first ranks, but nonetheless as a man with a public role who speaks in the name of the people and who exercises impor- tant duties. This cannot be forgotten. Something of Sade belongs to the Terror, as something of the Terror belongs to Sade. One may recall this famous text that resembles an Epinal illustration: "It is said that when Robespierre, when Cou- thon, Saint-Just, and Collot, his ministers, were weary of murders and condem- nations, when those hearts of bronze felt some remorse at the sight of the numer- ous arrests they had to sign and the pen slipped from their fingers, they would go read a few pages of *Justine* and then return to sign." Written in 1797 by Villers, this text was not written simply to denounce Sade as an immoral writer, but to compromise him by making him an accomplice of the masters of the Revolution. For all its stupidity, this text nonetheless says something fitting inasmuch as men who were otherwise opposed are here drawn together by what was equally exces- sive in their free movement and through their common conviction that the ex- perience of liberty always passes by an extreme moment. Whoever does not know this movement knows nothing of freedom. What, then, distinguishes these men, all reputedly infamous? This would at first seem evident. When, for the last time, Saint-Just gets up before the Tribunal of the Assembly prior to 9 Thermidor and sketches a portrait of revolutionary man composed of unshakable maxims (the revolutionary man is inflexible, judicious, frugal, simple; he is the irreconcilable enemy of every lie, every indulgence, and every affectation; he is a hero of com- mon sense and probity),[10] this moral portrait does not resemble the one that could be drawn of the integral man, except for the inflexibility of their principles (al- though the great masters of debauchery are also sober from surfeit, cold from an excess of sensibility, austere from too much pleasure, and simple for having stripped away all hypocrisy). When Saint-Just, accusing Desmoulins, reproaches him for having said that honor is ridiculous, that glory and posterity are a stupid- ity, this reproach would also befit Sade. But to my mind, it would speak in praise of him. For the word glory, found in every discourse of the time and also on the lips of Jean-Paul Marat, is almost never encountered in Sade's writings; he sees in it but another illusion, just as he sees in posterity a cold imposture.[11] (In fact, we ought to put this more precisely by noting that Saint-Just's reproach is aimed at the amiable skeptic in Desmoulins, whereas it is Sade's horror of prejudice, which will later be called the exigency of critical reason—that is, pure negative

passion—that prohibits him from adhering to these too easily acknowledged values.) When, finally, Saint-Just denounces the corruption of morality brought about by an atheism of the mind,[12] we find perhaps the firmest difference between these two philosophies, if not between the two men; and here again, we must dare to say it, it is to Sade's advantage. *"We are inundated with unnatural writings that deify intolerant and fanatic atheism—one would believe that the priest had become an atheist, and the atheist a priest. Let us speak no more of this! What we need is energy; what is suggested to us is delirium and weakness."* An accusation that is aimed at the already incarcerated suspects among whom, and precisely at this date, is the Marquis de Sade. It is true, and probable, that he was arrested for the relations he had in 1791, or for his opposition to measures he judged too radical (for example, the establishment of a revolutionary army within Paris, a sort of Praetorian guard, which, according to him, would have risked becoming an expedient for the ambitious who wanted to usurp power; another time, as president of his section, he refused to take a vote on "a horror," "an inhumanity") or else simply because, being imprudent and an aristocrat, he constantly drew denunciation. But I am willing to believe that he may also have made himself suspect by his atheist fanaticism: three weeks before being arrested, he takes the floor at the Convention to support the project of a cult of the virtues that would have been celebrated with hymns and incense on the disaffected altars of Catholicism. And in what terms does he speak? In a scarcely veiled manner, he speaks of himself: *"The* Philosophe *had for a long while been laughing in secret at the apish antics of Catholicism; but if he dared to raise his voice, it was in the dungeons of the Bastille where ministerial despotism was soon to constrain him to silence. And indeed, how could tyranny not have given its support to superstition?"* And just before this, we find the following: *"The reign of philosophy has now finally annihilated the reign of imposture; at last man is becoming enlightened and is destroying with one hand the frivolous toys of an absurd religion, while with the other he erects an altar to the Divinity most dear to his heart. Reason replaces Mary in our temples."* This project of an unmistakable atheism (not the least allusion was made to a Supreme Being) received honorable mention, but it did not fail to draw the hostile attention of those who held the reigns of government, nearly all Deists, who moreover feared that an idolatrous cult, exasperating the general population, which remained Catholic, would serve as a pretext for counter-revolutionary initiatives.

It is always by one's strengths that one perishes. This must have been true of Sade. Atheism was his essential conviction, his passion, the measure of his liberty. During his imprisonment in the Bastille, Mme. de Sade entreats him to veil his sentiments; he answers that he would rather die a thousand deaths than feign, even in personal letters, being what he is not. One of his first writings is the famous *Dialogue between a Priest and a Dying Man*, where he gives the strongest expression to what he will at all times and up to the end maintain: the certitude of nothingness. *"This has never frightened me and I see in it only a consolation and something very simple; all the rest is the work of pride, this alone is the work of reason."* A declaration that must be joined with that of one of his characters: *"If atheism wants martyrs, let it say so; my blood is wholly ready."* And finally, also, with this affirmation, one of Sade's most decisive and one of the keys to the system: *"The idea of God is the one fault I cannot forgive man."* God as the original sin: the lapse that explains why one cannot *govern* innocently.

(10) The scaffold just missed having Sade's head, but this was due solely to error; had it not missed him, the Terror would indeed have offered us a martyr of atheism—through yet another misunderstanding, it is true. Freed in October 1794, after an inquiry and after testimony from the Piques Section (which at the time of Robespierre had first attacked him, reproaching him for having said that democratic government was impracticable in France,[13] but now commending his good citizenship and his patriotic principles), Sade begins his last life as a free man. But now what does he do? All he can to ruin the liberty he holds so dear. Not that he conducts himself improperly; having separated in 1790 from the austere Renée de Sade, who, after having been for a time liberated by him from her virtue, had fallen back into coldness, he lives conjugally with a sweet and tender young woman who will never leave him. His demon is not that of lubricity, it is more dangerous. It is the demon of Socrates, a demon Socrates always resisted and to which Plato would have preferred not to yield: the madness of writing, a movement that is infinite, interminable, unceasing. It was for a long time believed that when Sade was arrested in 1801, it was for having defied Bonaparte in an anonymous pamphlet. Gilbert Lely has dealt with this too allegorical tradition as it deserved.[14] Prisoner at Vincennes and in the Bastille under royal tyranny, detained in Saint-Lazare and Picpus under the Rule of Liberty, taken to Sainte-Plélagie, to Bicêtre, and to Charenton under the heel of despotism that was soon to be crowned—all of this is true, and yet it should be noted (and I find it remarkable) that it was not a political adversary, but solely the author of *Justine* who was condemned to be confined for life by the high morality of the First Consul, that is to say, by society as a whole. For this is surely Sade's truth. A truth all the more dangerous for being clear, lucidly proposed, simply expressed—and in the most legible form precisely on the last page of *The Prosperities of Vice:* "HOWEVER MUCH MANKIND MAY TREMBLE, PHILOSOPHY MUST SAY EVERYTHING." Say everything. The line alone would have sufficed to render him suspect, the project to condemn him, and its realization to imprison him. And it is not Bonaparte alone who is responsible. We always live under a First Consul, Sade is always pursued, and always by reason of the same exigency: the exigency to say everything. One must say everything. Freedom is the freedom to say everything, a limitless movement that is the temptation of reason, its secret vow, its madness.

X

The Speech of Analysis

When we consider Freud, we have no doubt that with him we have a late reincarnation, perhaps the last, of the venerable Socrates. What faith in reason! What confidence in the liberating power of language! What virtues accorded to the most simple relation: one man speaks and another listens! And thus are healed not only minds, but bodies. This is admirable, it surpasses reason. To avoid every crude and magical interpretation of this marvelous phenomenon, Freud had to strive relentlessly for its elucidation—something all the more necessary since his method (originating very close to magnetism, hypnosis, and suggestion) came from a very mixed background. Even if these relations were reduced to the relations of language that exist between patient and doctor, would they not remain essentially magical? Magic does not always require ceremony, a laying on of hands or the use of relics. There is already magic when one individual acts in an imposing manner with regard to another; and if between one who is simply sick and his doctor there are relations of authority that always allow the latter to take advantage of his importance, the situation lends itself all the more to such abuse when the patient considers himself or herself (or is considered to be) unreasonable. The onlooker in any psychiatric clinic whatsoever is struck by this impression of violence; moreover, he adds to it by being its spectator. Speech is not free, gestures deceive. Everything that is said, everything that is done (whether by the patient or the doctor) is ruse, fiction, or illusion and deception. We are fully in the realm of magic.

And when Freud, with great unease, discovered the phenomenon of "transference"—bringing him again before relations equivalent to the fascination proper to hypnosis—he might well have sought there the proof that what occurs between the two persons who are brought together involves either obscure forces or the relations of influence that have always been attributed to the magic of the passions. Yet he admirably abides by his sense that the doctor plays not an enchanted role, but one more hidden—perhaps none at all, and because of this very positive: that of a presence-absence over and against which some ancient drama, some profoundly forgotten event, real or imaginary, comes again to take form and expression, truth and actuality. The doctor, therefore, would be there not as himself but in the place of another. By his presence alone he plays the role of another, is other, and is the other [*l'autre*] before becoming an other [*autrui*]. Freud at this point, and perhaps before he knows he is doing so, attempts to substitute dialectics for magic, but also for dialectics the movement of another speech.

Yet if he knew this, it quickly fell by the wayside. We might regret it, but we might also consider it a matter of luck. For rather than using an established philosophical vocabulary and precise notions that had already been elaborated, Freud was led to an extraordinary effort of discovery and to the invention of a language that in an evocative and persuasive manner permitted him to retrace the movement of human experience, its knots, and the moments at which a conflict, insoluble yet demanding resolution (each time the same conflict, but each time at a higher stage), carries further along the individual who either learns in this movement, is altered or broken.[1]

*

What is striking is the way in which Freud is animated by a kind of passion for the origin—which he also first experiences in reverse form as a repulsion with regard to the origin.[2] He thus invites each of us to look back behind ourselves in order to find there the source of every alteration: a primary "event" that is individual and proper to each history, a scene constituting something important and overwhelming, but also such that the one who experiences it can neither master nor determine it, and with which he has essential relations of insufficiency. On the one hand, it is a matter of going back again to a beginning. This beginning will be a fact; a fact that is singular, lived as unique, and, in this sense, ineffable and untranslatable. But this fact at the same time is not one: it is rather the center of a fixed and unstable set of oppositional and identificatory relations. It is not a beginning inasmuch as each scene is always ready to open onto a prior scene, and each conflict is not only itself but the beginning again of an older conflict it revives and at whose level it tends to resituate itself. Every time, this experience has been one of a fundamental insufficiency; each of us experiences the self as being insufficient. It is as though we had access to the various forms of existence only as deprived of ourselves, and deprived of everything. To be born is, after having had everything, suddenly to lack everything, and first of all being, inasmuch as the infant exists neither as an organized, self-contained body or as a world. For the infant, everything is exterior, and he himself is scarcely anything but this exterior: the outside, a radical exteriority without unity, a dispersion without anything dispersing. This absence, which is the absence of nothing, is at first the infant's sole presence. And each time he believes he has conquered a certain relation of equilibrium with the environment, each time he once again finds a bit of immediate life, he is to be deprived of it anew (weaned, for example). It is always around lack, and through the exigency of this lack, that a presentiment of the infant's history, of what he will be, is formed. But this lack is the "unconscious": the negation that is not simply a wanting, but a relation to what is wanting—desire. A desire whose essence is eternally to be desire: a desire for what is impossible to attain, and even to desire.

We know that it is man's luck to be born prematurely and that he owes his force to his weakness; a force that is the force of weakness, in other words, thought. As Pascal no doubt wished to say, man first had to become a reed in order to become capable of thought. But this original lack from which everything has come to him, this "wanting" that is experienced as a fault, the interdicts that preserve this lack and keep us from filling it so we can never have or be, being always separated from what is close to us and always destined to the foreign—these vicissitudes, fortunate difficulties and frightful episodes with which the history of our culture is filled, are first of all the expression of our own experience. Strange experience: as purely as we believe we think, it is always possible to hear resound in this pure thought the accidents of the thinker's originary history and to hear this thought, to understand it, on the basis of the obscure accidents of its origin. At least we have this: this certainty about ourselves, this knowledge of what is for us most particular and most intimate. And if we no longer have pure thought, in its place we have and know the thorn that is still in the flesh, having gone back toward these primary moments where something of us has remained fixed and where we have unduly lagged behind. Here, then, is where everything would have begun. Yes, if it would be a matter of moments that were truly first. But the force of analysis lies in the way it dissolves everything that seems first into an indefinite anteriority: every complex always dissimulates another. And as for the primordial conflict, we have only lived it as though having always already lived it, lived it as other and as though lived by another, consequently never ever living it but reliving it again, unable to live it. It is precisely this lag in time, this inextricable distance, this redoubling and indefinite uncoupling that each time constitutes the substance of the episode, its unfortunate fatality as well as its formative force, rendering it ungraspable as fact and fascinating as remembrance. And did it ever truly take place? It does not matter; for what counts is that, through the pressing interrogation of the psychoanalyst's silence, we should little by little become able to speak of it, give an account of it, make of this narrative a language that remembers and make this language the animated truth of the ungraspable event—ungraspable because it is always missed, a lack in relation to itself. A liberating speech wherein the event becomes incarnate—precisely as lack—and thus realizes itself.

*

The analytical situation, as Freud discovered it, is an extraordinary situation that seems borrowed from the enchanted world of books. There is this putting into relation, as we say, of the couch and the armchair; this naked conversation where, in a space that is separate, cut off from the world, two persons, each invisible to the other, are little by little called upon to merge with the power of speaking and the power of hearing, and to have no relation other than the neutral intimacy of the two faces of discourse. For the one, there is the freedom to say anything at all; for the other, that of listening without attending, as though without knowing it and as though he were not there. And there is this freedom that becomes the cruelest of constraints: an absence of relation, which, in its very absence, becomes the most obscure, the most closed and most open of relations. There is the one who, in some sense giving expression to what is unceasing, ought not to cease speaking, saying not only that which cannot be said, but little by little speaking as though on the basis of the impossibility of speech; an impossibility that is always already in the words as much as on their hither side, an emptiness and a blank that is neither a secret nor something passed over in silence but rather something always already said, silenced by and in the very words that say it—and thus everything is always said and nothing said. And there is the one who seems the most negligent and absent of auditors, someone without a face, scarcely someone; a kind of anyone at all who makes a counter-weight to the anything-might-be-said of the discourse and who, like a hollow in space, a silent emptiness, is, nonetheless, the real reason for speaking: incessantly disturbing the equilibrium, making the tension of the exchanges vary, responding by not responding and insensibly transforming the monologue without issue into a dialogue where each of them has spoken.

One may be astonished—without real astonishment—at discovering the scandal that Jacques Lacan provoked in certain psychoanalytical quarters when he identified (an identity of difference) the research, the knowledge, and the technique of psychoanalysis with the essential relations of language. For it seems evident that Freud's principal merit lies in having enriched "human culture" with a surprising form of dialogue; a dialogue in which, perhaps—perhaps—something would come to light that would enlighten us about ourselves when we speak by way of the other.[3] A dialogue that is nonetheless strange and strangely ambiguous due to the situation without truth of the two interlocutors. Each one deceives the other and is deceived with regard to the other. One is always ready to believe that the truth of his or her case is already present, formed and formulated in the other who listens and simply demonstrates his ill will in not revealing it.[4] The other, who knows nothing, is always ready to believe that he knows something because he has at his disposal a vocabulary and an allegedly scientific framework with which the truth has but to fall into line. He therefore listens from a position of strength, no longer as pure ear or as a pure capacity to hear, but as a knowledge informed from the outset that judges the patient, sizes him up, knowingly hears and cleverly deciphers in this immediate language another language of complexes, hidden motivations, and forgotten memories. The analyst's aim is to enter into communication with this other language so that, through a system of locks and barriers, this speech still mute in the one who is speaking may, from level to level, rise up to the decisive point of manifest language. But as nothing prohibits the patient from having read the works of Freud, he may from the outset be no more innocent than the learned man of the armchair. And even if the one speaking does not use Freud to resist Freud, it will not be easy to arrive at the more profound dissimulation that is summoned to appear between these two persons in such an encounter.

The requirement that the psychoanalyst be psychoanalyzed is traditionally an exigency to which he is always prepared to submit; but he less willingly submits what he knows and the form in which he knows it. How can he psychoanalyze himself with his knowledge, and precisely on the basis of this knowledge itself? If, however, psychoanalysis has become an "objective science" like the others, a science that pretends to determine the interior reality of the subject, to maneuver him with the help of tested techniques and reconcile him with himself by making him an accomplice of satisfying formulas, this has come about not only from the natural weight of things, from the need for certainty and the desire to immobilize the truth so as to have it comfortably at hand—a need, finally, to have more than a second-class science; it comes about also because in the doctor, and in response to the errant speech he brings forth, there is a profound anxiety that he tries to make up for by appealing to a ready-made knowledge, by a belief in the explanatory value of certain myths, and also by the illusion that, beyond language, one can truly enter into relation with the intimate life of the subject, with his true history, and with a whole pedantic and futile jumble of bric-a-brac that can be scrambled or sorted out at one's pleasure in order not to find oneself, exposed, in an unknown relation of inequality with this empty speech (empty even when full) that simply asks to be heard. We know, moreover, that in many cases psychoanalysis has above all become an auxiliary discipline, and that many of those who claim kinship with it do not hesitate to employ the customary procedures of medical observation. Perhaps this is inevitable. But how can one fail to see that the "relation" proposed by Freud is then destroyed in its very essence? How can one hope to reconcile a psychoanalysis that always puts one into question (questioning the very place one occupies as an observer or thinker, knowing or speaking) and a psychoanalysis that suddenly takes itself to be the naively absolute affirmation of a scientifically certain knowledge that would explain an objectively determined reality?

Jacques Lacan's effort is precisely to try to bring us back to the essence of psychoanalytic "dialogue," which he understands as a form of dialectical relation that nonetheless challenges (disjoins) the dialectic itself. He employs formulas such as this: *"The subject begins analysis by speaking of himself without speaking to you as you—or by speaking to you without speaking of himself. When he is able to speak to you of himself the analysis will be over."* He shows that what is essential in analysis is the relation with the other [*autrui*], within the forms that language's development make possible. He frees psychoanalysis from all that makes it an objective knowledge or a kind of magical act. He denounces the prejudice that leads the analyst to seek beyond words a reality with which he would strive to come into contact: *"Nothing could be more misleading for the analyst than to seek to guide himself by some so-called contact experienced with the reality of the subject. . . . Psychoanalysis remains a dialectical relation in which the nonaction of the analyst guides the subject's discourse toward the realization of his truth; it is not a phantasmatic relation where two abysses brush against each other." "There is no need to know whether the subject has remembered anything whatever from the past: he has simply recounted the event. Made it pass into verb or more precisely into the epos by which he brings back into present time the origins of his person." "In psychoanalytic anamnesis it is not a matter of reality, but of truth."* This effort to purify, which is only beginning, is assuredly an important undertaking, and not only for psychoanalysis.[5]

*

The originality of psychoanalytic "dialogue," its problems, its risks, and perhaps, in the end, its impossibility appear in this way only the more clearly. Such a liberation of speech by speech itself represents a moving wager made in favor of reason understood as language, and in favor of language understood as a power to collect and gather in the midst of dispersion. The one who speaks and who consents to speaking beside another will little by little find the paths that turn his speech into a response to his speech. This response does not come from an outside; it is neither an oracular speech nor the word of a god, neither the response of the father to the child nor of the one who knows to the one who wants not to know but to obey—a petrified and petrifying speech one wishes to carry like a stone in place of the self. Even coming from without, the response must come from within; come back to the one who hears it as the movement of his own discovery, permitting him to recognize himself and know himself recognized by this strange, vague, and profound other [*autrui*] who is the psychoanalyst, and in whom all the interlocutors of the patient's past life who have not heard him become at once particularized and universalized. The twofold characteristic of this dialogue is that it remains a solitary speech destined to find its paths and its measure on its own; and yet, expressing itself alone, it can come about only as a veritable relation with a veritable other [*autrui*]: a relation in which the interlocutor—the other [*l'autre*]—no longer weighs down on the word spoken by the subject (who is then separated from his self as from the center), but rather hears it, in hearing responds to it and, through this response, makes the subject responsible for it, making him truly speaking, and making it so that he will truly and in truth have spoken.

The word truth that arises here, and that Jacques Lacan uses in preference to the word reality, is, of course, the most easy to belie, it being always out of place, *misunderstood* by the knowledge that disposes of it in order *to know*. It would (perhaps) be better to renounce it if it did not pose the problem of time, and first of all that of the duration of the treatment; for we must not forget that the subject is not always a dilettante in search of himself, but may be someone deeply wounded whom it would be fitting to "cure." When, then, is the cure over? One can say: when both the patient and the analyst are satisfied. A response that can leave one reflecting. Inasmuch as it cannot be a matter of the kind of satisfaction depending upon mood or humor but rather of the contentment that is wisdom, this amounts to saying that one must wait for the end of the story and the supreme contentment that is the equivalent of death, as Socrates already suggested. This is not a criticism. One of the impressive aspects of analysis is that it may be tied to the necessity, following Freud's own formulation, of being always both "finite and infinite." When it begins, it begins without end. The person who submits to analysis enters into a movement whose term is unforeseeable and into a reasoning whose conclusion brings with it, as though it were a new capacity [*pouvoir*], the impossibility of concluding. For, to say this quickly, what begins to speak here is what is unceasing and interminable: the eternal going over, and over and over again, whose exigency the patient has encountered but has arrested in fixed forms henceforth inscribed in his body, his conduct, and his language. How can the interminable be brought to term? How will speech be able to complete itself precisely as infinite, and find precisely its end and signification in always recommencing its movement without end? And doubtless, we are told that it is a matter, to begin with, of a limited message that will have to be expressed (deciphered) when the proper time comes. But this makes the task all the more difficult since against the ground of the interminable, which must be preserved, affirmed, and accomplished all at the same time, a particular speech must take form and become a limit that will be right only if it falls at the right moment. In fact, the moment of the response is no less important than the direction it takes. A "true" response that intervenes too early or too late will not have the power to respond; it merely closes the question without rendering it transparent, or becomes the indefinitely surviving question's phantom. Another appearance of the eternal rebeginning wherein what appears (in dissimulating itself) is the fact that there is neither beginning nor end. A movement that is not dialectical, that threatens every dialectic, and that also speaks in language itself—a speech that is neither true nor false, neither sensible nor senseless but always both the one and the other: the most profound speech, but speech that speaks as a depth without depth. Perhaps it is the dangerous duty of the psychoanalyst to seek to suppress this speech, suppressing that which in fact opposes all supposedly normal conduct and expression—but also suppressing himself, thereby meeting up again with death, his truth.[6]

XI

Everyday Speech

The everyday: what is most difficult to discover.

In a first approximation, the everyday is what we are first of all and most often: at work, at leisure, awake, asleep, in the street, in private existence. The everyday, then, is ourselves, ordinarily. At this first stage, let us consider the everyday as without a truth proper to it: our move will then be to seek to make it participate in the diverse figures of the True, in the great historical transformations, and in the becoming of what occurs either below (economic and technical change) or above (philosophy, poetry, politics). Accordingly, it will be a question of opening the everyday onto history, even of reducing its privileged sector, private life. This is what happens in moments of effervescence—those we call revolution—when existence is public through and through. Commenting upon the law regarding suspects during the French Revolution, Hegel showed that each time the universal is affirmed in its brutal abstract exigency, every particular will and every thought apart falls under suspicion. It is no longer enough to act well. Every individual carries within himself or herself a set of reflections and intentions, that is to say reticences, that commits each one to an oblique existence. Being suspect is more serious than being guilty (hence the seeking of confession). The guilty party relates to the Law to the extent that he manifestly does everything he must in order to be judged; that is, in order to be suppressed, returned to the void of the empty point that his self conceals. The suspect is this fleeting presence that does not allow recognition, and through the part always held back that he figures forth, he tends not only to interfere with the work of the State, but also to place it under accusation. From such a perspective each governed is suspect; yet each suspect accuses the one who governs and prepares him to be at fault since he who governs must one day recognize that he does not represent the whole, but a still particular will that only usurps the appearance of the universal. Hence the everyday must be thought as the suspect (and the oblique) that always escapes the clear decision of the law, even when the law seeks by way of suspicion to track down every indeterminate manner of being: everyday indifference. (The suspect: anyone and everyone, guilty of not being able to be guilty.)

But critique (in the sense that Henri Lefebvre, by bringing forth "the critique of everyday life" has used this principle of reflection),[1] at another stage, is no longer content with wanting to change day-to-day life by opening it onto history and political life: it seeks rather to prepare a radical transformation of *Alltäglich-keit*. A remarkable change in point of view. The everyday is no longer the average, statistically established existence of a given society at a given moment; it is a category, a utopia and an Idea, without which one would not know how to get at either the hidden present or the discoverable future of manifest beings. Man (the individual of today, of our modern societies) is at once engulfed within and deprived of the everyday. And a third definition: the everyday is also the ambiguity of these two movements, the one and the other hardly graspable.

From here, we can better understand the various directions by which the study of the everyday might orient itself (bearing now upon sociology, now upon ontology, at another moment upon psychoanalysis, politics, linguistics, or literature). To approach such a movement one must contradict oneself. The everyday is platitude (what lags and falls behind, the residual life with which we fill our trash cans and cemeteries: scrap and refuse); but this banality is also what is most important if it brings us back to existence in its very spontaneity and as it is lived—at the moment when, lived, it escapes every speculative formulation, perhaps all coherence and all regularity. We can evoke here the poetry of Chekhov or even Kafka, and affirm the depth of the superficial, the tragedy of nullity. The two sides always meet: the everyday with its tedious, painful, and sordid side (the amorphous, the stagnant); and the inexhaustible, irrecusable, constantly unfinished everyday that always escapes forms or structures (particularly those of political society: bureaucracy, the wheels of government, parties). And that there may be a certain relation of identity between these two opposites is shown by the slight displacement of emphasis that permits passage from one to the other; as when the spontaneous, the informal—that which escapes form—becomes the amorphous and when, perhaps, the stagnant merges with the *current* of life, which is also the very movement of society.

*

Whatever its other aspects, the everyday has this essential trait: it allows no hold. It escapes. It belongs to insignificance; the insignificant being what is without truth, without reality, and without secret, but also perhaps the site of all possible signification. The everyday escapes. In this consists its strangeness—the familiar showing itself (but already dispersing) in the guise of the astonishing. It is the unperceived, first in the sense that we have always looked past it; nor can we introduce it into a whole or "review" it, that is to say, enclose it within a panoramic vision; for, by another trait, the everyday is what we never see for a first time but can only see again, having always already seen it by an illusion that is constitutive of the everyday.

Hence the exigency—apparently laughable, apparently inconsequential, but necessary—that leads us to seek of the everyday an always more immediate knowledge. Henri Lefebvre speaks of the Great Pleonasm. We want to be abreast of everything that takes place at the very instant that it passes and comes to pass. Not only are the images of events and the words that transmit them instantaneously inscribed on our screens and in our ears, but, finally, there is no event other than this movement of universal transmission: "the reign of an enormous tautology." The disadvantages of a life so publicly and immediately displayed can now be observed. The means of communication (language, culture, imaginative output), in never being taken as more than means, are wearing out and losing their mediating potential. We believe we know things immediately, without images and without words; in reality we are dealing with no more than an insistent prolixity that says and shows nothing. How many people turn on the radio and leave the room, satisfied with this distant and sufficient noise. Is this absurd? Not in the least. What is essential is not that one particular person should speak and another hear, but that, with no one in particular speaking and no one in particular listening, there should nonetheless be speech, and a kind of undefined promise to communicate guaranteed by the incessant coming and going of solitary words. One can say that in this attempt to recapture it at its own level, the everyday loses any power to reach us; no longer what is lived, it is rather what can be seen or shows itself, spectacle and description, without any active relation whatsoever. The whole world is offered to us, but by way of a gaze. We are no longer burdened by events as soon as we behold their image with an interested, then simply curious, then empty but fascinated look. Why take part in a street demonstration if at the same moment, secure and at rest, we are at the *demonstration* [*manifestation*] itself thanks to a television set? Here offering itself wholly to our view, produced-reproduced, we are allowed to believe that it is taking place only so we might be its superior witness. Substituted for practice is the pseudo-acquaintance of an irresponsible gaze; substituted for the movement of the concept—a task and a work—is the diversion of a superficial, uncaring, and satisfied contemplation. Well protected within the four walls of his familial existence, man allows the world to come to him without peril, certain of being in no way changed by what he sees and hears. "Depoliticization" is tied to this movement. And the man of government who fears the street—because the man in the street is always on the verge of becoming political man — is delighted to be no more than an entrepreneur of spectacle, skilled at putting the citizen in us to sleep while keeping awake, in the half-light of a half-sleep, only the tireless voyeur of images.[2]

*

Despite massive development of the means of communication, the everyday escapes. This is its definition. If we seek it through knowledge we cannot help but miss it, for it belongs to a region where there is still nothing to know, just as it is prior to all relation inasmuch as it has always already been said even while remaining unformulated, that is to say, not yet information. The everyday is not the implicit (of which phenomenology has made broad use); to be sure, it is always already there, but that it should be there does not guarantee its actualization. On the contrary, it remains always unactualized in its very realization, which no event, however important or however insignificant, is ever able to produce. Nothing happens; this is the everyday. But what is the meaning of this stationary movement? At what level is this "nothing happens" situated? For whom does "nothing happen" if, for me, something is necessarily always happening? In other words, what corresponds to the "Who?" of the everyday? And why in this "nothing happens" is there at the same time the affirmation that something essential would be allowed to go on?

What questions these are! We must at least try to hold onto them. Pascal offers a first approach, which is taken up again by the young Lukács and by certain philosophies of ambiguity. The everyday is life in its equivocal dissimulation: "life is an anarchy of light and shadow. . . . Nothing is ever completely realized and nothing proceeds to its ultimate possibilities. . . . Everything, without discretion, interpenetrates in an impure mix, everything is destroyed and broken, nothing flowers into real life. . . . It can only be described through negation." This is Pascalian diversion, the movement of restlessly turning this way and that; the perpetual alibi of an ambiguous existence that uses contradictions to escape problems and remain undecided in a disquiet quietude. Such is quotidian confusion. It seems to take up all of life; it is without limit and strikes all other life with unreality. But here there arises a sudden clarity. "Something lights up, appears as a flash on the paths of banality . . . it is chance, the great instant, the miracle." And this miracle "penetrates life in an unforeseeable manner . . . without relation to the rest, transforming the whole into a clear and simple account."[3] By its flash, the miracle separates the indistinct moments of day-to-day life; it suspends nuance, interrupts uncertainties, and reveals to us the tragic truth, that absolute and absolutely divided truth whose two parts solicit us from each side and without pause, each of them requiring everything of us and at every instant.

Nothing can be said against this movement of thought, except that it misses the everyday. For the ordinary of each day is not such by contrast with some extraordinary; it is not the "null moment" that would await the "splendid moment" so that the latter would give it a meaning, do away with it, or suspend it. What is proper to the everyday is that it designates for us a region or a level of speech where the determinations true and false, like the opposition of yes and no, do not apply—the everyday being always before what affirms it and yet incessantly reconstituting itself beyond all that negates it. An unserious seriousness from which nothing can divert us, even when it is lived in the mode of diversion. As we discover through the experience of boredom when indeed boredom seems to be the sudden, the insensible apprehension of the quotidian into which we slide in the leveling out of a steady slack time, feeling ourselves forever sucked in, yet feeling at the same time that we have already lost it and are henceforth incapable of deciding whether there is a lack of the everyday or too much of it—thus held by boredom in boredom, which develops, says Friedrich Schlegel, just as carbon dioxide accumulates in a closed space where too many people find themselves together.

Boredom is the everyday become manifest: consequently, the everyday after it has lost its essential—constitutive—trait of being *unperceived*. Thus the everyday always sends us back to that inapparent and nonetheless unconcealed part of existence that is insignificant because it remains always to the hither side of what signifies it; silent, but with a silence that has already dissipated as soon as we keep still in order to hear it and that we hear better in idle chatter, in the unspeaking speech that is the soft human murmuring in us and around us.

The everyday is the movement by which man, as though without knowing it, holds himself back in human anonymity. In the everyday we have no name, little personal reality, scarcely a figure, just as we have no social determination to sustain or enclose us. To be sure, I work daily; but in the everyday I am not a worker belonging to the class of those who work. The everyday of work tends to draw me apart from that membership in the collectivity of work that founds its truth; it breaks down structures and undoes forms, even while endlessly reforming itself back behind the form whose ruin it has insensibly brought about.

The everyday is human. The earth, the sea, the forest, light, night—these do not represent everydayness, which belongs first of all to the dense presence of the great urban centers. We need these admirable deserts that are the world's cities for the experience of the everyday to begin to overtake us. The everyday is not at home in our dwelling places; it is not in offices or churches any more than in libraries or museums. If it is anywhere, it is in the street. Here again, one of the beautiful moments of Lefebvre's books comes to mind. The street, he notes, has the paradoxical character of having more importance than the places it connects, more living reality than the things it reflects. The street renders public. "The street tears from obscurity what is hidden and publishes what happens elsewhere, in secret; it deforms it, but inserts it into the social text." And yet what is published in the street is not really divulged; it is said, but this "it is said" is borne by no word ever really pronounced, just as rumors are reported without anyone transmitting them and because the one who transmits them accepts being no one. Hence there results a perilous irresponsibility. The everyday where one lives as though outside the true and the false is a level of life where what reigns is a refusal to be different, a still undetermined stirring: without responsibility and without authority, without direction and without decision, a storehouse of anarchy in that it discourages all beginning and dismisses every end. It's the everyday. And the man in the street is fundamentally irresponsible: while having always seen everything he is witness to nothing. He knows all, but is unable to answer for it—not through cowardice, but because he takes it all lightly and because he is not really there. Who is there when the man in the street is there? At most a "Who?," an interrogative that settles upon no one. Always the same, always equally indifferent and curious, busy and unoccupied, unstable and immobile. And these opposing but juxtaposed traits do not seek reconciliation, nor, on the other hand, do they counter one another, all the while still not merging; it is this very *vicissitude* that escapes all dialectical recovery.

To which we must add that the irresponsibility of rumor—where everything is said, everything heard, incessantly and interminably, without anything being affirmed and without there being response to anything—rapidly grows weighty when it gives rise to "public opinion." But only to the extent that what is propagated (and with what ease) becomes the movement of propaganda; that is to say, when in the passage from street to newspaper, from the everyday in perpetual becoming to the daily transcribed (I do not say inscribed), it becomes informed, stabilized, *valorized*. This translation modifies everything. The everyday is without event; in the newspaper this absence of event becomes the drama of the news item. In the everyday everything is everyday; in the newspaper everything is strange, sublime, abominable. The street is not ostentatious. Passersby pass there unknown, visible-invisible, representing only the anonymous "beauty" of faces and the anonymous "truth" of those essentially destined to pass, without a truth proper to them and without distinctive traits. (When we meet someone on the street it comes always by surprise and as though by mistake, for we do not recognize ourselves there; in order to go forth to meet another one must first tear oneself away from an existence without identity.) But in the newspaper everything is announced, everything is denounced, everything has become image.[4] How then does the non-ostentatiousness of the street, once published, become a constantly present ostentation? This is not fortuitous. One can certainly invoke a dialectical reversal. One can say that newspapers, incapable of seizing the insignificance of the everyday, are able to render its value apprehensible only by declaring it sensational; incapable of following the process of the everyday insofar as it is inapparent, the newspaper seizes upon it in the dramatic form of proceedings. Incapable of getting at what does not belong to the historical, but is always on the point of bursting into history, newspapers keep to the anecdotal and hold us with stories [*histoires*]. Having thus replaced the "Nothing happens" of the everyday with the emptiness of the news item, the newspaper presents us with History's "Something is happening" on the level of what it claims is the day-to-day, and which is no more than anecdote. The newspaper is not history in the guise of the everyday, and in the compromise it offers us it doubtless betrays historical reality less than it misses the unqualifiable everyday — the present without particularity that it contrives in vain to qualify, that is, to affirm and transcribe.

*

The everyday escapes. Why does it escape? Because it is without a subject. When I live the everyday, it is any man, anyone at all who does so; and this anyone, properly speaking, is neither me nor, properly, the other; he is neither the one nor the other and, in their interchangeable presence, their annulled irreciprocity, both the one and the other — yet without there being an "I" or an "alter ego" able to give rise to a *dialectical recognition*. At the same time, the everyday does not belong to the objective realm. To live it as what might be lived through a series of separate technical acts (represented by the vacuum cleaner, the washing machine, the refrigerator, the radio, the car) is to substitute a number of compartmentalized actions for this indefinite presence, this connected movement (which is not, however, a whole) by which we are *continually*, though in the mode of discontinuity, in relation with the *indeterminate* set of human possibilities. Of course the everyday, since it cannot be assumed by a true subject (even putting in question the notion of subject), tends unendingly to weigh down into things. Any-man presents himself as the common man for whom all is appraised in terms of common sense. The everyday is then the medium in which, as Lefebvre notes, alienations, fetishisms, and reifications produce their effects. He who, working, has no other life than everyday life is also he for whom the everyday is most heavy; but as soon as he complains of this, complains of the burden of the everyday in existence, one immediately responds, "The everyday is the same for everyone," and adds, as did Büchner's Danton, "There is scarcely any hope that this will ever change."

There must be no doubt about the dangerous essence of the everyday, nor about the uneasiness that seizes us each time that, by an unforeseeable leap, we stand back from it and, facing it, discover that precisely nothing faces us: "What? Is this my everyday life?" Not only must we not doubt it, we must not dread it; we should rather seek to recapture the secret destructive capacity in play in it, the corrosive force of human anonymity, the infinite wearing away. The hero, while still a man of courage, is he who fears the everyday; fears it not because he is afraid of living in it with too much ease, but because he dreads meeting in it what is most fearful: a power of dissolution. The everyday challenges heroic values; but this is because, even more, it impugns all values and the very idea of value, ruining always anew the unjustifiable difference between authenticity and inauthenticity. Day-to-day indifference is situated on a level at which the question of value is not posed: there is [il y a] the everyday (without subject, without object), and while there is, the everyday "he" does not have to be of account; if value nonetheless claims to step in, then "he" [or "it," il] is worth "nothing" and "nothing" is worth anything through contact with him. To experience everydayness is to undergo the radical nihilism that is something like its essence and by which, in the void that animates it, everydayness does not cease to hold the principle of its own critique.

Conclusion in the form of a dialogue

"Is not the everyday, then, a utopia—the myth of an existence bereft of myth? We no more have access to the everyday than we touch this moment of history that could represent, historically, the end of history.

— That can, in fact, be said, but it opens onto another meaning: the everyday is the inaccessible to which we have always already had access; the everyday is inaccessible, but only insofar as every mode of acceding is foreign to it. To live in the way of the quotidian is to hold oneself at a level of life that excludes the possibility of a beginning, the very possibility of access. Everyday experience radically questions the exigency of the initial. The idea of creation is inadmissible when it is a matter of accounting for existence as it is borne by the everyday.

— To put this another way, everyday existence never had to be *created*. This is exactly what the expression *there is the everyday* [il y a du quotidien] means. Even if the affirmation of a creating God were to impose itself, the *there is* [il y a] (what there is already when there is not yet being, what there is still when there is nothing) would remain irreducible to the principle of creation: the there is is the human everyday.

— The everyday is our portion of eternity: the eternullity of which Laforgue speaks. The Lord's Prayer, in this way, would be secretly impious: give us our daily bread, give us to live according to the daily existence that leaves no place for a relation between Creator and creature. Everyday man is the most atheist of men. He is such that no God whatsoever could stand in relation to him. And thus one understands how the man in the street escapes all authority, be it political, moral, or religious.

— For in the everyday we are neither born nor do we die: hence the weight and the enigmatic force of everyday truth.

— In whose space, however, there is neither true nor false."

XII

Atheism and Writing
Humanism and the Cry

1

How can we regard this double title with anything but mistrust? What does it convey? How far does it claim to go? And why a text that will be a kind of response to a still absent question? What is questioning in this absence of question? A surplus of question. The here-lies on the tomb, it, too, is the epigraphic truth: as though, with the exception of these few words cast back, all the language within had been consumed, used up, rendered unemployable: the debris of a shipwreck. And we well know that in the immense and vain destruction that is culture, what most often remains of a book is its title, and only a few among an infinite number: nonetheless far too many.

But let us not believe that one can read in a title the question it poses. And let us not believe that it would suffice to render the absent question present through commentary in order that it might be restored to us in the questioning it would assign to us. I will take as example the work entitled *The Order of Things: An Archeology of the Human Sciences*. Let us assume that, struck and perhaps irritated by the complacent interest that is brought to the word man via the detour of the so-called human sciences, as well as by everyday and even political chatter, Michel Foucault asked himself: Really, why are we still speaking of "man"? And what is this "man"? Let us assume that in writing a book so learned and well thought out he sought to lend form, force, and power to affirmations such as this (which I cite from memory): "*Man, as the archeology of our thought demonstrates, is a recent invention.*" Or this: "*It is reassuring and profoundly calming*

246

*to think that man is no more than a recent invention, a simple fold in our knowl-
edge, and that he will disappear as soon as he has found a new form.*" Yes, let
us assume that this sentence was given to us so it might momentarily withdraw
us from ourselves and remind us of our proper, ephemeral name. Yet the fact remains that it is only proposed in the guise of a comforting remark and as an indirect consequence of the knowledge with which we are in other respects satisfied
and in which we take pride. And it is also true that it is the commentators, refusing
to be comforted—taking fright on the contrary and deeply unhappy, asking "is this
the end of humanism?"—who are alone responsible for this question they themselves made emerge by provisionally arresting the book at it, thereby obliging us
to ask from this basis in turn: Why this scandalized murmur? Why this sensitivity
of a paranoiac character—which indeed seems to be the essence of the human Self
and immediately leads some particular individual to feel he is being targeted, provoked, assailed, and wounded each time it is a question of "man"? The end of humanism? As though ever since Feuerbach, who gave it its most energetic form,
humanism had not been constantly knocked about and rejected by all important
research. Why then this uneasiness, this indignant rumor?

1. *Humanism: a theological myth*

We shall have to go back to Nietzsche: "*All gods are dead; now we want the
overman to live.*" The death of God leaves a place for man, then man's death a
place for the overman. Thus far from going beyond this word, Nietzsche retains
it, giving it additional value. Going beyond finds its point of gravity in what is
gone beyond. Even when he proposes to the future "*the earth*" and "*the eternal
return*" as enigma, it is still man as future, a future that always returns, that he
sets out to decipher and to bear through a frightful concern. Perhaps it is only
when he inquires into "*the play of the world*" that he orients us toward an entirely
different question: the very one held in the interrupted movement of fragmentary
writing.[1]

The theme of the death of God explains this mythical jump from which the idea
of the human benefits under the form that "humanism" procures for it. Feuerbach
says: Man is truth; the absolute being, the God of Man, is the very being of man:
religious man has taken his own nature as object. Feuerbach therefore shows that
man has thought himself, realized and alienated himself in God's name, and that
it suffices to negate the subject of Christian predicates to reconcile man with his
truth. God disappeared or disappearing, it is as a finite and earthly being, but also
as a being who has a relation to the absolute (having the power to found, and to
found oneself, to create and to create oneself) that we direct ourselves to the self
that is already there but simply separated from ourselves by egoism. All the
Promethean powers we attribute or allow to be attributed to ourselves by this double trait—finitude, the absolute—belong elementarily to theology. Be he God's ri-

val, his replacement, or his heir, creator of himself or in the process of becoming toward the point omega, man is but the pseudonym of a God who dies in order to be reborn in his creature. Humanism is a theological myth. Hence its attraction and usefulness (God is in turn called up in human form so he may work at constructing the world: compensation for the long while man lived in working for the other world), but also its weighty simplicity. To meddle with man is to meddle with God. God is there as sign and as future each time the same categories that have served in thinking the divine logos, be they profaned, are turned over to the understanding of man at the same time as they are entrusted to history.[2]

2. The "finite," a vanishing object

God is dead. This means that sovereignty, in the words of Georges Bataille, passes to death: "*The sovereign is no longer a king: he is hidden in our great cities, he surrounds himself with silence.*" Whence it follows that God still preserves, and even in death, the meaning of Sovereignty, thus preserving from death the Sovereignty that declares itself in it. Only now it falls to man to die. The right to death that he claims as a power is most ambiguous. On the one hand—and notwithstanding the necessary ingratitude of Marxist commentators with regard to Hegel, whose heirs we all are—it is clear that if man did not end, if he were not in relation to his end and, through this relation, in relation with the negative, man would know nothing, not knowing the power to negate that founds the possibility of knowledge. Man knows because he dies; and the most ordinary speech, like the most positive, speaks only because in it death speaks, negating what is, and in this negation paving the way for the work of the concept.

Yet man has always died and has always known that he will die. Why had we to wait for the modern epoch in order that man's knowledge of the end should give rise to an ambiguous positivity capable of taking man as the object of its research? Let us for a moment admit the commonplaces, however worn they may be. That the end is no longer appropriated by a beyond. That the possibility of living ideally, one's sights set on an earthly or a non-earthly ideal, no longer has sufficient authority to serve as an alibi for the certainty that man will end. But also that our mistrust with regard to ideology—the inherited set of representations by which we rule our conduct, nearly independently of the more real relations upon which they depend—leads us to go beyond the certainty of our end (always overlaid by clouded sentiments), and to seize this certainty as that which merely delimits the diverse regions of the "finite." The "finite": namely, what is known or is to be known as finite, and receiving from this trait—a "finite being"—the possibility of being knowledge. That is to say, once more: the finite, inasmuch as it is finite, always gives itself as a vanishing object. (The finitude that founds the new sciences, let us again note, is an essentially theological notion.)

3. *Absent from the human sciences*

Death offers possibility, all the while withdrawing it; this indicates the status of the figure that the disciplines we call the human sciences cause to rise up in the field of knowledge by determining more and more exactly its contours. This figure is scarcely designated before it vanishes. Indeed, of what is it a question in these sciences? Is it a question of man? Not at all. This would presuppose that there is a human reality determinable as such, and capable of becoming the object of a global scientific knowledge. Where is man when we encounter a man? We have renounced asking questions of this kind, just as the idea of elaborating a "philosophy of man" long ago disappeared from the great philosophical schemas — assuming it ever had a place in them at all (except, as it happens, with Feuerbach).[3]

This absence is perhaps significant. Kant, most assuredly, does ask the question: what is man? But the response he gives does not appear in the "anthropology" of his later years. It is rather affirmed in the necessity that spans his entire work: to wit, that a knowledge can be founded only if man is given to this knowledge as its principle, but on condition that one forever renounce finding through a *direct* knowledge the answer to the question: what is man?

If such a question is never a question for knowledge in the global sense, there are regions or, as one says, fields that are delineated on the basis of a certain form of human activity. Without a doubt. And again these regions are, *stricto sensu*, never given as immediately real; they exist on the basis of the knowledge it is possible to have of them. Which also means that what we encounter in these regions are not, in themselves, objective realities or, even less, facts one could already call scientific. The human sciences do not have as their object a particular region of being that is empirically observable and produced by men speaking or acting over the course of the ages; what man does — in a particular and well-determined zone of his activity — only concerns knowledge and in a sense only exists when "what is done" can be regarded as being a system (of forms and laws) that precedes and goes beyond the empirical acts that are delineated or inscribed in this zone. This reversal is the principal feature of the new sciences. Foucault significantly calls it the redoubling of the empirical into the transcendental. Redoubling — repetition — is the important word here. One could even say it is the possibility of redoubling that constitutes transcendence itself by opening the fact to the principle. But how is the "repetition" that opens this very possibility itself possible? How can the empirical redouble itself and, in so doing, become possibility? To say this differently, how does rebeginning — the non-origin of all that begins — found a beginning? Would it not first of all ruin it? And is there not here in the very success of the new sciences a defeat that precedes this success like their shadow?

But let us leave these questions and observe that it is not simply a matter of the ambiguous situation in which the human sciences would find themselves by being applied to man—man who is at the same time the object of a knowledge and the subject who knows. For here the *a priori* is not the *a priori* of a subject, that is, of a transcendental subjectivity. It is rather the constituted field of knowledge itself, which, forming the *a priori*, holds in it the "subject" who has knowledge; a field formally constituted and therefore always to be constituted, for otherwise there is the risk of a formidable dogmatism. So that, in a rigorous sense, there is a science only on the basis of a theory of the constitution of science, which itself can only be arrived at through an investigation devoted to knowing whether a scientific discourse is possible. But what is a scientific discourse if not a discourse that requires writing, and requires of writing a form able to guarantee it its own specificity? Finally, what is called "transcendence" (certainly a misplaced word) is given in and through writing, and through writing's aptitude (a necessarily unstable one) to depart from ideology.

Man is absent from the human sciences. This does not mean that he is elided or suppressed. On the contrary, it is his only way of being present in them in a way that makes that which affirms him neither an object—some sort of natural reality—nor a subjectivity, nor, yet again, a pure moral or ideological exigency: in a way, therefore, that is not empirical, anthropomorphic, or anthropological. But this absence is not pure indetermination; it is also always and each time (according to the zones envisaged) determined, that is to say, determining. The formal operations by which the multiplicity of presence remains always in advance both held on to and absent, the *sive* of human activity, characterize the space in which the human events that give rise to knowledge are produced. These operations are always more or less dissimulated by the "results" that serve to support them and by which they become alienated in becoming "things," that is to say, empirical realities. This shifting ambiguity of a transcendence or an *a priori* (that does not wish to declare itself) and of a positivity (that does not fail to disavow itself) constitutes the originality of the new human sciences in which man seeks himself as *absent*.

4. *Always light, meaning*

Let us here, at least in a word, quickly note that without the phenomenology of Husserl it is very unlikely that knowledge would have been so directly able to grasp the space that is proper to it, and that defines the idea of a *sui generis* relation. On the one hand (how can this be forgotten?), phenomenology contributed to the task of removing man, the psychical, from the status of a natural causality; then to removing consciousness itself from its naive characterization as a site of conscious states: intentionality empties consciousness of consciousness, and makes of this emptiness a relation that is always distinct from and superior to the terms in relation, thus ready as well to define that which does not have the trait of being conscious. Intentionality, conceived perhaps in order to guarantee judgment, can very well rediscover itself under the name of desire: desiring intention; as a type of process, therefore, that is strictly non-thought and non-conscious.

These and other misconceptions that transform phenomenology undoubtedly misrepresent it, but what can be done? They are henceforth at work, and they are important. On the other hand, by showing there is a rigorous correlation between the determinations of the object and the steps of the "consciousness" that intends them or takes up their evidence, phenomenology made thought familiar with the idea of a relation that is empirical and transcendental. Or, to state this more clearly: it is intentionality that maintains the empirical and the transcendental within a powerfully structured relation—an alliance that is essentially modern, that is to say, explosive. As a result, the empirical is never in and of itself the empirical: no experience can claim of itself to be in itself knowledge or truth. And also as a result of this, the "transcendental" will find itself nowhere localized: neither in a consciousness that is always already outside itself, nor in the so-called natural reality of things (which must always be suspended or reduced). Rather, it will reside in the emergence of a network of relations that neither unite nor identify but maintain what is in relation at a distance, and make of this distance, recaptured as a form of alterity, a new power of determination.

Phenomenology maintains—it is true—the primacy of the subject: there is an origin. This origin is light, a light that is always more original from the basis of a luminous primacy that makes shine in all meaning the summons of a first light of meaning (as Emmanuel Lévinas says it so magnificently). Phenomenology thus accomplishes the singular destiny of all Western thought, by whose account it is in terms of light that being, knowledge (gaze or intuition), and the logos must be considered. The visible, the evident, elucidation, ideality, the superior light [clarté] of logic—or, through simple reversal, the invisible, the indistinct, the illogical or silent sedimentation: these are the variations of Appearance, of primary Phenomena. And language will receive from these its character. The act of speech remains one of expression; it is a matter of expressing the meaning that always precedes, then of preserving it as much as possible in its luminous ideality. Or if, in fact, scientific truth must be *said* in order to constitute itself by freeing itself from the psychological singularity of the one who is supposed to have brought it to light, if, therefore, language has a certain constitutive power, one must immediately add that it is the speaking subject itself that holds this power. Speech would not therefore take the place of the subject in this act that is constitutive (phenomenologically speaking, this would be scandalous)—the subject speaks, and one cannot even say as a subject, since subjectivity itself is mute, inaccessible to the address of a language capable of rigorously expressing it.

Language, the expression of a meaning that precedes it, that it serves and safeguards: meaning, the ideality of light; a primary light that originates in the

Subject with which a beginning occurs; finally, experience (an experience that is rather difficult to determine; at times empirical, at times transcendent, and yet neither the one nor the other): source of signification. Now commonplaces, these are the affirmations that phenomenology transmits to all reflection, even if oriented differently.

It would seem that knowledge—in its effort to assert itself in the sciences we call human—retains much more from phenomenology than it would wish to acknowledge. First, the putting into question of its own positivity (its dread of positivism), and the necessity that it be internally at issue with itself (a dispute it maintains by the tracking down of ideologies). Science is in a state of crisis. This crisis does not threaten it; but science has an essentially critical function. Another sign: the role played by the *a priori*, which founds the possibility of scientific experience; however—and this is a decisive modification—the transcendental field is without subject: it manifests itself in forms, laws, and systems that phenomenology would not have recognized as having the value of authentic norms. Finally, what directs inquiry remains the exigency or the seeking of a meaning: what does this mean? why is there meaning? or, what is more curious, how is meaning made? These questions are always dangerously on the horizon. And the importance of linguistics—called a model science—contributes to this danger, which structuralist methods are far from eliminating in any case.

5. How is atheism possible?

Man, bearer of meaning: reduced to the idea of the meaning that is light. (Already Homer chose to give man the very name of light.) Knowledge: gaze. Language: medium wherein meaning remains ideally proposed to the immediate reading of a look. These are the traits that, within atheism, perpetuate what is essential to the divine logos. At this level atheism remains pure pretension. One may call oneself an atheist; one may say one is thinking man, but it is always God as *light* and as *unity* that one continues to recognize. One of the problems would be, therefore: what are the conditions of a true atheism? This amounts perhaps to excluding any response in the first person. I can very well tell myself, and believe with a strong conviction in so doing, that every form of affirmation in which the name or the idea of God would arise is foreign to me; yet "I" am never atheist. The ego, in its autonomy, secures or constitutes itself by way of the unmitigated theological project. The self as a center who says "I am" says its relation to an "I am" of height who always is.[4] But if the affirmation "I am an atheist" is no more than a biographical decision, this means as well that this decision is not a necessary one. Nietzsche already recognized in "The Death of God" something very different from a personal eventuality. Saying that the death of God is a historical event will in no way suffice, however, if, in doing away with God, history itself ends by laying claim to the privileges of a transcendent relation. Atheism is therefore not simply a moment or a thought of history, any more than it could be the simple project of a personal consciousness.

I do not know whether atheism is possible, but I assume that insofar as we suspect, and with good reason, that we are in no way done with the "theological," it would be of great interest to seek whence this possibility of atheism that always eludes us might come to us, and from whom. Let us note that the contrary is also true; the Churches continue to fear that under the thought of Transcendence a foreign affirmation is introduced—a decisive heresy that makes an atheist of the very one who thinks he "believes in God." And, in the church's view, it is always closest to the thought of God that danger threatens; one admits science, one admits consideration of man, and, with some reservation, one even admits humanism and converses with materialist communism. Yet why then do we suspect ourselves (and with good reason) of being drawn into a movement whereby to speak of God would be to say something quite different, and already to deliver speech over to that which will never let itself be heard on the basis of the unity of the Unique?[5]

A double suspicion that might well be suspected of being only one. On two levels: let us admit that where there is man with his divine attributes—consciousness in the first person, the transparency of light, a speech that sees and says meaning, a speaking gaze that reads it—there the theological has already been preserved, and without any relation of authentic transcendence (such as monotheistic faith requires) ever having had to designate itself explicitly. The theological will therefore be maintained; that is to say, also suspended. The ambiguity will sustain its indecision as long as the presence of man excludes—because it includes it—all Presence that is radically other; or if, by this inclusion, it attests to an Absence henceforth present in an immediate form and, as a consequence, immediately suppressed. Just as with the famous argument—opposed even to Sade—according to which all atheism, every negation of God (that is to say, affirmation of the absence of God) is still always a discourse that speaks of and to God in God's absence—it being even the sole discourse capable of keeping divine transcendence pure. For this argument itself turns about and obliges the affirmation of God to efface and forget itself, even to the point of breaking every relation with Being, as with language; otherwise one risks transforming the name of God into a concept, then into a word in our vocabulary or, still less, into an "operator" (in the mathematical sense of this term).

Then let us say, at first glance, that atheism falls short to the extent that this same failure attends every possibility of affirming the Presence of what would be above any present, as it does the possibility of affirming the Unique that would still be Other. So that, seeking the true atheists among the believers (always necessarily idolatrous) and the true believers among those who are radically atheist, we will, perhaps, exchanging the one for the other, happily come to lose the two figures they perpetuate.[6]

6. *Order and order*

For a long time knowledge seemed to be an answer. To know in the scientific mode; to know rigorously through a univocal language excluding all difference. Pascal already challenged the libertine atheists by calling upon them *"to say things perfectly clearly."*

But a language having a single voice that says the Same and represents it identically would have the feature of being unlike language. Classical language, Foucault states in the clearest formula, "does not exist, but functions." It represents thought in identical fashion, and in it (which is not), thought represents itself according to identity, equality, and simultaneity. Such is the magnificent decision of classical language. The response to Pascal's challenge comes in the project of a universal tongue, the *mathesis universalis*: a discourse in which order is to dispose itself in the simultaneity of space, that is, the hierarchized equality of all that is representable; it comes in the analytical vocation of this functional language that does not speak but classifies, organizes, and makes order. Rhetoric—the product and refined expression of the humanities since the Greco-Roman age—contributes both to giving a definition of humanism that is seemly, and, under cover of this seemliness, to diverting thought from any secret that would outstrip it or from any truth that is not of the order of judgment. In this sense, rhetoric (the garden of flowers) is also the "delicate blossom" of atheism: it presupposes a profane language that says the order of knowledge, and in which knowledge is always equal to the order in which it represents itself. The discourse of method is a discourse on the order of discourse.

*

An Ideal that has never disappeared, but will reverse itself (and, in truth, several times). The project of a universal discourse that organizes in order to put everything in order will dangerously extend itself to what requires order, but does not let itself be called to order—an order whereby all truths, as soon as they are named and thereby put in place, become equalized, albeit hierarchically. The Encyclopedia, by means of its multiple references, introduces within a system of names what escapes every name and thus reduces God to being merely a word in the dictionary: a word appearing in an alphabetical classification that offers it neither at the beginning nor at the end—an effect of language that cannot be without consequences. But this inventory (and the difficulties that render it infinite) will not simply reduce to an order—an order that, by a significant pleonasm, one could call ordinary—what cannot submit to it; it will run up against forces—life, work, time—that will disrupt it and render it problematic. By a concomitant movement and as the order of a possible science, however, this order that tended to distance itself from the theological will become Order, and will gather unto itself the domination of a Capital letter by alluding to a sort of transcendence whose vocation is to reproduce and to confirm a particular social and spiritual structure.

Moreover, it is clear that the classical order, so dangerous for religion when it authorizes the organization of a profane knowledge, is only tolerated because it speaks in favor of an Order that is supreme—an Order, therefore, always having two faces: the disorder of the passions, of the unorganized and the inarticulate, being neither in the sky nor on earth, cannot by rights enter the social space. These are closeted or reduced, just as one shuts up madness and represses the illogical, the essential evil. Thus is announced the double movement that will profane the divine by altering transcendence and alienate the profane by endowing it with divine attributes. Transcendence is brought down, the empirical rises up, the modern era is ushered in.

7. *The ultimate reservation: the One*

It remains nonetheless true that the Sovereignty of Order, represented by a wholly ordered language, risks, on the one hand—representation vanishing—being no more than an order of language, and also rendering language sovereign; on the other hand—representation becoming more dense—it risks affirming itself in this obscure thickness that, escaping expression, will cease being representable and will give primacy to silent interiority.

This can (very crudely) be schematized as follows: let us start with the idea that the power to speak, the right to language, belongs first to the Sovereign (celestial and terrestrial): the Verb is always from on high, and this because speech is only first, and in the first person, on the basis of eminence; in other words, because all ordinary speech preserves in itself the memory of a more original anteriority, because I can speak in this anteriority before speech—that is, *think*. As though this supreme, transcendent and absolutely originary Self, speaking always before me and above me, a royal and solar Self, Zeus, master of words, were leaving me this latitude, giving me time to think before speaking, and thereby opening me to a non-speaking thought: a pure consciousness that, as such, in me, is foundational. It results that the divine guarantee, so necessary to Descartes's triumph over the malin Génie and deceitful obscurity will, beyond Descartes, permit this obscurity situated at the level of a thought anterior to expression to attribute to itself the very power of origin. For it is understood that if thought, speech, and art coexist in God in a substantial unity, man must first, and in sequence, think, speak, and act: an anteriority that immediately becomes primacy. Thought subordinates speech; thinking is the great dignity. But what is thought before language? Either a luminous evidence before the formulation that obscures it or the still unordered depth: an obscurity still deprived of the order that will alone determine and inform it by rendering it possible.

By a prodigious decision, Kant's transcendent egology will join these two traits. The *a priori* forms of knowledge, destined to found science in determining the objectivity of phenomena, are nothing other than language reduced to the order of judgment in which this word-rule, the concept, designates itself. And, at the same time, if it is certain that we know only what we ourselves as a "subject in general" have established, this "subject," this "I think" that is unique and common to all, and from which comes all light, remains in itself what is most obscure and most mysterious. And the debate will go on. At times it is obscurity, no longer only that of romantic interiority, but the obscurity of the new forces—the forces that are Life (and desire), need (and Work), the dynamic of time (or History)—that will stop the advance of the intelligible Order, which is always more or less well represented by a language that is also, and par excellence, order, truth, and beauty. (And now it is the obscure that threatens in its nonrecognition the sovereignty of an integral light. The ambiguity no longer testifies for Pascal, but for the libertine; and knowledge, by becoming knowledge of life, of work and of time, will provide itself with explanatory schemas that no longer answer to what is given but to the obscurity represented by the dynamism of a causality always more or less borrowed from a philosophy of will.) At other times, it will be the theological that lays claim to "depth," "subjectivity," and "unrepresentability" in order to shield transcendence from the progress of enlightenment and to return to it the dimension of the inaccessible—but *never*, and this is decisive, going so far as to offer itself silently to the *Other*: to what would be *excluded* not only from the Same, but from the *One*. For God can very well be the Other and the Wholly Other, but he remains ever and always the unity of the Unique.

This ultimate reservation—the impossibility of freeing the Other from the One—marks the point at which atheist discourse (that of the learned, humanist logos) and theological discourse rejoin and confirm one another by furtively changing places. As a result, the obscurity claimed or taken over by the two discourses remains an obscurity that is measured, and always tributary to a more original light or clarity, just as all speech attributes to itself the silence that makes it speak.

8. *Writing*

Let us now attempt to ask of discourse what would happen to it if it were possible for it to break free of the domination exercised by the theological, be it in the humanized form of atheism. It may well come down to asking whether *to write* is not, from the start and before anything else, to interrupt what has not ceased to reach us as *light*; to ask as well if *writing* is not, always from the start and before all else, to hold oneself, by way of this interruption, in relation with the *Neutral* (or in a neutral relation): without reference to the Same, without reference to the One, outside everything visible and everything invisible.

I will not, however, return directly to these two "theses," which have been taken up in other texts and, moreover, fraught with writing, are as though always set up against the writing in which they come together in dispersing. Let us say calmer things.

2

9. *From writing to voice*

Let us say calmer things, and again take up this historical progression at its most classical moment. Language now represents. It does not exist, but functions. It functions less to say than to order. And in this language that essentially writes and that writes in order not to exist, speech—as murmuring orality, as a personal "self," as inspiration and life—disappears. Certainly, orators, those of the pulpit and the salons' conversationalists, keep up the oral tradition; but precisely in referring it back to He from whom it comes, the Most High. As though God were reserving the voice for himself, and spoke only in the word's highest places just as the Sovereign is by right the only one to speak, the art of conversation existing only to multiply the echoes of his speech, which gives rise to intrigue and to infinite rehearsal. Thus, only vocal speech relates to the sovereign logos. Writing, that is to say literature, escapes this obscure dictation, turns away from the detestable Self, spurns temporal change, and doubtless represents: but what? Representing by way of an order of its own, it tends to represent only this very ordering and the perfection of the disposition it enjoins.

In this sense, the classical age would be the first age of "structuralism": now everything is visibly form and rhetoric completes its self-constitution, preparing its keys for the decoders of the future. Furthermore, impersonality—a noble impersonality intended to eliminate all base particularity, all unseemly proximity, the unidentifiable—affirms itself as the mark of both writing and rationality. Yet the stable or impersonal order produced by a language that does not exist fails to carry through the operational task reserved for it. To put into an order and to classify is not to put into *relation* by way of *measuring operations* whose function would be to identify by equalizing, and by this equalization make successive transformations possible (this is why, let us add immediately, "structuralism" lacks the instruments essential to it, and even those rendering its operations possible). Descartes invents analytical geometry; this means he renounces constructing figures, renounces making the figure visible as a solution to the problem. Rather, he seeks its equation, that is to say, he *writes* it, even if the plotting of the figure remains unfigurable. Descartes thus directly proposes to writing a decisive change by "reducing" what is still natural in it, and by making it escape its ideal of visibility.

But writing, far from recognizing itself in this proposition whose aridity frightens it (and that would also fix writing as the sole measure of the Same by removing the Other, that is to say, all transcendence, even mathematical transcendence, which, in fact, Descartes refuses to consider), will, under the pressure of other exigencies, compromise itself and make a pact with the speech that in speaking gives voice to the origin. In this way, however, writing will also hasten its fate. Michel Foucault reminds us that in the eighteenth century, with the approach of romanticism, language quite literally takes its distance from the letter to seek itself in the sonorous (Grimm, Bopp). One could say that literature, in horror of the order it has served, separates from itself; what is written makes appeal to what will never be written because it is foreign to any possibility of being represented: speech without word, the eolian speech that was already heard at Dordona, not obscurely pronounced by the Sibyl but forever announced in the ramifying murmur of the tree, and that Socrates rejected no less than he did writing.

10. *The voice, not speech*

One has to wonder why, at an epoch when literature tends to take power in a declarative manner through the romantic exigency, it is the voice that is nonetheless privileged and the privilege of voice that imposes itself upon the poetic ideal. The voice, but not speech. The voice that is not simply the organ of subjective interiority but, on the contrary, the reverberation of a *space* opening onto the *outside*. Certainly, the voice is a natural mediation, and through this relation with nature it denounces the artificial order of socialized language. It is also responsible for the faith in inspiration that reestablishes the divine logos in its position of eminence, making the poet no longer one who writes verse according to the order of the beautiful, but one who hears and is himself consumed in this hearing of an immediate communication. This privileging of the voice nonetheless brings to literature a vague experience to which it awakens as though at the threshold of strangeness. The voice sets free from speech; it announces a possibility prior to all saying, and even to any possibility of saying. The voice frees not only from representation, but also, in advance, from meaning, without, however, succeeding in doing more than committing itself to the ideal madness of delirium. The voice that speaks without a word, silently — in the silence of a cry — tends to be, no matter how interior, the voice of no one. What speaks when the voice speaks? It situates itself nowhere, neither in nature nor in culture, but manifests itself in a space of redoubling, of echo and resonance where it is not someone, but rather this *unknown* space — its discordant accord, its vibration — that speaks without speaking. (Hölderlin, in his madness "declaiming" at the window, gives this voice an organ.) Finally, the voice has the characteristic of speaking in a way that does not last. Fleeting and destined to the forgetting in which it finds its end, without either trace or future, what it prefers thereby breaks with the book's perpetuity, its closure, its proud stability: its pretension to enclose and to transmit the true by making into its possessor the very one who will not have found it. A speech that has vanished when it has scarcely been said, always already destined to the silence it bears and from which it comes; a speech in becoming that does not keep to the present but commits itself and the literature it animates to its essence, which is disappearance. The voice is also perhaps always, at least apparently, outside or to the side of the rules, as it is beyond mastery, always to be won back, always once again mute.

This experience of vocality, an imaginary experience since with very few exceptions the romantics write (unless they put romanticism in their life, which is also their death), will modify literature's relation to itself and put it to the test. What it imposes, and dangerously (because there is a delving into the depths that will be difficult to surmount), is the idea of origin (the impersonality of the voice is a silent appeal to a presence-absence to the hither side of every subject and even every form; anterior to beginning, it indicates itself only as anteriority, always in retreat in relation to what is anterior). It imposes as well the idea of the symbol (and we know what prestige it will have; the symbol restores the power of meaning, it being the very transcendence of and the surpassing of meaning, that which both frees the text from all determined meaning since, properly speaking, it means nothing, and frees the text of its force as text since the reader feels entitled to set the letter of the text aside in order to find its spirit—hence the ravages wrought by a symbolic reading, the worst way to read a literary text). But the result of this experience, paradoxically, will also be that literature, as writing— the sole medium of vocality—will be invested by writing with a power of insubordination that is first exercised with regard to all order, as with regard to the visible ordering by which literature manifests itself. Writing ceases to be a mirror. It will constitute itself, strangely, as an absolute of writing and of voice. A *"mute written orchestration,"* Mallarmé will say: time and space united, a successive simultaneity, an energy and a work wherein energy gathers (*energeia* and *ergon*); a tracing wherein writing breaks always in advance with *what is* written. Born of this pressure, beyond the book, is the project of the Work, in its very realization always yet to come; a Work without content since always going beyond what it seems to contain and affirming nothing but its own outside, that is to say, affirming itself—not as a full presence but, in relation to its absence, the absence of (a) work, worklessness.

11. *Lacunary interlacing (cloud of intermittencies)*

Thus there will come strange jolts, paradoxical mutations, flights that are returns. Hence the voice, always ready to merge with a promise of speech, will tend to support writing's habit of engaging in an irreversible, successive movement that proceeds in the same direction or sense (namely, meaning), if it is true that one does not speak by moving backward. But at the same time, situated in the origin's retreat, the voice does not let itself be drawn forth following the simple and homogeneous line required by a progressive writing, it gathers the Work in the original space that would be proper to it. Yet through the experience that writing undergoes in the work itself, both against the voice and nonetheless in accord with it, writing holds the Work to the disposition of being a surface or a distant evenness: enrolling and unrolling without ceasing to be superficial, turning back upon itself without ceasing to be slack, and in this twisting movement that conceals it, only manifesting the turning about of a space without depth, always entirely outside.

What more will we learn at other stages from this spatial movement that is in relation with the becoming of writing that neither transcribes nor inscribes, but designates its own exteriority and the effraction of an outside that expels itself? That this naked distance should not in any way be considered as a homogeneous expanse, continuous and limited to offering a framework for the simultaneity of a global reading; that it is not a homogeneous time, a line that progresses or a homogeneous space, a picture presented to the immediate apprehension of a gaze that seizes a whole. One could call it multidimensional (if one wanted to entertain metaphors flattering to science), in order to indicate that this network—a lacunary interlacing[7]—is neither figurable nor unfigurable (in the manner of a spiritual reality), remaining just as foreign to equality as to inequality, and thus rather more comparable to a point that is non-punctual, a cloud of intermittencies where the curve of the universe only curves back because it is in advance always already broken.

Thus one comes to conceive of writing as an interruptive becoming; the moving interval that perhaps designates itself on the basis of interdiction, but by opening the latter to discover in it not the Law, but the *speaking-between [l'entre-dire], inter-diction* or the vacancy of discontinuity.

12. *The break: writing outside language*

Let us stop right away. For we sense that, leaving possibility, we have in a sense left ourselves. If this movement of writing emerged from the affirmation of the Work (that of Mallarmé, let us say, in order to assign it a name—but without forgetting that Mallarmé is also a future that is entirely other)—the Work where the vocal exigency and the written exigency gather in the isolation of the absolute—it does so only to break with both exigencies; not to allow their reconciliation by way of a complicitous opposition, but to break, via this rupture, with what authorized their unification: *discourse* itself, or, let us say it with still less restraint, *language* itself.

This is the decisive break not yet accomplished, and in a certain sense impossible to accomplish, but always decided. Let us then affirm it, beyond any proof.

Writing begins only when language, turned back upon itself, designates itself, seizes itself, and disappears. Writing conceives of itself on the basis neither of vocal nor of visible manifestation, these being merely opposed through a complicitous opposition that is roused where Appearing [*l'Apparaître*] reigns as meaning, and light as presence: the pure visibility that is also pure audibility. And this is why Heidegger, in his faithful belonging to the ontological logos, can still affirm that thought is a seizing by hearing that seizes by way of the gaze. Let us on the contrary assume—at least as a postulate, and as an exigency that is difficult to accept, but so pressing that it will always go further than its own postulation— that writing has ever and always, nonetheless never now, broken with language, whether it be a discourse that is spoken or written. Let us admit what this rupture entails: a rupture with language understood as that which *represents*, and with language understood as that which receives and gives *meaning*; therefore also with this composite of the signifying-signified that today has replaced, in the distinctions of linguistics (already outmoded, it is true), the old division of form and the formulated: a duality always ready to become unified and such that the first term receives its primacy only by immediately restoring it to the second term into which it necessarily changes. Valéry thus characterizes literature by way of its form, saying it is form that makes meaning or signifies; but this signified that is proper to form also makes form that which has no other task than that of expressing this new meaning: the seashell may well be empty; it receives from this emptiness the presence that informs it. A rupture then with the "sign"? At least with all that would reduce writing to conceiving of itself, as Foucault puts it, on the basis of a theory of signification.

Writing is not speaking. This brings us back to the other exclusion: speaking is not seeing, and thus leads to rejecting everything—hearing or vision—that would define the act that is at stake in writing as the immediate seizing of a presence, be it of an interiority or an exteriority. The break required by writing is a break with thought when thought gives itself as an immediate proximity; it is also a break with all *empirical* experience of the world. In this sense, writing also entails a rupture with all present consciousness, it being always already engaged in the experience of the non-manifest or the unknown (understood as neutral).[8] But let us understand then why this advent of writing could take place only after the end of discourse (which Hegel represented, at least as a metaphor, in absolute knowledge); and then after the accomplishment of man freed from his alienations (which Marx represented, at least as a practical possibility, while at the same time preparing the theory of this practice): that is, through the founding of a communist society, which is the just aim of all humanism.[9] And we will understand why, today, speaking and writing, we must always speak *several times and at the same time*; speaking according to the logic of discourse, and therefore under the sway of a nostalgia for the theological logos; speaking also to make possible a speaking communication that can only be achieved on the basis of a communism of the relations of exchange, thus of production—but also not speaking, writing, by way of a rupture with every language spoken and written, and therefore renouncing the ideal of the beautiful Work as well as the riches of transmitted culture and the validity of a sure knowledge of the true. Writing then but not writing, for no trace, no proof of this writing that is always exterior to what is written is visibly inscribed in books—only perhaps here and there upon walls or on the night, just as at the beginning of man it is the useless notch or the chance groove marked in stone that, unbeknownst to him, caused him to encounter the illegitimate writing of the future, a nontheological future that is not yet ours.

13. *The cry, the murmur*

But we finally understand why we are bound to pass by the mediation of a "humanist" speech or writing (if only to rub it out and efface it), theological insofar as it is still only atheist. Ideology is our element: that which causes us to breathe and, at the limit, asphyxiates us. Writing, except in the hyperbolic writing we have tried to discern, is never yet free from ideology because there is still no writing without language. To believe oneself sheltered from ideology, even if it is a matter of writing in accordance with the demands of the knowledge that is proper to the sciences called human, is to give oneself over, without the possibility of choosing, to the worst ideological excesses. Therefore we will choose our ideology. This is the only choice that might lead us to a nonideological writing: a writing outside language and outside theology. Let us shamelessly call this choice humanist. A humanism of what kind? Neither a philosophy nor an anthropology: for to tell nobly of the human in man, to think the humanity in man, is quickly to arrive at an untenable discourse and (how to deny this?) more repugnant than all the nihilist vulgarities. What, then, is this "humanism"? How can it be defined so as not to engage it in the logos of a definition? Through what will most distance it from language: the cry—that is to say, the murmur; cry of need or of protest, cry without words and without silence, an ignoble cry—or, if need be, the written cry, graffiti on the walls. It may be that, as one likes to declare, "man is passing." He is. He has even always already passed away, inasmuch as he has always been adapted to and appropriated by his own disappearance. But in passing, he cries out: in the street, in the desert; he cries out in dying; he does not cry out, he is the murmur of this cry. So humanism is not to be repudiated: on condition that we recognize it there where it adopts its least deceptive mode; never in the zones of authority, power, or the law, not in those of order, of culture or heroic magnificence, any more than in the lyricism of good company, but rather such as it was borne even to the point of the spasm of a cry. Among others by he who, refusing to speak of himself as a man, evoked only *the mental animal*, and yet of whom one can nonetheless say that he was a "humanist par excellence"—being without humanity and nearly without language. *"For in fact, I realized I'd had enough of words, even enough of howling, and what was needed were bombs and I had none either in my hands or my pockets."* And the same person, by the same movement, was such that he always lived only to affirm *"a high measure of equity without secrets,"* which is also the wait without hope that breaks up in the "humanist" cry.

XIII

On a Change of Epoch:
The Exigency of Return

"Will you allow as a certainty that we are at a turning point?

— If it is a certainty it is not a turning. The fact of our belonging to this moment at which a change of epoch, if there is one, is being accomplished also takes hold of the certain knowledge that would want to determine it, making both certainty and uncertainty inappropriate. Never are we less able to get around ourselves than at such a moment, and the discrete force of the turning point lies first in this.

— Can we be so sure? I mean, were this the case, that would not be certain either. You have in mind Nietzsche's words: 'The greatest events and thoughts are comprehended last; the generations that are contemporaneous with them do not experience such events—they live right past them.' Nietzsche also says, in a phrase frequent citation has come to exhaust: 'Thoughts that come on doves' feet guide the world; it is the stillest words that bring on the storm.' But note that Nietzsche does not say the storm will be silent.

— For Nietzsche the storm is speech, the speech of thought.

— When the French revolution occurs, everyone knows it except Louis XVI. Today when it is manifestly a matter of a change much more important—one by which all the previous overturnings that have occurred in the time of history come together to provoke a break in history—everyone has a presentiment of it, even if each of us cannot affirm that we know it. This is a knowledge that is not within the scope of any particular individual.

— Yet you yourself affirm it.

— Because I am no more than an episodic voice, a speech without contour. And of course I affirm more than I know. But what I mean to say is not without signs: it goes about in the streets and this steady, anonymous current runs strong; we must try to hear it.

— And it says we have arrived at the time of a break that separates times?

— It says this, perhaps, in the manner of the ancient oracle, when Pythia spoke in a language of violence and of the elements that the poet-interpreter — transcribing, describing — was to elevate to the calmer and clearer language of men.

— An obscure language.

— Not obscure, but open to that which is not yet truly divulged, though nonetheless known to all. A language into which passes precisely the indecision that is the fate of the turning — an individual turning point and a turning of the world.

— An uncertain, indecisive fate that therefore remains always unaccomplished.

— Uncertain today for a very different reason: because this accomplishment is of a kind such that it escapes our historical measures. Recall Herodotus, who is known as 'the father of history.' One enters his books as into a country upon which day is about to dawn. *Before this there was something else, it was mythical night. This night was not obscurity. It was dream and knowledge; between men and event relations other than those of historical knowledge and its separating force. Herodotus stands on the crest that separates night from day: not two times, but two kinds of clarity. After him there falls upon men and things the clear light of historical knowledge.*

— You speak like a book.

— Because I am citing one.[1] And I will cite again the question it formulates: would this light that begins with Herodotus and becomes steady with Thucydides not also have its time? And if in reading Herodotus we have the sense of a turning, have we not, in reading our years, the certainty of a change even more considerable, a change such that the events that offer themselves to us would no longer be bound together in the manner we are accustomed to calling history, but in another with which we are not yet familiar?

— Is it the end of history that you claim to announce — at this moment when history becomes universal and speaks imperiously in the consciousness of everyone?

— I am not proclaiming it, nor does it proclaim itself directly. What is proclaimed, in fact, is apparently the contrary: the all-powerfulness of historical science that penetrates down to the most profound layers, those that have never before been historical. This discovery is itself a sign. We discover that there was a time without history, a time for which the terminology proper to historical times is unsuited — terms and notions with which we are familiar: freedom, choice, person, consciousness, truth, originality, and, in a general sense, the state as the affirmation of a political structure. Just as the originary eras were characterized by the importance of elementary or telluric forces, so today the event we are encountering bears an elementary character: that of the impersonal powers [*puissances*] represented by the intervention of mass phenomena, by the supremacy of a machinelike play of these forces, and by the seizure of the constitutive forces of matter. These three factors are named by a single term: modern technology. For the latter includes collective organization on a planetary scale for the purpose of establishing calculated planning, mechanization and automation, and, finally, atomic energy—a key term. What up to now only the stars could do, man does. Man has become a sun. The astral era that is beginning no longer belongs to the bounds of history. Are you in agreement with this presumption?

— There's a fitting word. And how can one not agree with something necessarily so vague that to oppose it would be the sign of a thought just as confused? I recognize that to hear talk of the end of history is always pleasurable. I can see that the domination of values and of the historical sciences could go hand in hand with the exhaustion of the forces making history (if these words have a meaning). I grant that when walking in the street, one breathes in thoughts such as these. But one breathes them in, one does not think them; as soon as they are formulated they lose their storybook charm. I have heard it said that we are in the process of crossing the time barrier. This kind of metaphor abounds in the work of Teilhard de Chardin, who does not fail to add, with the naïveté proper to him: it is as a scholar that I speak; I have not left the terrain of scientific observation.

— Is it a metaphor? It suggests to us something important and troubling: that we are at the end of one discourse and, passing to another, we continue out of convenience to express ourselves in an old, unsuitable language. That is the greatest danger. It is even the only one. The street is therefore much wiser than the painstaking thinkers who wait until they have new categories with which to think what is happening. I would remind you that theologians have sometimes spoken of 'the smell of the end of time,' a sort of *sui generis* experience that, amid real historical phenomena, would allow one to discern the breakthrough: being heading for its end.

— No doubt the smell of atomic explosion. Nietzsche, another theologian, already asked us: 'Do we smell nothing as yet of divine decomposition?' And Heraclitus said before anyone else: 'If all things turned to smoke then we would discern things with our nostrils.' But he did not make the nose into a theological organ. Note that I have nothing against the smell of the end of time. It is even possible that the kind of mixture of vague science, confused vision, and dubious theology one finds in the writings of Teilhard may also have value as a symptom, and perhaps a prognostic: one sees this kind of literature develop in periods of transition. What is distressing is that this sincere and courageous man is unaware of the horrible mix with which he must content himself; while speaking in the name of science, he speaks as an author of science fiction.

— Now here is a title with which, in his place, I would not be displeased.

Something in these authors speaks that I do not always find in the greatest books. And don't forget that Kant himself wrote a treatise on 'the end of all things.'

— It is precisely in strong, forcefully systemized thinking that undertakes to think everything, and history as a whole, that a possibility such as the end of history can have meaning. So it is with Hegel and Marx: in the case of Hegel, it is the development of absolute knowledge, the final achievement of a coherent discourse; in the case of Marx, the advent of the classless society in whose final state there will no longer be any power [*puissance*] of a properly political form. Here, at least, we have a dividing line, a criterion by which to judge things. We more or less know of what we speak.

— I have nothing as coherent to offer you, it is true, and this lack of a rigorous system is not necessarily an advantage. But must we take advantage of this to diminish Teilhard by designating him as a poor man's Hegel or a vestry Marx, as do, I think, certain pious men? Criticism has little hold on me. What is weak does not need us to grow weaker, but we ought to preserve and reinforce what is strong. What counts in the case of Teilhard is that he was a competent prehistorian, and it is as a prehistorian intimate with the ancient earth (one who has weighed ancient crania and delved into the profound layers) that he learned to form an idea of man's future. One might say that this beginning prior to the beginning, this language prior to speech that the images of an originary time speak, everything we now see and have never been able to see, give a certain clairvoyance with which to discern the invisible future, suggesting relations with the spirit of the earth and an understanding that is not disconcerted or frightened by the great metamorphoses that are being accomplished today.

— Your very language is becoming obscure — a sign, in fact, of clairvoyance. But what relation is there between the ancient knowledge of the earth that romanticism so generously ascribed to early times and modern technology, which is thought to direct against nature an inordinately destructive power of attack and negation? Can one say anything serious in taking such a tack?

— Nothing. Moreover, I am simply speaking in the name of Jünger's book, which meets up with Teilhard in a striking way. It is perhaps the same romanticism, the same magical sense; to wit, that the earth, finally unified and open to its depths, will become animate and, merging with the humanity gathered on it, become *a living* star capable of a new brilliance. Teilhard speaks of a noosphere. Jünger says that our planet has acquired a new skin, an aura woven of images, of thoughts, melodies, signals, and messages. This, he says, is a higher degree of spiritualization of the earth. It passes above nations and their languages, above word and sign, war and peace. The stone ax extended the arm; technology is the projection of mind. To be sure, technology first of all glorifies matter; but the materialism affirmed here by Jünger is neither empty nor superficial (as his mediocre adversaries contend), it is depth itself. And in undertaking the most profound penetration of matter, in no longer simply using matter but arriving at a manipulation of the processes that command the genesis of matter, intelligence has embarked upon an extreme adventure of unforeseeable consequences — consequences of which it has an intimation each time Mother Earth begins to tremble and each time man is able to take this shaking in hand and capture it. This shaking and this grasp put the entire traditional structure into question, along with the ancient rights, ancient customs, and freedom; they precipitate the decline of the paternal gods and develop every anonymous force — a movement to which correspond an insatiable hunger for energy, a Promethean ardor of means and methods, vulcanism (fire and radiance), the emergence of unwonted forces, and a stirring of the serpent of the earth, but also the withdrawal of the heroic forces in favor of the titanic ones, as is natural when the technician takes precedence over the useless warrior. You have no objections?

— No, none.

— That's not a good sign. Does this alliance of romanticism and technology, or this romantic interpretation of technocracy, seem to you to play on the weak parts of the imagination? But even taken this way, it is not without meaning. The philosophy of nature, whose significance Hegel did not fail to recognize, tapped here a hundred and fifty years ago one of its sources. That it should emerge anew today, spanning history, shows that it represents an enduring presentiment and knowledge. Reduced to their simplest terms, what do these views signify? That, hidden in what is called modern technology, there is a force that will dominate and determine all of man's relations with what is. We dispose of this force at the same time as it disposes of us, but we are ignorant of its meaning; we do not fully understand it. Jünger draws out and makes this mysterious dimension of technology shine with the help of the old images of magic romanticism, as Teilhard also does with his manner of speaking of a science that is but a foreknowledge. Far from being frightened by this mystery, both of them rejoice in it and put their trust in it. Both have faith in the future, and they love the future: a future not only of years but of superior states. That is good.

— I wonder whether, on the contrary, your authors don't have a kind of horror of the future since they refuse to entertain the incompletion that it necessarily holds in it. One could say they do everything to turn away from the simple truth of our death: the fact that it is always premature and before term. Hence their haste to affirm that an epoch has ended, a time is over. There is surely something barbaric in this end of history that you, that your authors, announce.

— Yes, barbaric, I would agree. It is a foreign truth: it flatters curiosity, but runs against it as well. Let's consider this for a moment. Naturally, if historical values pass and come to an end, this signifies their dominion in this end that only begins. We do not think absolutely the idea of the end, we think it only in relation to the idea of beginning. The end revokes the beginning. But what was the beginning of history? The end of mythico-heroic times, the end of Homer and Heracles; nonetheless an end that has never ended but prolonged itself in history. This trait is easily brought forth. Historical man is bound up with the myths of heroic times insofar as he sometimes affirms himself by combating them, at other times by identifying with them. In originary time (the time of prehistory) there are no heroes; man is without a name, without a visage. He belongs to living nature and lives in the pleasure and pain of the earth. The mythical hero already has a name and a genealogy; he no longer takes pleasure in nature, he wants to conquer it: he struggles, he annihilates. With him are born the virile gods, and he himself seeks to complete himself in becoming a half-god. Historical man preserves myth and preserves himself from it. Certainly, his principal task is to conserve his dignity — his humanity — against the mythical powers. But within history the moral of heroic myths does not cease to act as a model: that of the great personality, appearing in wartime, in the sacrifice of the hero for the fatherland, and in state governance where the great man as father, as guide, and as providential man belongs, even during history itself, to the world of heroes and gods. The decline of the heroic myth that characterizes our time is therefore another sign of this end of history whose dawning clarity you do not wish to accept, seeing in it only twilight. The hero disappears from universal consciousness; just as the name disappears, so the personality. What new cult did the Great War engender? Only one: that of the unknown soldier. And the unknown soldier is the glorification of the anti-hero; he is the unperceived, the obscure, ghostly stranger who abides in the memory of a people by virtue of being forgotten. This memorial of non-remembrance, this apotheosis of namelessness is an invitation to recognize that the time of the hero — and of heroic literature — is past. I don't miss it.

— You prefer the myth of the end of time, the fear of worldwide catastrophe that shakes men's imaginings day and night.

— It is not a preference that I wish to indicate. But the possibility to which you allude is naturally a sign of the greatest magnitude. When, for the first time in the history of the world, one has at hand the material power to put an end to this history and this world, one has already departed historical space. The change of epoch has occurred. This can be simply expressed: henceforth the world is a barracks that can burn.

— You seem to rejoice in this. But are you sure it's the first time? Perhaps you've forgotten the Bible. Biblical man constantly lives from the perspective you describe as new, warned by Jahweh that if men persevere in their practices they will be annihilated and creation abolished. History is born under this threat, the very threat of historical time.

— Then the fire came from above. Today it comes from here below.

— I could easily respond that when God promises to destroy humanity, should it continue to behave badly, he turns the decision over to humanity. Everything always finally depends upon man, whether there be God or whether there be the atom.

— Be there God or the atom, the point is precisely that everything does not depend on man. In God's time this was very nearly clear — also offensive, I grant it. Today the danger comes from the illusion in which we live of being the masters of what is carrying itself out under the englobing name of modern technology. I do not rejoice in this power to end that is conferred on us in a still scarcely intelligible manner. I have no liking for the bomb. I simply note that it is but a sign, a crude sign, of the extreme peril that necessarily marks the passage from one time to another, and perhaps from history to a transhistorical epoch. I allude here to a thinker with whom you are familiar: he often says that each time, denouncing the danger of the bomb, we hasten to invite knowledgeable men to put nuclear energy to peaceful use we do no more than procure for ourselves an alibi and bury our heads in the sand. The bomb gives visible notice of the invisible threat that all modern technology directs against the ways of man. The American chemist Stanley, a Nobel Prize winner (as you can well imagine), made this statement: 'The moment draws near when life will be no longer in God's hands but in those of the chemist who will modify, form, or destroy every living substance at will.' We read such statements every day, statements made by responsible men, and we read them along with other news items in the papers with negligence or with amusement, and without seeing that through the force of modern technology the way is being paved for an attack that makes the explosion of the bombs signify little in comparison.

— In fact, the end of everything isn't much. And what do you conclude from this? That we must preach a crusade against the world of technology, condemn it as an *opus diabolicum* and prepare huge fires upon which to burn learned men? Must we begin by destroying the contemporary world out of fear that it may not take this task upon itself?

— Were we able, I would not wish to. Fortunately, we belong to this world; we will not escape it. And in its lack of measure, which frightens us, we are frightened because not only the threats but also the hopes it holds in store for us are beyond measure. We must simply be clearsighted, or try to be. The danger does not really lie in the bomb. It is not in the unwonted development of energy and technology's domination; it is first of all in our refusal to see the change of epoch and to consider the sense of this turning. The threat will grow as long as we have not determined it as a risk. I would even say that the danger is perhaps solely provoked by our old language, a language that obliges us to speak in the style of history and the discourse of representation where the word war continues to be in use, and along with it the old mythical images, the pretensions of prestige, frontier customs and the habits of a politics of heroics, whereas we sense that the very idea of war, as well as the traditional idea of peace, have fallen into ruin. Hence there results a new state of affairs without war or peace, an unsettled strangeness, an errant and in some sense secret, vast space that has little by little overgrown our countries and where men act mysteriously, in ignorance of the change they themselves are in the midst of accomplishing.

— When I listen to your ambitious nocturnal evocations, I wonder if the real danger does not also lie in suggesting in a vague sort of way that we no longer run the risk of war, on the pretext that such a word belongs to an anachronistic vocabulary. It may well be anachronistic. We will die necessarily, and in any case in an anachronistic manner, whether we belong to history or to this beyond of history whose existence you have argued for. But, in reality, you do not believe in the risk of absolute catastrophe. Father Teilhard de Chardin, with the logic of his lyrical optimism, already stated that the danger of a nuclear explosion capable of blowing up the world seemed to him negligible. Negligible! It is true, he took comfort in invoking, in his terminology, 'a planetary instinct of conservation'— he, too, probably ashamed of the old ecclesiastical language that would have obliged him to speak of Providence. Perhaps you yourself, along with Jünger and the romantics, have faith in some technocratic providence or some unknown harmony into whose sphere you think that man, crossing history, cannot fail to fall?

— I shall answer simply: I love the future that you do not love.

— I love the future more than you: *I love being ignorant of it.*"

*

± ± *Ignorance of the future: the end of history: the law of return.* — To speak of the "end of history" is simply to pose the question of the place of such words, henceforth without content since, as soon as history comes to a close, speech loses the direction and meaning that alone give speech the possibility of becoming historically realized.

"History is over." Who can say this when "the end of history" still belongs to discourse, moreover to the very discourse that this end alone makes possible? The end determines the coherence of the discourse; or rather it is the coherence of discourse that allows us to set down as an acceptable term "the end of history."

The fact remains that the "end of history" belongs also to eschatological language: Christ is only possible because he bears the end of time. The death of God, in the "Christic" sense, in the Hegelian sense, and in the Nietzschean sense, is always a passage to the limit: the transgression that marks the imperceptible divergence by which knowledge, becoming absolute, would reverse itself into a non-knowledge (in an immobile movement such that the "no," losing its negative character, is simply that which allows a dash [*tiret*] to be inscribed: the mark, in no way oriented, that still permits knowledge to be named while setting it aside). Nonetheless, transgression, the end of history, and the death of God are not equivalent terms. But each indicates the moment at which the logos comes to an end, not in negating itself but in affirming itself and always again anew, without novelty, through the obligation—the madness—of repetition.

± ± Whoever asks "what is transgression?" asks nothing and can only indefinitely repeat in this form or, more obliquely, in another: what is transgression?

"I too am ready to say it, thus to repeat it and, even more surreptitiously, in repeating it, make of the question a response—if repetition and transgression echo one another.

— *Then repetition would be transgression?*

— *On condition that transgression in this very way is able to repeat itself.*

— *But is able only to free repetition, thus making it impossible."*

Repetition is transgression insofar as transgression displaces transgressive repetition, rendering it impossible.

± ± The end of history. It is not history that comes to an end with history, but certain principles, questions, and formulations that will from now on be prohibited through a decision without justification, and as though with the obstinacy of a game. Let us therefore suppose that we renounce the question of origin, then all that makes of time the power of continuity and mobility—that which surreptitiously makes thought advance in that it also sets speech into motion. Let us suppose we give ourselves (with the obstinacy of a game) the right to a language in which the categories that up until now have seemed to support it would lose their power to be valid: unity, identity, the primacy of the Same, and the exigency of the Self-subject—categories postulated by their lack, and from the basis of their absence as the promise of their advent in time and through the work of time. Let us suppose that, supposing the end of history, we were to suppose all these categories not abolished, certainly, but realized, comprehended and included, affirmed in the coherence of a discourse from now on absolute. The book now closed again, all questions answered and all answers organized in the whole of a sufficient or founding speech—*now*, writing, there would no longer be any reason or place for writing, except to endure the worklessness of this *now*, the mark of an interruption or a break there where discourse falters, in order, perhaps, to receive the affirmation of the Eternal Return.

± ± *Affirmation of the Eternal Return.* — Through this affirmation, and through the difficulty it proposes, the limit-experience finds itself at grips with what always steals it away from thought. Let us first recall briefly in what ways such an affirmation, one that shakes everything, was received:

First thesis: the affirmation of the Eternal Return testifies to the shattering of a mind already ill, not because the affirmation would be mad, but because of the vertigo of thought that seizes Nietzsche when it declares itself to him. Out of a modesty of thought, better to disregard it. This is the conclusion of the first commentators, and later of many others. Even Bertram, despite his idolatry, speaks of the "monomania of the Eternal Return, the pseudo-Dionysian mystery of the Solitary One."

Second thesis: be it as a paradox, the affirmation belongs to what in Nietzsche is most important, either inasmuch as nihilism recognizes itself and confirms itself in it, or, on the contrary, overcomes itself by accomplishing itself therein. Thus Löwith intends to show that Nietzsche's true thought constitutes a system: first, the death of God; then in the middle, its consequence, nihilism; finally, the Eternal Return, which is the consequence of nihilism and its overturning.

Third thesis: the Eternal Return and the Will to Power must be thought together. In the series of lectures given in Freiburg from 1936 to 1939, Heidegger meditates on Nietzsche's "fundamental position," which he delimits by two propositions: the trait of being as a whole: Will to Power; Being: the Eternal Return of the Same. Heidegger says further: the Will to Power is the ultimate fact; the Eternal Return is the thought of thoughts. But in arguing that Nietzsche still belongs to metaphysics, and even completes it by bringing it to its end, Heidegger also introduces the thought of the Eternal Return back into metaphysics: eternity is thought as instant, and the instant is thought as the instancy of presence.

Fourth thesis: I would not want to conclude anything from conversations bearing on the Sils Maria experience, but which left no trace. It nonetheless seems that Georges Bataille did not feel drawn to such an affirmation: he gave it little emphasis, despite the courteous assent he accorded to the research of certain of his interlocutors. What was important and, to say it more precisely, beyond importance, was not the affirmation itself (which in any case Nietzsche was mistaken in presenting as a doctrine) but the vision at Surlei, a preeminently sublime vision by which a sovereignly atheist thought, and by its very atheism, opened onto the most gripping of mystical experiences. In its discursive formulation, the thesis is no more than its laborious translation and debris: as after a great fire, the charred wood of thought. Nietzsche's obstinacy in imposing, and even in scientifically giving proof of, an affirmation escaping all knowledge only testifies, poorly, to what for him had been the untransmissible experience in which, in an instant of empty sovereignty, the whole of being and of thought was attained.

Fifth thesis: Nevertheless, how can one not ask of this affirmation whether there might not be some relation between it and the fact that it gave rise to a "highly mystical experience"? What relation? What possibility of relation? The question was unfolded in all its rigor, its breadth, and its authority by Pierre Klossowski. It is not only Nietzsche who is done a new justice with this questioning; through it, there is determined a change so radical that we are incapable of mastering it, even of undergoing it.

± ± Affirmation of the Eternal Return. This is a thought of the highest coherence insofar as coherence itself is thought in it as that which institutes it and such that nothing other than this coherence can ever be thought; nonetheless also such that this coherence could not but exclude the coherent thought that thinks it; thus always outside the thought that it affirms and in which it is affirmed: the experience of thought as coming from Outside and in this way indicating the point of disjunction, of non-coherence, at which the affirmation of this thought, ever affirming it, already unseats it. Such is the sign—from now on inscribed at night on our walls—to which Pierre Klossowski gave such a dazzling quality: *Circulus vitiosus deus.*[2]

Is Nietzsche, with his affirmation of the Eternal Return, simply struggling with one of those pseudo-thoughts (analogous to those of a dream) under whose attraction, through the evidence that radiates from it, one cannot resist falling as soon as one falls into it? Further, is not the affirmation of the Eternal Return not only one of those pseudo-thoughts (impossible to think and impossible not to think), but also its "explanation," its "truth" in the sense that, as a semblance of thought, it denounces in all thought its simulacrum, which alone would make it true?

At this point, the difficulty Nietzsche does not master is perhaps the very one that exalts him. To think, to affirm the Eternal Return—to affirm such an affirmation in making the instant at which it affirms itself the great moment wherein *time turns*—is either to overturn this affirmation by recognizing in the fact that it declares itself, at the same time as it strikes forgetting, the possibility of breaking with the affirmation radically, or else it is to acknowledge the insignificance of this declaration since, having already occurred and having to occur an infinity of times, it does not cease to occur and, henceforth, is struck with insignificance, as it strikes with nullity the one who proclaims it as sovereignly decisive.

But Nietzsche does not shirk from this consequence. A consequence entailing multiple paths: the Sils Maria revelation is not that of Nietzsche, not that of a unique individuality arriving at a unique truth, at a unique site, at an instant of singularity and decision; it is affirmation itself, an affirmation that does no more than affirm, that affirms affirmation and, in the latter, maintains together repetition and difference, forgetting and waiting, eternity and the future. The revelation at Sils Maria not only frees Nietzsche from his limited singularity by repeating him indefinitely, it not only frees the revelation from itself since it reveals nothing that does not reveal itself without end, but the revelation at the same time commits Nietzsche to that singularity without which what would come would not already be a return, just as it condemns the revelation's insignificance to the ridiculous exaltation of its decisive importance.

But let us question this revelation again. What is new (for Nietzsche) at Sils Maria? Well before this hour the thesis had been mentioned both by the Greeks and, in this same century, by Goethe, Schopenhauer, and Nietzsche (according to the testimony of Rhode and Overbeck). But it was a thesis: a proposition of thought, not yet related to itself by the aleatory necessity of its declaration. At Sils Maria, the affirmation wherein everything is affirmed disperses as it takes place: the very place of its affirmation, the thought that bears it, the existence that causes it to exist, the unity of the instance of its occurrence, and the still indispensable coherence of its formulation. But at the same time (which time?), while it disperses in affirming itself, ceaselessly differing from itself through the repetition that disavows it, it gathers itself in this difference that can only defer and, in reproducing itself as difference, eternally return, and, in returning, differentiate itself through repetition—in this way distinguishing anew, as unique, Sils Maria, the instant, the thought, the lucidity of an individual perhaps named Nietzsche, but as such already deprived of a name, of memory, and of reason.

So why the "return," and why the "same"? If it is the "same," why must it be thought as *Wiederkunft* (*Wiederkehr*), a turning that repeats itself, a repetition that produces itself through its own detour? And why, if it returns, is it the "same"? Is it the "same" because it returns, and through the force of return; or is it the same in any case, therefore without return, therefore a single time and forever the same, thus impossible to recognize as the same since the "same" must be several times—an infinity of times—the same in order to identify itself as the "same"? But if it is the "same" through its return, is it not the return alone that would give rise to the same? And thus it would necessarily happen that the "same" has deferred through an infinity of rounds and times, only returning to the same by the law of return. Is it therefore not the case that nothing in this same comes back to the same, except *the return itself* (turn, detour, overturning); and is it not the case that the affirmation of return leads to affirming together—but without constituting a whole—the difference and the repetition, thus the non-identity of the same?

But does affirming the return mean to come around, to circulate, to make of the circle an accomplished sovereignty? Clearly not. If only because the eternity of the return—the infinite of the return—does not permit assigning to the figure a center, even less an infinity of centers, just as the infinite of the repetition cannot be totalized in order to produce the unity of a figure strictly delimited and whose construction would escape the law it figures forth. If the Eternal Return can affirm itself, it affirms neither the return as circle, nor the primacy of the One, nor the Whole, and not even by way of the necessity that through the Eternal Return "everything returns," for the circle and the circle of all circles do not give it a figure any more than the Whole can encompass the Eternal Return, or coincide with it. Even if "everything returns," it is not the whole that returns, but rather: it returns, the return returns (as neutral).

± ± "The end of history." We should listen carefully to what this limit-concept allows to be said: a critical operation, the decision to put totality itself out of play, not by denouncing it but by affirming it, and by considering it as accomplished. The end of history: the total affirmation that cannot be negated since negation is already included in it (just as, on the basis of the discourse that contains its own silence, no silence of this discourse can be attested to, hoped for, or dreaded).

"Saying it differently": what exceeds the whole, what (forever) exceeding the whole, can "say" itself "differently"?

"We know by hypothesis that this — this speech or this non-speech — still belongs to the whole.

— *Certainly, by hypothesis.*

— *But, by hypothesis, it marks itself off from it.*

— *Yes, by hypothesis.*

— *We therefore have something that is of the whole, that totalizes itself therein, and, as such, marks itself off from it."*

Is this not what the Eternal Return says (neither hypothetically nor categorically)?

± ± The Eternal Return is for Nietzsche a mad thought. It is the thought of madness, and he dreads it to the point of fright at the idea that he shall have to bear it; to the point also that, in order not to be alone in bearing up under it, he must free himself from it by seeking to express it. A dangerous thought if, in revealing it, he does not succeed in communicating it — in which case he is mad; more dangerous still if he makes it public, for it is the universe that must recognize itself in this madness. But what does this madness of the universe mean if not, first, that this madness could not be universal? On the contrary, it is removed from all general possibility, even if Nietzsche comes to write that such a thought will *little by little* be thought by everyone.

An allegory: the thought of the Eternal Return, a madness of the Universe that Nietzsche, in assuming it as a madness that would be proper to him — that is, in madly deciding to give an account of it — accepts saving the universe from. He thus takes on the role of Christ, but by going further than the Messiah in accepting what Christ could not: not the ignominious though still tragic and finally glorious death on the Cross, but rather a senile death, watched over by the devoted and abusive Saintly Women, mother and sister, and even the atrocious exaltation (his Resurrection) by he who in the twentieth century represented horror itself. The Crucified against Dionysus: Nietzsche crucifies himself on his madness in order that the jubilant dissolution, beyond sense and non-sense, the excess without goal and without rules that finds its sign in Dionysus, may remain just: a pure generosity to which is suited only a thought that sacrifices itself in it while resisting it in order to remain a thought.

± ± Everything is played out in the manner in which the thought of the Eternal Return is communicated. A troubled and troubling game. One could say that Nietzsche undertakes to speak in five ways: (1) through *Zarathustra*; (2) impersonally, in having recourse to a practice of language that imitates that of knowledge; (3) personally, in confiding to friends in the mode of a mute murmuring (Lou, Overbeck); (4) in entrusting this thought to the future by imagining a secret conjuration; (5) in proposing it, apart from all science, all metaphysics, and all historical practice, as the simulacrum of an ethical speech, beyond Good and Evil: would I will it in such a way that I should will it infinitely?

Why does no communication seem able to respond or to correspond to the exigency of the Return? Because all communication already belongs to the exigency and, inasmuch as communication does belong to it, could only break in on it if, in producing itself, communication claims to help it realize itself. The question constantly poses itself to Nietzsche: why this revelation that isolates him from what is revealed? Why such a revelation—the revelation of detour—and such that it turns away from every identity and, by way of this exception, makes either the revelation derisory or he who reveals it mad, because divine? The circle is in any case vicious, being so first inasmuch as it condemns Nietzsche to this exaltation beyond the circle signified by the name of God: *circulus vitiosus deus*. The "vice," the fault in the circle, lies in the fact that the knowledge that repeats it breaks it, and in this rupture establishes a faulty God. "*Whoever does not believe in the cyclical process of the Whole must believe in an arbitrary God.*"

± ± Nietzsche is there in order to maintain together "detour" and "return," and if he speaks of "the eternal return of the same" it is perhaps so as not to have to speak of the "perpetual detour of difference"—in relation to which there is never anyone to make remembrance of it, or to make it the center of a circular affirmation. "*To the paralyzing sense of general disintegration and incompleteness I oppose the Eternal Return.*" A formulation that prompts this reading: maintain the law of the Return if you are not capable of entering by way of it into what always turns you away from it, turning you away from yourself as it turns you away from maintaining yourself in it, that is to say, the perpetual neutrality of Detour.

± ± But the law of Return is without exception; it cannot be gotten beyond, everything repeats itself, everything returns: the limit of thought. To think or to affirm this law is also to speak *at the limit*, there where the speech that affirms affirms speech as that which transgresses every limit: setting down every mark, that is, all writing, on the basis of a line of demarcation that must be gone beyond inasmuch as it is impossible to exceed. "Saying it differently," to write in the return, is always already to affirm detour, just as it is to affirm by repetition difference without beginning or end.

± ± Through *Zarathustra* Nietzsche maintains a zone of silence: everything is said of all there is to say, but with all the precautions and resources of hesitation and deferral that the one writing knows (with a disquieting lucidity) are necessary, if he wants to communicate that which cannot be communicated directly; and if he wants, further (under the accusation of unreason that he foresees), to preserve for himself the alibi of ridiculousness. If, however, between the thought of the Eternal Return and its affirmation, Nietzsche interposes intermediaries always ready to allow themselves to be challenged (the animals, Zarathustra himself, and the indirect character of a discourse that says what it says only by taking it back); if there is this silent density, it is not due simply to ruse, prudence, or fear, but is also because the only meaning of *news* such as this is the exigency to differ and to defer that bears it, and that it bears: as though it could be said only by deferring its saying. The deferral therefore does not mark the waiting for an opportune moment that would be historically right; it marks the untimeliness of every moment since the return is already detour—or better: since we can only affirm the return as detour, making affirmation what turns away from affirming, and making of the detour what hollows out the affirmation and, in this hollowing out, makes it return from the extreme of itself back to the extreme of itself, not in order to coincide with it, but rather to render it again more affirmative at a mobile point of extreme non-coincidence.

± ± When Nietzsche, ill and drawn by the attraction of a formidable speech that devastates him, confides in Lou or Overbeck, this can be treated as an anecdote; and it is one, however moving it may be. A man in bed who is delirious betrays himself lugubriously without realizing that he is compromising his thought in delirium. That he does not realize it is in fact probable, and unimportant. But the relation of the delirium to the thought of the Eternal Return that the delirium communicates is more important, and perhaps not anecdotal. Nietzsche can only speak (in that direct-indirect manner, in the mode of a mute murmuring) by forgetting—in forgetting himself, and in this memory that is a forgetting in which he disappears to the point of giving way to the sinister murmuring voice that Overbeck, out of the modesty of friendship, will refuse to remember up to and including the final catastrophe. Overbeck, quite literally, did not hear this voice—it remained without a hearing. The "delirium" most assuredly does not constitute that deliberate (or non-deliberate) simulation with which later, at the moment of manifest madness, Nietzsche's reason was credited: the "delirium" is the form of absence in which Nietzsche's identity destroys itself—that Nietzsche who, formulating the *everything returns*, thus opens the circle, marks its point of singularity (point at which the non-circularity of the circle would be defined) by means of which closure and rupture coincide.

± ± God, that is to say Nietzsche, that is to say the "communication" that imperfectly, viciously closes the Circle into a non-circle by the hiatus constituted by this "communication" or revelation.

± ± The fragment: *"Do I speak like someone under the sway of revelation? In that case, have only scorn for me and do not listen! Would you be like those who still have need of gods? Does your reason not feel disgust in allowing itself to be nourished in such a gratuitous, mediocre fashion?*"[3] Let us understand, then, better than Overbeck, better than Lou, and better also than ourselves, readers of Nietzsche, that what we call the "exigency of Return" was not revealed at Sils Maria and could not have been communicated in an experience that would have occurred at a particular moment or for the gain of an individual. Not only because it is not a matter of a religious truth, fallen from above and received through grace in order to be spread abroad by faith, but because this "thought" cannot but escape every mode of "knowledge," active or passive: this is its characterizing trait. No passivity whatsoever, no activity whatsoever would be able to receive or grasp it. Then would it be forever outside revelation and outside knowledge? And of what am I speaking when I speak of it? Exactly: it is related to speech if it changes all relations of speech and writing, placing them under the decision of repetitive difference. Each time Nietzsche (to retain this name for him that is just as much our own, that is, the name of no one) has recourse to a particular formulation (lyrical, metaphysical, existential, or practical) it is not in order to privilege the one he momentarily chooses, but to challenge all the others. If he happens to express himself in a mode that appears to be "scientific," is it not simply to say: I am not speaking like someone who is under the sway of revelation? And if he speaks of this to Overbeck like a lightning-struck prophet, is it not also to warn him: be attentive, remain vigilant, for what is at stake here imperils all reason and modifies the possibilities—indifference, objectivity, unity—of every exercise of thought?; it is true, I speak as an unreasonable man, but it is because unreason here is less the lapse of thought than the excess of lack that the exigency of another reason—or of the Other as reason—calls for and desires.

Through the Return we do not only *desire* that which turns us away from every desired, but here there is desire without anyone desiring and by way of a detour from all desire, as from all that is desirable.

± ± "*If the thought of the eternal return of all things does not subjugate you, this is in no way a failing on your part, just as there would be no merit if all the same you were subjugated by it.*" This means: the infinite of the repetition determines innocence, and for all the more reason, therefore, the thought or the non-thought of repetitive possibility is still innocence. This means then: you are innocent, all the more so as, through this innocence, there is nothing in you that is you; you are therefore not even innocent. That is why you are hereby responsible for what is most weighty: the irresponsibility that comes to you from that which, turning you away from yourself, always (never) makes you come back. That is why, also, to the question of what sort of discourse would befit the enigma of the Return the response, if there must be one, is: an "ethical" discourse, beyond Good and Evil. Will to live this instant of life in such a way that you can accept having already *desired* it and having always to desire it *again* without beginning or end, even if it be as you yourself, without identity and without reality: the extreme of insignificance. *Will*.

± ± "*I love my ignorance of the future*." Now we return to this phrase, responding to it quite differently, for the desire it proposes to us must be set in relation with the thought of the Eternal Return, and called up at this moment when something like "the end of history" is pronounced. This ignorance does not free us from knowledge, but holds it still in reserve when everything is already known. Ignorance: uncertainty. And in another (posthumous) fragment from *The Gay Science*: "*I love the uncertainty of the future*." Applied by Nietzsche to Nietzsche, this signifies: do not be impatient to the point of anticipating by a too resolute seeking what is in store for you. Do not simplify. But there is this uncertainty: the ignorance borne by the hazardous trait of the future; the chance that implies either infinite detour through the return or the rebeginning again through the absence of end.

Let us gamble on the future: let us affirm the indeterminate relation with the future as though this indeterminacy, by the affirmation that confirms it, were to render the thought of the Return active. For there is *the future*, the one within the ring that offers itself to repetition as a temporal instance, and there is *the future* itself of "Everything returns"—the to-come now carried to the greatest power of lack; that to which, in its uncertain non-coming, we who are not in it, being henceforth deprived of ourselves, as of all present possibility, say: welcome to the future that does not come, that neither begins nor ends and whose uncertainty breaks history. But how do we think this rupture? Through forgetting. Forgetting frees the future from time itself. Forgetting is this lack that is lacking to desire, not only so as to permit desire, but in such a way that desire is lacking and forgotten in desire. Forgetting is the manner in which the "*chaos sive natura*" opens, the "*chaos of everything*," which, Nietzsche says, does not contradict the thought of the circular course. But what else does he say? "*Excluding the return*, there is nothing identical." There is nothing identical except for the fact that everything returns. "Everything returns" does not belong to the temporality of time. It must be thought outside time, outside Being, and as the Outside itself; this is why it can be named "eternal" or *aevum*. "*I love my ignorance of the future*": this desire to be ignorant by which ignorance becomes desire is the waiting welcomed by forgetting, is the forgetting traversed by waiting, *annulus aeternitatis*: the desire of the "Everything returns" that alone makes desire return, without beginning or end.

± ± The affirmation of the return: an affirmation that is itself without return, excluded from every site of affirmation. Where would this affirmation that is without return be situated? There is no moment—no instance—for the affirmation of all affirmation, any more than for he who would affirm it since its presence means:

a lack whose lack no mark could indicate without thereby annulling itself. It therefore never affirms itself. This "never" is the sole fault in such a thought; it is also its "verification," the sign of its absolute seriousness, and precisely what prevents it, whatever the speech that may bear it, from being taken seriously—the limit-experience. But of this as well, Nietzsche warns us, so as to have done with it: *"Thus you prepare yourself for the time when you must speak. And then perhaps you will be ashamed to speak . . . "*

III

THE ABSENCE OF THE BOOK
the neutral, the fragmentary

I

The Final Work

If Rimbaud brings his relations with literature to a close in drafting *A Season* and the "Farewell" with which it ends, this does not mean that in the month of August 1873, on a particular day and at a particular hour, he rose from his desk and retired. A decision of a moral order can, strictly speaking, be arrived at in an instant: such is its abstract force. But the end of literature once again involves all of literature, since it must find in itself its necessity and its measure. Let us suppose — as it is possible, and I think probable — that Rimbaud continued to write poetry after having *buried* his *imagination* and his *memories*. What would this continued activity, this survival mean? First, that his break was not simply "a duty" as he may momentarily have thought, but responded to a more obscure, more profound, and, in any case, less determined exigency. Secondly, that for one who wishes to bury his memory and his gifts, it is still literature that offers itself as ground and as forgetting.

I think that by his studies, his challenges, and his exactitude, Bouillane de Lacoste has done us a great service: precisely in deterring us from giving this end a simplicity pleasing to our imagination, but only befitting a moral decision. We were tempted to forget that it takes time to disappear, and that the poet who renounces being one is still faithful to the poetic exigency, if only as a traitor. An exigency that passes by way of literature and must lead back to it. In any case, despite the fact that Rimbaud wrote not only the *Illuminations* but also the thousands of lines one may from time to time find in Harrar, *A Season* indeed remains the final work, even if it was not written last and even if it needed the maturity of the other prose pieces to open out in a truer and more tried fashion upon silence.

We have no decisive proof whether in London a year after the break, or later, Rimbaud still carried on as a poet. On two occasions, however, he assumed the role of a man of letters: a first time (if here we credit Bouillane de Lacoste's material observations) by transcribing a clean copy of his poems while in the company of Germain Nouveau; then in 1875, in Stuttgart, in having Verlaine deliver some "prose poems" to Nouveau "to have them printed." We know, then, that through 1875 he kept up certain literary concerns. Even if he is not writing he takes an interest in what he has written; going back over the paths he has traced, he keeps them open as a possibility of communication with his friends. Already with the *Season*, which he took care to have published, we sense that he was not directing against his work a will that is simply aggressive and destructive. What he let become words have also to become printed words, after which he is apparently no longer concerned with the part of himself that has ceased to belong to him.

The relations between the *Illuminations* and *A Season in Hell* are clearly difficult to ascertain: not for anecdotal or stupidly mythical reasons, but because these two works (let us refer to them in this way since they are ordinary volumes in our libraries) are not written by the same hand, nor at the same level of experience. The *Season*, on the one hand, says everything: it is in this sense that it is written quite at the end, with only one exception. From this final perspective, the poet of the *Illuminations*, and the undertaking he assumed in writing them, find their place and are necessarily affirmed in the past. Most of the traits he uses there to define and denounce his endeavor (I recall them in rough outline: the supernatural powers, the ambition of reaching the whole and, first of all, the whole of man, the power to live a plurality of lives, the unveiling of the mysteries, study, the approach and description of every possible landscape, the force of rhythm, the use of hallucination and poison), as well as the entire history of his mind—all this experience he describes as vain—allude precisely to the plans at work in the prose fragments, allude to them as something that has already taken place, and that he takes to be over.

Whence, it seems to me, the assurance with which commentators have affirmed the anteriority of the *Illuminations*; not necessarily out of a love for the myth, but because it seems difficult to situate after the *Season* the composition of a work this latter examines and casts back into the past.

I think this truth must be taken into account. Even if written afterward, the prose poems belong to a time that is "anterior," the time particular to art that the one who writes would have done with: *"No more words"*—a prophetic being, seeking by every means a future and seeking it on the basis of the end already come. The "Farewell," in other words, takes as accomplished (and over) the possibilities that are those of art in general; those the *Illuminations* have set, or will set to work. The question we find posed is roughly this one: in this instant at which poetry comes to an end and literature is finished—each of these being not simply an aesthetic activity, but representing the decision to extend man's powers to the extreme limit by liberating him first of all from the divisions of morality and returning him to a relation of mastery with the primary forces — in this instant when he must dismiss poetry as a future, a future that is the "release" and unfolding of every human possibility through poetry, what will be left to him, what issue might there be? The *Season* is the search for a response that, as we know, is of an astonishing and enigmatic firmness.

Now this last book does not say that its author will no longer write; from its first preamble (probably written last) it says the contrary with a phrase that qualifies in advance the future literary accomplishments to which he foresees committing himself (perhaps also because they are already in progress): *"and while awaiting the few small belated cowardices, you who love in a writer the absence of descriptive or instructive faculties, I tear out for you these few hideous pages from my notebook of a damned soul."* I think these disparaging words characterize in what state of mind a man who is situated at the end of poetic time (the end, also, of the illusions of poetic magic) considers his next and last work: he sees in it a lack of rigor, he judges it anachronistic. But conversely, if *"the few small cowardices"* he still must finish in order to have done with poetry are "belated," it is because the affirmation of the end is anticipatory and prematurely announces a new hour — the grueling hour that will truly mark for him history's turning, the *Season* itself being this speech of the turning where, in a vertiginous manner, time turns.

*

Have we thus definitively shed light on the relations between the *Illuminations* and the "Farewell"? No. For if it is true that the prose poems are in advance included in the final settling of accounts, be it as an oeuvre still outstanding, it is no less true that even as they respond to the idea of a condemned art (condemned as *"lie"* and as *"stupidity"*), they belong to a different region from which a new force, a sovereign affirmation, comes to us — even and perhaps especially as it expresses the necessity of failure. We are here before a mysterious movement we cannot approach by relating it to biographical incidents (which, moreover, we do not even know). Bouillane de Lacoste says that in 1874, with Germain Nouveau, Rimbaud found stability and health, a health still associated with drugs if, as Yves Bonnefoy understands it, *"the assassins' hour"* does indeed belong to his second stay in London. This time the experience is successful, whereas in the preceding years it was but stupor, madness, hell.[1] But why such a change? By whatever name we call it, it constitutes the inexplicable. In studying the poems entitled "Youth," "Lives," "War," "Genie," "Sale," and in relation to "Morning of drunkenness" (an apotheosis of drugs), Yves Bonnefoy wonders whether the change may not have come from the newly discovered relation between "poison" and "music," the latter being one of the keys to the *Illuminations* insofar as there is affirmed there "a kind of symphonic fulfillment of man's nature, a rhythmic, coherent, danced unleashing of the virtualities of his essence." In these passages, says Bonnefoy, "everything is organized around two essential notions: that of a new undertaking, an *invention*, and of a *harmony*" that a calculation would seek to master. This is an analysis that perhaps rightly characterizes the endeavor, but in what way would it be new? In "Vagabonds," a prose piece that, whatever its date of composition, evokes the time when Rimbaud lived with Verlaine, we find clear allusions to the same research: on the one hand, to the undertaking (the "*pitiful brother*" reproaches him for not seizing it "fervently" enough); on the other hand to music, to creating through music the phantoms of a future nocturnal luxury, such as various poems of the *Illuminations* in the flash of an instant render visible ("*I was creating, beyond a country haunted with bands of rare music, the ghosts of future nocturnal luxury*"). Rimbaud ironically qualifies this exercise as a "*vaguely hygienic distraction*," hence Bonnefoy's conclusion that the moment of triumph celebrated by "Morning of drunkenness" has not yet come. But one can just as well say that at this late moment of lucidity and sobriety from which it is judged the triumph is already past. It is toward this conclusion that other commentators incline; in particular a most recent one in whose view the kind of "progressivist" optimism evident in poems such as "Genie," "To a reason," and "Motion" sends us back to a much earlier period, when social illuminism allowed a humanity in movement to glimpse for an instant a future of reason and love. "An optimism that will hardly be timely at the moment of his spiritual and moral crisis of 1873."[2]

I shall refrain, however, from adopting such a conclusion. It seems to me that in listening to these poems there can be no doubt that what "Genie" says, what "War" says, what "To a reason," "Departure," and even "Sale" say, has a fullness of affirmation, a decisive assurance, also a measure and an authority that depend upon no analogy and are consonant with no known period of Rimbaud's life. A certainty that one might express by saying simply: the *Illuminations* belong to a time that is other, whether this time be anterior to, posterior to, or contemporaneous with the *Season*. Or, to put this more clearly: these two works each time gather the whole of his experience from beginning to end around a different center; and this repetition, because it is accomplished in forms and at levels that are incomparable, makes of each an exclusive space, an affirmation that pushes the other back into the past. When we read the pages written from April to August 1873, we cannot doubt that we are reading what he wrote last, and we must believe him since he takes the precaution of telling us. The *Illuminations*, in a sense, appear supernumerary; of a time already rejected, drafted here and there in the interstices of days, and much too literary (in the sense of a certain preciousness in the words) to find their place in a life from now on without literature, unless it be out of "cowardice." But should we arrive at this other word and draw ourselves up to the height to which it invites us, we then reach a day so dominant, so far-reaching, and so impersonal that it is the whole of an entire existence still unknown that it seems to illuminate, as if the whole of life and experience were written from one end to the other anew, covering over, effacing, and annulling every other possible version.

*

One book overlays another book, one life another—a palimpsest where what is below and what above change according to the measure taken, each in turn constituting what is still the unique original. This obligation to read Rimbaud at times from the final perspective of the *Season* and at other times from the ultimate perspective of the *Illuminations* necessarily belongs to the truth that is proper to him, all the while making the ambiguous outcome of poetry perceptible to us—if indeed poetry must each time include its failure. But this failure is one time the abrupt ending of the "Farewell" (its decisive contestation excluding it from the truth it signifies), and another time the solemn and serene dismissal of "Genie," which one must "know how" to *send away*; it—spirit, genie, or genius—being there only in the movement, the clarity, the detour of its disappearance. How could we, from without and by means of erudite discoveries (useful, of course), choose one of these two endings over and against the other? How, from within, can we even approach what the necessity of this contradiction signifies?

Through analysis, certainly, we can always move a few steps ahead and thus better orient ourselves toward the center of these two works. The center: the needle, the point of secret pain that, far from allowing this figure to become circumscribed according to a relation determined from the outset, harries it with haste and without pause. What would the center be? If it is not within the commentator's scope to decide the matter by authority or knowledge, we can attempt an approach in interrogative form, asking: what in each case is the relation between the center and the present self of Rimbaud? And we sense that it is not the same self, for the one saying I at times says it (as in the *Season*) with a personal urgency, which, even through the metaphorphoses sketched out in "Bad Blood," preserves a violent relation to presence, while at other times it is said impersonally, from out of a distance or an irrevocable forgetting, even when in "Youth" or "Vagabonds" the speaker decidedly refers to himself. In these two works where everything comes to an end, where does the affirmation of a future that obstinately holds itself in reserve come from? And is it the same future? We sense that if the word each time speaks by anticipation, a word from a present in which a future is said, what comes is not of the same coming: at times granted in a waiting that is in the end awakened, and in fact is "the vigil," that vigilance of promise where, the silence won, Rimbaud destines himself victoriously to the seizable "truth," while at other times it is granted in the fulfillment of everything possible to man, that immense possibility where it is no longer important that Rimbaud be present. It is as though, in other words, the future of the *Season* offered itself as personally accessible to he who renounces impersonality and the magic sweep of poetic speech; but also as though the *Illuminations* designated that infinite future where no particular individual can have a place, and that even only allows itself to be said by one who has already desisted in this speech. In both cases there is renunciation: but in *A Season* the renunciation of poetic speech seems to promise a personal future of truth, while the renunciation of the *Illuminations* is a renunciation of every individual salvation in favor of the already impersonal speech that holds in it the possibility of all that comes.

Finally this last question, which again takes up the other two: it is manifest that in both these works rapidity is the word's essential trait, its power to attain and the chance of speaking truly.[3] So why is the movement of these two writings such that they will not submit to the same measure? For in *A Season* precipitation is a vital necessity. The fact that the writer feels the need to respond at the same time to opposing summons, also the transport that alone permits him to confront the contrary exigencies of his life as a whole, make this the most critical text that a literature can offer us. But if in the *Illuminations* the promptitude of the thought that displaces itself is less visible, it is not because its movement is less rapid, nor the sweep won by this movement less vast; on the contrary, the space that is occupied includes in its future the entire space of humankind, only coiled back up within the strictest limits. The poet's hand closes upon what it has seized: each fragment, then each word, compresses the distance covered in every time, in every manner, and everywhere into a unique site; all the humanly possible, which is not only the possible of active knowledge and reflective thought but, as Yves Bonnefoy so happily puts it, also a glorious possible, draws back through the contraction of form ("the formula") into the unity of a central "site"—a site of concentration that is less the center than its immobile shattering.

In however scattered a fashion circumstances have restored them to us, however foreign they remain to the structures of an ordered composition, and however unstable they may be, the *Illuminations* have as their movement the most direct and most decisive attraction toward a *possible* center; a lightning flash that in illuminating draws back to its originary site. The *Season*, on the other hand, a simultaneous affirmation of all the contradictory positions held to and an ordeal undergone with the most acute contrariety, is the experience of a thought driven and expulsed from its center; a center it discovers to be "the *impossible*" and to which it draws impossibly near, precisely in the divergence that pushes it away, dispersed, toward the outside. But what do the words "possible," "impossible" convey? It is less Rimbaud's secret than our own—I mean our task and our aim. It is, of course, easy to say that these names are the two ways of naming "the *unknown*," two modes of acceding or relating to what is other. And it is again easy to suggest that "turning toward . . . " "turning away from . . . ," these two movements that can be neither separated nor reconciled, already designate by their meaning the future of possibility and impossible presence. Movements that the direction of these two poetic works would help us begin to recognize.

*

Yves Bonnefoy says more than this, however, and in ending I would like to restate his reflections, for they are of the greatest value. Rimbaud, naming fire, affirms or promises immediate participation in the flame of what is. *"I lived as a golden spark of this light*, nature." But elsewhere:

> *Live, and to the fire*
> *Leave obscure misfortune.*

Yves Bonnefoy comments: There is, then, the *fire* of being or of the search for being; but what is *obscure pain?* What is this affliction obscurely associable with fire, and from which whoever wishes to live must distract himself? It may be that "poetry, engaging us wholly in the quest for unity, in a relation as absolute as possible with the very presence of being, . . . does nothing other than separate us from other beings." Thus, "having wanted . . . to find reality again in its depth, in its substance, the poet loses it all the more as harmony and communion." Rimbaud expressed this fundamental contrariety in diverse ways and at different levels, in accordance with the movements that were proper to his life and his research: the contradiction within him of a force and a lack. The force is his uncontrollable energy, the power of invention, the affirmation of everything possible, and untiring hope (drunkenness, the Vision in its Happiness); the lack, after the "stolen heart," is infinite dispossession, destitution, ennui, separation, affliction (sleep). But, once again, and from out of this essential default, poetry in Rimbaud sees itself charged with the duty of transforming lack into a resource, the impossibility of speaking that is affliction into a new future of speech, and the privation of love into the exigency of "a love to be reinvented"; to take up another of Yves Bonnefoy's expressions, it is as though the degradation of being to something inert and produced (objects, stratified society, stupra, moralizing religion) had to be borne and assumed by the poet, brought into relation with that which is always of the future in poetic presence. But the contradiction remains: a contradiction between the personal search for salvation (in the sense of a truth to be possessed in one soul and in one body, the search proper to communication) and the impersonal experience in which the neutral hides. That is to say, the contradiction between the need for communication that must affirm itself from the basis of affliction and through the *"ardent patience"* of the man who suffers, and the need for communication that is affirmed on the basis of fire and through the knowing, impatient, ecstatic and glorious seizing of the man who conquers.

But here, I believe, we must evoke Hölderlin, for whom, as for Rimbaud, the word *fire* and the word *light* represented "Happiness" and "obscure misfortune."

What Hölderlin says of *"the immediate"* —which is *"the impossible"* —ought to help us enter into the obscurity of this day that is nonetheless the common day, common to everyone and to every instant—for all communication comes from fire, but fire is the incommunicable. Calling to memory this knowledge that is for us necessarily still very abstract, let us listen to the simple words:

> *Come now fire!*
> *We wish*
> *To see the day . . .*

II

Cruel Poetic Reason
(the rapacious need for flight)

We are not yet able to attend as well as we should to the destiny of Antonin Artaud. Neither what he was, nor what happened to him in the domains of writing, of thought, and of existence—none of this, even if we knew it better, could provide us with signs that would be sufficiently clear. There are, however, some partial truths we should establish for the moment: that he had the gift of an extreme lucidity that tormented him; that he was constantly concerned with poetry and thought, and not with his person in the manner of the romantics; that he exposed himself to an exigency of disruption that put into question the givens of every culture, and in particular those of the contemporary world.

We shall forgo, in order to gain access to him, the conventional image of the lightning-struck genius. We shall not forget the space of suffering, of contraction, and of cries in which he remained, but we will never see him bring a complacent gaze to bear solely upon himself. If he examined the enigma that he represented with suspicion, it is because this enigmatic existence constantly required him to struggle with the new conditions and relations exacted by the spirit of poetry with which he was obliged to dwell without relying upon traditional social or religious forms. That he did not succumb, that he found himself among us a stranger, but with a strangeness that was pure and preserved and with an authority his language did not betray, this alone is what astonishes us and ought to help us discern in him the force of poetic reason.

This reason was never confused, but of a necessity so trenchant and of a firmness so rigorous that he had to fashion for it the word *cruelty*. It is this cruel poetic reason, following the paths of a particular kind of suffering, that first made him extremely hard on his own thought; then, at a later stage, dangerously induced him to seek in the communication of art and the sacred a new consciousness of the sacred and a new form of art.

It is somewhat arbitrary to interpret his experience and his life as though they were apportioned into distinct tasks and periods. This division is nonetheless useful because, even if arbitrarily, it helps us understand the different and complex meaning of the critical events to which he was destined.

The first period is represented by the *Correspondence* with Jacques Rivière, *Umbilical Limbo*, *Nerve Scales*, *Art and Death*, and nearly all the texts collected in the first volume of his *Complete Works* in French. These texts constitute the richest and most subtle meditation on the essence of thought. They constitute the most burning approach to this singular *lack* that is thought when it realizes itself as the center of literary creation. With a force of image and a refinement of abstraction, Artaud here tells us more and tells us more precisely about the relations between thought and poetry than do most thinkers and, in general, the most painstaking creators. Twenty years after writing them, he himself will bring this judgment to bear upon *Umbilical Limbo* and *Nerve Scales*: "*At the moment, they seemed to me full of cracks, fissures, platitudes and as though they were stuffed with spontaneous abortions, with abandonments and abdications of every kind, moving always off to the side of what I wanted to say that was essential and enormous, and which I said I would never say. But after a lapse of twenty years they appear stupefying to me, not a success in relation to me, but in relation to the inexpressible.*"

The experience of poetic thought as a lack and as a suffering is overwhelming. It engages whoever undergoes it in the violence of combat. Artaud, mysteriously, was the site of this combat: a combat between thought as lack and the impossibility of bearing this lack, between thought as nothingness and the plenitude of upsurgence that hides in thought, between thought as separation and life as inseparable from thought. In 1946 Artaud says again of this combat: "*and I never wrote but to say that I had never done anything, could never do anything and that in doing something I was doing nothing. My entire work was built and could only be built on this nothingness   on this carnage, this fray of extinguished fires, of crystals and slaughter; one does nothing, one says nothing, but one suffers, one despairs and fights, yes I think that in reality one fights — will one appreciate, judge, or justify this combat? No   Will it be given a name? not either   to name the battle is, perhaps, to kill the nothingness. But above all to stop life   one will never stop life.*"[1]

*

Neither literary art as he finds it, despite his admiration for surrealism, nor life as it manifests itself in the world in which he lives, even that of the churches, seem to him able to approach what is at stake in this combat. During a period of transition when he participates with more ease in the movements of his era, he is led to seek the conditions for a true art, a new language, and, more radically, a renewed culture. The importance of these preoccupations for Artaud cannot be overstated. Certainly he is not a professor, an aesthetician, or a man of serene thought. He is never on sure ground. He says what he says not through his life itself (this would be too simple), but through the shock of that which calls him outside ordinary life. Thus delivered over to an inordinate experience, he measures himself against it with a mind that is steady, difficult, and fiery, but ever seeking light in the flame.

Artaud left us a major document that is nothing other than a treatise on poetics. I grant that in it he speaks of the theater, but what is in question is the exigency of poetry, an exigency that can only be answered through a refusal of the limitations of genre and the affirmation of a more original language *"whose source is taken at an even more buried and remote point in thought."* The themes and discoveries of his reflections, to my mind, hold true for every creative act: (1) That poetry is *"a poetry in space"* insofar as it is language that *"aims at encompassing and using expanse, that is, space, and by using it, making it speak."* Thus it is not simply a matter of the real space that the stage presents to us, but of a space that is *other*, closer to signs and more expressive, more abstract and more concrete; the very space prior to all language that poetry attracts, makes appear and releases through words that dissimulate it: *"The intellectual space, the play of the physical and the silence, molded by thoughts, which exists between the members of a written sentence are traced [in the theater] in the scenic air between the members, the air, and the perspectives of a certain number of cries, colors, and movements."* (2) That poetry *"springs from the need for speech rather than from speech already formed."* (3) That *"the highest possible idea of theater is one that reconciles itself philosophically with Becoming."* (4) That art does not tell of reality, but of its shadow—that it is the darkening and deepening through which something other announces itself to us without revealing itself. *"For theater, as for culture, the problem remains one of naming and directing the shadows."* (5) That true theater, "true" art, *"incites to a sort of virtual revolt that can only be of value if it remains virtual"*: the experience of art as the accomplishment of that which cannot be accomplished, the realization of what is nonetheless always other than the real.

The idea of poetry understood as space, a space not of words but of the relations of words that—always preceding them and nonetheless given by them—is their moving suspension, the appearance of their disappearance; the idea of this space as a pure becoming; the idea of image and of shadow, of the double and of an absence *"more real than presence"*; that is, the experience of being that is image before it is object, and the experience of an art that is gripped by the violent difference that is prior to all representation and all knowledge; the idea, finally, of art as revolt—but the most grave revolt, although apparently not real. These are some of the themes we owe to Artaud, themes he developed with the clear rigor that is the rigor of poetic consciousness.

*

This rigor is proper to Artaud. It is the violence that never allowed him to think without danger. He immediately recognized that if, on the level of artistic realization, it signifies "*implacable purity, a culmination at whatever price*," and if, on another level, it requires the pursuit of intense movement, a passionate, convulsive life and also a moral rigor, a determined and resolute consciousness on a level that he calls cosmic or metaphysical, this rigor is marked by "*the unbridling of pure forces*," the shock of what is without limit and without form, "*the initial viciousness*" of that which, while it remains inviolable and safe, never leaves us untouched: a dismembering violence that from out of the open depths makes an ignoble body, at once closed and fissured, and from out of the fragmentary an absolute morcellation by bursts, tearings, organic and anorgic explosions: the prior dissociation or decomposition that is released in the fury—the flesh heap—of writing. Whence this sentence devoid of morality: "*all writing is a spilling of guts.*"

At about the same time as he is writing the texts destined to find a place in *The Theatre and Its Double*, Artaud writes *Heliogabale*, where the research he will not cease to sustain up to the end of his life begins to find expression: it is that of the "*sacred spirit.*" The sacred: not the sky separated from the earth, but the violent communication that does not disjoin force and god, that does not "*nail the sky in the sky and the earth to the earth*," that remains in contact with the whole and with "*the crushing multiplicity*" of things, their shattering contradictions, their "*aspect of flaming discord*," and their unity. In all the texts that are to follow, as in his whole bearing, we will recognize the same endeavor and course: the decision to take over from non-Christian civilizations the essential form of the sacred; the advent of the divine through "*the god-liaisons of the earth . . . who play in the four ringing corners of the atmosphere and at the four magnetized knots of the sky*": the "spasmodic" manifestation of being.

Much more than by his blasphemy and invectives, this understanding of the sacred, a stormy identification with the whole, marks the irreducible divergence from Christian religion and idealism. I think this trait must be remembered if we wish to understand why his conversion in 1937 was the most dramatic of alienations. He is a Christian, if this is the meaning of his conversion, but he is unable to *think* in Christian terms; the speech and the poetry in him unendingly affirm what renders his faith absurd and his life impossible. Evoking Nietzsche here cannot fully clarify matters. Nonetheless, we see Nietzsche collapse at the point where Dionysus, the pagan revelation of the divine, collides in him against the affirmation of the Crucified. Hölderlin, also, says the Unique that is the Christian god, and says the sacred that is the convulsion that engulfs the Unique. There are many differences between these three destinies. But even if we ought not let ourselves become fascinated by what is common to them, we glimpse in the event by which they are struck the violent collision of two irreconcilable forms of the sacred—a contradiction that is its very essence, and the impossible division between the gods of the return and the God of the decline. For an existence belonging historically to a monotheistic civilization, what does such an appeal to the gods signify? Nothing that can be reconciled with the historic sojourn they have in common. And why the gods? Why are they *gods?* The response is perhaps suggested by Hölderlin: the gods are gods in order to be not only unique, but alone in their plurality.

*

We are not ready to place in their true light the last ten years of Artaud's life. What is staggering is that, delivered over to the spirit that is flame, Artaud never frees himself from the faithfulness to light that is spirit. Nor does he betray the one for the other. He was, nonetheless, perhaps the closest witness to the spirit of flame ever to appear since Böhme (and here again, by way of, or even beyond, the enigmatic way it is recalled by Hölderlin, Rimbaud, and Heraclitus):

> *Wicked fire that rises*
> *perfect projection and symbol of*
> *the irritated will rebelling*
> unique *image of rebellion*
> *fire separates, and separates from itself*
> *it disjoins and burns itself*
> *what it burns is itself*
> *punishing itself*

When he speaks of life it is of fire that he speaks; when he names the void it is the burning of the void, the ardor of raw space, the incandescence of the desert that he names. Evil is what burns, forces, excoriates. If in the intimacy of his thought and the violence of his speech he always felt the attack of something wicked, he recognized in this Evil not sin, but cruelty, and the very essence of the spirit that *"the true heart of the suffering poet"* is destined to shelter. It is indeed true that Artaud's suffering is of the mind and by the mind. It is true that his thought was pain, and his pain the infinite of thought. But this violence he suffers with a strange innocent torment, like the revolt affirmed by his speech, far from representing a particular and personal impulse, indicates the insurrection that comes from the depths of being: as though being were not simply being, but already in its depths *"the spasm of being"* and the *"rapacious need for flight"* that constantly swept the life and the poetry of Antonin Artaud.[2]

III

René Char
and the Thought of the Neutral

I shall start by noting what might seem to be no more than a detail. Certain important words in René Char's language are grammatically neuter, or border on the neutral. *"The foreseeable, but not yet formulated," "the absolute inextinguishable," "the impossible living," "pleasure's moaning," "Chilling"* [*Transir*], *"Bordering," "the great unformulated distant (the unhoped-for living)," "the essential intelligible," "the half-open," "the impersonal infinite," "the obscure," "Leaving."* These reminders are meant not to prove anything, but simply to orient our attention. A technical analysis, moreover, would show the different—and nearly each time different—functions of these various expressions. But this is not what is important. The neuter is not merely a question of vocabulary. As, for example, when René Char writes *"the passing"* (and even when he does not, we often sense it inhabiting what he writes): "furrowed passing," an intransitive passing. Were we content to translate this by "the man passing" or "he who passes," I think we would alter the neuter designation this word would bring to language, as when René Char names the *"star of the destined"* or *"the rumors of the hostile."* But what is the neuter, the neutral?

Let me also cite, from the "Argument" of *Poème pulvérisé*, a question each of us may recall: *"How can we live without the unknown before us?"* The word "unknown," whether or not expressed, is also constantly present in the language of these poems. True, it is rarely alone: *"equilibrating unknown," "the unknown that hollows out,"* yet unknown all the same. Let us now ask: why this exigency of a relation with the unknown? An answer will link the two questions. From a verbal point of view, the unknown is neuter. The discretion of the French language, which does not possess a neuter gender, is awkward but finally not without its virtue, for what belongs to the neuter is not a third gender opposed to the other two and constituting for reason a determined class of existents or beings. The neuter is that which cannot be assigned to any genre whatsoever: the non-general, the non-generic, as well as the non-particular. It refuses to belong to the category of subject as much as it does to that of object. And this does not simply mean that it is still undetermined and as though hesitating between the two, but rather that the neuter supposes another relation depending neither on objective conditions nor on subjective dispositions.

Let us pursue this a bit further. The unknown is always thought in the neuter. Thought of the neuter or the neutral is a threat and a scandal for thought. We recall, however, assisted by Clémence Ramnoux's book, that a primary trait of one of the first languages of Western thought, that of Heraclitus, is to speak in the neuter singular: *"the-one-thing-wise," "the-not-to-be-expected," "the-not-to-be-found," "the-not-to-be-approached," "the common."* What we must immediately remember is that Heraclitus's words (*"the wise-thing," "the common-thing,"* or *"this-the-wise," "this-the-one," "this-the-common"*) are not concepts in the sense of either Aristotelian or Hegelian logic, nor are they ideas in the Platonic sense or, to be precise, in any sense at all. Through this neuter nomination, which French translations cannot directly render, something is given to us to say for which our modes of abstracting and generalizing are incapable of advancing any sign.

So we find ourselves again before the question of knowing what is being proposed to us when the unknown takes this neuter turn; that is, when we sense that an experience of the neutral is implied in every relation with the unknown. But let me open yet another parenthesis. By a simplification that is clearly abusive, one can recognize in the entire history of philosophy an effort either to acclimatize or to domesticate the neuter by substituting for it the law of the impersonal and the reign of the universal, or an effort to challenge it by affirming the ethical primacy of the Self-Subject, the mystical aspiration to the singular Unique. The neutral is thus constantly expelled from our languages and our truths. This is a repression that Freud in his turn brought to light in an exemplary manner by interpreting the neuter in terms of drive and instinct, and then finally in a perspective that is perhaps still anthropological,[1] before Jung came along to recuperate it under the name of archetype, retrieving it on behalf of a respectable spirituality. Heideggerian philosophy can be understood as a response to this examination of the neuter and as an attempt to approach it in a non-conceptual manner; but this must also be understood as a new retreat before that which thought seems only able to entertain by sublimating it.[2] It is the same thing when Sartre condemns what he calls "the practico-inert," speaking of it as theologians speak of evil and seeing therein (rightly, as it happens) not a moment of the dialectic, but a moment of experience capable of undoing all dialectics, for it is again the neuter that thought approaches, this time by belittling it; that is, precisely in refusing to think it as neutral.

"How can we live without the unknown before us?" In the evidency of this question-affirmation there is something that summons us; a difficulty that, holding us in its sight, nonetheless steals away in a nearly reassuring form. It has to be sought. The unknown is neutral, a neuter. The unknown is neither object nor subject. This means that to think the unknown is in no way to propose it as "the not yet known," the object of a knowledge still to come, any more than it would be to go beyond it as "the absolutely unknowable," a subject of pure transcendence, refusing itself to all manner of knowledge and expression. On the contrary, let us (perhaps arbitrarily) propose that in research—where poetry and thought affirm themselves in the space that is proper to them, separate, inseparable[3]—the unknown is at stake; on condition, however, that it be explicitly stated that this research relates to the unknown as unknown. A phrase all the same disconcerting, since it proposes to "relate" the unknown inasmuch as it is unknown. In other words, we are supposing a relation in which the unknown would be affirmed, made manifest, even exhibited: disclosed—and under what aspect?—precisely in that which keeps it unknown. In this relation, then, the unknown would be disclosed in that which leaves it under cover. Is this a contradiction? In effect. In order to bear the weight of this contradiction, let us try to formulate it differently. Research—poetry, thought—relates to the unknown as unknown. This relation discloses the unknown, but by an uncovering that leaves it under cover; through this relation there is a "presence" of the unknown; in this "presence" the unknown is rendered present, but always as unknown. This relation must leave intact—untouched—what it conveys and not unveil what it discloses. This relation will not consist in an unveiling. The unknown will not be revealed, but indicated.

(In order to avoid any misunderstanding, we should make it clear that if this relation with the unknown sets itself apart from objective knowledge, it does so no less from a knowledge that would arise out of intuition or a mystical fusion. The unknown as neutral supposes a *relation* that is foreign to every exigency of identity, of unity, even of presence.)

Let us return to our reflections, and let us even hasten them. We have spoken of relating to the unknown without unveiling it through a relation of non-presence that would not be an uncovering. In very precise terms, this means that the unknown in the neuter, in the neutral, does not belong to light, but rather to a region "foreign" to the disclosure that is accomplished in and through light. The unknown does not fall before a gaze, yet it is not hidden from it: neither visible nor invisible; or, more precisely, turning itself away from every visible and every invisible.

These propositions risk having no meaning unless they achieve their end, which is to put into question the postulate under whose sway all Western thought stands. Let me again recall this postulate: knowledge of the visible-invisible is knowledge itself; light and the absence of light are to furnish all the metaphors for the means by which thought goes out toward that which it proposes to think; we can "set our sights" (still an image borrowed from optical experience) only on what comes to us in the presence of an *illumination*; finally, inasmuch as all sight encompasses a view of the whole, inasmuch as the experience of sight is an experience of panoramic continuity, we must always submit not only comprehension and knowledge but also every form of relation to a perspective *of the whole*.

*

"But if the unknown as unknown is neither visible nor invisible, what relation with the unknown — one we have supposed to be in play in poetry itself (a relation non-mystical and non-intuitive) — might still indicate itself?'

— Yes, what relation? The least exceptional, the relation that poetry has the task of carrying: poetry, which is to say, also, the most simple speech, if speaking is in fact the relation through which the unknown designates itself in a relation other than the one accomplished in illumination.

— Then it would be in speech — in the interval that is speech — that the unknown, without ceasing to be unknown, would indicate itself to us such as it is: separate, foreign?

— Yes, speech; but nonetheless only insofar as it responds to the space that is proper to it. 'How can we live without the unknown before us?' The unknown excludes all perspective; it does not remain within the circle of sight, it cannot belong to a whole. In this sense, it also excludes the dimension of a 'going out ahead.' The unknown of the future with which we can have a prospective relation is not the unknown that speaks to us as unknown; on the contrary, it cannot but hold in check and ruin every hope of a future.

— Then ought we say that to offer oneself to the experience of the unknown is to put oneself radically to the test of the negative or of a radical absence?

— No, we cannot say this. With the thought of the neutral the unknown escapes every negation as it does every position. Neither adding to nor withdrawing anything from what affirms it, it is neither negative nor positive. The unknown does not find its determination in the fact that it either is or is not, but only in the fact that relation with the unknown is a relation that is not opened by light or closed by light's absence. A neutral relation. Which means that to think or to speak in the neuter, the neutral, is to think or to speak apart from every visible and every invisible, that is, in terms that do not answer to possibility. *'How can we live without the unknown before us?'* The pressing form of this questioning, then, comes from the following: (1) to live is necessarily to live ahead of oneself;

(2) to live 'authentically,' 'poetically,' is to have a relation with the unknown as such, and thus to put at the center of one's life *this-the-unknown* that does not allow one to live ahead of oneself and, moreover, withdraws every center from life.

— Assuredly, the 'unknown' of which René Char speaks is not the simple unknown of the future: the latter is always already given to us and is but a 'not yet known.' Every individual life has this future, even in a world become entirely commonplace.

— The unknown to which poetry alerts us is much more unforeseeable than the future can be, even *'the future unforetold'* for, like death, it escapes every hold.

— Except the hold that is speech.

— Except speech, but insofar as speech is not a hold, affords no purchase. Here is the essential. To speak the unknown, to receive it through speech while leaving it unknown, is precisely not to take hold of it, not to comprehend it; it is rather to refuse to identify it even by sight, that 'objective' hold that seizes, albeit at a distance. To live with the unknown before one (which also means: to live before the unknown, and before oneself as unknown) is to enter into the responsibility of a speech that speaks without exercising any form of power; even the power that accrues to us when we look, since, in looking, we keep whatever and whomever stands before us within our horizon and within our circle of sight — thus within the dimension of the visible-invisible. Here let us recall René Char's now long-standing affirmation, which will bring forth everything we have just tried to say: '*A being of which one is ignorant is a being that is infinite — capable, in intervening, of changing our anguish and our burden into arterial dawn.*' The unknown as unknown is this infinite, and the speech that speaks it is a speech of the infinite.

— It is in this sense, then, that we are permitted to say: to speak is to bind oneself, without ties, to the unknown.

— Speaking, writing."

*

I will close these initial reflections here. They do not pretend to offer a commentary on René Char; they rather point to a path previously neglected so as to attempt approach to one part of his work. A part that is perhaps growing. What was written at the margin is no longer simply marginal. Hence — at least so it seems to me — the lack of recognition and the kind of violence with which, "at this hour of nightfall," certain critics seek to guard against this work in seeking to immobilize it, assign it limits, and reduce it to their tranquil measure. "*I am going to speak and I know what saying is, but what is the hostile echo that interrupts me?*"

Parentheses:

± ± "*The neuter, the neutral: What are we to understand by this word? —* "*Perhaps there is nothing in it to be understood.*" — "*So we should first exclude the forms by which, traditionally, we are most tempted to approach it: the objectivity of some knowledge; the homogeneity of a milieu; the interchangeability of elements; or fundamental indifference, where the absence of ground and the absence of difference go hand in hand.*" — "*In that case, where would such a word apply?*"

± ± "*Let us continue to exclude and erase. Neutral—this comes to language through language. However, the neuter, or neutral, is not simply a grammatical gender—or as a gender and a category, it orients us toward something else, the* aliquid *that bears its mark. To give a first example, let us say that the one who does not enter into what he says is neutral; just as speech can be held to be neutral when it pronounces without taking into account either itself or the one who pronounces it, as though, in speaking, it did not speak but allowed that which cannot be said to speak in what there is to say.*" — "*Neutral, then, remarkably, would send us back to the transparency whose ambiguous and non-innocent status would be marked in this manner: there would be an opacity of transparency, or something even more opaque than opacity since that which reduces this opacity does not reduce the depth of transparence, which, as an absence, carries it and makes it be.*" — "*Precisely, its being: the being of transparence.*" — "*This is just what I would not say, saying rather: the neutral of what we call being, which already places being in parentheses and in some sense precedes it, having always already neutralized it less by a nihilating operation than by an operation that is inoperative.*" — "*Let us then also say that if transparency has the neutral as its trait, the neutral does not belong to it; it is not a neutral of transparency.*" — "*Let us remember that what is neutral is given in a position of quasi-absence, as an effect of non-effect—analogous (perhaps) to the supposed position that each radical of a word, or a series of words, holds in a same family of tongues or across differing inflections, a 'fictive' radical; in a sense, the meaning that comes to be glimpsed without ever either presenting itself or disappearing, thus impassive and as though imprescriptible, nonetheless deprived of and free of any proper meaning since it only conveys meaning through the modalities that alone give it value, reality, a 'sense.' *" — "*Thus the meaning of meaning would be neuter, neutral?*" — "*Let us for the moment assume this: neutral if, already, both affirmation and negation leave it intact in its position of meaning. (Or better: let us say that meaning is not posed, neither positive nor negative, yet affirming itself as though outside every affirmation and every negation. This would be the force and the inanity of the ontological argument: God, whether he is or he is not, remains God; God: sovereignty of the neutral, in relation to Being always in excess, empty of mean-*

ing, and through this emptiness absolutely separate from all meaning and non-meaning.)" — "Again neutral, if meaning operates or acts through a movement of retreat that is in some sense without end, through an exigency to become suspended and by an ironic outbidding of the épochè. It is not simply the natural position or even that of existence that is to be suspended so that meaning, in its pure disaffected light, might appear; meaning itself can only bear meaning by placing itself in brackets, in parentheses or quotation marks, and this through an infinite reduction; thus finally remaining outside meaning like a phantom that dissipates by day and that nonetheless is never lacking, since to be lacking is its sign." — "Meaning would therefore only exist by way of the neutral." — "But insofar as the neutral would remain foreign to meaning — by which I mean, first: neutral as far as meaning is concerned; not indifferent, but haunting the possibility of meaning and non-sense by the invisible margin of a difference." — "From which one might conclude that phenomenology had already moved obliquely toward the neutral." — "As has all that we call literature if one of its characteristics is to pursue indefinitely the épochè, the rigorous task of suspending, and suspending even itself, without it being possible, however, to ascribe this movement to negativity." — "Neutral would be the literary act that belongs neither to affirmation nor to negation and (at a first stage) frees meaning as a phantom, a haunting, a simulacrum of meaning; as though literature were spectral by nature, not because it would be haunted by itself, but because it bears the preliminary of all meaning, which is its obsession. Or, more simply, because it would itself be reduced to engaging in nothing other than simulating a reduction of the reduction, whether or not this be phenomenological; and thus, far from annulling this reduction (even should it appear to do so), it would rather, following the interminable, increase it by all that disperses it and hollows it out."

± ± *The neutral would thus be related to that which in the language of writing gives "value" to certain words, not by bringing them forward but by placing them in quotation marks or parentheses, through the singularity of an effacement that is all the more efficacious for the fact that it does not signal itself — a subtraction subtracted and dissimulated without, however, resulting in duplication. The italics the surrealists used as a sign of authority and decision would, with relation to the neutral, be outstandingly misplaced, although placing in parentheses, between dashes, or under the too-visible Saint Andrew's cross has perhaps no other effect and is only more hypocritical. Let us therefore say that it is not through the operation of placing between parentheses that the neutral would come about, but rather that this operation nonetheless corresponds to one of the neutral's sleights of hand, its "irony."*

± ± Neutral, *a word apparently closed but fissured, a qualifier without quality, raised (according to one of the customs of our time) to the rank of a substantive with neither substance nor subsistence, a term in which the interminable, without situating itself, would gather: bearing a* problem *without* response, *the neutral has the closure of an* aliquid *to which no question corresponds. For can the neutral be interrogated? Can one write: the neutral?; what is the neutral?; what can be said of the neutral? Certainly one can. But the neutral is not broached by this questioning that leaves it and does not leave it intact, that traverses it through and through or, more probably, lets itself be neutralized, pacified, or passified by it (the neutral's passivity: the passive that is beyond, and always beyond, any passive voice; the passion proper to it enveloping its proper action, an action of inaction, an effect of non-effect).*

± ± *When an act qualifiable as passive seems to lack direct relation to a subject who would accomplish it, we believe we can already speak of the neutral, the neuter: it [ça] speaks; it [ça] desires; one [on] dies. Certainly, the drive of the enigma that Freud, in naming the Unconscious, does not cease to designate but cannot fasten down—and by using as a kind of reference point capable of delimiting it, a word that is in some sense mute and whose strangeness the French ça, at once crude and refined, marks even better; as though there arose from the "vulgar" street the murmur of an unmasterable affirmation in the manner of a cry from the lowest depths—is first understood by way of the neuter, and in any case makes it so that one limits oneself to understanding the neutral as the pressure of this very enigma. But one of the traits of the neutral, which slips away as much from affirmation as from negation (and perhaps through this turn maintains the ça in the problematic position that keeps it from being either subject or object), is to harbor, yet without presenting it, the thrust of a question or questioning, not in the form of a response, but as a withdrawal with regard to whatever in this response would come to respond. The neutral questions, but it does so not in the usual manner by interrogating; while seeming to hold none of the attention that is directed toward it, and while letting itself be traversed by every interrogative force while neutralizing it, it pushes always further the limits within which this force might still exercise itself, when the very sign of questioning fades and no longer leaves affirmation either the right or the power to respond.*

± ± *The neutral: that which carries difference even to the point of indifference. More precisely, that which does not leave indifference to its definitive equalization. The neutral is always separated from the neutral by the neutral, and, far from allowing itself to be explained by the identical, it remains an unidentifiable surplus. The neutral: surface and depth, casting its lot with depth when the surface seems to rule, and with the surface when depth seeks to dominate (that is, become a dominating will), thus rendering it superficial all the while pushing it under. The neutral is always elsewhere than where one would situate it; not simply always on the hither side and always beyond the neutral, not simply devoid of a proper meaning and even of any form of positivity and negativity, but also preventing either presence or absence from proposing it with certainty to any experience whatsoever, even that of thought. And yet every* encounter *—where the Other suddenly looms up and obliges thought to leave itself, just as it obliges the Self to come up against the lapse that constitutes it and from which it protects itself—is already marked, already fringed by the neutral.*

IV

The Fragment Word

That René Char, with a more vigilant relation than any other writer to the *"night leisurely recircled"* of the neutral, should be the one who, liberating discourse from discourse, but always according to a measure, calls upon it to respond in fragmentary speech to *"the tragic, tumultuous nature of human beings, in interval and as though suspended"*: this (although already mysteriously) is what teaches us to hold together, like a doubled vocable, the fragmentary the neutral — even if this doubling is a redoubling of enigma.

Fragment word [*parole de fragment*]; a term that is hard to approach. "Fragment," a noun, but possessing the force of a verb that is nonetheless absent: brisure, a breaking without debris, interruption as speech when the pause of intermittence does not arrest becoming but, on the contrary, provokes it in the rupture that belongs to it. Whoever says fragment ought not say simply the fragmenting of an already existent reality or the moment of a whole still to come. This is hard to envisage due to the necessity of comprehension according to which the only knowledge is knowledge of the whole, just as sight is always a view of the whole. For such comprehension, the fragment supposes an implied designation of something that has previously been or will subsequently be a whole — the severed finger refers back to the hand, just as the first atom prefigures and contains in itself the universe. Our thought is therefore caught between two limits: the imagining of the integrity of substance and the imagining of a dialectical becoming. But in the fragment's violence, and, in particular, the violence to which René Char grants access, quite a different relation is given to us — at least as a promise and as a task. *"What is reality without the dislocating energy of poetry?"*

We must try to recognize in this *"shattering"*[1] or *"dislocation"*[2] a value that is not one of negation. It would be neither privative nor simply positive; as though the alternative and the obligation to begin by affirming being if one wished to deny it had here been finally, mysteriously broken. *Poème pulvérisé* is not a diminutive title. *Pulverized poem*: to write and to read this poem is to accept bending our listening to language toward the experience of a certain breaking up, an experience of separation and discontinuity. Think of *dépaysement*. Being out of one's element does not mean simply a loss of country but also a more authentic manner of residing, a habitless inhabiting; exile is an affirmation of a new relation with the Outside. The fragmented poem, therefore, is not a poem that remains unaccomplished, but it opens another manner of accomplishment—the one at stake in writing, in questioning, or in an affirmation irreducible to unity.

Fragmentary speech is never unique, even should it want to be. It is not *written* in view of unity, or by reason of unity. Taken in itself, it is true, it appears with its sharp edges and broken character like a block to which nothing seems able to attach. A piece of meteor detached from an unknown sky and impossible to connect with anything that can be known. Thus it is said that René Char employs "the aphoristic form." A strange misunderstanding. The aphorism is closed and bounded: the horizontal of every horizon. By contrast, what is important and exalting in the sequence of nearly separate "phrases" that so many of his poems (text without either pretext or context) propose is that while they are interrupted by a blank, isolated and dissociated to the point that one cannot pass from one to the next—or only by a leap and in becoming conscious of a difficult interval—they nonetheless convey in their plurality the sense of an arrangement they entrust to a future of speech. A new kind of arrangement not entailing harmony, concordance, or reconciliation, but that accepts disjunction or divergence as the infinite center from out of which, through speech, relation is to be created: an arrangement that does not compose but juxtaposes, that is to say, leaves each of the terms that come into relation *outside* one another, respecting and preserving this *exteriority* and this distance as the principle—always already undercut—of all signification. Juxtaposition and interruption here assume an extraordinary force of justice. Here all freedom finds its order on the basis of the (uneasy) ease it accords us. An arrangement at the level of disarray. An immobile becoming.

It should be understood that the poet in no way plays with disorder, for incoherence knows only too well how to compose and arrange things, albeit in reverse. Here there is a firm alliance between rigor and the neutral. René Char's "phrases," rather than being coordinated, are posed one next to the other: islands of meaning with a powerful stability, like that of the great stones of the Egyptian temples that stand without any connection between them, of an extreme density and yet capable of an infinite drift, offering an evanescent possibility, destining the weightiest to the lightest, the most abrupt to the most tender, the most abstract to the most living (the youth of a morning face). We could analyze this: a verbal privilege given to substantives; a condensation of images so rapid (a ravishment and uprooting) that the most contrasted signs—more than contrasted, without relation—are in the least space made contiguous. And finally, in the syntax of phrases, a tendency to a paratactic order; when words having no articles defining them, verbs without a determinable subject (*"Alone dwell"*), and phrases without verbs speak to us without any preestablished relations that organize or connect them.

Each of René Char's collections of poems, and each advancing on the basis of the others, sets out an always different manner of welcoming the unknown without detaining it. We each time discover a fresh relation between the poem and thought, and the error we would make in interpreting this language as though it still belonged to discourse, whether dialectical or not. The rigorous incongruity this language proposes—at times so difficult that we experience it as speech carried away or in suffering—cannot be made to enter the forms of the old categories (the tension and resolution of opposed terms). It calls upon us to surpass the false delight of scintillating ambiguity, then the torment of contrariety that opposes one term to another, but not in order to arrive at a totality where the for and the against are reconciled or merge: rather he makes us responsible for irreducible difference.

Because for René Char, as for Heraclitus, for whom (as from one solitude to another) he always felt a fraternal bond, what speaks essentially in things and in words is Difference; secret because always deferring speaking and because always differing from that which signifies it, but also such that everything makes a sign and becomes sign because of it: sayable but not silent, at work in the detour of writing.

*

Speech as archipelago: cut up into the diversity of its islands and thus causing a surging of the great open sea; this ancient immensity, the unknown always still to come, designated for us only by the emergence of the earth's infinitely divided depths. The eternal wish once again finds its force: *"But who can re-create around us that immensity, that density that was really created for us and, once, though not divinely, bathed us on all sides?"*

"Not divinely." We hear now as echo: *"The gods are back, comrades. They have just penetrated this life, but the word that revokes beneath the word that unfolds has also reappeared so that, together, they might make us suffer."* Is this a response?

Then these words: *"Suppressing distance kills. The gods only die in our midst."* Is this the response?

Let us nevertheless listen again. Let us learn to read by reading words that offer a resource to forgetting; there where writing, a writing without discourse, a tracing without trace, takes up again the always aleatory truth into the neutrality of its own enigma: *"The west lost behind you, presumed to be swallowed up, touched by nothing and outside memory, tears itself from its elliptical bed, climbs without losing its breath, at last rises and catches up. The point melts. The springs pour out. Upstream bursts forth. And below the delta turns green. The frontier song reaches the vantage point downstream. Easily content is the alder's pollen."*

Thus, through fragmentary writing, the return of the hesperic accord is announced. It is a time of decline, but a decline of ascendancy, pure detour in its strangeness: that which, permitting to go from one deception to another (as René Char states elsewhere), leads from one courage to another. The gods? Returning, having never come.

Parentheses:

± ± *The neutral does not seduce, does not attract: this is the vertigo of its attraction from which there is no safeguard. And to write is to bring this unalluring attraction into play, to expose language to it and to disengage language from it through a violence that will once again deliver language over to it—to the point of the fragment word: the suffering of an empty morcellation.*

± ± *"But isn't the neutral what is closest to the Other?"* — *"But also the most remote."* — *"The Other is in the neuter, even when it speaks to us as* Autrui, *then speaking by way of the strangeness that makes it impossible to situate and always exterior to whatever would identify it."* — *"Will we not have to grant that the* eteron *comes with the* neutral, *not like the positive with the negative, or the right side with the wrong, but rather as dissimulated in it; finding in the neutral the non-appearance of its own separation and the lure that conceals the infinity of the relation through which it is in play?"* — *"But would this not mean that the Other, always under threat of the neutral, and even marked by it, would also be in a still unmastered relation of vicissitude, and thus what demarcates itself from the neutral absolutely?"* — *"Let us first of all say that the Other and the neutral relate by, and relate to, the very thing that ought to prohibit them from ever being thought together— were it possible (but it cannot be entirely) to affirm that the Other and the neutral, but necessarily each in a different manner, do not fall under the jurisdiction of the One any more than they allow themselves to be implicated in the nonetheless inevitable belonging to Being."* — *"Each in a different manner: one through excess, the other through lack or default?"* — *"Perhaps, but all the while recalling that the difference between excess and lack—this difference that would like to become an opposition—will come to nearly nothing if it cannot be fixed: in the one case the default or the lack being excessive, just as the excess is founded upon the immensity of a lack."* — *"We can no longer, nor as easily, be content with this challenge to the One: all the more so because such a challenge cannot but fall short if it is accomplished in a mode that would simply be negative, and because it cannot—perhaps—play itself out solely through a passing 'to the limit.' "* — *"In any case, it will fall short, we can be sure of this."* — *"But wouldn't death play this role? Coming as Other, having the false appearance of the neutral, not allowing itself to be seized as unified; attaining only inasmuch as it remains inaccessible (and thereby rendering inaccessible what it reaches), nevertheless touching only what it has always already touched; having no actuality and only allowing itself to be encountered by the 'Self' that it haunts when the Self, stand-in for the Other, is no more than the already broken* fictive partner *that the Other offers itself and receives as a gift."*

± ± *Inscribe your death, then, in a region where it would not be marked as a lack; a region that would be so separate from the other regions of discourse that they would be unable to recapture this separation, even in order to designate it as such, and, in designating it, relinquish or resign it. For discourse in general, that is to say, in the region where death is inscribed as a zero of meaning (a subtraction subtracted), the lack that is marked by death would not fail to touch—all the while leaving intact—the concept of "truth," as well as the concepts of "subject" and "unity," which are deposed by it from their primary position. In this way, and at this very moment, discourse nonetheless maintains for itself the illusion of the true and the illusion of the subject; illusions with which it plays so that the ungraspable true and the subject always supposed alienated can still ensure discourse of its perpetual falling short.*

± ± *I seek the distance without concept in order that death without truth may be inscribed there—which tends to say that dying, rather than signifying failure, might delimit a region in which the effect of truth would not even be marked as a lack. Admitting a notion of science, then, as an exact writing that lacks nothing, we would suppose it capable, and solely capable, of specifying at what site writing and dying would be superimposed, or articulated together. But Science* ["la" science]: *how could it, of itself, admit this simple unity that ideally totalizes it and gives it once again over to "ideology?"*

± ± *In discourse, through discourse, and at a distance from discourse, the line of demarcation invisibly traces itself; a line that, withdrawing from discourse any power to totalize, assigns it to multiple regions; a plurality that does not tend to unity (be it in vain), nor that is constructed with relation to unity—as lying to its hither side or beyond—but that has always already set it aside. The scientificity of science does not consist in its reflection on a unity of essence but, on the contrary, in a* possibility of writing *that, each time distinct, frees the word* science *from every prior unity of essence and of meaning.*

Nonetheless "literature," through which there is no speech that is not already destined to writing, sets itself apart from science by means of its own ideology (which it can only have the illusion of deposing by reinforcing it); but also, and above all—here is literature's always decisive importance—by denouncing as ideological *the faith that science, through an implacable allegiance and for its salvation, pledges to identity and to the permanence of signs. A lure*, irreprochable decoy.

± ± *Thus we have—perhaps—better indicated the neutral's provocation. The neutral: a word* too many *that withdraws either by reserving a place for itself from which it is always missing, all the while marking itself there, or by provoking a displacement that is without place, or else by distributing itself in a multiple manner in a supplement of place.*

The word too many: it would come from the Other without ever having been heard by a self—nonetheless the sole auditor possible since it is meant for him; less to disperse or break him than to respond to the breaking or dispersal that the "I" conceals, making of itself a self by this movement of hiding that seems the beating of an empty heart. Where there is, or would be, a word too many, there is the offense and the revelation of death.

± ± *Will you, as a self, accept taking this self as problematic, as fictive, and nonetheless therefore more necessary than if you were able to close up around yourself like a circle sure of its center? Then, perhaps, in writing, you will accept as the secret of writing this premature yet already belated conclusion that is in accord with forgetting*: that others write in *my* place, this place without occupant that is my sole identity; this is what makes death for an instant joyful, aleatory.

V

Forgetful Memory

Poetry is memory; this is the classical assertion. Memory is the muse. The singer sings from memory, and grants the power to remember. The song itself is *mé-moire*, the space where the justice of memory holds sway: *Moira*, that portion of obscurity according to which right and regard are laid out.

The most ancient of the ancients already protested against the exorbitant power of the singers who, establishing themselves as masters of the memorable, had the power of death over the dead and could reward with a false renown those who ought to have disappeared without recall. Thus was Homer often blamed for the glory bestowed upon Ulysses, a man of ruse, not of deed.

Nonetheless, this protest, aimed at the caste of singers and serving the sacred shrines and their rivalries, thus the gods, is not a protest against the arbitrary flights of fancy of the poets, guilty of exalting or debasing the great silent events at their pleasure. In the first place, no one dreams that works and songs could be created out of nothing. They are always given in advance, in memory's immobile present. Who would be interested in a new and non-transmitted speech? What is important is not to tell, but to tell once again and, in this retelling, to tell again each time a first time. In the august sense, to hear is always already to have heard: to take one's place in the assembly of prior listeners and thus permit them once again to be present in this enduring hearing.

Song is memory. Poetry makes remembrance of what men, peoples, and gods do not yet have by way of their own memory, but in whose keeping they abide even as it is entrusted to their keeping. This great impersonal memory, the memory without memory of the origin that is approached by the poems of genealogy, with their terrifying legends in which the first gods are born (both within the account itself, and from out of its narrative force), constitutes the reserve to which no individual in particular, either poet or listener, has access. This is the remote. Memory as abyss. In certain Greek poems where the gods are engendered and where, still divine, they engender one another as names that are already powerful and in some sense metaphysical, Forgetting is the primordial divinity, the venerable ancestor and first presence of what, in a later generation, will give rise to Mnemosyne, mother of the Muses. The essence of memory is therefore forgetting; the forgetfulness of which one must drink in order to die.

This does not simply mean that everything begins and ends with forgetting, in the weak sense we give to this expression. Here forgetting is not nothing. Forgetting is the very vigilance of memory, the guardian force thanks to which the hidden of things is preserved, and thanks to which mortal men—like the immortal gods, preserved from what they are—rest in what of themselves is hidden.

With the modesty that is his—a modesty that in no way implies a lesser dimension of thought—Supervielle tells us, at least tells me, something of this sort. The muse is not Memory, it is Forgetful Memory. Forgetting is the sun: memory gleams through reflection, reflecting forgetting and drawing from this reflection the light—amazement and clarity—of forgetting.

> But with so much forgetting how can we make a rose,

I recall, when at present I have with Supervielle's work almost no ties other than those of memory and forgetting, the tenderly painful radiance of this central line. Memory is first confusion; it is "dim memory," "fleet memory," the altering force that establishes in us, at a surprising proximity, the enigma of an indefinite change.

> Am I here, am I there? My customary shores
> Change on every side and leave me wandering.

This interior migration, which must be lived as risk before it can be experienced as resource, is the "immobility" behind which the poet "knows what is happening." What is forgotten is a marker enabling a slow advance: the arrow designating direction. What is forgotten points at once toward the thing forgotten and toward forgetting, the most profound effacement where the site of metamorphosis is found. A passage from the outside to the inside; then from the inside to something still more inward, where intimacy and the outside of all presence, say Novalis and Rilke, are gathered within a continuous-discontinuous space.

But there is a double temptation and a risk that is hard to conceal. Forgetting is no more than the things forgotten; nonetheless, by a power of forgetting that surpasses us and greatly surpasses them, it leaves us in relation with what we forget. Philosophers would say that to forget is to possess the secret of the mediating force since what is thus effaced of us should come back to us, enriched by this loss and augmented by this lack, idealized as they say.

> *The oak becomes again tree and the shadows, plain,*
> *And here is this lake that has grown before our eyes?*

Forgetting is mediation, a happy power. But in order that this function be realized in its poetic dignity — in order that it cease being a function and become an event — what is means, intermediary, a forgetting that is simple and instrumental, an always available possibility, must be affirmed as a depth without path and without return; it must escape our mastery, ruin our power to dispose of it, ruin even forgetting as depth, and all of memory's comfortable practice. What was mediation is now experienced as separation; what was a bond now neither binds nor unbinds; what used to go from the present to a presence recalled — a productive becoming that brought all things back to us as image — is now the sterile movement, the unceasing coming and going through which, having descended into forgetting, we do not even forget: suspended between any memory and any absence of memory, we forget without the possibility of forgetting.

This trial is the trial of poetry where, as always, we rediscover the moment when reversal freezes into an errant immobility: a destiny to which, in a work of simplicity and wonder, Supervielle responded by writing what he considered his purest narrative, "The Child of the Open Sea." Here we approach, and in a manner scarcely hoped for, this life of forgetting; here something is forgotten and yet for this forgetting all the more present. A presence of forgetting and in forgetting; the power to forget without end in the event that forgets itself, but forgetting without the possibility of forgetting: forgetting-forgotten without forgetfulness. We owe a great deal to the one who with such measure made us familiar with this experience, and who succeeded in giving it to us in a single image.

But now we see better the risks between which we are held by the muse Forgetful Memory. Either it is simply a matter of a memory able to forget, and we do not succeed in descending to the shore where beings would come toward us in their metamorphoses, as we ourselves would in this strange body changed into its own unknown space; or else forgetting makes us forget everything — but then how can we rejoin things? How will we return to presence?

> *But with so much forgetting how can we make a rose,*
> *With so many departures how can we make a return,*
> *A thousand birds taking flight do not make one that lands*
> *And so much obscurity simulates poorly the day.*

There is in memory a relation we can no longer term dialectical, since it belongs to the ambiguity of forgetting that is at once the mediating site and a space without mediation — indifferent difference between depth and surface; as though to forget were always to forget profoundly, but also as though the depth of forgetting were profound only by the forgetting of all depth. Hence this question that Supervielle leads us to hear:

> *O lady of the depths,*
> *What are you doing at the surface,*
> *Attentive to all that passes,*
> *Watching the clock at my hour?*

> *For what obscure deliverance*
> *Do you ask my alliance?*

> *O you, always ready to end,*
> *You would like to hold me back*
> *On the very edge of the abyss*
> *Of which you are the strange summit.*

This summit of the abyss, memory.

There is the same secret relation, but one hard to fix, between the distant and the near, as the dialogue of the bird reveals—a dialogue almost terrifying in its sweetness:

> *— Bird, what are you seeking, fluttering over my books?*
> *All is foreign to you in my narrow room.*

> *— I do not know your room and I am far from you,*
> *I have never left the woods, I am in the tree*
> *Where I have hidden my nest. Find another explanation.*
> *For all that happens to you now, forget a bird.*

And this end where the mortal approach in its distancing is expressed to us in the most simple words:

> *— But what horror was hiding in your obscure sweetness*
> *Oh! You have killed me I fall from my tree.*

> *— I need to be alone, even the gaze of a bird . . .*

> *— But since I was far away in the depth of my woods!*

To you the force, he says to the tree, *to me the accent*. The accent of this voice is the accent of memory, always restrained, at times stifled, yet calm and limpid; a simple response to what was lived under the pressure of strangeness. If the tale's truth is at every moment given to him, it is because of this relation with that profound, immemorial memory that originates in the time of the "fabulous," at the epoch when, before history, man seems to recall what he has never known. It is the same with Supervielle: the poet speaks as though he were remembering, but if he remembers it is through forgetting.

VI

Vast as the night

I recall this passage from a letter Kafka wrote to Brod: "*The writer is the scape-goat of humanity; thanks to him men can innocently, or nearly innocently, take pleasure in a sin.*" This nearly innocent pleasure is reading. The writer is guilty; he delivers himself radically over to evil. (I suppose that Christian writers, often so happy to write and at times quite proud of what they write, easily ignore this; Graham Greene remarks that a true Christian surely would not write.) But what he creates in sin becomes happiness and grace for the reader. Let us exaggerate these traits: creation, essentially unhappy, gives rise to an essentially happy reading. The book is a night that would become day: a dark star, unilluminable and calmly giving light. Reading is this calm light. Reading transforms into light that which is not of the order of illumination.

Everything nonetheless contributes to making the reader lose such a fine innocence. First the author, who, unable to come to the end of his task, publishes books still unwritten and into which the reader enters less by reading than by being obliged to prolong, imaginarily and anxiously, the passion of writing (which, in turn, produces between author and reader relations of a singular intimacy, as we see from romanticism on). But still further, there is the existence of that bizarre, illegitimate, encumbering, superfluous, and always ill-willed character (if only by excess of his goodwill and "comprehension") that is the critic. The critic is there to come between book and reader. He represents the decisions and the paths of culture. He prohibits the god's immediate approach. He says what we must read and how we must read it, finally rendering reading useless. But is he, at least, the happy man who reads happily? Not at all, since he dreams only of writing what he reads. Hence the result that if perhaps there has never been written as much as there is today, we are nonetheless gravely and painfully deprived of reading.

This situation is not new. Socrates poked fun at the rhapsodes who, rather than being content with reciting Homer's poems, also claimed to interpret his "thought." *"I have often envied the profession of a rhapsode, Ion; you are obliged to learn Homer's thought and not merely his verses! Now that is something to envy! . . . The rhapsode must interpret the poet's thought to his audience."* To which Ion, insensitive to irony, responded: *"That's true, Socrates. And that's the part of my art that took the most work. I think I treat Homer better than any man. . . . "* − *"I'm glad to hear you say so, Ion."* Thus were assigned the ways of reading that are called allegory, symbol, and mythic deciphering. When Plato so rudely chases Homer from his city, it is less Homer he expels than allegorical exegesis, which sets the poet's words aside to make way for truths and messages. Plato cuts short this undermining by affirming that there is nothing to extract from a poet inasmuch as he is enclosed in a world of reflections and surface. I wonder whether he is not thereby defending the truth that is Homer's better than the exalted grammarians who found in him an account of every physical, moral, and metaphysical certainty. Late antiquity, then the first Christian eras, are responsible for this allegorical intemperance; but there has always been strong opposition. Plutarch: *"By means of what the Ancients called 'hidden signification,' which today we call allegory, one wished to do violence to Homer's accounts."* And Tatien: *"You shall apply allegory neither to your myths nor to your gods."*

How the symbol follows allegory (mysteriously in the case of Plato, deliberately with Plotinus or the romantics), then how psychoanalytic reading takes over from symbolic reading (as a more learned and reflective form of the latter[1]) constitute a history of which only the broadest outlines are known, even in the West. The differences between these movements, no matter how firm, cannot make us forget the identity of approach. It is a matter of a reading that is a textual explication or commentary; this commentary seeks beneath the apparent meaning another that is hidden, and beneath this meaning still another, in order to reach the obscure center whose direct revelation is uncertain since it always needs either translation or metaphor to be formulated. "Psychoanalysis," in the end, designates the unconscious whose mode of expression is the symbol, not only as it is bound to language, but as language itself. (The entire question remaining that of knowing to what level of speaking relation such a putting into question of speech introduces us.) This is what the young Schelling was already ready to affirm of allegory when he called it a "redoubled language"; for the most simple speech disguises, saying something other than it says, otherwise it would not speak. Allegory is therefore that which concentrates expression upon its principal characteristic, the duality of a meaning that is manifest and a meaning that is latent.

Schelling's evolution is characteristic. He very quickly perceived that by destroying literal appearance allegory destroyed poetry, since it did away with the image, that is to say, the original expression of the poet in favor of another, unexpressed expression that was declared to be the only important or true one. Even the symbol, which is concerned with a meaning that is more remote, richer, and perhaps necessarily secret, has the same shortcoming if there is always a moment at which it invites us to go beyond the text in order to hear or to contemplate something else. Hence Schelling, refusing all division between figure and meaning, nature and surnature, arrived at his famous idea of a mythology in which the gods signify only what they are.[2]

At the risk of applying an unfair metaphorical treatment to Bachelard himself, I believe one could say that he might pass for the Schelling of psychoanalysis. He always had the finest passion for images and the books in which they have their truth and their life. He thus became more and more wary of a proud and comprehensive technical knowledge constituted in the course of very different kinds of experiments and ready to verify its method in relation to the productions of art, considering these as cases among others, and providing an explication of them so profound (in relation to the forces called profound) that it is no longer the work that counts but only what is behind it, and not what the writer writes but what the psychoanalyst finds, which, moreover, he had already found elsewhere and in advance.[3] This way of reading, magisterial though very approximate, is doubtless justified but does not correspond to the simple truth of reading. Reading is ignorant. It begins with what it reads and in this way discovers the force of a beginning. It is receiving and hearing, not the power to decipher and analyze, to go beyond by developing or to go back before by laying bare; it does not comprehend (strictly speaking), it attends. A marvelous innocence. But in refusing all exegesis and in taking the image such as it offers itself, does not such a simplicity, without a past and without certainties, do an injustice to the richness of literary invention? Would it not be disdainfully rejected by the specialists of knowledge, commentary's technicians, and by "every philosophy of poetry"?

In order to restore our good conscience, Bachelard will here step in with the caution of his own approach. Knowing many things and master of an "active rationalism," he often said how he had to forget his knowledge and break with his habits of thought in order not to betray what seems to him to be the essential poetic act. "Here," he says, "the cultural past does not count." In order to enter into the presence of the image, the philosopher has nothing more to do than what the most simple reader does: be present to the image through a total adherence to its solitude and its newness as image. How liberating these assertions are. The poetic image, to cite Bachelard again, has no past; it is not under the sway of some inner drive, nor is it a measure of the pressures the poet sustains in the course of his early life, and that are brought to light by psychoanalysis. To affirm that there is a constitutive relation between the singularity of the image and the history of the man in whom it originates is to bring the image back to metaphor (which is there to transmit a prior signification, already active or completely formed). The trait proper to the image is suddenness and brevity: it springs up in language like the sudden springing forth of language itself. *"The poetic image places us at the origin of the speaking being . . . it is young language, . . . it is the property of a naive consciousness."*

To seek its antecedents is thus the sin par excellence, the sin against the spirit of the image (and the mark of an infamy that used to be called psychologism). The poet is born of the figure to which he opens, each time the first time, and is renewed in this brief newness that introduces an interval in duration and inaugurates an other time. So it is with the reader, and in a manner still more striking, since the reader cannot claim the problematic name of creator. What happens to the one who is reading? If I say the reader understands the poem, I confuse him with the interpreter who is essentially reductive, and who reduces the irreducible by bringing it back to the profound forces, to sleeping archetypes, to the values rooted in our depths. But perhaps the reader understands in a different manner: not by turning back toward a vulgarized knowledge, but in slackly descending toward the resonances the poem awakens in him (that is to say, adding himself to the image and going beyond it toward the already lived realities of his world)? Employing here an expression borrowed from E. Minkowski, Bachelard makes us attentive to a very fine and very precious distinction. *Resonance* does no more than bring us sentimentally back to our own experience. What alone places us at the level of poetic power is *reverberation*, the image's summoning to what in it is initial, an instant summons to leave ourselves and to move in the shaking of its immobility. This "reverberation" is not, then, the image that resounds (in me, the reader, and on the basis of my self), it is rather the very space of the image, the animation proper to it, the point of its springing forth where, speaking within, it already speaks entirely on the outside.

One senses, then, why a predisposition to the image finds in us, and in so many ways, a being ill-disposed to it. To put a thought in its place, to translate it, is but the least offense; and, it must be added, the penchant for allegory or myth of so many ancient and modern readers does not necessarily imply such crudeness. Even Aristotle's praise for this inclination has an almost religious character: *"Love of myth,"* he says, *"is love of Wisdom, for myth is a marvelous assemblage."* And when Plato, the Plato of the letters, writes to Denys *"I must, then, speak to you about this, but in enigmas,"* we see clearly that it is not a matter of a profane prudence, but rather of the reserve that holds dear the exigency of truth and respects its approach. Let me also cite a later author, Maxime de Tyr, for the delicate manner in which he justifies the image by the restraint and discretion that characterizes all just language: *"All is full of images in the case of poets as well as philosophers: the modesty with which they surround truth seems to me preferable to the direct language of recent authors."* And this: *"More mysterious than discourse but clearer than enigma,*[4] *holding the mean between science and igno-*

rance, rallying approval through pleasure but baffling it through strangeness, myth leads the soul as though by the hand to seek what is, and urges its exploration still further beyond." Here the guilty word would be the word *beyond*: the image is now no more than the occasion or the springboard for an ulterior leap that is outside every figure and perhaps all writing. But "reverberation," such as Bachelard invites us to hear it, is the image's very tension, its range and the overture of its apparition, which opens us to the force of what appears. The obstacle, therefore, would be our stiffness, that is, the certitude of our world and the obstinacy of our culture. "It is a matter of passing to images that have not been experienced, that life does not prepare, and that the poet creates; of living the unlived and opening oneself to an opening of language." Let us retain these last words: they indicate what would distinguish this praise of the image from a mysticism. Origin of language rather than its abyss, the image is a speaking beginning, not an ecstatic end; rather than elevating that which speaks toward the unsayable, it puts speech in a heightened state. As Pasternak suggests: "*Man is silent, the image speaks.*"

*

I think every reader will have experienced the joyful sentiment that corresponds to such affirmations; affirmations for which Bachelard asks less our consent than that we should give them life through our freedom as readers. In reading, among his other books, *The Poetics of Space*, we never feel ourselves confined by judgments so true that we can do no more than appropriate them; rather, we are encouraged—and this is a trait nearly unique today—to pursue another direction, knowing full well that all encounter supposes a diversity of paths. I will admit that in the poems to which I am closest I find everything that Bachelard so perfectly sheds light on when he speaks of the poetic image—with the sole reservation that in them I find no image. Never, in the surprise of their discovery, does the sentiment of the image as such, brief and distinct, come to impose itself; on the contrary, there is a profound and an overwhelming absence of image, and in this absence—in the refusal of each to emerge and to show itself—is the very presence of the space of writing (qualified sometimes as imaginary), the evidence of its reality in the poem's unreal (non-positive) affirmation. Naturally, other readings can take place that will detach from the poem "images," which will now have their imaged truth, but these are readings of an entirely different character, no longer receiving the poem in the collectedness proper to it, but accompanying it and diverting one or several of its moments in order that they should live apart. Also, naturally, it often happens that the poem escapes us, either because it does not yet exist (through a lack this "not yet" promises to the accomplishment of no future) or because we are unable to encounter it (unable to place ourselves in its outside space, amenable to its detour), capable only of encountering in it beautiful images that suffice and illuminate us with a light that does not come from us.

Thus I wonder whether, as soon as they appear, images do not usurp a power that alters them and, more gravely, alters the becoming proper to the work. If rhythm and measure, if the as yet unlit secret of poetic rhythm and measure, belong to what is most essential in each poem, how can images be heard outside the dimension they take from this measure — a dimension, in its uneven regularity, that makes them pass one into another, or, on the contrary, abruptly separates them because their separation is the very measure of the poem's "unity"?

I know that Bachelard intentionally limited his research, yet what he says precisely on this point gives us pause: "By limiting our inquiry to the poetic image in its origination from the basis of pure imagination, we leave aside the problem of the *composition* of the poem as a grouping of multiple images." Running into the word composition brings to mind the protest Goethe made to Eckermann: "Composition, what an ugly word. We owe it to the French and should get rid of it immediately. How can one say that Mozart 'composed' *Don Juan?* Composition!" Bachelard, it is true, adds that it is his modesty as reader that keeps him at the level of separate images: "Indeed, it would seem to me immodest to assume personally a power [*puissance*] of reading that would recapture and relive the organized and entire power [*puissance*] of creation implied by the whole of the poem. . . . It is therefore on the level of detached images that we can 'reverberate' phenomenologically." A moving (and generous) modesty. But does it not also have the disadvantage of humbling ever so slightly the image by reducing it to being no more than an image, that is, a modest component of the poem? Here I would gladly complement my preceding remarks by turning them around: just as I see no images in the poem, for in the poem everything is image and everything becomes image, so must we say that every image is as well the poem in its *entirety*; its unique center, its absolute and momentary appearance, its discrete advance, and its restraint (and thus we again find the sense of modesty to which Bachelard so rightly recalls us). Nothing in the poem, then, is more glorious than the image since it is the poem's secret and its depth, its infinite reserve.[5]

Reading *Poetics of Space* well, I think (and this is surely what we owe such an exemplary reader), we shall not take exception to this book, but rather move in the direction it indicates by asking it to support assertions that seem to contradict it. This work apparently follows in the wake of Bachelard's celebrated series on water, air, earth, and fire. The spatial, like the aerial and the igneous, would be a district of the substantial imagination attributable to the imaginary, or a theme to orient the dreams of the reader when he encounters specialized and spatialized images. What is at stake is something very different, however, as indeed we see in the last three essays entitled "Intimate Immensity," "The Dialectics of Outside and Inside," and "The Phenomenology of Roundness." That a certain image may house us or dislodge us, give us a feeling of happy or unhappy abode, surround and shelter us or take us off course and transport us does not simply mean that the imagination takes over experiences of space that are real or unreal, but rather that we approach through the image the very space of the image, the outside that is its intimacy: *"this horrible inside-outside that real space is,"* as Henri Michaux says in terms we cannot forget once we have grasped them. It would therefore follow that there is no image of immensity, but rather that immensity would be the possibility of image or, more precisely, the manner in which it meets up with and disappears into itself: the secret unity according to which the image unfolds, immobile, in the immensity of the outside and at the same time holds itself in the most interior intimacy. This space of the image, a site engendered in measure and through measure, is also entirely imageless, an imaginary speech rather than a speech of the imaginary, where the imaginary speaks without speaking either of or through images: a level at which, in truth, these three words, image, imaginary, and imagination, no longer have distinct signification.[6] Thus, in Baudelaire's work, the word "vast" becomes figure on its own, and suffices to carry the entire "force of speech." *As vast as night and light.* In this case, where would the image be, if there were one? In the word *vast*, where night spreads to attain its nocturnal dimension, where light destines itself to light by way of the always unilluminated expanse, yet without night and clarity mixing or merging, being never "vast" enough to measure the birth in this word of the image, which is each time the entire presence of this counter-world that is, perhaps, the imaginary.

*

The image becomes enigma when, by our indiscreet reading, we make it emerge in order to display it by tearing it away from the secret of its measure. At this moment an enigma, it poses enigmas. It does not lose its richness, its mystery, or its truth; on the contrary, by its air of question, it calls up all our inclination to respond by bringing forward the assurances of our culture and the interests of our sensibility. As a question, the image is no longer simple; but it is also response, reverberating in us as that which draws out from us the response it engages us to be. This redoubling seems, then, to be its path and its nature: it is essentially double, not only sign and signified but figure of the unfigurable, a form of the nonformal, an ambiguous simplicity that addresses itself to what in us is double, reanimating the duplicity through which we divide and reassemble ourselves indefinitely. Can one say that this movement by which the image departs from its simplicity is a fortuitous betrayal, an awkward and foreign derogation? If it is a betrayal, it belongs to the image. The image trembles, is this trembling of the image, the shiver of that which oscillates and vacillates: it constantly leaves itself, for always already outside itself and always the inside of this outside, there is nothing in which it can be itself, being at the same time of a simplicity that renders it more simple than any other language, and in language being like the source from which it "departs"—but because this source is the very force of a "setting out," the streaming of the outside in (and through) writing.

Image, imagination: subordinating the image to perception and the imagination to memory, and making of consciousness a small world reflecting poorly the big world, we have for a long time represented by these words the play of our imitative fantasy. More than anyone else, and because he was able to reestablish relations between the image and "matter," dream and substance, Bachelard has helped us question this ensemble. Indeed we now feel that the words image, imaginary, and imagination designate not only an aptitude for interior phantasms, but also access to the proper reality of the unreal (its unlimited non-affirmation, the infinite position of its negative exigency) and, at the same time, the recreative and renewing measure of the real, which is the opening of unreality. And yet, possessing this rich and promising knowledge, have we really come close to what the image is before it becomes enigma, in the sobriety of its non-appearance and in the simplicity of the work in its absence? That we must, at best, conclude this research in the interrogative shows clearly that each time it is a question of the image, what we are seeking to hear is the question, but not yet the image, in which the neutral emerges.

VII

Words Must Travel Far

"Is it reasonable to continue speaking of books or about books? I am astonished that every work of criticism, even the most traditional, does not begin with a lengthy apology.

— If it began that way it would never get around to beginning. Criticism must be taken for what it is: a modest activity, a useful auxiliary, at times a necessary betrayal.

— Criticism is not modest. Every 'literary' activity, even of the most modest appearance, is inordinate; it brings the absolute into its game, always and at every moment it says something final, saying also that every critical illusion should be eliminated.

— Is that true even of the notice to the reader?

— Even the briefest note. Otherwise how would any censurer assume the right to judge, to decide that a book is admirable or worthless? But in fact, he is simply making use of the extreme affirmation that passes through every literary exercise. For a moment holding in his hands the essence of literature, he is no less than all authors and all books. Indeed he is more; everyone and no one, he is the last to arrive, the one who speaks last.

— Having the last word is an advantage that may please those engaged in argument; others would step back from such an unfortunate privilege. Moreover, if there is this back and forth of words between us — we who are ourselves nothing but the necessity of this back and forth — perhaps it is to avoid the arrest of a last word.

— Do you mean that while one of us speaks the other has already gone beyond these words or countered them?

— I would not much care for such a movement. It would lead to no more than idle chatter, which, I admit, is a great delight, but only in the truth of life where one is always on the verge of discovering how hard it is: one would have to be an insensitive pedant, stupid in one's intelligence, to become irritated by chatter where words are going to be lacking. But here we are out in the open; we accept as our starting point the difficulty of things to be lived, and this impossibility of saying them that in the course of the everyday we must forget by means of a more considerable gift.

— But we ourselves forget it nonetheless. Otherwise we would limit ourselves to standing before the absurdity of our double immobile voice.

— This double anonymous voice behind which, under an assumed silence, there is someone standing apart who indeed ought to answer for it.

— Then why does he not speak directly?

— Because, I imagine, he cannot: in literature there is no direct speech.

— Then here would be a first justification for this movement: the simple reminder that literature, which is perhaps without truth, is nonetheless the sole truth of the author. Between the latter and what he says there is a margin that should be made apparent. Words must travel a long way.

— Far enough to efface their tracks, and above all the authoritarian presence of a man who is master of what should be said. Criticism, then, would err for being at times too abrupt or quick, too short-winded.

— But not because it judges with too few words.

— Simply because it appropriates for itself the kind of absolute that is at stake in literature, immediately making it into a power. The critic is a man of power. Hence it can seem so easy, so pleasant to become one, and can happen that the first arms handed over to the young inexperienced writer are this bow and these arrows.

— Juvenile weapons, nearly those of a game and wounding only those who wish to be wounded. To go quickly, let us grant that criticism belongs to the epochs in which art, disengaging itself from the paths of the sacred, appears in its own name and as a particular technique; but we thereby also grant that the appearance of the critic merely sanctions and confirms this change in art itself—its entry into the world, its approach to power, and its aspiration to its means. The poet, on the one hand, dons a sacerdotal cloak and hides behind the clouds of the absolute; on the other hand, he intervenes in the affairs of his century as either prebendary or censurer. He can hardly complain if he encounters in the guise of the critic this other man of the world who counts his verses and reminds him of the rules.

— Hardly significant, indeed. Encountering the critic, the poet encounters his shadow, the image slightly dark, a bit empty, and vaguely counterfeit of himself—

moreover, a faithful companion. Let us nonetheless consider the following: criticism judges according to the means of knowledge, of custom, and according to the values proper to an epoch and a society; but the entire force of this judging speech comes to it from literature taken as an absolute—from literature, therefore, withdrawn from all judgment (in the end withdrawn from itself). Therein consists its equivocacy, its troublesome bearing. At bottom, the critic's judgment has only the form of a judgment; it is always already something else. He may very well provide reasons and take every sort of precaution, but even after lengthy negotiations he precipitately and suddenly decides. For the critic, too, is literature; he says literature, which says nothing—a judgment perhaps, but a last judgment. This is why the frivolity of so many critics is not unpleasant, it is princely caprice, the royal prerogative.

— The reader nonetheless retains only the preemptory verdict, the serious conclusion of a speech without seriousness.

— He does not retain it for long. More grave than the peculiarities of any particular judgment is this waiting for judgment, the desire to read only good books, the concern with their value: a normative illusion, even if it is concealed in interpretive research.

— Aren't you attributing too much importance to the qualifying terms that the critic avails himself of? And who still says a book is good or bad; or if he does, does not know that he speaks without having the right to? In truth, what can one say of a work? In praising Beckett's *How it is*, would we dare promise it to posterity? Would we even wish to praise it? Which does not mean that it surpasses, but rather discredits all praise, and that it would be paradoxical to read it with admiration. We have, then, a category of works that go unrecognized more through praise than through disparagement: to deprecate them is to come into contact with the force of refusal that has rendered them present and also with the remoteness that gives them their measure. If the strongest attraction, the deepest concern could be expressed through indifference, then indifference would indicate to what level these lead.

— It would be better not to speak of such works, even to read them, as happens in any case.

— Reading is often a too-wise completion that risks betraying the still unaccomplished movement to which one should respond. I think the pure happiness of reading, what in reading is necessarily chaste and virtuous, cannot but be in disaccord with the books of Sade—at times rendering them more innocent than they are, at other times, on the contrary, lending them a meaning that is simply and unequivocally corrupt and very remote from the true scandalous power that prompts them: a power that passes precisely by way of what we disdainfully call their unreadability. Yes, unreadable—capable of putting into question the honest act of reading.

— But Sade wished to be read.

— He did, his books did not.

— Nevertheless they are read, read outside reading. Let us say, perhaps, that works such as these, and first of all Beckett's, come closer than is customary to the movement of writing and to the movement of reading, seeking to combine them in an experience that, if not common to both, is at least scarcely differentiated—and here we meet up again with the idea of indifference, of a neutral affirmation, equal-unequal, eluding all that would give it value or even affirm it.

— The term hearing would befit this act of approach better than reading. Behind the words that are read, as before the words written, there is a voice already inscribed, not heard, not speaking; and the author, close to this voice, is on an equal footing with the reader—each nearly merged with the other, seeking to recognize it.

— Yes, and thus we find justified in Beckett's case the disappearance of every sign that would merely be a sign for the eye. Here the force of seeing is no longer what is required; one must renounce the domain of the visible and of the invisible, renounce what is represented, albeit in negative fashion. Hear, simply hear.

— And this goes for the pure movement of writing.

— With what clarity and in what a simple manner the voice offers itself to the one who holds himself or herself within the space of such a book, ready to hear; how distinct the rumor is in the indistinct. Reduced to the essential, but rejecting only words that are useless to listening, with a simplicity that at times divides and redoubles itself, the voice speaks eternally.

— And yet this is not in the least a spoken language, the oral style of a non-written speech. Even though we are at the limit of effacement, a long way from all that makes a din, and even though this murmur is close to monotony, saying in an even, equal manner the uneven equality of all speech, there is an essential rhythm, a modulation, a slightly accentuated movement or cadence marked by returns and at times by refrains. It is a tacit song.

— Something attractive, insensibly but incessantly alluring; the attraction of the indifference of which one of us spoke. In a certain sense we have returned to the source of the novel: *How it is* is our epic, a narrative of the first citation in three parts, with stanzas and verses, the back and forth that by nearly regular interruptions gives us a sense of the necessity of this uninterrupted voice.

— Everything, in fact, begins in a way as it does in the *Iliad*, with an invocation of the Muse, a call to voice and the desire to give oneself over to this speech of the outside that speaks everywhere. Between this being—just barely living and also not living, no more than its own panting at the level of the mud—and the anonymous voice, there are established relations that in their laughable insignificance are more important than the various peripeteia of the story. To begin with, this panting keeps the voice from being heard; thus *this breath token of life must die down* so that life can be heard, so this being can say *I hear my life*. And it is always with a certain happiness that he says it, as though hearing remained the ultimate passion even if, or because, it interrupts life.

— To hear, simply hear: *my life a voice without quaqua on all sides words scraps then nothing then again more words more scraps the same ill-spoken ill-heard then nothing vast stretch of time then in me in the vault bone-white if there were a light bits and scraps ten seconds fifteen seconds ill-heard ill-murmured ill-heard ill-recorded my whole life a gibberish garbled six-fold*

— But what is this voice?

— That is the question not to ask, for the voice is already present in one's hearing of the question one asks about it. A voice that is old, older than any past, and that seems to speak intimately of the remote figures proper to each one who hears it. Thus two or three images of childhood and adolescence are still affirmed in the beginning; images, in this narrative where there is almost nothing to see, that have a fascinating force, as do the rare words corresponding to things that are representable and still capable of evoking them: *the sack the tins the mud the dark.* Strange, this need we have to see and to give to be seen that survives nearly all else.

— But what is this voice?

— At the end there is a kind of hypothesis: it is perhaps the voice of all of us, the impersonal, errant, continuous, simultaneous and alternating speech in which each of us, under the false identity we attribute to ourselves, cuts out or projects the part that falls to him or to her: *rumor infinitely transmissible in both directions*, a procession, not stopping, that holds in reserve a certain possibility of communication: *there he is then at last not one of us there we are then at last who listens to himself and who when he lends his ear to our murmur does no more than lend it to a story of his own devising ill-inspired ill-told and so ancient so forgotten at each telling that ours may seem faithful that we murmur to the mud to him*

— *and this life in the dark and mud its joys and sorrows journeys intimacies and abandons as with a single voice perpetually broken now one half of us and now the other we exhale it pretty much the same as the one he had devised*

— *and of which untiringly every twenty or forty years according to certain of our figures he recalls to our abandoned the essential features*

— This is biblical speech: extending from generation to generation, it runs on. Only here the duty is not to prolong it but to put an end to it, to bring the movement to rest; and in order to do this, the solo reciting voice asks himself if there would not be *a formulation that would eliminate him completely and so admit him to that peace at least while rendering me in the same breath sole responsible for this unqualifiable murmur of which consequently here the last scraps at last very last*

— *responsible for this unqualifiable murmur*: responsible for this irresponsibility. Even at the level of mud, then, this remains the exigency from which no being who hears can stand entirely apart. Strange, strange.

— And there is also this singular reminiscence of a world that has to be called spiritual, the interminable time without sleep where Maldoror (often evoked by Beckett's tale) had already found the equivalent of damnation—the eternity that is hell, even if it bears the name heaven: *prayer in vain to sleep I have no right to it yet I haven't yet deserved it prayer for prayer's sake when all fails when I think of the souls in torment true torment true souls who have no right to it no right ever to sleep we're talking of sleep I prayed for them once if I may believe an old view it has faded*

— A memory of childish things in the course of the voyage of the first part, which is perhaps the voyage of birth or prior to birth, in the infinitely slow migration that is this epic's Odyssey until Pim, the companion, is encountered—last vestige of the characters of another time, last avatar of the couple of the victim-tormentor. But these words, as it is said, are too strong here, *almost all a little strong I say it as I hear it.* And it is true, the raspy speech of humor fades, the parody slackens; the picturesque scrapes away vainly against the absurd. One might say that speech turns into a soft specter of speech, at times nearly appeased.

— Would this be a calm?

— Calm perhaps, never calm enough. But naturally there are becalmed moments; those, sadder than all the others, that recall the *Texts for nothing.* '*Yes, I was my father and I was my son, I asked myself questions and answered as best I could, I had it told to me evening after evening, the same old story I knew by heart and couldn't believe, or we walked together, hand in hand, silent, sunk in our worlds, each in his worlds, the hands forgotten in each other. That's how I've held out till now. And this evening again it seems to be working. I'm in my arms, I'm holding myself in my arms, without much tenderness, but faithfully, faithfully. Sleep now, as under that ancient lamp, all twined together, tired out with so much talking, so much listening, so much toil and play.*'

— Then at times the voice would fall silent?

— '*And were the voice to cease quite at last, the old ceasing voice, it would not be true, as it is not true that it speaks, it can't speak, it can't cease. And were there one day to be here, where there are no days, which is no place, born of the impossible voice the unmakable being, and a gleam of light, still all would be silent and empty and dark, as now, as soon now, when all will be ended, all said, it says, it murmurs.*'

— So we must still wait. And in waiting what is there to be done?; what do we do?

— Well, waiting, we chat.

— Yes, listening to the voice. But what is this voice?

— Not something to hear, perhaps the last written cry, what is inscribed in the future outside books, outside language.

— But what is this voice?"

VIII

Wittgenstein's Problem

Flaubert

No one doubts that Flaubert marks an epoch in the history of writing — if we suppose that the pursuit of *the act of writing*, the silent, absent, and perverse demon that makes every writer of the modern age a Faust without magic, can take the form of a history.

And yet almost every time he gives expression to his theoretical concerns, exalting Art, but affirming form or exhausting himself through Work, we are at once fascinated and disappointed by what he says: as though in what he wanted to say there were something else acting, something more essential though unformulated whose attraction and torment he undergoes. This is why he always felt that his correspondents misunderstood him, why he had to repeat and contradict himself until, finally, the only thing that asserts itself is the disproportion of an absurd passion or the unreason of an unworking labor. Thus he glorifies prose; this is one of his important discoveries. He says that prose is more difficult than poetry, that it is the summit of art and that French prose could attain a beauty as yet unimagined. But what does he mean by prose? Not just the space of the novel (which, even after Balzac, is for the first time raised to some kind of absolute existence), but rather the enigma of language as it is written, the paradox of a direct speech (*prorsa oratio*) bent by the essential detour, the perversion of writing. It is the same with form: he wants beautiful form, he wants to write *well*, he tracks down repetitions and disharmonies in his sentences, he believes that exact prose should speak up. An ideal we have moved far away from. Then he suddenly corrects himself: form is nothing but idea — and here he understands it in the classical sense, as someone who was taught Boileau; write well in order to think well,[1] form and substance are inseparable, even indistinguishable. Then he once again turns the exigency around the other way: "I try to think well *in order to* write well. But my aim is to write well, I don't deny it." And what does it mean to write well? When George Sand reproaches him for his apparent dedication to beautiful and sonorous, well-rounded sentences, he immediately answers: "The accomplished turn of a sentence is nothing, but to write *well* is everything" — and then he again equivocates with this explanation borrowed from Buffon: "To write well is at once to feel well, to think well, and to speak well" (let us note that writing is conceived as a totality of which expression would be only one moment or component, perhaps a secondary determination). Finally, as almost always happens, the temptation of capital letters leads him to a veritable Platonism where salvation by Form opens onto a new heaven: "Fact is distilled in form and rises up as a pure incense of the Spirit toward the Eternal, the Immutable, the Absolute, the Ideal."

Pure plastic manifestation, destined to make the sentence a beautiful thing both visible and audible: the phrased; or again, a sure means of mastering the formlessness that always threatens it. Art, reduced to its formal values, oriented solely toward euphony, seems to us quite foreign to the power Mallarmé will seek to discover and that, in relation to ordinary language, will be designated as another language, purer but also more effaced, and capable of bringing into play — in order to disappear in it — the very Other of all language; an Other, however, that is nothing but a language that also has an Other in which it will have to disappear — and so on indefinitely. From such a perspective, then, we are tempted to say that Flaubert is not yet Mallarmé. And as we read the collection of texts taken from his correspondence,[2] we are tempted to recognize how difficult it is for a writer, even though he may be quite conscious of himself and of what is at stake in his task, to grasp the experience with which he is struggling so long as he tries to understand it by referring to notions that are still warped by a tradition and obscured by the particular conditions of a society.

For us everything is clear, almost too clear, in the process we find described in these uncertain words. We hasten to reinterpret this dim past using the intelligence of the future, and, in the Hegelian manner, we distinguish between the writer's experience as it was for him and that same experience as it presents itself to us. It thus seems to us that it is Literature itself in its capital truth that progresses in this way, extricates and unfolds itself, or else closes around its own center, a center ever more inward, more hidden and absent. But is this really how it is? Are we not harboring an illusion? Are we not taking as legible what has not yet even been written? Are we not forgetting that while Flaubert was certainly at a turning point, we, too, are exposed to the demands of a "turning point" — this movement of turning about by turning away for which we do not yet have sufficient theoretical means of elucidation; at times apprehending it as the movement of historical becoming, at other times becoming aware of it in terms of structures and recognizing in it the enigma of every relation, that is, in the end, of every language?

*

It is the anguish of form that is important in Flaubert, and not the signification he now and then lends to it; or to put it more exactly, this anxiety is infinite, proportionate to the experience in which he feels himself engaged, and with only very unsure reference points to delimit its direction. The engagement of the writer Flaubert is an engagement—a responsibility—to a still unknown language he makes every effort to master or subject to some kind of reason (that of a value, a beauty, a truth), the better to undergo the hazardous power that the unknown in this language forces him to confront. He is not in any sense unaware of this. He says very precisely that his search for form is a method ("the concern for external beauty with which you reproach me is for me a *method*"), which certainly means that form has the value of a Law that is arbitrarily predicated, but also that it responds to what is arbitrary—to the risk, the chance—in all speech, that is, to its essentially problematic character.

The more sumptuous, splendid, and dazzling art is, the more will it manifest itself in solely exterior artifices; and, denouncing by this too-glorious appearance the void that is hidden within it, the more will it also seek to become one with its own effacement. This is a movement Flaubert certainly does not accomplish willingly, but whose ruinous meaning is revealed in his last book. The question being no longer that of knowing whether B. and P. are "imbeciles through and through" or, on the contrary, are perfectly human men, at once mediocre and sublime, destined to effort and failure—predecessors of Bloom and successors of Ulysses; the question is rather how nullity becomes a work and how, at the level of literature, the totality of encyclopedic knowledge (therefore a maximum of substance) can coincide with this nothing without which Flaubert suspects there can be no literary affirmation. (*Bouvard et Pécuchet* will therefore paradoxically realize the hope of the young Flaubert: *"What seems beautiful to me, what I would like to make, would be a book about nothing, a book without any exterior attachment."*) After having demanded that style be governed by the law of numbers, that it be pleasing to the ear because of its so-called musical qualities (understood in a completely external sense), he also knows very well and as though in spite of himself that "Art must be a 'good fellow' ": not let itself be seen, give up everything pleasurable, confine itself to the austerity of nonappearance where there rules an *"unwitting poetics"*—a revealing formulation. The same goes for work. No writer has worked harder than he did or done more to reduce those who write to the condition of "horrible workers." To listen to him and see him toil away, we assume that a book is made in the same way a beautiful object was made long ago: with care, with skill, and through time. But it is also immediately apparent that Flaubert's work has nothing in common with Boileau's; this is not the honest and tranquil labor of an artisan who possesses a trade and a certain technical knowledge, who brings the work to perfection in conformity with a tradition and according to a model. At the very time when work becomes the sign for every value, here it is without value and properly tragic.[3] It is something excessive, a kind of madness: an encounter with the terrifying, a confrontation with the inhuman, the practice of the impossible, a torment set to work. And what is one working for? A work that does not exist—a beautiful unreal book? Not even that. A sentence, and a sentence that cannot be written: "The simplest sentence, like 'he closed the door,' 'he went out,' requires incredible artistic ruses"; which no doubt means that the most ordinary actions are very hard to formulate, but also that in a more profound sense, at the level of literature, the sentence "he closed the door" is, as such, already impossible.

Hence the many declarations that were found laughable or merely pathetic, until one began to take them seriously: "I have come to the conclusion that it is *impossible to write*" (the italics are Flaubert's). "Writing is more and more impossible," and for this reason "despair is [his] normal state"; a state from which he can emerge only by means of some violent distraction, exhausting himself, "unceasingly gasping for breath" in this exercise of writing that exceeds life because writing is this very excess. ("Art exceeds.") Then why persist in this unhappiness, why not rest from it? "But how can I rest? And what to do while I am resting?" "There is a mystery beneath this that escapes me"; a mystery, however, that he helps us approach when to one of his correspondents he writes the following, which must be understood unreservedly: *"What is diabolic about prose is that it is never finished."* Because of this, all the works he undertakes to write are extravagant; with each one he shatters against "horrifying" difficulties, each time he promises himself that the next will be easy, happy, more suited to his talent, and each time he chooses the only one he is unable to write: "I must be absolutely mad to undertake a book like this one. . . . I must be crazy and completely out of my mind to undertake such a book! I am afraid that in its very conception it is radically impossible. . . . What terror! I feel as though I'm about to embark on a very long voyage toward unknown regions, and that I won't be coming back." This is the reason for the dry and somber conclusion with which, five years before he dies, he begins his patient, malicious wait for death: "I don't expect anything more from life than a succession of sheets of paper to blacken with ink. It feels to me as though I were crossing an endless solitude, going I know not where. And I am at once the desert, the traveler, and the camel." (To George Sand, March 27, 1875, after having noted: "Perhaps it is the work that is making me ill, for I have undertaken an extravagant book.")

*

We cannot but see from the following that Flaubert was attracted by the search for a new meaning to give the word "writing": "I would like to make books in which it would only be a matter of *writing* sentences." In underlining the word writing Flaubert was not trying to enhance its status, but make it appear, wishing to indicate that this verb is not exhausted by its transitive power and that the work proper to it is a work of intransitivity. Books and sentences are only particular modes of what is at stake when one writes. One writes, and one writes (sentences), but the result remains in parentheses; the result—sentences, a book—does not even serve to give validity to "the act of writing," to bring out the value that is proper to it, or to transform it into a value (as, for example, the Creation would bring God forward as a creative power). One writes sentences so that the sentence's visibility will cover up and preserve the privilege of invisibility and the power to disclaim and efface that do not allow "writing" to be anything but a neutral word.

Roussel

When Michel Foucault, considering Raymond Roussel, designates the central void Artaud bore witness to with his cries as the common site for madness and the work of art[4]—how can we not recall the accusatory formulation that Flaubert used just a hundred years ago when he confided his difficulties to Louise Collet: "*The plasticity of style is not as broad as the whole idea, I know. But whose fault is it? The fault is that of language. We have too many things and not enough forms. This is what tortures those who are conscientious.*" A striking coincidence. Yet what is truly striking is not the coincidence, but the long route that literary activity has had to travel from one to the other of these coinciding reflections. Flaubert does not rush to rejoice in it, but he clearly sees the truth of language in this "too many things" and this "not enough forms," and he regards this lack as the writer's reason for being since the writer is called upon to make up for it through labor, skill, and cunning. "Too many things," "not enough forms," a poverty he deplores since it obliges him to give only limited expression to so much wealth. This corresponds to Lévi-Strauss's hypothesis that art is essentially reduction, the elaboration of a reduced model. Except that, far from feeling distressed by this, Lévi-Strauss cheerfully describes all the advantages afforded by the reductive power of both the plastic arts and (as he implies) language. ("Being smaller, the totality of the object seems less formidable; because it is quantitatively diminished, it seems qualitatively simplified; this quantitative transposition increases and diversifies our power over a homologue of the thing.")

But let us reflect on this. I wonder if Flaubert's uneasiness is not justified— providing, however, that we turn his formulation around, saying "always too many forms"; that is, there is always too much of what we never have enough of. The problem, as we sense, is that the inadequacy of language—once we recognize it as the essence of speaking — risks being never sufficiently inadequate. This lack of language means (to begin with) two things: a lack with respect to what there is to be signified but, at the same time, a lack that is the center and the life of meaning; the reality of speech (and the relation between these two lacks is itself incommensurable). To speak, as we know today, is to bring such a lack into play, to maintain it and deepen it so as to have it at our disposal; but to deepen it is also to make it be more and more, and finally to put in our mouths and our hands no longer the pure absence of signs, but the prolixity of an indefinitely and indifferently signifying absence: a designation that, although bearing nullity within itself, remains impossible to annul. If it were not this way we would all have been long ago satisfied with silence. But this very silence — the lack of signs — itself remains always significant and always excessive in relation to the ambiguous lack that speech brings into play.

Let us reflect a bit more. "Too many things," then, would be the Other of language, which is itself considered as consisting in "forms," these latter taken as being finite in number (as Flaubert and Lévi-Strauss postulate) whereas things would correspond to some sort of infinite (or indefinite). But what is proper to a form of language is that it contains something only as long as it contains nothing. Which amounts to concluding that the statement that there are "not enough forms" would only be true of a language that considers form to be already and only a thing. In other words, even if the number of structures is finite, that is, if there are only a defined number of kinds of relations, as long as one of them is such that it expresses (contains) the infinite, Flaubert's statement can be turned around the other way, and one ought not complain that there are "too many things," but rather "never enough things": now the universe in its entirety does not suffice to fill the Danaids' barrel.

Finally, and to go quickly: the problem defined by Flaubert is the question of the *Other* of speech. Now, ever since Mallarmé, we have sensed that the other of a language is always posed by this language itself as that by way of which it looks for a way out, an exit to disappear into or an Outside in which to be reflected. Which means not only that the Other is already *part* of this language, but that as soon as this language turns around to respond to its Other, it turns toward another language; a language that, as we ought not ignore, is other, and also has its Other. At this point we come very close to Wittgenstein's problem, as corrected by Bertrand Russell: every language has a structure about which we can say nothing *in* this language, but there must be another language that treats the structure of the first and possesses a new structure about which we cannot say anything, except in a third language — and so forth. Several consequences follow from this, among them the following: (1) what is inexpressible is inexpressible in relation to a certain system of expression; (2) although there may be reason to regard the ensemble of things and of values as a whole (for example, within a given scientific and perhaps political conception), the virtual ensemble of the different possibilities of speech cannot constitute a totality; (3) the Other of any speech is never anything but the Other of a given speech or the *infinite movement* through which a mode of expression—always ready to unfold in the multiple exigency of simultaneous series—contests itself, exalts itself, challenges or obliterates itself in some other mode.[5]

*

Bearing these remarks in mind, I would like to return to the work of Roussel, which Michel Foucault's book has once again made speak to us. Yes, if we bear these remarks in mind, it seems to me that we will understand more fully the prodigious effect this work produces on us (independently of its actual inventions). For in its passage from description to explanation and then, within this explanation, to a narrative account that, though scarcely begun, opens so as to give rise to a new enigma that must in turn be described and then in its turn explained (something that cannot be done without the enigma of a new narrative account), Roussel's work—through this series of intervals perpetually opening out one from another in a coldly concerted, and for this reason all the more vertiginous, manner—represents the infinite navigation from one kind of language to another; a movement in which there momentarily appears in outline, and then endlessly dissipates, the affirmation of the *Other* that is no longer the inexpressible depth but the play of maneuvers or mechanisms destined to avert it. This is why descriptions, explanations, narratives, and commentaries function as though of their own accord, flatly and mechanically, in order better to channel the void or lack through a system of openings and closings that this lack alone sets in motion and keeps in motion. We cannot but observe—and not without a somewhat frightened surprise—that in this respect there is a kinship between *Locus Solus*, *L'Etoile au Front*, and his early works, which are constructed around a play of parentheses. One is inevitably tempted to ascribe the obsession involved in this process to the perversity of some kind of madness, and in this there is nothing scandalous; but since madness itself —of whatever sort—is only a language of a particular kind, and one we will endeavor if we are learned to transpose into another, we will be doing no more, however vigilant we may be, than simply—blindly—embarking in our turn on this navigation that ends neither in a harbor nor in some shipwreck: all of us delivered over, with more or less pomposity or simplicity, to the play of displacement without place, of redoubling without duplication, of reiteration without repetition— processes that fold into and unfold within one another infinitely and without moving, as though the word that is in excess could in this way be exhausted.[6]

IX

A rose is a rose . . .

"Alain used to say that true thoughts are not developed. To learn not to develop would thus be one part, and not the least, of 'the art of thinking.'

— It would therefore be a matter of thinking by separate affirmations. Someone says something and goes no further. Without proof, reasoning, or logical sequence. I fear that such a manner of saying comes back to the imperious declaration: *sic dico, sic jubeo*.

— Generally, when someone says something, he or she relates it (implicitly or not) to an ordered set of words, experiences, and principles. These connections of coherency, this search for a common order, and the methodical progression through which thought transforms itself while remaining the same belong to the exigency of reason. A developed thought is a reasonable thought; it is also, I would add, a political thought, for the generality it strives for is that of the universal State when there will be no more private truth and when everything that exists will submit to a common denominator.

— A great and a fine exigency. Let us develop our thoughts.

— We will most certainly never say anything against reason, except to provoke it, for it easily falls asleep — but still, we must develop completely, and we know how very far we are from this total development. Consequently, let us be aware of the fact that today when our children develop an argument in three steps and when our teachers develop a beautiful rhetorical discourse, they simply consecrate the arbitrariness of a particular political state of things. And consequently, to learn not to develop is to learn to unmask the cultural and social constraint that

339

is expressed in an indirect yet authoritarian manner through the rules of discursive 'development.'

— Or it's to risk giving the forces of unreason free reign. A cry is not developed.

— Madness, however, is. And the anti-intellectualist philosophies, such as that of Bergson, refer us back to a fluid continuity, to a supposedly living progression that only goes development one better. Alain was speaking of thoughts that are true thoughts, not the manifestations of a somber self or the movements of an illogical existence. Let this be precisely stated. True thoughts are thoughts of refusal: refusal of natural thought, of the legal and economic order, which imposes itself like a second nature, and of the spontaneity, without research and without caution, which is merely a habitual movement that pretends to be a movement that is free. True thoughts question, and to question is to think by interrupting oneself.

— Thinking against time and thinking against the intemporal.

— It seems to me, however, that there is something else in Alain's phrase: 'true' thoughts, vigilant thoughts, reach us by surprise but also in such a way that, once expressed, they leave us the power to resist them freely and even test the astonishment that comes to us from them. Developed thoughts, however, are thoughts that impose themselves through the order by which they unfold, and this order, first of all, is never purely intellectual but necessarily political in the broadest sense; secondly, their effect is to efface surprise and at the same time leave us disarmed before them. Thoughts that are developed do not develop according to the movement and reason that inhabit them, but rather always seek allies in a mode of exposition whose principal merit is to conform to our habits or our cultural ideal. Listen to a sermon or a televised address: we know perfectly well that their 'truth' lies not in the least in the ideas that are expressed, but wholly in their oratorical development and gesticulation.

— Certainly, but no one would dream of looking for true thoughts in a sermon of the Church or the State.

— Let us consider this differently: if true thoughts are not developed, it is not because they would be immutable, eternal, perfect in their unique formulation, but because they do not wish to impose themselves. Far from being statements of authority, scorning proof and requiring blind obedience, true thoughts shun the violence that is inherent in the art of demonstrating and arguing. The violence of the unreasonable man who gives himself over to some passion is no more menacing than the violence of the man who wants to be right and wants reason to be his. The development against which Alain cautions us is that of a will to power: intellectual will is legitimate only in judgment; to judge is to stop, to suspend, to interrupt and make a void, that is, to put an end to the tyranny of a speech that is continuous and well connected. Enter a room where people are speaking, each one taking a discussion as far as it will go, as though each were alone with his own reasoning and seeking to include everything in its development: this is odious.

— Then you would have people give up arguing and begin fighting.

— I would have men speak, but without making their language into a form of war — or at least not always, for speech must also be struggle. Let us say that development is the pretension of holding onto speech, not through the volume of a powerful voice, but by the breadth of a continuum logically organized (in accordance with a logic held to be the only right one) so as to have the last word. A speech that does not develop has on the contrary, and from the outset, renounced having the last word, either because it is supposed to have already been stated or because to speak is to recognize that speech is necessarily plural and fragmentary, always capable of maintaining difference beyond unification. Someone says something and goes no further: this means that someone else has the right to speak and that a place for him is to be left in discourse.

— I recall being present at a conversation between two men who were very different from one another. One would say in simple and profound sentences some truth he had taken to heart; the other would listen in silence, then when reflection had done its work he would in turn express some proposition, sometimes in almost the same words, albeit slightly differently (more rigorously, more loosely, or more strangely). This redoubling of the same affirmation constituted the strongest of dialogues. Nothing was developed, opposed, or modified; and it was manifest that the first interlocutor learned a great deal, and even infinitely, from his own words repeated — not because they were adhered to and agreed with, but, on the contrary, through the infinite difference. For it is as though what he said in the first person as an 'I' had been expressed anew by him as 'other' [*autrui*] and as though he had thus been carried into the very unknown of his thought: where his thought, without being altered, became absolutely other.

— A thought exchanged.

— Rather a thought withdrawn from exchange, by which I mean from transaction and compromise. Just as there was no relation between these two repeated instances of speech, these two men had in a certain sense nothing in common, except the movement (which brought them very close) of turning together toward the infinite of speech, which is the meaning of the word conversation. Having listened to them, I said to myself that men are very wrong to fear repetition, providing they seek in it not the means of convincing through stubbornness, but the proof that, even said again, a thought does not repeat itself — or, to say this another way, repetition only makes what is said enter into its essential difference.

— Saying two times the same thing, not through a concern with what is identical but by a refusal of identity, and as though the same phrase, in being reproduced but displaced, in some sense developed of itself and in accordance with the very traits of the space engendered by displacement rather than according to the exterior organization of rhetorical development.

— So we arrive at the idea that 'true thoughts' are not developed, but repeat themselves? A conclusion rich in misunderstandings.

— I would propose three clarifying formulations. First, true thoughts are not developed because true thoughts come about only at the end of a long development they resume as they do away with it: limit-thoughts, thoughts of the end of a world. Secondly, true thoughts do not develop because they preserve the infinite development that inhabits them. Thirdly, thoughts are spoken in discrete words that are also discreet; they do not impose and, once said, they interrupt themselves: discontinuous, a speech of fragments, reserving between being and nothingness the possibility of a discrete reasoning.

— Words without connection, given to incoherence.

— Not without connection, for an interval can also become relation.

— I wonder whether Alain, a literary genius, was not audaciously seeking in poetic formulation the model of these thoughts that should be said without being developed. Poetry and literature do not bear up under the insistence of something signified, or of an ensemble of significations already constituted and organizing themselves through the coherence of a solely logical discourse. In the most traditional sense, a narrative is a manner of speaking continuously while refusing the continuity of developed speech; one is content to add separate events one to another. Except that the organization of these events into a story, around a character or an 'idea,' underhandedly takes up again the principal traits of a continuous development: the linear development of temporal sequence. All of the contemporary efforts could pass for a refusal of development's resources, even when the author has recourse to the admirable excesses of what is in every sense a massive continuity. To write without developing. A movement that was first recognized by poetry.

— All the same, this was a late requirement.

— Because for a long while literature concerned itself only with the world insofar as the world seemed to bear a response, and what literature represented — as well as the other figurative arts of the time — is this response. But as soon as literature affirmed itself as a question, question of the world and question of itself, manifestly suspending any response, it had to break as well with all the habits of a rhetoric of development, for the question insists but is not developed.

— We should think of repetition, then, as the insistence of a questioning that interrogates at various levels, without, however, affirming itself in the terms of a question. A repetition repeating not in order to cast a spell over speech, but rather to disenchant speech with speech itself, to tone it down rather than stifle it.

— Let us recall in passing that repetition responds to the 'death drive'; it responds, that is, to the necessity or counsel of this discretion that sets between being and nothingness the interval that is proper to speech. Repetition effaces saying and demystifies it. This is the meaning of Marx's reflection on those tragic events that are repeated as farce; but what if the farce is in its turn repeated? What if what occurs always returns, and always anew? What if what has been said one time not only does not cease to be said but always recommences, and not only recommences but also imposes upon us the idea that nothing has ever truly begun, having from the beginning begun by beginning again—thereby destroying the myth of the initial or the original, to which we remain unreflectively subject—and tying speech to the neutral movement of what has neither beginning nor end: the incessant, the interminable? I am reminded of a line by Gertrude Stein: *a rose is a rose is a rose is a rose.*[1] Why does this phrase trouble us? Because it is the site of a perverse contradiction. On the one hand, it says that one can say nothing of the rose but the rose itself, and that in this manner the rose declares itself to be more beautiful than if one were to call it so; but on the other hand, through the emphasis of reiteration, it withdraws from the rose even the dignity of its name, which, unique, claimed to maintain it in its beauty as essential rose. The thought, the thought of the rose, quite resists any development—it is even pure resistance. *A rose is a rose*: this means that one can think it, but can represent nothing of it and not even define it (so that, as we suggested, tautology may be no more than the stubborn refusal to define). But *a rose is a rose is a rose . . .* comes in its turn to demystify the emphatic nature of nomination and the evocation of being: the 'is' of the rose and the name that glorifies it as rose are both forever uprooted—they fall into a multitude of chatter, the chatter that in turn arises as the manifestation of every profound speech, speaking without beginning or end.

— The work of Samuel Beckett in every way reminds us of this, and I believe the secret force of certain of Nathalie Sarraute's works also resides here in the enigmatic space of repetition. The coming and going of opinion regarding the fictitious book *Les Fruits d'or*, about which we know nothing but that it is sometimes exalted and sometimes repudiated, may very well give the impression of being a simple social comedy; but the flux and reflux, the strangeness of this movement of attraction and withdrawal, of affirmation and recession, of folding back in and exhibition through which something (but what?) timidly advances and immediately withdraws, appears and disappears, then again disappearing when it reappears and nonetheless maintaining itself in its disappearance; yes, what lies in this movement, if not the very speech of the work, a speech that requires remembrance and forgetting, forgetting and rememoration, insistence and efface-ment but, finally, asks nothing and thus comes forward as the most vulnerable and most easily negated affirmation; nevertheless always intact, always innocent, always used up and unusable in this wearing away until the moment at which, un-perceived, it delivers up its final truth—surely marvelous, surely deceptive.

— *Tropisms* was already a model of this discontinuous, brief and infinite speech, the speech of thoughts that are not developed, and nonetheless more suited than any other to making us enter through interruption, and at the same time through repetition this movement of the interminable that comes to be heard beneath all literature.

— Yes, the unceasing, the discontinuous, repetition: literary speech mysteriously seems to respond to these three exigencies that are opposed to one another, all three nonetheless opposing themselves to the pretension of an invincible unity.

— Alain used to say that true thoughts are not developed: they resist, insist, and are said in discreet, discrete phrases that from the outset are interrupted, then tacitly and interminably repeated, until they are only pure figures of phrases. Now what have we ourselves done but develop this refusal to develop, thus contradicting it and contradicting ourselves in the very demonstration?

— At least this should signal to us that there are no thoughts that do not end up, as they are developed, and even within a rigorous and sequential logic, by presupposing new postulates that are indispensable to this development and that are nonetheless incompatible (or whose compatibility cannot be demonstrated) with the initial postulate. So we would probably do best to go no further. Since it is only at the end of a development, however, and in order to suppress it that a thought has the right to propose itself, I will now propose this semblance of a thought in the form of an aphorism:

To identify by separating, speech of understanding,

To go beyond by negating, speech of reason,

There remains literary speech that goes beyond by redoubling, creates by repeating, and by saying over infinitely, says a first and unique time even this word too many where language falters."

X

Ars Nova

In *Doctor Faustus*, Thomas Mann consigns the musician Adrian Leverkühn to damnation. Not only to eternal damnation – this would be little – but also to the more grave malediction that makes him the symbolic image of German destiny as it sinks into the madness of the Third Reich. Leverkühn's story follows rather closely that of Nietzsche, and his art borrows many traits from Schönberg. Mann moreover informs us of some of these evident correspondences. We know of his relations, and then his differences, with the musician; we also know it was Adorno who introduced him to twelve-tone music; we know too (through a book by Adorno published some time ago) that the latter is not in the least ready to damn Schönberg, even less to relate the fate of this new music to the aberration of German national socialism.

Let us set aside Thomas Mann's work itself, which is preserved from conclusions that are too simple by its narrative ambiguity. The musical system lent to Leverkühn's execrable invention is, nonetheless, the serial system; thus a form that is decisive for the whole development of music is proposed as a symbolic symptom of the Nazi perversion, without great scruples and without much caution. Thomas Mann writes in his journal that behind the beloved name of Adrian Leverkühn is to be read in filigree the abhorred name of Adolph Hitler.

The *Ars nova* from which all the music to come originates could therefore, to some degree, be qualified as a music politically and socially tainted. Other critics, speaking in accordance with the principles of an aesthetics erroneously called socialist, have spoken of a reactionary music. The same thing has happened with non-figurative art. But let us return to Thomas Mann. The motives for his judg-

345

ment are complex. On the one hand, as he recognizes, his understanding of music stops with Wagner; he displays with regard to the new adventure the mistrust and intolerance of a man still devoted to the traditional forms of an art that he loves — an intolerance that is comprehensive and interested, but all the more closed-minded for it. Here there is a rupture that seems to him to be a rupture with order itself. On the other hand, however, he cannily senses in atonal music the element of change and innovation that he needs in order to give authority to Adrian Lever-kühn's genius. He suggests, moreover, that the invention attained through the personal madness of a man and the general madness of the time is not a fortuitous error, but represents the madness proper to an art arrived at its term. He says in his journal that Schönberg's music supplies everything he needs to describe the general crisis of civilization and of music, and thus to delineate the principal theme of his book: the approach of sterility, the innate despair predisposing to a pact with the devil.

In the condemnation pronounced by Thomas Mann (a condemnation in which the word damnation predominates) there is the judgment of a man of culture. It is as a man of culture that he fears the *Ars nova*, just as it is as men of culture and not as political theoreticians (I believe this must be said simply) that certain socialist leaders level harsh judgments against non-figurative art. The same is true with Lukács and, in general, with the men of taste who, in the name of a supposed Marxism, qualify as reactionary every form of art and literature that their culture, inherited from a long history, does not allow them to receive without uneasiness. Let us say more precisely: what they deny and (rightly) dread in artistic experience is that which renders it foreign to all culture. There is an a-cultural part of literature and of art to which one does not accommodate oneself easily, or happily.

*

Adorno says with regard to this "new music" — let us keep this designation, which is in fact quite unsatisfactory — the following: "If atonality may well originate in the decision to rid music of every convention, it by the same token carries within itself something barbaric that is capable of perturbing always anew the artistically composed surface; dissonant harmony sounds as though it had not been entirely mastered by the civilizing principle of order: in its breaking up, the work of Webern remains almost entirely primitive."[1] Affirmations like these have to be read with prudence. The words "barbarous" and "primitive" are hardly appropriate. The composer's efforts to make possible the total organization of sonorous elements, and specifically in order to disavow the idea of a natural aesthetics (according to which sounds or any particular system of sounds would in and of themselves have signification and value), is contrary to, and in a decisive manner contradicts, the most barbaric conception of music — even if such a barbarity borrows, as it always does, the appearance of an ideal. And as for technique, whose use is condemned as being excessive (and, once again, condemned as being barbaric—the barbarity of an integral rationalism), it in no way gives itself as the whole of music, but only as that which must necessarily and momentarily predominate in order to "break the blind constraint of sonorous material" or suspend the already organized meaning of the musical object; in a word—we will come back to this—to destroy the illusion that music, in and by its nature, would have a value of beauty independent of historical decision and of the musical experience itself.

From this point of view, then, what seems "barbaric" in the *Ars nova* is everything that ought to keep it from being taken as such: its critical force, its refusal to accept as eternally valid the worn-out forms of culture, and above all its violent intention to empty natural sonorous material of any prior meaning, and even to keep it empty and open to a meaning yet to come. A violence that, in doing violence to nature, has something despotic and dangerously uncivilized about it.

What, then, does Adorno mean when, in the judgment just cited, he states that the breaking up of sonorous space makes Webern's music an event that is almost entirely primitive? Without entering into any learned analysis, it is clear that if the musician renounces with an austere rigor the continuity of a unified work or the fluid development of what Walter Benjamin called the "auratic" work of art (a work of ambiance), he does so not in order to deny all coherence or the value of form, or even to oppose the musical work considered as an organized whole (as sometimes appears to be the case with Stravinsky); on the contrary, it is because he places himself beyond aesthetic totality. More precisely, in a language that is first rendered indeterminate by the rejection of traditional conventions, and then on this basis restructured in such a way as to possess virtually all the essential elements of a later thematic elaboration, what is already given (or pre-formed) is the whole of the musical composition, which is able to move forward only by analysis and by division into structures that are more and more subtle; that is, through a form of composition that will involve differentiation and dissociation. If, therefore, musical language seems to break up and even disperse into always more parceled forms, it is because the analysis truly becomes creative, just as variation is no longer a procedure for developing a theme it would be a matter of enriching, but a principle of disenvelopment through which the totality already virtually present in the choice and in the preparatory work of the series becomes free of itself by giving itself over to a veritably torturing question—a question that, through the obstinate return of the identical, as again Adorno makes clear, seeks to engender an unceasing renewal. Finally, when it is said that Webern's last works have "liquidated" even contrapuntal organization, I think it would be better to say, in his own terms, that Webern in no way breaks with a rigorous counterpoint, but rather decides to have us hear it only as a reference, via its traces, as a memorial of a rigor that no longer imposes itself upon us except as a recollection or an absence, which leaves us always free, dangerously free, in our listening.

*

The fragmentary work — the fragmentary exigency of the work — therefore has a very different meaning depending on whether it appears as a renouncing of the act of composing, that is, an aggressive imitation of a pre-musical language (which expressionism attempted to arrive at with sophistication) or, on the contrary, as the seeking of a new form of writing that would render the finished work problematic. Problematic not because it refuses accomplishment, but because it explores with an inexorable rigor — beyond the conception of the work as something unified and closed upon itself, as organizing and dominating the values transmitted by a tradition already established and attained — the infinite space of the work, though with a new postulate: namely, that the relations of this space will not necessarily satisfy the concepts of unity, totality, or continuity. The problem the work of the fragment poses is a problem of extreme maturity: first of the artist, and also of society. Walter Benjamin remarks that in the history of art last works are catastrophic: "For the great masters, the works that are finished weigh less heavily on them than those fragments on which they work all their life. In the fragmentary work they trace their magical circle." Why? Because the works by which their skills are tried are not open to a global response; or rather because, for them, it is a matter of beginning at the moment when "composition" itself is in some sense already over, thus leaving them only with the suffering of a work that is apparently negative and with the pain of a dis-location that is nonetheless empty of meaning only because it is a promise of meaning, or refractory to the order of meaning.

These remarks are offered in an attempt to resolve a misunderstanding by recalling that if there is an essential difference between art and culture it is not because art is retrogressive — I mean turned toward a primitiveness without culture or tempted by the nostalgia of an originally natural harmony. It is rather because art has always surpassed every acquired cultural form, to the point that art might best be qualified as postcultural. What frightens Thomas Mann in the *Ars nova* (and frightened no less the masters of the Third Reich, since they hastened to prohibit atonal works, preferring an aesthetics of grandeur, pretentious accomplishment, and monumentality) is frightening, in effect, due to the infinite exigency to which the artistic experience requires us to respond, an experience that can be realized only in works given over to the fragment, whose presence suffices to unsettle the entire future of culture and every utopia of happy reconciliation.

*

This new music does us the service of making us "hear" the gap between artistic affirmation and cultural affirmation in an almost immediate fashion. It compromises the notion of a work, whereas culture wants finished works that, in their immobility of eternal things, can be admired as perfect and contemplated in the preserves of civilization: museums, concerts, academies, libraries, record and film archives. The new music works to "desensitize" language, to rid it of all the intentions and significations that make it a kind of natural knowledge. Rigid, hard, austere, with no spirit of play and without nuance, this music wants to concede nothing to the "human" that society is always ready to appeal to as an alibi for its own inhumanity. Humanism is the trait that bears culture: the idea that man must naturally recognize himself in his works and is never separate from himself; the idea that there is a constant movement of progress, a continuity impossible to interrupt that assures the joining of the old and the new, culture and accumulation moving apace. As a consequence, culture requires answers from art and from speech because answers alone can be accumulated in the great silos of culture; hence a problematic art, an art that gives itself as pure question, and also puts into question the very possibility of art, can only appear to be dangerous, hostile, and coldly violent. Cold, insensitive, inhuman, sterile, formalist, abstract; these reproaches addressed to the *Ars nova* always reveal the man of culture who formulates them, and who does so with all the more force and sincerity for feeling himself put into question precisely with regard to what in him is "good," "valuable" and fortunate, and put in the presence of his real distress, which he does not wish to acknowledge. For culture is "good"; how can we deny it? And it is legitimate to work to increase it. What writer is not also a man of culture? We all are, when we are not writing and even when we are writing, not writing. When Alban Berg speaks of the joy he experiences whenever, through chance (through rigor), a series happens to produce tonal relations, there is surely in this joy the impulse of a consolation found in returning to the realm of established cultural achievement: suddenly exile has ended, we have returned, prodigal son, to the familial bosom of the whole and of unity.

The new music condemned by the man of culture is at once rigorously constructed and yet such that (and herein lies its most decisive research for the other arts and for speech itself) it is not constructed around a center; such even that the idea of a center, of unity, is as it were expelled from the field of the work, which is thereby, at the limit, rendered infinite. A painful and scandalous exigency for all culture and all comprehension. "In music in which each particular sound is determined in a transparent manner by the construction of the whole, the difference between the essential and the accidental disappears." And Adorno adds: "At each of its moments such music is close to the center, and thus the formal conventions that had up to now ruled proximity and distance from the center lose their meaning." Since everything gives itself as essential, there is no longer any inessential transition between stressed elements, just as there is no longer any development, or any theme to be developed but, in their place, a perpetual variation that varies nothing, a force of non-repetition that only succeeds in bringing itself about through an indefinitely reiterated affirmation within difference itself.

Yes, a painful exigency; and, in effect, what presents itself in this particular mode of accomplishment is indeed like a pain that makes itself heard and is painful to hear—insensible, nonetheless: the very ordeal of thought seeking to escape the power of unity. At about the time when Schönberg begins to be discovered, Worringer and certain German painters assign to the plastic arts the task of seeking a field or a surface without privilege, one setting forth no possibility of orientation and realizing itself through movements whose areas would all have equal value. Still later, Klee dreams of a space where the omission of every center would at the same time do away with any trace of the vague or the indecisive. And later. . . But let us not ask that a comparison of the different arts furnish the traits of a common research: common precisely in that they would all affirm relations without unity, relations thus withdrawn from any common measure. And yet reading Georges Poulet's book,[2] where all the adventures of speech and thought are brought into relation with the power of the circle, inscribing themselves always in relation to a center and to a circumference, and always attempting to break it the better to coincide with it, then having closed it—a book in which the simplest figure (and because it is the most finished) permits us to recapture without alteration and without monotony all values and the most diverse riches—I asked myself why, along with this book, the very history of criticism and culture closed and why, with a melancholy serenity, it seemed at the same time to send us off and to authorize us to enter a new space. What space? Not to answer such a question, certainly, but to show the difficulty of approaching it, I would like to invoke a metaphor. It is nearly understood that the Universe is curved, and it has often been supposed that this curvature has to be positive: hence the image of a finite and limited sphere. But nothing permits one to exclude the hypothesis of an unfigurable Universe (a term henceforth deceptive); a Universe escaping every optical exigency and also escaping consideration of the whole—essentially non-finite, disunited, discontinuous. What about such a Universe? Let us leave this question here and instead ask another: what about man the day he accepts confronting the idea that the curvature of the world, and even of his world, is to be assigned a negative sign? But will he ever be ready to receive such a thought, a thought that, freeing him from the fascination with unity, for the first time risks summoning him to take the measure of an exteriority that is not divine, of a space entirely in question, and even excluding the possibility of an answer, since every response would necessarily fall anew under the jurisdiction of the figure of figures? This amounts perhaps to asking ourselves: is man capable of a radical interrogation? That is, finally, is he capable of literature, if literature turns aside and toward the absence of a book? A question the *Ars nova*, in its neutral violence, has already addressed to him (and in this a diabolical art: Thomas Mann was finally right).

XI

The Athenaeum

In Germany, and secondarily in France, romanticism had political stakes, though its fortunes were varied: at certain times the most retrogressive regimes laid claim to it (in 1840 Frédéric-Guillaume IV, and then the Nazi literary theorists), at others, it was clarified and taken as a renovating necessity (this was the task of Ricarda Huch and Dilthey, among others). After the war, Lukács irrevocably condemned it as an obscurantist movement; only Hoffmann, whose work Marx was fond of, escapes this severe judgment. It is remarkable that in France such abhorrence is manifest only in critics who are linked to a school of thought on the extreme right, a school that rejects German romanticism on two counts—because it is romantic and because it is German: irrationalism threatens order; reason is Mediterranean; barbarism comes from the North. Surrealism, on the contrary, recognizes itself in these great poetic figures and in them recognizes what it rediscovers on its own: poetry, the force of absolute freedom. At the same time and slightly later, the work of numerous French Germanists (that of Albert Béguin, the publications of the *Cahiers du Sud*, research on the young Hegel and the young Marx, then the reflections of Henri Lefebvre, which constantly seek to free within Marxism its romantic source) contributes not only to a knowledge of this movement but, through this knowledge, to a new feeling about art and literature that paves the way for other changes, all oriented toward challenging the traditional forms of political organization. Consequently, if romanticism has an ambiguous status in Germany, in France the romanticism that has come from Germany plays a critical role and implies an often radical negation; as though the night—a night without illusion or abatement, but not without perversity—were here taking the place of the *Aufklärung*, whose lights men as responsive as Lessing (and who were closer to Shakespeare than to Voltaire) made shine in a dawn of crisis above a literature still to come.

This particular way of seeing things expresses a deliberate choice. One decides to consider certain traits as unimportant, while considering others as the only authentic ones: to consider the taste for religion accidental and the desire for revolt essential; to consider the concern with the past episodic and the refusal of tradition, the appeal to the new, and the consciousness of being modern as determinant; to consider nationalist penchants as a momentary trait and as decisive the pure subjectivity that has no fatherland. And finally, if all these traits are recognized as being equally necessary, inasmuch as they are opposed to one another, what then becomes the dominant tone is not the ideological meaning of any one of them in particular, but rather their opposition: the necessity of contradiction, the scission and the fact of being divided—what Brentano calls *die Geteiltheit*. Thereby characterized as the requirement or the experience of contradiction, romanticism does no more than confirm its vocation of disorder—menace for some, promise for others, and for still others, futile threat or sterile promise.

This difference of perspective becomes accentuated depending on whether one decides to define romanticism by its premises or its results, at the moment it begins or when it ends. Friedrich Schlegel is the symbol of such vicissitudes: as a young man he is an atheist, a radical, and an individualist. The freedom of spirit he displays, the intellectual richness and fantasy that each day lead him to invent new concepts, not irreflectively but in the high tension of a consciousness that wants to understand what it is discovering, are surprising to Goethe himself—who feels less intelligent, less learned and free than those Wieland names "the proud seraphim," and who feels grateful to know he is honored by them. Some years pass: the same Schlegel, converted to Catholicism, a diplomat and journalist in the service of Metternich, surrounded by monks and pious men of society, is no longer anything but a fat philistine of unctuous speech, lazy, empty, his mind on food, and incapable of remembering the young man who had written: "A single absolute law: the free spirit always triumphs over nature." Which is the real one? Is the later Schlegel the truth of the first? Does the struggle against a bourgeois who is banal engender no more than a bourgeois who is exalted, then weary, and finally only contribute to an exaltation of the bourgeoisie? Where is romanticism? In Iena or in Vienna? Where it manifests itself, rich in projects, or where it dies out, poor in works? Where it is master of a productivity without impediment (according to Schelling's definition)? Or there where it seems that the sublime capacity to produce, precisely by its refusal of impediment, has produced nearly nothing, while the pure creative force that has not remained pure has nonetheless still not created anything? But then, once again, everything turns around. Romanticism, it is true, ends badly, but this is because it is essentially what begins and what cannot but finish badly: an end that is called suicide, madness, loss, forgetting. And certainly it is often without works, but this is because it is the work of the absence of (the) work; a poetry affirmed in the purity of the poetic act, an affirmation without duration, a freedom without realization, a force that exalts in disappearing and that is in no way discredited if it leaves no trace, for this was its goal: to make poetry shine, neither as nature nor even as work, but as pure consciousness of the moment.

To which one can easily reply that, under such conditions, the romantic author fails twice over since he does not really succeed in disappearing (even if, as Lukács affirms, German literature between Goethe and Heine remains empty, setting aside Hoffmann) and since the works through which he cannot help claiming to realize himself remain, and in a sense intentionally, unfinished. Thus Novalis will die, almost symbolically, without having written the second part of *Heinrich von Ofterdingen*, the part that should have been entitled "Accomplishment." And there is always Goethe's morose murmur: unfinished books, works unaccomplished. Perhaps. Unless precisely one of the tasks of romanticism was to introduce an entirely new mode of accomplishment, and even a veritable conversion of writing: the work's power to be and no longer to represent; to be everything, but without content or with a content that is almost indifferent, and thus at the same time affirming the absolute and the fragmentary; affirming totality, but in a form that, being all forms — that is, at the limit, being none at all — does not realize the whole, but signifies it by suspending it, even breaking it.

If one wanted to receive these first romantic assaults as though they were new (an effort still to be undertaken), what perhaps would be surprising is not the glorification of instinct or the exaltation of delirium, but, quite the contrary, the passion of thought and the almost abstract demand posited by poetry that it reflect itself and accomplish itself through *its* reflection. Naturally, it is no longer a matter here of poetics, a subsidiary knowledge: it is the heart of poetry that is knowledge; it is of its essence to be a research and to be a search for itself. Just as consciousness is no longer simply moral but poetic, poetry no longer wants to be a natural spontaneity but solely and absolutely consciousness. (Hence, once again, the acute discontent of Goethe, who means to keep the secret and the truth of creation at the level of nature: if we want to know what creation is, study the natural sciences.) Romanticism is excessive, but its first excess is an excess of thought. An abuse for which Schlegel alone cannot be held responsible since Novalis is stirred by the same intellectual fervor and the same dizzying theoretical investigation, since Hölderlin is consumed by thoughts that are not only thoughts of poetry and by poetry, but also thoughts on the meaning of poetry and art,[1] and, lastly, since romanticism unceasingly gathers around philosophers, be they a Fichte or a Schelling, or else proposes and engenders others, at times somewhat eccentric, that are its own. But here is the striking trait: it is the romantic writers themselves who, because they write, feel they are the true philosophers, feeling themselves no longer called upon to know how to write, but bound to the act of writing as to a new knowledge they are learning to take up anew by becoming conscious of it. Each of them says it in a way that is his own, and in every case says it with an overwhelming obstinacy. Novalis: *"To distinguish the poet from the philosopher is to wrong them both." "Today spirit is spirit by instinct, it is a spirit of nature; it ought to become a spirit of reason, spirit through reflection and through art." "Poetry is the hero of philosophy. Philosophy elevates poetry to the rank of a principle. It is the theory of poetry." "The poetic philosopher is 'in a state of being an absolute creator.' "* Schlegel: *"The history of modern poetry is a perpetual commentary on this philosophical axiom: all art must become science, all science, art; poetry and philosophy must unite." "If the poet, finally, has little to learn from the philosopher, the philosopher, on the other hand, has much to learn from the poet."* And Schelling: *"An action necessarily and at every instant reflective, such is art's constant act."*

Hence, contrary to the idea that is now current, we observe as well that romanticism (at least in its first generation) may be regarded as a protest against the turbulence of genius. Novalis said that what is important is not the gift of genius, but the fact that genius can be learned, and he said also: *"To become a writer, one ought for a time to have been a professor and an artisan."* Valéry, apparently very far from the romantics' conception of things, seems not to know that he shares with them an admiration for Leonardo da Vinci, in whom both recognize a model of the true artist because *"he thinks more than he can do,"* and because *"this superiority of intelligence over the power of execution"* is the very sign of authenticity. The great and pure artist is one who *"pursues all the demands of art with the obstinacy of science and the strength of duty."* Thus *Don Quixote* is the romantic book par excellence, in the degree to which it reflects upon and unceasingly turns back upon itself with the fantastic, agile, ironic, and radiant mobility of a consciousness in which plenitude seizes itself as a void, and seizes the void as the infinite excess of chaos.

These commentaries can be read in several of the six issues of *The Athenaeum*, a journal that did not last long (from 1798 to 1800), but long enough for romanticism to reveal itself there, and even determine its future as an autorevelatory force. This is another of its very striking characteristics. Literature (by which I mean all its forms of expression, which is to say also its forces of dissolution) suddenly becomes conscious of itself, manifests itself, and, in this manifestation, has no other task or trait than to declare itself. Literature, in short, declares it is taking power. The poet becomes the future of humankind at the moment when, no longer being anything—anything but one who knows himself to be a poet—he designates in this knowledge for which he is intimately responsible the site wherein poetry will no longer be content to produce beautiful, determinate works, but rather will produce itself in a movement without term and without determination. To put this differently, literature encounters its most dangerous meaning—that of interrogating itself in a declarative mode—at times triumphantly, and in so doing discovering that everything belongs to it, at other times, in distress, discovering it is lacking everything since it only affirms *itself* by default. There is no need to insist upon what is well known: the French Revolution is what gave the German romantics this new form constituted by the declarative demand, the brilliance of the manifesto. Between these two movements, the "political" and the "literary," there is a very curious exchange. When the French revolutionaries write, they write, or believe they are writing, as the classical writers do; thoroughly imbued with respect for the models of the past, they in no way wish to interfere with the traditional forms. It is not, however, to the revolutionary orators that the romantics will turn for lessons in style, but to the Revolution in person, to this language become History that signifies itself through declarative events. The Terror, as we well know, was terrible not only because of its executions, but because it proclaimed itself in this capital form, it making terror the measure of history and the logos of the modern era. The scaffold, the enemies of the people who were presented to the people, the heads that fell uniquely so they could be shown, the evidence (the grandiloquence) of a death that is null—these constitute not historical facts but a new language: all of this speaks and has remained speaking. When *The Athenaeum* publishes this announcement: "*You will not waste your faith or your love on political things, but reserve yourself for the divine domain of science and art*" or this: "*The national gods of the Germans are not Hermann or Wotan, but art and science,*" it dreams not at all of rejecting the conquests of liberty (this is the moment at which Schlegel intervenes in the history of criticism by showing the relations between the French Revolution, Fichte's *Lessons in Science*, and *Wilhelm Meister*) but, on the contrary, of giving the revolutionary act all its decisive force by establishing it as close as possible to its origin: where it is knowledge, creative word, and, in this knowledge and this word, the principle of absolute liberty.

Literary manifestos, certainly, were not lacking before the romantics, but this time it is an event of an entirely different sort. Art and literature, on the one hand, seem to have nothing other to do than manifest, that is to say, indicate themselves in accordance with the obscure mode that is proper to them: manifest, announce, in a word, communicate themselves. This is the inexhaustible act that institutes and constitutes the being of literature. But, on the other hand—and herein lies the complexity of the event—this becoming self-conscious that renders literature manifest, and reduces it to being nothing but its manifestation, leads literature to lay claim not only to the sky, the earth, to the past, the future, to physics and philosophy—this would be little—but to everything, to *the whole that acts in every instant and every phenomenon* (Novalis). Yes, everything. But let's read carefully: not every instant such as it occurs, nor every phenomenon such as it produces itself, only the whole that acts mysteriously and invisibly in everything. This is the ambiguity. Romanticism, the advent of poetic consciousness, is not simply a school of literature, nor even an important moment in the history of art.

Romanticism inaugurates an epoch; even more, it is the epoch in which every epoch reveals itself for, through it, the absolute subject of all revelation comes into play: the "I" that in its freedom adheres to no condition, recognizes itself in no thing in particular, and is only in its element—its ether—in the *whole* where it is free. The world, says Novalis, must be romanticized. The past is already romantic in its greatest creators (Shakespeare, Dante, Cervantes, Ariosto, Leonardo da Vinci); furthermore, antiquity becomes eternal presence and the Olympus of art only through romanticism's act of recognition, for, says Schlegel, *"one must be essentially modern to have of antiquity a transcendental point of view."* Finally, the future belongs in its entirety to romanticism because romanticism alone founds it: *"Romantic creative art is still in the process of becoming, and it is even its essence proper never to obtain perfection, to be always and eternally new; no new theory can exhaust it, it alone is infinite just as it alone is free"* (Schlegel). This seems to ensure a joyous and temporal eternity for romanticism and, in effect, it does; but this is an eternity threatened by immediate disappearance, as will be seen when Hegel draws disastrous consequences from this tendency of romanticism to universalize itself historically—that is, on the day he decides to name all the art of the entire Christian era romantic, while recognizing in romanticism proper only the dissolution of the movement: its mortal triumph, the moment of decline when art, turning the principle of destruction that is its center against itself, coincides with its interminable and pitiful end.

Let us acknowledge that, from its beginnings and well before Hegel's *Lectures on Aesthetics*, romanticism—and this is its greatest merit—is not unaware of the fact that such is its truth. Dissolved in the whole, even if at times (and equivocally) it seeks to establish its empire over the totality of things, romanticism has the keenest knowledge of the narrow margin in which it can affirm itself: neither in the world nor outside the world; master of everything, but on condition that the whole contain nothing; pure consciousness without content, a pure speech that can say nothing. A situation in which failure and success are in strict reciprocity, fortune and misfortune indiscernible. By becoming everything poetry has also immediately lost everything, thereby reaching that strange era of its own tautology where it will inexhaustibly exhaust its difference by repeating that its essence is to poeticize, just as the essence of speech is to speak. As Novalis discerns as early as 1798, in a text of angelic penetration: *"There is something strange in the fact of writing and speaking. The laughable and astonishing error people make is to believe they speak in accordance with things. They are all unaware of what is proper to language: that it is concerned only with itself. This is why it constitutes a fertile and splendid mystery. It is precisely when someone speaks simply to be speaking that he is able to say the most original and truest things. . . . Only he who has a profound feeling for language, who feels it in its application, its suppleness, its rhythm, and its musical spirit—only he who hears it in its inner nature, and seizes in himself its intimate and subtle movement . . . yes, he alone is prophet."* And Novalis adds: *"If I think I have in this manner clearly specified the essence and the function of poetry, I also know . . . , having wanted to say it, that I have said something quite stupid from which all poetry is excluded. Yet what if I had to speak? What if, pressured to speak by speech itself, I had in myself this sign of the intervention and the action of language? Then it might well be that there was some poetry without my knowing it, and that a mystery of language was rendered intelligible. . . . And also, therefore, that I am a writer by vocation, since only a writer is inhabited by language, inspired by speech.*[2] Or again: *"To speak for the sake of speaking is the formula for deliverance."* One can indeed say that in these texts we find expressed the non-romantic essence of romanticism, as well as all the principal questions that the night of language will contribute to producing in the light of day: that to write is to make (of) speech (a) work, but that this work is an unworking; that to speak poetically is to make possible a non-transitive speech whose task is not to say things (not to disappear in what it signifies), but to say (itself) in letting (itself) say, yet without taking itself as the new object of this language without object (for if poetry is simply a speech that claims to express the essence of speech and of poetry, one will, and scarcely more subtly, return to the use of transitive language—a major difficulty through which one comes to discern the strange lacuna at the interior of literary language that is its own difference, in a sense its night; a night somehow terrifying, and analogous to what Hegel believed he saw in gazing into men's eyes).

A question is henceforth posed. In order to keep it intact, romanticism, as we know, will give this answer: speech is the subject. From this will come strange discoveries, marvelous works and destructive difficulties. To begin with, the one I have emphasized: the penchant for forgetting that poetic omniscience (*"the true poet is omniscient"* says Novalis) is not a particular knowledge of the whole any more than poetic power is a magical power. Then the following: if true speech is the subject, free of every objective particularity, this means that it is so only in the existence of the poet in which the pure subject affirms itself by saying "I." The "I" of the poet, finally, is what alone will be important: no longer the poetic work, but poetic activity, always superior to the real work, and only creative when it knows itself able to evoke and at the same time to revoke the work in the sovereign play of *irony*. As a result, poetry will be taken over not only by life, but even by biography: hence the desire to live romantically and to make even one's character poetic—that character called "romantic," which, moreover, is extremely alluring inasmuch as character is precisely what is lacking in that it is nothing other than the impossibility of being anything determined, fixed, or sure. Hence the frivolity, the gaiety, the petulance, the madness, and, finally, the extravagance—everything Novalis will lucidly condemn when he reproaches the romantic soul for becoming too weak through dispersion and for being effeminate, while others (like Wackenroder) will speak of the literary bad faith that consists in believing oneself to be sublime and at the same time *"of no use what-soever to the world, being much less active than an artisan."*

From these and many other contradictions in whose midst romanticism unfolds — contradictions that will contribute to making literature no longer a re-sponse, but a question — let us, in ending, retain this one: the romantic art that concentrates creative truth in the freedom of the subject also defines for itself the ambition of a total book, a kind of Bible, perpetually growing, that will not repre-sent the real but replace it, for the *whole* can only be affirmed in the non-objective sphere of the work. This Book, say all the great romantics, will be the novel. Schlegel: *"The novel is the romantic book."* Novalis: *"The novel alone is able to absolutize the world, for the idea of the whole must dominate and entirely shape the esthetic work."* And Solger: *"All the art of today rests not with drama but with the novel."* But this total novel of which most of the romantics are content to dream in the manner of a fable, or by realizing it in the fabulous form of the *Mär-chen*, in a strange synthesis of abstract innocence and ethereal knowledge, will be undertaken only by Novalis. And here is the remarkable trait: not only will Novalis leave this novel unfinished, but he also will sense that the only way he could have accomplished it would have been to invent a new art: that of the frag-ment. As I observed in beginning, this is one of romanticism's boldest presenti-ments: it is what prompts the search for a new form of completion that mobilizes — renders mobile — the whole through its interruption and through inter-ruption's various modes. This demand for a fragmentary speech, not in order to trouble communication but to render it absolute, is what causes Schlegel to say that only future centuries will know how to read "fragments." It is also what leads Novalis to write: *"The art of writing books has not yet been discovered, but it is about to be: fragments like these are literary seeds."* From this same perspective, both Schlegel and Novalis will affirm that the fragment, in monologue form, is a substitute for dialogical communication since *"a dialogue is a chain or a garland of fragments"* (Schlegel) and, more profoundly, an anticipation of what one could call a plural writing; the possibility of a writing that is done in common, an inno-vation whose signs Novalis recognizes in the development of the press: *"Newspapers are already books made in common. The art of writing jointly is a curious symptom that makes us sense a great progress in literature. One day, per-haps, we will write, think, and act collectively."* Just as genius is nothing other than a multiple person (Novalis) or *a system of talents* (Schlegel), what is impor-tant is to introduce into writing, through the fragment, the plurality that in each of us is virtual, in all of us real, and that corresponds to *"the unceasing, autocrea-tive alternance of different or opposed thoughts."* Discontinuous form: the sole form befitting romantic *irony*, since it alone can make coincide discourse and si-lence, the playful and the serious, the declarative, even oracular exigency and the indecision of a thought that is unstable and divided, finally, the mind's obligation to be systematic and its abhorrence for system: *"Having a system is as mortal for the mind as not having one: it must, then, decide to lose both these tendencies"* (Schlegel).

In truth, and particularly in the case of Friedrich Schlegel, the fragment often seems a means for complacently abandoning oneself to the self rather than an attempt to elaborate a more rigorous mode of writing. Then to write fragmentarily is simply to welcome one's own disorder, to close up upon one's own self in a contented isolation, and thus to refuse the opening that the fragmentary exigency represents; an exigency that does not exclude totality, but goes beyond it. When with great frankness he writes, *"I can conceive for my personality no other pattern than a system of fragments, because I myself am something of this sort; no style is as natural to me and as easy as that of the fragment,"* he declares that his discourse will not be a dis-course, but a reflection of his own discordance. As when he notes, *"A fragment, like a miniature work of art, has to be isolated from the surrounding world and be complete in itself like a porcupine,"* he leads the fragment back toward the aphorism, that is to say, the closure of a perfect sentence. This inflection is perhaps inevitable and comes down to: (1) considering the fragment as a text that is concentrated, having its center in itself rather than in the field that *other* fragments constitute along with it; (2) neglecting the interval (wait or pause) that separates the fragments and makes of this separation the rhythmic principle of the work at the structural level; (3) forgetting that this manner of writing tends not to make a view of the whole more difficult or the relations of unity more lax, but rather makes possible new relations that except themselves from unity, just as they exceed the whole. Naturally, this "omission" or inflection is not explained by the simple failings of personalities that are too subjective or too impatient to reach the absolute. It is also explained (at least in the original sense of this verb, and more decisively) by the orientation of history, which, become revolutionary, places at the forefront of its action work that is undertaken in view of the whole and the dialectical search for unity. It remains nonetheless true that literature, beginning to become manifest to itself through the romantic declaration, will from now on bear in itself this question of discontinuity or difference as a question of form—a question and a task German romanticism, and in particular that of *The Athenaeum*, not only sensed but already clearly proposed—before consigning them to Nietzsche and, beyond Nietzsche, to the future.

XII

The Effect of Strangeness

± ± Poetry: dispersion that, as such, finds its form. Here a supreme struggle is engaged against the essence of division, and nonetheless from this very basis; language responds to a summons that brings its inherited coherency back into question. It is as though language were torn from itself: everything is broken, shattered, without relation; passage from one sentence to another, one word to another is no longer possible. But once the internal and external ties are broken, there arises in each word as though anew all words; not words, but their very presence that effaces them, their absence that calls them forth — and not words, but the space, appearing and disappearing, that they designate as the moving space of their appearance and disappearance. I read this, this force of continuity engendered on the basis of discontinuity, in the poems of André du Bouchet and at times in those of Jacques Dupin. Poems gravely and tenderly nocturnal that ask one to say of them what they say of the night: *"This night that waits for us and fills us, we must go on disappointing its waiting so that it be night."* The waiting is borne in this poetry by each and every word, and in each there is response to the inexpressed, its refusal and its attraction. *"And the landscape disposes itself around a word tossed out lightly that will come back laden with shadow."*

± ± Theater is the art of playing with division by introducing it into space through dialogue. Dialogue is a late notion. In the most ancient forms of theater, words speak in solitude, turned only toward the men who have religiously come together to hear them; there is no lateral communication, and the one who speaks addresses himself to the public out of a plenitude that excludes all response: a speech from on high, a relation without reciprocity. But as soon as speech divides so as to move back and forth on stage, relations with the public change, the distance widens. Those who sit below in order to hear no longer hear immediately, but as guarantors: their attention carries and supports everything. Silence is henceforth present as a *third party*, until the time when one ends by forgetting it, the ideal being to carry on a dialogue naturally as one would in company. Now discontinuity is lost in favor of a continuity of surface. (The art of Jean Genet's theater, on the contrary, is profoundly discontinuous.)

And Brecht? Brecht: the one who became conscious of fascination and wants to break with it by turning it back against itself.

± ± In Brecht everything is seductive, everything calls up the sympathy against which he did not cease to caution us. A great simplicity, the most natural alliance with the simplicity of song, the power to make simple words speak and also to do justice to affliction, to suffering, and to human beings, simply by making them speak. This is something powerful, living, and perhaps, finally, happy. All these qualities are evident. And nonetheless this naive man is a cunning author. This natural simplicity is composed also of study, research, and constraint, just as it gives practice its place and is tempted by pedagogy. Here is a writer who has the gift of images, who knows the power of light, of gesture, of movement and who is quite ready to animate for us the enchantment of space — but no, it is to judgment that he is addressing himself, and the freedom he seeks to awaken is a freedom of mind he oftentimes understands very abstractly. Exuberant and austere, moving, but with a horror of moving and a mistrust of good feelings, just the same open to simple convictions, to heartfelt certainties, to hope; a Marxist, but perhaps in the manner of the nineteenth century. And was Brecht such a happy man? His youth belonged to the war he detested; then to the liberty of disorder he mistrusted; then to the threat of tyranny that he loathed. His maturity belonged to the exile he was never able to bear. His last years are obscure. Everything indicates that in spite of costly compromise these were the most brilliant and fortunate, if not the most fruitful, years of his life. But must we add that this fundamentally free man, spared by a premature death from the events to come (from which he would have intimately suffered) had, in this sense, a happy end? A sad happiness, in accordance with our time.

A writer for the theater, passionate about the theater, he seems to have felt an early distaste for theatrical success and its means. Poe, in a famous passage, sought the means for writing a poem by defining beforehand the points of sensibility upon which the poem most surely must act. Brecht sought the contrary. When he enters the auditorium of a theater, he is horrified and grieved by the spectacle of those fascinated people who listen but do not hear, who stare but see nothing: sleepwalkers immersed together in a dream that stirs them, deprived of judgment, bewitched and fundamentally insensible. (Is it really this way? Is not the spectator rather often frivolous, that is, only slightly interested, as incapable of fascination as of attention?)

No matter; this is indeed the kind of influence that the author, the actor, and the director would like to exert. If the actor performs well, he will identify with his character and powerfully attract souls; not in the manner of a man who is real, but as a dreaming force or an unreal existence in which we, the others seated below in our seats, will for an instant incarnate our hopes and actualize our dreams in order to satisfy them passionately, without peril and without truth. This participation and sympathy, this almost revolting contact between merged sensibilities, these immediate relations in which nothing is in relation, this manner of loving without love are what seem to have offended Brecht from the outset; and all the more so inasmuch as, with their expressionist disorder and brutality, his first works have recourse to incantatory means that provoke, it is true, more resistance than adherence.

Then why does he persist in writing and working only for the theater, where failure seems to him more honorable than this sort of success? Probably because he has a malevolent gift for theater; perhaps because an artist and a writer feel all the more called to exercise an art the less they can bear it as it is; because there is in Brecht a great concern for being in relation with the world of men, for telling them what he knows, but, even more, for listening to them and leading them to the threshold of speech. For him the theater will be less the place where marvelous phantoms stir than the still vaster site where real or nearly real men and women, the spectators, will not lose themselves in dreams, but rather rise up to thought and soon have their say.

*

Brecht's apprehensions are many. Everything in the theater is to be feared, and above all the illusory movement that makes us believe there are not actors but characters on stage, and that what is being acted out, far from being simply a game, would be a kind of event accomplished a single time and forever in a tragic or exalting permanency that is removed from any change. The spectator identifies with this speaking figure, with this mute, inexorable action in which he participates through a magical sympathy that, throwing him outside himself, makes him consent to everything through an obscure obedience from which he leaves thinking: so it is, and so it shall eternally be. The theater, whatever the content of the play, instinctively makes us believe in an immutable human kind, in an eternal order and inordinate forces before which, ceasing to be ourselves, we are turned into shadows or heroes—which means that the theater is guilty of making us believe in theater.

How can these perils be avoided? The formulations that are the focus of Brecht's short "Organum"[1] (which, moreover, were already being elaborated in

Berlin during the course of the tumultuous years following the First World War), the fruit of his own experience and of the collective experience of those working in the theater, are today well known—too well known; and yet they still remain surprising in the degree to which they belong to the very dangers they denounce. Hence their importance, for they show that Brecht does not draw them from theoretical, political, or philosophical ideas. What he wants, therefore, is to propose to the spectator images and a way of acting that will allow him, or even bestow upon him, freedom, movement, and judgment. What profoundly shocks Brecht is the sort of *immediate* relation that the traditional theater establishes between actor and spectator. The one is fastened to the other like the hypnotized to the hypnotist, yet this abject adjacency does not even have the truth of "real" relations, as may happen in relations of passion. Here passivity is at its height; we are our own shadow, steeped in obscurity and avid for a pale blood that flows from no wound. Brecht will therefore do everything to place an interval between the different elements that make up the theater: interval between the author and the "tale," between acting and event, between actor and character, and then the widest, between the actor and the public, the two halves of the theater. This process received a name now become almost too celebrated, and for which Brecht, without any pedantic impulse (though he is a bit pedagogical), chose a slang designation: *V-Effekt*, *Verfremdungseffekt*: the effect of strangeness, of distancing or foreignness.

At this point our interest grows, and since the name *V-Effekt* has acquired such prestige, we have to be persuaded that Brecht chose it knowingly: it is a strong word, rich and charged with various powers. How does it tie in with his preoccupations? First, it calls attention to the kind of rupture that, in the new theater, is to make the sympathetic interest through which every happy spectator fades into what he sees (and is thereby truly *touched*) more difficult. The image through which the effect of strangeness is realized, says Brecht, is one that, while permitting us to recognize the object, will make it appear strange and foreign. This effect therefore seeks to abstract the thing represented from the instinctive adherence through which understanding and meaning perish. What happens up there on the stage is not natural, and we are not to take it for real coin. We must, on the one hand, always be able to remind ourselves that in front of us is a fiction obtained by artificial means and that the actor is an actor and not Galileo Galilei; he is rather a man who has studied this role: first read it, then annotated it, then droned his way through it and is now reciting it, perhaps living it, but always from a distance. For when the action begins he knows very well, although we do not, how it ends, and he must act in such a way that we are advised that he does. In the same way, the sun that shines on him is not the light of day but a projector; so let us show it, and let the theater no longer dissimulate what it is: a coordinated but unstable set of dissembling appearances, a foreign space that can render foreign and remote the things that come about in it and in such a way that, as familiar and as consecrated as these things may appear to us, we can take our distance from them, cease taking them as natural, and, on the contrary, regard them as unheard of, even unjustified. Thus, we will no longer say: so it is, so it will always be, but rather: so it was, it could also be otherwise.

Brecht's great concern is the weight of things: the frozen, stable appearance of human relations, their pretense of being natural, the certitude that preserves them, our faith in custom, and our incapacity to imagine change — to aspire to it and prepare for it. All his works could well open with the interpolation that the actors, in a memorable warning, address to us at the beginning of *The Exception and the Rule*: "*Find it estranging even if not very strange / Hard to explain even if it is the custom / Hard to understand even if it is the rule / Observe the smallest action, seeming simple, / With mistrust / Inquire if a thing be necessary / Especially if it is common / We particularly ask you— / When a thing continually occurs— / Not on that account to find it natural / In an age of bloody confusion / Ordered disorder, planned caprice, / And dehumanized humanity, lest all things / Be held unalterable!*"[2]

This concern may appear more philosophical than artistic insofar as it is a matter of arousing surprise so that the spirit of questioning, then of observation, then freedom of judgment and, if need be, the spirit of revolt may be born. But the power of art, even more than that of Galileo, can designate in everything something else: beneath the familiar the unheard of, and in what is, what may not be. It is a power that sets things apart so as to render them sensible to us and always unknown, from out and by means of this separation that becomes their very space.

Now it is precisely this separation, this distance, that Brecht is seeking to produce and maintain through the effect of strangeness. The new artistic image, let us repeat this along with him, does not simply represent the thing, but shows it to us by the light of the distant and as transformed by the force of the distant, other than it had the habit of appearing to us — thus withdrawn from the usual appearance of familiarity in which we believed we saw its true nature and its eternal substance. This is particularly so of human relations. Able to produce the effect of strangeness, the image therefore effects a kind of experiment by showing us that things are perhaps not what they are, that it falls to us to see them otherwise and, by this opening, render them first imaginarily other, then really and entirely other.

*

But if we sense that what Brecht is saying here is right, we also sense that his way of thinking entails (and dissimulates) a grave, a difficult, perhaps an essential problem; as though we found ourselves here at the limit on which our power turns. He wants, on the one hand, to break the immediate relation upon which the traditional theater establishes its influence and, at best, turns those in the audience into powerless and distracted spectators, terrified or enchanted, rapturously accepting this magical loss of self. It is a matter of distancing the spectacle from the spectator so that, escaping a paralyzing contact, he can recover the distance and breathing space, the possibility on the basis of which will come to him a freedom of judgment and a power of initiative that he is lacking even in the real world. For, on the other hand, the Brecht who wants fascination to reign no longer in the theater wishes even more that it would cease to alter human relations. In the world it is the fascination of the everyday, the familiar, of what goes without saying, to which we are bound; this is what renders us incapable of seeing that what appears to us as reality is arbitrary and can be modified. The theater, with its strange representation of things, will therefore give us the means to escape our fascination with the "natural" and, by the strangeness and distance it puts at our disposal, give us access to a freer view both of the things represented and of representation itself. Thus in a sense we will be dealt a double blow, and a double windfall.

A too satisfying solution; and Brecht does not fail to sense the difficulties it holds in store for him. Is he not, first of all, wrong to attribute solely to the technique of sympathy and to the illusion of proximity the stupor that, according to him, is responsible for riveting the spectator to the spectacle? Might he not instead see in these an effect of the distance—a reduced and yet irreducible distance—that separates in such a prodigious manner the two halves of the theater? What is represented and brought close to us by illusion acts upon us because it is at once absolutely distant from us and without relation to us; and this absence of relation, this living and moving void is the medium in which, through a leap, we move to encounter one another and where the perilous metamorphosis is accomplished. When, therefore, Brecht would wish to distance the spectacle from the spectator by the effect of strangeness, does he not risk augmenting the spectacle's fascinating power insofar as this power is founded precisely upon the remote and upon separation—thus delivering the spectator, and in an even more insidious fashion than before, over to the spell that is cast upon each of us by the familiar becoming foreign, becoming the inaccessible image that always in advance doubles it, becoming this double both familiar and strange, and making each of us into our own double, deprived of ourselves?

This is certain, and Brecht is far from being unaware of it since he finds (and condemns) in the theater of antiquity, as well as in medieval and Asian theater, all sorts of *V-Effekte* (which he nonetheless employs: the use of human and animal masks, music and pantomime) that assuredly have the advantage of impeding sympathy, but also the inconvenience of reinforcing hypnotic suggestion by acting through impassiveness itself, and exerting the influence of what cannot itself be influenced. But if this is so, how can he keep the effect of strangeness from stupefying the mind rather than waking it, from making it passive rather than active and free? Although he does not reveal it directly, his thought is clear. There is a "good" strangeness and a "bad" strangeness. The first is the distance that the image places between ourselves and the object, freeing us from the object in its presence, making it available to us in its absence; permitting us to name it, to make it signify, and to modify it: a mighty and a reasonable power, the great driving force of human progress. But the second strangeness to which all the arts owe their effects is the reversal of the first one, which, moreover, is its origin; it arises when the image is no longer what allows us to have the object as absent but is rather what takes hold of us by absence itself: there where the image, always at a distance, always absolutely close and absolutely inaccessible, steals away from us, opens onto a neutral space where we can no longer act, and also opens us upon a sort of neutrality where we cease being ourselves and oscillate strangely between I, He, and no one.

Brecht, quite clearly, plays upon this duplicity of the imaginary. He plays with it all the more insofar as, a great artist and a great poet, he not only seeks to free the theater from fascination, but even more to free the social world from the fascination that custom (as a result of economic causes and class structures) exerts on us. To succeed in this he needs the power of defamiliarizing and unsettling that art offers to him. This means that he struggles pathetically, stubbornly, and nobly against fascination, but with fascination's help: at times designating by the term *V-Effekte* the means proper to countering the theater's magic and illusion, at times seeking in these everything that in the theater, and through the very magic of the strangeness of theater, is able to change things by representing them, and able to make us reflect upon this change.

Must we not, then, reproach Brecht for promoting a certain confusion, and also for a certain wiliness that permits him to use this confusion and the double meaning that his formula—it, too, magical—dissimulates beneath its powerfully equivocal name? We have to admire his cunning, but also the vigilance he demonstrates in constantly pursuing the fleeting point where the image brings forward this power of absence it holds within itself and where, also, this absence can awaken the spectator's freedom (in giving the spectator space and breathing room) just as much as it can encroach upon it through the alluring and engaging force of the imaginary: the power to give meaning, the power to metamorphose itself into this meaning, and thus the risk of being lost there. Constantly, Brecht seeks to animate this distance between spectacle and spectator, seeking to render it workable and available and to keep it from becoming frozen—from becoming the space across which the words addressed to us and the images that reflect us change into being (into the absence of being), and, rather than speaking to us and representing us, absorb us and draw us out of ourselves. And thus if the play tends to become a narrative—thereby distancing itself—the actors, on the contrary, do not fail to turn to us, to call upon us and speak to us directly—thus drawing us near. Yet as Brecht does not want to impose his view of things on us, but on the contrary wants to augment our freedom and our spirit of initiative, it is through the enigmatic simplicity of song and the ambiguous force of poetry that the interpolation is addressed to us; and once again it is the distant that seizes us, the strangeness and defamiliarization necessary in order that everything that does not speak in habitual words may at last break the silence and prepare us for a new, for a first hearing.

A study of Brecht's plays would perhaps show us the various forms that this debate took for him (a debate that was first a conflict within him); and we would see that for the most part he relies upon the actor and the director to apply his formula—while the writer in him, and the work, far from exalting the voluntaristic part of life and its stimulating powers, express events in their passive succession and men in a sort of absence from whose depths they scarcely wake.

This is because, for Brecht, speech in the theater must not cease being space; and this space of speech, the part belonging to the stage, is destined more to recount than to produce either the violence of action or the inactive violence of dialogue. It is as though, to a certain extent, passivity should be reserved for the stage and activity for the public; as though, moreover, in order that a nascent dialogue take form between spectator and actor, the space that is the stage was not to exhaust and concentrate within itself (by dispersing it between the loquacious characters who think only of speaking among themselves in closed company) this power of communication that is always yet to be born. Let us recall that Jean Vilar, the great interpreter of Brecht (but whose ideas are apparently different)[3] also, and with expressive severity, calls into question the kind of tyranny exercised by dialogue, along with its attendant consequences: plot, scenes to be crafted, purple passages, deeds of daring, virtuosity, heroic chatter. The universal form of bourgeois drama has made us forget what we noted a while back: that the theater, at its origin, is not in the least a place of conversation, nor is it born of the need to place beings on stage so they may indefinitely exchange answers back and forth. The first great figures of the stage, still merged with an original silence, scarcely speak; they speak to each other only exceptionally and in an almost fortuitous way by means of an encounter that is unexpected, violent, and sudden. As though speech remained a rare event, marvelous and perilous, and as though the speech of the theater were still midway between the silent impassivity of the gods and the speaking and suffering activity of men. A tragedy without a hero, a language almost without a subject.

XIII

The End of the Hero

It is true, the myth of the hero is not easily erased. There is the space hero, the hero of the stadium, or the hero of comic books. And we are apt to praise some state leader by calling him the most illustrious of history's heroes.

The hero is the ambiguous gift literature bestowed on us before becoming conscious of itself. Hence the fact that the hero, despite his simplicity, is divided between doing and saying. First, if he belongs to the earliest epochs, he does not belong to the most ancient times. What the Germans call *das Märchen*, a term we translate (poorly) by tale [*conte*], goes back to an age of the world without heroes and nearly without a face: no attention was paid at that time to names, and the premythical character, even if he has a name, is not separated from the material forces — plants, water, earth — that common nouns suffice to designate. The era depicted by the tale is exempt neither from perverse beings nor from violent deeds; but, as Jünger remarks, when we meet up with dwarfs, ogres, and witches, we do not meet either Siegfried or Heracles. Even the hunter who takes on the natural environment at the same time belongs to it, merely availing himself of a right that does not belong to him personally, but that he exercises in a zone of collective and magical safety, originally delimited and moreover protected by sacred compensatory acts. This is not the golden age. Rousseau nonetheless helps us understand why we may be spellbound upon entering the caves of prehistoric man, yet remain free of heroic exaltation. No hero ever lived in one.

The appearance of the hero marks a change in man's relations with nature. There is Hercules, Achilles, and Roland, there is the Cid and Horace. This list nearly tells it all. In the age of the tale there continues to exist a malicious complicity with the earth or the sky that is not one of unity, but supposes a common horizon: we are almost never on the vertical plane but on the horizontal. And if man struggles against the beings of the various natural realms, he does so not by a clearly warlike action but by ruse, the shrewd exchange or magical transformation that permits him to take the truth and the knowledge of these adverse forces in hand. Hercules opposes the nature from out of which he monstrously emerges, though he does so through force; his exploits are nonetheless enterprises, one might even say labors, and this renders his situation equivocal. Hercules is not a hero of the sun, he is too strong; and this force is neither virile nor divine but natural—it is nature forcefully separating from herself. There is something sad about Hercules, as though he represented a kind of betrayal; the division by which splendid nature renounces her grandeur but, as mastered, deprives us of that enchanted knowledge that allowed us to acquiesce to her monstrous appearances. Force domesticates force and becomes servile. It is curious that Chiron, the centaur, is the bearer of wisdom and Hercules, the man, the bearer of brutality. Indeed, Chiron is not a hero.

The hero fights and conquers. Where does this conquering virility come from? From himself. But where does he himself come from? This is the beginning of the hero's difficulties. He has a name that is proper to him, one he has often even appropriated—a surname [*surnom*], just as we speak of a superego [*surmoi*]. He has a name, he is a name. But if he has a name, he has a genealogy; the ascendancy he exerts and owes to his deeds of valor is at the same time a sign of the ascendancy that he owes to his origin, which makes him come naturally from above. He will never free himself from this contradiction. The hero who owes nothing to anyone but himself is for this reason divine—but thereby always and forever a god; thus it is no longer his action that is glorious, but his glorious essence that is affirmed and proven by his acts, consecrated and proclaimed in his name. The hero teaches us something in this. First, our invincible propensity to essentialize: the hero is solely action and action makes him heroic, but this heroic doing is nothing without being; being alone—essence—satisfies us, reassures us, and promises us the future. For ignoble obscurity is frightening. Glory is suspect if it comes from the night. The heroic act must therefore be always already anterior to itself, just as the hero, the first man par excellence, must be a man come from afar, a hereditary marvel, recognized and transmitted. Achilles, hidden and disguised as a girl, is nonetheless already Achilles. He is so by his origin, which is divine: his waiting (for himself) is merely a waiting for his manifestation. Not unknown, but dissimulated. Suddenly this occultation ceases and there he is in broad daylight, entirely visible, bearer of a clarity that not only triumphs over the night but has also in advance negated it, already made it the coming of day.

Between origin and beginning, nonetheless, there are dark relations that precisely the hero helps us to grasp. The origin is not the beginning; between the two there is an interval, and even an uncertainty. The origin secures us against obscurity but is itself obscure, either because it dissimulates itself or because, in doing so, it retains in itself the part of inhumanity that genealogies endeavor to make historical. Even with a divine origin one must be born as a man: he is awaited, he waits for himself, and when he declares himself it is easy to say that he could not have failed to appear. Yet before he proved himself nothing had established him as a child from on high; on the contrary, he was but a bastard without sure parentage—his illegitimacy is even what prompts him to make himself known. He thus comes to possess an origin only at the moment when he bestows upon himself a beginning and, without lineage, without belonging, makes his appearance on the basis of a non-appearance that only hid the plenitude of being.[1]

Achilles is the hero, but Agamemnon is the king of kings. This difference, this distance setting the hero apart, will forever continue to exist, obliging him to be unique in order not to be second. Nephew of the emperor, paladin and necessarily noble, the hero is close to power, and often stronger than power, but his strength is excentric, it represents another center that could not, even should it claim to do so, unfold into a system without disappearing. He therefore incarnates in his radiance, that is, in the most direct manifestation, something that is nonetheless indirect, an oblique affirmation, an equivocacy from which the frankness of his exploits will not succeed in clearing him. Even if he does not lie, he is on the verge of falsehood, his essence deceptive. His simplicity, indeed the most simple—that of a braggart showing off—is vitiated by a duplicity that gnaws at him: he is thus divided between origin and beginning, between being and doing, magic and strength, strength and sovereignty, glory and the throne, rank and blood. That is not all. One must add: between saying and doing.

The hero is nothing if not glorious. The word exploit marks this relation with the outside: heroism knows nothing of conscience, as it knows nothing of the virtual and the latent. Glory is the shining forth of immediate action, it is light, it is radiance. The hero shows himself; this dazzling manifestation is that of a being's being, the transfiguration of origin into beginning, the transparency of the absolute in a decision or an action that is nonetheless particular and momentary. But this glorious disclosure that leaves nothing to disclose (the hero's soul is the most empty) and at the same time claims to be inexhaustible, is the privilege of his near namesake, the herald: he who announces and makes resound. Heroism is revelation, the marvelous brilliance of deed that joins essence and appearance. Heroism is the act's luminous sovereignty. Only the act is heroic, and the hero is nothing if he does not act—nothing outside the clarity of the act that illuminates and brings him to light. This is the first form of what will later be affirmed by the name praxis (with a complete reversal of meaning). Therefore, heroic authenticity—if there is such a thing—should be determined as a verb, never a substantive. And yet the hero in the plenitude of his name is all that counts, all that is important. This means also that if there is heroism only through action, there are heroes only in and through speech. Song is his privileged abode. The hero is born when the singer comes forward in the great hall. He is told. He is not, he is merely sung.

The hero, the active man par excellence, owes his existence solely to language. But it must immediately be noted that between the roving bard and the forceful man who is without power and without place there is both a complicity of fate and a similarity of function (we praise Roland rather than Charlemagne). For both are marginal, or at least represent a presence that is at once frontal and lateral. The singer recognizes himself—from a distance—in the hero, and in this way thinks he is making himself recognized by proposing recognition of the hero. Not that the poem, in recounting the marvelous action, is content to celebrate it: in celebrating it the poem produces it, rehearses it in the strongest sense of the term and accords it the power of redundancy that comes from the name and unfolds in renown, *the rumor of glory accompanying the name*. The obscure hero does not exist. Pindar will say: "*Honor is accorded solely to those for whom the gods make arise a fine discourse come to assist the dead.*" Measured speech and heroic lack of measure have this in common: both affront death. But speech is more profoundly engaged in the movement of dying because it alone succeeds in making of dying a second life, an enduring without duration. In this sense, and granting that the hero is master, the man who seems to possess speech as a power will be this master's master.

*

But is the hero the master? This is the question Serge Doubrovsky's book poses and helps us to pose.[2] It is his thesis that Corneille's entire theater amounts to a study, or better, a profound exploration of the project of mastery, of mastery as it was brought into the truth of philosophical discourse by the Hegelian schema. The only difference is that Corneille has no interest in the slave, being interested only in the master: what are the latter's relations with his equals? Don Diego gives the answer: *Die or kill*. Death—the risk of death given or received, lived in anguish, that is to say, in the movement by which the natural man changes nature—this is indeed the truth of the master. But the master is not alone in confronting this truth. The Self who has vanquished death, and has vanquished by death, encounters other Selves that are in like manner victors. Will he have to enslave them—but the man who has instantaneously acquired superiority by turning against nature through the ultimate act of violence will only make a deteriorated phantom, never a good slave—or must he annihilate them? Mutual extermination would be the just solution, but would bring as a consequence the ruin of the State, the failure of power, an absurd collapse. To avoid this, Cornelian tragedy seeks other outcomes that are political and historical: it is a matter of seeing whether, heroism having become an institution, the master can form a society with other masters and the sovereign Self found a sovereign order of Selves.

If there are seemingly happy tragedies in which the master as hero and the master as monarch find an equilibrium and concord, thus promising a long future of security and brilliance, the oeuvre taken as a whole fails and says nothing other than its defeat: there is no salvation through heroism. The failure Corneille's oeuvre bears in itself as its proudly dissimulated knowledge (its secret defect) expresses the meaning of mastery in its relations with impossibility. The hero is not without a progressive role to play: at a certain moment, he represents the impatient decision to defy nature. The hero does not want to be natural, nor does he want nature to triumph in him, even if it does so in order to make him triumph. *Out of my heart, nature* is what Cleopatra superbly cries, and they all say it or keep it to themselves in their own way. The decidedly heroic act could not but be an antiphysical act: a crime, a denatured crime, a crisis by which man not only negates what opposes him but negates the natural part within himself—happy spontaneity, easy courage, good fortune without virtue. It is not a question simply of carrying off the act, then, but rather of carrying it off in such a way that nature is vanquished: this is the sublime act, doing not only the impossible, but willing what one has done:

He is free, he is master, he wills all he does.

Let us admit this definition. It makes of the hero an inaugural Self, and of the heroic Self a will mustered in an act that owes nothing to being. But where does this will that we still call free spring from; what is the origin of the infinite it bestows upon us in the face of a limited nature? If it is a gift, the sign and signature of our essence, then it still comes from nature, even if it is from a transcendent nature that we receive this exceeding by which we rise above her. To be naturally free, naturally antinatural; how could the hero be content with such a parody? *Out of my heart, nature*. This ardent wish is pathetic but above all laughable, as Serge Doubrovsky remarks, for in the one who formulates it, nature is long gone, and Cleopatra, who kills her sons as others might kill flies, need make no effort. This monstrosity proves nothing, nor does the difficulty of the act or the hesitation in accomplishing it—an indecisive hero is a comic hero; as for this burst of energy by which the admirable act—an act against nature and above nature—proposes itself and is immediately accomplished, where could it come from, if not still from nature? Sade, through his cries and ordeals, indicated much more lucidly than Corneille, but in the same vein, the contradiction that threatens every free will that sets itself against nature. He also recognized in which direction a response might be sought: it is that free will does not belong to being and, as a consequence, *is* not, unless it succeeds in coinciding with a transcendent power of negation. One is not free, one makes oneself free and does so only by refusing; but one only refuses by an action—an affirmation—that is decidedly negative.[3]

Born like everyone from nothing, and nonetheless wanting to make of this nullity the sign of an exceptional origin; born from nothing, but not an ignoble nothing—rather from an already illustrious and, as it were, ancient void; uniquely present, but of a presence so brilliant that its present light retrospectively sheds light on all his past as it illuminates the future; declaring himself in a trial wherein he must choose himself once and for all and absolutely by choosing between everything and nothing—death, triumph—through a forceful act that is a toss of the dice (but that offers itself also as supreme reason): therefore master of everything in this nothing that he assumes and produces in the brilliance of a decisive action—the hero-master has no intention of returning to nothing. On the contrary, he wants to affirm himself beyond himself through a unique glory that assures the mythical survival of his name; he wants, moreover, on the basis of a uniquely personal action in which nothingness has for an instant become being, to found an impersonal order capable of unfolding infinitely in time and in space the invincible caste of the master. But there are too many contradictions here, too much bad faith as well. The fact remains that these are precisely the contradictions that define the heroic project from the moment when, on the one hand, the hero is no longer content to represent extraordinary action but wants to rise up as the extraordinary agent of action, as an "I" in and by itself sublime (*Master of the universe without being master of myself, I alone rebel against that sovereign power*), and when, on the other hand, the hero who thus seems to interiorize heroism and place himself outside the ordinary, not by what he does but by the manner in which he does it, intends to pass from heroism to mastery, realize himself in history by becoming the master of action, and, through this action that has become partial, exteriorize and impersonalize this undertaking since in the end it is History, and no longer the singular self, that becomes the pure hero.

Corneille, that is to say Corneille's oeuvre, accomplishes itself as such in this uncertainty. Hence the uneasiness, in some sense healthy, it produces in us. For if it discloses all the consequences of this uncertainty, the work itself hides from it, plunges into it, and at times becomes entangled in it in a manner that might be called exemplary. Thus heroism appears: at times as the exercise of valor and the affirmation of prowess; at times as the will to establish an order that will endure; at times as a pure anachronism, fitted out with all the old ingredients—exploits, glory, brilliance, and the brilliant speech that is challenge or boastful provocation; at times as pure moral exigency, voluntary ascesis, silent delving, infinite subjectivity; at still other times as the seeking of power, cunning empiricism, objective and political domination when it is no longer a matter of losing oneself, but of reigning—even if, sadly, this can only occur by making a good marriage—and finally valorization and exaltation of the crime of the State:

All crimes of State, committed for the throne,
Heaven pardons when it makes us mount thereon,
And on the sacred dais where the emperor sits,
The past turns just, the future all permits.

This uncertainty, this equivocity, is perhaps especially revealed in the meaning that death acquires, or fails to acquire, in Cornelian tragedy. Don Diego's *Die or kill* shows that death is sovereign; a dilemma that allows no way out, for it is not even an alternative, but a cruel or deceptive redundancy. It amounts to saying: die or die; die as ego, die as alter ego; kill the master in yourself or in the other in order that, through death, the master-power, that is, death as mastery and the unique mastery of death, will be affirmed. This, in a sense, says everything. Death is the presence in the form of a shadow that from beginning to end takes up the entire stage, speaks when the hero speaks, and responds to him when he is silent. The tragedy of identity, of a mortal tautology, death is always suicide whether it be immediate or (preferably) the doing of an intermediary. Except that this identity is empty, and empty even of death itself. For one dies there without having died, dies without alteration or suffering in an act that eludes, effaces, or suppresses all the infinite passivity of mortal experience. Heroes have problems, certainly, but death is never one of them. The anguish involved in the Hegelian schema (the only instructive one) is for the hero necessarily absent; how could heroes ever be troubled? So it is not from death confronted as a risk that they acquire mastery; they die always already masters of death and masters of themselves in this mortal game. They know how to die, and they expect no knowledge from death:

If one knows how to die, one knows how to evade everything.

The meaning of the death called heroic is its escape from death; its truth is its making of death a fine lie. *Where are you leading him? — To death — To glory.* This is the secret, the naive avowal. In dying the hero does not die, he is born; he becomes glorious, he accedes to presence and establishes himself in memory, a secular survival. Or else, through a refinement that is in fact quite superior to this vain martyrdom, he arranges it so that his final ostentation, even as he is vanquished, can be another vengeance, a triumphant defiance:

Before my eyes she dies, but she dies with ease,
And in dying displays with pomp a wrath
That seems less to die than to triumph over us.

There is no death for the hero but only pomp and ceremony: a superb, a supreme declaration, repose in visibility.

Nonetheless—and this is one of the most important traits of the Cornelian oeuvre that Doubrovsky brings forward—it sometimes happens that death ceases to be pure brilliance in order to become impure horror, no longer glorious instantaneousness but monstrous approach. This occurs when the death of an instant is no longer enough to satisfy the master's desire for extremity, when he must have a death that lasts and will not end. Such is the project of the surprising heroine Marcelle, who, not content with sending the virgin Theodore into prostitution, dreams of an interminable death for her:

> *If my hatred at its pleasure could*
> *Inspire the torturers it would know how to choose,*
> *And feed my pains with a hard and slow death,*
> *Returning it to you at once cruel and drawn out,*
> *And amidst the torments hold out to you your fate,*
> *Causing you each day to feel another death!*

The aged Corneille here rises to the level of Sade;[4] and even if it is still only a matter of the bliss of vengeance rather than negativity experienced as sovereignty, something essential is designated at this moment: death takes but an instant while dying is without end, just as it provokes in the being who dies not his promotion to being, not his exaltation in a permanent identity, but his dissolution—his infinite alteration in the form of suffering or sexual pleasure. This same Marcelle thus literally decomposes in the pleasure of the death she gives and the suffering she inflicts, in making the "beloved" die in front of her "lover":

> *At times full of their last breath,*
> *At times feasting her eyes on their fatal distress,*
> *And measuring there her joy, she finds more charm*
> *In the pain of the lover than in the beloved's death.*

Here, finally, is a ray of truth. Death is not something clean, neat, and valorous, it is not the keen edge of death, the pure activity of a Master-Act: it is passivity and obscurity, the infinite of a suffering given or received, abject affliction, extinction without brilliance. How will the hero accommodate himself to such a discovery? How can he survive it? He does not survive it, he collapses in it, disappears into it, and this is the end we get with the admirable *Surenas*, where Corneille takes his departure from himself, departing from the myth.

Admirable *Surenas*, perhaps precisely for the fact that the admiration always aimed at and required by Corneille for acts that are no more than gestures here no longer finds employ. To die, yes, but wretchedly, in disarray and distress; to die, an unsuitable word since it is a matter of dying without death, of this impotent death that is suffering. Eurydice:

> *I want a dark despair to waste me slowly*
> *And make me deeply taste its bitterness;*

> *I want without the untimely aid of death,*
> *To be always loving, suffering, dying.*

The ternary rhythm of the final line, destined to augment infinitely its duration, strangely enough provokes a slight nausea, as though a slackness, a sickening rocking motion had come into play. A very harmonious nausea, it is true. Let us also consider that if it is indeed a question of an infinite suffering, this suffering is always introduced by an *I want* twice affirmed that claims to prevail over the audacity of death — *without death daring* — as though weakness could only present itself under the mask of a power. We know how Surenas, the glorious general, the conquering hero covered with trophies, will die: he is to be cut down in sinister fashion on a street corner.

> *Hardly had we gone out into the street*
> *When from an unknown hand an arrow sped;*
> *Two others followed; and I saw that conqueror —*
> *As though all three had lodged within his heart —*
> *Fall dead in public in a stream of blood.*

This is no longer a death but a liquidation. "Like a dog" Kafka's "hero" will later say. There is no longer any ceremony, pomp, struggle, or burst of energy, not even the resource of a public that would make this end, even if infamous, memorable. This is a death that is neutral, solitary, anonymous — any death at all; the death that does away with the name and undoes courage, the true death without truth: a fall into the silent void. As Serge Doubrovsky says very well, the arrow that assassinates Surenas does not kill a man, it effaces a myth: this is the death of the Hero — even if, once again, Corneille tries in advance to give this oblique end the value of an open defiance. Surenas, to whom prudence is counseled, responds that he prefers a decisive death to one left to chance:

> *If the king seeks my death, be it now or later,*
> *Then let it be a flagrant crime, not chance;*
> *May none ascribe it to the general law*
> *Imposed by nature and decreed by fate.*

A last, indeed very characteristic defense: to escape nature and the common lot in seeking a death that is intentional and, having been willed (even if by someone else) capable of receiving a final meaning, of still taking on a value, and thus capable of remaining human. A death that is still an act and therefore in some sense exemplary, or at least significant — this is the last ardent wish of the last hero. And so if Eurydice fades away rather than dies (although the discretion of this death without tears can also be interpreted as a willfully sublime bearing wherein pain is transfigured: *You cause his death and cannot even cry! / — I am not crying, Palmis, I am dying*), the line that brings the tragedy to an end will not consecrate death but promise vengeance:

> *Stay, mighty Gods, this pain that hastens to die!*
> *And in your crowding ills in which I'm plunged,*
> *Ah, do not let me die until I'm avenged!*

Hence it must be concluded: dying does not bring action to its end, the will does not die.

*

Neither does the hero, he simply outlives himself, survives himself, which is the worst ruin for what he claims to represent. In Corneille's work, as we have seen, the hero already undergoes a mutation because he wants to interiorize himself (the heroic seeking of a beautiful Self that will become the sickly satisfaction of the beautiful soul), and yet he wants to make of heroism the movement of History: to reach the inordinate, on the one hand, through the affirmation of an empty "I" that will consist in an arrogant delirium, and, on the other, through the advent of a new form of political domination. In both cases the hero has already lost himself. If the word heroism has a meaning, it lies entirely in a certain overvaluation of the *act* taken in itself; when the act, dazzling exploit, affirms itself in the instant and seems to be radiating light, this dazzling is *gloire*—a splendor, a glory that does not last and cannot become incarnate. Thus, as we have seen, the hero always seems more or less to exploit the heroic act: he substantializes it and makes his career out of it. In truth, heroism represents at a particular moment, and represents no more than, astonishment before the power to act, astonishment before what is no longer the magical power bestowed by nature, but the *marvelous human* that is given impersonally in conquering action: What! That could be done! And let us note that the true hero is not always the man who acts; he is also the instrument of action, not only Achilles but his weapons, not Roland but Durandal.

Perhaps we must conclude that there can be no tragic hero, and the only genre suitable to this sort of enterprise is epic rhapsody. The epic recounts an unparalleled action and untiringly reiterates it. The repetition of the unique does not impoverish admiration: the exploit must be renewed or, more exactly, begin anew, even if it is still the same story (novelty is useless). The exploit is exhausted in the instant, but since in this genre exhaustion (with all the misery this word entails) is forbidden, everything must start up again unceasingly and with an evenness of success that suffers no interruption. The epic has neither beginning nor end. And so it must be with the hero: appearing, disappearing, simple and gracious material support for a marvelous act that is inscribed in legend but not in history. His action is for nothing, and efficacy is not one of its qualities: it is a beautiful flash in the sky, not the crude furrow plowed in the earth. In this sense, as we see, the hero's action is very close to the aesthetic category that it will for a long while harbor, and even in the ambiguity that is proper to it. An action for nothing, but an action all the same; a feat of valor, but a victory that often corresponds to some real event one may remember. And this hero, appearing — without birth — and disappearing — without death — in the truth of his brilliant act (there is thus no room for sadness on the listener's part about an end that is not one), does not content himself with this destiny that traverses time in a sterile burst, exactly as is effaced, scarcely said, the most beautiful speech. From this death without trace, a death neither wholly private nor truly historical (putting in question neither a dynasty nor the sovereignty of a State), the hero makes himself into a superior, quasi-intemporal duration — the one given by victorious memory, and on the basis of what is most discontinuous; a dazzling appearance, he achieves the surest continuity, finding again without difficulty in legend all that he lacked in history. Thus one could say that he represents the first form of what will later be meant (but in a sense still scarcely elucidated) when one speaks of an existence that is public, for he has no other presence than an exterior presence, and seems turned solely toward the outside; hence also corresponding to the speech that quite wholly produces him and that he in turn translates.

Literature, heroism, each the other's accomplice and dupe, for centuries exchanging their gifts. The song bestows glory and guarantees the name by its renown, while the singer himself is obscure and remains anonymous. Then the hero becomes *his* hero; the artist in his turn lays claim to immortality, not indirectly but directly; the work of art eternalizes, and itself becomes eternal in the manifestation of a quasi-presence, which, in history itself, believes it represents possibilities that are more than historical. At this moment candidate-heroes can be seen as hesitating between writing and dominating, shining by the redundancy of a literary style of prestige and by the prestige of a personage that is by nature redundant. But as two certainties are better than one, heroes become their own herald, providing themselves with a legend by writing their story and wanting to make each of their words a feat, as they want to make each decision a gesture that is already oratorical. Finally — and this is indeed curious — it is the pride of speech, the concern with aesthetic staging that wins out. The hero becomes the adventurer, and the adventure the feat of a prudent and well-articulated discourse. Thus the circle closes upon itself once again. In the meantime, it is true, literature has discreetly retired, having at last discovered that where it is in play it cannot be a question of immortality, of power, or of glory.

XIV

The Narrative Voice
(the "he," the neutral)

I write (I pronounce) this sentence: "The forces of life suffice only up to a certain point." As I pronounce it, I think of something very simple: the experience of weariness that constantly makes us feel a limited life; you take a few steps on the street, eight or nine, then you fall. The limit set by weariness limits life. The meaning of life is in turn limited by this limit: a limited meaning of a limited life. But a reversal occurs that can be discovered in various ways. Language modifies the situation. The sentence I pronounce tends to draw into the very inside of life the limit that was only supposed to mark it from the outside. Life is said to be limited. The limit does not disappear, but it takes from language the perhaps unlimited meaning that it claims to limit: the meaning of the limit, by affirming it, contradicts the limitation of meaning, or at least displaces it. But because of this, the knowledge of the limit understood as a limitation of meaning risks being lost. So how are we to speak of this limit (say its meaning), without allowing meaning to un-limit it? Here we must enter into another kind of language, and in the meantime realize that the sentence "The forces of life . . . " is not, as such, entirely possible.

*

Nevertheless, let us hold onto it. Let us write a narrative in which it has a place as an accomplishment of the narrative itself. What is the difference between these two—identical—sentences? The difference is certainly very great. I can represent it roughly as follows: the narrative would be like a circle neutralizing life, which

379

does not mean without any relation to it, but that its relation to life would be a neutral one. Within this circle the meaning of what is and of what is said is indeed still given, but from out of a withdrawal, from a distance where all meaning and all lack of meaning are neutralized beforehand. A reserve that exceeds every meaning already signified, without being considered either a richness or a pure and simple privation. Like a speech that does not illuminate and does not obscure.

Often in a bad narrative—assuming that there are bad narratives, which is not altogether certain—we have the impression that someone is speaking in the background and prompting the characters, or even the events with what they are to say: an indiscreet and awkward intrusion. We say it is the author speaking, an authoritarian and complacent "I" still anchored in life who breaks in without restraint. This is indiscreet, also indiscrete, it is true—and this is how the circle is effaced. But it is also true that the impression that someone is talking "in the background" is really part of the singularity of narrative and the truth of the circle: as though the center of the circle lay outside the circle, behind it and infinitely far back; as though *the outside* were precisely this center that could only be the absence of any center. Now this outside, this "in back," which is in no way a space of domination or a lofty space from which one might grasp everything in a single glance and command the events (of the circle), would this "in back" not be the very distance that language takes from its own lack as its limit?—a distance certainly altogether exterior, but that inhabits language and in some sense constitutes it; an infinite distance such that to hold oneself within language is to be always already outside, and such that, if it were possible to entertain this distance, to "relate" it in the sense that is proper to it, then one would be able to speak of the limit, that is, bring to the point of speech an experience of limits and the limit-experience. Now considered from this point of view, narrative would be the hazardous space where the sentence "The forces of life . . . " can be affirmed in its truth, but where in turn all sentences, even the most innocent, risk assuming the same ambiguous status that language assumes at its limit. A limit that is perhaps the neutral.

*

I will not hark back to "the use of personal pronouns in the novel," which has given rise to so many remarkable studies.[1] I think we must go further back. If, as has been shown (in *The Space of Literature*), to write is to pass from "I" to "he," but if "he," when substituted for "I," does not simply designate another me any more than it would designate aesthetic disinterestedness—that impure contemplative pleasure that allows the reader and the spectator to participate in the tragedy through distraction—what remains to be discovered is what is at stake when writing responds to the demands of this uncharacterizable "he." We hear in the narrative form, and always as though it were extra, something indeterminate speaking;

something the evolution of this form works round and isolates, until it gradually becomes manifest, although in a deceptive way. The "he" [or "it," *il*] is the unlighted event that occurs when one tells a story. The distant epic narrator recounts exploits that happened and that he seems to be reproducing, whether or not he witnessed them. But the narrator is not a historian. His song is the expanse where, in the presence of a remembrance, there comes to speech the event that takes place there; memory, muse and mother of muses, holds truth within itself, that is to say, the reality of what takes place. It is in his song that Orpheus really descends to the underworld—which we translate by adding that he descends to it through the power of his singing. But this song, already instrumental, signifies an alteration in the institution of narration. To tell a story is a mysterious thing. The mysterious "he" of the epic institution very quickly splits: the "he" becomes the impersonal coherency of a *story* (in the full and rather magical sense of this word). The *story* stands alone, preformed in the thought of a demiurge; and since it exists on its own there is nothing left to do but tell it. But the *story* soon becomes disenchanted. The experience of the disenchanted world that Don Quixote introduced into literature is the experience that dissipates the *story* by contrasting it to the banality of the real; this is how realism seizes on the form of the novel that for a long time to come will be the most effective genre of the developing bourgeoisie. Here the "he" [*il*] is everyday life without adventure: what happens when nothing is happening, the course of the world as it escapes notice, the passing of time, life routine and monotonous. At the same time—and in a manner more visible—the "he" marks the intrusion of the character: the novelist is one who forgoes saying "I," but delegates this power to others; the novel is peopled with little "egos"—tormented, ambitious, unhappy, although always satisfied in their unhappiness; the individual is affirmed in his subjective richness, his inner freedom, his psychology; the novel's narration, that of individuality, is already marked—leaving aside the content itself—by an ideology to the extent that it assumes that the individual, with his particular characteristics and his limits, suffices to express the world: it assumes, in other words, that the course of the world remains that of individual particularity.

Thus we can see that the "he" has split in two: on the one hand, there is something to tell, the *objective* real such as it is immediately present to an interested gaze; on the other hand, this real is reduced to a constellation of individual lives, of *subjectivities*—a multiple and personalized "he," an "ego" manifest under the cloak of a "he" that is apparent. In the interval of the narrative, the narrator's voice, sometimes fictive, sometimes without any mask, can be heard more or less accurately.

What has given way in this remarkable construction? Almost everything. I will not dwell on it.

*

There is something else that should be said. Let us draw a comparison (while remaining aware of the clumsiness of such an unduly simplistic procedure) between the impersonality of the novel as it is rightly or wrongly attributed to Flaubert, and the impersonality of a novel by Kafka. The impersonality of the impersonal novel is the impersonality of aesthetic distance. Its watchword is imperious: the novelist must not intervene. The author—even if Madame Bovary is myself—does away with all direct relations between himself and the novel; reflection, commentary, and moralizing intrusion, still brilliantly authorized in Stendhal or Balzac, become mortal sins. Why? For two reasons that, although they nearly merge, are different. The first: what is recounted has aesthetic value to the extent that the interest one takes in it is an interest from a distance; disinterestedness—an essential category in the judgment of taste since Kant and even Aristotle—means that the aesthetic act, if it wishes to create a legitimate interest, ought to be based on no interest whatsoever. A disinterested interest. Thus the author must take and heroically keep his distance so the reader or the spectator can also remain at a distance. The ideal is still the form of representation of classical theater: the narrator is there only to raise the curtain. The play is performed down on the stage, from time immemorial and as though without him; he does not tell, he shows, and the reader does not read, he looks, attending, taking part without participating. The other reason is nearly the same, although quite different: the author must not intervene because the novel is a work of art, and the work of art exists quite by itself; an unreal thing in the world outside the world, it must be left free, the props removed, the moorings cut, in order to maintain its status as an imaginary object (but here Mallarmé, that is, an entirely different exigency, is already being announced).

Let us for a moment call to mind Thomas Mann. His is an interesting case because he does not respect the rule of non-intervention; he constantly involves himself in what he is telling, sometimes through interposed characters, but also in the most direct way. What about this unwarranted intrusion? It is not moralizing, it is not a stand taken against a certain character, nor does it consist in illuminating things from the outside—the print of the creator's thumb as he shapes figures to his liking. It represents the intervention of the narrator challenging the very possibility of narration; an intervention, consequently, that is an essentially critical one, but in the manner of a game, a malicious irony. Flaubert's kind of impersonality, contracted and difficult, still affirmed the validity of the narrative mode: to tell is to show, to let be or to make exist, without there being reason—despite the great doubts one may already have had—to question oneself about the limits and the workings of the narrative order. Thomas Mann knows very well that we have lost our naïveté. He therefore tries to restore it, not by passing over illusion in silence but, on the contrary, by producing it, by making it so visible that he can play with it, just as he plays with the reader and in so doing draws him into the game. Thus with his great sense of the narrative feast, Thomas Mann succeeds in restoring it as a feast of narrative illusion; giving back to us an ingenuousness twice removed, that of the absence of ingenuousness. One could therefore say that if aesthetic distance is denounced in his work, it is also proclaimed, affirmed by a narrative consciousness that takes itself as a theme, whereas in the more traditional impersonal novel it disappeared, placing itself in parentheses. Storytelling was a matter of course.

Of course storytelling is not a matter of course. As we know, the narrative act is generally taken in charge by a certain character; not that this character, by telling it directly, makes himself the narrator of a story that has already been lived or is in the process of being lived, but because he constitutes the center around which the perspective of the narrative is organized: everything is seen from this point of view. There is, therefore, a privileged "I," if only the "I" of a character referred to in the third person who takes great care not to exceed the possibilities of his knowledge and the limits of his position: this is the realm of James's ambassadors, and it is also the realm of subjectivist formulas in which the authenticity of the narrative depends upon the existence of a free subject. These formulas are correct insofar as they represent the decision to stick to a certain bias (obstinacy and even obsession are among the rules that seem to impose themselves when it is a matter of writing—form is obstinate, this is its danger), but they are in no way definitive: on the one hand, they wrongly assert some sort of equivalence between the narrative act and the transparency of a consciousness (as though to tell were simply to be conscious, to project, to disclose, to cover up by revealing), and on the other hand, they maintain the primacy of an individual consciousness that could only in the second place, and even secondarily, be a speaking consciousness.

*

In the meantime, Kafka wrote. Kafka admires Flaubert. The novels he writes are marked by an austerity that might permit a distracted reader to rank them among Flaubert's descendants. Yet everything is different. One of these differences is essential to the subject that concerns us. The distance—the creative disinterestedness (so visible in Flaubert inasmuch as he must struggle to maintain it)—which was the writer's and the reader's distance from the work and authorized contemplative pleasure, now enters into the work's very sphere in the form of an irreducible strangeness. No longer questioned or reestablished as something denounced, as in Thomas Mann (or Gide), this distance is the medium of the novelistic world, the space in which the narrative experience unfolds in its unique simplicity—an experience that is not recounted but is in play when one recounts. This distance is not simply lived as such by the central character who is always at a distance from himself, just as he is from the events he experiences or the beings he encounters (which would still only be the manifestation of a singular self);

this distance keeps him aloof from himself, removing him from the center, because it is constantly decentering the work in an immeasurable and indiscernible
way, while at the same time introducing into the most rigorous narration the alteration occasioned by another kind of speech or by the other as speech (as writing).

The consequences of this kind of change will often be misinterpreted. One consequence, immediately evident, is noteworthy. As soon as the alien distance becomes the object and, in a sense, the substance of the story, the reader can no
longer be disinterested in it; he who up to now has been identifying from afar with
the story in progress (living it, for his part, in the mode of contemplative irresponsibility) can no longer take a disinterested pleasure in it. What is happening? What
new exigency has befallen the reader? It is not that this concerns him: on the contrary, it concerns him in no way, and perhaps concerns no one; it is in a sense
the *non-concerning*, but with regard to which, by the same token, the reader can
no longer comfortably take any distance since he cannot properly situate himself
in relation to what does not even present itself as unsituatable. How, then, is the
reader to set himself or herself apart from the absolute distance that seems to have
taken all distance up into itself? Without any bearings, deprived of the interest
of reading, he is no longer allowed to look at things from afar, to keep between
things and himself the distance that belongs to the gaze, because the distant in its
non-present presence is not available either close up or from afar; it cannot be
the object of a gaze. Henceforth it is no longer a question of vision. Narration
ceases to be that which presents something to be seen through the intermediary
of, and from the viewpoint of, a chosen actor-spectator. The reign of circumspect
consciousness—of narrative circumspection (of the "I" that looks at everything
around itself and holds it by its gaze)—has been subtly shaken, without, of course,
coming to an end.

*

What Kafka teaches us—even if this formulation cannot be directly attributed
to him—is that storytelling brings the neutral into play. Narration that is governed
by the neutral is kept in the custody of the third-person "he," a "he" that is neither
a third person nor the simple cloak of impersonality. The narrative "he" [*il*] in
which the neutral speaks is not content to take the place usually occupied by the
subject, whether this latter is a stated or an implied "I" or the event that occurs
in its impersonal signification.[2] The narrative "he" or "it" unseats every subject
just as it disappropriates all transitive action and all objective possibility. This
takes two forms: (1) the speech of the narrative always lets us feel that what is
being recounted is not being recounted by anyone: it speaks in the neutral; (2)
in the neutral space of the narrative, the bearers of speech, the subjects of the
action—those who once stood in the place of characters—fall into a relation of
self-nonidentification. Something happens to them that they can only recapture

by relinquishing their power to say "I." And what happens has always already happened: they can only indirectly account for it as a sort of self-forgetting, the forgetting that introduces them into the present without memory that is the present of narrating speech.

This, of course, does not mean that the narrative necessarily relates a forgotten event, or even the event of forgetting that dominates lives and societies, which, separated—or as one still says, alienated—from what they are, move as though in their sleep seeking to recapture themselves. It is narrative (independently of its content) that is a forgetting, so that to tell a story is to put oneself through the ordeal of this first forgetting that precedes, founds, and ruins all memory. Recounting, in this sense, is the torment of language, the incessant search for its infinity. And narrative would be nothing other than an allusion to the initial detour that is borne by writing and that carries it away, causing us, as we write, to yield to a sort of perpetual turning away.

The act of writing: this relation to life, a deflected relation through which what is of no concern is affirmed.

The narrative "he" [or "it," *il*], whether absent or present, whether it affirms itself or hides itself, and whether or not it alters the conventions of writing—linearity, continuity, readability—thus marks the intrusion of the other—understood as neutral—in its irreducible strangeness and in its wily perversity. The other speaks. But when the other is speaking, no one speaks because the other, which we must refrain from honoring with a capital letter that would determine it by way of a majestic substantive, as though it had some substantial or even unique presence, is precisely never simply the other. The other is neither the one nor the other, and the neutral that indicates it withdraws it from both, as it does from unity, always establishing it outside the term, the act, or the subject through which it claims to offer itself. The narrative (I do not say narrating) voice derives from this its aphony. It is a voice that has no place in the work, but neither does it hang over it; far from falling out of some sky under the guarantee of a superior Transcendence, the "he" [*il*] is not the "encompassing" of Jaspers, but rather a kind of void in the work—the absence-word that Marguerite Duras evokes in one of her narratives: "a hole-word, hollowed out in its center by a hole, the hole in which all the other words should have been buried." And the text goes on: "One could not have spoken it but it could have been made to resound—immense, endless, an empty gong."[3] This is the narrative voice, a neutral voice that speaks the work from out of this place without a place, where the work is silent.

*

The narrative voice is neutral. Let us rapidly consider the traits that characterize it at first approach. For one thing, it says nothing, not only because it adds nothing to what there is to say (it knows nothing), but because the narrative voice subtends this nothing—the "silencing and "keeping silent"—in which speech is here and now already engaged; thus it is not heard in the first place, and everything that gives it a distinct reality begins to betray it. Then again, without its own existence—speaking from nowhere, suspended in the narrative as a whole—neither does it dissipate there in the manner of light, which, though itself invisible, makes things visible: radically exterior, it comes from exteriority itself, from the outside that is the enigma proper to language in writing. But let us consider still other traits, traits that are actually the same. The narrative voice that is inside only inasmuch as it is outside, at a distance without there being any distance, cannot be embodied. Although it may well borrow the voice of a judiciously chosen character, or even create the hybrid function of mediator (the voice that ruins all mediation), it is always different from what utters it: it is the indifferent-difference that alters the personal voice. Let us (on a whim) call it spectral, ghostlike. Not that it comes from beyond the grave, or even because it would once and for all represent some essential absence, but because it always tends to absent itself in its bearer and also efface him as the center: it is thus neutral in the decisive sense that it cannot be central, does not create a center, does not speak from out of a center, but, on the contrary, at the limit, would prevent the work from having one; withdrawing from it every privileged point of interest (even afocal), and also not allowing it to exist as a completed whole, once and forever achieved.

Tacit, the narrative voice attracts language indirectly, obliquely and, under this attraction of an oblique speech, allows the neutral to speak. What does this indicate? The narrative voice bears the neutral. It bears the neutral insofar as: (1) To speak in the neutral is to speak at a distance, preserving this distance without *mediation* and without *community*, and even in sustaining the infinite distancing of distance—its irreciprocity, its irrectitude or dissymmetry: for the neutral is precisely the greatest distance governed by dissymmetry and without one or another of its terms being privileged (the neutral cannot be neutralized). (2) Neutral speech does not reveal, it does not conceal. This does not mean that it signifies nothing (by claiming to abdicate sense in the form of non-sense); it means that the neutral does not signify in the same way as the visible-invisible does, but rather opens another power in language, one that is alien to the power of illuminating (or obscuring), of comprehension (or misapprehension). It does not signify in the optical manner; it remains outside the light-shadow reference that seems to be the ultimate reference of all knowledge and all communication, to the point of making us forget that it only has the value of a venerable, that is to say inveterate, metaphor. (3) The exigency of the neutral tends to suspend the attributive structure of language: the relation to being, implicit or explicit, that is immediately posed in language as soon as something is said. It has often been remarked—by philosophers, linguists, and political analysts—that nothing can be negated that has not already been posited beforehand. To put this another way, every language begins by declaring and in declaring affirms. But it may be that recounting (writing) draws language into a possibility of saying that would say being without saying it, and yet without denying it either. Or again, to say this more clearly, too clearly: it would establish the center of gravity of speech else-where, there where speaking would neither affirm being nor need negation in or-der to suspend the work of being that is ordinarily accomplished in every form of expression. In this respect, the narrative voice is the most critical voice that, unheard, might give to be heard. That is why, as we listen to it, we tend to confuse it with the oblique voice of misfortune, or of madness.[4]

XV

The Wooden Bridge
(repetition, the neutral)

If every narrative, under summons of the neutral or in citing it, is already a site of extravagance, we understand why *Don Quixote* so evidently opens the tormented age that will be ours — not because it sets loose a new kind of eccentricity, but because, trusting ingenuously in the sole movement of recounting, it gives itself over to "extravagance," and by the same token puts on trial (denounces) what, after it (but perhaps only for a short time), we still call literature.[1] What is this Knight's madness? It is our own, the madness of everyone. He has read a great deal and he believes in what he has read. In a spirit of perfect coherence, and faithful to his convictions (he is clearly someone engagé), he abandons his library and decides to live rigorously, the way one does in books, in order to learn whether the world corresponds to literary enchantment. We have, therefore, and undoubtedly for the first time, a created work that deliberately offers itself as an imitation. The hero who is central to all this may well present himself as a character of action who, like his peers, is capable of accomplishing feats of valor; but his feats are always already a reflection, just as he himself cannot but be a double, while the text in which his exploits are recounted is not a book, but a reference to other books.

Upon reflection, it is clear that if there is some madness in Don Quixote, there is an even greater madness in Cervantes. If Don Quixote is not reasonable, he is nonetheless logical in thinking that the truth of books may also hold for life. And if he sets out to live like a book, this is a marvelous and deceptive adventure since the truth of books is deceptive. For Cervantes things are different because, unlike Don Quixote, he does not set out into the street to put the life of books into practice; rather, it is still into a book that he puts all his efforts, not leaving his library and doing nothing while he lives, acts, and dies other than writing—without living, and without either moving or dying. What does he hope to prove, and prove to himself? Does he take himself for his hero who, for his part, takes himself not for a man but for a book, and who nonetheless claims not to read but to live? A surprising madness, a laughable and perverse unreason that all of culture dissimulates, but that is also its hidden truth, the truth without which it would be unable to edify itself and upon which it does so majestically and vainly.

But let us consider things more simply from another angle. We have read a book, we comment upon it. In commenting upon it, we perceive that this book is itself no more than a commentary: a setting into book form of other books to which it refers. We write our commentary and elevate it to the rank of a work. Become a thing published, a public thing, it will in turn attract a commentary, which, in turn . . . Let us acknowledge this situation, so natural to us that it seems tactless to formulate it in these terms. As though, in bad taste, we were divulging a family secret. So be it, let us own up to such indelicacy. But I take one of the great merits of Marthe Robert's book to consist in the questioning to which she leads us by an interrogation that is double or can be formulated twice: What about the speech that is commentary? Why are we able to speak about an instance of speech? Furthermore, *can* we, except by injuriously taking it to be silent, that is to say, by taking this beautiful work we revere as being incapable of speaking on its own? And what about those creative works that constitute for themselves their own exegesis? Do they reveal an impoverishment of literature, the advent of a decadent, belated, and exhausted civilization, the "sentimental" fastidiously repeating the "naive"? Or are they not, rather than more distant, closer to the literary enigma; not more reflective but more within the movement of thought and thus not duplicating literature, but accomplishing themselves by virtue of a more initial doubling that precedes and puts into question the supposed unity of "literature" and of "life"?

*

The speech of commentary: not all criticism is involved here in the various, though still confused, senses this word allows. It is a matter of repeating the work through a pretense that perhaps, in effect, envelops all criticism. But to repeat the work is to grasp—to hear—in it the repetition that establishes it as unique. Now this repetition—this originary possibility of existing doubly—will not be reducible to the imitation of an interior or an exterior model, be it the book of another writer or life (the life of the world, of the author) or the kind of project that would be the work in the writer's mind, already entirely written, but in a reduced model he would be content to transpose on the outside by enlarging it or reproducing it, taking dictation from the little man in him who is god. Replication presupposes a duplicity of another kind, the following: a work says what it says by silencing something (although not by affecting a secret: the work and the author must always say everything they know; hence literature can admit to no esotericism that is exterior to it—the only secret doctrine of literature being literature). Literature moreover says this by silencing itself. There is in literature an emptiness of literature that constitutes it. This lack or distance, unexpressed because covered over by expression, is that on the basis of which the work, while said one time, said perfectly and incapable of being said again, nonetheless irresistibly tends to say itself over again, requiring the infinite speech of commentary where, separated from itself through the beautiful cruelty of analysis (which, in truth, does not separate the work arbitrarily, but by virtue of the separation already at work in it—a non-coincidence that would be its faint heartbeat), it awaits the silence that is proper to it to come to an end.

A waiting that is naturally disappointed. This repetition of the book by commentary is the movement thanks to which a new speech, new and yet the same, introduces itself into the lack that makes the work speak, claiming to fill it in or make it good. This is an important speech; finally we will know what is what—we will know what is behind the great Castle and whether the phantoms of *The Turn of the Screw* are mere phantasms born in the feverish mind of a young girl. A revealing, a usurping speech. For if the commentary—this is only too manifest—fills in all the interstices, or through this omnisaying speech even completes the work, but, having abolished its space of resonance, renders it mute and is consequently in its turn struck dumb, or if it is content by its repetition to repeat the work on the basis of the distance within the work that is its reserve—not obstructing it, but, on the contrary, leaving it empty, designating it by circumscribing it from afar or translating it in its ambiguity through an interrogation henceforth still more ambiguous since it bears this ambiguity, bears upon it, and ends by becoming dissipated in it—then what good is commentary?

Yes, what good is it. Yet this "what good is it" is itself also superfluous; whether we judge it unavailing or dangerous, the necessity of repeating can in no way be eluded since it is not superadded to the work nor imposed solely by the habits of social communication. When commentators have not yet imposed their reign (as, for example, at the time of the epic), this work of redoubling is accomplished within the work itself and we have the rhapsodic mode of composition; that perpetual repetition from episode to episode, an interminable amplification of the same unfolding in place, which makes each rhapsode neither a faithful reproducer nor an immobile rehearser but the one who carries the repetition forward and, by means of repetition, fills in or widens the gaps, opens and closes the fissures by new peripeteia, and finally, by dint of filling the poem out, distends it to the point of volatilization. A mode of repetition that compromises the work no less than the first. The critic is a kind of rhapsode, this is what has to be seen: a rhapsode upon whom we rely, the work hardly done, to distract it from its capacity to repeat itself—a power that comes from its origins and that, left to itself, would risk indefinitely undoing it. Or else the critic is a scapegoat, banished to the confines of the literary space and charged with every faulty version of the work so that the work itself may be affirmed, intact and innocent, in the sole copy we hold to be authentic—unknown, in fact, and probably nonexistent—and that we conserve in the archives of culture: the unique work, complete only if it is lacking something, where this lack is its infinite relation to itself, a plentitude in the mode of deficiency.

But what, then, of those modern works that are their own commentary, and that refer not only to what they are but to other books; or, better yet, to the anonymous, unceasing, and obsessive movement from which all books come? Do works such as these, which are thus commented upon from within (like *Don Quixote*, which is not simply an epic poem but the repetition of every epic and, consequently, also its own repetition—and derision), not run the risk (if it is a risk and not a chance) of rendering difficult, impossible, or vain the exercise of every other commentary by virtue of the fact that in recounting they recount themselves at one remove? Indeed, might not the proliferation of such works entail a sort of end of criticism? The response is reassuring, for the contrary is the case. The more a work comments upon itself, the more it calls for commentary; the more it carries on relations of "reflection" (of redoubling) with its center, the more this duality renders it enigmatic. Such is the case with *Don Quixote*. Even more evidently, it is also the case with *The Castle*. Who will not remember adding something to it and feeling guilty for having done so? What an abundance of explications and a frenzy of interpretation; what exegetical fury, be it theological, philosophical, sociological, political, or autobiographical; how many forms of analysis, allegorical, symbolic, structural, and even (anything can happen) literal! And so many keys: each employable only by the one who forged it, each opening one door only to close others. Where does this delirium come from? Why is reading never satisfied with what it reads, incessantly substituting for it another text, which in turn provokes another?

It is because, Marthe Robert states, the same thing happens with a book by Franz Kafka as with a book by Miguel Cervantes. The book does not consist in an immediate narrative, but in a confrontation of this narrative with all the books of the same type, which, though they may be of dissimilar age, origin, signification, and style, in advance occupy the literary dimension in which it, too, would like to find a place. To put this differently, the Surveyor does not survey imaginary and still virgin countries but the immense space of literature; he thus cannot keep from imitating—and thereby reflecting—all the heroes who have preceded him into this space. In this way, *The Castle* is no longer simply the unique work of a solitary writer but a kind of palimpsest in which can be read—juxtaposed, intertwined, and at times distinct—all the versions of a millenary adventure: a sum and thus a résumé of the Universal Library where at times one sees K. as the hero of a social novel (a failure who wants to get ahead via women), at other times as the hero of a serialized novel (the hero with a big heart, defender of the weak against the tyranny of a privileged caste), and at still other times as the hero of a fairy-tale and, more precisely, of a new cycle of the saga of King Arthur's court, waiting, as rehearser of *The Odyssey* and as Ulysses' successor, to find his true role, which is to put to the test the epic of epics, and along with it, the great Homeric order, that is to say, Olympian truth. This is a design Marthe Robert boldly attributes not to the fatality of reading that condemns every cultivated man to see everything through the decomposing prism of culture, but to Kafka himself, also a very cultivated man. A man, she says, who was attracted by the success of the Greeks at a critical moment of his life: that moment when, having converted to Zionism and ready to leave for Palestine, he took on the task of understanding and classifying the monstrous archives of Western culture from which he could not exclude his own works.

*

Let us reflect for a moment on this remarkable and, I think, entirely new thesis: that the meaning, the ultimate secret of *The Castle* would lie in the fact that it is an imitation of *The Odyssey* and a critique of Olympian bureaucracy[2] — a thesis that certainly has a strange ring at first. Let us reflect on it less to accept or refuse it than to grasp its principle, and to ask whether it might not be possible to apply it differently. Let us assume then that the Surveyor, in an indirect and invisible manner, is struggling not only with the Forces that the Castle and the Village represent, but also, through these forces and behind them, with the supreme instance that is the book, and with the infinite modalities that its approach, through oral and written exegesis, entails. We know very well that for Kafka the space of the Book, due to the tradition to which it belongs and, in particular, due to the tormented epoch in which he writes his narrative, is a space that is sacred, dubious, forgotten, and at the same time a space of unlimited questioning, study, and research, since it has been the very fabric of Jewish existence for thousands of years. If there is a world where, in seeking the truth and the rules of life, what one encounters is not the world but a book, the mystery and the commandment of a book, this world is indeed Judaism: a world where the power of the Word and of Exegesis is affirmed as lying at the beginning of everything, where everything starts from a text and comes back to it — a unique book in which a prodigious sequence of books is rolled up, constituting a Library that is not only universal but that stands in for the universe, and is even more vast, more profound, and more enigmatic. A writer in Kafka's situation and with the concerns that are his, whether he elude or lay himself open to them, cannot escape this question: how can a literary man, a man without a mandate, enter the closed — the sacred — world of the written? How, author without authority, can he claim to add a strictly individual word to that Other, old, terrifyingly old Word that covers, comprehends, and encompasses all things, all the while remaining hidden in the depths of the tabernacle from which it has perhaps disappeared? How can he add a word to this Word that is infinite, that has always in advance said everything and in regard to which, ever since it was first pronounced, the Messieurs of speech are no more than mute depositories — left only with the task of keeping it by repeating it, while others have only to listen to it by interpreting it? As a writer, he must — this is the irreducible exigency — go all the way to the source of the written since he will only begin to write when he succeeds in engaging in a direct relation with this originary speech. But he has no means of approaching this high place, other than speaking, that is to say, writing — and writing in this way in advance; running the risk through this speech that is premature, without tradition and without justification, of obscuring still more the, for him, impenetrable relations of the Word and its Meaning.

· But in proposing these remarks, let me immediately add that I am in no way proposing a new interpretation of *The Castle*. Nor am I suggesting that K. is purely and simply the writer Franz Kafka, the Castle the biblical word, the Offices the Talmudic commentaries, the Village the site of the faithful where the repeated word would be at the same time living and dead, in the same way that a commandment is just and authentic if one belongs to it from the inside, but otherwise deceptive, even absurd, should one approach it from the outside — pretending moreover to judge it, and to speak of it without having received prior instruction (as necessarily happens to the writer of today who has no legitimacy other than the exigency of writing, which allows neither reference nor guarantee, just as this writing is not content with any relative satisfaction). It is simply fitting to note that: (1) in writing, and in questioning oneself about writing — we know with what breadth and what seriousness — it is not, first of all, against the academic space of Homer's epic that Kafka must measure himself, but against three thousand years of Judaic writing; (2) if, contrary to *Don Quixote*, *The Castle* does not have the preexisting world of books as its subject (K. is a land Surveyor, neither a reader nor a writer), and if it does not directly ask the question of Writing, it nonetheless contains this question in its very *structure* since the essential element in the narrative — that is, the essential aspect of K.'s peregrination — consists not in K.'s going from place to place, but from exegesis to exegesis and from commentator to commentator, listening to each of them with impassioned attention, then breaking in and arguing according to an exhaustive method of examination that could easily be compared with certain turns of the Talmudic dialectic (let us name it this way for the sake of simplicity, and in specifying that according to those who are competent, the latter would be even more demanding than the one with which K. has to be satisfied).

This, it seems to me, is all one has the right to propose. *The Castle* does not consist of a series of events or peripeteia that are more or less linked, but of an ever-expanding sequence of exegetic versions that finally only bear upon the very possibility of exegesis itself—the possibility of writing (and of interpreting) *The Castle*. And if the book stops unfinished, unfinishable, it is because it bogs down in commentary; each moment requiring an interminable gloss, each interpretation giving rise not only to a reflection (*midrash halachah*), but also to a narration (*midrash haggadah*) that must in turn be heard, that is to say interpreted at different levels; each character representing a certain level of speech, and each instance of speech, at its level, saying what is true without saying the truth. We are given assurance that K. might have put an end to the narrative by his half-justified death; but of what death could he have died? Not his own handsome death, but rather an exegetical death, the commentary of his death, and on condition of having been able to discuss and in advance refute all the possible interpretations of this end that is not personal (private), but merely general (official), registered in some text that is eternal and eternally forgotten. (His march toward death and his march toward the word entail the same steps: an advance toward death through speech and an advance toward speech through death, each anticipating and annulling the other.) When one night, the last night of the narrative, he finds himself suddenly face to face with the possibility of salvation, is he truly facing his own salvation? Not at all: he is in the presence of an exegesis of salvation to which he can respond only through his weariness, an infinite weariness that is of the same measure as an endless speech. And in this there is nothing absurd: "salvation" can only come, if it comes, through the decision of a word; but the word of salvation will assure only a salvation in speech, one that is valid only in general (be it even an exception) and therefore incapable of applying to the singularity of existence—the latter reduced by life itself, and by the weariness of life, to speechlessness.

Of course *The Castle*, I insist once again, is not only this, it is just as much the force of its images, the fascination of its figures, and the decisive appeal of its narrative; these constitute its unique truth, a truth that seems always to say of itself more than anything one could say about it, thereby engaging the reader, but above all the narrator, in the torment of an endless commentary.[3] Thus we come back to our point of departure, which was to question ourselves about the necessity of repeating that the work contains within itself, precisely in the part of it that is silent, the unknown side that underlies the speech of commentary, this speaking about speaking, vertiginous pyramid constructed on a void—a tomb—covered over and perhaps long ago forgotten. There is, of course, between the interior and the exterior commentary this evident difference: the first employs the same logic as the second but, on the inside of a circle traced and determined by literary enchantment, it reasons and speaks on the basis of a spell; the second speaks and reasons about this spell, and about the logic that is haunted by it and grafted onto it. But it seems that *The Castle*—and this is what makes for the force of such a work—holds within itself, as its center, the active and unilluminated relation between what is most "interior" and most "exterior," between the art that sets into play a dialectic and the dialectic that claims to encompass art. In other words, it would seem to hold in itself the principle of all ambiguity, and to hold to ambiguity itself as a principle (ambiguity: the difference of the identical, the non-identity of the same): the principle of all language and the infinite passage from one language to another, as from art to reason and from reason to art. Hence the fact that all the hypotheses one might develop about this book appear as sound and as powerless as those that are developed within it—providing they preserve and prolong its infinite character. Which amounts to saying that in some sense all books from now on pass by way of this book.

But let us attempt to come to a better understanding of what this means. In general, in reading this narrative, we allow ourselves to be caught up in the mystery that is most visible, the one that descends from the inaccessible site that is the hill of the count; as though the entire secret—the void from out of which the commentary is elaborated—were situated there. But if one reads more attentively, one soon notices that the void is situated nowhere and is spread out equally over every point of the narrative to which inquiry is directed. Why do all the responses bearing upon the relation between K. and the Castle always seem insufficient, and such that they seem infinitely to exaggerate and infinitely to invalidate the meaning of this site that the most reverent and the most denigrating judgments do and do not suit? It is strange; one can go looking for the supreme designations that humanity has been perfecting for thousands of years to characterize the Unique. One may well say: "But the Castle is Grace; the *Graf* (the Count) is *Gott*, as the identity of the capital letters proves; or it is the Transcendence of Being, or the Transcendence of Nothingness, Olympus, or the bureaucratic administration of the universe."[4] Yes, one may well say all this and, of course, in saying it endlessly delve deeper. The fact nonetheless remains that all these profound identifications, the most rich and sublime we have at our disposal, do not fail to disappoint us: as though the Castle were always infinitely more than this—infinitely more and thus also infinitely less. What, then, is above Transcendence, what below Transcendence? Well (let us hasten to respond, as haste alone will caution the response) it is that before which all evaluation reveals itself to be inadequate, be it the highest or the lowest; that which, therefore, strikes all possibility of evaluating with indifference and, in so doing, challenges all the guardians of value, whether they be celestial, terrestrial, or demonic and whether their authority derive from reason, unreason, or surreason. Is this very mysterious? Certainly it is, but at the same time, I think, without mystery, since each time we speak we put it into play, even though we end up when we try to speak of it by making it retreat, covering it over by our very expression. Let us choose for the moment to call it by the most modest, the most effaced, and the most neutral of names: precisely the neutral, because to name the neutral is perhaps—is surely—to dissipate it, but necessarily still to the neutral's benefit. Given these conditions, have we the right to suggest that the Castle (the count's residence) would be nothing other than the sovereignty of the neutral and the site of this strange sovereignty? Unfortunately, one cannot say this so simply, although the most profound part of Marthe Robert's book, at least the one to which I most respond, is the part where she shows that the sovereign power is neither transcendent nor immanent;[5] she shows that it is neutral, limiting itself to "registering all the facts, and also the judgments that precede and follow them—the thoughts, the dreams, and all of this with a neutrality and passivity that the individual feels strangely as a weight and as an injustice." An important, perhaps a decisive remark. Only one cannot limit oneself to it because the neutral cannot be represented, cannot be symbolized or even signified; moreover it is everywhere, inasmuch as it is borne by the infinite indifference of the entire narrative (just as everyone, says Olga, belongs to the Castle; from which it must be concluded that there is no Castle). It is as though it were the infinite vanishing point from which the speech of the narrative, and within it all narratives and all speech about every narrative, would receive and lose their perspective: the infinite distance of their relations, their perpetual overturning and annulment. But let us stop here, for fear of engaging in our turn in an infinite movement. The fact remains that if *The Castle* contains within itself what we call the neutral, contains it as its center (and the absence of any center), the act of naming it cannot remain entirely without consequences. Why this name?

*

"Why this name? Indeed is it a name?
— *Might it be a figure?*
— *Then a figure figuring only this name.*
— *And why can a single person speaking, a single speech, despite appearances, never succeed in naming it? We are obliged to be at least two to say it.*
— *I know. We have to be two.*
— *But why two? Why two instances of speech to say a same thing?*
— *Because the one who says it is always the other."*

XVI

Literature One More Time

"We should try one more time to grasp, perhaps not the traits proper to what literature is understood to be, but those that have ceased to belong to it.

— At the risk of being a bit crude.

— Necessarily so. But a simple inventory might suffice: for example, the idea of the masterpiece has disappeared. When we speak of a masterpiece it is always out of convenience, facility, or respect for the past. Literature, in its obscure self-assertion, excludes the promotion of the work of art called a *chef d'oeuvre*.

— Perhaps because it also excludes the idea of a work, an *oeuvre*.

— At least a certain idea of the work. Thus we know that the work counts less than the experience of the search for it, and that an artist is always ready to sacrifice the work's accomplishment to the truth of the movement that leads to it.

— Or that prohibits attaining it. Then what counts? The artist, the writer?

— The artist as a creative personality, the literary figure as an exceptional existence, the poet as genius — the hero — these fortunately no longer have a place even in our myths. Vanity, of course, remains; the literary 'I' continues to be in evidence. We still speak of great writers and artists. Yet no one attaches any importance to this; these old echoes are beginning to die out. Consider what the theme of immortality signified for so many centuries — the hope of posterity's acclaim and the word glory (already degraded in the desire to be known by all and for all time). Who today would dare to feel justified by the good fortune of having his ashes tomorrow in the Pantheon?

— Yes, who would? Many perhaps: but let's disregard them. The idea of immortality has become devalued, while at the same time the belief in a beyond is wearing away. I grant that we are indifferent to the idea of survival. One who is conscious of what is at stake in becoming will be happy to disappear; Nietzsche already attempted to teach us this. Are we then, by way of compensation, to exalt the idea of actuality (as has been done), that is, seek the meaning of literature and art in the exigency of the present?

— *One must be absolutely modern*. Rimbaud's and Baudelaire's summons, which inaugurated a new age or corresponded to a mutation in the arts by putting them in relation with the secret essence of something that would be the 'modern,' certainly had great meaning; but even if the new retains its prestige, even if the provocative seeking of what lies ahead can still play a critical role for us, it represents nothing binding. The thought of being modern seems to us almost as strange as the idea of becoming classical or of falling in with a secure tradition. Why? We could try to find out, were it worth the trouble.

— Some words no longer suffice to convey what they are a sign of. 'The modern era' presupposes relations that have been maintained between the present, the past, and the future, be these relations of opposition or of contrast. But let us imagine changes such that these relations would no longer have a directing force. We will now no longer be conscious of belonging to modern times, nor of opposing ourselves to an age that is past; the modern will in its turn be outmoded as a mode of becoming. When history turns, this movement of turning that implies even the suspension of history (in the name of a utopian truth) also revokes 'the tradition of the new.'

— A rupture such that this interruption would constitute an event uninscribable in the continuity of a memory, and would signify the interruption of the memorable, if not the birth of a new memory. And one would have to think of literature as being bound up with this interruption, yet necessarily almost ungraspable by means of the categories that continue to be ours. So literature could no longer be content with simply being modern, even in the sense Baudelaire and Rimbaud intended, and even considering the gain that comes to us from what we call modern art.

— We therefore also have to renounce the exigency of the alternative: 'Literature will be modern or it will not be.'

— But by the same movement, renounce seeking to base our efforts on some tradition, and on the hope—always secretly entertained, even by the most innovative—of forming a happy synthesis between what was and what will be. Being classical insofar as one is modern is a seed that will no longer germinate.

— One could perhaps say more precisely that by the secret constituting it, literature remains distinct from culture. To make a poetic work is not to make a cultural work, and the writer does not write to enrich the cultural patrimony. Culture can doubtless lay claim to literary acts; it absorbs them by introducing them into the ever more unified cultural universe that is its own, and where works exist as spiritual, transmissible, durable, comparable things that are in relation with the other products of culture. Here the work seems to have found its certainty and consistency; books are added to books in order to constitute that beautiful Alexandria no flame will ever reach, that always finished, always unfinished Babel that is the world of literature and literature as world. Let us recognize that the immense work of culture, which makes a whole of literature and makes literature an element within a larger whole, constantly furnishes us with an alibi. The consolidation of culture allows all writers and artists, in the current of ordinary life, to feel themselves still of use amidst the values they uphold by putting them in question. But let's maintain the idea that Kafka does not write to make a cultural work (nor does he write to check culture), any more than did Homer, any more than would the last writer that we all for a moment suppose ourselves to be.

— To write to . . . or not to write to . . . is not sufficiently determining. Let us put it better by saying that, on the one hand, literature belongs to culture (since it can be studied as a fact of culture) but, on the other hand, what is affirmed on the basis of literature not only contests culture in what it values, but also escapes it and deceives it—if what literature communicates to culture with regard to its substantial contents is only an empty becoming, or if what culture succeeds in extracting from literature in order to study it immediately becomes substantialized, and thereby falls outside literature.

— Let us try to put this still more precisely. Literature is a language. Every language (as we formulate it today) is constituted by a signifier, a signified, and the relation of the one to the other. It is not sufficient to say, as Paul Valéry for a long time affirmed, that form has more importance in literary language than in ordinary languages; it must first be said that in literary language the relation between signifier and signified, or between what one calls form and (erroneously) content, becomes infinite.

— Which means?

— Which means many things, too many for us to delimit them. It means essentially that this relation is not a relation that unifies: form and content are in relation in such a way that all comprehension, all efforts to identify them, to relate them one to the other, or to a common measure in accordance with a regularly valid order or with a natural legality, alters them and necessarily fails. From which follow consequences so difficult to ascertain that we could never discover them all. Here is one of them: the signified can never be taken as being a response to the signifier, or as its end, but rather as that which indefinitely restores to the signifier its power to give meaning and to constitute a question (the reality of the 'content' is there only to recharge form, to reestablish it as form, a form that, in its turn, is exceeded by a 'meaning' that conceals itself and cannot fill it). Here is another: this infinite relation—bearing the exigency of an infinite distortion—will accomplish itself all the more as the terms between which it is produced give themselves as more distant, entailing from one to the other the strongest element of disjunction so that the relation between them does not have the effect of unifying them, but on the contrary prohibits all synthesis, thus affirming through the strangeness of this relation only the improbable becoming of signification in its infinite—that is to say, infinitely empty—plurality. Hence one is able to conceive why this relation of strangeness seems to precede and to deceive every signification, and, at the same time, seems to signify infinitely and signify itself as infinite, and why the innermost meaning of every literary work is always 'literature' signifying itself.

— As though, in literary language, the signifier's emptiness functioned as positive and the content's 'reality' as negative, so that the greater the difference of potential between the two conductors and the stronger the resistance—to the point of tending to the infinite—the closer the work would come to signifying itself as literature. Let us suppose this, although there is much here to object to. But it seems to me that in limiting ourselves to this we have forgotten our point of departure, which was to establish why culture is able to lay claim to literature while the literary experience, at the limit, falls outside the field or the jurisdiction of culture.

— Perhaps we have not forgotten it. Perhaps now we are better able to say something about this difficult problem. For culture tends to conceive of and to establish as relations of unity relations that, on the basis of literature, give themselves as infinite, that is, irreducible to any unifying process. Culture works for the whole. This is its task, and it is a good one. Having the whole as its horizon, it retains all that contributes to the movement of the whole. A cumulative process. It therefore privileges results. For culture, a work's signification is its content, and what is set down and deposited in literary works, their positive side, is the representation or reproduction of an exterior or an interior reality. Literature communicates society, human beings, and objects to us in a manner that is proper to it. It is a volume in the encyclopedia. The ideal of culture is to bring off pictures of the whole, panoramic reconstitutions that situate in the same view Schönberg, Einstein, Picasso, Joyce—throwing Marx into the bargain, if possible, or better yet, Marx and Heidegger. Then the man of culture is happy; he has lost nothing, he has gathered up all the crumbs of the feast.

— Well, now we have kept our promise of being crude. I shall add this remark. A while back we evoked masterpieces; it is culture that loves and perhaps invents them; it needs them to simplify and facilitate reception of the contributions of the centuries. A masterpiece is a kind of concept, gathering together and resuming the reality of the numerous works for which it stands; and it is from the perspective of culture that certain books rise above the others to become at this altitude the visible sign of a whole. And yet, at the same time, culture aims to destroy the notion of the work: what interests culture is, properly speaking, what does not belong to the work of art.

— Because these two tendencies go hand in hand. Whoever wants masterpieces has never discerned what is at stake in the idea of the work—its secret difference, what constitutes it as always unperceived, non-produced, not set into work; the strangeness of its unworking.

— Let us then conclude that literature is not simply a manifestation of culture, which only holds onto results, and above all those that correspond to an established state of the world — some would say its most alienated part. But perhaps we might have avoided this lengthy detour simply by remarking that what is proper to the literary work is being creative, whereas what is proper to culture is to receive what has been created. The first gives; the second has to do only with what is already given, its work being to constitute in a kind of new natural reality the initiatives and the beginnings that, procured by the arts, tend to modify the state of things.

— So that when one speaks of culture one would do better to speak of nature. Still, the idea of creation, though compelling, remains problematic. What does it mean to create? Why would the artist or the poet be the creator par excellence? Creating belongs to the old theology, and we are content to transfer the most common divine attribute to a privileged individual. To create something from nothing is the sign of power. To create a work: in so doing, not only to imitate the demiurgy of divinity, but also to prolong and reestablish the creative forces that once made the world, thus to take over for God. All these myths are indistinctly implied by the word creation when, as though by rights, we apply it to the labor of the artist. To which is added, mixed in with this word, the idea of natural growth, the power of unfolding and springing forth that belongs to nature. To create, to grow, to increase; to participate in the divine secret that created nature, or in the secret of nature that creates itself in the play of metamorphoses — I wonder why we accept, almost without question, such an inheritance of imposing ideas.

— Imposing, and perhaps excessively so. Upon further reflection, it might well come out that we use the term 'creator' or 'creation' only as a commonplace. In the romantic period the artist takes his place at the summit and as though outside any social role: for what at this moment counts in the work of art is neither the work, nor art, but the artist and, in the artist, his brilliance and genius. The creator can even create nothing. He is the divine and absolute self that in itself bears the highest sovereignty, and this sovereignty need be neither socially recognized nor humanly productive. But just as the prestige attributed to inspired subjectivity has worn away, so has the idea of the creator become less distinct and with it, perhaps, the idea of creation as what properly characterizes art.

— Or it has been modified. What does it mean to create? We don't know, or no longer know, how this term would apply to literature. We might say that it seems too strong to us, too charged with received and poorly defined ideas, and also too laden with pretension — in a word, too positive. We have become very modest.

— That is to say, very mistrustful. Because the more the values of this world impose themselves upon us by their natural appearance and their look of positivity, the more we mistrust them; we mistrust their very power to posit, let alone create, processes by which something more is added to a reality that does not satisfy us. Whoever creates risks doing no more than conserving what is by enriching it, and even though he is admired, he already attracts our suspicion. Consequently, the interest we bring today to literature goes, if it goes anywhere, to its critical force, let us say more precisely: to its mysteriously negative forces. Nietzsche, for whom the word creator retained all its attraction, already said that the true creator has the face of the destroyer and the malice of the criminal.

— Is this not to suggest that literature—foreign to culture, repugnant to the order of established values, revoking the criteria of tradition and even that of the modern, refusing to be creative in a world in which creating has no admissible signification—dangerously opens itself to a nihilist perspective, as certain important contemporary literary movements have shown?

— We could say so, if in speaking of nihilism we had the sense that we knew of what we were speaking. But nihilism is precisely one of those words that no longer suffices to convey what it points to. Perhaps what hides beneath this word and escapes every direct hold has its essence in this very movement of slipping away.

— Which amounts to sensing that nihilism, indistinguishable from its masks and nothing other than the false appearance of its false appearances, threatens us precisely when it reassures us, and never poses the most dangerous threat when the threat is most manifest. When, for example, nihilism joined forces with what was called nazism or fascism, it was doubtless not due to what in this movement had an openly negative signification (it never wanted to be seen as destructive; the destroyers were the others, the decadent, the Jews, the atheist Marxists), but rather through the positive values it advanced and that roused other values that are opposed, but related (the values of race, nationalism, force, the value of humanism, and, on both sides, the value of the West); at the same time, this movement claimed kinship with Nietzsche, not the Nietzsche who knew nihilism profoundly, but the Nietzsche who wanted to go beyond it, and precisely by caricaturing such possibilities of going beyond (the overman, the will to power).

— So it would be a matter of coming to maintain ourselves face to face, through an always more direct search, with what only assails us indirectly: as though Orpheus, as long as he did not turn around, thus accepting the infernal law of detour, had done nothing other than let himself be seduced by the nihilist illusion, incarnate, as is fitting, in his art and in its pretension to triumph over nothingness, that is to say, to assure the triumph of nothingness by carrying along in its wake all the forces of dispersion of hell. But he had the courage to look face-on at the fascinating and fascinated thing, and he saw it was nothing, that the nothing was nothing: at which moment hell was really vanquished. An interpretation of the myth so reassuring and so tempting that I would be ready to see in it the very temptation to which Orpheus succumbed. Nihilism has always sought to lure us into challenging it immediately and to suggest we would come more openly to the end of it if we were to dare notice, looking straight-on at the Medusa's head, that she herself is no more than a beautiful face with empty, already petrified eyes.

— Hence you would be inclined to conclude that at this moment nihilism itself is speaking through us.

— When two partners in speech, renouncing all controversy, and through the play of redoubling and alternance, attempt to bring even the unknown to resound, one of them perhaps necessarily assumes the role of nihilism. Only which of the two enters into this game? The one who admits it? The one who does not? Where is the other when two men come to speak, speaking in accord with what they cannot say directly? One of the two is the other, which is neither the one nor the other. As for nihilism, this dry and in any case Latin word, I think it has ceased to reecho in the direction of what it cannot reach. So let us renounce employing it to situate what might come to us from literature—that is, if what came from literature did not itself always in some sense hold itself back in it, and did not hold literature itself back and as though in retreat. At bottom, if to say plainly of literature that it is creative seems to us to be an indiscreet claim, to say that it is nihilist, or in league with some force of nothingness, is no less pretentious and indiscreet. To state it is sufficient to realize this.

— There is still too much positivity in nothingness. The enormity of this word, like the enormity of the word being, has made both of them collapse beneath their ruins (ruins moreover still too easily turned to advantage). These are terms one would do well to be wary of. Literature, we discern, holds itself at a distance from any determination that is too strong: hence it is averse to masterpieces, and even withdraws from the idea of the work to the point of making the latter a form of worklessness. Literature is perhaps creative, but what it creates is always recessed in relation to what is, while this receding only renders what is more slippery, less sure of being what it is, and because of this as though attracted to another measure: that of its unreality where in the play of infinite difference what is affirms itself, though all the while stealing away under cover of the no. Thus not really 'creative,' but also not destructive through the violence of a decisive negation, for the absence literature produces is a kind of overfullness with regard to the 'real,' and this effacement that comes from it, which is also within it as the movement that would efface it—its own infinite questioning—does not really succeed in making it disappear, but rather affirms it through this disappearance, leading it back toward the strangeness of that which gives origination and, at times, perhaps always, allows it in turn to become a thing, a thing full of itself, a self-imposing reality that claims to be of value in consolidating the reign of values.

— When I hear the word origin pronounced, a word the habits of time push toward us, I wonder why we so willingly call it to assist us when, concerning art, speech, and thought, we have some enigma in view. Is it because it is itself enigmatic? Is it because it would hold within itself the word of the enigma—its answer?

— If it holds it, it does not hand it over. Note that as regards the notions we have stirred up so as to seize this possibility that is literature, we have each time sensed that it was ready to rouse itself in the background. Were it a matter of the tradition, we could have said with a certain philosopher: tradition is the forgetting of the origin. Or we could have called it a forgetting of the modern, and then we could have said with another: to live in the modern world is to detach the real from its origin. Or again, were it a matter of the idea of creation, we would have rediscovered behind this idea, before any theological reminiscence and justifying its prestige, the relation with the origin. And it is not merely this power of destruction or effacement at work in literary speech that would lay claim to this obscure origin: not only because, in relation to every thing established, an originary perturbation ruins and prevents any subsistence, but because the origin itself, excluding in its unrecoverable anteriority all that is born of it, is, not being, but rather what turns away from it—the harsh breach of the void out of which everything arises and into which everything sinks and gives way, the very play of the indifferent difference between Arising and Giving-way.

— So when we pronounce the word *origin,* we do no more than gather into a privileged word all the traits that constitute the enigma in our research.

— All these traits perhaps converge, in fact, toward this word, which is in turn the center of all divergence—or, to state this more precisely: divergence itself as the center of every relation.

— A center that in this case is the absence of any center, since it is there that the thrust of all unity comes to be shattered: in some sense the non-center of non-unity. This amounts to maintaining the origin itself under the harsh interrogation of the absence of origin, which, as soon as the origin poses as the cause, the reason, and the word for the enigma, immediately deposes it and speaks as a more profound enigma: the Arising that, as such, sinks down, is engulfed and swallowed up.

— Which amounts therefore to rejecting this reference to the origin to which we had hoped to limit ourselves. I cannot help but remark that we have overturned and effaced, one after another, and in a rather disappointing movement, all the traits we have evoked in order to grasp what is at play in literature.

— Perhaps because literature is essentially made to disappoint, being in some sense always wanting in relation to itself. And, it is true, the word masterpiece, then the words work, posterity, glory, and culture, the words creation and being, destruction and nothingness, and finally the word origin have each in turn offered themselves and retired—but perhaps each time not being entirely erased, leaving in this movement of withdrawal a trace and an almost ineffaceable trait. Thus the masterpiece disappeared, leaving in its place the work understood as its own self-elevation; and in its turn the work disappeared, leaving in its place the affirmation of the work as non-produced, idle, the experience of worklessness; in the place of the idea of the modern there was left the idea of a more profound rupture signifying the suspension of anything memorable; as for culture, it has helped us to conceive of literature as the language in which the relation between form and content becomes infinite (that is to say, the most rigorous and the most aleatory, the affirmation of a rigor and an arbitrariness); finally, the idea of creation and destruction has led us to the idea of origin, which has seemed almost by itself to efface itself, leaving us, as a sign, the idea of difference, of divergence as a first center. This is little, I admit. Nonetheless, it seems to me that an indication remains, an Ariadne's thread that, at each turn of the labyrinth, has allowed us not to lose ourselves definitively. This idea, so many times proposed and always displaced, is that there would be at play in literature some affirmation irreducible to every unifying process, not permitting itself to be unified and itself not unifying, not provoking unity. This is why we can grasp it only indirectly through a series of negations, for it is always in terms of unity that thought, at a certain level, composes its positive references. This is also why literature, if it is made to disappoint all identity and to deceive comprehension as a power of identification, is not really identifiable. That beside all the forms of language in which the whole constructs and speaks itself—speech of the universe, speech of knowledge, of labor and of salvation—one shall always sense an entirely different speech, liberating thought from being always only a thought in view of unity—this is perhaps what would still remain for us at the bottom of the crucible.

— At least momentarily."

± ± *After the last momentary word, let us suppose, by a decision that is clearly illegiti-mate and of pure pretension, that* literature *is dismissing us, which would also mean that* literature *(here unemphasized) has hold of us in this movement of illusion and belonging. This was surrealism's reason, and its madness: in interrogating it no longer in relation to what comes to an end, but with the question of the future that designates itself in this end that is infinite, we will be outside the closure of time; also more enclosed than ever by this opening of the space where are inscribed anew the names that define it as they indetermine it:* concepts that would like to escape all conceptualization (*at the very moment when knowledge, already rediscovering them, recuperates them and even turns them back over to culture—it is true, after the discretion of a long silence*).

I place them here in the "safekeeping" of the absence of the book *that is their ruin as well as their advent.*

XVII

Tomorrow at Stake

One cannot speak of what was neither a system or a school, nor a movement of art or literature, but rather a pure practice of existence (a practice of the whole bearing its own knowledge, a practical theory) in a determinate temporal modality.[1] In the past tense, it would constitute a history, a fine story (the history of surrealism is only of scholarly interest, particularly if the conception of history is not modified by its subject, and nothing up to now has appeared to justify evoking such a possibility). And as for the present or the future, just as one cannot claim that surrealism has been realized (thus losing more than half of what names it: everything in it that goes out ahead of it), neither can one say that it is half real or on the way to realization, in becoming. What constitutes surrealism as an absolute summation, and a summons of such urgency that through it (be it in a most fortuitous manner) waiting opens itself to the unexpected, also prohibits us from trusting solely to the future for it to be accomplished or take form.

To speak of surrealism — and each of us would like to understand it — is to speak of it without authority and in a subdued tone, addressing no one, though still perhaps he who crossed the frontier and broke the last solitude. This is not to speak of it as of a common good (common to whom?) or as a property — it is not the good and it belongs to no one. I presume only that those who are perilously invested with the power to represent it know that even if it possesses no present, no future, and no past, surrealism can at any moment rise up before them and demand justice, requiring a form of accomplishment in accordance with the meaning they will have given it. There is no last judgment other than this exigency by virtue of which the invisible, something that does not exist, will be measured by the works, the actions, the silence, and the practical resolution, that is to say, the joined play of life and death of all those who will have claimed to have given it evidency. A manifestation of the non-manifest.

*

Surrealism—we cannot sense its destination otherwise—is and has always been a collective experience. This is its first trait. Here we may suspect that André Breton's role was different from the one that is recognized through admiration, affection, or personal ill will as having been his. He was neither a master nor a guide, neither the leader of a party nor the head of a religion, any more than a simple arbiter or genius who would have taken the place of all the others through his innocent superiority, founding a coherence and an existence where, without him, there would have been only the stirring of a few dreams or a confrontation of ardent wishes. If he was predominant, he was so outside the group, through his books, his prestige, and his radiant authority: his manner of being truthfully present everywhere. Perhaps, however, within surrealism, he had the particular power not of being the *one* any more than the others, but of making surrealism each one's Other, and in the attraction of this Other taken as a living presence-absence (a *beyond the day* at the horizon of a space unknown and without a beyond), of living it with friendship in the most rigorous sense of this exacting term: making the surrealist affirmation, in other words, a presence or a work of friendship.

Were the surrealists, then, no more than a group of friends? And should their mutual understanding, as well as their separations, be considered simply as the vicissitudes belonging to human relations, where what is involved is first a question of persons? Not in the least. Let us try to understand this more fully. Surrealism is always a third party in the friendship; an absent third term through which passes and through which issues this relation of tension and passion that effaces characters as it gives rise to and motivates initiatives and attractions. Whoever falls short of surrealism (its coldest rules as well as its most burning affirmations) falls short of this friendship and excludes himself from any possibility of encounter, no matter whether he be companion or brother. It is not in the name of betrayed friendship that the exigency in play strikes those who place themselves outside the game; it is rather this exigency itself, making possible or impossible the relations that the rapprochements, encounters and exchanges determine at the level of the everyday, that leads them to a rigorous friendship, but a friendship always revocable, always short of what the surrealist demand might ask of it.

Let us think these things differently. Surrealism: a collective affirmation; a strange plurality. Of what kind? It is hard to be several. Speech does not suffice, unless one is content with the pure chatting (a melancholic alibi) it sometimes consents to become. But in this case one speaks so as not to speak—or, at best, one exchanges information, comments upon and prepares events and public demonstrations, all mediocre forms of sociability. Let us admit to seeing in the surrealist initiatives – the sleep, the games, and the various forms of its experience – an entirely new means of communicating and such that, thanks to these, one can communicate without passing through ordinary speech and without isolating oneself in writing. Of course it is not simply a matter of using up time while being together. Communication – to employ this dubious word – is communication with the unknown. But communicating with the unknown requires plurality.

*

Let us continue with this hypothesis. From the unknown – what is neither the pure unknowable nor the not yet known – comes a relation that is indirect, a network of relations that never allows itself to be expressed unitarily. Whether it be called the marvelous, the surreal, or something else (that which, in any case, disavows transcendence as well as immanence), the unknown provokes – if in fact (in what way?) it is provoked – a non-simultaneous set of forces, a space of difference and, to speak like the first surrealist work, a *magnetic field* always free of the itinerary it calls forth, embodies, and nonetheless holds in reserve. The surrealist affirmation thus affirms this multiple space that does not allow itself to be unified and never coincides with the understanding that individuals, grouped around a faith, an ideal, or a labor, might sustain in common. Perhaps the future of surrealism is bound to this exigency of a plurality escaping unification and extending beyond the whole (while at the same time presupposing it, demanding its realization), untiringly maintaining, in the face of the Unique, contradiction and rupture.

What would therefore distinguish this group from other groups – political cells, religious sects, study groups, literary or philosophical associations, *collèges* come together around a name or persuasion, or groups forming only to give momentary rise to group neuroses (perhaps also in order to study them) – is surely this trait: being several not to accomplish something, but without any reason (even one hidden) other than to make plurality exist by giving it new meaning. A meaning that is betrayed by all the words indicating the movement of gathering: "collectivity," "association," "re-ligion," and, first of all, "group." Let us say: surrealism, an affirmation that is not collective, but plural or multiple.[2]

*

This perpetual affirmation, perpetual dissuasion and dissidence, involves in the first place language ("*It should therefore come as no surprise to see surrealism almost exclusively concerned first with the question of language*"),[3] not because the surrealists would simply be impenitent literary types but because speaking, that is to say, writing, presupposes this space, just as living – desiring – at every moment either frees it or reduces it, according to the conditions of existence that are offered to human beings, and first of all by society. Surrealism—*"it should come as no surprise"*—thus encounters writing, and through this encounter defines itself. But this is a writing of another kind. That the first "purely surrealist" attestation was produced in a kind of anonymous fashion through a double movement of writing that had no other aim than a freeing of the space (*the magnetic field*) that was affirmed by so-called automatic writing—this is what André Breton, despite the disappointments and with a profound understanding of the radical change it provoked, always rightly held to be the essential initiative, the inaugural decision. *"Language has been given to man so he may make surrealist use of it."* Automatic writing, a writing freed from the logic of the logos, refusing everything that puts it to work and that makes it available to a work, is the very proximity of thought, also the affirmation that affirms it, always already inscribed without transcription, a tracing without traces: the *textual*.

Hence a network of necessarily contradictory formulations. Here are a few of them. Thought dictates. Automatic dictation means not that saying reproduces what is thought, but rather: (1) Thinking is always already a saying, a sign of what in advance destines itself to writing. (2) It is a matter of thought (*"the actual [réelle] functioning of thought"*), not of a self who thinks; and thus this saying, without interdiction and without reference to a unique power or capacity to say, does not take its resources from the initiative of the subject, but rather refuses the notion of talent, as it does that of the magisterial work (the masterpiece) and also the notions of oeuvre, of culture, and even of reading. For writing is not reading, a giving to be read or making legible: no one knows ahead of time whether or not automatic writing will be situated at the level of pure unreadability. (3) The *real* functioning of thought. The word "real" is most unfortunate when it is a matter of proposing the surreal; "real" must be put in relation with the expression that defines it more precisely, as when, further on, allusion is made to *the disinterested play of thought*. This disinterest signifies that exterior preoccupations—aesthetic (saying well), as well as moral (acting well, willing well)—are suppressed, and then, with them, everything that constitutes the self as it is protected by censure and the guarantee of repression. Disinterested play is pure passion, the thought that stands under the allurement of desire and as the intensity of what cannot appear, cannot transpire. But *real*? Authentic thought? Non-distorted, non-enclosed, non-alienated? Primitive thought? The *real* is the temptation to which surrealism risks succumbing when it lends itself to a search for the immediate. André Breton says with a magnificent humility: *"I believe more and more in the infallibility of my thought as it relates to myself, and this with good reason. Nonetheless, in the writing of this thought, where one is at the mercy of the least external distraction, one may also fall into 'the soup.' It would be inexcusable to try to hide this. Thought, by definition, is strong and incapable of catching itself at fault."* By definition—but when is thought equal to its definition? When is it what is essentially strong, the force that cannot fail, the very energy that not only passes into writing but, dispersing in it, becomes the movement of writing in its infinitude? Can one then affirm of thought that it "is," or that it is "real"? Such words are too weak to designate the thought that is strong and never fails since they only refer us back to what, within surrealism, will constantly be on trial: not only vulgar realism but also empiricism and, through empiricism, all the customary forms of experience (one of the great surrealist initiatives is precisely to have separated empiricism and experience, reality and knowledge).

It nonetheless remains a fact that the equivocacy of the word *real* and the temptation of what is apparently easy in the immediate is responsible for the link that will be established between automatic writing and a demand for continuity. As though thought—an *inexhaustible murmur*, a self-presence in even, uninterrupted becoming, a voice from the moment of awakening and even in sleep, always speaking and always to be heard—did not cease communicating, and were in unceasing communication with everything, continuous with the whole. And how, when speaking of the real, can one imagine that there might be holes in what is, a lack in the universe, a void that would not be repugnant to nature? Hence this ideology of the continuous from which we are just beginning to disengage ourselves, and for which surrealism (reduced by some to a kind of Bergsonism) is less responsible than it is its victim, as was Freud and as were so many scientific, political, and sociological conceptions. An ideology easy to summarize inasmuch as it consists of two propositions: the world—the real—is continuous; the discontinuous is the continuous such as it comes to man, who has insufficient means to know it and formulate its expression. The continuous refers to the plenitude of being; the discontinuous comes from knowing, sign of our destitution (whereas, understood more rigorously, both the continuous and the discontinuous are signs of different problematics: one surreptitiously identifying reality with a model—the continuous—that it takes not as a model but as what alone is really real; the other affirming that knowing is not the alteration and diminishment of being, being less something, but rather the *less* that, coming forth under determined conditions of language and thought, produces this new modality, this radical change and prodigious *surplus* that is the effect of speech and a knowledge that has never yet been known).

André Breton may well say, but in vain: *"Perhaps the surrealist voice will be stilled, I have given up trying to keep track of those disappeared."* The flux, the linear continuity of words, uninterrupted poetry, will be attributed to surrealist efforts and will thereby risk thwarting the search for an affirmation that stands in a distant relation with the unknown: that which is not measured by unity, and be it even interior to it, always extends beyond, separates from and dis-arranges the whole.

*

Automatic writing: a writing without anyone writing, passive; that is to say, a writing of pure passion, indifferent because bearing in itself every difference: thought writing (not thought written),[4] and over which there can be no master since it excludes mastery, just as it refuses any possibility of being brought into play other than as a disinterested play of thought; thought representing nothing, a fortuitous presence that plays and that permits play.

Play: a word designating the only seriousness of any worth. Play is the provocation by which the unknown, allowing itself to be caught up in the game, can come into relation. One plays with the unknown, that is to say, with the unknown as the stakes. Chance is the sign. Chance is offered by way of encounter. The aleatory introduces into thought as well as into the world, into the real of thought as into exterior reality, what is not found, what is encountered only through encounter. Automatic writing, then, is the *infallibility* of the improbable: what by definition does not cease coming about and yet only comes about exceptionally, in uncertainty and outside every promise: at all times but in a time impossible to determine, that of surprise.

Through the aleatory a relation is therefore produced that is no longer founded on continuity. André Breton and Paul Eluard say this in their joint note on poetry — "*What is created are hiatus and lack*"[5] — thereby discrediting the conception of a homogeneous plenitude that would in some way *really* be transported into language and that language would immediately give to be read. Rupture, lack, lacuna; this is the textual web (that of the inside and the outside, the "*capillary tissue*") to which we accede through poetry's inaccessibility. The search for the immediate (terms that carefully contradict each other) passes by way of the indirect.[6] "*I say that subjective emotion, whatever its intensity, is not directly creative in art, that it has value only insofar as it is reinstated in, and incorporated into, the emotional depths that the artist is called to draw upon.*" And further on: " . . . *providing it avoids the temptation to communicate the emotional process directly*" ("Political Position of Today's Art, 1935").

*

When we evoke *Nadja*, *Communicating Vessels*, and *Mad Love*, written of course by André Breton and on the basis of himself, but subject to surrealism's intervention — which constantly announces itself in them as a danger impossible to bear alone — we immediately discover the changes of which these texts are the site. In refusing, on the one hand, the genre of the novel (guilty of inventing without invention) and, on the other hand, refusing every other genre (guilty of not inventing, and also without saying the true), it is not to an aesthetic concern that André Breton wishes to respond; it is rather a much more decisive mutation he has in view. In this sense, *Nadja* is the grand adventure that we are far from having considered in all it asks of us, and in all that it promises.

There is first this difficulty: the text (let us call it a narrative) has the character of an account that records. What occurs in the narrative has occurred in actual fact. Something takes place there that took place at a time sometimes specified by a date (as one tears a page from a calendar) and in places photographs render present (while withdrawing them from verbal fluctuation). The narrative excludes fiction, it belonging to the category of *"books that are left ajar, like doors, and whose keys don't have to be sought."* Consequently, everything is simple: the author makes known to us a particularly important moment of his life, which means that what is important is the real event whose "poetic" evocation is the book. Perhaps through simplicity and the marvelous transparency that at certain times was his privilege, André Breton would have accepted such a version of things. Yet even in accepting it he would not have consented to it, and even less would the book. We say: a real event, but of what sort? Such that, having been lived and continuing to be lived, it could only find its site in the space opened by the movement of writing. (A book, a simple book, one will say: yes, but one that is neither a book of fiction nor that simply imparts information; so already from this point of view a book that is other, absent.) This event is the encounter. The encounter with Nadja is the encounter with encounter, a double encounter. Naturally, Nadja is real [*vraie*] or, more precisely, she is not real [*vraie*]; she remains apart from every interpretable truth, signifying only the unsignifying particularity of her presence; and this presence is that of encounter—brought forth by chance, taken back again by chance, as dangerous and fascinating as it is, and finally vanishing in and of itself, in the frightening *between-two* opened by the aleatory between reason and unreason. But this encounter that necessarily takes place in the continuity of the world is given precisely in such a way that it breaks this continuity and affirms itself as interruption, interval, arrest, or opening. *Real*, this young woman without a name, very shabbily dressed, walking with her head held high and so fragile that she scarcely touches the ground as she goes. The present of the description is not there to represent her, but to accentuate in a decisive manner the "entrance on stage" of presence; namely, the arrival on the scene of what is simply there, without justification, without proof, and on the basis of which the condition of real and present things will be definitively or momentarily changed. As though the encounter—its chance, the chance of Nietzsche or of Mallarmé: be this the hiatus between several levels of reality, between several systems of determination, between the outside and the inside, or between diverse fields of knowledge; or else the impossible return to unity and the paradoxically unique manifestation of difference (given in a single stroke, a *single* moment and in *one* place)—opened in this world in which things come about a distance without term wherein what arrives in an abrupt manner and like by lightning (Mallarmé would say) is the non-coming itself. But this unarriving of the encounter, this knot in space impossible to undo, and all the more so as its center is emptiness, the spacing that renders intercalary everything that claims to fill it, is the space where writing maintains, unfolds, and again refolds the difference—the essential plurali-ty—that has been entrusted to it, and in a sense consciously, by surrealism. To such a degree (or so fatally) that the encounter with Nadja, a real encounter with a real young woman, a young woman really delivered over to the unreality of what is called madness, is, as though in advance and in the brilliance of a ravaging fate, destined to the exigency of writing—even to the point that this marvelous moment of life, a toss of the dice that will not come about a second time, is staked, and fatally lost, in a preliminary Narrative whose master (as he well knows) is not in the least André Breton, who is merely the lure of the trap in which he him-self just missed being caught.

*

The encounter: what comes without advent, what approaches face-on, and nonetheless always by surprise, what requires waiting and what waiting awaits but does not attain. Even at the innermost heart of interiority, it is always irrup-tion of the outside, exteriority shaking everything. The encounter pierces the world, pierces the self; and in this opening, everything that happens, not happen-ing (coming about with the status of what has not arrived) is the reverse side that cannot be lived of what on the right side cannot be written: a double impossibility that by a supplementary act—a fraud, a kind of falsehood, also a madness—must be transformed in order to adapt it to living and writing "reality." As when one pretends to bring death into the game—for surely one of the most certain and the most indecisive forms of encounter is dying's stealing away.

The encounter encounters us. "Objective chance," fortuitous necessity, in the Hegelian sense, is certainly insufficient to account for what is at stake in this sen-tence. As in the Hegelian totality, what is separated—contraries—gives evidence of an anterior identity and announces a terminal identification, time being nothing but the passage of the first simplicity to the second; so in the same way the chains of distinct causalities, constituting a kind of sequence without relation, come to intersect at a point that appears to be fortuitous because the knowledge of the whole determining it is lacking, even though these chains of causality are nonetheless ideally one, never being foreign to the principle of unity that makes their coinciding not an irreducible *strangeness*, but a promise of coherence or a reminder of concordance.

The encounter encounters us. What is striking is not (as Cournot said in a de-finition that was famous at school) that two independent series—the tile, the passerby—emerging from out of the furthest improbability, should meet via the independence of their conditions; it is not even that the supposed consequence—death—while being rigorously determined, should, as such, remain without a proper determination, without the determination capable of accounting for its meaning. Or perhaps this has to be expressed differently (to say nevertheless the same thing). The encounter designates a new relation. At the point of juncture – a unique point – what comes into relation remains without relation, and the unity that thus comes to the fore is but the surprising manifestation (a manifestation by surprise) of the un-unifiable, the simultaneity of what cannot be together; from which we have to conclude, even should this ruin logic, that where the junction takes place it is disjunction that reigns over unitary structure and causes it to shatter. Therefore chance – the aleatory – does not simply put in question two determinations of a different order (a causality, a finality) or two locally autonomous and qualitatively distinct series (nature, history). These two series (it may be a matter of the meeting of two instances of freedom: Nadja and her companion), whether homogeneous or not, cease being so at their point of intersection. It is this heterogeneity of phenomena, their radical *distance* at the very site of their crossing, that sanctions the brilliance of their difference. Or if one prefers to formulate it differently: infinite exteriority, the non-contemporaneity of what is given in the unity of presence is the mystery of chance, its revelatory element.

The encounter, therefore, designates a new relation because at the point of coincidence – which is not a point but a divergence – it is non-coincidence that intervenes (that affirms itself in the inter-vening [*l'inter-venue*]).

To again refer back to the deceptive example of the tile and the passerby, there is a level of reality at which the two movements, that of the fall, that of the passing, are but two trajectories that come to intersect. Now, in this schema, what falls never kills anyone because the idea of death is not involved. To put this differently, the object as such never reaches the passerby as such, but only an arbitrary moving object; it is *elsewhere*, in *another time* that the passerby passes and dies; dying, in the proper sense of this word, by chance, and through chance, as though at the end of a game of dice whose outcome for him would have been unfavorable (supposing death was not his wish). A curious formulation. Let us accept it for the moment. It has the merit of showing the hiatus that holds the two fields apart even as they coincide; thus what introduces the thought of chance is this hiatus wherein is lodged, through recurrence, and for the sake of filling it in, the mortal possibility called the stroke of fate. So in this case, in order to kill there must be: (1) a determining cause; (2) the absence of a determinate cause – and it is the absence of cause that always causes death, this lack that signifies a rupture of continuity.

And thus chance: the indeterminant that indetermines.

It is in this lack that obscure desire, the desire that cannot realize itself as desire, seeks and finds its site. Who would not be tempted to believe that where clear intention slips away it is the hidden interference of desire that denounces itself, belatedly claiming necessity as though it had itself established it and set it in place ahead of time? Chance is desire; which means either that desire desires chance, inasmuch as it is aleatory, or that desire seduces chance so as to render it unconsciously similar to what is desired – a form of magic, therefore, that for a time was surrealism's temptation. But Nadja withdraws precisely from magical reconciliation, just as she slips out of amorous reach. This is why her adventure is the most decisive. The fascinating, enigmatic point: her companion, he who walks beside her, is unable to come to an understanding with her in the allure that comes from her presence.

*

There is a dissymmetry in the encounter, an essential discordance between the "terms" that come face to face. What approaches face-on is also absolutely turned aside. It comes by surprise, arbitrarily and necessarily: the arbitrariness of necessity, unexpected by reason of the waiting. "*I don't know why it should be precisely here that my steps take me, here that I almost always go without specific purpose and without anything determining it other than this obscure clue: namely that it (?) will happen here.*" It (?) [*Cela (?)*]; the very specification of what is in the encounter: the neutral of the unknown. The neutral of the unknown that is always in play in encounter allows the encounter to come about only in order immediately to put its realization at stake. This is the breathless, exhausting pursuit. Nadja is always encountered—one must always recommence encountering her—always withdrawn as soon as she offers herself, destined to slip away, and even in her disappearance that is as uncertain and even more obscure than her manifestation, which does not abolish the event, but takes place in the same space—the nonplace—of encounter.

Hence this thought, this questioning hope: would not Nadja, this name that is but a half-name, giving her a visage, a voice, a presence—would she not be this indecisive *cela(?)*, the very unknown that, in the world, but disturbing the world, would allow itself to be observed so as to make the surrealist affirmation, in the full light of day, tangible and real? How simple this would be, and how well one understands why André Breton would wish to believe this, and would wish also to convince her of it—but in vain: the unknown is never but an interloper, that is, a third party in default, ever exterior to the horizon against which it seems to stand out, always different from the enigma by which, enigmatic, it would give itself over to knowledge. In the relation thus offered neither of them encounters what they encounter: André Breton is for her a god, the sun, the dark and lightning-struck man close to the sphinx; for him, she is the genie of the air, inspired-inspiring, she who always departs. The unknown thus acquires its character of beauty and height, which fixes it at a certain level—a level both reassuring and stirring—of irreality. But that Nadja should also be Mlle. D. who makes idle, tiresome remarks, who persists in misplaced coquetteries and low, lamentable adventures from which her dignity does not emerge intact, that she, in a word, is the one who "falls"—at this moment the unknown, perhaps precisely at this time closest to being lived, steals away and revokes itself without leaving any other trace than this deranged everydayness (and here the common sense of the word "derangement," which is also the most impressive, comes appropriately to name the event in completing its alteration).

What does all this signify? The misunderstanding—let us immediately set aside all that might be offered to account for it in the way of differences of character or even, due to their personalities, the protagonists' incapacity to be up to the event—is not the accidental and regrettable effect of an encounter in every other respect marvelous; misunderstanding is its essence and, as it were, its principle. Where no understanding is possible, where all that happens happens outside understanding and is therefore fascinating—terrible or marvelous—and with no relation other than the intimacy of the absence of relation, it is here that the experience of encounter deploys its dangerous space: a field that is non-unified, non-legalized, and without set paths, where life is no more given at the level of the real than writing, accomplice of that life, is present in the language where the real is articulated. The experience—danger itself: a gap through which life, far from interrupting itself in the living being so that the latter, as a good writer, can do his work, rather doubles itself in a sense in order to expose itself to this interruption; being then free for an instant of its conditions of stability and security, that is to say, free of its order and its future—as from its present and past—so that one may live it, without, however (since it is only a matter of a burning nonpresence and a violent lack), ever being able to claim having lived it: an interruption that the one who writes receives and retains without knowing, for his part, whether the silence found there—but is it silence?—was from the outset given to him in this suspended and heightened moment of life, or, on the contrary, whether he writes only in order that this silence might occur, a silence without which the encounter—did it take place, will it take place?—would be deprived of all communicable reality.

An *experience* that is therefore not only an experimentation (the action of writing on life), but an experience of that which does not obey the reigning order of experience, and, without taking the form of a new order, holds itself *between* the two—between two orders, two times, two systems of signification and of language: the ordeal, therefore, of what is given neither in the arrangement of the world nor in the form of the work, and thus announcing itself on the basis of the real as *derangement*, and on the basis of the work as *unworking*—a practice of life and of writing in which we thought we recognized one of the characteristic traits of the surrealist project.

*

Derangement (or becoming as the energy of intermittence) is at work, but produces no work. It is not outside what can be attested, but its attestation is always an attestation of default so that attestation, in its case, does not consist in observing it as though it were inscribed in a perceptible state of the world or a reality and, as such, adhering in an object offered to a gaze, or to the introspection of a subject. Disarrangement, derangement is invisible; this means that it blocks the direct relation light seems to authorize and that unduly organizes knowledge, just as it reduces all speech to the model of sight and the thing to be seen; this means as well that it never merges with the trace it leaves or with the phenomenon that bears it — a trace or a phenomenon always belonging to one or another time, to one or another system. When one remarks it, it cannot be established; when one makes it speak, it refers to a "without speech" that is nonetheless language inasmuch as the latter only speaks in preceding itself or in tearing itself away from itself. "It interrupts itself," "it turns aside" are still falsifying propositions since they give interruption as being a sort of mysterious and secondary withdrawal from a phenomenon, and also because they make this withdrawal or this detour into a phenomenon — even though absent — of the same order as presence, always already regulated and brought to order.

Unworking is at work, but does not produce the work. Thus when we analyze and comment on the work, we have a tendency either to determine this movement of unworking as the originality of a new order, one harmony breaking with another, or to grasp it as the autonomous principle of the work's engendering, its unity at work, whereas worklessness is always outside the work: that which has not let itself be put to work, the always un-unified irregularity (the non-structure) that makes it so that the work relates to something other than itself, not because it says or enunciates (recites, reproduces) this other thing — the "real" — but because it only says itself in saying this *other* thing, saying it through this distance and difference, this play between words and things that is also between things and things, between one language and another. This outside of difference makes it so that the real never seems to be in the real, but in the knowledge that elaborates and transforms it, thus always appearing more in the work's discourse than in life — but as soon as we have it, it is life (by way of the exteriority it represents and that it opposes to the work as its supposed model) that seems to embody the moment of unworking, and independently of what has come of it in the relation established by the work.

The surreal of surrealism is thus perhaps offered to the future as this between-two of difference; a field infinitely plural, a point of curvature where irregularity decides. The surreal is not a region, it is not situated: not in the real or above the real, above reason in unreason or beneath consciousness in the unconscious; nor is it the reconciliation always still to come of these irreconcilable possibilities. The surreal may well seek to constitute for itself imaginary objects, indicate itself in the margins, discover itself close to the unwonted through what is stunning and fascinating. These indications still have no more than a distancing value: reminders of the *unseemly* whose law is not only to disorder the order of the appropriate, but also to be unable to suit itself, concern itself, or conform to itself by assuming a form. The non-coinciding, the non-concerning—these are indeed what cause the surreal radically to change the meaning of what we have called the *experience* in which it is in play, not only separating it from all empiricism, but leading it to touch on everything at once: life, knowledge, thought, speech, love, time, society, and the whole itself; putting everything in question (ejecting the whole from the order of the whole) not by a stormy tumult or a purely capricious negation, but through this concerted, non-concerted seeking that remains without assurance and without guarantee since it aims at the other that is always other. An other "field," without unity and without itinerary, which, although being there, is never given, remains to be opened and, once opened, opens onto danger and the marvelous—before again closing itself, perhaps always already closed upon a new order, a tradition, a new culture; or, to limit ourselves to particular fates: for Nadja the asylum, and for André Breton that absence of the book dissimulated in a book—the "narrative," in other words, that she herself who passed had wanted and, according to her desire, should not have carried the name of an author but instead a name for fire: for *"be careful: everything fades, everything vanishes."* And here the man's name itself also begins to be effaced, drifting alone, far from our understanding, indifferent to remembrance, foreign to admiration and refusing to be this glorious name on an appointed tomb, already too *unknown* to let itself be borne even by the anonymous force of surrealism: the trace of steps having never yet passed.

*

Nadja: we must not take our distance from this book, a book "always in the future," not only because it opened a new path for literature—how, when the future's future is at stake, can one be content with such an innovation?—but because, perhaps, from now on committing to each of us the task of seizing the absence of work that designates itself as the work's center, it imparts to us the obligation to experience on the basis of what lack and in view of what default all writing bears what is written. This absence—already aimed at by the thinking, writing in which it becomes necessity (and presence) through chance—is such that it changes the possibility of every book, making of the work what always ought to put itself out of work, unworking itself as it modifies the relations between thought, discourse, and life.

"Life is other than what we write." How does this *other than* manifest itself in *Nadja*? Rather than in the way of this sentence, it is in lacuna, in silence, in the impossibility of saying where the provocation of danger is revealed. Misunderstanding—another name for derangement—is one of its signs. This enigmatic allusion as well: "Whatever desire or even illusion I may have had to the contrary, perhaps I was not up to what she was offering me. *But what was she offering me? It doesn't matter.*" Here the work turns, one could even say turns short, on condi-

tion that one hear in this arrest what holds the work back before it accomplishes itself, also before it undoes itself. Then comes madness (*"I was told, several months ago . . . "*), which is challenged via society's assumed right to take legal action against her—without its force of revelation being refused, and without the mental deterioration that it perhaps signifies being refused either. Then the final query—*"Who goes here? Is it you, Nadja? . . . Is it only me? Is it myself?"*—so strange, so faltering, and responding as an echo to the first words of the book—*"Who am I?"*—so that the whole narrative is but the redoubling of the same question maintained in its spectral difference. Finally, the most surprising: as the book is coming to an end, it begins again only to destroy itself, obscuring the one who was Nadja (she who is excluded from understanding, enigmatic passerby) by another figure who is celebrated as the only one living since loved, and thus free of enigma. A most troubling betrayal; an anxious attempt to make disappear from the life of time and from the life of life what always divides time and turns aside from living, what in effect excludes itself from every remembrance as from every possibility of ever having one time been lived: the encounter, that is the appearance-disappearance, the space of greatest danger. It is through this appearance-disappearance, and through the appeal of danger, that Nadja signals the future of surrealism: no longer the title of a book, but *tomorrow in play* and as a player; the aleatory that would always shatter the book, break up knowledge, and derange even desire by making the book, knowledge, and desire—when there is no time but between-times—response to the unknown.

*

Let us isolate by way of a single trait a few names, a few concepts escaping every conceptualization.

Worklessness, the absence of (the) work. As Michel Foucault has reminded us in the strongest terms, the absence of work is used by the current ideology to designate as "madness" what it rejects. But the absence of work, confined in the asylum, is also always walled up in the work. If the work is elaborated on the basis of the work's absence, it will not rest until it has reduced this absence to insignificance, or, what is worse, rendered it proper to the understanding of a new order or the harmony of a new accord. The absence of the work nonetheless always cites the work outside itself, calling it always in vain to its own unworking and making the work re-cite itself, even when it believes it has its sights on "the outside" that it does not fail to include—rather than working to exclude it. The absence of work, the aleatory that lies between reason and unreason, is not "madness," but madness plays the same role as the work since it permits society, as the work permits literature, to retain the absence of work—inoffensive, innocent, indifferent—within the firm limits of a partitioned, cellular space.

Disarrangement, disarray. Surrealism has always taken itself, and certainly with reason, to be a subversive movement (André Breton: *"Surrealism could only die out if another more emancipatory movement were to be born"* — in other words, surrealism itself). But this would hardly suffice to allow us to grasp its truth, nor explain the fact that in having a relation to everything it cannot content itself with this whole — the accomplishment of the whole, man as everything — that it nonetheless socially and politically demands through an energetic struggle at the most sensitive points, and through decisions always precise and firm. Surrealism is not a philosophical discourse, not a political action, a morality turned inside out, or an enterprise of literary renewal. No more than it is all of these at once; if it has a relation to everything as a whole, on the whole, it has no determinate object, and not even this whole. The surrealist experiment [*expérience*] aims (it seems to me) at the point of divergence on the basis of which all knowledge, as every limited affirmation of life, escapes itself in order to expose itself to the neutral force of derangement. The surrealist experience [*expérience*] is the experience of experience, whether it seeks itself in a theoretical or practical form: an experience that deranges and deranges itself, disarranges as it unfolds and, in unfolding, interrupts itself. It is in this that surrealism — poetry itself — is the experience of thought itself. And a kind of blindness would be needed to recognize in *Nadja* or in *Mad Love* works in which a certain didacticism intervenes to corrupt the poetic act or the "pure beauty" of the narrative. What misunderstanding. In works such as these thought is experience inasmuch as the written comes to thought in the movement of writing. Knowledge does not exist before writing, and writing, by its detours, its decisions, and its interruptions, knows itself always responsible for a latent knowledge, as it knows itself responding to another possibility; a possibility that is the other of all knowledge and whose attraction carries the act of writing, but carries it to the point of becoming risk. *Danger*: the danger by which, in the place of the work, is introduced the *play* of the absence of (the) work.

The game, the aleatory, the encounter. These words designate, without defining it, the new space, a space that is the vertigo of spacing: dis-tance, dis-location, dis-course, from out of which — be it in life through desire, in knowledge through the by no means uncontrolled expression of an absence of knowledge, be it in time through the affirmation of intermittency, or in the whole of the Universe through the refusal of the Unique and through the accord of a relation without unity, finally, in the work through the liberation of the absence of the work — the *unknown* announces itself and, outside the game, comes into play. A space that is never more than the approach of another space: the neighboring of the distant, the beyond, but without either transcendence or immanence. A field "at the confines of art and of life," a site of tension and difference where every relation is a relation of irreciprocity, a multiple space that could be affirmed, apart from every affirmation, solely by a *plural speech*; the speech that, giving a new meaning to plurality, would in turn receive from plurality the silent possibility: death finally lived.

XVIII

The Absence of the Book

Let us try to question, that is to say, welcome in the form of a question what cannot reach the point of questioning.

1. — *"This insane game of writing."* With these words, simple as they are, Mallarmé opens up writing to writing. But these simple words are such that it will take a great deal of time—a great variety of experiments, the work of the world, countless misunderstandings, works lost and scattered, the movement of knowledge, and, finally, the turning point of an infinite crisis—for us to begin to understand what decision is being prepared on the basis of this end of writing that is announced by its coming.

2. — Apparently we read only because what is written is already there, laying itself out before our eyes. Apparently. But the first one to write, the one who cut into stone and wood under ancient skies, was hardly responding to the demands of a view requiring a reference point and giving it a meaning; rather, he was changing all relations between seeing and the visible. What he left behind was not something more, something added to other things; it was not even something less—a subtraction of matter, a hollow in relation to a relief. Then what was it? A gap in the universe: nothing that was visible, nothing invisible. I suppose the first reader was engulfed by this non-absent absence, but without knowing anything about it. And there was no second reader because reading, from now on understood as the vision of a presence immediately visible, that is to say intelligi-

422

ble, was affirmed precisely in order to make this disappearance into *the absence of the book* impossible.

3. — Culture is bound to the book. The book as a repository and a receptacle of knowledge becomes identified with knowledge. The book is not only the book found in libraries, that labyrinth where all the combinations of forms, words, and letters are rolled up in volumes. The book is the Book. Still to be read, to be written, always already written and thoroughly penetrated by reading, the book constitutes the condition for every possibility of reading and writing.

The book admits of three distinct investigations. There is the empirical book. The book acts as a vehicle of knowledge; a given, determinate book receives and gathers a given, determinate form of knowledge. But the book as book is never simply empirical. The book is the *a priori* of knowledge. We would know nothing if there did not always exist in advance the impersonal memory of the book and, more essentially, the prior disposition to write and to read contained in every book and affirming itself only in the book. The absolute of the book, then, is the isolation of a possibility that claims to have originated in no other anteriority. An absolute that will later tend to be affirmed with the romantics (Novalis), then more rigorously with Hegel, then still more radically (though in a different way) with Mallarmé as the totality of relations (absolute knowledge, or the Work) in which would be accomplished either consciousness, which knows itself and comes back to itself after having exteriorized itself in all its dialectically linked figures, or language, closing upon its own affirmation and already dispersed.

Let us recapitulate: the empirical book; the book: condition for all reading and all writing; and the book: totality or Work. But with increasing refinement and truth all these forms assume that the book contains knowledge as the presence of something that is virtually present and always immediately accessible, if only with the help of mediations and relays. Something is there that the book presents in presenting itself, and that reading animates and reestablishes through its animation in the life of a presence. Something that, on the lowest level, is the presence of a content or a signified; then, on a higher level, the presence of a form, of something that signifies or operates; and, on a still higher level, the development of a system of relations that is always already there, if only as a possibility to come. The book enfolds time, unfolds time, and holds this unfolding in itself as the continuity of a presence in which present, past, and future become actual.

4. — *The absence of the book* revokes all continuity of presence just as it eludes the questioning borne by the book. It is not the book's interiority, nor its continuously elided Meaning. Rather it is outside the book, although enclosed within it — not so much its exterior as the reference to an outside that does not concern it.

The more the Work assumes meaning and acquires ambition, retaining in itself not only all works, but also all the forms and all the powers of discourse, the more the absence of the work seems about to propose itself, without, however, letting itself be designated. This occurs with Mallarmé. With Mallarmé, the Work becomes aware of itself and thereby seizes itself as something that would coincide with the absence of the work; the latter then deflecting it from ever coinciding with itself and destining it to impossibility. A movement of detour whereby the work disappears into the absence of the work, but where the absence of the work increasingly escapes by reducing itself to being no more than the Work that has always already disappeared.

5. — The act of writing is related to the absence of the work, but is invested in the Work as book. The madness of writing — *this insane game* — is the relation of writing; a relation established not between the writing and production of the book but, through the book's production, between the act of writing and the absence of the work.

To write is to produce the absence of the work (worklessness, unworking [*désoeuvrement*]). Or again: writing is the absence of the work as it *produces itself* through the work, traversing it throughout. Writing as unworking (in the active sense of the word) is the insane game, the indeterminacy that lies between reason and unreason.

What happens to the book in this "game" in which worklessness is set loose in the operation of writing? The book: the passage of an infinite movement that goes from writing as an operation to writing as worklessness; a passage that immediately impedes. Writing passes by way of the book, but the book is not that to which it is destined (its destiny). Writing passes through the book, accomplishing itself there even as it disappears there; yet we do not write for the book. The book: a ruse by which writing goes toward *the absence of the book*.

6. — Let us try to gain a clearer understanding of the relation of the book to *the absence of the book*.

a) The book plays a dialectical role. In some sense it is there in order that not only the dialectics of discourse can be accomplished, but also discourse as a dialectic. The book is the work language performs on itself: as though there had to be the book in order for language to become conscious of itself, in order for language to grasp itself and complete itself in its incompletion.

b) Yet the book that has become a work — even more, the whole literary process, whether it affirm itself in a long succession of books or manifest itself in a single book or in the space that takes the place of that book — is at once more a book than other books and already outside the book, outside the category of book and outside its dialectic. *More* a book: a book of knowledge scarcely exists as a book, as a volume unfolding; the work, on the other hand, claims to be singular: unique, irreplaceable, it is almost a person. Hence the dangerous tendency for the work to promote itself into a masterpiece, and also to essentialize itself, that is to say, designate itself by a signature (not merely signed by the author, but also—and this is more grave—in some sense by itself). And yet it is already outside the book process: as though the work only marked the opening—the interruption—through which the neutrality of writing passes and were oscillating, suspended between itself (the totality of language) and an affirmation that has not yet come about.

Moreover, in the work, language is already changing direction—or place: the place of its direction; no longer the logos that participates in a dialectics and knows itself, it is rather engaged in a relation that is other. So one can say that the work hesitates between the book (vehicle of knowledge and fleeting moment of language) and the Book raised to the Capital Letter (Idea and Absolute of the book), and then between the work as presence and the absence of the work that constantly escapes, and where time deranges itself as time.

7. — The end of the act of writing does not reside either in the book or in the work. Writing the work, we come under the attraction of the absence of the work. We necessarily fall short of the work, but we are not by this reason, by this failing, under the necessity of the absence of the work.

8. — The book: a ruse by which the energy of writing—which relies on discourse and allows itself to be carried along by the vast continuity of discourse in order, at the limit, to separate itself from it—is also the ruse of discourse, restoring to culture the mutation that threatens it and opens it to the absence of the book. Or again, a labor through which writing, modifying the givens of a culture, of "experience" and knowledge, that is to say, discourse, procures another product that will constitute an entirely new modality of discourse as a whole and will become integrated with it, even as it claims to disintegrate it.

The absence of the book: reader, you would like to be its author, being then no more than the plural reader of the Work.

How long will it last—this lack that is sustained by the book, and that expels the book from itself as book? Produce the book, then, so it will separate, disengage from itself in its dispersion. This will not mean you have produced *the absence of the book*.

9. — The book (the civilization of the book) affirms: there is a memory that transmits, there is a system of relations that orders; time ties its knot in the book where the void still belongs to a structure. But the absence of the book is not founded on a writing that leaves a mark and determines a directional movement— whether this movement unfolds in linear fashion from an origin toward an end or unfolds from out of a center toward the surface of a sphere. The absence of the book makes appeal to a writing that does not commit itself, that does not set

itself down, and that is not content with disavowing itself or with going back over its tracks to erase them.

What is it that summons us to write when the time of the book, determined by a relation of beginning-end, and the space of the book, determined by deployment from a center, cease to impose themselves? The attraction of (pure) exteriority.

The time of the book: determined by the beginning-end (past-future) relation, on the basis of a presence. The space of the book: determined by deployment from a center, itself conceived as the search for an origin.

Wherever there is a system of relations that orders or a memory that transmits, wherever writing gathers itself within the substance of a trace that reading regards in the light of a meaning (referring this trace back to an origin whose sign it is), and when emptiness itself belongs to a structure and allows for adjustment, there is the book: the *law* of the book.

As we write, we always write from out of the exteriority of writing and against the exteriority of the law, and always the law draws upon what is written as a resource.

The attraction of (pure) exteriority — the place where, since the outside "precedes" any interior, writing does not set itself down in the manner of a spiritual or an ideal presence, inscribing itself and then leaving a mark, a trace, or a sedimentary deposit that would allow one to track it down, that is, restore it to its ideal presence or ideality, its plenitude, its integrity of presence on the basis of that mark as lack.

Writing marks but leaves no trace; it does not authorize us to work our way back from some vestige or sign to anything other than itself as (pure) exteriority — never given, never constituting or gathering itself in a relation of unity with a presence (to be seen, to be heard), with the totality of presence or the Unique, present-absent.

When we begin writing, we are either not beginning or we are not writing: writing does not go along with beginning.

10. — Through the book, the disquiet — the energy — of writing seeks to rest in and accrue to the work (*ergon*); but the absence of the work always from the outset calls upon it to respond to the detour of the outside where what is affirmed no longer finds its measure in a relation of unity.

We have no "idea" of the absence of the work; not as a presence, certainly, but also not as the destruction of what would prevent it, even if only as an absence. To destroy the work, which itself is not, to destroy at least the affirmation and the dream of the work, to destroy the indestructible, to destroy nothing so the idea that destruction would suffice — an idea that is out of place here — will not impose itself. The negative can no longer be at work where the affirmation that affirms the work has taken place. And in no case can the negative lead to the absence of the work.

To read would mean to read in the book the absence of the book, and, as a consequence, to produce this absence precisely where there is no question of the book being either absent or present (defined by an absence or a presence).

The absence of the book is never contemporaneous with the book, not because this absence would announce itself from out of another time, but because from this absence comes the very non-contemporaneity from out of which it, too, comes. The absence of the book, always diverging, always without a relation of presence with itself, and in such a way that it is never received in its fragmentary plurality by a single reader in the present of a reading—unless, at the limit, with the present torn apart, dissuaded—

The attraction of (pure) exteriority or the vertigo of space as distance; a fragmentation that sends us back to nothing more than the fragmentary.

The absence of the book: the prior deterioration of the book, its dissident play with reference to the space in which it is inscribed; the preliminary dying of the book. To write: the relation to the *other* of every book, to what in the book would be de-scription, a scriptuary exigency outside discourse, outside language. To write at the edge of the book, outside the book.

This writing outside language: a writing that would be in a kind of originary manner a language rendering impossible any object (either present or absent) of language. This writing would never be the writing of man, that is to say, never God's writing either; at most the writing of the other, of dying itself.

11. — The book begins with the Bible in which the logos is inscribed as law. Here the book attains its unsurpassable meaning, including what exceeds its bounds on all sides and cannot be gotten past. The Bible refers language to its origin: whether it be written or spoken, this language forms the basis for the theological era that opens and endures for as long as biblical space and time endure. The Bible not only offers us the preeminent model of the book, a forever unparalleled example, it also encompasses all books, no matter how alien they are to biblical revelation, knowledge, poetry, prophesy, and proverbs, because it holds in it the spirit of the book. The books that follow the Bible are always contemporaneous with it: the Bible doubtless grows, increases on its own through an infinite growth that leaves it identical, it being forever sanctioned by the relation of Unity, just as the ten Laws set forth and contain the monologos, the One Law, the law of Unity that cannot be transgressed, and that negation alone cannot deny.

The Bible: the testamentary book where the alliance, the covenant is declared, that is to say, the destiny of speech bound to the one who bestows language and where he consents to dwell through this gift that is the gift of his name; that is to say, also, the destiny of this relation of speech to language that is dialectics.

It is not because the Bible is a sacred book that the books deriving from it—the entire literary process—are marked with the theological sign and cause us to belong to the theological realm. It is just the opposite: it is because the testament—the alliance or covenant of speech—was enfolded in a book and took the form and structure of a book that the "sacred" (what is separate from writing) found its place in theology. The book is essentially theological. This is why the first manifestation of the theological (and also the only one that continues to unfold) could only have been in the form of a book. In some sense God only remains God (only becomes divine) inasmuch as He speaks through the book.

Mallarmé, faced with the Bible in which God is God, elevates the work in which *the insane game of writing* sets to work and already disavows itself, encountering indeterminacy's double game: necessity, chance. The Work, the absolute of voice and of writing, unworks itself [*se désoeuvre*] even before it has been accomplished; before, in accomplishing itself, it ruins the possibility of accomplishment. The Work still belongs to the book and therefore helps to maintain the biblical character of every Work; yet it designates (in the neutral) the disjunction of a time and a space that are *other*, precisely that which no longer affirms itself in relation to unity. The Work as book leads Mallarmé outside his name. The Work in which the absence of the work holds sway leads he who is no longer called Mallarmé to the point of madness. If we can, let us understand this *to the point of* as the limit that, once crossed, would be decisive madness; from which we would have to conclude that the limit—"the edge of madness"—conceived as the indecision that does not decide, or else as non-madness, is more essentially mad: this would be the abyss—not the abyss, but the edge of the abyss.

Suicide: what is written as necessity in the book denounces itself as chance in the absence of the book. What the one says the other says over, and this reiterating speech, by virtue of its redoubling, contains death, the death of the self.

12. — The anonymity of the book is such that in order to sustain itself it calls for the dignity of a name. The name is that of a momentary particularity that supports reason, and that reason authorizes by raising it up to itself. The relation of Book and name is always contained in the historical relationship that linked the absolute knowledge of system with the name Hegel: this relation between the Book and Hegel, identifying the latter with the book and carrying him along in its development, made Hegel into a post-Hegel, a Hegel-Marx, and then a Marx radically foreign to Hegel who continues to write, to bring into line, to know, and to affirm the absolute law of written discourse.

Just as the Book takes the name of Hegel, in its more essential (more uncertain) anonymity, the work takes the name of Mallarmé, the difference being that Mallarmé not only knows that the anonymity of the Work is his (its) trait and the indication of his place, not only withdraws in this way of being anonymous, but also does not call himself the author of the Work: at the very most he proposes himself, hyperbolically, as the power—the never unique or unifiable power—to read the non-present Work, in other words the power to respond, by his absence, to the always still absent work (the absent work not being *the absence of the work*, being even separated from it by a radical break).

In this sense, there is already a decisive distance between Hegel's book and Mallarmé's work; a difference evidenced by their different ways of being anonymous in the naming and signing of their work. Hegel does not die, even if he disavows himself in the displacement or turning about of the System: since every system still names him, Hegel is never altogether nameless. Mallarmé and the work are without relation, and this lack of relationship is played out in the Work, establishing the work as what would be forbidden to this particular Mallarmé, as it would be to anyone else bearing a name, and as it would be to the work conceived as the power of accomplishing itself in and through itself. The Work is freed from the name not because it could be produced without anyone producing it, but because its anonymity affirms it as being always and already outside whatever might name it. The book is the whole, whatever form this totality might take, and whether the structure of this totality is or is not wholly different from what a belated reading assigns to Hegel. The Work is not the whole, is already outside the whole, but in its resignation it still designates itself as absolute. The Work is not bound up with success (with completion) as the book is, but with disaster: although disaster is yet another affirmation of the absolute.

Let us say briefly that if the book can always be signed, it remains indifferent to whoever would do so; the work—Festivity as disaster—requires resignation, requires that whosoever claims to write it renounce himself as a self and cease designating himself.

Then why do we sign our books? Out of modesty, as a way of saying: these are still only books, indifferent to signatures.

13. — The "absence of the book," which the written thing provokes as the future of writing—a future that has never come to pass—does not constitute a concept, any more than does the word "outside," the word "fragment," or the word "neutral," but it helps conceptualize the word "book." It is not some contemporary interpreter who, in giving Hegel's philosophy its coherence, conceives of it as a book and thus conceives of the book as the finality of absolute Knowledge; Mallarmé does it already at the end of the nineteenth century. But, through the very force of his experience, Mallarmé immediately pierces the book in order (dangerously) to designate the Work whose center of attraction—a center always off-center—would be writing. The act of writing, *the insane game*. But the act of writing has a relation (a relation of alterity) with the absence of the Work, and it is precisely because Mallarmé has a sense of this radical mutation that comes to writing through writing with the absence of the Work that he is able to name the Book, naming it as that which gives meaning to becoming by proposing a

place and a time for it: the first and last concept. Only Mallarmé does not yet name the absence of the book, or he recognizes it simply as a way of thinking the Work, the Work as failure or impossibility.

14. — The absence of the book is not the book coming apart, even though in some sense coming apart lies at the origin of the book and is its counter-law. The fact that the book is always undoing itself (dis-arranging itself) still only leads to another book or to a possibility other than the book, not to the absence of the book. Let us grant that what haunts the book (what beleaguers it) would be the absence of the book that it always falls short of, contenting itself with containing it (keeping it at a distance) without being able to contain it (transform it into a content). Let us also grant the opposite, saying that the book encloses the absence of the book that excludes the book, but that the absence of the book is never conceived only on the basis of the book and solely as its negation. Let us grant that if the book carries meaning, the absence of the book is so foreign to meaning that non-meaning does not concern it either.

It is very striking that within a certain tradition of the book (as it is brought to us through the Cabalists' formulation, and even if it is a matter of sanctioning with this usage the mystical signification of literal presence), what is called the "written Torah" preceded the "oral Torah," the latter then giving rise to an edited version that alone constitutes the Book. Thought is here confronted with an enigmatic proposition. Nothing precedes writing. Yet the writing of the first tablets becomes legible only after they are broken, and because they are broken—after and because of the resumption of the oral decision that leads to the second writing, the one with which we are familiar: rich in meaning, capable of issuing commandments, always equal to the law it transmits.

Let us attempt to examine this surprising proposition by relating it to what might be an experience of writing yet to come. There are two kinds of writing, one white, the other black: one that renders invisible the invisibility of a colorless flame; the other that is made accessible in the form of letters, characters, and articulations by the power of the black fire. Between the two there is the oral, which, however, is not independent, it being always involved with the second kind of writing inasmuch as it is this black fire itself, the measured obscurity that limits and delimits all light and makes all light visible. Thus what we call oral is designation in a present of time and a presence of space, but also, first of all, the development or mediation that is ensured by a discourse that explains, receives, and determines the neutrality of the initial inarticulation. The "oral Torah" is therefore no less written than the written Torah, but is called oral in the sense that, as discourse, it alone allows there to be communication, that is, allows the word to be enunciated in the form of a *commentary* that at once teaches and declares, authorizes and justifies: as though language (discourse) were necessary for writing to give rise to general legibility, and perhaps also to the Law understood as prohibition and limit; as though, as well, the first writing, in its configuration of invisibility, had to be considered as being *outside speech*, and as turned only toward the *outside*; an absence or fracture so originary it will have to be broken to escape the savagery of what Hölderlin calls the anorgic.

15. — Writing is absent from the Book; writing being the non-absent absence from out of which the Book, having absented itself from this absence (at both its levels: the oral and the written, the Law and its exegesis, the interdiction and the thought of the interdiction), makes itself legible and comments upon itself by enclosing history: the closure of the book, the severity of the letter, the authority of knowledge. What we can say of this writing that is absent from the book, and nonetheless stands in a relationship of alterity with it, is that writing remains foreign to legibility; illegible, then, inasmuch as to read is necessarily to enter through one's gaze into a relation of meaning or non-meaning with a presence. There would therefore be a writing exterior to the knowledge that is gained through reading, and also exterior to the form or the requirements of the Law. Writing, (pure) exteriority, foreign to every relation of presence, as to all legality.

As soon as the exteriority of writing *slackens*, that is, as soon as, in response to the appeal of the oral force, it accepts taking form in language by giving rise to the book—written discourse—this exteriority tends to appear: at the highest level as the exteriority of the Law, and, at the lowest, as the interiority of meaning. The Law is writing itself, writing that has renounced the exteriority of interdiction [*l'entre-dire*] in order to designate the place of the interdict. The illegitimacy of writing, always refractory in relation to the Law, hides the asymmetrical illegitimacy of the Law in relation to writing.

Writing: exteriority. Perhaps there is a "pure" exteriority of writing, but this is only a postulate already unfaithful to the neutrality of writing. In the book that signs our alliance with every Book, exteriority does not succeed in authorizing itself, and, in inscribing itself, inscribes itself in the space of the Law. The exteriority of writing, laying itself out and stratifying itself in the form of the book, becomes exteriority as law. The Book speaks as Law. Reading it, we read in it that everything that is, is either forbidden or allowed. But isn't this structure of authorization and interdiction a result of our level of reading? Might there not be another reading of the Book in which the book's other would cease to proclaim itself in precepts? And if we were to read this way, would we still be reading a book? Would we not be ready then to read *the absence of the book*?

The initial exteriority: perhaps we should assume that its nature is such that we would be unable to bear it except under the sanction of the Law. What would happen if the system of prohibition and limitations ceased to protect it? Or might it simply be there, at the limit of possibility, precisely to make the limit possible? Is this exteriority no more than an exigency of the limit? Is the limit itself conceived only through a delimitation that is necessary at the approach of the un-limited, a delimitation that would disappear if it were ever passed—for this reason impassable, yet always passed over precisely because it is impassable?

16. — Writing contains exteriority. The exteriority that becomes Law falls henceforth under the Law's protection; the Law, in turn, is written, that is to say, once again falls under the custody of writing. We must assume that this redou-bling of writing, a redoubling that from the outset designates it as difference, does nothing more than affirm in this duplicity the trait of exteriority itself, which is always becoming, always exterior to itself and in a relation of discontinuity. There is a "first" writing, but inasmuch as it is first, it is already distinct from it-self, separated by that which marks it, being at the same time nothing but this mark and yet also other than it if it thereby marks itself: so broken, distanced, denounced in this disjunctive outside where it announces itself that a new rupture will be necessary—a brisure that is violent but human (and in this sense, definite and delimited) so that, having become a text that shatters, and the initial fragmen-tation having given way to a determined act of rupture, the law, under the veil of interdiction, can offer a promise of unity.

In other words, the breaking of the first tablets is not a break with a first state of unitary harmony; on the contrary, what the break inaugurates is the substitu-tion of a limited exteriority (where the possibility of a limit announces itself) for an exteriority without limitation—the substitution of a lack for an absence, a break for a gap, an infraction for the pure-impure fraction of the fragmentary: that which, on the hither side of the sacred separation, presses in the scission of the neutral (the scission that is the neutral). To put it yet another way, it is neces-sary to break with the first exteriority so that with the second (where the logos is law and the law logos), language, henceforth regularly divided, in a reciprocal bond of mastery with itself and grammatically constructed, might engage us in the relations of mediation and immediation that guarantee discourse, and then with the dialectic, where the law in its turn will dissolve.

The "first" writing, far from being more immediate than the second, is foreign to all these categories. It does not give graciously through some ecstatic participa-tion in which the law protecting the One would merge with it and ensure confu-sion with it. The first writing is alterity itself, a severity and an austerity that never authorizes, the burning of a parching breath infinitely more rigorous than any law. The law is what saves us from writing by causing writing to be mediated through the rupture—the transitiveness—of speech. A salvation that introduces us to knowledge and, through our desire for knowledge, to the Book where knowledge maintains desire in dissimulating it from itself.

17. — The proper nature of the Law: it is infringed upon even when it has not yet been stated. Of course, it is henceforth promulgated from on high, at a dis-

tance and in the name of the distant, but without there being any relation of direct knowledge with those for whom it is destined. We might conclude from this that the law—as transmitted and as bearing transmission, thus becoming the law of transmission—establishes itself as law only through the decision to fall short of itself in some fashion: there would be no limit if the limit were not passed, revealed as impassable by being passed.

Yet does not the law precede all knowledge (including knowledge of the law), which it alone inaugurates in paving the way for its conditions by a prior "one must," if only on the basis of the Book in which the law attests to itself through the order—the structure—that it looms over as it establishes it?

Always anterior to the law, neither founded in nor determined by the necessity of being brought to knowledge, never imperiled by anyone's misunderstanding, always essentially affirmed by the infraction that supposes reference to it, drawing into its trial the authority that removes itself from it, and all the more firm for being open to facile transgression: the law.

The law's "one must" is first of all not a "thou shalt." "One must" applies to no one or, more determinedly, applies only to no one. The non-applicability of the law is not merely a sign of its abstract force, of its inexhaustible authority, of the reserve it maintains. Incapable of saying "thou," the law never aims at anyone in particular: not because it would be universal, but because it separates in the name of unity, being the very separation that enjoins with a view to the unique. Such is perhaps the law's august falsehood: having "legalized" the outside in order to make it possible (or real), the law frees itself of every determination and every content in order to preserve itself as pure inapplicable form, a pure exigency to which no presence can correspond, even though it is immediately particularized in multiple norms and through the code of alliance in ritual forms so as to permit the discrete interiority of a return to self, where the infrangible intimacy of the "thou shalt" will be affirmed.

18. — The Ten Commandments [*lois*] are law only in reference to Unity. God—the name that cannot be taken in vain because no language can contain it—is God only in order to uphold Unity and in this way designate its sovereign finality. No one can assail the One. And thus the Other bears witness, testifies to nothing Other than the Unique; a reference that unites all thought with what is not thought, keeping it turned toward the One as toward that upon which thought cannot infringe. It is therefore of consequence to say: not the One God but Unity, strictly speaking, is God, transcendence itself.

The exteriority of the law finds its measure in responsibility with regard to the One: an alliance of the One and the many that thrusts aside as impious the primordiality of difference. There nonetheless remains in the law itself a clause that retains a memory of the exteriority of writing, when it is said: thou shalt make no images, thou shalt not represent, thou shalt reject presence in the form of resemblance, sign, and mark. What does this mean? First, and almost too clearly, interdiction of the sign as a mode of presence. Writing, if to write is to refer back to the image and to invoke the idol, is inscribed outside the exteriority that is proper to it; an exteriority writing then rejects by attempting to fill it with the emptiness of words and with the pure signification of the sign. "Thou shalt make no idol" is thus, in the form of law, not a statement about the law, but about the exigency of writing that precedes every law.

19. — Let us grant that the law is obsessed with exteriority, by that which beleaguers it and from which it separates via the very separation that institutes it as form, in the very movement by which it formulates this exteriority as law. Let us grant that exteriority as writing, a relation forever without relation, can be called an exteriority that *slackens* into law precisely at the moment when it is *most taut*, when it has the tension of a gathering form. It is necessary to know that as soon as the law takes place (has found its place), everything changes; and it is the so-called initial exteriority that, in the name of the law henceforth impossible to denounce, gives itself as slackness itself, an undemanding neutrality, just as the writing outside the law, outside the book, seems now to be nothing more than the return to a spontaneity without rules, an ignorant automatism, an irresponsible movement, an immoral game. To put this differently, one cannot go back from exteriority as law to exteriority as writing; in this context, to go back would be to go down. That is to say: one cannot "go back up" save by accepting the fall, and being incapable of consenting to it; an essentially indeterminate fall into inessential chance (what the law disdainfully calls a game—the game in which everything is each time risked and everything lost: the necessity of the law, the chance of writing). The law is the summit, there is no other. Writing remains outside the arbitration between high and low.[1]

I would like to state that this book, in its articulated-inarticulated, mobile relation — that of its play — brings together texts for the most part written from 1953 to 1965. This indication of dates, referring to a long period of time, explains why I take them to be already posthumous, that is to say, regard them as being nearly anonymous.

Thus belonging to everyone and even written, always written, not by a single person, but by several: all those to whom falls the task of maintaining and prolonging the exigency to which I believe these texts, and with an obstinacy that today astonishes me, ceaselessly seek to respond, even unto the absence of the book *they designate in vain.*

Notes

Part I. Plural Speech (the speech of writing)
I. Thought and the Exigency of Discontinuity

1. Or let us say rather: poetry, the novel, are form—a word that, far from clarifying anything, now carries the whole of the interrogation.

2. At least this is Clémence Ramnoux's interpretation, *Héraclite ou l'homme entre les choses et les mots* (Paris: Les Belles Lettres, 1959).

3. This is expressed in tragic-parodic form in the last letter to Burckhardt: "Dear Professor, all things considered, I would rather be a professor at Basel than God."

4. But we must immediately add that one of the traits of philosophy as it manifests itself in Heidegger can be expressed in this way: Heidegger is essentially a writer, and therefore also responsible for a writing that is compromised (this is even one of the measures of his political responsibility).

5. This fault, if it is one, is explained in part by the fact that we do not possess the texts of Aristotle, but notes from courses, students' "notebooks."

6. See below the text devoted to "the future of surrealism": it appears that the surrealist demand, to the extent that it calls forth the unknown through chance and play, invites a relation that is foreign to the ideology of continuity.

7. When it is supposed (most often implicitly) that the "real" is continuous, and that only knowledge or expression would introduce discontinuity, it is first of all forgotten that the "continuous" is no more than a model, a theoretical form that, through this forgetting, passes for pure experience, pure empirical affirmation. But the "continuous" is only an ideology that is ashamed of itself, just as empiricism is merely a knowledge that repudiates itself.

Permit me to recall what set theory has allowed us to posit: contrary to what has long been affirmed, there is an infinite *power* that raises infinity beyond the continuous; or, the continuous is only an eminent case of infinity. Or again, as Jules Vuillemin has put it, "the infinite is the genus of which the continuous is a species," *La Philosphie de l'algèbre* (Paris: Presses Universitaires de France, 1962).

II. The Most Profound Question

1. See the second chapter of Dionys Mascolo's book, where he states: "There remains nothing more in reality but a question of the whole," *Le communisme* (Paris: Gallimard, 1953).

2. When, in Sophocles' *Oedipus the King*, the blind man and the clairvoyant man confront one another — the seer who knows by way of a non-knowing and the man of mind who mortally solves the riddle, the one who bears the sacred word and the one who clears space by deciphering (by reducing) this word, but who also draws the unspeakable into this void — there is issued this challenge (Oedipus to Tiresias): *"When the dark singer, the sphinx, was in your country, did you speak word of deliverance to its citizens? And yet the riddle's answer was not the province of a chance comer. It was a prophet's task and plainly you had no such gift of prophecy from birds nor otherwise from any God to glean a word of knowledge. But I came, Oedipus, who knew nothing, and I stopped her. I solved the riddle by my wit alone. Mine was no knowledge got from birds."* Here is precisely the opposition between two forms of response, that is to say, between two kinds of question. Why, in fact, was Tiresias — he *"who is versed in everything, things teachable and things not to be spoken, things of the sky, heaven, and of the earth"* — speechless before the riddle? To reply that he speaks only when the gods speak will not suffice; for with regard to Oedipus's secret, it seems that Tiresias needs neither birds nor rites to discover it, but only Oedipus's presence, reading his secret through the violence he discovers there and that constrains him to speak. Creon, who is Tiresias's ally, gives, as though in his place, this sign: *"The riddling Sphinx induced us to neglect mysterious crimes and rather seek solution of troubles at our feet."* Tiresias, the blind one, sees the mystery but does not fathom it. This also means that he fixes it in its place, there where it is, for fear that if he draws it out of its distance and its strangeness he will identify it and, through this identification, render it common and identical to the community, a community that from then on would no longer be separated from it, but mingled with that which separates, the pious impiety of separation. On the one hand, it is evident that the riddle of the Sphinx is meant for Oedipus alone (no one but he would know how to decipher it); on the other hand, it is evident also that Oedipus, in giving an answer that is valid for everyone, makes the riddle clear by a luminous universality, on the condition that he seem to keep for himself alone (taking it upon himself and appropriating it) the obscure horror that escapes revelation — as though in reserving being Oedipus for himself, he authorized us henceforth to be tranquilly "men." But in his challenge, what does he say to Tiresias?: *"Your life is one long night so that you cannot hurt me or any other who sees the light."* An arrogance of clear speech that comes from confidence in knowledge; hence the violence proper to him, that of an excess of knowledge. This too-much knowledge, having in one sweep attained the full form of universality (man as universal), makes him forget the reserve that he bears within himself and from which he excepts himself by forgetting — that part he cannot recognize as being true since it also has the status of being the non-true, the idle rupture, the radical infidelity marked by a double withdrawal of the divine and the human: non-presence itself. Let us add that Jocasta, the mother-spouse, reveals to Oedipus with a prodigious tranquillity, and precisely through the excuse of generality, the insignificance of the interdict against which his singularity must at once shatter and determine itself to the point of madness. For to Oedipus's avowed torment (*"But surely I must fear my mother's bed?"*) she responds by announcing desire without law via a recommendation (*"trust to fortune"*) that surely must be read as an invitation to transgress everything; a temptation meant to seduce the law itself in order that it in turn become enticing, seductive, deceptive: sovereignly impure. *"Why should man fear since chance is all in all for him, and he can clearly foreknow nothing? Best to live lightly, as one can, unthinkingly. As to your mother's marriage bed, — don't fear it. Before this, in dreams too, as well as Oracles, many a man has lain with his own mother. But he to whom such things are nothing bears his life most easily."* This is the same Jocasta who, through an indication intended for each of us, mysteriously designates in Oedipus his belonging to limit-speech, since for him there is no other speech than that where horror and terror speak and become

speech. "*He* (Oedipus) *is always at the speaker's mercy, when he speaks of terrors.*" Jocasta: the only one who possesses in her being the words of truth. This is why she bears the death that she begets, as though her true child were death, a child with whom she then by rights couples, just as her son does not fail to couple with this death each time that, coupling with his mother through want of knowledge, he returns to the anteriority of origin. [*Oedipus the King*, ed. D. Grene and R. Lattimore, trans. David Grene, *Greek Tragedies* vol. 1 (Chicago: University of Chicago Press, 1960).]

3. It would seem that this long text succeeds in one thing only: it indicates that there is a question that the question of the whole (dialectical accomplishment), the question that bears everything, does not include. And it also indicates that this question that escapes is not to be confused with the problematic of being.

Question of the whole, question of being: rather than being opposed, each question takes over the other. The question of being is for the dialectic only a moment — the most abstract and empty — of the way in which the whole realizes itself by becoming a question. From the perspective of ontology, the dialectic cannot pronounce on the being of the dialectic itself, any more than on the *this is* that is prior to the work of negation: the dialectic can begin only on the basis of a given that is devoid of meaning, and out of which it can then make meaning; the meaning of non-meaning is that without which there could be no meaning. One can only *negate* what was first *posited*, but this "positive" and this "first" remain outside the question. A more fundamental ontology claims to take up this question beyond question anew by transforming it into a question of the difference between being and what is (the "whole" elaborated by the work of the dialectic involves not being, but what is). Several difficulties have nonetheless immobilized ontology, putting it in question in its turn: (1) It has not found a language in which it can be said; the very language in which it speaks remains a language that belongs to the domain of what is. This supposed ontology is thereby formulated in the language of metaphysics. (This is the same problem Kant had already come up against in using the language of objectivity to speak of the conditions of objectivity in general.) (2) The thought that asks about being, that is to say, about the difference between being and what is — the thought that thus bears the very first question, renounces questioning. Heidegger says initially: "*questioning is the piety of thought*"; he then takes back his assertion and later substitutes another one for it: questioning is not what authentically bears thought; only hearing is authentic, the fact of hearing the saying wherein what must come into question announces itself. A decisive remark. It signifies: (a) that the question of being is not authentic, at least is not the most authentic question inasmuch as it is still a question; (b) that in whatever manner we question being, this question must have announced itself as speech, and that this speech must have announced itself, been transmitted to us by way of the voice; (c) that only *hearing* is authentic and not questioning. We begin by hearing; piety is no longer in questioning, but in hearing: piety is that which responds to the first exigency. But how is hearing to be understood? Is it the immediate reception of the immediate that admits no question? To hear, *hören*, hear [*ouir*], is also *hörig sein* — to obey. Hearing is submission to what is accorded according to what is. In *The Essence of Reason*, Heidegger says: Man speaks only when he responds to language according to what is meted out. But in the same work, he says that to hear is to seize by sight, to enter into seeing; "in Greek thought to say signifies to bring to show, to make a thing appear in the figure that is proper to it, to show it in the manner in which it regards us, and this is why, saying it, we see (understand) it clearly." (Compare this formulation: thought is an apprehending by hearing that apprehends by looking; compare also Goethe's remark: *if the eye were not akin to the sun*. And Heidegger denies the metaphorical character of this appeal to seeing for the reason that there is metaphor only where there is a distinction between the sensible and the non-sensible; that is to say, in metaphysics.) This corresponds to the idea that "being is shining." Hence the inordinate privilege accorded to sight: a privilege originally and implicitly presupposed not only by all metaphysics, but by all ontology (and, needless to add, all phenomenology), and according to which everything that is thought, everything that is said, has as its measure light or the absence of light. (3) This hearing that looks, this play of hearing and seeing is a play wherein there is at play "what is most high and most profound": The One. The question of being that dies away as a question is a question that dies away in hearing the One. The One, the Same, remain the first and the last words. Why this reference to the One as the ultimate and unique reference? In this sense, the dialectic, ontology, and the critique of ontology have the same postulate: all three deliver themselves over to the One: be it that the One accomplishes itself as everything, be it that it understands being as gathering, light, and unity of being, or be it that, above and beyond being, it affirms itself as the Absolute. With regard to such affirmations, must we not say: "the most profound question" is the question that escapes reference to the One? It is the other question, the question of the Other, but also a question that is always other.

IV. The Great Refusal

1. I am following here the movement by which Yves Bonnefoy—in a book already mysteriously illuminated by its title, *L'Improbable* (Paris: Mercure de France, 1959)—seeks to designate the place from which poetry speaks to us and realizes itself; a place that must therefore be situated "in the general economy of being." Thus we come again to the question of questions, the one that escapes the questioning of discourse.

2. [From Hölderlin's "As on a holiday . . . " ("Wie wenn am Feiertage"). I have translated *das Heilige* here as "the holy" (as is customary for these verses in English). Blanchot uses *le sacré*, which is more appropriately translated in English as "the sacred."]

3. Heidegger, commenting on Hölderlin.

4. In a beautiful text by Philippe Jaccottet, published in no. 23 of *Botteghe Oscure* (Rome: DeLuca Editore, 1959), I find once again established—or called for in the poem—the same mysterious relation between what might seem the most simple reality (or the simplicity of the real) and the footstep, the passing of a god. Likewise, Claude Vigée, a poet of exile and a poet in exile, seeks to say the reality of presence: "All poetry, fundamentally, is but a sign of recognition to what is." But he says also: "The poem is not being. It first reflects back your effort toward it, then bears witness, through you, to the one who is hidden among so many faces. Worship none of these languages." *Journal de l'été indien* (Paris: Gallimard, 1957).

5. I do not believe, however, that one is ever justifed in expressing oneself in this way. Poetry is not a means, any more than an end: it cannot belong to the order in which such an articulation of concepts has its place.

6. "La solitude essentielle," in *L'Espace Littéraire* (Paris: Gallimard, 1955). ["The essential solitude," in *The Space of Literature*, trans. Ann Smock (Lincoln: University of Nebraska Press, 1982); also "The essential solitude," in *The Gaze of Orpheus*, trans. Lydia David (New York: Station Hill Press, 1981).]

7. "Immediate" presence—presence (of) the immediate: an expression in which the predicate clause has no acceptable meaning. For in what way could this presence actualize what is called the immediate, as though it could ever be said to be non-present? And at the same time, how could it be said to be present, even by pleonasm? Does it not ruin all possibility of arrest in a present? A presence without present, without determinable content, without assignable term, but that is nevertheless not a form; a neutral, an empty or an infinite presence. The immediate as non-presence, that is to say, the immediately *other*.

8. Entirely different in character, this division is never made nor once and for all decided, just as one cannot confine the relations between two terms within a simple opposition—thinking, for example, that possibility is won from impossibility as day from night and that, at the end, when everything will have been affirmed in the evidence of light, impossibility cannot but be definitively mastered and the obscure resolved into clarity. This is a way of looking at things from which it would follow that someone who is concerned with the "impossible" is the enemy of possibility, and vice versa. I mention

these somewhat childish conceptions because they convey the untroubled certitudes of good sense for which clarifying and obscuring are decisively opposed, as are light and its absence. And to observe that, on the contrary, if ever one day everything were understood, as Lenin hoped, and if ever freedom, the heart of the possible, succeeded in affirming itself manifestly as the consummation of our power, then far from losing the measure of what is secret in it, we would be ready to respond to the summons of its hidden essence. This is what escapes those who want only to struggle for the possible, as it does those who would like to keep disdainfully apart from it.

Perhaps it is necessary that everything appear so that the meaning of the relation with the obscure might become more essential. Perhaps it is necessary that what we call light and what we call logos at last reign totally and realize themselves as the whole in order to be received in the affirmation that keeps them outside of the whole. Perhaps. But one cannot say this so simply, nor hasten to conclude that possibility and impossibility are held together in a mutual belonging that would already allow us to maintain them together, with difficulty, but happily, at the same time. How could it be thus?

V. Knowledge of the Unknown

1. Emmanuel Lévinas. *Totalité et infini, essai sur l'extériorité* (The Hague: Martinus Nijhoff, 1961). [*Totality and Infinity*, trans. Alphonso Lingis (Pittsburgh: Duquesne University Press, 1969, 1979).] [The French word *autrui* will consistently be left in French to differentiate it from *l'autre*. *Autrui* designates other people, neighbor (*prochain*), or fellow man. It is most generally used in French as a complement, as, for example, in "les enfants d'autrui."]

2. "Context" here, as Jacques Derrida very aptly observes, is a word that Lévinas could only deem inappropriate – just as he would the reference to theology. [Derrida, "Violence et métaphysique, essai sur la pensée d'Emmanuel Lévinas," in *L'écriture et la différence* (Paris: Seuil, 1967); *Writing and Difference*, trans. Alan Bass (Chicago: University of Chicago Press, 1978).]

VII. The Relation of the Third Kind (man without horizon)

1. Let me recall that Emmanuel Lévinas gave this turn of speech its determinant signification: "The curvature of space expresses the relation between human beings."

VIII. Interruption (as on a Riemann surface)

1. I have found something on this topic in Judith Robinson's book *L'Analyse de l'esprit dans les Cahiers de Valéry* (Paris: José Corti, 1963). Montel relates the following anecdote: "Mathematicians use a tool called a Riemann surface: it is an ideal note-pad made up of as many pages as necessary, fastened together according to certain rules, and whose total thickness amounts to nearly nothing. Upon this leaved surface numbers are inscribed, some of which occupy the same place upon different sheets. In the course of a conversation, Valéry said to me: 'Don't you find that conversations occur on a Riemann surface? I make a remark to you, it is inscribed upon the first sheet; but at the same time I prepare on the second sheet what I will say to you next, and even on a third sheet what will come after. From your side, you respond to me upon the first sheet, while at the same time putting in reserve on other sheets what you intend to say to me later.' " Of course the image remains very unsatisfying since here discourse, instead of implying a true dehiscence of language, only calls upon what one might name the principle of deferred speech.

2. Or let us say this again more simply: the protagonists of a dialogue speak in a divided manner not only because each of them bears a personal, limited, and different affirmation that would like to become common (this is the dialectical perspective); but also because they speak in order to make speech speak as difference – which is also to realize the very interruption that alone decides difference as speech.

Part II. The Limit-Experience
I. Heraclitus

1. I would like to express the gratitude I am not alone in feeling to the authors of works like Clémence Ramnoux's *Héraclite ou l'homme entre les choses et les mots* (Paris: Les Belles-Lettres, Guillaume Budé 1968, c. 1959). A thesis; therefore something put together with severe erudition, a network composed of pure research, a report on studies undertaken in the course of entire lifetimes on some few words by very learned scholars — for a thesis, it is true, this is necessary. But this thesis is also a simple meditation, lively yet profound, and fascinating in that it responds to the force of fascination of texts that speak to us in words of evidence and obscurity of something essential. Here we share not only a knowledge but also a passion and a kind of intimacy of reading to which a whole life was devoted, and not simply out of a taste for work. To have lived close to Heraclitus while other, very close dangers were traversing the times bespeaks the choice by which "this proud genius, stable and anxious," as René Char names her, is still, and in response to immediate necessities, capable of soberly guiding our lives.

I will indicate the course of thought to which the project of such a book responded. In this thesis it is a matter not of a thesis but of a concern; the desire to read texts in the most simple manner possible, and without the resources a philosophical language that was established afterward put dangerously at our disposal. To understand these ancient words is to let them speak on their own, but in the way they speak to us in our free belonging to what is most proper to us. There are thus two dangers, both of them inevitable; one is to read Plato, Christian spirituality, and Hegel in place of Heraclitus, the other is to hold to a historical research capable, through erudition, of making us masters of a world that has disappeared and of a dead truth. This makes two already serious difficulties. And when it is a question of a text in shreds and an enigmatic author, then it is to the superabundance of enigmas that we must loyally give ourselves so as to support our reading — a reading that with clarity and naturalness must always hold in reserve more meaning than we can lend it.

2. Fragment 32: "*One Thing, the only Wise Thing, is unwilling and willing to be called by the name Zeus.*" [My translation of the fragments Blanchot cites has followed those proposed by T. M. Robinson in *Heraclitus, Fragments* (Toronto: University of Toronto Press, 1987), with slight modification where it seemed indicated for consistency with Blanchot's readings.]

3. For Heraclitus, as Abel Jeannière notes, the divine is in the neuter. This is a most important trait, and one whose meaning is most difficult to approach.

4. Let me cite these examples as illustration: "Life-Death" is coupled with "Wakefulness-Sleep" [fragment 21]: "Death is what we see awake, Sleep what we see while sleeping." In this fragment a place seems reserved for the word Life, which is absent, but which calls up the word Death, so that one can read (one possibility) "It is Life-and-Death that we discover in waking" and interpret it to say, as does Clémence Ramnoux, that to awake is to discover that life and death are necessarily linked, while men asleep continue to live-and-die a false appearance of life belied. Unless Life and Death become interchangeable as reciprocally changing functions, at times verb and at times complement; this offers us the remarkable formulation "living death," "dying life," which is found in several fragments. Entering into composition with the couple "men-gods," such formulations give us this extreme movement of language: "Immortal Mortals, Mortal Immortals: living their death and dying their life" [fragment 62]. A game of exchange whose general formulation is indicated in fragment 88: "For the latter, having changed round, are the former, and the former, having changed round, are again the latter."

5. Heraclitus's formulations obey strict arrangements that are unmodifiable and yet constitute the form for a whole series of possible modifications. Reduced to their form, they can be read in this way: any two contraries whatsoever, taken as subject, have as attribute "the One," "the Same," "the Thing in common." Or else two contraries are attributed to a common subject. Or a subject attributes to itself its own contrary. Or two verbs having contrary meanings, or employed with yes and no, go with the same subject ("is unwilling and willing to be called"; "We step and do not step into the same river").

6. It is true that this is a reproach Socrates, in the *Theatetus*, puts in the mouth of a supposed adversary, meaning to exclude himself from it; but there are other passages in which Socrates ironically praises himself for knowing how to turn in a circle and lazily lose himself on the longest circuits: this, he says, is our path. I imagine Ramnoux would not allow herself to lead us to this comparison. In seeking what Heraclitus most highly prized, however, she almost always responds: "It is intelligent conversation . . . conversation between friends able to understand one another." The idea of teaching, in the strict sense, becomes so preponderant that she proposes we translate logos by the word lesson. She nonetheless does not forget to set "conversation" back into an institutional framework: perhaps teaching took as its model the transmitting of formulas during ceremonies of initiation. According to tradition, it would appear that Heraclitus's work was a *written* work, and that he himself left it in the temple in the care of the goddess (perhaps because this work addresses itself no less to the gods than to men). In fragment 1, there is allusion to a work of distinguishing words and things [*découpage*]; one wonders whether this task did not have a precise technical meaning at a time when Greek was written without separating words and without punctuation.

7. Fragment 18: "If (one) does not expect (the Thing) unexpected, (one) will not discover (it); for (it) is not to be found out and impenetrable" (it is undiscoverable and offers no access). Ramnoux here notes that the Thing is designated solely by negatives—neuter and privative nouns. One must turn one's waiting toward a Thing determinable solely by negative attributes. (But does the negative have the same value for Heraclitus as for us? That is, do we know whether in writing we may not be playing with a difference that undoes the alternative of positive and negative?)

8. What opposes one term to another is the passage from scintillating ambiguity to hard contrariety. One may live in indifference and as a sleepwalker between night and day, but as soon as the severe difference day-night has become present the tragic choice begins. To choose wakefulness over sleep, to choose the gods of clarity and do an injustice to the nocturnal forces: this is each time the tragic choice, as the for and the against are equal. One of Heraclitus's responses: one must choose Difference, not one of the differing terms.

9. René Schaerer, *L'Homme antique et la structure du monde intérieur, d'Homère à Socrate* (Paris: Payot, 1958). Schaerer also says of Greek man: "He equalizes the for and the against, waiting for the heavens to make the scales lean to one or the other side. And the sky, before making the scales tip, waits for man to balance them." This indicates that equality is necessary so the inequality of discourse, a difference of level, cannot be interpreted as a simple refusal of what is equal.

10. Fragment 93: "*The lord whose oracle is at Delphi neither speaks nor conceals, but gives a sign.*"

II. Measure, the Suppliant

1. Edmond Beaujon has devoted to this theme an essay from which we learn a great deal in *Le Dieu des Suppliants: poésie grecque et la loi de l'homme* (Neuchâtel: Baconnière, 1960).

2. Through his body bowed low to the ground rather than prone—postures that are moreover both designated by the word *prostrate*—and without first releasing his voice from silence so as to let the immobility in which he holds himself speak, the suppliant announces his state of mourning, prefigures his death, assumes his condemnation, and gives himself up to waiting; a waiting that awaits nothing and thus purifies and initiates (as Marcel Detienne has shown in *Les Maîtres de vérité dans la Grèce archaïque* (Paris: Maspéro, 1967).

3. It is true, the refusal of a meal signifies a great deal: refusal of fraternity, repugnance at entering into domestic friendship. It is as though Priam wanted to remain the stranger, the interdicted, and were thus giving grave offense to Hestia, the divinity through which is expressed and confirmed the sacred permanence of the home. See Jean-Pierre Vernant's *Mythe et pensée chez les Grecs* (Paris: Maspéro, 1965). [*Myth and Thought among the Greeks*, trans. Paul Kegan (Boston: Routledge, 1983).]

III. Tragic Thought

1. "Faith embraces many truths which seem self-contradictory—*a time to laugh, to weep*, etc. *Responde; ne respondeas*, etc. The source of this is the union of the two natures in Jesus Christ, and also of the two worlds (creation of a new heaven and a new earth; new life, new death; all things doubled, yet the same names persisting). And finally the two human types in the righteous (for they are the two worlds, and a member of Jesus Christ and His image. And so all names are appropriate to them: righteous and sinners; dead, living; living, dead; elect, condemned, etc.)" (Fragment 462, Lafuma edition; "Adversia," Fragment 175). [I follow for the most part the English translation proposed by H. F. Stewart in *Pascal's Pensées* (New York: Pantheon, 1965). The numbering of the fragments thus appears as follows: first, that of the Lafuma edition, as indicated by Blanchot; then the numbering employed by Stewart. Fragment numbers are indicated when they appear in the French text.]

"The two contrary reasons. We must begin with that: otherwise we understand nothing, and everything is heresy; and even when one truth is established, we must add that we remember the opposite truth" (Fragment 460; "Apology," Fragment 619). In the same vein, *Source of contradictions* (Fragment 448; "Apology," Fragments 559 ff).

2. "We possess truth and good, but only partially and mixed with evil and falsehood" (Fragment 298; "Apology," Fragment 197).

3. Lucien Goldmann. *Le dieu caché* (Paris: Gallimard, 1959). [*The Hidden God*, trans. Philip Thody (New York: Humanities Press, 1964).] One will hardly be surprised that Goldmann's interpretation does justice to the rigor of Pascal's thought and the saintliness of his research better than do most Christian commentaries. It is true that Goldmann does not in the least believe all problems are solved because some key phrases of the great Marxist interpreters might offer a response to them. His approach to questions and his examination of difficulties always show both prudence and liberty, even a robust simplicity. Let us add that Goldmann is not the first to have recognized in Pascal a form of thought as distinct from Cartesian rationalism as it is different from skeptical contestation; a thought that remains, despite the word heart, an exigent reasoning. The most simple reading indicates this. The opposition to Descartes is invincible. Moreover, it is a majestic phenomenon that thought, not content with affirming itself as sovereignly as it does in Descartes, should, at nearly the same moment, find a mind as imperious in which it shows itself capable of a very different sovereignty that, over and against the other, discovers the uncertainty of principles and discovers in this uncertainty an entirely new necessity. And these two possibilities will remain inexhaustible and nearly unshakable. The power to begin, the initial clarity, the liberty of a first and evident decision belong today, as they did three centuries ago, to the force of the *Cogito*. But when a different reason finds it impossible to be satisfied with this beginning; when it perceives only the absence of any point of departure and the incessant necessity of infinitely beginning anew; when it already sees the against in the for, and in the reversal of the for and the against a still stronger force; when it finds in this seeking of contraries that it is not merely divided but also affirmed and as though gathered back together—such a reason will know itself under Pascal's mask of authority.

4. This expression was borrowed from Georg Lukács.

5. Goldmann explains in this manner certain contradictions in Pascal's life, adding that it is at the moment when Pascal is writing the *Pensées*, that is, when he is inclining to the greatest religious rigor, that he returns to a certain scientific activity; then, the latter ceasing around 1660, probably for reasons of health, he returns to certain worldly activities such as the enterprise of public five-penny carriages. Not expecting "anything essential from the world any more than from the militant Church," Pascal "saves his exigency for totality through an *outward* submission to political and ecclesiastical power, and through a life in the world and in a scientific activity that are *at the same time* a radical refusal of every compromise with power through paradox, tragedy, and a call to God." Goldmann differentiates very well this attitude from two others that are extreme (that of Jacqueline Pascal and that of Barcos).

6. Etienne Souriau, *L'ombre de Dieu* (Paris: Presses Universitaires de France, 1955).

7. As does the following, commented upon by Goldmann: "Learn from those who have been bound like you, and who now stake all they possess." Wagering, says Goldmann, has the sense of believing. This equivalency seems too simple.

8. Souriau concludes quite differently that "God is justified because he exists; in showing himself, he absolves himself." For Souriau, the wager would be an attempt to engage God in the wager.

9. " . . . nor, on the other hand, was it right that He should come in so hidden a manner that He could not be known by those who sought Him sincerely. He wanted to render Himself perfectly knowable to these; and thus, willing to appear openly to those who seek Him with all their hearts and to remain hidden from those who shun Him with all their hearts, He modified knowledge of Himself to the extent of bestowing visible marks thereof upon those who seek Him, but not upon those who do not. There is light enough for those who only desire to see, and darkness enough for those who are contrary-minded" (Fragment 309; "Apology," Fragment 249).

10. One must wonder whether, in the *Memorial*, Pascal himself did not leave us a clearly mystical document. One must also wonder whether it is not possible for tragic thought, as such, to become a mystical movement. I read in an essay by Georges Bataille: "The atheistic mystic, self-conscious, conscious of having to die and to disappear, would live, as Hegel *obviously said concerning himself*, 'in absolute dismemberment'; but for him, it is only the matter of a certain period: unlike Hegel, he would never come out of it, 'contemplating the Negative right in the face,' but never being able to transpose it into Being, refusing to do it, and maintaining himself in ambiguity" ("Hegel, la mort et le sacrifice," *Deucalion* 5, 1955. ["Hegel, Death and Sacrifice," in *Yale French Studies* 78, 1990, trans. Jonathan Strauss, ed. Allan Stoekl.] If we replace the word ambiguity with the word paradox, the movement that Georges Bataille takes to be mystical corresponds to that of a tragic thought.

11. Another translation, that is to say, another interpretation of this fragment is possible: "*What is God? Unknown to him, yet / rich with his qualities is the aspect / of the sky. Lightning in fact / anger of a God. All the more invisible, is what is destined (delegates itself) to strangeness.*"

12. Cf. Heidegger's commentary, " . . . Dichterisch wohnet der Mensch . . . " [in *Vorträge und Aufsätze*, 4th ed. (Pfüllingen: Neske, 1959)]: "For Hölderlin, God, as the one who he is, is unknown and it is just as *this Unknown One* that he is the measure for the poet. . . . What is the measure for human measuring? God? No. The sky? No. The manifestness of the sky? No. The measure consists in the way in which the god who remains unknown is revealed *as* such by the sky. . . . Thus the unknown god appears as the unknown by way of the sky's manifestness. This appearance is the measure against which man measures himself." [" . . . Poetically Man Dwells . . . ," in Martin Heidegger, *Poetry, Language, Thought*, trans. Albert Hofstadter (New York: Harper & Row, 1975).]

13. What form would suit tragic thought? A paradoxical form, and an expression that is fitting only in the *fragment*, says Goldmann. Paradoxical: which means that this thought always carries to the extreme the contrary affirmations it must maintain together, even though, unable to avoid paradox, it cannot accept it either, for what it seeks is the accomplishment of the synthesis that it affirms absolutely, but as absolutely absent. Paradoxical is thus the contrary of ambiguous. Paradox always demands the greatest clarity in the greatest contrariety; its words are always extremely strong, and are understood only when heard in all their force, although this understanding can only impose itself as broken. The fragment: if, for Goldmann, the *Pensées* remained in the form of thoughts, it is because the fragment is the only form of expression suited to a paradoxical work, affirming that man is a paradoxical being who encounters truth only in the obscurity of the mystery that is paradox. "To seek the 'true' plan of the *Pensées* thus appears to us to be an eminently anti-Pascalian enterprise." And it is indeed true that one could not read this book without being bothered by every logical plan and without recognizing as essential the abrupt separation of its parts, which, while without relation, are yet strongly bound by this absence of relation that is never disorder. For the *Pensées* are also, essentially,

the search for an order and the exigency of order, and, because of this, thoughts that will find no plan satisfactory. But if such is the tragic work, what is tragic art? Is there a single *work* that is tragic?

IV. Affirmation (desire, affliction)

1. Let us, however, recall what she wrote in her notes from America: "*In any case, a new religion is needed. Either a Christianity so modified as to have become a different thing, or something else.*" ["New York Notebook, 1942," in *First and Last Notebooks*, trans. Richard Rees (London: Oxford University Press, 1970).] Irregularity is even more difficult to maintain in the case of mystical thought, for it is in its essence irregular. Moreover, references abound: in the admirably varied domain of religious minds, there is always someone one resembles and this resemblance then seems sufficient to account for everything. Finally, the dispersal of Simone Weil's writings, the fact that the most important among them are notes in still uncertain form or, even more troubling, occasional writings that received from the occasion their provisional orientation, all of this allows one to attribute to her — or take away from her — a part of what she said, and without too much bad faith. With the exception of some texts written before her departure from France, it seems she is most completely herself in the fragments and short *pensées*. (The book she envisioned, and for which the brief mystical account entitled "Prologue" was to constitute a beginning, would have been, it seems, a book of meditations.) In this respect she is no less close to Nietzsche, whom she did not like, than to Pascal, whom she also did not like.

2. Thus, there is more "reality" (naturally this word causes difficulties) in the idea of the Good, even if it be illusory, than in all that exists. We ought therefore to turn ourselves absolutely away from what is falsely good here below and live turned absolutely toward the idea of the Good, without worrying about knowing whether this idea is an illusion from the point of view of existence, for it is superior in dignity to everything, preferable to everything, even if it is an illusion. The category of existence, in any case, is not suited to the Good. But Simone Weil does not seek to think, or succeed in thinking, the ontological status of the Good. Is the Good that is outside existence above Being, as Plato affirmed? And then what is the meaning of our speech when it claims to formulate this relation by which the Good would renounce Being, renounce existing? Would not the thought of the Good break with transcendence, as with immanence, and provoke in thought itself a discontinuity by which there would be no "good" other than that of a discontinuous, that is to say infinite, speech?

3. Jacques Cabaud, *L'expérience vécue de Simone Weil* (Paris: Plon, 1957). [Jacques Cabaud, *Simone Weil: A Fellowship in Love* (New York: Channel Press, 1964).]

4. As far as we know (but we do not know everything), Simone Weil spoke of this to two people: Father Perrin and Joë Bousquet, and the latter because he questioned her. The account of her experience (the "Prologue"), which is found in her *Notebooks* and is a mythic transposition of this same event, deliberately avoids putting it in question.

5. Gershom G. Scholem, *Les grands courants de la mystique juive*, trans. M.-M. Davy (Paris: Payot, 1950). [*Major Trends in Jewish Mysticism*, trans. George Lichtheim (New York: Schocken, 1961, c. 1941).]

6. The identity of God and man, in this common movement of disappearance in the "nothing," is the obstacle that does not permit Simone Weil to choose between the natural and the surnatural paths of salvation, nor does it permit her to think through the meaning of this choice. We are naturally supernatural in our hidden depth that is in this movement, now and from here in our nature, God in us, us in God.

7. I refer to the essay "How to Discover the Obscure?" which appears in Part I of the present collection.

8. It is for this reason that Robert Antelme's account of man reduced to the extreme affliction of need in the world of the German deportation camps can be given the title *L'espèce humaine* (Paris: Gallimard, 1978, c.1957). He says: "I relate here what I lived." "The horror was not of gigantic

proportion. At Gandersheim there were neither gas chambers nor crematories. There the horror was obscurity: an absolute lack of reference, solitude, ceaseless oppression, slow annihilation. The motive of our struggle, finally, was only the ruthless demand, itself almost always solitary, to remain up to the end men." As we will see, this book is of an exceptional significance.

9. This is what she writes: "*Attention consists in suspending one's thought, in leaving it detached, empty and ready to be penetrated by the object; it means holding in our minds, within reach of this thought, but on a lower level and not in contact with it, the diverse sorts of knowledge we have acquired and which we are forced to make use of. But above all, our thought should be empty, waiting, not seeking anything.*"

10. I have testimony, however, that says something else: some of her friends have written to tell me how often in her life she could be silent, reserved, and as though without movement.

V. The Indestructible

1. Albert Memmi. *Portrait d'un Juif* (Paris: Gallimard, 1962).

2. André Neher. *L'existence juive* (Paris: Seuil, 1962).

3. See the work of Isaac Heinemann, adapted by Charles Touati, *La loi dans la pensée juive* (Paris: Albin Michel, Collection Présences du Judaisme, 1962).

4. Without any further conclusions, let me anticipate an objection. I can indeed understand why many who are horrified by anti-Semitism wish to silence those who accuse the Jews by attenuating the importance of the question that comes to us from them. They protest against what they call the metaphysics of the Jewish question; they say it feeds hate for the Jews because this hate is nourished by a myth that has nothing to do with the real conditions of existence. One must therefore deny this question any meaning that would not be simply historical and seek the means to respond to it only in the history that brought it to us. No doubt. But here distinctions must be made. I observe, on the one hand, that anti-Semites, too, seek fundamentally only to avoid the metaphysical exigency that Judaism poses to each of us by way of Jewish existence, and that it is in order better to suppress this question that they want to suppress all Jews (that is to say, radically denounce being-Jewish). To neglect this aspect of anti-Semitism is to renounce coming to grips with its gravity, to renounce finding in it one of its roots, and therefore to refuse to see what is at stake when, in the world, in whatever form it may take, anti-Semitism affirms and strengthens itself. But on the other hand, certainly, the relations that link being-Jewish to a people or to a specific nation are also historical relations that must not be considered as being outside history; and these are relations that the work of men in history is called upon to change. At the end of his book, Albert Memmi asks: "Is this all in the past? I think it is, in part. It is possible that we have entered into an entirely new period of history that will see the progressive liquidation of the oppression undergone by the Jew. But in addition to the fact that regression is always possible, this process has only begun. And it has already begun several times." The rebirth of the State of Israel, as well as our greater consciousness of what conditions of oppression are may cause us to advance along this path. It ought to remain clear, however, that the question expressed by the words "being-Jewish" and by the question of the State of Israel cannot be identical questions, although each modifies the other. I recall Hermann Cohen's remark regarding the Zionists, as cited by Rosenzweig, who neither criticizes it nor assents to it: "These hearty souls want to be happy." After the advent of Hitler he would not have been able to entertain this reflection so simply. For then it became manifest that it was not a question of being happy, but of being. But the hunger for life implies, precisely as Rosenzweig says it does, the metaphysical obligation to live (and perhaps also to be happy), so that to ensure the possibility of a free existence to a people—be it by the reconstruction of a "place of sojourn," and by the perhaps dangerous means of a national claim—is still the most urgent task. Yet if this task itself, which passes by way of the edification of a dwelling place and, finally, of a state, partially responds to the question of safeguarding the Jews, it cannot constitute a response to the question that being-Jewish poses, which is a universal question. We can be assured that this

task only produces the question in a new light. Here I will cite a remark of André Neher. He notes that Theodor Herzl, and in a general way Zionist ideology, have proposed a purely Western solution for a situation that is specifically Oriental (perhaps it would be better to say: a situation exceeding all determined historical signification); this solution entails a State, as though the entire movement carried by Judaism ought to tend toward nothing other than the foundation of a State conceived on the nineteenth-century model, claiming for itself the reality of the Law, and affirming the whole, transcendence. I cite again André Neher: "The question of whether the State of Israel shall be religious or laic—whether it will be capable of realizing itself in a sharing or in a synthesis of these two dimensions (or even in being neither laic nor religious)—does not fall within the province of political parties but of philosophers: the entire Jewish vocation is in question." I would be tempted to conclude by saying that in the society that is being tried in Palestine—a society caught up in struggle, under threat and also threatened by nothing less grave than the necessity of this struggle for "safeguarding" (as is also the case in the societies that have issued from Marxism or been liberated from colonial bondage)—it is philosophy itself that is being dangerously measured against power inasmuch as this society, like the others, will have to determine the meaning and the future of "nomadic truth" in the face of the state.

5. Robert Antelme. *L'espèce humaine* (Paris: Gallimard, 1978, c. 1957).

6. See below: "Reflections on Hell."

7. Why collective? Because it is a question of coming back to truth as the affirmation and the question of the whole; totality cannot be posited, either in knowledge or in action, unless the subject does so in and as a movement toward that "totality," and is, himself, already a form of the whole.

8. But this (should it be necessary to state it explicitly) is the most difficult: first because there is a kind of irreducible opposition between the man that is Other [*l'homme Autre*], the absolutely deprived, and any kind of force, even if this force is protective. Robert Antelme says this with a decisive simplicity: "A suspicion always hangs here over the man who is still strong. . . . He does not defend us by the means that are ours, but with the force of muscle that no one here possesses. And this man, doubtless useful, effective, does not seem to be one of us."

9. With the experience that he draws from himself and from his learning, Gerschom Scholem has said, speaking of the relations between the Germans and the Jews: "The abyss opened between us by these events cannot be measured. . . . For, in truth, it is impossible to realize completely what happened. Its incomprehensible nature has to do with the very essence of the phenomenon: it is impossible fully to understand it, that is to say, integrate it into our consciousness." Impossible, therefore, to forget it, impossible to remember it. Also impossible, in speaking about it, to speak of it—and finally, as there is nothing but this incomprehensible event to say, it is speech alone that must bear it without saying it.

VI. Reflections on Nihilism

1. F. Nietzsche, *Werke in drei Bänden* (*Works in Three Volumes*), ed. Karl Schlechta (Munich: Carl Hanser, 1956). Schlechta gathered his commentaries in a short volume entitled *Der Fall Nietzsche* (*The Nietzsche Case*) (Munich: Carl Hanser, 1958). I might note that these reflections go back more than a dozen years. The works of Nietzsche have since been published in France by Gallimard under the direction of Colli and Montinari, thus making available to us, in their entirety and in their integrity, the texts that came out during Nietzsche's lifetime and posthumously.

2. A word must be said concerning yet another of Mme. Förster-Nietzsche's initiatives, one less grave but more sordid. Certainly one had learned to mistrust her. Overbeck, Bernouilli, and Podach had made it known that she was capable of altering texts. Her intrigues in the painful Lou affair were known. Nonetheless, to those who contested her right to speak for Nietzsche and to assume with regard to his thought the power of exclusive decision, she responded by presenting a whole series of letters in which her brother treated her as his privileged confidante. The originals of these letters had

disappeared, but one could not doubt their authenticity. It was after her death, in 1935, that Schlechta, assisted by E. Thierbach and W. Hoppe, threw light on this mystery by finding the drafts of some letters. The letters were indeed by Nietzsche, but addressed to his mother or to Malwida von Meysenburg. This strange sister had thus appropriated the expressions of confidence that had not been meant for her in order to find in them the moral and intellectual guarantee she needed for her enterprise. She had destroyed the original letters and touched up the drafts rather crudely. (Why had she not destroyed them? Doubtless because they authenticated the letters; an ink spot wasn't out of place on a draft, nor surprising on Nietzsche's part inasmuch as his myopia made him clumsy.) All these falsifications required a persevering spirit and a good deal of energy, and this formidable woman lacked neither. It is almost certain that she suppressed important biographical documents, notably the medical prescriptions that would have shed light on Nietzsche's illnesses. See the work by R. Blunck that mentions the treatment Nietzsche underwent in Leipzig for syphilis. (But must we add that it is not, finally, the person of Elisabeth Förster-Nietzsche that is important in this still obscure story? For some commentators have judged that it would be unjust to make too much of a role that was not always unfortunate, and that familial devotion explains all too easily. What to my mind remains decisive is that, for those who were subject to Hitler's advent, the use of Nietzsche's name does not belong to a history that is conjectural; it was rather a part of everyday political experience. It could be read in the newspapers. Some of us, on November 4, 1933, were made aware of the following information, which appeared in the press: *"Before leaving Weimer to travel to Essen, Chancellor Hitler paid a call on Mme. Elisabeth Förster-Nietzsche, sister of the famous philosopher. The elderly lady gave him a walking-stick with a sword that had belonged to her brother. Mr. Hitler listened with interest to a reading of the report that Doctor Förster, Nietzsche's brother-in-law and an anti-Semite propagandist, had addressed to Bismarck in 1879, and who from that date continued to direct attention to the dangers 'that the preponderance of the Jewish spirit posed to Germany.' Holding Nietzsche's walking-stick in his hand, and amidst much applause, Mr. Hitler made his way through the crowd and then left in his car for Essen, via Efurt."* That same day, November 2, 1933, in Weimar, Hitler had a photograph taken of himself next to a statue of Nietzsche, a photo that Richard Oehler reproduced shortly afterward in his book *Nietzsche et l'avenir de l'Allemagne* [*Friedrich Nietzsche und die deutsche zukunft* (Leipzig: Armanen-Verlag, 1935)], in which he turns Nietzsche into something like the prefacer of *Mein Kampf*. Richard Oehler, related to the Nietzsche family, played at this time an important role in the "Nietzsche-Archiv" and beside Elisabeth Förster, whose advanced age – she was 86 – frees her in part from responsibility, at least as regards this ceremony.)

3. This was already affirmed in 1906 by A. Lamm who, from that date on, protested against overestimation of the posthumous texts. But as only a part of them were known to him, this affirmation must also be taken as polemical. Lamm (like Schlechta) fails to recognize – a misreading of the gravest sort – not only what the reworked or repeated versions of a same "idea" bring forth that is new, but also the meaning of repetition itself: its new relation to meaning.

4. I think it should be recalled that, well before Schlechta, and at least from 1936 on (in a series of lectures on Nietzsche that were in part given from 1936 to 1939, and published in 1961 in two volumes [(Pfüllingen: Neske, 1961); these have been published in English by Harper & Row, edited by David Farrell Krell: vol. 1, *The Will to Power as Art* (1979), trans. Krell; vol. 2, *The Eternal Recurrence of the Same* (1984), trans. Krell; vol. 3, *The Will to Power as Knowledge and as Metaphysics* (1987), trans. Frank A. Capuzzi; vol. 4, *Nihilism* (1982), trans. Capuzzi]), Heidegger questioned in the firmest and most authoritative manner, if not the editors, at least the publication of the text of Nietzsche for which they were responsible. Under the heading (which in itself is significant) *"das sogennante 'Hauptwerk,' "* Nietzsche's "so-called 'major work,' " Heidegger denounces in an important chapter (p. 481 ff., vol. 1) the arbitrariness in choice and classification of the notes borrowed from the years 1884–88 and published under the title *The Will to Power*, "even though the thought of the Will to Power was only *now and again* foremost for Nietzsche." "By this arbitrary choice,

which bases itself in fact on plans that for Nietzsche are very sketchy, Nietzsche's philosophy became the philosophy of the Will to Power" (at the expense of the thought of the Eternal Return).

What then, asks Heidegger, about this work entitled *The Will to Power?* We must oppose to it uncontestable facts: (1) despite what he announced, Nietzsche never produced this work; (2) he later abandoned both the plan and the title. . . . That is why, to come back to the essential of Nietzsche's thought that remained unpublished during his lifetime, the work entitled *The Will to Power* could not have a determining value. Even the plan is but a passing phase within the work that is evolving. Heidegger further adds, which is essential: the "Hauptwerk" was never finished; not only was it not completed, but it never became a "work" in the sense of modern philosophical works (Descartes, Kant, Hegel).

Why were the steps of the thought that was destined to lead to the "Will to Power" never able to lead to a work of classical structure? The answer is all too readily given: one says that a single thinker, alone, could not measure up to the task of mastering such a subject, which involves logic, ethics, aesthetics, the philosophy of language, and political and religious philosophy. Or one says that Nietzsche did not have the aptitude for forming a systematic philosophy; moreover, that he himself made his mistrust known regarding every systematic thinker. One says as well that Nietzsche was the victim of a disproportionate pressure, both interior and exterior—a pressure such that he was unable to escape the temptation of acting or of immediately showing off to advantage. One adds that, precisely during the years when Nietzsche's task was to "systematize" the reflections on the Will to Power, he lacked the force to work and to concentrate. Heidegger then remarks: These explanations are right *on condition* one presupposes that, in what was being prepared, it was a matter of a *work*, and most particularly a work in the form of the philosophical *Hauptwerk*. This presupposition is unfounded and is even without truth (*unwhar*), because it contradicts what is at stake in the very thought of the Will to Power. Even if Nietzsche, in his letters (and especially those to his sister), speaks of a "Hauptwerk," this does not suffice to justify such a "prejudice." Nietzsche saw all too well that those who were close to him were incapable of measuring the exigency to which he found himself exposed. "Incompleteness" is thus a word that is out of place, for it can only mean that the inner form of this unique thought would have refused itself to the thinker; but perhaps it did not refuse itself: perhaps this refusal (*Versagen*) is only encountered in the work of those who bury (*verschütten*) the movement of thought under premature and circumstantial interpretations. It is only through the arbitrary presupposition of a work wrongly supposed to be destined to completion that one can take for a "sketch," a "preliminary labor," a *"Bruchstück"* or *"Fragment"* what Nietzsche left behind him without having it published. There is no other choice. If this presupposition is entirely without foundation and does not accord with the fundamental thought of this thinker, *then* the traces of the posthumous thoughts take on an entirely different character. Or, to speak more prudently: the question that should first be asked is how these traits or these leaps of thought are to be taken so we can think them without accommodating them to our intellectual habits. Heidegger concludes: "Therefore this book is not a 'work' of Nietzsche. . . . This work can of course serve as a basis for attempting to think this unique thought—*on condition* that we free ourselves, in advance and completely, from the order that was established for the published book." Heidegger observes that he, in any case, will also follow an *apparently* arbitrary order, but that he will at least avoid the jumble (*Durcheinandermengen*) of pieces borrowed from entirely different periods, which is the rule for the publication of the posthumous texts then available. Elsewhere (at the beginning of his lectures) Heidegger says further: (1) Without their having intended to do so, but by publishing one after another, and in sequence, notes borrowed from different manuscripts or from different places in a same manuscript, the editors mislead us. (2) The only edition that can be taken as being definitive is the one that follows the chronological order.

I think Heidegger's judgments should put an end to the doubts that certain commentators, through an unreasonable attachment to the past, continue to oppose to the critical edition of Nietzsche's texts as a whole, an edition that is clearly important: we have not finished with Nietzsche, nor even with the publication of his texts. I should add that, in these lectures by Heidegger, one can hear phrases that constitute a warning against any exploitation of Nietzsche's philosophy by the masters of the regime. I recall this phrase in particular: *"We do not have the right to exploit Nietzsche in order to make him serve contemporary enterprises of spiritual counterfeiting"*; and Heidegger, who is lecturing, speaks of the political interpretations of the Will to Power that are possible only if one "flattens" the thought, or purely and simply strikes it out. In 1939 this should have rung out clearly, as a warning and a call, to the ears of some of the listeners in the audience. It is appropriate that it should be recalled by those who are unable to take as negligible Heidegger's principal "political" text of 1933 (unknown to many until its publication by Guido Schneeberger in 1960) [*Die Selbstbehauptung der deutschen Universität* (Breslau: Korn, 1933); a translation by Karsten Harries of this essay appears in *Review of Metaphysics* 38, no. 3 (March 1985)]—a text, it is true, that is in every respect frightening, but above all for the following reason: with the aim of recommending a decisive vote in favor of national socialism, it put in Hitler's service the *very* language and the *very* writing through which, at a great moment in the history of thought, we had been invited to participate in the questioning designated as the most lofty—that which would come to us from Being and Time.

5. This essay appeared in the volume entitled *Beiträge zur Geschichte der Aesthetik* (Berlin: Aufban-Verlag, 1954) (*Contributions to the History of Aesthetics*).

In another work, *La Destruction de la Raison*, trans. S. George, A. Gisselbrecht, E. Pfrimmer, R. Girard (Paris: L'Arche, 1958), [*The Destruction of Reason*, trans. Peter Palmer (London: Merlin, 1980); *Die Zerstörung der Vernunft* (Berlin: Aufban-Verlag), 1953], Lukács devoted a chapter to an analysis of Nietzsche's work as a whole. The essay accuses and indicts Nietzsche. The subject of the book is polemical in nature. Lukács seeks, in the domain of philosophy, the paths by which Germany had arrived at Hitler and become the chosen fatherland of the enemies of reason. One often has the curious impression that one is reading a book written not by Lukács, but by Maurras.

6. In *Le problème de la vérité dans la philosophie de Nietzsche* (Paris: Seuil, 1966), Jean Granier cites various sources for this term: Jacobi, Jean-Paul, Turgenev, Dostoyevski, and Paul Bourget. Others should be added, but this is of little consequence. The word itself is flat. Turned into a system, it contradicts itself. The contradiction only brings out its barrenness. The semantic play between the void, or nothingness [*le néant*] and nothing [*rien*] shows that it is apparently difficult to negate what has not first been affirmed. But the term's lack of density does not reduce it to inaction. Descartes, Kant, Hegel, and Bergson not only refused to think nothingness apart from being, but became irritated (except, perhaps, Hegel, who identifies nothingness with the sovereign malice of the immediate, thus making the immediate into nothingness) by what, for one, is the sign of the will's range (thus a mark of perfection), for another, the lack of a concept or a concept that is empty and without object, and for still another, an emptiness without object and without concept, that is to say, a word, that is to say, the illusion of a word; or to put this differently, nothing but a nothing, which is all the same something. But all these reductions (which are founded on the masked exigency of continuity and plenitude that philosophy bears) have served for "nothing"—not even for deciding whether the language that contains the nothing speaks (or not) for nothing, or whether the nothing is there to permit speech.

7. Science as a theory of science, as a theory of the constitution of science, requiring "writing," that is to say, a form of writing freed from ideology, has barely emerged, let us not forget, from the horizon of scientific truths. Let us say that it is yet to come.

8. I note that the affirmation of the Eternal Return, here considered only in relation to nihilism, will give rise—on the path opened and followed by Pierre Klossowski—to another series of remarks, found below: "On a Change of Epoch: The Exigency of Return."

9. Hence one can conclude that nihilism identifies itself with the will to surmount it *absolutely*.

10. *Ueber die Linie* can signify "Over the Line" or "Considerations on the Line" (the zero parallel). Henri Plard translated Jünger's text by the title *Passage de la ligne* (Rocher). Heidegger's text was published by this other title: *Zur Seinsfrage* (Frankfurt am Main: V. Klostermann, 1956).

11. Nietzsche, in particular, saw that Platonic dualism presupposes the experience of the specular: that of light, the Idea, and of its reflection, the sensible.

12. Jacques Derrida ["Force et signification," *L'écriture et la différence* (Paris: Seuil, 1967)].

13. He says elsewhere *"The will to power interprets,"* but the Will to Power cannot be a subject.

14. *"Are we, further, to suppose that the interpreter is behind the interpretation? That would already be poetry, hypothesis."*

15. Let us keep in mind what Nietzsche points out: *"the universe must be broken up."*

16. These pages are written at the margins of books by Michel Foucault, Gilles Deleuze, Eugen Fink, and Jean Granier—*Les mots et les choses* (Paris: Gallimard, 1966) [*The Order of Things* (New York: Vintage, 1970)]; *Nietzsche et la philosophie* (Paris: Presses Universitaires de France, 1973 [*Nietzsche and Philosophy*, trans. Hugh Tomlinson (New York: Columbia University Press, 1983)]; *La philosophie de Nietzsche*, trans. Hans Hildebrand and Alex Lindberg (Paris: Minuit, 1965); *Le jeu comme symbole du Monde*, trans. Hildebrand and Lindberg (Paris: Minuit, 1966); *Le problème de vérité dans la philosophie de Nietzsche* (Paris: Seuil, 1966)—and of several of Jacques Derrida's essays, collected in *L'écriture et la différence* (Paris: Seuil, 1967) [*Writing and Difference*, trans. Alan Bass (Chicago: University of Chicago Press, 1978)]. [Since Blanchot most often cites Nietzsche in French, only exceptionally providing the German, I have in some instances chosen to base my renderings of the Nietzsche passages on the French translation that Blanchot cites, thereby giving the reader a sense of what Blanchot would have heard in Nietzsche's words. I sometimes therefore cite Walter Kaufmann's English translation of Nietzsche without modification, while at other times (when the latter seems very different from the French), I remain close to the French translation of Nietzsche.]

VII. Reflections on Hell

1. Kafka nonetheless says of the law, the inner law: *"Why do you compare the inner law to a dream? Does it seem as absurd* (sinnlos, *deprived of meaning), as incoherent, as inevitable . . . as a dream? All of that—absurd, first of all, for it is only when I do not observe it that I can continue to exist here."*

2. This is why dialogue is the greatest danger. *"Dialogue is an instrument of evil,"* states Kafka. It is therefore evil, the wood louse itself, who wishes to draw us into dialogue. We converse with evil in order to reduce it or master it, but this conversation is already evil.

3. *Tu peux tuer cet homme; scènes de la vie révolutionnaire russe*, ed. and trans. Lucien Feuillade and Nicolas Lazarevitch (Paris: Gallimard, 1950). In the pages that introduce this collection, Brice Parain has stated, with the sobriety and concern for truth that are his, what the Russian nihilists sought to impart to us.

4. *"Nothing amuses, nothing excites the mind as do large numbers"* (Sade).

5. Micheline Sauvage, *Le cas Don Juan* (Paris: Seuil, 1953).

6. Isolde: *"We have lost the world, and the world has lost us."*

7. The sword of power is between them. But it would be naive to interpret this as the interdict of I know not what purity, or as an allusion to impotency. It is nevertheless true that the mere decision of virile mastery can only open what knows no mastery and is never commensurable with the erotic relation, as is indeed illustrated by Sade's enormous attempt to exhaust (through the reversal of activity into passivity and suffering into pleasure) a relation he would nonetheless only want to appropriate in terms of power—unless it be by recapturing it through the neutrality of writing.

VIII. Forgetting, Unreason

1. Michel Foucault, *Histoire de la folie à l'âge classique* (Paris: Librairie Plon, 1961). [Foucault, *Madness and Civilization: A History of Insanity in the Age of Reason*, trans. Richard Howard (New York: Vintage, 1973, c. 1965).]

2. It was for a long time customary to *show* the insane, and I wonder whether the exhibition ses-

sions in psychiatric hospitals, useful no doubt in teaching (and today made by television massively public), do not also prolong this ancient practice.

3. I refer here to *L'espace littéraire* (Paris: Gallimard, 1955), where the category of worklessness, the absence of the work, begins to emerge. [Blanchot, *The Space of Literature*, trans. Ann Smock (Lincoln: University of Nebraska Press, 1982).] See as well "The Absence of the Book," which concludes the present collection of essays. It seems to me that in the narrative Louis-René des Forêts has entitled *Le Bavard* (Paris: Gallimard, 1946), which is in every way staggering, the same situation is already set forth.

IX. The Limit-Experience

1. We see again to what extent the problematic of the absurd is but an easy way to hand oneself over to meaning, to "making sense."

2. "Belongs?" Yes, if this is a belonging without appurtenance; again, a relation that withdraws from relation.

3. This is the problem that Georges Bataille also poses in another form when he relates human movement to the play of interdict and transgression (a passing beyond the limit that cannot be gotten beyond). *The interdict marks the point at which power ceases.* Transgression is not an act of which the force and the mastery of certain men, under certain conditions, would still be capable. Transgression designates what is radically out of reach: assailment of the inaccessible, a surpassing of what cannot be surpassed. It opens to man when power ceases to be man's ultimate dimension.

4. What the one speaking—the "self"—seeks to say in all the rigor of speech and against chance (the dice fall), the "Other" at the same time affirms on the basis of the indefinite itself, on the basis of the unknown, which is always linked to the ungraspable strangeness of an end (the dice are tossed). Thus, as we see, there is simultaneity of these two discursive gestures: in a sense, the dice of speech (obeying the gravity that renders words necessary) must fall so that the dice will be thrown; and it is the very falling of the dice (their falling at the appointed time) that, transformed into a limitless fall, coincides with the impetus capable of calling chance forth.

5. The passages that concern us appear in Sade's *Philosophy in the Bedroom*, in the section entitled "Yet Another Effort, Frenchmen, if You Would Become Republicans"; the "political writings" appear in volume 8 of Sade's *Oeuvres complètes* (Sceaux: J.-J. Pauvert, 1948-). [*The Complete Justine, Philosophy in the Bedroom and Other Writings*, trans. Richard Seaver and Austryn Wainhouse (New York: Grove, 1968); *Juliette*, trans. Austryn Wainhouse (New York: Grove, 1968).]

6. This is an expression Sade applies to himself: "*Happy French, this you felt in reducing to dust those monuments of horror, those infamous prisons from which philosophy in chains cried out to you, before it had an intimation of the energy that would cause you to break the chains by which its voice was being silenced.*"

7. Let us not immediately evoke Nietzsche, but Blake: "Energy is the only life. Energy is Eternal delight" and even Van Gogh: "There is good in every energetic movement," for energy is thought (intensity, density, the sweetness of thought pushed to its limit).

8. Saint-Just says to the contrary, but in the same vein: "Revolutions proceed from weakness to audacity, and from crime to virtue."

9. Helvétius formulates the same idea: "One becomes stupid as soon as one ceases to be impassioned."

10. In yet another speech Saint-Just says: "*Simple common sense, energy of soul, a cool mind, the fire of a pure and ardent heart, austerity, unselfishness: these are the traits of a patriot.*"

11. Saint-Just will express nearly the same thought in his silent speech of 9 Thermidor: "*Renown is a vain rumor. Let us lend our ears to bygone centuries—nothing more is heard.*"

12. He does so in one of his most beautiful speeches, where we find this sentence: "*Those who make only a half revolution do no more than dig their own graves.*"

13. It is likely that Sade spoke in this way, and it would have been a sign of his sincerity and his lack of prudence. The text says, "in private conversation he was constantly drawing comparisons from Greek and Roman history to prove the impossibility of establishing a democratic and republican government in France." Impossible "without an effort and yet another effort"; this is the theme of our treatise: it was not a crime, it was said everywhere. Saint-Just was also of this opinion, believing that after Lycurgus there always come the oppressors who destroy his work: "*sad truths.*"

14. *Vie du marquis de Sade*, vol. 2 (Paris: Gallimard, 1957, c.1952). [*The Marquis de Sade, a Biography*, trans. Alec Brown (London: Elek Books, 1961).] Gilbert Lely has shown that this pamphlet could not have been written by Sade. Need we recall here all that we owe to the considerable work of Lely, who has carried on that of Maurice Heine?

X. The Speech of Analysis

1. In the correspondence that Freud kept up with Fliess from 1887 to 1902, which has only recently been translated into French under the title *La naissance de la psychanalyse, lettres à Wilhelm Fliess, notes et plans, 1887-1902* (Paris: Presses Universitaires de France, 1979, c. 1956), one can follow these tentative efforts, detours, and vain attempts; one notes as well the renunciations, and the silences, and the need to know that precipitously gives form to thoughts and definitions. And there are moving words: in 1893, when he is still far from what is to be psychoanalysis, Freud writes to his friend, "I am too old and lazy and overwhelmed with daily tasks to be able to learn anything new at this stage." But in 1897: "We shall not be shipwrecked. Instead of the passage we are seeking, we may find oceans to be fully explored by those who come after us; but, if we are not prematurely capsized, if our constitutions can stand it, we shall make it. *Nous y arriverons.*" [Sigmund Freud, *The Origins of Psycho-Analysis, Letters to Wilhelm Fliess*, trans. Eric Mosbacher and James Strachey (New York: Basic Books, 1954).]

2. The correspondence with Fliess indeed confirms what we knew: it was the self-analysis undertaken after his father's death that alone allowed Freud to seek the source of neurosis no longer in a real scene of seduction (it happened, strangely, that all his patients had a father, an uncle, or a brother who had seduced them in childhood) and to arrive at the idea of the complex, in particular the Oedipus complex, whose configuration had been dissimulated by the strange structure of Freud's own family. "My self-analysis is really, for the moment, what is most essential and promises to be of the greatest value to me if I succeed in bringing it to completion." "Something from the deepest depths of my own neurosis has opposed any further advance in the understanding of neurosis." "This analysis is harder than any other, and it is also the thing that paralyzes the power of writing down and communicating what I have already learned." But is self-analysis even possible? "A true self-analysis is really impossible, otherwise there would be no more illness." That Freud should always need a friend to whom he can make his thoughts known as they are being discovered indeed seems to be in keeping with the method of analysis: a friend who often and quickly becomes an enemy. With Freud one observes as well a fascinating back and forth movement of thought, which in part explains the fact that, no matter how firmly he holds to the principles of his method, he can so freely and easily renounce the various explanatory schema that his disciples so willingly turn into dogma: "At times ideas whirl through my head that promise to explain everything . . . then they disappear again, and I make no effort to retain them since I know that both their coming to consciousness and their subsequent disappearance are no real indication of their fate."

3. *La psychanalyse: sur la parole et le langage*, vol. 1 (Paris: Presses Universitaires de France, 1956). In 1953, a certain number of French psychoanalysts formed the French Society of Psychoanalysis. The volume published under this title in 1956 (an important event) constitutes the first collection of their work. Jacques Lacan's contribution, "Fonction et champ de la parole et du langage en psychanalyse," a report that was read and discussed in Rome in September 1953, became the (already decentered) centerpiece of this collection. The remarks I published then, and here reproduce, thus

refer only to this particular text by Lacan. At the time I added this question: is it a matter of a new psychoanalytical orientation? Doubtless, it is a matter of a turning point that would constitute a return to Freud's thought such as certain forms of philosophy and contemporary knowledge, freed from themselves (thus from science itself as possible), would illuminate and confirm it. [Jacques Lacan, *Ecrits* (Paris: Seuil, 1966); *Ecrits, a Selection*, trans. Alan Sheridan (New York: Norton, 1977); *Speech and Language in Psychoanalysis*, trans. Anthony Wilden (Baltimore: Johns Hopkins University Press, 1968).]

4. Lacan says in a striking manner: *"The illusion that impels us to seek the reality of the subject beyond the language barrier is the same as that by which the subject believes that his truth is already given in us and that we know it in advance."*

5. On condition, it is true, that the word dialectic and the analyses of Hegel do not in their turn give rise to magical formulas capable of answering everything. Research on language is itself deceptive to the extent that language is always more and always less than language, it being first of all also writing and then, in the end, in a future that has not come about, a writing outside language. I wonder if the example of Freud, who with such liberty invented a vocabulary and the most varied schemes of explanation to account for what he was discovering, does not show that every experiment would do well to follow itself through, to understand and formulate itself first in relation to itself.

6. Psychoanalysis — as we well know — is at once a technique and a knowledge: a power, an action, and a comprehension always within the horizon of science. In this sense, it is very close to Marxism. The power of technique is the power to understand; but is it comprehension that gives power, or is it power that clears the way for comprehension? Both the one and the other, but in a manner that remains obscure and equivocal. The doctor does not claim to act upon the one who is ill. Power is situated in neither one; it is between them, in the interval that separates them by bringing them together and in the fluctuating relations that found communication. Yet, practically speaking, there is a sick person to be cured, a knowing technique having no end other than this cure, and the doctor who has this responsibility. "Psychoanalytic communication" is most often (in its still always predominant form) conceived of in terms of power, and the speech that it secures is the power to speak within the normal conditions of a given society. So that psychoanalysis, itself become under these conditions an *institution* (whether or not willingly), risks serving the institutional forms that alone, historically, have a hold on speech.

XI. Everyday Speech

1. Henri Lefebvre published a first book by this title in 1947 (*Critique de la vie quotidienne*, Paris: Grasset); then, in 1958, as a preface to another edition of this first essay, a second study of different orientation. A third volume took up these questions again in a new light (Paris: l'Arche). Since I first published these remarks, Lefebvre has continued to extend his reflections (see *La vie quotidienne dans le monde moderne*, Paris: Gallimard, 1962). [*Everyday Life in the Modern World*, trans. Sacha Rabinovitch (New York: Harper & Row, 1971); (New Brunswick, N.J.: Rutgers University Press, 1984).]

2. See Edgar Morin's *L'esprit du temps* (Paris: Grasset, 1975, c. 1962). In this book Morin does not deal directly with the problem of information, but studies what he calls Mass Culture: "that is to say, produced according to the large-scale standards of industrial output and distributed by techniques of mass circulation; addressed to a social *mass*, that is, to a gigantic agglomerate of individuals existing before and beyond the internal structures of society (class, family, etc.)." It is indeed a matter of a culture with its myths, its symbols, its images. It "tends to corrode, to break down other cultures. . . . This is not the only cultural form of the twentieth century, but it is the truly massive and new current of the century." Morin sometimes opposes this culture to others, for example, to humanist culture — wrongly, it seems to me. I mean that the importance of "mass culture" is that it puts into question the very idea of culture by realizing it in such a manner as to expose it to view.

3. Georg Lukács, *L'Ame et les formes* (Paris: Gallimard, 1974), as cited by Lucien Goldmann in *Recherches dialectiques* (Paris: Gallimard, 1959). [Georg Lukács, *Soul and Form*, trans. Anna Bostock (London: Merlin, 1974, c. 1971).]

4. Photography—mobile, immobile—as exposition: the bringing to the fore and setting up of the conditions for the appearance of a human presence (that of the street) that does not yet have a countenance and that one can neither approach nor fully look at face-on. Photography, in this sense, is the truth of daily publication where everything is to be put in the limelight. See Roland Barthes's study "Le message photographique" in *Communications*, vol. 1 (Paris: Seuil, 1961). [Barthes, "The Rhetoric of the Image," in a collection of his articles entitled *Image-Music-Text*, trans. Stephen Heath (London: Hill and Wang, 1978)].

XII. Atheism and Writing. Humanism and the Cry

1. Nietzsche: "*This pose, man as measure of the world and judge of the world . . . , is in prodigiously bad taste. . . . We laugh as soon as we encounter the juxtaposition of 'man' and 'world,' separated by the sublime presumption of this little word 'and.'* " We must add, as nearly goes without saying, that if the Eternal Return brings us face to face with the enigma of recommencing and thereby ruins the thought of Unity, it thereby diverts us, in the final affirmation, from every humanist ideal. See the text that follows, "On a Change of Epoch: The Exigency of Return."

2. Stirner, responding in his trenchant way to Feuerbach, will say something like this: when God is interiorized to the point of giving his divinity over to man, the latter is more of a slave of the divine than ever.

3. And yet on this subject, and against this designation, there is much to be said. When Feuerbach speaks of anthropology, of anthropotheism, and of practical atheism, does he appeal to humanism precisely when he wants to name "the new philosophy"? I do not recall. But humanism is born in his vicinity; it is a political word. Arnold Ruge (as Jean-Pierre Faye recalls with ironic timeliness), who gave the word "humanism" its radical signification (a word formed in France some fifty years earlier, and having the sense of humanity, human generosity), is very close to Feuerbach, the name with which Ruge opens his famous *Annales de Halle* [*Hallischen Jahrbücher für deutsche Wissenshaft und Kunst*]. However, when Feuerbach, speaking of himself in the third person, wishes to characterize himself, he does not say Feuerbach is a humanist, but "Feuerbach is neither a materialist, an idealist, nor a philosopher of identity. What is he then? He is in his thoughts what he is in fact . . . : a man; or rather . . . Feuerbach is a communitary man, a communist." "Communist" therefore preceded and basically effaced in advance "humanist." Let us also add that if Feuerbach uses the word "man," it is as a first and a new name, bearing also a new principle: a name destined to unsettle and (perhaps) replace every name. "To think, to speak and to act in a purely human manner is given only to the generations to come. Today it is not yet a matter of exposing man, but of drawing him out of the mire into which he has sunk." [*Principles of the Philosophy of the Future*, trans. Manfred H. Vogel (Indianapolis, Ind.: Bobbs-Merrill, 1966); *Grundsätze der philosophie der Zukunft* (Zurich: Verlag des literarischen Comptoirs, 1843).] Let us then not drag the thought of "humanism" into a debate where this word's use would suffice for its understanding. Even Hölderlin, so far from this thought, rallies "to the point of view of what is called humanism" (to "what makes the bond, the community of human natures and of their tendencies," as he explains), and proposes to found "a humanist journal of a poetic nature." This occurs during the period of *Empedocles*, when he is attempting to break free of his separation.

4. In this sense where there is an "I," the identity of a self, "God is not dead." This is also why Nietzsche's decisive contestation has to do with "consciousness" or the identity of the "I." Consider this text drawn from Nietzsche's unpublished writings, cited by G. Colli and M. Montinari in the *Cahiers de Royamont* no. 6 (Paris: Minuit, 1967), devoted to Nietzsche: "*I rather take the I itself as a construct of thought, of the same order as 'matter,' 'thing,' 'substance,' 'individual,' 'goal,' 'number,'*

thus as a regulative fiction *thanks to which one introduces a sort of constancy, and therefore a sort of 'intelligibility' into a world of becoming. Faith in grammar, in the linguistic subject and in the object, has up to the present held metaphysics under its yoke: I teach that one must renounce this faith."*

5. When Feuerbach declares that "atheism is the secret of every religion," meaning that where man conceives, adores and loves God, it is necessarily the human being—though a being that is absolute and sacred—that one senses and loves, he shows quite well (it is true, without knowing it) that, inasmuch as one transposes the divine, but does not efface it—where effacing it does not simply consist (this is the essential) in negating it or setting it aside, but in substituting for it a still unperceived possibility, that is to say, in opening a dimension that is radically other—it is ridiculous to claim to have broken with the theological era. It ensues as a consequence that under the name of God it is always also man as Unique that one continues to adore.

6. Already for Nietzsche the problem poses itself in the most radical manner, in the sense that for him atheism is always problematic, and is itself an anachronistic expression. It would be a question, therefore, as Karl Löwith says very well, of passing from the a-Theism of the nineteenth century to A-theism, which is what occurs with a recognition of the world as the "play of the world."

7. Novalis already speaks of *"reticular form."* A notation I find in the beautiful translation of Novalis's *L'Encyclopédie* (Paris: Minuit, 1966) by Maurice de Gandillac, to whom we already owe several translations of rare and important texts. [Novalis, *Werke, Briefe, Dokumente*, vol. 3, ed. Ewald Wasmuth (Heidelberg: L. Scheider, 1957).]

8. This is why the discovery of the unconscious, understood as the dimension of that which cannot be discovered, is, along with a writing that does not speak, one of the principal steps toward liberation with regard to the theological: on condition, however, that one does not take the Un-conscious to be the un-Conscious, and realizes that here neither the term presence, nor the term absence, nor the terms affirmation or negation is fitting. In other words, we do not yet have a word for the "unconscious."

9. Humanism—humanity, as Kant already said, *"is communicability itself."*

XIII. On a Change of Epoch: The Exigency of Return

1. This book, first published in German, is by Ernst Jünger, *An der Zeitmauer: Zum Weltgeist des Atomzeitalters* (Stuttgart: Ernst Klett Verlag, 1959); *Le Mur du Temps, Essai sur L'âge atomique*, trans. Henri Thomas (Paris: Gallimard, 1981, c. 1963).

2. Heiddeger also cites and comments upon this "sign," borrowed from fragment 56 of *Beyond Good and Evil*. Pierre Klossowski, *Un si funeste désir* (Paris: Gallimard, 1963), and *Nietzsche et le cercle vicieux* (Paris: Mercure de France, 1969).

3. This fragment of *The Gay Science* is taken from the notes in which Nietzsche questions himself for the first time on the nature of the "event."

Part III: The Absence of the Book (the neutral, the fragmentary)
I. The Final Work

1. I refer here to Yves Bonnefoy, so close to the subject he treats in his circumspect reflection: *Rimbaud par lui-même* (Paris: Seuil, 1961). [Yves Bonnefoy, *Rimbaud*, trans. Paul Schmidt (New York: Harper & Row, 1973).]

2. See Suzanne Bernard's introduction, biographical summary, and notes in *Oeuvres de Rimbaud* (Paris: Classiques Garnier, 1981, c. 1960). [I have followed frequently, but not exclusively, the translations proposed by Wallace Fowlie in *Rimbaud, Complete Works, Selected Letters* (Chicago: University of Chicago Press, 1966), and Paul Schmidt in *Rimbaud, Complete Works* (New York: Harper & Row, 1976).]

3. René Char: "In Rimbaud's case, *diction* precedes *contradiction* by a farewell. Its discovery, its incendiary date is rapidity."

II. Cruel Poetic Reason (the rapacious need for flight)

1. I refer here to what appeared in "Artaud" in *Le livre à venir* (Paris: Gallimard, 1986, c. 1959).

2. What he feared, finally, was that madness, speech, and the cry, immediately dispersed, would be no more than the elements of a strategy. This is what occurs, precisely in his regard (and already in this text), through a renown that happily exhausts his name.

III. René Char and the Thought of the Neutral

1. This, of course, is much too quickly and unfairly said. [The French *neutre* means in English both neuter and neutral. Since the first term refers to an effect of language, and the second to that of thought, relation, or experience, I have attempted to render *le neutre* in such a way as to bring forward whenever possible both this distinction and the fact that it cannot hold.]

2. Reflection upon the difference between being and beings—a difference that is not the theological difference between the Transcendent and the finite (less absolute and at the same time more original than the latter), a difference that is also entirely other than that between the existing being and its manner of existing—seems to call upon thought and upon language to recognize in *Sein* a fundamental word for the neuter or neutral; in other words, it calls to think in the neutral. But it is also necessary to rectify this immediately and say: the dignity accorded to being in the summons that would come to us from it, everything that relates in an ambiguous manner Being and the divine, the correspondence between *Sein* and *Dasein*, the providential fact that being and the comprehension of Being go together—being being that which illuminates itself, opens, and destines itself to beings that become an opening of clarity; the relation, therefore, between *Sein* and truth, a veiling unveiling itself in the presence of *light*—all of this does not prepare us to seek the neutral as it is implied by the unknown.

3. In truth—as René Char's example persuades us—poetry, speech, and thought are all the same name under an apparent duality. But if two names, several names, are needed to name that which comes about as one in research, this is because the latter has as its center only a unity that is without unity.

IV. The Fragment Word

1. "*In the breakup of the universe we experience, prodigious! the pieces that drop are* living."

2. "*Heraclitus, Georges de la Tour, I am grateful to you . . . for having rendered my dislocation agile and admissible.*"

VI. Vast as the night

1. At least in a hermeneutic conception of psychoanalysis, to which objection can be made. In order to avoid any misunderstanding, let us recall that the symbolic, as Jacques Lacan would have us understand it, is not to be read as a symbol with reference to a symbolized, but rather through elucidation of the law that founds this instance and orders it, even as a disorder.

2. I refer here to the learned and pleasurable book by Jean Pépin, *Mythe et Allégorie* (Paris: Montaigne, 1958). This book studies the ways in which the first Christian theologians reacted to the myths of antiquity and their allegorical treatment. In the first part of his study he also sheds light on the Greek theory of expression and allegorical interpretation, as well as Jewish allegorism as elaborated by the Alexandrian Jews. A more summary introduction alludes to Schelling and certain modern conceptions of mythology.

3. It is Jung (although we may find this astonishing) who denounced the violent character of such a critical method: "Interest is diverted from the work of art and loses itself in the inextricable chaos

of psychological antecedents; and the poet becomes a 'clinical case,' an example bearing a specific number in the *psychopathia sexualis*. Thus the psychoanalysis of a work of art moves away from its object and carries the discussion to a domain of general human interest that is in no way particular to the artist and, notably, has no importance for his art."

4. In a chapter of his *Art poétique* (Paris: Gallimard, 1958), Roger Caillois has studied the relations between image and enigma. The enigma has a ritual signification and is not divined: one must have mastered a secret knowledge in order to respond to it; the response is part of the initiation and is initiation. "The enigma is liturgical and immutable, whereas from the beginning, the value of the poetic image lies at least in part in its novelty, that is to say, its capacity to shock. In one case it is a matter of knowing, in the other of creating." The Greeks, clearly the late Greeks, are as though midway between these two kinds of figure: enigma is simply a more obscure allegory, but allegorical expression is not the free play of fantasy. The Delphic oracle expressed itself through images, at times qualified as enigma, at other times as metaphor. Let us recall the later remarks by Plutarch (a priest of the Delphic Apollo) when he speaks in praise of the Pythia for having renounced figure and verse and adopting a more direct language: "With this clarity of the oracles an evolution in opinion in their regard has been produced that is parallel to other changes: their strange, singular, oblique, and periphrastic style used to fill the crowd with admiration and with a religious respect, and was a motive for their belief in the oracles' divine nature; but later one wished to learn each thing clearly and easily, without bombast or stylistic affectation, and the poetry that surrounded the oracles was accused of opposing the knowledge of truth by mixing obscurity and shadow with the god's revelations; one even suspected that the metaphors, enigmas, and ambiguities of expression were routes of escape and refuge, permitting the diviner to withdraw into them and hide there in case of error." Plutarch nonetheless recognizes the usefulness of poetic half-light: "By putting truth in poetic form—as one would a ray of light by reflecting and dividing it several times—the god takes from it what may be wounding and hard." But Sophocles said: *"The wise one always understands the god's enigmas; for one who is unreasonable, the god's lessons, no matter how clear, are in vain."* And Heraclitus: *"The lord whose oracle is at Delphi neither speaks nor conceals, but gives a sign."*

5. In isolating the image, in making us attentive to those "brief, isolated, live transactions" that are for Bachelard the pure essence of poetry, I also think he means to limit himself to what in a literary work would most escape the jurisdiction of psychoanalysis as he believed he knew it, as well as indiscreet cultural research. Discourse, at the level of the image, would not yet be alienated, it being the moment at which the power to communicate escapes the uses of force. "The communicability of a singular image is a fact of great ontological significance." A question that goes, perhaps, beyond the interrogative resources proper to ontology. Yet in its purity as element, the image seems to *lend itself* to writing at the same time as it would like to remain foreign to it; hence, once again, the necessary mistrust one harbors with regard to it, unless we recall that its distinctive trait is to belie its appearance, that is, to never be able to appear [*apparaître*] without also *seeming* [*apparaître*] to be in excess. This anteriority of the image in relation to the image rejoins, while not coinciding with, the anteriority of writing.

6. Bachelard arrives very directly at this site of the image, where the image is no more than its site: "If we could analyze impressions of immensity, images of immensity, or what immensity brings to an image, we should soon enter into a region of phenomenology of the purest sort—a phenomenology without phenomena; or, stated less paradoxically, one that, in order to know the productive flow of images, need not wait for the phenomena of the imagination to take form and stabilize into complete images." And further on: "In analyzing images of immensity, we should realize within ourselves the pure being of pure imagination." [Gaston Bachelard, *La poétique de l'espare* (Paris: Presses Universitaires de France, 1989, c. 1957); *The Poetics of Space*, trans. Maria Jolas (New York: Orion Press, 1964). The translation of Bachelard Jolas proposes has been slightly modified when it seemed indicated for consistency with Blanchot's reading.]

VIII. Wittengenstein's Problem

1. *"The word is never lacking when one possesses the idea."*

2. A collection that Geneviève Bollème has carefully selected and entitled *Extraits de la correspondance; Préface à la vie d'écrivain* (Paris: Seuil, 1972, c. 1963)—a preface, we must add, that consumes the life itself.

3. It is as though Flaubert were trying to use the surplus value in work (available as soon as the writer, the editor, the critic, the reader, and the finished work all become its proprietors) in order to captivate and compensate for this strange minus-value that works so that the more one says the less one speaks.

4. *"This solar hollow . . . is the space of Roussel's language, the void he speaks from, the absence through which the work and madness communicate and exclude one another. And I don't mean this void metaphorically: it is a matter of the insufficiency of words that are less numerous than the things they designate, and that owe to this economy the fact that they mean something."* Further on, Michel Foucault alludes to *"an experience that surfaces in our time, teaching us that what is lacking is not 'meaning,' but the signs that nevertheless only signify through this lack."* [*Raymond Roussel* (Paris: Gallimard, 1963); *Death and the Labyrinth: the World of Raymond Roussel*, trans. Charles Ruas (Berkeley: University of California Press, 1987, c. 1986).]

5. When Flaubert says, with naïveté and malice, "too many things," "not enough forms," he is not contrasting a richness (the richness of the unsayable real) to a poverty (the poverty of words that are too few and too awkward to say it). Although he does not know it, all he is doing is contrasting one language with another: one fixed at the level of its content and semantically full, the other reduced to its formal values and fixed in its pure signifying decision. This is an opposition he cannot affirm in either of these two languages, but using a third, and thus speaking from higher up, he pronounces his judgment: "too many things," "not enough forms."

6. Wittengenstein, Flaubert, and Roussel say the following: if there were a discourse—scientific, for example—such that lack could not find a place in which to inscribe itself and exercise its effect as a deficiency, it would nonetheless *already* be inscribed there, if only by the necessity of or the demand for *another* language called upon to determine the meaning and the theoretical possibility of this discourse without lack. Language owes its perpetual failure to this lack; but the lack in its turn owes to language, through the infinite passage from one mode of saying to another, and even if it is not marked in any given region of discourse, the fact that it attains in language, at its limit (dispersing itself there in the moving plurality of an always unoccupied place), an excess of place, "the word that is in excess." It is perhaps this "word too many" that constitutes (while immediately unseating him) the invisible partner, the one that does not play, in relation to which Roger Laporte's books are ceaselessly written.

IX. A rose is a rose . . .

1. [Stein wrote,"Rose is a rose is a rose is a rose." Blanchot uses an initial article: "A rose is a rose . . . "]

X. Ars Nova

1. Theodore W. Adorno, *Philosophie de la nouvelle musique* (Paris: Gallimard, 1979, c. 1962). [*The Philosophy of Modern Music*, trans. Anne Mitchell and Wesley Blomster (New York: Seabury, 1973).]

2. Georges Poulet, *Les métamorphoses du cercle* (Paris: Plon, 1961); (Paris, Flammarion, 1979). [*The Metamorphoses of the Circle*, trans. Carley Dawson and Elliott Coleman (Baltimore: Johns Hopkins University Press, 1967, c. 1966).]

XI. The Athenaeum

1. But it must immediately be added: Hölderlin does not belong to romanticism; he is not part of any constellation.

2. Armel Guerne, from whom I borrow this text (he has translated it in *Les romantiques allemands*, [Paris: Desclée de Brouwer, 1963, c. 1956]), recalls its title: *Monologue*. He comments: "Essentially, everything written is a monologue within language." Let us recall that already in 1784, Hamann wrote to Herder: "*Were I as eloquent as Demosthenes, I could not but repeat three times, as a single word: reason is language, logos. This is the marrow-filled bone that I am gnawing, and will until my death. A profundity that remains still obscure to me, and I await the angel of the Apocalypse who would deign to bring me the key to such an abyss.*"

XII. The Effect of Strangeness

1. "Kleines Organon für das Theater," in *Gesammelte Werke*, vol. 7 (Frankfurt am Main: Suhrkamp Verlag, 1967). Composed, Brecht says, in 1948. ["A Short Organum for the Theater," in *Brecht on Theatre: The Development of an Aesthetic*, ed. and trans. John Willett (New York: Hill & Wang, 1964).]

2. ["The Exception and the Rule," in *The Jewish Wife and Other Short Plays*, trans. Eric Bentley (New York: Grove, 1965); "Die Ausnahme und die Regel" in *Gesammelte Werke*, vol. 1 (Frankfurt am Main: Suhrkamp Verlag, 1967).]

3. To the extent that Vilar does not reproach theater for misusing its incantatory function but for having lost it; a function or a force that, for him, must go hand in hand with the concentration of thought and the intensification of consciousness. Jean Vilar, *De la tradition théâtrale* (Paris: L'Arche, 1955); (Paris: Gallimard, 1975).

XIII. The End of the Hero

1. Oedipus is the victim of precisely this plot between origin and beginning. Who is he? The pure hero, the man who, having won power solely by merit, proudly considers himself to be author of himself; born from nothing, he makes this his glory: "*But I account myself a child of Fortune, beneficent Fortune, and I shall not be dishonored. She is the mother from whom I spring.*" Strange mother that scandalously reintegrates him with legitimacy and unites him with the origin to such a degree that, in order to separate from it, he will have to withdraw from everything and leave every site: an outlaw precisely in that he is the legal heir, but an heir without inheritance who believed he could use noble violence to become king, while it is violence that used him solely in order to break the right of inheritance and henceforth designate in every son the violated origin.

2. Serge Doubrovsky, *Corneille et la dialectique du héros* (Paris: Gillimard, 1982, c. 1963). This is a very rich essay in which specific assertions are as worthy of consideration as the thesis as a whole. Doubrovsky sheds light on Corneille by way of Malraux and on the hero by way of the adventurer, not without justice; he also wants to bring in Sartre and this, to my mind, is less pertinent. Regarding Nietzsche, he repeats the time-worn interpretation ("*Nietzschean history sinks in its entirety into a vast biologism*" or again: "*Nietzschean salvation willingly seeks itself on the side of biology*"): I believe he is wrong, even if he is right not to wish to relate the Cornelian hero to the Overman. Regarding Corneille, I would like to recall the beautiful study by Jean Starobinski, *L'oeil vivant* (Paris: Gallimard, 1989, c. 1961) [*The Living Eye*, trans. Arthur Goldhammer (Boston: Harvard University Press, 1989)], which teaches us a great deal about the myth of the hero. Let me mention as well Bernard Dort's *Pierre Corneille dramaturge* (Paris: L'Arche, 1972, c. 1957).

3. It is precisely in Sade's work that we find represented for the first time and with all its conse-

quences the confrontation of masters, and see exposed in all its cruel clarity the problem of the relations between Power and power.

4. *And how many deaths I suffer without dying even once*, Creusa already says, as she is consumed by the pestilential robe given her by Medea. This grand gesture of a hyperbolic death thus traverses Corneille's entire work. [No English translation exists for some of the tragedies Blanchot cites; when they are available, I have used those proposed by Samuel Solomon in *Pierre Corneille, Seven Plays* (New York: Random House, 1969).]

XIV. The Narrative Voice (the "he," the neutral)

1. I am referring to Michel Butor's *Répertoire II* (Paris: Minuit, 1964).

2. The "he" [or "it," *il*] does not simply take the place traditionally occupied by a subject, a mobile fragmentation; it modifies what we mean by place: a fixed location, unique or determined by its placement. Here we should once again (confusedly) say that the "he," dispersing after the fashion of a lack in the simultaneous plurality—the repetition—of a moving and diversely unoccupied place, designates "its" place as both the place from which it will always be missing and that will thus remain empty, but also as a surplus of place, a place that is always too many: hypertopia.

3. *Le Ravissement de Lol V. Stein* (Paris: Gallimard, 1964). [*The Ravishing of Lol Stein*, trans. Richard Seaver (New York: Grove, 1966) and (New York: Pantheon, 1979, c. 1966).]

4. It is this voice—the narrative voice—that I hear, perhaps rashly, perhaps rightly, in the narrative by Marguerite Duras that I mentioned a while back. The night forever without dawn—the ballroom where the indescribable event occurred that cannot be recalled and cannot be forgotten, but is retained in forgetting: the nocturnal desire to turn around in order to see what belongs neither to the visible nor to the invisible, that is, to remain for a moment, through one's gaze, as close as possible to strangeness where the rhythm of revealing-concealing has lost its rectifying force; then the need (the eternal human wish) to place in another's charge, to live once again in another, in a third person, the dual relation, the fascinated, indifferent relation that is irreducible to any mediation, a neutral relation, even if it implies the infinite void of desire; finally, the imminent certainty that what has once taken place will always begin again, always give itself away and refuse itself. Such are, it seems to me, the "coordinates" of the narrative space, the circle by which, as we enter it, we incessantly enter the outside. But who is telling the story here? Not the one who is relating it, who formally—and also a little shamefully—does the speaking, actually usurping speech to the point that he seems to be an intruder; it is rather the one who cannot recount because she bears—this is her wisdom, her madness—the torment of the impossible narration, knowing herself (by a closed knowledge anterior to the scission of reason-unreason) to be the measure of this outside where, as we accede to it, we risk falling under the attraction of a speech that is entirely exterior: pure extravagance.

XV. The Wooden Bridge (repetition, the neutral)

1. We say "so evidently." Yet, in a work devoted to *Don Quixote* whose second part treats Kafka's *The Castle*, and in pursuing by means of these two books a reflection on literature, Marthe Robert brings forth better than any other commentator the devastating enterprise of Cervantes, through which the Spanish Golden Age comes, or begins to come, to an end. I refer to the very rich work *L'Ancient et le nouveau: de Don Quichotte à Franz Kafka* (Paris: Grasset, 1963), whose movement I am "doubling."

2. Marthe Robert states explicitly: "Like Don Quixote, tempted rather late in life by the model the least Don Quixotesque and perhaps the most suited to providing an immediately useful norm, Kafka thus attempts to come close to Homeric thought and devotes his *last* novel to this task."

3. I will refrain here from entering into all the glosses to which *The Castle* might give rise. It should be noted, however, that if all these interpretations are (more or less) justified, they can be so

only if they remain at the level the method to which they claim to adhere has established, and if they remain consistent with it—if they show, in other words, that they cannot. In the same way, one may very well look for all the work's antecedents, all the myths it repeats and all the books to which it refers. But this repetition—a repetition that in itself is true and true for we who are reading—cannot be true in the same manner if one also decides to make it the book's truth, the truth as it proposed itself to Kafka, and in a sense as its future. In reality, we know very well that Kafka borrowed the story of the Castle from a novel that had charmed him in adolescence. Entitled *The Grandmother*, this novel by the Czech novelist Bozena Nemcova relates the difficult relations between the Castle and the village that is dependent upon it. Czech is spoken in the village, German is spoken in the Castle, the first sign of distance. The Castle is governed by a princess who is very amiable but unapproachable; between her and the peasants is a dark horde of lying servants, narrow-minded officials, and hypocritical bureaucrats. And this is the remarkable episode: a young Italian courtier assiduously pursues Christel, the innkeeper's pretty daughter, and makes indecent propositions to her. Christel feels lost: her father is a good man, but timid, and what can he do against the people of the Castle? The Princess is just, but one can neither reach nor inform her; moreover, she is most often away and one never knows where she resides. Thus the girl ends up feeling guilty, already touched by the fault that seeks and covets her. Her only hope lies with the other functionaries, providing that she succeed in attracting their interest. "It is," she says, "our only hope. Since they questioned him, perhaps they will help us. But it often happens that an affair is looked into without anyone really offering help. One is simply told it is not possible and no satisfaction is obtained." Now what is the name of this immoral courtier in Nemcova's novel? This is the surprise. His name is *Sortini*. It is therefore evident that we have here, at the same time, the first particulars of *The Castle* and the first sketch of the strange Amalia episode; it is also evident that, in keeping the name Sortini, Kafka wished to recall its model. Of course the difference between these two works is enormous. The Czech narrative is idyllic; the book's central character, the grandmother, breaks the spell, triumphs over obstacles, and manages to reach the Princess, from whom she obtains justice and reparation for the persecuted. In short, she succeeds where K. fails, thus playing (as Max Brod, from whom this information comes, remarks) the role of the righter of wrongs that K., being moreover incapable of assuming it, refuses. The comparison between the two works helps us, I think, to understand the following: in Kafka's work the decisive invention, and the most enigmatic, bears perhaps not upon the Castle but upon the village. If K., like the grandmother, belonged to the village, his role would be clear and as a character he would be transparent; either the man in revolt, resolved to bring an end to the injustices of the privileged class, or the man of salvation, devoted to putting symbolically to the test the infinite distance between the world here below and the world on high. But K. comes from a third world. He is doubly, even three times a foreigner: a stranger to the strangeness of the Castle, a stranger to the strangeness of the village, and a stranger to himself since, in an incomprehensible manner, he decides to break with his own familiarity, as though pulled ahead toward these sites nonetheless without allure by an exigency he is unable to account for. From this perspective, one would almost be tempted to say that the entire meaning of the book is already borne by the *wooden bridge* that leads from the main road to the village and upon which "*K. stood for a long while, gazing into the illusory emptiness above him.*"

4. Incidentally, I would note that for Kafka bureaucracy is not simply a late development (as though the gods, the first forces, were pitifully ending their reign by becoming functionaries) nor simply a negative phenomenon, any more than is exegesis in relation to speech. To his friend Oskar Baum he writes the following, which demands reflection: "Bureaucracy, if I judge it from my own perspective, is closer to original human nature than any other social institution." (This in a letter of June 1922, the period of *The Castle*.)

5. It is true that Marthe Robert says there is nothing transcendent about the Castle, and that it constitutes an immanent force. But this can be only an approximate way of putting things. One of the essential traits of the neutral, in fact, is that it does not allow itself to be grasped either in terms of immanence or in terms of transcendence, drawing us into an entirely different sort of relation.

XVII. Tomorrow at Stake

1. For myself, I cannot erase the memory that this text was written in the shadow of André Breton's death. Why, then, in the face of the "absolute impropriety" of this death that filled us with grief, evoke "the future of surrealism?" I reproduce here, not as response but as excuse, these lines destined to erasure: "*Surrealism was unique in Breton insofar as he brought it to the light of day, loaned it the passionate truth of an existence and made it begin, without origin, in a living manner as a life begins (when does it begin?): bound to an epoch, to this power of suspense and interruption that makes an epoch less something that lasts than the interval disordering duration. In this sense alone surrealism is the phenomenon of an epoch. Through it something was interrupted. There was a hiatus, a caesura of history—in every sense a derangement, a disarray that negation is incapable of defining (hence the impossibility of giving, through laziness and as one might wish, preponderance to dadaism); nonetheless a negation that does not accord with any affirmation ready to become law, institution, or a firmness one can proffer. Those who nevertheless think they are doing justice to André Breton by arresting surrealism at the hour of death, saying that his end brought everything to an end, are allowing themselves to be deceived by sorrow's counsel. Others, with even more haste, already reproach him for having been weak enough to prolong a movement that had for a long time been over. Let us ask why surrealism, whether it bear this name or none at all and as indissociable from Breton, is summoned by the very force he gave it to affirm itself as always still to come, or as the limit it never reached: and yet without future, without present, without past.*"

2. With Artaud the surrealist exigency in a sense turned about, affirming itself against itself. Artaud was excluded because he rejected Revolution in the communist sense of the word, rejecting even more fiercely all that (in his view) adherence to communism dissimulated in the way of a desire for action and immediate efficacity. Artaud could not without fraud allow his "powerlessness"—which was the point of departure for his protest—to be taken from him any more than his solitude, without which, for him, there would be no communication. How could he engage himself beyond himself? He could, but by powerlessness. This powerlessness, then, could not permit itself to be diverted from its own "force"—a paroxysm—by a search for compensatory results. "*It is for having refused to engage myself beyond myself, for having demanded silence around me and for being faithful in thought and in deed to what I felt to be my profound, my irremissible powerlessness that these gentlemen judged my presence among them to be inopportune. But what seemed to them above all condemnable and blasphemous was that I should wish to take solely upon myself the task of determining my limits.*" This powerlessness is therefore not pure negation; it is what affirms itself as a limit determining limits. Artaud, necessarily excluded from surrealism, is the absence—an absence André Breton qualifies as abstract and Artaud as weak, moronic, useless, abnormal, and vile—that always gives an uneven contour to surrealist plurality, keeping it from being pure presence and yet making it necessary "*at the edge of the abyss.*"

3. We know, but forget, that surrealism, as much as Mallarmé, restored power to language: "*Language can and ought to be torn from its bondage.*" "*Doesn't the mediocrity of our universe depend essentially on our power of enunciation?*" "*The problem of social action is only one of the forms of a more general problem that surrealism set out to deal with: the problem of human expression in all its forms.*"

4. Another formula, nonetheless the same: "SURREALISM is writing negated."

5. Even if they intend this playfully. Valéry: "Lack and lacuna are what create."

6. André Breton speaks as well of "the search for surprise": "*Surprise ought to be sought out for itself, unconditionally.*"

XVIII. The Absence of the Book

1. *I dedicate* (and disavow) *these uncertain pages to the books in which the absence of the book is already producing itself as promise in keeping its word; books written by—, but let no more than the lack of a name designate them here, for the sake of friendship.*

Index

Compiled by Hassan Melehy

Theory and History of Literature

Maurice Blanchot is a French critic, theorist, and novelist and the author of numerous works. Among these are *Faux pas* (1943), *L'Arrêt de mort* (1948), *La Part du feu* (1949), *Thomas l'obscur* (1950), *L'Espace littéraire* (1955), *Le Livre à venir* (1959), *L'Attente l'oubli* (1962), *L'Amitié* (1971), *La Folie du jour* (1973), and *La Communauté inavouable* (1983), some of which have been translated into English.

Susan Hanson is a professor of French in the Department of Foreign Languages at Drake University.